WORLD PHILOSOPHY

WORLD PHILOSOPHY

Essay-Reviews
of
225 Major Works

5

1932 - 1971

Edited by
FRANK N. MAGILL

Associate Editor
IAN P. McGREAL
Professor of Philosophy
California State University
Sacramento

SALEM PRESS
Englewood Cliffs, N.J.

Library of Congress Catalog Card Number: 82-060268

Complete Set: ISBN 0-89356-325-0
Volume V: ISBN 0-89356-330-7

First Printing

Some of the material in this work also appears in *Masterpieces of World Philosophy in Summary Form* (1961)

PRINTED IN THE UNITED STATES OF AMERICA

CHRONOLOGICAL LIST OF TITLES
IN VOLUME FIVE

WORLD PHILOSOPHY

PERCEPTION

Author: Henry Habberley Price (1899-   )
Type of work: Epistemology
First published: 1932

PRINCIPAL IDEAS ADVANCED

Sense-data are the given elements in our sense experience, the colors, odors, noises, and pressures of things as they are met in consciousness; such sense-data are particulars, not universals.

Material objects are spatially complete, three dimensional objects; but sense-data are spatially incomplete and private, and they are free from the causal relations which characterize material objects.

Sense-data which fit together to form solids are said to be constructible, and solids perceptually constructed within a mediate range of vision in which perfect stereoscopy is possible and said to be constructed from perfectly constructible sense-data.

The material object, known by reference to constructible sense-data, has causal properties which could not belong to any family of sense-data; consequently, phenomenalism is false.

In a book which might well be a model of procedure for such special studies, H. H. Price undertakes to examine existing theories of perception, reject what is bad, retain what is good, and by adding original reflections construct a new, more adequate theory avoiding the difficulties of the old. Price phrases the problem of perception in two separate questions: (1) What is perceptual consciousness and how is it related to sensing? (2) What is the relation of "belonging to" when we say a sense-datum "belongs to" a thing?

Consciousness contains givens—color expanses, pressures, noises, smells. These givens are *sense-data*, and the act of apprehending them intuitively is *sensing*. There are other data of consciousness, such as of introspection or memory. Sense-data differ from these solely in that they lead us to conceive of and believe in the existence of material things (whether such things *actually* do exist). By accepting sense-data as given, we do not commit ourselves to believing (1) that they persist when not being sensed (but only that they exist when sensed); (2) that the same sense-datum may be a datum of more than one mind; (3) that sense-data have some particular status in the universe; or (4) that they originate in any particular way.

Price examines and rejects naïve realism, its offshoot termed the selective theory, and the causal theory. He makes some use of the theory of phenomenalism and gathers the apparatus with which to exclude it only after stating most of his own theory. He never loses sight of his two basic questions, and all his very thorough and detailed arguments and rebuttals keep constant contact with them.

Naïve realism asserts that (1) perceptual consciousness is knowing that there exists an object to which a sense-datum now sensed belongs, and (2) for a visual or tactual sense-datum to belong to an object is for that sense-datum to be part of the surface of a three-dimensional object. Those who oppose the naïve realist usually regard hallucinations and perceptual illusions as ample refutation—but they commonly assume in their premises the theory they profess to upset. Price argues that the argument which actually disposes of naïve realism is simply that the many surfaces as seen, if they were really surfaces, simply would not fit together to construct the sort of three-dimensional solid the naïve realist believes in. From the controversy, we can rescue the facts that the *totum datum* (the sum of all the data of all the senses at a particular time) has main parts, the somatic sense-data and the environmental, and that in certain respects these vary concomitantly. They are always co-present and covariant; that is, the *totum datum* is *somato-centric*. Similarly, from the remains of the effort to establish an improved form of realism which he names the selective theory, Price draws the lessons that we must account for abnormal and illusory sense-data as well as normal ones; that to various persons the same material things may be present to the sense in various ways; and that obtainable as well as actual sense-data will have to be provided for.

The causal theory of perception states, as answers to Price's initial questions, that "belonging to" means "being caused by" a material thing, and that perceptual consciousness is fundamentally an *inference* from effect to cause. While Price expects to refute the theory readily, he notes that it seems to be the official foundation for the natural sciences. The only plausible version of the causal theory is, if every event has a cause and if sense-data are events, something other than sense-data must exist: the *causes* of sense-data. But we can know nothing of the character of the causes, and cannot prove them to be material. The fact is that from the first, we are "on the look out" for sets of sense-data of the sort that we already expect to adumbrate solids. We already have a notion of the material thing before being capable of formulating ideas of causality. This notion seems not only innate but *a priori*, a necessary condition of certain kinds of experience. This must be a whole complex notion of thinghood, including the factor of causality.

Price then sets out toward his own theory. Sense-data are not universals but particulars; not redness, but instances of red. They are not facts, but the bases for judging facts. Visual and tactual sense-data are the primary ones for establishing the existence of material things. A visual sense-datum can be called a colored expanse, but to call it a colored surface assumes too much. Sense-data are not substances; when suitable bodily and external conditions are present; they are created out of nothing and, when these conditions disappear, vanish into nothing. They have a finite, usually very small, duration. They take up no space and do not have causal characteristics, such as inertia or impenetrability. They are not so much like mechanical processes as *vital* processes. They are generated in neither the brain nor the mind alone, but in the substantial compound of the two, having certain characteristics which neither would have by itself.

The primary form of perceptual consciousness of our sense-data is perceptual acceptance. With the arising of a sense-datum there also arises a state of taking for granted the material thing to which it belongs. The question whether to believe simply does not enter with the first sense-datum, though it may be introduced later. Other than the datum itself, perceptual acceptance has no content. While I take for granted that the front surface of what I see has a back, I leave it until later to determine the nature of the unseen part. Moreover, the first sense-datum does not completely specify the details of the accessible side, but rather it simply limits the possibilities to some extent. Further observation adds greater detail. I therefore do not actually take my first datum as identical with the front surface of the object, but simply take it that a thing now exists which has a certain general character.

Unlike the transitory sense-datum, a material thing persists through a period before and after the sense-datum. It is spatially complete in three dimensions, whereas a sense-datum is spatially incomplete. It is public and accessible to many minds, whereas a sense-datum, being somato-centric, is private. "Belonging to" it are sense-data of many, usually all, of the different senses. Finally, it has causal relations, whereas the relation between a sense-datum and the awareness of that sense-datum is not causal.

Price accounts for error, illusion, and even mere peculiarities of interpretation by referring to the difference in nature between sensing and perceptual consciousness. Sensing is undoubted and perfectly intuitive reception of the given. Perceptual consciousness is a mode of *taking as* existing a material thing, although that thing is not *necessarily* present; it *seems* intuitive only because it is instantaneous, not discursive, and is yet the raw material of judgment, not the product. But the claim of any ostensibly sensed object to exist, and have a certain character, may be tested and corrected.

The further development of perceptual consciousness is *perceptual assurance*. This leads our primary acceptance through additional perceptual acts to a settled conviction of the existence and nature of the material thing that first gave rise to sense-data. With succeeding acts of perception the mode of reception is no mere acceptance, as with the first. Conditioned by the first sensing, it is now a *progressive confirmation* of the thinghood of what is sensed, a continual further specification of previously unspecified detail and addition of other parts not at first sensed. For we take the initial sense-datum as confirmable by other obtainable sense-data, which will fit together in a unified, enduring something that is spatially complete and has causal characteristics. As further acts of perception provide such confirmations, the existence of the thing and the specifications of its nature become settled rational beliefs. (Those cases with some confirmation but in which the way to adequate confirmation is blocked may be said to bring *perceptual confidence*, our ordinary state regarding most things.)

Price carries out a subtle and complex analysis of the relation of sense-data to one another. From the separate sense-data of sense-fields, as both change, we gain our beliefs in the existence of individual things. The theory that sense-data which resemble one another comprise a class, and that the thing is simply the class of resembling data, is inadequate since many of the data of an individual thing do not resemble one another in any sensible way. A better theory is that of gradual transition, which accounts not only for the changing of sense-data with motion of the observer, but also for distorted data (as in perspective viewing) as well as for changing qualities (while, it is assumed, the thing itself does not change). According to this view, the whole group of changing data gathered as we move about a thing to get further specification of it, "belong to" the particular thing. But shapes, sense-data apprehended as spatial, must be related not only geometrically but also *locally*. We need an account of the manner in which sense-data "fit together" to form a solid. Price calls data which thus fit together *constructible*.

Price cites certain empirical facts. While optical theory has not recognized it, vision has two types of stereoscopy, *perfect* and *imperfect*. The familiar sort associated with perspective seeing is the imperfect; it allows us to construct solid objects from its data, but incompletely. Immediately before the eyes there is a range of depth in which the usual perspective effects are reversed—the parallel edges of a matchbox when held against the nose seem closer together at the nearer rather than farther end. Between this nearest range and the outer one, there is a range of perfect stereoscopy, in which the visual sense-data of any object small enough to lie within it *actually do coincide*, approximately, with the surfaces of the particular thing. In this range, things are seen without distortion. The rectangular sides of the matchbox are seen as rectangular, not trapezoidal, even though the three sides seen at once are facing in quite different directions.

These facts allow Price to conclude that the thing seen within the range of perfect stereoscopy is seen virtually as it is ("as it really is," in common language). The solid perceptually constructed in this range is constructed from *perfectly constructible sense-data*. He calls it a *nuclear solid*. Around it we can arrange all constructible sense-data, in order from the least deviation to the greatest. The variations in perspective order will form a *perspectival distortion series*, and those varying concomitantly with that series from greatest to least specification will form a *differentiation series*. The members limiting these series at the position of the nuclear solid are their *nuclear members*. The nuclear solid provides the ground for uniting both continua, and indeed the continua of all sense-data both of spatial and nonspatial senses. The nuclear members with respect to a single sense are standard forms—the nuclear visual sense-datum, for example, gives the *standard figure* and *standard color*. The nuclear solid constructed from the perspectival distortion series, emended by the best presentation (that with most specific detail) of the differentiation series, gives us the *standard solid*. The collection of all sense-data unified by a standard solid is a *family of sense-data*.

To establish the validity of the construction of material things from sense-data, Price cites three propositions that seem obviously true, although he cannot imagine a way to prove them. First, some sense-fields are not momentary, but have a finite duration; second, some two sense-fields must be continuous, rather than discrete, in time and quality; and third, two successive sense-fields sometimes overlap in time—have a part of their durations in common. These are the logical requirements of three-dimensional construction. If granted that they actually occur, then, given two sense-fields, one containing a pair of sense-data AB and the other containing a pair BC, each pair sensibly adjoining and also arranged in a spatial relation R (such as "to the right of"), we can know that A and C are also related by relation R. This *method of progressive adjunction* is our validation of the "beyond"—the existence of unseen surfaces.

It is easily seen that the nonnuclear data do not exist in space. The tabletop which is narrower at the far end exists in sense only, as a member of the family of sense-data of the table, not as a constituent of the standard solid of the table. The nuclear sense-data are not parts or surfaces of the standard solid, but may be said to *coincide* with it. Position in physical space is not a characteristic of a single sense-datum, but rather a *collective* characteristic of a whole group of sense-data constituting a standard solid.

A family of sense-data perhaps should not be said to *exist* in time and undergo change, but to *prolong* itself through time and differ through time. The point of view of the observer, and its motion, are definable in terms of the space of standard solids. Obtainable sense-data are definable in terms of changes of the observer's point of view.

So far, it might seem that the theory of perception Price has offered is an elaborated phenomenalism, identifying a material thing with the family of sense-data. He shows, however, that this is not his theory. A material thing *physically*, as well as sensibly, occupies a space. By this we mean that it manifests in that space certain *causal* characteristics, most notably that of impenetrability. When a chestnut drops on a stone and bounces away, it is a causal characteristic of the stone, not a sense-characteristic, that has acted on the chestnut. An obtainable sense-datum, on the other hand, is not an existent particular, but a fact of the form "If any observer were at such and such a point of view, such and such a sense-datum would exist." Since an individual observer can occupy only one point of view at a time, he can realize only one of the alternatively obtainable sense-data at a time. The family of sense-data thus has a peculiar mode of existence, as a collection of actual sense-data, plus an infinite number of obtainable sense-data existing as contemporary alternatives, centering on a standard solid. This is not the kind of entity to which causal characteristics may belong. Further, in many instances, a family of sense-data is manifested in only one part of a region when a causal characteristic is being manifested in many parts of that region. Again, causes continue to be manifested during times when no sense-data are obtained. There is no necessary concomitance of caused events with sense-data, though there is concomitance among sense-data themselves. Accordingly, the causative physical occupant and the family of sense-data are not identical, and phenomenalism is false.

Now we see that for a sense-datum *s* to belong to a certain material thing M, first *s* must be a member of a family of sense-data prolonging itself through time and centering in a standard solid having a certain place in the system of standard solids; and second, that the place must be physically occupied—causal characteristics must be manifested there. This is Price's theory, the Collective Delimitation Theory. It stresses that the primary relation of "belonging to" is between an entire family and a material thing, the relation of a single sense-datum to the thing being derivative; moreover, that the family is related to the material thing by coinciding with the physically occupative portion of the thing.

Probably we get our first hint of the relation of causation to sense-data by observing other people's changed behavior in the face of certain evident changes in their environment. More important is the influence of the fact of our having several senses. By reflection on the data of one, we discern how the data of another sense originate. Concomitant changes in our tactual sense-data, for example, with the introduction of objects of the visual field to the skin, are a source of knowledge. The *complete thing* is the physically occupative thing with causal properties plus the family of sense-data. A changing complete thing is not the cause of changes in our sense-data, for the data are part of the thing. But a change in the thing *as physical occupant* of space may entail changes in the sense-data that depend upon the presence both of it and its observer. The laws of sense-data are of a different order from ordinary causal laws. We can define a given type of physical occupant only by reference to the kind of family of sense-data it is coincident with and to all those foreign ones whose mode of prolongation it influences. But of the intrinsic qualities of physical occupants, we have no knowledge at all.

Price's *Perception* perhaps represents our farthest point of advance in its area. Whether his position is adopted, his close study of the problems and his careful solutions have much that is useful. For the introspective part of his procedure, Price asks of us only the accordance with our own experience, a reasonable enough request. And he seems to begin with the perhaps intuitive preconceptions which have made us suspicious of some of the stranger theories of perception, and to exhibit and justify these conceptions. Finally, Price's convincing exposition of the differences between the separately certifiable orders, sense-data and the manifestations of causality, seems by correcting the "emptiness" of phenomenalism to be a considerable contribution.—*J. T. G.*

PERTINENT LITERATURE

Hirst, R. J. "The Difference Between Sensing and Observing," in *The Philosophy of Perception*. Edited by G. J. Warnock. London: Oxford University Press, 1967.

The Philosophy of Perception is a very useful collection of articles on the problem of perception, containing articles by O. K. Bouwsma, R. J. Hirst, Richard Wollheim, Anthony Quinton, H. P. Grice, Alan R. White, and F. N. Sibley. The volume also contains an introduction by G. J. Warnock, the editor, and a bibliography of works on perception other than those dealt with in the articles.

Hirst (Professor of Logic, Glasgow University) in "The Difference Between Sensing and Observing" describes H. H. Price's *Perception* as a version of the "classical theory of sense-data." Hirst follows Price in adopting the terminology "perceptually conscious of a book" to use in cases when one does not intend to suggest that the mode of consciousness consisting in (presumably) being aware of a book entails the presence of a book of which one is aware. The terms "perceive" and "observe" are used by Hirst to imply sense awareness and also the existence of the physical object that one perceives or observes. His article is concerned with the difference between "sensing" and "observing."

According to Hirst's understanding of Price's *Perception*, Price would distinguish sensing from observing by making reference to sense-data ("colour patches, sounds, smells, etc.," as Hirst puts it) of which one is directly aware. When one is merely aware of sense-data, one is merely sensing; but when, in addition to being aware of sense-data, one presupposes or rationally believes that there is a material object which one senses, then one "perceives" or "observes."

For Price, Hirst maintains, sensing is fundamental and is regarded as a form of knowing having as its essential features immediacy and certainty. (One may be uncertain that it is a tomato one is observing; one may even doubt that a physical object that one is observing is present; but under certain circumstances one cannot doubt, for one knows immediately and with certainty "that there exists a red patch of a round and somewhat bulgy shape . . . ," as Price describes the kind of sense-datum involved.) Hirst contends that Price's analysis is not the only analysis possible and that there are more plausible analyses that avoid the difficulties of Price's theory of perception.

The first difficulty in Price's theory, according to Hirst, is that introspection during such an experience (as that involved in being aware of the round, red, bulgy sense-datum) reveals nothing about the *existence* of an *object* of which one is aware. *Apparently* one is aware of a "red existent" under such circumstances; but one cannot be certain that there is an existent that is red and of which one is aware, Hirst points out. It is possible, he suggests, that the experience that Price presumes to be the experience of a sense-datum can be understood "adverbially"—that is, that one is sensing "redly."

The second difficulty is that it is not at all evident that the kind of experience one has when actually perceiving something could be identical in kind, as experience, to the experience of hallucinating. The third difficulty with Price's theory, according to Hirst, is that the contention that the "red patch" is an existent, a private red particular, is to go beyond what experience reveals and to hypostatize the "look."

Hirst charges Price with a kind of circularity in argument. Price argues that since physical objects may not have the color they appear to have, there must be something, namely a sense-datum, that does have the color of which one is aware. But Hirst argues that one cannot legitimately deduce from the fact that something red exists that the "something" is a sense-datum possessed of privacy, transitoriness, and lack of causal properties. Only on the assumption of the theory Price advocates could one conclude any such thing.

Hirst argues that the having of hallucinations is not a case of "sensing sense-data." Such an experience is not a case of observing; it is more akin to dreaming or imagining. Analogously, in the having of after-images one is not observing sense-data but undergoing the after-effects of certain perceptions. Nor, Hirst argues further, does one have to posit sense-data to account for illusions or to explain how it is that a penny looked at partly from the side looks elliptical. A penny looked at obliquely *looks* elliptical; one does not have to presume that there is an elliptical existent, private and transitory.

Objects often look different from what they are, Hirst maintains, but when they do it is simply because the observer's view is affected by distance or interference or because there is something wrong with his sense organs. To presume, as Price does, that one is always incorrigibly aware of sense-data requires that in cases of the various kinds discussed "a host of unnecessary existents," each incorrigibly sensed, succeed one another (as the view improves, for example, the organs are corrected).

Price is faced with the further difficulty of having to account for the fact that a change in attention reveals information not previously secured. If sense-data are incorrigibly sensed, then how is it possible to err or to miss something? If, on the other hand, one attempts to explain the results of a change in attention by maintaining that the object of attention changes, the explanation is implausible. Consequently, Hirst rejects Price's attempt to explain sensing by reference to sense-data: sensing is neither the awareness of a private object, nor a purely adverbial experience, nor something that can simply be explained alternatively by the use of a "sense-data" language having no theoretical implications.

Hirst's own account of sensing is that it is "a postulated constant element within observing," while observing involves the interpretation and adjustment of sensing. Sensing is basic but it cannot be divorced from the awareness of public objects.

Grice, H. P. "The Causal Theory of Perception (1)," in *The Philosophy of Perception*. Edited by G. J. Warnock. London: Oxford University Press, 1967.

H. P. Grice, Fellow of New College, Oxford, attempts in "The Causal Theory of Perception" to construct the outlines of a plausible causal theory. He points out that causal theories of perception have received little attention for quite some time, perhaps because it has been supposed that such a theory involves the assumption or consequence that material objects are unobservable. Grice regards such an interpretation of the CTP (as he calls the "causal theory of perception") unfair or unsympathetic.

A theory counts as a causal theory of perception, Grice contends, only when the theory in elucidating perception makes some reference to the material object perceived as having some role in the "causal ancestry" of the perception (or sense-impression or sense-datum). It is not enough simply to believe that there is some causal process involved in perception, and it is not the task of a CTP to redefine perceptual terms so as to devise an ideal or scientific language; nor should the effort to construct an elucidatory CTP be confused with the attempt to explain causal properties of material objects.

Grice then refers to H. H. Price's *Perception* as offering a formulation of the CTP in which the effort is made to explain the causal role of the material object. As Grice represents Price's position, Price holds that "*M* [a material object] is present to my senses" is equivalent to "*M* causes a sense-datum with which I am acquainted" and consequently that perceptual consciousness is an inference from effect to cause. (Grice explains that Price uses the expression "present to my senses" as indicative of one of the senses of "perceived by me.") Grice concentrates on the claim that "perceiving a material object involves having or sensing a sense-datum," noting that unless this proposition can be defended there is no point in discussing other features of the CTP.

Grice considers at some length criticism directed against the effort to understand the use of the term "sense-datum" by the use of some such locution as "So-and-so looks (for example, blue) to me." The criticism is that there is no sense in saying "looks to me" unless there is some doubt or denial that calls a description into question. Grice argues that if one were to say, while looking in clear daylight at a red firebox, "It looks red to me," what is said might be misleading or boring, but literallly true. Such a statement, used for the purpose for which it *is* used, would be very important, perhaps in part because it is misleading (in that there is no doubt or denial).

Grice concludes his lengthy discussion of possible objections to the use of such locutions as "It looks _____to me" in explicating perception by contending that the objections do not survive careful analysis and that such locutions are likely to be useful in explaining the notion of a sense-datum. He suggests, however, that the term "sense-datum" be restricted to such "classificatory labels" as "sense-datum sentence." (For brevity's sake, however, Grice uses the term sense-datum as a noun.) The author suggests that his interpretation of what is involved in perception and in the use of "looks _____to me" locutions makes possible an acceptable version of the theory that perceiving involves having a sense-datum ("involves its being the case that some sense-datum statement or other about the percipient is true").

Grice then undertakes an inquiry to decide whether it is a necessary or sufficient condition of the perception of a material object that the perceiver's sense-impression be causally dependent on some state of affairs involving the material object. Such a condition certainly appears to be a necessary condition: if a sense-impression is not causally related to a material object, no such object could correctly be regarded as having been perceived by way of that impression.

Grice argues that for the causal condition to be accepted as a sufficient condition of perception, the kind of causal connection involved must be made clear. The only satisfactory way of making such a connection clear is by the use of examples, for any explanation that involves the kind of technical analysis a specialist (in light waves and vision) might offer would not elucidate the ordinary notion of perceiving. Grice then proceeds to reject the suggestion that the CTP involves the claim that material objects are unobservable. Such a claim is either false or, if true, true in a sense that makes it acceptable but does not make it run counter to the conventional notion that material objects are observed.

The proposal Grice makes in his conclusion (as taking off from but not necessarily staying within the spirit of Price's theory of perception) is that a person perceives a material object if and only if some present-tense sense-datum statement is true as reporting what the material object is causally responsible for. The justification of such a claim is by way of showing that one must assume the material object if what the sense-data statements report is to be accounted for.—*I.P.M.*

ADDITIONAL RECOMMENDED READING

Armstrong, D. M. *Perception and the Physical World*. New York: Humanities Press, 1961. A defense of Direct Realism. Involves some discussion of Price's descriptions of sense-data.

Chisholm, Roderick. *Perceiving: A Philosophical Study*. London: Oxford University Press, 1957. A brilliant analysis, well worth reading for its sensitive exploration of linguistic pitfalls involved in the effort to describe and explain perception. A number of references to Price are made along the way.

Hirst, R. J. *The Problems of Perception*. New York: Macmillan Publishing Company, 1959. A book-length statement of Hirst's position.

Price, H. H. *Belief*. New York: Humanities Press, 1969. Price's Gifford Lectures, delivered at the University of Aberdeen in 1960 but subsequently extensively revised for publication. Lecture 4 is concerned with belief and perceptual evidence.

White, Alan. "The Causal Theory of Perception (2)," in *The Philosophy of Perception*. Edited by G. J. Warnock. London: Oxford University Press, 1967. A lively and well-considered response to Grice's paper discussed above.

AN IDEALIST VIEW OF LIFE

Author: Sarvepalli Radhakrishnan (1888-1975)
Type of work: Ethics, metaphysics
First published: 1932

PRINCIPAL IDEAS ADVANCED

The ideal world, which alone is real, lies beyond the phenomenal world of appearance, yet dominates it; the center of the universe is the transcendent, the Absolute, Brahma.

Intuition is the way to an integral apprehension of ultimate reality; it is a knowledge by identity which transcends the distinction between subject and object.

Scientific certainty is not the only kind of certainty available to men; but in considering the mystical revelation as a source of certainty, one must distinguish between the content of the experience and the interpretation of it, for interpretation is historically conditioned and liable to error.

The scientific view of the inorganic world and of life and mind is more compatible with idealism than with naturalism.

An Idealist View of Life has a marked mystical foundation in theory of knowledge. In this regard, it may be said to express the main Hindu tradition in philosophy. This is one reason for its importance. The other is the author's familiarity with Western philosophy and science. Though his general standpoint guides him, there is no turning away from crucial problems.

Sarvepalli Radhakrishnan recognizes that the term idealism needs definition. It is clear that he is not a subjective idealist of the mode of the early Berkeley. Nor does he much concern himself with Hegelian rationalistic idealism. Rather, his emphasis is on the relation of value to reality. The truly real is replete with value. The alignment is with the *Upanishads* in India and the outlook of the Platonists, especially that of Plotinus, the father of the Western tradition of mysticism.

As suggested, the book is peculiarly interesting because it does reflect the meeting of the East and the West along these lines. The broad sweep of Radhakrishnan's thought brings together Hindu classic thinkers with Plato and Aristotle, and with the Anglo-American idealists, Bradley and Royce. As one might expect, less attention is paid to Western naturalism and realism. That is both the strength and the weakness of the book. It stands out as an excellent example of its perspective. And it does have scope and verve.

The general argument is to the effect that the ideal world, which alone is real, lies beyond the phenomenal one of appearance yet is tied in with it and dominates it. Spirit is working in matter that matter may serve spirit. In a sense, matter is an abstraction and not a concrete reality, such as spirit. That is why materialism can be absorbed and transcended. It is doubtful whether Western materialists would accept this thesis; but it goes quite logically with the author's outlook. For him, the center of the universe is the transcendent, the Absolute, Brahma, that which has *aseity*, being. But, despite this assurance—rather, because of it—he is sympathetic with other points of view because they have their partial truth.

The first of the eight lectures concerns itself with the modern challenge to the religious outlook on the universe as a result of scientific and social thought. Here the author confronts Freud, John B. Watson, and Émile Durkheim. The second lecture notes contemporary movements such as humanism, naturalism, and logical positivism. These are tied in with science. In all this, the author is frank and well informed. He is not trying to defend specific orthodoxies. Like the Buddhist, he has no tradition of particular doctrines in geology and biology. Science is to be accepted but has its limits. It is fascinating to note how he draws the line.

It is in the third lecture that Radhakrishnan states the basic claims of the religious consciousness, especially at the mystical level. Here we have the introduction of *intuition* as a way of knowledge other than that of sense perception or discursive conception. He puts forward the claim for an integral apprehension of ultimate reality. It is a knowledge by identity which transcends the distinction between subject and object. Here, of course, is where dispute arises. Those who do not have the mystical vision are likely to deny its significance.

In the fourth lecture, Radhakrishnan develops the idea that scientific certainty is not the only kind of certainty available to us. A query may, of course, be raised as to the scientific claim which is usually more modestly put as an affair of working hypotheses. But the author is ready to admit that, in the mystical revelation, we must distinguish between the kernel of it and the interpretation given, which is historically conditioned. Thus Hindu, Moslem, and Christian mystics have different accounts of the meanings of their experiences.

The fifth lecture takes up the nonconceptual, intuitive, imaginative, and affective ingredients of morality, art, and religion. The element of creativity is noted with reports from mathematicians, scientists, and poets. Just how do new ideas arise? What part does the subconscious play? It is generally agreed that there must be preparation. It takes a trained mathematician to have relevant ideas and to solve mathematical problems. There is a big literature on this question and Radhakrishnan is familiar with it. He is at home in aesthetics and art and quotes freely from Croce, Dante, Keats, Shakespeare, and Browning. The stress, it is to be noted, is on creativity. The suggestion is that this is something higher in nature than perception and conceptual reasoning. Does it link up with his third kind of knowledge?

The sixth and seventh lectures are devoted to a brief formulation of the scientific view of the inorganic world, of life, and of mind. It was written in an era in which Eddington and Jeans were the avowed spokesmen of science. A semi-idealistic, semi-agnostic note was in the air. Relativity and quantum mechanics were transforming science away from Newtonian mechanics. Scientists were finding the world a more subtle and complex sort of thing than had been supposed earlier. The question at issue was whether naturalism could do justice to this development or whether it implied idealism. If these are the alternatives, there is no question as to which side Radhakrishnan adopts. He sees the development as favoring idealism. And it is well to have this alignment so beautifully carried out.

In the eighth, and last, lecture, the turn comes for metaphysics and its basis in an integral intuition of ultimate reality. Here we have an excellent example of transcendental metaphysics, something to which the logical positivist is so opposed with his insistence that sensory verification is essential for the meaningfulness of empirical statements. It is clear that much depends upon the certainty and value of the mystical experience. It is upon this foundation that Radhakrishnan builds. Nothing could be more desirable than such a confrontation.

Let us now go over the movement of Radhakrishnan's argument in more detail to bring out its scope and its point. Even a person who remains skeptical of the mystical insight will be impressed by the idealism to which it leads. Though Nehru is more of an agnostic, one can note in him something of the same elevation of spirit.

The essential thing, Radhakrishnan argues, is to know what the problem is. Freud's queries help to bring this home. Is religion an illusion? That there have been illusory ingredients is undeniable. Popular religion has been too anthropomorphic and has laid too much stress on special providences. On the other hand, Newtonian rationalism led to deism and the absentee God. But of what use is an absentee God? Surely, that is not the sort of God the religious consciousness requires.

The influential feature of science has been its attack on parochialism and narrow ideas. Watson's behaviorism, for instance, has forced us to think more clearly about mind. These challenges must be met. For instance, the French school of sociology represented by Durkheim stresses the pressure of society but does not do justice to personality and self-consciousness. Again, the study of comparative religions should have the effect of enlarging our horizon. The so-called higher criticism of the Scriptures ought to have the same effect. Such a critical attitude is fairly common among thoughtful Hindus and Buddhists. And it is doubtful that the traditional proofs for theism are convincing. Radhakrishnan stresses an internal religious approach. It would appear that he regards the materialistic atmosphere of technology as the greatest enemy. It is not the mastery of nature as such that is at fault but the industrial and utilitarian climate.

The result of this frank approach is the contention that nothing can be true by faith if it is not true by reason. But then reason must not be taken as limited to deduction from fixed premises. Radhakrishnan believes in a source of insight of a higher order.

But what are the substitutes for religion offered these days? One is an atheistic naturalism. It appears that Radhakrishnan has in mind Russell's early protest against a supposedly alien nature composed of blind atoms ruled by mechanical laws. This would be, in effect, a malign nature which might well be defied. Such an outlook would represent a mixture of naturalism, stoicism, and paganism. The stoicism reflects man's innate dignity.

Humanism is an old tradition which goes back to the Greeks with their doctrine of inner harmony and to the Romans with their sense of decorum. There are elements of it in Chinese thought and in Kant. Such humanism tends to be religion secularized and separated from a larger reality. It lacks *élan*. It sets up boundaries. It is these boundaries which religion oversteps. On the other hand, it cannot be denied that humanism is humanitarian and stresses social reform.

Pragmatism is more an American development which emphasizes will and practice. It is a protest against the separation of knowledge and active planning.

Modernism, on the other hand, is a halfway house. It seeks to revise religious tradition. It is confronted by the revival of authoritarianism. This regards itself as an escape from anarchy. But loyalty to tradition should not involve bondage to it. There is often a secret skepticism in authoritarianism.

All these movements seem to Radhakrishnan to lack something of the spiritual. There is a lack of profundity. What is needed is a synoptic vision.

We come now to the positive position. Religious experience is factual in its own right. Philosophy of religion explores this domain and differs from dogmatic theology. For religion is not a form of knowledge. It is more akin to feeling. It is inward and personal. It is the response of the whole man in an integral way to reality. It expresses an incurable discontent with the finite and seeks the transcendent.

It is now that the Hindu tradition comes to the front, though it is soon connected with the mystical note in the West. The Vedic seers stressed the eternal and sought to raise themselves to this plane. In this respect, Plato, Augustine, and Dante are examples of the same direction. Can this massive evidence be illusory? But it involves a higher kind of knowledge or insight. That is the problem for philosophy of religion. The justification of this claim is taken up in the conclusion. This constitutes the debate with scientific empiricism and naturalism.

One must be very careful here, Radhakrishnan warns us. There is danger in a purely negative approach. It is so hard to translate the mystical experience. Its note is timelessness and unity. When we use language to bring out the contrast, we call this ultimate reality the Absolute. The term "God" is of the nature of a symbol.

There goes with the experience a sense of harmony and unity. Self-mastery is involved. From this flows idealism and denial of what is selfish. The danger in this concentration is, perhaps, disregard of social ties. This should be guarded against.

If all knowledge were of the scientific type, as some empiricists hold, then the challenge to the religious outlook on the world could hardly be met. Hence comes the importance of the question of intuitive knowledge, something which cannot be expressed in propositions, yet is justifiable. It is well to recall that sense qualities are confused and that logic and mathematics are essentially analytic and do not give us factual information.

In Hindu thought, in Plotinus, in Bergson, there is emphasis upon direct intuition. The facts of telepathy, for example, prove that one mind can directly be aware of another's thoughts. It would seem that intuition is the extension of a sort of perception beyond the senses. Bergson sets limits to the intellect. He thinks it useful rather than true. Hegel criticizes immediacy and tends to ignore the importance of feeling and will. Yet he is opposed to the abstractions of the understanding. But is not the unity of nature coordinate with the unity of the self? Kant emphasized the "I think" at the phenomenal level and believed in a noumenal world beyond. Faith and spiritual experience make their demands. It is well to look at the creative spirit in man.

Scientific discovery is more like intuition than people ordinarily realize. Henri Poincaré's account of mathematical imagination is a case in point. There is something creative about it. We prove deductively but invent by intuition. There is here a kind of integrative passivity. Michael Faraday is another case of unpredictable invention. The whole self is involved. When philosophers devote themselves to abstruse analysis, this creative factor may escape them.

If we turn from science to poetry and the plastic arts, intuition stands out even more clearly. The poet feels himself to be inspired. This should not be taken too literally, yet it has meaning. There is emotional value and this has significance. It would seem that Croce connects intuition and expression too closely. There must be room for communication. It is well to recall the testimony of Plato and Carlyle. Emotional intensity goes with a sense of deep insight. Too much modern literature tends to be trivial and to avoid the agonies of spirit. Has it given us one genuine epic?

Creativity is a path to discovery and is to be connected with knowledge. It involves understanding of life and brings us into accord with it. It is true that Juliet dies, but only after making us realize the greatness of love.

If we turn to ethics, Radhakrishnan maintains, we find something similar. The moral hero, or saint, tends to be somewhat antinomian. He does not keep to conventions. It is because of this that moral heroes can make fools of themselves in the eyes of the world.

Modern science stresses abstraction and statistics. For Eddington and Jeans, matter tends to be reduced to thought. In terms of relativity and quantum mechanics, it is a term for a cluster of events possessing habits and potencies. The traditional idea of substance is in abeyance. There is a touch here of the Hindu notions of Samsara. All is becoming. There is another respect in which science suggests idealism. What we know is the effect things produce in us; all is experience and possible experience. This is the idealistic note.

If we turn to life, we find it to be of the nature of a dynamic equilibrium. The theory of evolution developed from Georges de Buffon and Chevalier de Lamarck to Darwin and is still subject to improvement. Natural selection is a sifting process. Herbert Spencer made it too quickly into a philosophy.

Mind is under study in comparative psychology. The nature of nervous integration is under study. Pavlov and Watson were pioneers, but we now have *Gestalt* principles opposed to purely mechanical notions.

Radhakrishnan then turns to human personality. Atomistic psychology is obsolete. The person is a unity and more than the sum of his parts. He is an organized whole. We must give up the notion of a changeless soul. The self is a growth constantly interacting with its environment.

And now we come to the term "subject." William James and James Ward differed in their views on this topic. James thought of it as the passing thought. This concept seems inadequate; there must be something more enduring. The subject, by its very nature, cannot be an object. Why not hold it to be one with the simple, universal spirit? Here we are beyond the lower order of existence and are confronted by such problems as those of freedom and *karma*. Eastern and Western thought have long pondered these problems. It seems to Radhakrishnan that mere predestination is unethical. Freedom is not a matter of caprice nor is *karma* mere necessity. Suppose we take freedom to be a term for self-determination. It is the whole self that is involved in choice. The will is the active side of the self. It is not something in itself. *Karma* means, literally, action or deed. It is the principle of causal continuity. Thus, it is not opposed to creative freedom, unless one takes causality to demand mere identity or repetition.

There is a good side to the idea of *karma* which is not always recognized. It involves sympathy. People may be more unfortunate than wicked. There is tragedy in the world.

While there is a demand for a future life and personal immortality, people hardly know what they want. There are those who hold that immortality is a prize to be won. This is called conditional immortality. But the idea seems to favor the more fortunate and to be semi-aristocratic in motivation. It is certain that the modern mind cannot accept the idea of endless punishment which is not justified by improvement as a goal. Surely, no being is wholly evil. The Hindu idea of rebirth has its biological difficulties but these are not insurmountable. There would need to be some kind of selectivity.

All this leads up to the speculative climax of Radhakrishnan's argument. How are we to envisage ultimate reality? Radhakrishnan summarizes the results of his survey of the world. The world is an ordered whole; everything is an organization with its mode of connection. There is a development in the direction of greater union with surroundings. Nature is a domain of becoming without fixity. Yet these changes are not meaningless. Evolution goes with progress on the whole. And, lastly, the highest kind of experiences and personalities seem to indicate a goal of being.

These principles are opposed to traditional naturalism. It did not have a sufficient place for time. Radhakrishnan aligns himself in some measure with holism and Lloyd Morgan's emergent evolution. But, it would seem, he is most in sympathy with Whitehead's Platonism, with its primordial God and Consequent God. God is the home of universals, of possibilities, and of ideal harmony.

The Eastern note in the conclusion is interesting. The Absolute is also absolute freedom in activity. All else is dependent, created reality, *Maya*. One can speak symbolically of three sides of God's nature. In Hindu tradition, these are Brahma, Vishnu, and Siva. These must not be set apart.

It is clear that Radhakrishnan regards absolute idealism as representing the basis for a fusion of the Vedanta perspective in India and Western thought. It is debatable whether he has done justice to trends towards realism and analysis. But he would be the last to hold that human thought has finished its task. Probably the most intriguing element in his thought is his belief that mystical apprehension is a genuine form of knowledge, though it is evocative and does not lend itself to description. Here, he would hold, we are capable— a few of us at least—of contact with the absolute and the eternal.—*R. W. S.*

PERTINENT LITERATURE

Radhakrishnan, Sarvepalli. *Selected Writings on Philosophy, Religion, and Culture*. Edited by Robert A. McDermott. New York: E. P. Dutton, 1970.

Robert A. McDermott's anthology contains a representative selection of Sarvepalli Radhakrishnan's most important works in the areas of philosophy, religion, and culture. The selections are grouped under several headings, covering Radhakrishnan's ideas on such topics as the nature of Indian philosophy, the Hindu view of life, the East-West integration as personified by Rabindranath Tagore and Mahatma Gandhi, and the idealist philosophy drawn primarily from *Upanishadic* and *Vedāntic* sources. The anthology also contains McDermott's introduction of Radhakrishnan's ideas on all of the above topics. This review concentrates on the third part of the Introduction, which explains the main ideas and important presuppositions of Radhakrishnan's idealist philosophy, which finds its most creative expression in his *An Idealist View of Life*.

McDermott regards Radhakrishnan's epistemology as primarily a theory of intuition. Indian philosophy, according to Radhakrishnan, emphasizes intuitive experience, and in this respect it is unlike Western philosophy, which has a decided preference for discursive knowledge. Radhakrishnan, in his *An Idealist View of Life*, emphasizes intuition, but he also sees the need for conceptual expression, because, through the latter, intuition finds its cognitive significance. Hence he observes, somewhat inconsistently according to McDermott, that even though intuitive knowledge transcends the bounds of mediated knowledge, intuition and intellect are complementary. McDermott believes that Radhakrishnan's position would be more plausible if he explained more clearly the precise relation between intuitive experience and conceptual expression. However, McDermott notes that Radhakrishnan does spell out his general position, which is that intuitive knowledge can never adequately be expressed in conceptual terms, even though the latter is the only means of its expression.

In *An Idealist View of Life*, Radhakrishnan envisions the philosopher as living an integrated life of intuition and intellect. Such a philosopher's pursuit of truth should not be just an intellectual quest; rather, he should respond with his whole personality to the reality he encounters. Reality can be expressed, within limit, through myths and images, literature and art, and especially through the deep and rich lives of those integrated seers who partake in it spiritually and express it philosophically.

For Radhakrishnan, the real is the ideal which lies beyond the phenomenal and which finds its philosophical expression in the *Upanishads* and the *Vedānta*. McDermott thinks that such a conception of the levels of reality, including the phenomenal world of appearance and the ideal world of Brahman, has strong parallels in Plato. However, in the Advaitic tradition, unlike in Plato's philosophy, the world of appearance is explained away as a mystery which is due to *Maya*. But Radhakrishnan, through his own interpretation of the *Maya* doctrine, aims to give the world a more positive status than is accorded in the tradition.

Similarly, Radhakrishnan's interpretation of the Advaitic doctrine of *karma*, in *An Idealist View of Life*, attempts to reconcile *karma* with his own vision of history as creative evolution and man as the agent of his own destiny. The principle of *karma* gives man a continuity with the past and a possibility for the future. When man overcomes his *karmic* bondage through the practice of selflessness, he thereby helps enhance the collective situation of all mankind, because, as Radhakrishnan understands the Advaitic belief, a man is not saved until he regards other people's salvation as his own. Consequently, Radhakrishnan's interpretation of the *karma* doctrine provides a tie between individual spiritual advances and universal spiritual regeneration.

Raju, P. T. *Idealistic Thought of India*. Cambridge, Massachusetts: Harvard

University Press, 1953.

P. T. Raju thinks that idealism is particularly representative of the traditional Indian ways of thinking and living. Speculative Indian thought began with the *Upanishads*, which were mostly idealistic; later on, during its highest development, Indian philosophy remained idealistic. Raju's book studies the historical as well as the logical development of the systems of Indian idealistic metaphysics and, toward the end, contains two chapters on some contemporary idealistic Indian philosophers. Sarvepalli Radhakrishnan is one of them.

Raju states that Radhakrishnan understands the spirit of both the Eastern and the Western philosophies in a manner which very few scholars do. Through his various writings which attempt an East-West synthesis, Radhakrishnan strives to show that the spirit of man is essentially the same even though outlooks may vary. As an original interpreter of traditional Indian wisdom to Westerners, Radhakrishnan has, besides showing Westerners a new approach to philosophical problems, revealed to Indian thinkers new significance in their own ancient philosophies. In Raju's judgment, Radhakrishnan's *An Idealist View of Life* illustrates well the depth and originality with which he undertakes his task.

Even though Radhakrishnan is an Advaitic idealist in his philosophical outlook, he occasionally takes issue with S'añkara, the founder of the Advaita school of *Vedānta*. The latter takes God to be an unreal appearance of the Absolute, whereas Radhakrishnan, through his doctrine of intuition, tries to relate God to the Absolute in more positive terms. For Radhakrishnan, even though intuition transcends intellect, intellect is needed for its expression. In this sense he regards intuition and intellect as complementary to each other, one revealing the Absolute and the other translating it into the language of understanding. However, Radhakrishnan believes that to be able to understand the translation which, within its own discursive limitation, purports to express the Absolute, one must already have some direct apprehension of the truth.

For Radhakrishnan, the Absolute and God are related to each other in the same way as intuition and intellect are. The truth of intuition is the Absolute Brahman, whereas the ultimate object of intellect is God, who, in reality, is the same as the Absolute. Their apparent differences are, therefore, complementary.

Radhakrishnan cautions that even though intuition is nonconceptual, it is not nonrational. Because intuition is the response of the whole man to reality, it must also include reason. Were it not so, intuition could not have been immanent in the very nature of our thinking and be the basis of our thought. Self-consciousness is the highest intuition; at the same time, it is also the basis of all other conscious activities, including conceptualization.

In the same way that he relates the Absolute to God, Radhakrishnan also shows how the world and the Absolute are related. He thinks, not without justification according to Raju, that S'aṅkara's own writings contain passages which show a positive relation between the world and Brahman, but S'aṅkara's interpreters in the Advaita tradition have generally emphasized the unreality of the world and have explained the relation between the world and Brahman as a mystery (*Maya*). According to Radhakrishnan, we have to suspend our judgment regarding the reality of the world because our knowledge of the world is attained through the help of intellect, which cannot truly reveal the real. The real is known through the transcendental knowledge of intuition. However, just as intuition is the basis of thought, similarly, for Radhakrishnan, the finite world is presupposed by the infinite. In fact, according to him, the world is one of the infinite number of possibilities actualized. From our empirical point of view, the world is actual; but, in view of the fact that discursive understanding cannot reveal the real, the world as it appears to our understanding cannot be real. However, it is not unreal either, for anything that is actual is not unreal.

Datta, D. M. "Radhakrishnan and Comparative Philosophy," in *The Philosophy of Sarvepalli Radhakrishnan* (The Library of Living Philosophers). Edited by Paul A. Schilpp. New York: Tudor Publishing Company, 1952, pp. 659-685.

D. M. Datta thinks that in the area of comparative philosophy, which he considers to be still a relatively new field in philosophy, Sarvepalli Radhakrishnan is a bright star. The task of comparative philosophy is to study, understand, and integrate philosophies of all cultures and traditions, ancient as well as modern. This ideal also happens to be a great need in today's world, which cannot survive without a global consciousness based on mutual understanding and appreciation. Radhakrishnan's writings over the last few decades have helped to bring the East and the West closer by demonstrating the sameness of human spirit regardless of the difference in outlooks.

Radhakrishnan believes that persons or nations on their march forward cannot ignore the traditions in which they are rooted. Each tradition needs to be molded to suit human need and to keep pace with time, yet progress and tradition need not be at odds with each other. This same spirit is reflected in all of Radhakrishnan's writings. He bases his philosophy on the traditional Indian idealism of the *Upanishads* and the *Vedānta*; yet, through reinterpretation and change of emphasis, he helps the tradition to evolve into a modern system with a universal message. This philosophy is that of absolute idealism, which Radhakrishnan prefers to regard as a spiritual view of the world. In developing such a philosophy he has been profoundly influenced by the ideas of Western thinkers as well, most notably by Henri Bergson's dynamic and evolutionary world view and by his emphasis on intuition.

Datta distinguishes two broad periods in Radhakrishnan's philosophical career—one comprising his earlier writings, which mostly consist of scholarly, critical, and interpretative works in comparative and Indian philosophies, and the other culminating in a synthesis of scholarship and vision. Datta regards *An Idealist View of Life*, stemming from Radhakrishnan's Hibbert Lectures delivered at the Universities of London and Manchester in 1929, a major work of this second phase of philosophic development.

In *An Idealist View of Life*, Radhakrishnan not only attempts to trace the idealist trend in Indian and European philosophies but also tries to affirm idealism as the ultimate basis of all philosophy. He examines modern challenges and alternatives to the idealist or spiritual view of life and concludes that they will not be able to find answers to man's restlessness because, ultimately, man's dissatisfaction with himself is due to his failure to find meaning and value in his spirit. Man is presently externally oriented; however, the realization of the internal reality of the oneness of self with the Supreme is the basis for a life of the spirit. Such reality is revealed in intuition, which is the culmination of, rather than contrary to, intellect, and is the basis of all true religions. Radhakrishnan believes that only an integrated life of the spirit can save man from unrest.

In Datta's judgment, *An Idealist View of Life* is the first grand and constructive experiment in comparative philosophy because, along with solid scholarship and sympathetic understanding of various diverse traditions, it offers flexibility of structure and a universal vision. Unfortunately, the work may appear to be vague and discouragingly broad, especially to analytic philosophers, for these very same reasons. However, Datta thinks that Radhakrishnan's distinction between the relative spheres of intuition and intellect effectively answers such negative judgment. The importance of logical analysis in the realm of communication is not denied, but the role of intuition in the sphere of self-realization is emphasized. Moreover, Radhakrishnan himself admits that the world of the spirit can be better described through such devices as allegory, myth, and music than through precise statements. Finally, any constructive work in comparative philosophy, in Datta's judgment, must necessarily be broad because of its synthetic nature.

Radhakrishnan does not see himself as a prophet of a new age; rather, he considers himself to be just a philosopher presenting the very essence of idealism, which for him is the spirit. His original contribution lies in the way he depicts and relates the various modes of the spirit, which, in his system, are mainly the Absolute, the self, God, and matter.—*D.C.*

ADDITIONAL RECOMMENDED READING

McDermott, Robert A. and V. S. Naravane, eds. *The Spirit of Modern India: Writings in Philosophy, Religion, & Culture*. New York: Thomas Y. Crowell, 1974. Includes selections from Radhakrishnan's writings on ultimate reality, mysticism, and ethics, with the editors' introductory notes.

Naravane, V. S. *Modern Indian Thought*. Bombay: Asia Publishing House, 1964. Contains a chapter on Radhakrishnan's idealist philosophy.

Schilpp, Paul A., ed. *The Philosophy of Sarvepalli Radhakrishnan* (The Library of Living Philosophers). New York: Tudor Publishing Company, 1952. An authoritative volume on Radhakrishnan's philosophy, containing articles on various aspects of his philosophy by leading Indian and Western philosophers. Also includes a reply by Radhakrishnan to his critics.

Srivastava, R. P. *Contemporary Indian Idealism*. Delhi: Motilal Banarsidass, 1973. Includes a study of Radhakrishnan's idealist philosophy.

THE PHILOSOPHY OF PHYSICAL REALISM

Author: Roy Wood Sellars (1880-1973)
Type of work: Epistemology and metaphysics
First published: 1932

PRINCIPAL IDEAS ADVANCED

Human beings know external objects by being affected sensibly by them.

Be means of the organs of sense the brain is stimulated by objects in such a manner that particular sense-events occur.

The object is disclosed in the act of perception, and human knowledge is not mere inference but actual knowledge.

Only individual things are real; there are no universals.

Substance is a self-existent continuant which can enter into relations with other self-existents.

Consciousness is an emergent feature of a brain-mind process.

Values are understandable in terms of the power of things to become important to human beings.

Despite the fact that in the United States idealism has had a significant role to play in the development of American thought, the philosophy which confines reality to mind and its ideas has never been a direct expression of the American temperament. Pragmatism and realism, on the other hand, appear to be the intellectual equivalents of the frontier spirit, for they take the world as it presents itself, as a problem to be handled by plans of action put to the test. Although pragmatists and realists are not always happy in one another's company, they are alike in turning away from the habit of mind which, putting full faith in the use of reason, calls into question the existence of whatever is most tangible, most recalcitrant, most independent in the world of common sense and action.

It is customary to regard the American realists as innovators in epistemology, as philosophers who set out to show that to *know* is to confront the existence and character of something which is in no way dependent for either its existence or its nature on the fact of its being known. Put as directly as possible, a *realist* is one who believes that there are objects, known and unknown, which exist whether or not they are known; the *idealist*, on the other hand, supposes that to be, to exist, is either to be a thinking substance, a mind, or one of its ideas (or perceptions, sensations, emotions, beliefs). The argument between realists and idealists, then, has often taken the form of an epistemological argument: Is the act of knowing an act which involves the independent existence of the object of knowledge? The realists have argued that knowing does involve some kind of transcendence of the object, while the idealists have contended that the attempt to go beyond the mind's own content is not only futile but senseless.

Since it has been customary to regard the realistic account of the knowledge process as an epistemological venture, Roy Wood Sellars' *Critical Realism* (1916) has generally been interpreted as presenting his theory of knowledge, while his later defense of evolutionary naturalism, *The Philosophy of Physical Realism*, has been described as presenting "metaphysical" views. Thus, Joseph Blau speaks of Sellars' "version of the critical realist theory of knowledge," and then refers to Sellars' "metaphysical views to which we may assign such descriptive names as 'physical realism,' 'naturalism,' or 'materialism.'" Professor W. H. Werkmeister, writing in a similar fashion, speaks of Sellars' "evolutionary naturalism" or "physical realism" as "a metaphysical doctrine" developed after "the controversy over epistemological realism. . . ."

Nevertheless, although Sellars himself, in the Preface to *The Philosophy of Physical Realism*, speaks of the book as "an attempt at 'first philosophy,' . . . a development and defense of physical realism," and of critical realism as "an *elucidation of natural* realism in which the mechanism of knowing is studied and certain illusions about the nature of knowing are mastered," and goes on to state that "The epistemological task is not the replacement of natural realism but its development," it may very well be that all of these writers have erred, practically if not theoretically, in attempting to distinguish between critical and physical realism on the ground that the former is epistemological while the latter is metaphysical. Although critical realism presents itself as a theory of knowledge, it proceeds from a limitation of the use of the term "knowledge" to realistic contexts in which it is no longer meaningful to talk about the possibility that physical objects are, after all, merely complexes of ideas or sensations. Yet it is precisely such persistent philosophical restriction of language which justifies the application of the term "metaphysical." If this is so, Sellars' physical realism is best described as the metaphysical addition to his earlier critical realism, itself metaphysical. This is not to deny the value of his effort. It is only from a positivistic point of view—itself metaphysical—that metaphysical commitments are disreputable.

Sellars' philosophy in the volume under review is naturalistic, evolutionary, and critically realistic in its opposition to new or "naïve" realism. To understand these adjectives it is necessary to consider Sellars' philosophy as emerging from the realistic revolt against American idealism.

The New Realism (1912) appeared as a further defense of a program and platform already enunciated and supported by six American realists: E. B. Holt, W. T. Marvin, W. P. Montague, R. B. Perry, W. B. Pitkin, and E. G. Spaulding. As described by Montague in a retrospective essay, "The Story of American Realism," which appeared in *Philosophy* in April, 1937, the new realists supported a realism which was, at once, existential, Platonic, and presentative. It was existential (in a sense having no relation to existentialism) in holding that "Some, at least, of the *particulars* of which we are conscious exist when we are not conscious of them." It was Platonic in claiming that "Some, at least, of the *essences* or *universals* of which we are conscious subsist when we are not conscious of them." And it was presentative in its distinctive assertion that "Some, at least, of the particulars as well as the universals that are real are apprehended directly rather than indirectly through copies or mental images."

Clothed in its technical terminology, new realism is not surprising—nor is it, in any obvious way, a defense of common sense (as it is sometimes purported to be). But if we call the particular sensation we have upon perceiving a physical object a "sense-datum"—what is given to sense—then we may understand the new realist as claiming that sense-data sometimes exist when we are not conscious of them (existential realism), that the characteristics of sense-data (like mathematical relationships) sometimes exist when we are not conscious of them (Platonic realism), and that physical objects (ordinarily understood as complexes of sense-data in abstraction from any act of sensation) can be "apprehended" directly (presentative realism). Reduced to the language of ordinary discourse (thus accentuating the bizarre character of the new realist thesis), the new realism is a philosophy which regards the surfaces of physical objects as directly and immediately seen, smelled, touched, and so forth; colors, for example, are not to be understood as the causes of visual sensations, but as qualities of surfaces seen immediately and precisely as they are. Of course, such a view makes explanation of error or sense differences difficult.

Disturbed by a philosophy which made the naïve faith in the appearances of things a respectable doctrine, a group of American philosophers in 1920 issued *Essays in Critical Realism*. The authors were George Santayana, C. A. Strong, A. K. Rogers, A. O. Lovejoy, Roy Wood Sellars, J. B. Pratt, and Durant Drake. The opposition to new realism had grown in momentum over the years, as a result of work done by Santayana, Lovejoy, D. C. Macintosh, and others. The critical realists contended "that knowledge is *transitive*, so that self-existing things may become the chosen objects of a mind that identifies and indicates them; second, that knowledge is *relevant*, so that the thing indicated may have at least some of the qualities that mind attributes to it." This realism rested on a causal theory of perception which involved the claim that physical objects affect a perceiving subject who takes the content of his experience as an identifying sign of the presence and character of the object. Some realists, like Santayana, supposed it possible that, on occasion, the character (essence) of the object known might be identical with the character of the experience (sense-datum) by which it was known —but most were agreed that identity in character was perhaps limited to certain structural properties. In any case, for most critical realists, to know an object was to identify it by the character of its sensible effect and to be able to anticipate the character of subsequent sensible effects; the notion that objects could be "intuited"—known for what they are by some *immediate* perception, not by the conscious response to the sense stimulation of the physical organism—was rejected as naïve and as making an account of error impossible.

In what sense, then, is such a philosophical realism a metaphysical—and not merely an epistemological—point of view? In the sense that the causal theory of perception was assumed, not proved. But some realists—and Sellars is among them—maintain that we *do know* physical objects, and that we distinguish between the objects we know, which are the causes of our sensations, and the sensations of these objects. But to insist that we know *that* there are physical objects and that we also know *what* they are is to be persistently realistic—dualistically—in one's use of the verb "to know." There is nothing illegitimate or "mistaken" about this procedure; it is the linguistic way of being metaphysical.

The Philosophy of Physical Realism, therefore, may be considered an individual philosopher's extension of a metaphysical thesis which was developed in cooperation with others and in opposition to new realism which was, in turn, a manifestation of a critical opposition to American idealism.

In arguing against new realism and for his own variety of realism, Sellars contends that the proper epistemological method "is to begin with the actual cognitive experience and to examine it carefully in the light of its claims and of the relevant facts." He offers six general principles as the basis of a theory of knowing that would make sense out of the claim that in knowing the knower transcends himself:

"First principle: Human knowing is conditioned in a perfectly natural way as regards both external controls and internal operations. . . .

"Second principle: Though conditioned causally and resting on neuromuscular mechanisms, human knowing is yet knowing. . . .

"Third principle: The causal theory of perception should be restated as the causal theory of sense-data and not of perceiving. . . .

"Fourth principle: Knowing must be studied at its various levels as a characteristic claim of the human knower. . . .

"Fifth principle: The act of cognition is complex and appears in consciousness as an interpretation of an external object in terms of logical ideas. . . .

"Sixth principle: Things are selected as objects by the mind and not in the mind. This signifies that knowing involves a peculiar transcendence."

(In the text Sellars follows each principle with a defense and explanation of the point involved.)

Sellars is careful to point out that in perceiving we are ordinarily convinced that we are "in contact" with the perceived object and that the sensory presentation is the surface of the object—but to suppose this philosophically is to be naïve. Nevertheless, he objects to the claim made by many scientists that since perceiving involves interpretation, the physical object is inferred.

He suggests an idea of human knowing "which permits of degrees and approximations."

Sellars' theory of truth is based upon a distinction of three factors: the attitude of belief, the content of the belief, and the external state of affairs which is denoted. The attitude and the content are "features of the knower," but the third element, the external state of affairs, is not. A true idea is a "knowledge-giving" idea in that it discloses (whether or not one knows that it discloses) the denoted object. True ideas are *"such that* we can think the object as it is by means of them."

Sellars can be distinguished from some other critical realists by reference to his claim that sensory presentations are *particulars, not* essences. In other words, Sellars supposes that the brain-mind is stimulated by objects in such a manner that particular sense-events occur; these sense-events, or sensory presentations, are not characteristics which can belong to other events in other minds, nor are they predicates which can be attributed to objects. It is not surprising, then, that he rejects the theory of universals (Platonic realism) and accepts a nominalism which takes the form: "Only individual things are real; and these are real in their relations." When it is pointed out that we characterize objects by use of adjectives, suggesting that they are alike in kind, Sellars replies that "Ontologically, similarity is sufficient." Human beings make the mistake, he argues, of supposing that since there is organized stability in the world, there is an identity of features corresponding to the logical identities in our language.

The possibility of error is easily accounted for on Sellars' view. He argues that there are two ways of being mistaken in our reference to objects: (1) we may attempt to indicate an object when no object is present, and (2) we may describe an object incorrectly when one is present. To make a claim in regard to an object, to present a proposition concerning it, is to use a sense presentation as the basis of a meaning intended to disclose the object; if there is no object when we suppose there is, or if the object is not disclosed by our proposition, then we are in error, and truth and knowledge have been missed.

With Chapter XI of his book Sellars begins the development of what he calls his "ontology." We are prepared for this by his Preface in which he remarks, "I am an unashamed ontologist and a convinced believer in the ontological reach of science. And this in spite of pragmatist, Viennese positivist, or religious personalist." Nevertheless, despite his belief in "the ontological reach of science," Sellars is not inclined to regard the theory of relativity as having ontological significance; that is, he is not inclined to suppose that since, according to the physicist, there can be no absolute simultaneity of events, an account of simultaneity cannot be given. The scientist is interested in discourse that makes sense relative to measurement operations he and others can perform, but the philosopher—particularly when he is a realist—is not inclined to accept any such limitation upon his conception of things. According to Sellars, Newtonian physics confused ontological and operational questions—and to some extent so do modern physicists who take the theory of relativity as a theory having to do with a reality beyond measurement. The proper approach, according to Sellars, is to recognize that there are two approaches: measurement and ontology.

The extent of Sellars' philosophical courage can be seen in his defense of substance. He considers the objections advanced by Berkeley and Hume, and he argues that a cogent reply involves a reformulation of Locke's conception of substance. Like Spinoza, Sellars regards substance as a self-existent continuant, but he does not agree with Spinoza in denying substance the possibility of relations with other self-existents. He rejects the idea of substance as an inert focal "stuff" to which properties are somehow "attached."

In causal theory Sellars allies himself with C. J. Ducasse and others who reject a uniformity theory of cause in favor of a single event explanation. Thus, he opposes himself to Bertrand Russell's idea of cause as involving regular sequence. The point here appears to be that if an event can be known to be related to another event with which it is continuous and contiguous, it can be known to be causally related to that other event whether or not similar pairs of events are observed.

Without rejecting causality Sellars accounts for human freedom and moral import by emphasizing man's existence as an agent, a process, not as a fixed thing. He gives up predestination, but he gives positive content to his philosophy by calling attention to "the capacity of matter to organize into things like ourselves."

Sellars' evolutionary naturalism comes to the fore in his account of consciousness. In response to the question, "How precisely are we to think of consciousness as *in* the brain?" he answers that "Consciousness is in the brain as an event is in the brain, and is as extended as is the brain-event to which it is intrinsic." According to Sellars, judgment is the basic feature of cognition, and in judgment we form predicates based upon sense-data in order to describe objects. The sense-data provide the basis for judgments about objects, but they cannot accurately serve as the basis of judgments about the brain: for example, when an apple is judged to be red in virtue of the presence of a red sense-datum, it would be an error to judge the brain to be red. Throughout his account Sellars makes the effort to analyze consciousness as an emergent feature of a whole process which the brain-mind makes possible; there is no separate "thinking substance."

Sellars offers an objective, capacity theory of value; that is, he claims that the adjectives "good," "bad," "beautiful," and so forth, call attention to the capacity of objects "to enter human life with certain consequence of importance to the self or to a social group." He rejects the possibility of intrinsic value, but mostly because he takes the term "intrinsic" to be synonymous with "non-relational"; and since he supposes that goods are always goods *for* someone, it seems to him that no good could be intrinsic. Since Sellars emphasizes the descriptive use of value terms in propositions having truth-values, he is not sympathetic toward such a theory as Perry's, as developed in the latter's *General Theory of Value* (1926), dismissing it as a study probing "in a behavioristic way into the mechanism of interest and propensities."

Sellars closes grandly with the declaration that "I have tried to show that, with an adequate epistemology and ontology, most of the traditional riddles vanished and that then man could see himself as he is, a creature in one world, a creature strangely gifted to look before and after and to follow his desires and dreams on an earth partly plastic to his power." Although the author may be optimistic in hoping that *The Philosophy of Physical Realism* can lead to elimination of most of the traditional riddles, surely this work deserves reexamination as a lucid and meaningful defense of a critically responsible realism.—*I.P.M.*

PERTINENT LITERATURE

Delaney, C. F. *Mind and Nature: A Study of the Naturalistic Philosophies of Cohen, Woodbridge, and Sellars.* Notre Dame, Indiana: University of Notre Dame Press, 1969.

C. F. Delaney distinguishes between what he calls the "descriptive naturalism" of M. R. Cohen and F. J. E. Woodbridge and the "materialistic naturalism" of Roy Wood Sellars. He regards these three American philosophers as having attempted naturalistic reintegrations of mind and nature—Cohen by a philosophy of science, Woodbridge by a "realistic theory of experience," and Sellars by a theory of emergent evolution. According to Delaney, all three philosophers regard existence as given; the problems of naturalistic philosophy are problems of analytic explanation. It follows that a theory of man must be developed within a theory of nature. Finally, Delaney argues, all three philosophers agree in regarding nature as exhibiting a structural order that manifests itself in dynamic process (although there are differences in the emphasis on and the account of process).

As to the philosophy of man, Delaney writes, Cohen gave little attention to its development; Woodbridge emphasized the appetitive side of man's nature—his fearing, hoping, and praying; Sellars attempted a critical examination of knowing, culminating in an evolutionary naturalism which viewed perception as "a referential operation guided by sensations and founded on a biological mechanism of the sensorimotor type." Delaney charges Sellars with deferring to science in his effort to be specific in his account of man in nature. The naturalist's alignment with science must be defended, Delaney argues, and the only relevant line of defense would be a more developed and sophisticated philosophy of science. Sellars is a thoroughgoing materialist,

Delaney contends; Cohen and Woodbridge "shy away from that sort of explanation entirely."

Delaney distinguishes between a "transcendent" and "descriptive" metaphysics, and within the transcendent he distinguishes between a "genetic accounting" which aims at the identification of the origins and ends of the universe, and a "nontemporal" effort to identify ultimate principles, the ultimate ground of reality, whether it be atoms or God.

Sellars attempts to have it both ways, Delaney contends, in that Sellars moves from the temporal to the nontemporal form of transcendent metaphysics while assuming throughout a materialistic atomism. (In a footnote Delaney admits that Sellars' view is "tempered by his critical realism." Sellars regarded the categories of physics as fundamental in the understanding of the world; he did not argue that those categories reveal the fundamental character of the world. But Delaney argues that Sellars must be transcendent in metaphysics in that the categories of physics apply to "non-experiential entities.") Sellars' effort to found his materialism on the elemental particles of physics involves an "uncritical attitude toward science," Delaney insists.

In Chapter V, "R. W. Sellars: Mind as Organic Behavior," Delaney argues that Sellars adopts a three-stage approach to the problem of integrating mind and nature. Sellars begins with epistemological investigations that led him to reject idealism and new realism in favor of a commonsense position he called "natural realism." Natural realism also failed to survive critical examination, however; it could not be that physical events are given in perceptual experience. Hence, critical realism was developed as a kind of mean between the subjectivism of idealism and the absolute objectivism of new realism. The data of sense are not the objects of perception but means by which, through a complex behavioral operation, things are denoted as public, independent, and real.

According to Delaney, the fundamental ontological categories for Sellars are *"existence, substance,* and *matter."* Through perception one knows and accordingly denotes a public object; the object is denoted as existing. An existent is a substance; substance is "spatial, energy-containing, organized, movable, and formable" (as Delaney summarizes Sellars' position)—hence, substance is material. As for matter, it is best conceived as the physicist conceives it—in terms of energy systems.

Delaney then gives careful attention to Sellars' cosmology as emphasizing the dynamism, organization, and emergent novelty of physical systems. Through a process of emergent evolution living things emerge from inorganic nature; then mind (an organization of habits and tendencies that enable an animal to adjust itself in response to stimuli) becomes a novel reality; finally, civilizations emerge through the growth of social processes.

Sellars handles the problem of the relation of mind to body by developing his theory in three stages. According to Delaney, Sellars regarded the *or-*

ganism as the knowing self, the mind as a physical category, and consciousness as a unique coemergent. The mind, writes Sellars, "is the brain as known in its functioning," and consciousness is "the whole content and process of experience. . . ." Each "pulse of consciousness" is a feature of a mind-brain state. Hence, as Sellars developed his resolution of the mind-body problem, one finds an organically functioning physical system that has a qualitative dimension in consciousness. Hence, Delaney concludes, Sellars believed that the problems of dualism are avoided once a materialistic explanation is devised that rests on what Delaney describes as "a sophisticated epistemology and an emergent cosmology."

Drake, Durant, *et al. Essays in Critical Realism: A Co-operative Study of the Problem of Knowledge.* London: Macmillan and Company, 1920.

The *Essays in Critical Realism* is not simply a collection of essays written independently of one another, published in various places, and later drawn together as representing a general philosophical tendency. The essays included in this volume were written for it, modified in the course of discussion among the participants, and published as a joint expression of a consensus on the major points of a theory called "Critical Realism" to distinguish it from the "New Realism" of Edwin B. Holt, Ralph Barton Perry, W. P. Montague, and others, and from the traditional realism of John Locke and his successors. Roy Wood Sellars is one of the contributors, and consequently the appreciation of his work is enhanced by a reading of his views in the context of a collection of essays written in the cooperative effort to promote a distinctive philosophical position.

Durant Drake's essay, "The Approach to Critical Realism," opens the volume, perhaps because more than any other of the essays it provides an introductory overview of the area of controversy that Critical Realism entered with the intention of resolving the problem of empirical knowledge once and for all. Drake distinguishes between the objective and subjective philosophical approaches to the problem of knowledge. The objectivist supposes that the data of perception are themselves physical existents (Drake calls such a philosopher a "naïve realist") while the subjectivist regards the data of perception as psychological existents—that is, mental entities, "ideas."

Drake represents Critical Realism as a position that combines what is true and useful in the two radically opposed historic views while avoiding the errors of both. Both the subjectivist and objectivist views may be realistic in that both positions at least allow for the possibility of objects existing independently of mind and its data. But "epistemological monism," as Drake calls it, errs in identifying the data of perception with the aspects of physical objects (as in New Realism), while "epistemological dualism" errs in maintaining an absolute division between the data of perception and independently existing physical objects. Critical Realism relates the data of perception to physical objects in such a way as to explain how knowledge of physical objects is possible. (Drake suggests that Critical Realism itself not be described as a "dualism" if to do so would be to suggest that Critical Realists suppose that perceptual data are known and physical objects merely presumed; the Critical Realists insist that physical objects are *known* in perception. Of course, the view is "dualistic" in the sense that a distinction is made between data and physical existents, but since the physical existents are known by way of data, the emphasis is on the unitary character of the knowing situation.)

According to Drake, Critical Realists believe in the existence of physical objects because such a belief is pragmatically justifiable: it serves to account for the appearances and to make their order intelligible. The subjectivist is a realist in that he believes in independently existing mental existents. If one is to be consistent, Drake suggests, one should be thoroughly skeptical or thoroughly realistic.

As for naïve realism, Drake continues, whether the naïve realist supposes the sense data that constitute physical objects literally to be projected into the object or actually to be selected aspects of the physical object, difficulties arise. In the former case, one makes a radical assumption for which there is no evidence—namely, that each perceiver has a mechanism by the use of which he is able to place data in space; in the latter case, the naïve realist has to account for perceptual differences by presuming that perceiving organisms are selective, each taking from a field of independent data some but not others. It is much more credible, Drake writes, that differences in perception are the result of differences in perceivers, in how each is affected by physical objects.

The data by which we identify and know physical objects are sometimes called "sense-data," and one may thereupon be inclined to regard them as existents. But, Drake contends, the data *qua* data are "merely character-complexes, logical entities," not existents. In cognition one knows physical objects, or mental states, or physical processes; one does not *know* the given.

In his essay "Knowledge and Its Categories," Sellars writes that critical realism contends that knowledge of the physical world involves the givenness of character-complexes as a foundation of knowledge but certainly does not regard the objects known as intuited character-complexes. Nor is the realm of physical existents inferred. According to Sellars, we "affirm it through the very pressure and suggestion of our experience."

Sellars describes traditional representative realism as a "thwarted naïve realism." Such a realism presumes that the characters of sense data are similar to the characters of physical things, but Sellars suggests that there is no need to presume any similarity of character; it is enough if we know things as causes of the experiences we have in perception. Although Sellars denies that the characters of sensations are identical with or similar to the characters of physical things—or, at least, he denies the value of any such assumption—he does contend that in knowing one apprehends the "form" of a physical object. By "form" Sellars means the "position, size, structure, casual capacities, etc." of physical objects. Such formal features are "mediated" by the given elements in experience. To know such features is to know the thing—that is, to know formal features by way of data is to know the thing.

Of the remaining essays, George Santayana's "Three Proofs of Realism" is especially rewarding. Santayana offers a "biological" proof, a "psychological" proof, and a "logical" proof. In the biological proof, Santayana argues that the attitude of a child's body in reaching for something (say, the moon) is clearly an indication that the child's object is not his sensuous experience, for he *has* the experience; he does not have the object he strives for. All animals have "relevant and transitive knowledge of their environment," Santayana argues; and he maintains that realistic knowledge is "but another name for vital sensibility and intelligence." Santayana argues that even transcendental idealism is realistic in that minds are regarded as something more than present ideas, and although a strenuous effort is made to deny time, the belief in time, writes Santayana, "is the soul of introspective psychology."

Finally, Santayana argues that the relationships between and within essences are real in that they are not invented by minds; nor can they be denied except arbitrarily. The datum, Santayana writes, is an "ideal essence," and essences have a kind of being that is independent of intuition. An essence is a real entity even though it is not physical; it has an inalienable logical or aesthetic character. Santayana describes his proofs as "circular" in that unless realism is assumed, proof is impossible. But all "reasonable human discourse" presupposes realism, he argues, and any honest person can be shown that he is a realist at heart.—*I.P.M.*

ADDITIONAL RECOMMENDED READING

Bahm, Archie, Roderick M. Chisholm, *et al.* "A Symposium in Honor of Roy Wood Sellars," in *Philosophy and Phenomenological Research*. XV, no. 1 (September, 1954), pp. 1-97. A set of competent essays illuminating many of the issues discussed by Sellars.

Chisholm, Roderick M., ed. *Realism and the Background of Phenomenology*. Glencoe, Illinois: The Free Press, 1960. This volume includes selections by Franz Brentano, Alexius Meinong, Edmund Husserl, H. A. Prichard, Samuel Alexander, Bertrand Russell, A. O. Lovejoy, and G. E. Moore, and from *The New Realism* (1912). It also has an excellent bibliography, including books and articles by Roy Wood Sellars.

Delaney, C. F. *Mind and Nature*. Notre Dame, Indiana: University of Notre Dame Press, 1969. This book (reviewed above) offers an extensive bibliography of works by and about Cohen, Woodbridge, and Sellars specifically, and about naturalism in general.

Reck, Andrew. *Recent American Philosophy*. New York: Pantheon Books, 1964. A discerning survey of ten American philosophers, including (Chapter 7) Roy Wood Sellars.

ART AS EXPERIENCE

Author: John Dewey (1859-1952)
Type of work: Aesthetics
First published: 1934

Principal Ideas Advanced

When experience is satisfactory, when it combines memory of the past with anticipation of the future, when it is an achievement of the organism in the environment in which it functions, the experience is an *experience.*

Any experience which is, in this unified and consummatory way, an *experience is an aesthetic experience.*

Art is to be understood as an *experience made possible by the organizing and unifying process in which the artist engages; the spectator meets the interest of the artist with an interest of his own in the reciprocal process of going through a similar operation.*

Art supplies mediums of communication, making community of experience possible.

All arts share a common form: they are organized toward a unified experience; they all operate through sensory mediums such as stone, water colors, oil paints, and words; and they are all concerned with space and time.

Art as Experience is the most extensive and, many say, the best book on aesthetics from the pragmatic point of view. Dewey believed that aesthetic theory should attempt to explain how works of art come to be and how they are enjoyed in experience. How is it that something produced to fill a need becomes in addition a source of aesthetic enjoyment? How is it that ordinary activities can yield a particular kind of satisfaction that is aesthetic? These and like questions must be answered by an adequate aesthetic theory.

Dewey's interest in biology influenced his description of the aesthetic experience. An organism lives in an environment through which it fulfills certain needs. The process of fulfilling these needs is called *experience* and may be more or less satisfactory to the organism. When experience seems to be completely satisfactory, when it is a happy experience that combines memories of the past and anticipations of the future, when it is an achievement of the organism in the world of things, Dewey calls it "an experience." *An* experience, realized by a human being, is aesthetic. Thus, there is no sharp line between animal and human experience. Animals could have aesthetic experience, but we simply would not be likely to call it that.

Aesthetic experiences are not found in museums or in libraries alone. As a matter of fact, such settings often make enjoyment impossible by putting works of art beyond ordinary human activities and concerns. For Dewey, an intelligent workman doing his job, interested in it, finding satisfaction in doing it well, is having an experience. He is artistically engaged; he is finding aesthetic enjoyment. Consequently, everyday activities are the ones most meaningful to the average person. To him the most vital arts are popular music, comic strips, newspaper accounts of crime and love, articles on the intimate doings of popular entertainers. These things are a significant part of the concerns of an organized community, just as in the past rug, mat, and cloth making, dancing, music, and storytelling were an integral part of day-to-day living.

Modern museums and institutions segregate art and remove it from the concerns of most people. Dewey criticizes the modern artist for reflecting the view that art is isolated and for not attempting to reach anyone except those whom the artist regards as having a superior cultural status. The object that he produces may be thought of as a work of art, but the actual work of art is to be understood as what affects human experience. The problem of the artist should be to show that his activity can be connected with the actual processes of living.

Dewey points to other properties of the aesthetic experience. In his practical concerns with the real world, a person thinks in terms of effect and cause. He converts these for his own use into ends he wishes to achieve and devices for achieving them; that is, into consequences and means, organizing the world in terms of needs and environment. Art, too, involves organization and may be related to any activity of the living organism. The great work of art is a complete organization; and in this completeness lies the source of aesthetic pleasure.

No experience is a unity, Dewey says, unless it has aesthetic quality. The integrated, the well-rounded, the emotionally satisfying make up the artistic structure of the experience which is immediately felt. Because of its relation to experience, art is always a part of the process of doing or making something. Like all experience, it involves emotion and is guided by purpose. The artist organizes, clarifies, and simplifies his material according to his interest. The spectator must go though these same operations according to his own interests in order to have an aesthetic experience from his relation to the art object. He must be creative when confronted by the art object, just as the artist was creative when he produced it. What the spectator creates is an experience which is enjoyed and is satisfying for its own sake.

What are the characteristics of experience for Dewey? Experience begins with an impulsion of the whole organism, outward and forward. The organism moves to satisfy a need, but the nature of this motion is determined by the environment and the past experiences of the organism. Emotion always accompanies an experience. Without emotion there is no action.

A work of art does not simply evoke an emotion. The material in it becomes the content and matter of emotion when it is a part of the environment which satisfies a need in relation to the past experiences of an organism. Art objects may be inadequate or excessive in relation to the emotional needs of the spectator. Art is not nature; it is nature organized, simplified, transformed in such a way that it places the individual and the community in a context of greater order and unity.

Thus, for Dewey, the work of art represents nature as experienced by the artist. It organizes the public world by taking the scattered and weakened material of experience, then clarifying and concentrating it. But the work of art does not lead to another experience of the world; it is *an* experience. Only secondarily, as it becomes a part of the past experiences of a person does it transform his everyday existence. The painter, for example, perceives the world just as everyone else does. But to him certain lines and colors become important, and he subordinates other aspects of what he is perceiving to relations among them. What he takes as important is influenced by his past experiences, by his theories of art, by his attitudes toward the world, and by the scene itself.

One reason for the importance of art, claims Dewey, is that it supplies "the only media of complete and unhindered communication between man and man that can occur in a world full of gulfs and walls that limit community of experience." Since art communicates, it requires, like language, a triadic relation of speaker (the artist), the thing said (the art product), and the hearer (the spectator). All language involves what is said and how it is said—substance and form. In art, substance is the content of the work itself; form is the organization of this content.

Each art has its own medium, fitted for a particular kind of communication. When there is a complete set of relations within a chosen medium, there is aesthetic form. Form is relation, and relations are modes of interaction: pushes, pulls, lightness, heaviness. In a successful work of art, the stresses are so adapted to one another that a unity results. The work of art satisfies many ends, none of which is laid down in advance. The artist experiments. He communicates an individual experience through materials that belong to the public world. He means the work of art, and the work of art means whatever anyone can honestly get out of it.

In *Art as Experience* there is a difference between the art product and the work of art. The art product—the statue, the painting, the printed poem—is physical. The work of art is active and experienced. When the art product enters into experience it takes part in a complex interaction. It is the work of art with its fixed order of elements that is perceived. But the work of art is like an organism: it manifests movement, it has a past and present, a career, a history. Energy is organized toward some result. The spectator interacts with the work of art so that energies are given rhythmic organization, are intensified, clarified, concentrated.

The fact that art organizes energy explains its power to move and to stir, to calm and to tranquilize. Paintings that seem dead in whole or in part are those that arrest movement, rather than carry it forward toward a dynamic whole. Thus aesthetic perception differs from ordinary perception. The latter results in classification: those are rain clouds, so I must carry an umbrella. Aesthetic perception is full, complete, and rhythmical.

"What properties do all of the arts share?" Dewey asks. In the past it had been argued that they have a common subject matter. But the tendency in the arts is to go beyond limits. New artists have new interests and express them through new uses of material. Yet, the arts do share a common form to the extent that they are all organized toward a unity of experience. Further, all arts operate through sensory mediums. A material such as stone, water-color, oil paints, or words becomes a medium when it is used to express a meaning other that that of its commonplace physical existence. Different mediums give different qualities to works of art; pastel differs from oil. "Sensitivity to a medium as a medium is the very heart of all artistic creation and esthetic perception." The medium is a *mediator*; it relates the artist and the perceiver. The third property that all arts share is that they are concerned with space and time. The arts are dynamic, and all action must occur in space and time. Spatiality is mass and volume; temporality is endurance.

The aesthetic experience, Dewey contends, is located in the interaction between the spectator and the art product. Thus, art products cannot be classified into aesthetic categories. There can be as great a variety of works of art as there can be a variety of unified experiences. The work of art comes into existence when a human being cooperates with the art product. This cooperation results in an experience which is enjoyed because of its liberating and ordered properties. Thus, for Dewey, no art is inherently superior to any other. Every medium has its own power, its own efficacy and value. The important thing is that it communicates by making common, related, and available what had been isolated and singular.

Every work of art contains something of the particular personality of the artist. In practical action we must divide reality into subject and impersonal object. No such division characterizes aesthetic experience for Dewey. Art is a unity of subject and object. Like rite and ceremony, it has the power to unite men through shared celebration to all of the concerns and anticipations of life.

Aesthetic experience, indeed all experience, is imaginative. Imagination helps to adjust the old to the new, connecting the new with its physical past and the past of the person involved. Aesthetic experience is the paradigm of experience, experience freed from the factors that would impede and thwart its development.

Thus, if Dewey is right, it is to aesthetic experience that philosophers must turn if they are to understand the nature of experience itself. In the past, philosophers have explained aesthetic experience as but one type of experience. Rather, they should have taken experience in its most complete form, the fusion of the self with the objective order and law of the material that it incorporates, and used this—aesthetic experience—as the model for understanding experience in general.

Dewey uses the principles delineated in *Art as Experience* to solve what he takes to be some of the major problems of aesthetics. Does art express the universal or the unique and particular? In Dewey's opinion it does neither exclusively. It forms a new synthesis which is both. The expression is neither objective nor subjective, neither solely personal nor completely general.

Does art convey knowledge? It is true that it makes life more intelligible, says Dewey; but not through concepts in the way that knowing does. Art clarifies by intensifying experience. Both philosophy and art depend on the imaginative power of the mind. Art is a manifestation of experience *as* experience, of experience unalloyed. Because of this manifestation, it can provide a control for the imaginative ventures of philosophy.

Dewey has much advice for the critic. Criticism is a judgment about art. If we are to understand the nature of criticism in the arts, we must first understand the nature of judgment. The material which judgment uses is supplied by perception. This material in a mature judgment must be controlled and selected. In viewing a work of art, the spectator conducts a controlled inquiry, which requires an extensive background and developed taste. The spectator must discriminate and unify, but unlike the jurist he has no socially approved rules to apply. The law is conservative, but criticism must be sensitive to new forms of expression that stem from spiritual and physical changes in the environment.

At the opposite extreme from Dewey is the impressionistic critic. Mere impression can never organize experience; unification and discrimination always involve reference to some theory. If works of art are not to be judged by impressions, they are also not to be judged by fixed standards. In the primary sense, a standard is a physical object that measures quantitatively. The critic measures qualitatively.

How, then, can the critic make objective judgments? The qualities that he is judging are those of an object, and his judgment requires a hypothesis. It is his hypothesis that provides a criterion for judging him as a critic. His theory of criticism must be adequate to enable him to point to properties of the art object that will evoke an aesthetic experience. He must discuss form in relation to matter, the function of the medium, the nature of the expressive object. He must lead rather than dictate. He must discover a unifying pattern which pervades the work of art, perhaps not the only one, but one that can be shown to be maintained throughout the parts of the art object.

Art as Experience identifies two fallacies of aesthetic criticism. The first of these is reduction. The reduction fallacy occurs when some aspect of the work of art is taken as the whole. The work of art is a self-contained unity; it combines many things, none of which has aesthetic priority. The second fallacy results from a confusion of categories. Works of art provide data for students of art; for example, for the art historian. But to identify the historian's account of the work of art with aesthetic criticism is to be guilty of a confusion of categories.

Another type of category confusion concerns values. The most obvious example is found in moralistic criticism. A work of art may well make moral judgments, but these are not the sole criterion of its aesthetic value. Art is a medium of communication in its own right, not a substitute for religion, science, philosophy, or moral exhortation. The function of the critic is to delineate the aesthetic experience, which has its own inherent value, to reeducate so that others may learn from the criticism to see and to hear.

There is one problem that the artist, the critic, and the aesthetician must face. It is the relation between permanence and change. Human beings and their environments are continually subjected to change operating within a structure of laws. This structure is in turn subject to gradual change. Art must reflect such changes. Artists and critics have only begun to realize that the rise of industrialism is the source of new patterns and of new materials. Art can show that there is permanence in the changing and change in the permanent.

In a broad sense, aesthetic experience reveals the life and development of civilization. Art is a magnificent force that brings together conflicting elements found in every period of history. The customs and rituals of a people, all of their communal activities, unite the practical, social, and educative into an aesthetic unity.

The art of the past must have something to say to the present to be worthy of present consideration. An art can die just as can any other human institution. But great art, for Dewey, is a revelation of self and always has something to say to succeeding peoples under different environments; it tells of the ordered movement of the matter of some experience to a genuine fulfillment.

We often think of ancient civilizations in terms of their art products. To the elements of civilization which the art of the past reveals have been added two in the modern world. These are natural science and its application to industry and commerce through machinery. These new factors have yet to be absorbed into the attitudes of most people. Science has given us a new conception of our environment and of our relation to it. Science tends to show man as a part of nature and gives rational support to his desire to control himself and his environment. It enables him to understand himself in relation to his past, his present, and his future.

Industry creates an environment in which more and more people leave the rural world of nature for the man-made world of the machine. This new setting can have aesthetic quality. Objects with their own internal functional adaptions can be combined with man in a way that yields aesthetic results.

The artist can create a physical and moral environment that will shape desires and purposes, that will determine the direction of the interest and attention of human beings. Artistic experience, says Dewey, can and must shape the future.—*J. Co.*

PERTINENT LITERATURE

Gauss, Charles E. "Some Reflections on John Dewey's Aesthetics," in *Journal of Aesthetics and Art Criticism.* XIX, no. 2 (Winter, 1960), pp. 127-132.

A characteristic trait in John Dewey's philosophy is his reluctance to make sharp distinctions and his resolution to give explanations which emphasize continuity, process, interpenetration, interaction, and fluidity. This practice is especially so in his discussions on aesthetics. For people who have been trained to appreciate clear distinctions as a primary requirement for intelligent communication, reading Dewey may seem like a nightmare filled with endless ambiguities. Dewey talks about experience in general being aesthetic insofar as it is *an* experience; then he turns right around and discusses experiences he calls truly aesthetic in a distinctive sense. He objects to abstractly or otherwise separating art and science; yet he constantly refers to their separate functions. He defines art as having an essentially aesthetic dimension, but at the same time he stresses that there is a difference between art and the aesthetic. And so on. Charles E. Gauss in this short article gives perspective to Dewey's thought by clearing up some of the problems created by Dewey's seemingly ambiguous language.

One has *an* experience when the doings and undergoings which constitute the interaction of an organism with its environment have run full course, giving a unity characterized by a single quality. *An* experience is characterized by an upsurge of new meaning achieved as a result of internal integration (of organism and environment) and fulfillment. Using the example given by Gauss, a surgeon who has fought a running battle with death and who by overcoming the tensions and resistances of the situation has dramatically saved his patient on the operating table, thus bringing the situation to a satisfactory closure—this surgeon has undergone *an* experience. According to Dewey, any experience insofar as it is *an* experience has an aesthetic quality.

While admitting that any experience is capable of exhibiting an aesthetic quality, Dewey also recognizes that there are different kinds of experiences, and that the "distinctively aesthetic" is one of these kinds. What he means, according to Gauss, is that all experiences may in theory have aesthetic quality, "but in aesthetic experience this quality is emphasized." In describing how the aesthetic quality is emphasized, Dewey sticks to a fairly orthodox analysis of aesthetic experience: (1) it occurs on a perceptual level; (2) it involves a contemplation or attention to the material of experience for its own sake; (3) it is an organic organization of material; and (4) it yields a characteristic enjoyment.

Dewey defines art as any act of doing or making that is governed by aesthetic intent. Any type of act could conceivably qualify as art according to this definition. The surgeon in the above example could be considered an artist to the extent that his actions were done with the intention of bringing a situation to its satisfactory terminus. Still, Dewey wishes to distinguish between what he calls "aesthetic art" and "other art." This initially seems confusing, since he has already claimed that all art must be aesthetic in nature. If art must be aesthetic to be "truly" art, then how can "other art" be art at all? Gauss resolves the apparent predicament by explaining that when Dewey refers to "aesthetic art" he means fine art (in the ordinary sense of the term), and by "other art" he simply means all other acts of doing or making that are governed by aesthetic intent.

Another apparent perplexity stems from Dewey's discussion of the relationship between art and science. On the one hand, he distinguishes the two by saying that "science states meanings; art expresses them." On the other hand, he often speaks of the genuine artistry of the inquiring scientist. Gauss clears up the ambiguity by way of analogy. While it would be true to say that there is a difference between the act of doing or undergoing and the result or consequence of that act, just as there is a difference between what may be called the artistry and the physical vehicle of a work of art, there is a sense in which the act and the consequences cannot be separated; nor can the creative artistic activity and the art object be separated. Similarly, if we think of science as a procedure of inquiry, and distinguish an inquiry procedure from the completed results, and view art as a type of consummate experience, but essentially conjoined with preparatory activities, it makes perfect sense to distinguish science from art, yet to regard science as an artistic activity (of inquiry) moving toward an aesthetic terminus.

While Dewey's descriptions are not always clear, his ambivalent attitude toward distinctions is probably less a weakness than a strength of his thought.

Gotshalk, D. W. "On Dewey's Aesthetics," in *Journal of Aesthetics and Art Criticism*. XXIII, no. 1 (Fall, 1964), pp. 131-138.

D. W. Gotshalk's presentation centers on (1) Dewey's theory of aesthetic experience, (2) Dewey's theory of fine art, and (3) the relationship of Dewey's aesthetics to his general philosophy. From a critical point of view, the discussion of Dewey's theory of fine art is most worthwhile.

Dewey distinguishes between the *product of art*, which is the physical and external entity turned out by the artist, and the *work of art*, which "is what the product does with and in experience." The work of art requires a kind of creative collaboration between the artist and the spectator, each contributing to the total effect or total experience. In a sense, the work of art is perpetually created anew by each individual experiencer.

Gotshalk objects to this highly unconventional view of a work of art because of the odd consequences such a view implies. One implication is that, strictly speaking, there is no one work of art. A painting by Henri Matisse, for example, constitutes a single product of art, but corresponding to that product is an indefinitely larger number of works of art, for there are an indefinite number of people who might view the painting aesthetically. Since each person is different, and since each person's interaction with the painting creates a unique organic whole, the work of art will be something different in each case. This leads to the predicament that when any two people talk about the painting as a work of art, they cannot be talking about the same thing. Not only does this rule out the possibility of art criticism on a common basis, but it creates an infinite number of private aesthetic worlds, with no available bridge for discussion, communication, and sharing.

Another difficulty stems from Dewey's reference to the product of art as being something physical and external, such as a painting on canvas, a statue, or a poem on paper. Dewey seems not to recognize that since the product comes from the artist it is more than just a material object; the product of art also has a formal and expressive and functional dimension, and these dimensions can be discovered by properly oriented attention. Dewey's distinction between the product of art and the work of art detracts from what in general is a deeply provocative theory of art.

As to the nature of fine art, Dewey is correct, says Gotshalk, in claiming that a work of art is intended for human consumption and that an active process of interaction on the part of the spectator is required to consume it properly. Where Dewey goes wrong is in reducing what is ordinarily called a work of art to a pure potential, a potential which becomes actualized only through consumption (aesthetic appreciation) by some spectator. Gotshalk concludes that it would be much more accurate to say that the artist by himself creates an actual work of art which, as created, exists potentially as an object of appreciation for a potential consumer. The consequent result, then, of the spectator interacting with the work of art is not that the work of art is actualized, but rather that an aesthetic experience is actualized.

Zeltner, Philip M. *John Dewey's Aesthetic Philosophy*. Amsterdam: B. R. Grüner B. V., 1975.

In this book of 125 pages Philip M. Zeltner provides a capable guide to the salient features of John Dewey's theory of art as experience. Dewey's somewhat confusing terminology is clarified and his aesthetic theory is positioned within the framework of his general philosophy of experience. Zeltner's most novel contribution is a chapter aimed at developing a theory of meaning in music based upon Dewey's understanding of that medium of expression.

In the first two chapters Zeltner argues, contrary to some, that Dewey's aesthetic theory is in actuality the capstone of his entire philosophy. It might even be said that Dewey's aesthetics *is* his philosophy, in the sense that his undertakings in the areas of logic, metaphysics, epistemology, and psychology all point to and culminate in his analysis of aesthetic experience. At the same time, without a grasp of Dewey's provocative notion of experience, along with his theory of nature and doctrine of inquiry, it would be nearly impossible to comprehend or appreciate his aesthetics.

A distinction is drawn between Dewey's broader general theory which pertains to what he calls "aesthetic experience as a primary phase," and his more refined theory which centers on the "deliberate and intentional cultivation" of aesthetic experience. While the latter essentially concerns the fine arts and their elements, the former relates to ordinary life experiences. The failure to recognize this important distinction can lead to serious misinterpretations of Dewey's ideas. Because of its foundational status, Zeltner is interested mainly in laying out the broader theory.

Developing this broader theory, Dewey stresses that every normal, ordinary everyday type of experience is capable of being aesthetic, of exhibiting an aesthetic quality. This view is due to the fact that he regards every complete experience—with emphasis upon *complete*—as an aesthetic experience. Zeltner explains what Dewey means.

To begin with, Dewey conceives of experience and nature as inseparable, essentially an organic unity: experience *is* nature in one of its myriad forms. Using Zeltner's description, experience is "an aspect of nature which involves the human organism in interaction with the rest of nature." There are many differing forms of experience, including intellectual, emotional, and practical, all of which occur in "situations" or "contexts." The process of living proceeds *in* an environment and, more significantly, through interaction with it. The relationship of organism and environment is dynamic, not static, fundamentally characterized by ongoing activity, interaction, and change.

Every "situation" presents its own unique set of qualities ranging from *precarious* to *stable*. Organisms become caught up in situations of disequilibrium created by obstacles and elements of resistance; then through processes of recovery they achieve equilibrium, stability. Life's activites reflect the constant ebb and flow of interactions with nature, the facing of problems and the solving of them. Dewey further points out that since no state of affairs lasts forever, every situation has an end, or terminus. What he is referring to is a qualitative change in the situation, such that the very being of the situation is qualitatively altered; where, for example, an obstacle is overcome, a problem is solved, or an organism has adapted (or succumbed) to a unique set of circumstances.

Lastly, experience gives rise to *meanings*. For Dewey, meanings are not to be understood strictly in a cognitive sense, and they are not primarily or exclusively related to language. Basically, meanings characterize relationships between elements of nature. The experiential meaning of an object or event is a function of the situation in which it occurs, the interactions to which it has given rise, the consequences of those interactions, and the future possibilities it has occasioned. A glass of water means one thing to a person sitting in front of a television on Sunday afternoon; it means something totally different to a man lost in the desert.

All of this relates to Dewey's aesthetics in the following manner. People are continuously and dynamically interacting with their environment. Problematic situations arise which stifle the individual's activity and create a qualitative tension, or disequilibrium. The individual's natural response is to resolve the problem, to restore equilibrium. For this to happen a qualitative change in the situation must come about somehow; in short, the situation must reach its terminus. To the extent that the situation develops and changes, new meanings are created, since new relationships and modes of interaction are established. If the individual survives the qualitative change by recovering equilibrium with the environment, he will have changed and grown through an incorporation of new meaning. This phase in the life-process, characterized by the termination of a situation, the restoration of equilibrium, and the possession of new meaning, Dewey calls "*an* experience," or a "consummatory experience." It is also what he means by a *complete* experience. *And every consummatory experience has aesthetic quality*. In this way Dewey ties aesthetic experience to experience in general. Fine art, in turn, becomes defined as the intentional and deliberate cultivation and communication of aesthetic quality—namely, that quality in experience which manifests finality, consummation, completion, integration, unity, and fullness of meaning.

In a very informative chapter Zeltner considers the role of emotion in Dewey's theory of art, and how art functions as a means of expression. For Dewey, an artistic act is an act of expression. The question is, how and what is the artist expressing? Dewey's answer, as always, stems from his understanding of experience and nature. In any complete experience, as a result of the organism's falling out of step with its environment and subsequently regaining equilibrium, growth occurs and there is a movement forward of the organism in its entirety, an "impulsion" outward as the individual incorporates the meaning brought into being by the consummatory act. This impulsion outward, when accompanied by an emotional discharge, translates into an act of expression. Examples would include a mother's comforting smile, a lover's kiss of affection, and even a friendly handshake.

Zeltner carefully clarifies the point that Dewey does not equate expression with emotional discharge. "To discharge is to get rid of; to express is to carry forward in development, to work out to completion." So, while an emotional discharge is a necessary condition for an act of expression, it does not constitute a sufficient condition. Furthermore, it would be wrong to interpret Dewey as holding that what is expressed in art is emotion. Emotion is the cementing and driving force of artistic activity, explains Zeltner, but not the content of expression. The significant content of expression is meaning, as it has been defined above. The gist of the matter, in Dewey's view, is that art functions to intensify, clarify, and give expression to meanings engendered by consummatory experiences.

Other chapters deal with the interpenetration of substance and form in Dewey's aesthetics, the elements of rhythm and symmetry in works of art, the medium and meaning of music as an art form, and Dewey's views on art criticism. Without doubt this book qualifies as an excellent critical introduction to Dewey's aesthetic philosophy.—*R.A.S.*

ADDITIONAL RECOMMENDED READING

Hook, Sidney. *John Dewey: An Intellectual Portrait*. New York: John Day Company, 1939. A clear and nontechnical introduction to the central ideas in Dewey's philosophy. Chapter X, entitled "Art as Experience," focuses on Dewey's aesthetic theory. Hook's fine reputation as a philosopher and commentator is widely recognized.

Mathur, D. C. "A Note on the Concept of 'Consummatory Experience' in Dewey's Aesthetics," in *The Journal of Philosophy*. LXIII, no. 9 (April 28, 1966), pp. 225-231. A concise analysis of Dewey's notions of *"an* experience" and "consummatory experience" and an explanation of how Dewey uses these basic notions in discussing aesthetic experience.

Morgenbesser, Sidney, ed. *Dewey and His Critics: Essays from* The Journal of Philosophy. New York: The Journal of Philosophy, 1977. Included in this volume of reprinted articles by Dewey and his leading critics are two essays on Dewey's aesthetic theory by E. A. Shearer (1935), and a piece entitled "Art as Cognitive Experience" by James Jarrett (1953). All three articles contribute to a greater understanding of Dewey's conception of art as experience.

Pepper, Stephen C. "Some Questions on Dewey's Esthetics," in *The Philosophy of John Dewey* (The Library of Living Philosophers). Edited by Paul A. Schilpp. New York: Tudor Publishing Company, 1951, pp. 369-389. Pepper raises a number of noteworthy objections to the aesthetic theory presented in Dewey's *Art as Experience*. In particular, he tries to demonstrate the inherent inconsistency in any theory of aesthetics such as Dewey's that seeks to be both organistic and pragmatic.

MIND, SELF, AND SOCIETY

Author: George Herbert Mead (1863-1931)
Type of work: Philosophical psychology
First published: 1934

PRINCIPAL IDEAS ADVANCED

Mind and self can best be understood as emergents from a more basic social process.

There is no absolute separation between the social and the organic, and any pragmatic or behavioral account of human action which fails to recognize this fact is faulty.

Novelty of response is possible for individual selves which, by the use of memory, can take advantage of past experience within society.

How Professor Mead's book came to be published tells one something about the author's unusual stature as a teacher. The book's contents primarily represent the careful editing of several sets of notes taken down by appreciative students attending Mead's lectures on social psychology at the University of Chicago, especially those given in 1927 and 1930. Other manuscript materials also find some place in the book. For more than thirty years Mead taught at the University of Chicago, exerting a powerful scholarly influence on students, colleagues, and professional acquaintances. His written contributions during his lifetime were confined to articles and reviews for learned journals. Nonetheless, as a result of the devotion of some of those he influenced, Mead has left to the learned world four published books which bear his name. All of these appeared after his death. The other three books are *The Philosophy of the Present* (1932), *Movements of Thought in the Nineteenth Century* (1936), and *The Philosophy of the Act* (1938).

Mind, Self, and Society remains crucial for the manner in which its central concerns dominated all of Mead's philosophizing during the first three decades of this century. Its subtitle—"From the Standpoint of a Social Behaviorist"—indicates the theme. Mead thought that all aspects of human conduct, including those so often covered by terms like "mind" and "self," can best be understood as emergents from a more basic process. The four separate but related parts of the book present Mead's defense of a social behaviorism: "The Point of View of Social Behaviorism," "Mind," "The Self," and "Society."

Mead's attempt to state the nature of social behaviorism is related to the specific situation which he found on hand in the intellectual landscape. As a naturalist strongly influenced by the theory of biological evolution, Mead shows the usual suspicion of older dualistic accounts of the mind-body problem. He sets out to explain physical and mental events by one embracing theory. Thus, he rejects the view that a physico-psychological dualism exists which requires a theory to account for supposed differences between mental and nonmental forms of conduct or between human and nonhuman.

Mead's philosophical views are those of the pragmatists, for whom the function of intelligence is the control of actions rather than a supposedly disinterested description of metaphysical realities thought to be independent of experience. But how is the psychologist to avoid a dualist theory if he retains in his vocabulary words like "mind," "consciousness," "self-conscious-ness," and "self"? This was Mead's initial problem, stated here in the form of a simple question. One answer of the day had come from John B. Watson, sometimes called the father of psychological behaviorism. Watson had argued that the scientific study of human conduct must confine itself strictly to those aspects of behavior which are externally observable. Accordingly, Watson insisted that psychologists give up using terms like "mind" and "self," since what can be observed are brains and nervous systems in response to external stimuli.

Like Watson, Mead claims that any effort to understand human behavior by reliance on introspection of internal mental states produces a theoretical difficulty in that psychological explanations can never be subjected to exper-imental tests. Mead also insists that earlier philosophers made hasty and often illegitimate metaphysical capital out of the distinction between *external* and *internal* aspects of behavior. Thus, he shares Watson's general scientific aim— the statement of a thoroughly behavioral account of human action. But Mead criticizes Watson's physiological version of behaviorism as resting on too narrow a conception of what makes up an action. Words like "mind" and "self" must be kept in the psychological vocabulary, but they should never be thought of as referring to entities or processes which stand outside the subject matter of behavioral analysis. Watson's views result from a heavy reliance on mechanical models as well as from too restricted a notion of the nature of reflex activity. By *reducing* experiences of a mental kind to explicitly physiological correlates, Watson produced a psychological behaviorism which "leads inevitably to obvious absurdities."

Mead's claim is that psychologists need not "explain away" those features of conscious life which often prove embarrassing to strictly physiological an-alysts of conduct. There definitely are minds and selves. The narrow Wat-sonian model fails to take their existence into account. The reason is that the model depicts conduct as created by an organism (containing a brain and a central nervous system) responding to numerous stimuli (response-provoking objects which are external to that organism). Here lies the source of Watson's incorrect view of what action involves, according to Mead. This view lacks an adequate awareness of the *social* aspect of action, especially human action. To produce an adequate behavioral theory of action one needs a model demonstrating that the social aspects of human action *belong partly to* the organism itself rather than *result from* the relations between atomic organisms and external stimuli. What this means is that, in the case of human action, no absolute separation exists between the social and the organic.

The major problem for Mead is to explain how minds and selves appear in the social process. Minds and selves are exclusively features of human conduct. Mead admits that animals possess intelligence but denies that they have minds, even though animals also function in social contexts. The necessary conclusion is, then, that only social beings can be said to possess self-consciousness. Only human organisms are socially based emergents having this specific kind of mental life. How can this be explained? Mead answers in terms of the emergence in the social process of what he calls *significant* symbols. Such symbols are ultimately linguistic in form, but they evolve from the roles played in all organic conduct by gestures and responses to gestures. Certain gestures become significant symbols when "they implicitly arouse in an individual making them the same responses which they explicitly arouse, or are supposed to arouse, in other individuals, the individuals to whom they are addressed. . . ." Human organisms differ from other animal organisms in their ability to make use of significant symbols. For example, a dog which growls at another dog is making a gesture; but the dog cannot make use of a *significant* gesture since he can never take the role of the "other" in a process of communication the way men can and do. Communication involves this taking of the role of the other, self-consciously in a social context. It is this ability possessed by human organisms which makes language and communication possible.

Mead does not argue that "meaning" exists only in linguistic form, but he argues that language constitutes the most meaningful type of communication. For Mead, meaning is objectively *there* as a feature of social processes. "Awareness of consciousness is not necessary to the presence of meaning in the process of social experience." Communication involves making available to others meanings which actually exist to be discovered and talked about. Significant symbols function to make the user of them aware of the responses they call out in those to whom he directs them. The significant symbol not only calls out in the user the awareness of others' responses to it; the symbol functions to make those responses serve as stimuli to the user. This gives an anticipatory character to communication. The result is that users of such symbols can respond to them in novel ways, actually introducing changes into the social situation by such responses. In this view, ideas are anticipations of future expected actions made possible by the capacity to use significant symbols.

This capacity of the human organism to use significant symbols is a precondition of the appearance of the self in the social process. The self is not like the body, which can never view itself as a whole. The self emerges from a process of social communication which enables one to view himself, as a whole, from the perspective of others. Mead treats this problem in terms of the phases of the self, the "me" and the "I." His effort is to understand this human capacity to adopt the attitudes of others toward oneself. Each response to a significant symbol presupposes that one can associate himself with the set of attitudes making up the social group ("the generalized other") to which he belongs. In this manner the "me" emerges as a phase of the self, for the "me" *is* that set of attitudes appropriated by the individual. The "I" as a phase of the self is that which makes possible the organism's response. The "I" can respond to the "me" even in novel ways, meaning that, for Mead, social action is never simply imitative or literally repetitive. Mead makes use of the notions of the game and play to illustrate his thesis. Games and play require participants to adopt the roles of the others involved. Just as in a game one can never get beyond the set of attitudes associated with the various roles of the different players, so in the case of the human "mind" and "self" there is no getting beyond the social process which they presuppose. Without society involving a number of different roles there would be nothing in terms of which a self could arise. Without the viewpoints of others which form the "me" there would exist nothing to which the "I" could respond.

Mead's treatment of the nature of the self permits him to take seriously features of "depth" psychology which Watsonian behaviorism overlooks. To understand a self means to understand something about the roles and attitudes of others as productive of that self. Here Mead finds a difference between the social lives of animals and men. Animal and human social communities involve organization, but in human social systems the organization reflects the self-conscious adoption of a number of roles, a thing impossible in animal communities. The strict organizational patterns found in bee and ant societies do not lead to significant communication or to the creation of a language. While social life is necessary as a condition of the appearance of minds and selves, minds and selves do not always exist where there is social life. *What* emerges in the form of minds and selves *from* a social process is a genuine and an irreducible reality.

Because the self exists only when an individual can know the attitudes of others in a community, it is normal for a multiple self to be present in each person. These attitudes form the possibility of a "me" which can become an object and response-provoking stimulus to an "I." The self can become an object to itself in a way in which a body cannot. The nature of the social community in which the self arises obviously influences the nature of that self. "Normally, within the sort of community as a whole to which we belong, there is a unified self, but that may be broken up. To a person who is somewhat unstable nervously and in whom there is a line of cleavage, certain activities become impossible, and that set of activities may separate and evolve another self."

The pathological aspect of a multiple self concerns the possibility of "forgetting" forms of past experiences from which important elements of the self have emerged. In any existing social community, there must exist some fairly stable attitudes and roles if a self is to emerge at all; and it is the stable elements which permit language to possess a universal significance for communication. The symbols of a language permit a self to respond to the same meaning or object as others in the group using that set of symbols. Linguistic confusions reflect social instability in that meanings are hardly fixed at all. Personality is unable to develop when rapidly altering social attitudes and roles fail to permit language to capture relatively stable meanings. The reason is that there can be no completely individual self. "When a self does appear, it always involves an experience of another; there could not be an experience of a self simply by itself."

In Mead's analysis of the self, the "me" reflects those features which make up the stable habit patterns of an individual's conduct. In a sense, the "me" is the individual's character insofar as it can issue forth in predictable forms of behavior. But how does the "I" arise as a phase of the self which permits some novelty of response? Mead's answer is that the "I" appears only in the memory of what the individual has done. Mead claims that an individual usually knows what he has done and said only *after* he has acted and spoken. There is a retrospective stance to the self-awareness of the "I" which permits novel uses of this memory in new situations. Individuals are not compelled to respond in the same way they formerly did once there is a self. They can react in original ways to the attitudes of other members in the social community. In such reactions the "I" always acts in terms of an appeal to a widened social community if it reacts against the existing practices of the group. Mead claims that the moral importance of the reactions of the "I," as a phase of the self, resides in the individual's sense of importance as a person not totally determined by the attitudes of the others. "The demand is freedom from conventions, from given laws." Such a demand, when it occurs, implies that another community exists, if only potentially or ideally, in which a broader and more embracing self is possible of realization. The complete development of a self therefore requires both phases, the "I" and the "me"—established habits in a social situation which yet leave room for novel responses to new situations.

Each individual in a social community will have some element of a unique standpoint from which to react to the attitudes making up that community. The reason is that each individual can reflect on his own experiences within the social structure supporting his existence. Mead thinks that a rational social community will encourage development of self-responsible action rather than automatic responses by coercive external conditioning. Such a community will provide opportunity for the stereotyped kind of work which each person needs (if he is a healthy individual) plus opportunity for self-expression through unique responses to situations (so that the person does not feel "hedged in" and completely "the conventionalized 'me' "). A rational community differs from a mob or a crowd, for in a rational community the individual can become a determinant of aspects of the environment. Great personalities like Socrates, Jesus, and Buddha were able to influence the communities of their own day and age by their appeals to an enlarged potential community.

Mead's social behaviorism places him in opposition both to the individualistic and to the *partially* social explanations of mind. The individualistic theory argues that mind is a necessary logical and biological presupposition of any existing social process. Its adherents attempt to account for the social aspect of human existence in terms of contract theories of the origin of political and social life. The *partially* social theory admits that mind can express its potentialities only in a social setting but insists mind is in some sense prior to that setting. Mead argues that his social behaviorism is in direct contrast to these competing theories in that "mind presupposes, and is a product of, the social process." For Mead, the forms of social groupings tend either toward cooperative or aggressively competitive ones. Mead favors the former. He believes that the democratic ideal of full human participation in a variety of social situations (involving different roles) can best call out the wide range of human responses which mind makes possible. In a democratic society the twin quests after universality of experience, economic and religious, can best be harmonized. Such a society also makes available a wider range of roles from which an individual can develop a self. It is clear that, for Mead, democracy involves a society which permits a rich variety of primary groups to exist.

Mead's attempt to state a consistent theory of social behaviorism may have failed. In fact, his position is a metaphysical rather than a scientific one. However, his views form a metaphysical defense of the democratic ideal in terms of the behavioral hopes of psychologists to bring human conduct under rational control. Mead is at least on the side of reason and rationality. He is stubborn in his refusal to give up terms like "mind" and "consciousness," and he is equally unwilling to discard the behaviorist model of the psychologists. He tries valiantly to widen men's conception of the human act. The critical question remains, naturally, whether Mead or any man can have the best of two possible worlds.—*W. T. D.*

PERTINENT LITERATURE

Miller, David L. *George Herbert Mead: Self, Language, and the World.* Austin: University of Texas Press, 1973.

David L. Miller had been a student of George Herbert Mead at the University of Chicago and a coeditor of his mentor's notes and papers published in 1938 as *The Philosophy of the Act.* His book is a comprehensive reinterpretation of Mead's thought in the light of recent philosophy. Thus he relates Mead's themes to process philosophy, analytic philosophy, phenomenology, and existentialism. He situates and examines Mead's social psychology within the broader context of cosmology, metaphysics, and the natural and social sciences, fed by mathematics, astronomy, physics, biology, physiology, and neurology. Further, he locates Mead's entire philosophy within the American tradition of pragmatism. Miller's purpose is, in part, to stimulate others to develop Mead's suggestions in the philosophy of mind, social psychology, epistemology, metaphysics, and the philosophy of science.

Particular chapters of Miller's book are directly pertinent to Mead's *Mind, Self, and Society*. Chapters 1 and 2 touch on relevant concepts, while Chapters 3 and 4 are most crucially germane to the social psychology; the final chapter deals with Mead's ethical theory.

Chapter 1 is devoted to Mead's conception of biosocial man. Miller discusses the naturalistic basis of Mead's thought and amplifies the pragmatist theory of knowledge. He compares Mead's theory of the self with the theories of others—Sigmund Freud, René Descartes, and the existentialists. Instead of splitting the self into a Freudian id and superego, Mead proposed a functional dualism of the "I" and the "me," stressing the creative interplay of these two facets of the self in lieu of the repression or destruction of one by the other. Unlike the isolated Cartesian ego, Mead's self is social, capable of assuming the attitudes and roles of others, so that the individual is itself a product of social process. Nor is the self a passion, as Jean-Paul Sartre has taught, but essentially a thinking being engaged in the symbolic process of language use.

Chapter 2 is an exposition of Mead's basic terms and intentions. Especially noteworthy for understanding Mead's social psychology is Miller's account of the act, including the subconcepts of the primitive social act and the social act which involves the manipulating phase. In Chapter 3 Miller expounds Mead's concept of the self, traces the origin and development of the self, and explains how it functions in society. Miller compares and contrasts Mead's views with the theories of others, such as Charles Cooley, William James, and Immanuel Kant. And he draws upon another, unpublished set of notes taken from Mead's famous course in social psychology.

Chapter 4 recapitulates Mead's theory of language and of the significant symbol. Of course, theory of language has become a field more central to philosophy since Mead's time; but for Mead, who retained mentalistic terms in his social behaviorism, language was essential in mind and its operations. Miller discusses Mead's theory of language in connection with the more fashionable views of Ludwig Wittgenstein and the post-Wittgensteinians. Thus Mead, who would not have condoned the extensionalist picture theory of meaning espoused by Wittgenstein in his *Tractatus Logico-Philosophicus*, would perhaps have favored the Viennese philosopher's later strictures on private language, without succumbing, however, to the reductionism of orthodox behaviorism. Miller also probes Mead's theory of the significant symbol and examines, in a penetratingly original way, the doctrine of universals that is involved, and compares this theory with the rival conceptions of Gilbert Ryle, Wittgenstein, and Alfred North Whitehead. He closes Chapter 4 with a section on language use among lower animals.

In the final chapter Miller shows that Mead's ethical theory, which is central to the social psychology and social philosophy, has much in common with Kant's, although it is grounded in a naturalistic, evolutionist conception of man and society.

Metzger, Bernard N. *The Social Psychology of George Herbert Mead.* Kalamazoo: Center for Sociological Research, Western Michigan University Press, 1964.

This monograph is designed to serve as supplementary reading for courses in sociological theory and social psychology. It presents the main elements in George Herbert Mead's thought which inspired the theory of symbolic interactionism advanced by perhaps his most famous disciple in social psychology, Herbert G. Blumer. While Bernard N. Metzger mainly summarizes the essential contents of Mead's social psychology, he is guided by adherence to symbolic interactionism. Thus he maintains that Mead sought to explain human behavior not simply in biological terms, but rather by reference to socially interpreted and shared meanings. The "conversation of gestures," illustrated in the posture, facial movement, and snarls of fighting dogs—and also in the behavior of hens clucking at their chicks—is transformed in human behavior by the development of language, which involves intended meanings. Exclusively physical in the case of the lower animals, gestures become significant symbols when individual human beings, socially interacting with one another, form intentions and ascertain intentions on the part of others and, moreover, respond to one another in accord with these intentions.

Against Mead's social psychology Metzger raises three major lines of criticism. First, he finds some of Mead's crucial concepts vague. In particular he underscores various concepts for their fuzziness: impulse, meaning, mind, self, the "I," the generalized other, and so on. He attributes the vagueness of Mead's thought to two factors: incomplete and undeveloped conceptions and formulations and, in addition, uncritical adherence to an emergent evolutionist philosophy which induced him to emphasize the continuity of animal and human behavior while also stressing the novelty of the latter. Second, Metzger observes that Mead's theory is marred by broad substantive omissions. A purely analytical scheme, Mead's theory lacks empirical content, and it furnishes no basis for explaining specific human behavior. Moreover, Mead's theory neglects the affective components, sentiments, and emotions, so that it ignores the unconscious or the subconscious as a factor in human behavior and adjustment. Finally, Metzger charges that Mead's theory is defective methodologically. For the most part, the theory does not appear to be amenable to scientific research, since Mead, who never presented any systematic evidence for his theory, also never related how his analytical scheme could either be verified or employed in research.

Nevertheless, Metzger agrees with John Dewey in esteeming Mead to have been a seminal thinker of the first rank. He counts Charles Cooley, William I. Thomas, Robert E. Park, Robert L. Burgess, Ellsworth Faris, and Blumer the most prominent among the social psychologists whom Mead deeply influenced, and he concludes his monograph with an appreciative assessment of Mead's positive contributions to social psychology. He credits Mead with originating the symbolic interactionist theory, which distinguishes human behavior from other forms of behavior by virtue of its responsiveness to what situations signify (or symbolically signify) for organisms capable of thought and imaginative interpretation. Furthermore, he praises Mead for the following achievements: (1) adopting a sociological rather than a narrowly biological explanation of mind and selfhood, (2) clarifying the role of language as the mechanism for development of the mind and the self, (3) advancing a theory of the self which delineates the reciprocal influence of society and the individual, (4) interpreting mind as the internalization of the social process within the psychobiological individual, (5) construing the act as the dynamic principle by which individuals construct not only their ongoing activity but also the objects which constitute their environments, (6) describing how human individuals develop and form a common world, and (7) showing how human beings, instead of merely responding mechanically to one another's external behavior as the lower animals do, actually share one another's conduct and meanings.

Hansen, Donald A. *An Invitation to Critical Sociology: Involvement, Criticism, Exploration.* New York: The Free Press, 1976.

Donald A. Hansen invites the reader to become an involved, critical explorer of the possibilities for man and society. As a consequence of both the spread of a technological rationalism which undermines traditional human values and the pervasive relativism which erodes these same values, there is, according to this book, a crying need for critical sociology. The alternative offered by existentialism will not suffice, despite its natural grounding in human feelings. Whereas existentialism opens no avenues to social reconstruction, critical sociology is most promising in this regard.

Hansen concentrates on three pioneering sociologists: George Herbert Mead, Karl Marx, and Max Weber. Each is esteemed for having extended an invitation to critical sociology, although each has a different orientation. Mead invites us to self-and-other awareness, apprehended as the foundation of our personal freedom and responsibility, while entangling us in a social network involving others. Marx invites us to transcend self-and-other awareness and social involvement to engage in social criticism and action, and to question conventional interpretations of social organization and functioning. Weber invites us to conjoin social commitment with social criticism and to explore the possibilities and limitations of man and society. Throughout the book Hansen compares and contrasts the theories of these three sociologists. Part One of this tripartite book is devoted to Mead. Between two chapters on the invitation of Mead is sandwiched a chapter with the title, "The Beats: Images of Community and Change."

The first chapter on Mead's invitation opens with an exposition of his account of the genesis of the self. Although this account stresses the priority of the social process, the individual self, according to Hansen, is no merely passive social product. Analyzed by Mead to consist of an "I" and "me," the self displays in its "I" aspect the function of creative activity. Even the continuity of the temporal process, climactic in a present which incorporates the past and faces the future, is indispensable for the persistence and the stability of the self and society; yet, this fundamental temporal continuity is an achievement of the interpretations and reconstructions of creative selves within society. Operative throughout the social process, creativity is conspicuous in superior individuals. Hence individual creativity is indispensable to society.

In the chapter on the Beats, Hansen examines their search for communal brotherhood, revealing how their progress and defeat illustrate facets of the social process Mead had uncovered decades earlier at the theoretical level. The collapse of the Woodstock nation at the Altamount in California in late 1969 symbolizes a societal principle which Mead had recognized—namely, that divisive hostility accompanies communal cohesion.

The last chapter on Mead explores what American sociology has tended to ignore—in Hansen's words, "the tough Mead." The reader encounters a social thinker who, despite his general optimism about the ideals and possibilities of democratic society, nevertheless faced the ugly facts of human character. Society is inescapably fraught with conflict, and this breeds hostility. Yet, as Mead emphasized, social cohesion in turn is fed by hostility; the members of a society unify in their struggle against others. Hostility is evident, on the one hand, in the system of punitive justice, and, on the other hand, in war; and in both instances it enhances social cohesion. For Mead, therefore, there was no easily attained moral equivalent for the dark impulses of human nature upon which society rests. While he remained optimistic about the success of the democratizing processes of social interplay and sympathy, Mead failed to understand the economic substructure which underlies society and to apprehend the bureaucratic superstructure which overlies society. Hansen finds fault with Mead in this regard, and he looks to Marx and to Weber to supplement Mead's critical sociology.—*A.J.R.*

ADDITIONAL RECOMMENDED READING

Corti, Walter Robert, ed. *The Philosophy of George Herbert Mead*. Winterthur, Switzerland: Archiv für genetische Philosophie, 1973. A collection of papers, including two by Van Meter Ames, a former student of Mead, entitled "No Separate Self" and "Mead and European Philosophers—Husserl, Sartre, Buber."

Lee, Grace Chin. *George Herbert Mead: Philosopher of the Social Individual*. New York: King's Crown Press, 1945. A lucid, well-researched dissertation, with focus on Mead's social psychology.

Natanson, Maurice. *The Social Dynamics of George H. Mead*. Washington, D.C.: Public Affairs Press, 1956. A dense critical interpretation of Mead's social psychology and temporalist metaphysics from the standpoint of European phenomenology.

Pfeutze, Paul E. *The Social Self*. New York: Bookman Associates, 1954. A comparison of Mead's naturalistic social psychology and philosophy with Martin Buber's religiously inspired thought.

Reck, Andrew J. *Recent American Philosophy: Studies of Ten Representative Thinkers*. New York: Pantheon Books, 1964. Mead's social psychology considered within the framework of his constructive pragmatism and twentieth century American thought.

Rucker, Egbert Darnell. *The Chicago Pragmatists*. Minneapolis: University of Minnesota Press, 1969. Mead's life and work discussed in its institutional setting.

THE LOGIC OF SCIENTIFIC DISCOVERY

Author: Sir Karl R. Popper (1902-   )
Type of work: Philosophy of science and epistemology
First published: 1935 (German); 1959 (English)

PRINCIPAL IDEAS ADVANCED

The method of testing in the empirical sciences is characterized, not by inductive inference, but by deducing empirically testable claims from proposed theories.

Falsification, not verification, is crucial in science.

Scientific propositions are to be distinguished from nonscientific in that only the former are empirically falsifiable.

The asymmetry between verification and falsification makes it possible for a falsification criterion to succeed where the verification principle failed.

A scientist proposing a theory must state the conditions under which it will be appropriate to reject it.

Karl R. Popper's *The Logic of Scientific Discovery*, described by N. R. Hansen as without doubt one of the most important books ever written on the philosophy of science and by P. B. Medawar as "one of the most important documents of the twentieth century," begins with a consideration of the problem of induction. An inference is inductive, Popper explains, if it moves from a singular statement (roughly, a statement whose subject term refers to some particular concrete thing) to one or more universal statements (roughly, statements whose subject terms refer to all the members of a class of things). In science, such inferences occur when one passes from descriptions of particular experimental results to hypotheses or theories alleged to be justified by these results. *All observed swans have been white* sums up a set of particular statements which report observations of concrete particular items. *All swans are white* expresses a universal statement one might inductively infer from that summary.

Notoriously, Popper notes, such inferences are not deductively valid, and *the problem of induction* is the question of whether such inferences are ever rationally legitimate, and if so under what conditions. One widely held view, Popper notes, is that the universal statements which express natural laws, or laws of science, or well-confirmed scientific theories, or the like, are known by experience; that is, singular statements are statements known by experience from which the natural-law-expressing universal statements may somehow legitimately be derived. Hence, in this view, the problem of induction has some proper solution.

This alleged solution, Popper continues, is often expressed in terms of a *principle* of induction—a proposition known to be true which can be placed in inferences from singular to universal scientific statements and whose presence in such inference renders the inference rationally compelling. Some philosophers, Hans Reichenbach among them, have held that without some principle of induction, science would be without decision procedure and could no longer distinguish solid theory from superstition.

This alleged principle of induction, Popper notes, cannot be a logical truth or a statement true by virtue of its very form or structure (because no such proposition would legitimately lead one from *All observed A's are B* to *All A's are B*, or from singular to universal statement in any other case). It must rather be synthetic, or not contradictory to deny. How, though, Popper asks—consciously restating an argument offered by David Hume—shall we rationally justify our acceptance of this principle? It must be not a singular but a universal statement. We cannot certify its truth by logic alone. If, then, we try to justify it from experience we shall again face the very sort of derivation of universal from singular statements the principle itself was meant to sanction, and so on *ad infinitum* if we appeal to a higher-order inductive principle. Perhaps, as Reichenbach contends, an inductive principle is accepted by "the whole of science"; but, Popper asks, cannot "the whole of science" err? Nor, Popper continues, will it do to say that singular statements, while they do not *entail* universal conclusions, nevertheless render such conclusions probable, for then we should need some principle of probability, and while perhaps this would differ in content from a principle of induction, its justification would present exactly similar difficulties. Thus it is clear that Popper completely rejects the familiar inductivist view that, while not rendering universal statements certain or providing conclusive justification for them, true singular statements can provide good reason for universal statements or render them (at least to some degree) probable. Popper argues that, if some degree N of probability is to be assigned to statements based on inductive inference of some sort, then some sort of principle of induction must be somehow justified. How this is to be done remains utterly problematic, even if one weakens the alleged relationship between singular premise and universal conclusion ("providing some degree of reliability" replacing "inductively justifies") or the alleged status of the conclusion ("probable" replacing "true"). Other attempts to shore up induction, Popper feels, are equally unsuccessful.

Obviously, Popper also rejects the views that induction *needs* no justification and that universal statements are merely, albeit perhaps infinite, conjuncts of singular statements. In this respect, Popper's view agrees with an acid (but not for that reason incorrect) remark by Bertrand Russell to the effect that there are two kinds of reasoning: deductive and bad.

Rejection of inductive reasoning, Popper holds, involves much gain and no loss. Obviously, however, if he rejects inductive inferences and hence inductive confirmation of theories, Popper must replace this account of scientific method by some other. It is this positive, constructive task that is the central topic of *The Logic of Scientific Discovery*.

The basic task of the scientist, Popper contends, is to put forward, and then test, theories. Part of this task, of course, is the invention of theories, a matter Popper holds "neither to call for logical analysis nor to be susceptible of it." Study of the conditions, activities, and stages included in the invention of theories, he holds, is a matter for psychology, not philosophy. Philosophy, or the "logic of knowledge" as opposed to its psychology, is concerned with the *testing* part of the scientist's task.

This testing procedure, Popper tells us, begins by deducing consequences from the theory being tested; the theory, in effect, becomes a premise from which conclusions are deductively derived. This done, Popper continues, four lines of testing may be distinguished. First, the conclusions may be compared among themselves; this provides something of a test as to the internal consistency of the theory. Second, the conclusions may be examined to see if the theory has any empirical consequences, and so is scientific as opposed to tautological. Third, the conclusions may be compared to those of other theories to see whether the theory, if it survived empirical tests, is such that its acceptance would mean scientific advance. Fourth, the empirical conclusions or predictions, if any, are applied to experimental results to see if what the theory tells us will occur really does occur.

It is this fourth line of testing which is central for Popper. It is the *new* empirical consequences of a theory—empirical conclusions which follow from it but not from hitherto-accepted theories—that gain the assessor's attention. These predictions are compared with the results of relevant experiments, old or new; if the predictions of what would happen under certain circumstances are not correct descriptions of what did happen under those conditions, the theory, Popper notes, is falsified. (The form of deductive inference involved here is the simple and standard *modus tollens*: if p entails q, and q is false, then p is false.) If the predictions are correct, then the theory is (so far) verified. A theory which, often tested, is not falsified is *corroborated*, although this is fundamentally a matter of *not having been falsified*. This doctrine of testing procedure raises various questions, some of which we will discuss shortly. What Popper emphasizes most, however, is that the procedure outlined above contains no inductive procedures whatever, and yet—*contra* Reichenbach—does not leave the scientist, or the philosopher of science, without rational decision procedure when faced with a choice between incompatible theories.

Popper's "criterion of demarcation" requires that a genuinely scientific hypothesis must be (in principle) empirically falsifiable. Popper regards distinguishing the nonscientific (including what is logical, or mathematical, or metaphysical) from the scientific—a task he designates "the problem of demarcation"—as an epistemological problem, perhaps the most basic one. He holds that appeal to inductive reasoning provides no solution to this problem, and that his own testing-through-attempting-to-falsify account of scientific decision procedure solves it.

In contrast to traditional (for example, Humean) empiricism, which recognized as scientific only concepts analyzable in terms of sensory phenomena, Popper holds that statements, not concepts, are the basic elements of scientific theories. In contrast to contemporary empiricism, which at least to some degree replaced analysis of concepts by analysis of statements, but recognized as scientific only statements derivable from (or reducible to) elementary perceptual claims, Popper holds that any statement which entails a proposition which describes a possible experimental or observational result is scientific, whether it is itself entailed by some set of elementary perceptual claims. ("Scientific" here does not mean "part of science," and certainly not "true," but something like "within the scope of scientific interest." One might say that mathematical claims are those which, whether true or false, fall within the domain of mathematics in that they are decidable by its procedures; then one is using the word "mathematical" in a sense analogous to that in which "scientific" is used above.)

Popper is quite candid about a feature of his view which has given others pause. His criterion of demarcation, he admits, rests, if not securely, then at least squarely, on a *convention*. He distinguishes science from nonscience, he tells us, not on the basis of some discernible intrinsic difference between scientific and nonscientific propositions, but on the basis, in effect, of a decision that the science/nonscience distinction be made along the line of demarcation. This decision, he admits, is not beyond rational dispute; but he adds that any such dispute can be only among those who share his purposes, and whether one does that or not, he holds, *is* beyond rational dispute. Thus if Popper succeeds in marking off what is of scientific interest from what is not, he feels he will have been triumphant. The logical positivists, he contends, shared his purpose but, by appealing to the verification principle (which, roughly, asserts that a sentence has truth value only if it is either a tautology or is empirically confirmable or disconfirmable) as their principle of demarcation, failed to provide a basis for distinguishing science from metaphysics. The core of their failure, Popper suggests, is found in their acceptance of induction as a confirmation method. By contrast, and without claiming anything about whether metaphysical propositions have truth value, Popper holds that his own criterion does mark out the desired distinction. If one has some other end in mind, there is neither reason nor need to suppose his criterion will serve that end.

Popper, then, views science as an empirical theoretical system—a system of synthetic or nontautological statements which represents not only a possible but also our actual world of experience. That a system does represent our world is guaranteed only by its having been exposed to unsuccessful falsification attempts. This, Popper notes, falls short of the ideal of such philosophers as Moritz Schlick and Friedrich Waismann who require that meaningful statements be conclusively verifiable or in principle determined as true; it replaces this ideal by another—that a scientific statement be capable of being refuted by experience. Lest this seem to trivialize natural laws, Popper points out that the more ways there are of refuting a proposition, or the more ways there are of its going wrong, then the more information the proposition contains. Information content waxes proportionate to falsifiability potential.

The falsification strategy, Popper notes, is made possible by an asymmetry between verification and falsification; that a proposition cannot be verified or established does not entail that it cannot be falsified or refuted, and that a proposition can be falsified does not entail that it can be verified. Further, while even if we limit ourselves to propositions with empirical content, while no set of singular statements will entail a universal statement, a universal statement will entail singular statements. The failure of the verification principle, Popper asserts, is no reason to expect the falsification criterion to suffer a similar fate.

A complication, if not a problem, arises, however, when we note that, as Pierre Duhem and W. V. O. Quine have emphasized, rarely if ever does a theory all by itself entail any predictions; it does so only together with auxiliary hypotheses. Schematically, one has not that *T* (theory) entails *P* (prediction), but that *T and H* (auxiliary hypothesis) entails *P*. If, then, one deduces *P* from *T and H*, and discovers that under the relevant controlled experimental conditions, *P* turns out to be false, various alternatives remain open. One could reject the rule of inference by which *P* was derived, or claim that the experiment was not properly conducted, or deny that one's perception of the result was correct, although these alternatives may often seem (and be) radical. Or one could reject *T*, or else *H*. If one rejects *H*, one can retain *T* without recourse to any of the other alternatives noted. If one always rejects the auxiliary hypotheses, no theories will ever be falsified. To put it mildly, this would be inconvenient for Popper's perspective.

Popper, of course, is fully aware of the problem. To meet it, he specifies that, when a member of a scientific community proffers a theory, he or she also is to specify the conditions under which the theory itself (and not some other proposition, be it auxiliary hypothesis or whatever) is to be abandoned. In such fashion, as it were, those who play the game of science must be prepared to say when they will admit defeat.

Popper maintains that his view provides for the objectivity of scientific theories which, he contends, lies in their being intersubjectively testable. If science is to have an empirical basis, he continues, the propositions comprising this basis must themselves be objective, and hence intersubjectively testable. Thus they must entail predictions, and so on *ad infinitum* so that science can contain no ultimate statements. The infinite regress thus produced, he argues, is not vicious; true, every claim can be tested and testing must stop somewhere so that some claim is accepted which is not tested—some claims will be accepted as correct observational reports without their having run a falsification gauntlet. But this, Popper reminds us, violates no tenet of his philosophy of science, and (in principle) one can test any proposition one wishes. The net effect of this is that scientific knowledge is possible without its being required to rest on allegedly indubitable propositions. Popper explicitly rejects the view that science is comprised of propositions about which we are rightly epistemically certain—about which it is logically impossible that we are wrong—and his methodology in philosophy of science rules out science's having, or needing, indubitable foundations. In this important respect, as in others, he differs from classical empiricism.

It has been claimed that what Popper says often seems simple, even obvious. Perhaps it often is; but then it was not "obvious" until he said it. The above summary of Popper's views probably does not give much hint of their breadth and depth. A sense of that comes on the one hand from knowing something of the intellectual landscape he occupied—the issues and problems he dealt with and the light he threw on them—and on the other hand from reading the rich detail of *The Logic of Scientific Discovery* and the later *Conjectures and Refutations.—K.E.Y.*

PERTINENT LITERATURE

Toulmin, Stephen. "Conclusion: The Cunning of Reason," in *Human Understanding*. Vol. I. Princeton, New Jersey: Princeton University Press, 1972.

Stephen Toulmin in *Human Understanding* (as we shall see) deals with some of the same fundamental issues as Karl R. Popper does in *The Logic of Scientific Discovery*, so it is natural that Toulmin should discuss Popper's views. Toulmin argues that in science as well as in ethics the actual cultural diversity of human concepts, cross-culturally and historically, poses an intractable problem for those who view *rationality* as a property of particular propositional or conceptual systems. In this view, scientific rationality is a matter of inference within scientific theories, and the history of science becomes a story of one system of propositions being succeeded by another.

Recently, Toulmin reports, philosophers have sought to extend the notion of rationality beyond the meaning provided to it by formal logic, and to develop this notion in such a way that it has application to contexts involving conceptual change. Among such philosophers are Popper, as well as Thomas Kuhn and Imre Lakatos. His own view, Toulmin notes, might be seen as fitting within this general perspective, but Toulmin finds that his own argument, in one fundamental way at least, opposes the tendency these other philosophers share. Popper and the others, Toulmin reports, begin by taking a formal logician's perspective on science, and thus they find conceptual change somewhat anomalous. Toulmin rejects this choice of a beginning, as well as the consequences he takes to follow from it.

This view, Toulmin suggests, involves a confusion or makes a mistaken identification; it misconstrues the nature of rationality. Toulmin contends that instead of being identified with a property of conceptual systems, rationality should be seen in terms of the procedures by means of which persons change from one set of beliefs or concepts to another. Failure to do this—or continuing to view (scientific) rationality as a matter of inference within scientific systems—Toulmin argues, has led to viewing the basis for choosing between scientific systems to be not rational judgment but pragmatic preference.

Popper's treatment of the logic of scientific research, Toulmin notes, focuses on problems of formal proof or disproof. He held, Toulmin continues, that the universal and timeless criterion which any genuine scientific hypothesis must meet is that of being falsifiable by experience. Rational progress in science is for Popper a matter of elimination of hypotheses. Toulmin adds that although Popper later modified his position to the extent that hypotheses may achieve a degree of positive corroboration, having some higher status than merely failing to be rejected, it is still *whether propositions are acceptable*, rather than *whether concepts are applicable*, that is Popper's concern. Ultimately, Toulmin contends, Popper imposes on science a procedure not drawn from within its own procedures and proposes a definition of the scientific which is ultimately arbitrary.

One consequence of this approach, Toulmin contends, is that lines of theoretical advance, although justified in themselves, are closed off because they do not conform to the (arbitrary) criterion for being scientific. Paul Feyerabend, Toulmin reminds us, has strongly protested against this aspect, as he sees it, of Popper's thought.

If one is committed to making rationality a characteristic not of procedures of conceptual change but of systems of substantive scientific propositions, the only alternative to Popper's own account, Toulmin suggests, is to pay closer attention than does Popper to the actual history of science—to what scientists as scientists have actually done—and hope to discern in this history some illumination concerning scientific rationality. This, Toulmin says, Lakatos and Kuhn, each in his own way, has done. Toulmin is not satisfied, however, that either has succeeded in providing a satisfactory account of scientific rationality.

Lakatos, Toulmin finds, simply continues Popper's argument, discussing the history of science in terms taken over from formal logic. Even though Lakatos stresses the importance of the actual history of science (Toulmin thinks that Popper's interest in historical episodes does not prevent his philosophy of science from being fundamentally ahistorical), his shared beginnings with Popper lead him to expect, Toulmin contends, "knock-down dialectical victories" in scientific, and particularly in philosophy-of-science, disputes. Further, Toulmin continues, while Lakatos goes so far as to say that if a demarcation criterion is inconsistent with what practicing scientists will accept as the distinction between what is and what is not scientific, then the demarcation criterion should be rejected, he does not make clear how his own criterion (based on the notion of a research program) is concretely to be applied to actual instances so as to tell what is and what is not scientifically rational. In particular, Toulmin contends, we are not told how to recognize when even majority scientific opinion, or the judgment of the "scientific elite," is mistaken; nor are we given the grounds on which such judgment should be overturned.

Toulmin finds Kuhn's position, which he claims shares Popper's sort of starting point although it differs from Popper's view in important ways, is also a failure in its endeavor to offer a satisfactory account of scientific rationality. The core of Kuhn's position, according to Toulmin, involves appeal to *what scientists normally do*, and he finds this ambiguous between *what scientists habitually do* and *what scientists properly do*. The former meaning, Toulmin contends, leads to relativism and provides no appeal beyond sheer scientific practice. The latter meaning, he adds, has Kuhn depending on criteria such as maximum predictive accuracy, and thus imposing on scientific procedures standards not discovered from a study of actual scientific endeavors.

Toulmin, then, finds Popper's own approach to scientific rationality, as well as that of Lakatos and Kuhn, whom he sees as sharing Popper's starting point, to be inadequate. His basic purpose in *Human Understanding* is to provide his own alternative account.

Lakatos, Imre. "Popper on Demarcation and Induction," in *The Methodology of Scientific Research Programmes*. Edited by John Worrall and Gregory Currie. Cambridge: Cambridge University Press, 1978, pp. 139-167.

Imre Lakatos claims that Karl R. Popper's ideas represent "the most important development in the philosophy of the twentieth century," and compares his accomplishment to David Hume's, Immanuel Kant's, and William Whewell's. Popper, he reports, discussed two basic problems in *The Logic of Scientific Discovery*—the problem of demarcation and the problem of induction; the second problem, Popper contended, was an "instance or facet" of the former, although Lakatos disagrees with this. Lakatos reports that, according to Popper, the logic of scientific discovery is comprised of a set of rules for appraisal of already-stated theories; the rules are tentative and cannot be mechanically applied.

Given Popper's work, Lakatos notes, the term "normative" in the expression "normative philosophy of science" has come to refer not to rules for coming up with solutions, but to rules for appraising solutions. Popper, he continues, proposed that a theory should be taken seriously only when a crucial experiment has been devised for it, and rejected when it fails such an experiment. Thus theories are not established or made probable, but rather are eliminated, by appeal to experience; clash with, not confirmation by, experience becomes central. Lakatos thus describes the history of science, viewed in Popperian terms, as a duel between theories and experiences in which experiences can win but theories can only survive.

What is actually tested, as Lakatos tells us Popper was aware, is not isolated statements, or even isolated theories, but clusters of theories. (The relevance of this is that if theories T1, T2, T3 and T4 together lead to the conclusion that x will happen under condition C, and x does not happen under C, then, barring some error of inference or experiment, we must reject T1, or T2, or T3, or T4. But we do not yet know *which*.)

Lakatos reports Popper's view to be that we must decide, in advance of running a crucial experiment, which claim or theory will be abandoned if the experiment fails (that is, does not come out as the current theories require)— even should this involve a guess agreed upon by scientists. Such guesses are crucial to Popper's theory; moreover, they must be guesses as to what components of theories, not what statements of initial conditions, shall be rejected. This is required, Lakatos explains, because if whenever a theory entails that, under certain initial conditions, something x will happen, and x in fact does not occur under those conditions, we allow ourselves always to say that the descriptions of initial conditions were at fault (the actual initial conditions only *seemed* to fit the description of those under which, according to the theory, x would occur), then we shall never refute or eliminate any theory. Thus, Lakatos continues, Popper requires that a scientist who wishes his theories to be taken seriously to specify in advance of running them what crucial experiments there are whose failure to go as their theories requires will bring them to abandon those theories—and to abandon the basic assumptions they involve. This rule, he suggests, is basic among the conventions which, for Popper, define the "game of science."

Pursuing the metaphor, Lakatos notes that the opening move in the game involved the presentation of a logically consistent hypothesis or theory which, under agreed-upon conditions, would be falsified. The proposition, Lakatos continues, which expresses the experimental results which would falsify the hypothesis or theory is a *basic* proposition, and there must be unanimous agreement within the scientific community that some experimental results will yield knowledge as to the truth value of the basic statement. Then the crucial experiment is repeatedly run. If, Lakatos tells us, the experiment goes as the theory requires, the theory is corroborated, which only means that it lives to duel again; if it goes otherwise, it is falsified. Should there not be unanimity as to whether the results went as the theory requires, then either the hypothesis is withdrawn, or a new basic proposition is formulated; or perhaps unanimity is purchased at the price of expulsion from the scientific community of the members as one side in the dispute.

Lakatos adds that if a theory is falsified, its replacement must explain whatever success its predecessor had—account for what its predecessor succeeded in accounting for. Further, Lakatos explains, it must contain new empirical content over its predecessor. Once a new hypothesis of the indicated sort has been proferred, it is tested. Science, Lakatos indicates, progresses, in Popper's view, in the sense that the replacing hypotheses have more empirical content and pose deeper questions about the world than those they replace.

Lakatos' presentation makes it clear that Popper rests the demarcation of science from nonscience on conventions or (nominalistic) definitions. Popper suggests that only those who agree on what constitutes the purpose of science will be able to develop a rational procedure for assessing his conventions or definitions; and Popper, in turn, Lakatos explains, views the adoption of such purposes as nonrational, or beyond the scope of argument. Lakatos adds that Popper never specifies a purpose for the game of science that transcends the rules of that game, nor does he provide a procedure for assessing one logically consistent set of rules over another. Popper proposed, for the first time in 1957, Lakatos indicates, that the goal of science is truth, but in *The Logic of Scientific Discovery* this was classified as a (psychological) motive of scientists, "not a rational *purpose* of science." Thus, Lakatos contends, Popper has no theory of how noncontradictory conventions are to be assessed. Putting the matter in Popperian terms, Lakatos remarks that Popper has not told us under what conditions he would abandon his own criterion of demarcation. Lakatos concludes his essay by endeavoring to supply what he has argued that Popper failed to provide.—*K.E.Y.*

ADDITIONAL RECOMMENDED READING

Kuhn, Thomas. *The Structure of Scientific Revolutions*. Chicago: University of Chicago Press, 1970. Presents a major alternate approach to Popper's.

Lakatos, Imre. *Philosophical Papers*. Edited by John Worrall and Gregory Currie. Cambridge: Cambridge University Press, 1978. Collection of essays developing a Popperian type of approach.

Lakatos, Imre and Alan Musgrave, eds. *Criticism and the Growth of Knowledge*. London: Cambridge University Press, 1970. Discussion of Kuhn's views, including a contribution by Popper.

Magee, Bryan. *Karl Popper*. New York: The Viking Press, 1973. An introduction to Popper's thought; in the *Modern Masters* series.

—————. *Modern British Philosophy*. New York: St. Martin's Press, 1971. Contains contributions by Popper.

Popper, Karl R. *Conjectures and Refutations: The Growth of Scientific Knowledge*. London: Routledge and Kegan Paul, 1963. An account of Popper's views; variations on the theme that we can learn from our mistakes.

Schlipp, Paul A., ed. *The Philosophy of Karl Popper* (The Library of Living

Philosophers). La Salle, Illinois: Open Court, 1974. Thirty-three essays on Popper, plus Autobiography and Reply.

PHILOSOPHY AND LOGICAL SYNTAX

Author: Rudolf Carnap (1891-1970)
Type of work: Philosophy of philosophy
First published: 1935

PRINCIPAL IDEAS ADVANCED

Philosophy is the logical analysis of meaningful language.

Meaningful language is either the language of logic and mathematics (involving analytic sentences) or the language of science (involving empirically verifiable synthetic sentences).

Metaphysics and ethics are not legitimate parts of philosophy for their language is meaningless.

Logical analysis is logical syntax, and logical syntax is the study of the manipulation of signs in accordance with the rules of a language.

Rudolf Carnap's *Philosophy and Logical Syntax* is the substance of three lectures which he gave at the University of London in 1934. As a result, the book is short, presenting the essentials of the logical positivism of the Vienna Circle in outline form. It is perhaps as good an outline summary of the Vienna Circle views as is available, coming, as it does, from the pen of the best known—and perhaps the most influential—member of the group.

Logical positivism is certainly not an unknown movement to American and British philosophers. During the 1930's and early 1940's it seemed destined to sweep all other philosophical movements into the forgotten and insignificant areas of the past. Recent days, of course, have seen the movement called into question, but the ghost of the verifiability criterion of meaning and the emotive theory of ethics still stalks the philosophical world.

Logical positivism had its origin in a seminar conducted in the 1920's in Vienna by Moritz Schlick. A number of the members of this group, the original "Vienna Circle," were scientists reacting against those idealist philosophers who pontificated, sometimes in almost complete ignorance, about the aim and function of science. Part of positivism's program was the explicit rejection of this kind of irresponsible philosophizing. Another characteristic concern of the group was a strong interest in logic, an interest which grew out of their admiration for the work which had been done on the foundations of mathematics toward the close of the nineteenth century and in the early twentieth century, particularly the work of Whitehead and Russell in their *Principia Mathematica* (1910-1913). These interests quite naturally led the Vienna group to deliberate regarding philosophy's proper business. They decided that philosophy is properly the analysis and clarification of meaningful language. By meaningful language they meant the language of empirical science together with the language of mathematics; all other language, they held, lacked cognitive meaning. The Vienna Circle philosophers gave expression to this conviction in their criterion of empirical meaning, a widely known and vigorously debated tenet of logical positivism.

Carnap spends the first of the three chapters of *Philosophy and Logical Syntax* discussing the implications of the verifiability criterion. At one point he states that only the propositions of mathematics and empirical science "have sense," and that all other propositions are without theoretical sense. However, he does not do much in the book with mathematical propositions— with "analytic" propositions, as positivists sometimes labeled the propositions of logic and mathematics. He spends most of his time with "synthetic" propositions; that is, with propositions whose truth value cannot be determined simply by referring to their logical form. As examples of this analytic-synthetic distinction we might consider here the two propositions: (1) "The ball is red," and (2) "Either the ball is red or the ball is not red." We cannot know whether the first one is true or false without in fact examining the ball, but we can know that the second proposition is true without looking at the ball. It is true in virtue of its logical form. A sentence which is true or false in virtue of its form alone is analytic; a sentence whose truth value is determined by the (nonlinguistic) facts is synthetic.

Carnap holds the view that the only synthetic propositions which make sense are those propositions whose truth value can be determined by consulting the evidence of sense. And these propositions, he further believes, are all to be found within the domain of empirical science. He uses the word "verification" in the usual logical positivist sense; that is to say, a proposition is verifiable if its truth value can be determined by reference to sense experience. The only synthetic propositions which make sense, then, are verifiable propositions, and these are all scientific propositions. This is the verifiability criterion of empirical meaning.

It is Carnap's view, then, that philosophy is the logical analysis of meaningful language, and meaningful language is restricted either to analytic propositions (logic and mathematics) or to empirically verifiable propositions (natural science). This theory implies that certain traditional areas of philosophy are no longer to be regarded as legitimate. Carnap rejects what he calls traditional metaphysics since it is made up of propositions which he feels are neither analytic nor empirically verifiable. As examples of such illegitimate metaphysical sentences he mentions sentences about "the real Essence of things," about "Things in themselves," about "the Absolute," and "such like." In addition, Carnap rejects traditional philosophical ethics. He believes the usual utterances of ethical philosophers—such as "Killing is wrong"—mislead people in virtue of their grammatical form. They look like propositions, and so philosophers have given arguments to show that they are either true or false. Carnap, however, believes that what is grammatically an assertion, "Killing is wrong," is logically not an assertion at all, but rather a disguised command,

"Do not kill." However, commands are neither true nor false and hence cannot be propositions. Ethics, then, is necessarily ruled out of the domain of philosophy.

Ethics and metaphysics are thus ruled out of philosophy proper. But there must be something to them; otherwise why have people been so concerned about them? Here Carnap also has a simple answer. Metaphysical and ethical utterances express deep feelings and emotions. That is why people are so concerned about them. They express our emotions. But this, Carnap points out, is to say that they resemble the utterances of the lyric poet; that is, they express emotion, and they evoke a profound response in the reader, but they nevertheless do not make theoretical or cognitive sense—they are meaningless from a philosophical and scientific point of view.

But not only metaphysics and ethics suffer from Carnap's determination to rid philosophy of the senseless burden it has borne. Epistemology and psychology also suffer as a result of his reforming zeal. Insofar as there is a legitimate area of psychology, it is an empirical science which, as such, is not the philosopher's concern. And epistemology is, Carnap suspects, a hybrid of psychology and logic. Philosophers must continue to do the logic, but they should give over the psychology to the behaviorists. And now, finally, we reach the proper domain of the philosopher, after rejecting metaphysics, ethics, psychology, and epistemology. The philosopher is to do logical analysis on the language of the scientist. There can be no misunderstanding of Carnap's intention here, for he writes: "The only proper task of *Philosophy* is *Logical Analysis.*"

We should now try to determine what Carnap means by "logical analysis." As Carnap understands it, logical analysis is a concern with the logical syntax of a language. This claim needs elucidation.

In other of his writings, Carnap has taken some pains to identify what he means by logical syntax. In the *Foundations of Logic and Mathematics* (1939) he has perhaps made the distinctions most clearly. There he distinguishes pragmatics, semantics, and syntax as parts of the general philosophical concern with language which he calls "semiotic." The first distinction which needs to be made here is between language which is about language, and language which is not about language. One might, for example, assert the proposition: "The ball is red." In this case one would be using language to talk about the nonlinguistic world, to talk about a ball. But one might then go on to talk about the proposition which refers to the red ball; one might say: "The proposition 'The ball is red' has four words in it." In this case the proposition is not about objects such as red balls, but about language itself. Such language about language is called "meta-language"; language about objects is called "object language." The general theory of an object language, stated in a meta-language, is what Carnap means by "semiotic." But semiotic has three branches: pragmatics, semantics, and syntax. Pragmatics is an empirical study of three elements which can be distinguished in the use of a language—linguistic signs, the meanings (Carnap calls them "designata") of the signs, and the users of the signs. Pragmatics studies all three elements. Oversimplifying, pragmatics may be likened to the activity of an anthropologist constructing a dictionary for a tribe he is studying. The anthropologist studies and records how the tribesmen use words, how the words are spelled and combined, and what the words indicate.

Semantics is an abstraction from pragmatics. The semanticist (in the Carnapian sense—not to be confused with the so-called "General Semanticist") restricts his concern to the words or signs and their designata, their meanings. He abstracts from users to focus solely on the signs and their designata. There can be two kinds of semantics: descriptive semantics is an empirical study of signs and their matter-of-fact meanings in popular usage; pure semantics, on the other hand, is not an empirical study but a normative one which lays down rules regarding the signs and what their proper designata are. A pure semantical system is an artificial language consisting of rules specifying designata for a collection of linguistic signs. An example of a pure semantical sentence might be: "The predicate word 'large' designates the property of being large in a physical sense." This specifies how the word "large" is to be used in a given artificial language, and it implies that such common language expressions as "That's a large order" are incorrect in the semantical system in which the rule occurs.

Syntax represents yet another level of abstraction. Pragmatics includes signs, designata, and users. Semantics ignores the users and focuses its attention solely on signs and their designata. Syntax ignores the designata of the signs as well as ignoring the users. It is concerned only with the signs and the rules in accordance with which they can be combined and manipulated. Again we may oversimplify and say that the subject matter of syntax is the traditional rules of logical deduction, provided we add that the rules are formulated in a more abstract and formal way than is customary. Very roughly speaking, then, we may say that pragmatics may be likened to making a dictionary of usage, that semantics may be likened to specifying the exact and unambiguous definitions of words in, say, a technical treatise, and that syntax may be likened to constructing a formal set of rules of logic.

In his second chapter Carnap attempts to characterize and illustrate logical syntax somewhat more fully. In the first place, he says, syntax is a "formal" theory. He means by this that syntax abstracts from all concern with the sense or meaning of the signs and confines itself strictly to the forms of the signs or words. It consists entirely of rules specifying how signs—regarded simply as shapes or designs or sounds—may be combined and manipulated. Within this formal theory there are two kinds of rules: formation rules and transformation rules. The formation rules, in effect, define what is to be regarded as a proper sentence. The ordinary man's rejection of Russell's well-known

example of an ill-formed sentence—"Quadruplicity drinks procrastination"—
is made in virtue of an appeal to the implicit formation rules of the English
language. Ordinarily, of course, we all abide by the implicit formation rules
of English. Carnap's formation rules are intended to make explicit these
implicit rules that we follow. The other group of rules, the transformation
rules, specify what manipulations can be performed on the well-formed sentences identified by the formation rules. The transformation rules are the
rules of logical deduction expressed in syntactical terms. Carnap states that
the two primitive terms in a logical syntax are "sentence" and "direct consequence." That is to say, syntax is concerned to identify what are proper
sentences and also to specify how we are to draw their logical consequences.

There are other important syntactical terms in addition to "sentence" and
"direct consequence," however. Carnap spends a fair amount of time in the
second chapter defining and illustrating these additional syntactical terms. He
defines "valid" as the property a sentence has if it is a direct consequence of
the null class of premises. Putting this into a different logical terminology, we
could say that a proposition which is validly inferred from tautologies is itself
a tautology; Carnap means by "valid" what is often called "tautologous."
Carnap then defines "contravalid" so that it corresponds to the usual notion
of self-contradiction. These two classes of sentences, the valid and the contravalid, make up the class of "determinate" sentences; all other sentences
(sometimes called "contingent sentences" by other logicians) are called "indeterminate."

The syntactical transformation rules serve to isolate the valid and contravalid sentences. These rules are called "L-rules" by Carnap. But there are
other inferences that may be made which depend, not on these logical rules,
but on certain laws of natural science; for example, Newton's laws or the laws
of thermodynamics. Scientific laws, such as these, which also serve to justify
drawing the consequences of sentences, Carnap calls "P-rules" to distinguish
them from the L-rules. Carnap is then able to distinguish additional kinds of
sentences; namely, P-valid and P-contravalid sentences.

Other additional terms are defined in this second chapter. Enough have
been mentioned here, however, to enable us to see what it is that Carnap is
up to. He is making many of the usual distinctions and defining many of the
usual terms of traditional logic. But he is doing it in a slightly different way
from that characteristic of traditional logic. He has avoided the usual basic
logical terms "true" and "false," since they depend on the question of the
meaning of the propositions which are said to be either true or false. He has
also avoided the usual logical term "implication," and has replaced it with
"direct consequence." All of this is intentional and novel. Carnap sees it as
being implied by his definition of syntax as a *formal* theory. He can describe
a language and lay down rules for manipulating it without ever dealing with
the question of the meaning of the words and sentences, and, consequently,

without ever worrying about what the subject matter is that the language deals with. He is not doing physics or chemistry or biology; rather, he is manipulating symbols, symbols which might be assigned meanings later on so that they become words and sentences in a theory of chemistry or physics or biology. But, as Carnap sees it, he has sharply separated the work of the philosopher-logician from the work of the scientist. Furthermore, abstracting from the meanings of the words and sentences enables the philosopher-logician to concentrate on the properly logical matters and avoid the tangles that often impede progress in the sciences. Best of all, he has, as a philosopher-logician, a legitimate activity in which to engage, one which benefits the scientist and which also circumvents the morasses of much traditional philosophy.

Just how Carnap feels he has avoided the morasses of traditional philosophy is best seen by looking at his discussion of what he calls "pseudo-object sentences." (In his *The Logical Syntax of Language*, 1934, he calls these "quasi-syntactical sentences.") Carnap feels that many times philosophers have combined syntactical predicates with nonsyntactical subjects. The result is neither one thing nor another; they are not statements in the object language, nor are they statements in the metalanguage. They are, however, responsible for many of the disputes of traditional metaphysics about the reality or nonreality of entities such as universals. One example will perhaps illustrate Carnap's distinction fairly clearly. He distinguishes three sentences:

(1) The rose is red. A real object-sentence in the material mode of speech

(2) The rose is a thing. A pseudo-object sentence

(3) The word "rose" is a thing-word. A syntactical sentence in the formal mode of speech

No disputes arise over the first sentence. It is a sensible sentence which everyone understands and knows how to handle. Nor do disputes arise over the third sentence. Most people do not speak this way, but when they do (that is, when they are philosophical syntacticians), they make sense and avoid confusion. Unfortunately, philosophers have too often spoken in the manner of the second sentence. They then believe they are speaking about roses, and they begin debating and defining, getting further and further mired in the morass of bogus entities. One should speak either with the vulgar about red roses or with the sophisticated about thing-words. But one should beware of speaking with the metaphysicians about rose-things.

Pseudo-object sentences are likely to give rise to pseudo-questions. This is the burden of the final chapter of Carnap's book. Logical positivism offers hope, he feels, for genuine progress in philosophy because it identifies the errors of earlier philosophies, and it provides a technique for avoiding them. The problem of universals, for example, is not a real problem; it is a pseudo-problem which results from confusing the "formal mode" of speech and the "material mode" of speech, from being deceived by pseudo-object sentences such as "The rose is a thing." We should speak in the formal mode about "predicate words"; we should not speak in the material mode about universals as things.

The position Carnap staes in *Philosophy and Logical Syntax* has been stated much more fully in other of his works, especially in his earlier *The Logical Syntax of Language*. In some of his later works he has also modified some of his earlier views—most notably, perhaps, by admitting semantics to philosophical legitimacy along with syntax. But in its essentials the position is as stated in *Philosophy and Logical Syntax*. It is a view which has influenced contemporary philosophy greatly, and it is a view which is genuinely novel— a notable achievement in as ancient a discipline as philosophy. It probably has not had the influence outside philosophy which the intrinsic merit of the position deserves. This lack of widespread influence is quite probably the result of Carnap's tendency, in his more extended writing, to use a formidable and forbidding battery of technical apparatus including strange terms and Gothic script. He unfortunately has not completely rid himself of a Germanic fascination with architectonics and a tendency to identify the profound with the unfamiliar. He has also suffered from a tendency to oversimplify and trivialize the views he opposes. One can understand his rejection of the excesses of some idealist philosophers, but one finds it hard to move from that to the simple "resolution" of the problems the idealists wrestled with which defines them out of existence as "pseudo-problems." But when all is said about Carnap's lack of understanding and sympathy for any philosophical problems other than his own, one must still acknowledge the great skill he has brought to bear on the problems that did interest him. Carnap is a great innovator and an original thinker of enormous stature; one can forgive him if he is not the best twentieth century historian of philosophy. And when the history of twentieth century philosophy is written, surely Carnap's attempt to develop a logic which does not rest on any prior theory of meaning will be given a most prominent place, and deservedly so.—*R.E.L.*

PERTINENT LITERATURE

Quine, Willard Van Orman. "Two Dogmas of Empiricism," in *From a Logical Point of View*. New York: Harper & Row Publishers, 1963.

Modern empiricism, Willard Van Orman Quine suggests, has to a significant degree been founded on two assumptions. One, he says, is that there is a basic bifurcation between analytic truths (grounded in meanings) and synthetic truths (grounded in fact). The other (not our concern here) is reductionism—the view that each meaningful claim is constructed out of terms which refer to immediate experience. Quine rejects both; our concern will be with his critique of the former dogma.

Quine reminds us that David Hume distinguished between relations of ideas and matters of fact, Immanuel Kant between analytic and synthetic propositions, and Gottfried Wilhelm Leibniz between truths of reason and truths of fact. Leibniz held that truths of reason are true in all possible worlds, Quine notes, adding that this is tantamount to saying that they cannot be false. Analytic statements, Quine adds, are said to be those which have self-contradictory denials, although insofar as the concept of *being self-contradictory* is wide enough to serve the purpose of marking off analyticity, it is itself in equal need of clarification. Quine's view is that these various ways of marking off the analytic from the synthetic fail to do so with sufficient clarity to justify the dogma concerning them.

Kant's distinction, Quine argues, treats an analytic statement as one whose predicate conceptually contains nothing not already contained in its subject, and is thereby twice defective in that it applies only to subject-predicate statements, leaving the metaphor of containment unanalyzed.

With regard to singular terms, *meaning*, Quine contends, is one thing; *naming* another (as "nine" and "the number of planets" share referent but not meaning). An analogous distinction, he adds, arises with respect to predicates or general terms; general terms do not name, but are true of, items— the items a term is true of being its extension. But the extension of a general term is to be distinguished from its meaning, or intension, Quine insists, illustrating his point with the extensional identity and intensional distinctness of "creature with kidneys" and "creature with a heart."

Quine finds it a short step from distinguishing between meaning and reference, and theory of meaning and theory of reference, to viewing the theory of meaning as primarily focusing on analyticity of statements and synonymy of linguistic forms, and rejecting meanings as "obscure entities." So, Quine suggests, consideration of the (thus purified) theory of meaning leads us back to problems concerning analyticity.

Propositions viewed as analytic, Quine suggests, fall into two classes. One class is comprised of logical truths, such as *No unmarried man is married*; such truths remain true no matter what interpretation we give to their nonlogical components. The other class is composed of statements such as *No bachelor is married*—which can be turned into logical truths by trading synonym for synonym. But the content of "synonymous" is not more lucid than that of "analytic."

Rudolf Carnap, Quine notes, has explained analyticity in terms of "state-descriptions." A state-description is a complete assignment of truth-values (truth or falsity) to each atomic or noncompound statement of a language. Carnap assumes, Quine explains, that the truth values of compound statements in a language will be functions of the truth values of their components, and a statement is analytic if it remains true under every state description.

Quine points out that this rendition of analyticity succeeds only insofar as the atomic sentences of the language are logically independent, unlike, say, *Suzy is a spinster* and *Suzy is not married*. Without this qualification, one could assign *true* to *Suzy is a spinster* and *false* to *Suzy is not married*, so that *No spinster is married* becomes, not analytic, but synthetic. Thus, Quine continues, the state-description account of analyticity will do only for languages "devoid of extralogical synonym pairs" of the sort exemplified by *Suzy is a spinster* and *Suzy is not married*. Quine suggests that the net result is that the state-description criterion provides an account of logical truth, not of analyticity generally. Carnap, Quine reports, is not unaware of this, and uses his state-description account as a tool for approaching topics in probability and induction. Quine's point is that the state-description account could not be proffered as a successful general account of analyticity.

Appeal to definition—"an *analytic* statement is one true by definition"—Quine argues, will not help, since definitions other than stipulative depend on already recognized but quite unanalyzed synonymy. Passing over Quine's discussion, and rejection, of the "interchangeable in all contexts without change of truth value" criterion for synonymy, we now consider Quine's treatment of Carnapian strategies regarding analyticity.

It is sometimes suggested, Quine remarks, that problems in separating analytic from synthetic statements arise from vagueness in natural language which could be removed by the precision of artificial language. A statement S will then be *analytic for* a language *L*, and, Quine notes, the problem then becomes giving sense to *S is analytic for L*.

Carnap's work on artificial languages and semantical rules, Quine suggests, is the natural place to look for help in this regard. Quine argues as follows. Suppose we have an artificial language L* such that L*'s semantical rules explicitly specify all of L*'s analytic statements; they tell us that only such-and-such statements are the analytic statements of L*. Then the rules will contain the as-yet-not-understood term "analytic." To grasp "A statement is analytic for *L** if and only if. . . ," (where some specific analysis fills in the dots) we must first (where S and L, in contrast to L* are, not constants, but variables) understand "*S is analytic for L*." Hence, Quine concludes, appeal to a Carnapian artificial language whose semantical rules specify the language's analytic statements does not provide a proper analysis of analyticity.

Alternatively, Carnap continues, one could view the semantical rule, not as specifying analytic sentences of L*, but as a conventional definition of the simple symbol *analytic-for-L*. But this, Quine contends, will define neither *analytic*, nor *analytic for*, nor will it explicate "*S is analytic for L*," where S and L are variables—not even if we restrict the range of L to artificial languages.

Again, Quine suggests, we might appeal to the fact that analytic statements at least must be true, and consider a semantical rule R which simply states that such-and-such statements (along with others unspecified) are true. A statement may then be said to be analytic provided that it is not only true but also true according to *R*. But then, Quine claims, we must contend not with "analytic" but with "semantical rule," which is as yet unexplained. Were every rule that says that some statements are true to count as a semantical rule, Quine reports, one could easily turn all truths into analytic ones in the sense just characterized, thus ruining the strategy for marking off analytic from synthetic statements. Semantic rules, Quine suggests, at least so far as the present alternative goes, are but those which appear on a page beneath the meaningless heading "Semantical Rules."

In these (and other) ways Quine argues that appeals to semantical rules and artificial languages fail to provide a clear content to, or basis for, a clear division of all statements into the analytic, or else the synthetic, type. Indeed, he contends, that any such distinction to be made is a piece of unestablished empiricist dogma.

Bohnert, Herbert. "Carnap's Theory of Definition and Analyticity," in *The Philosophy of Rudolf Carnap* (The Library of Living Philosophers). Edited by Paul A. Schilpp. La Salle, Illinois: Open Court, 1963, pp. 407-430.

That there is a sharp division between analytic sentences and synthetic sentences, Herbert Bohnert notes, has been dubbed (by Willard Van Orman Quine) one of the "two dogmas of empiricism." Rudolf Carnap accepted the dogma, and his way of developing the distinction has had great influence among empiricists.

Bohnert holds that the analytic-synthetic distinction, while historically important and progressively more clearly articulated, was not made with precision until the late nineteenth century. One reason for this was that, at times, the motive for precision was weak, in that analytic propositions basically were discussed only to contrast them unfavorably with empirical propositions, as in John Locke and John Stuart Mill, or to distinguish them from alleged other sorts of necessary although nonanalytic claims, as in Immanuel Kant. The growth of a mathematical edifice housed with paradoxical and imaginary entities but lacking rigorous analysis was unfavorable to the offering of a lucid criterion for analyticity, as was the inclusion of geometry within mathematics, given a natural dependence on visualization in geometrical thinking. Another factor contributing to lack of precision, Bohnert notes, was the rise of psychologism, which involves taking propositions to be mental acts of judgment and supposes that such terms as "true," "valid," and "analytic" apply to states of mind, thus, in effect, putting off attempts to give precision to the notion of analyticity until the mind was better understood and, more importantly, sanctioning the mistaken view that analyticity was more a matter of psychology than of logic.

Then, Bohnert continues, mathematical analysis was scrutinized and purified, logic took great steps forward in the work of Gottlob Frege and Bertrand Russell, among others, and the view, proffered by David Hume, that mathematics did not include matters of empirical fact was reinforced by the effort to reduce mathematics to logic. Further, the creation of logically consistent non-Euclidean geometrics produced a sharp distinction between a postulate system and its interpretation, and the relativistic revolution in physics, which seemed to show that what had appeared to be self-evident geometrical truths were actually false empirical claims, distinguished geometry from the rest of mathematics. Geometrical claims, Bohnert reports, were viewed as synthetic by some, and analytic by others, of the interpretations of the systems in which they resided. The development of the concept of a (formal) language, and of the distinction between a (first order) language and a metalanguage (or second order language), matters which received their fullest treatment at Carnap's hands, provided a full escape from psychologism by replacing judgments with sentences. Carnap, then, Bohnert notes, endeavored to develop a rigorous and consistent empiricism which accounted for necessity in mathematics and limited the role of convention in the sciences. This program, Bohnert reports, required a sharp and rigid analytic-versus-synthetic bifurcation. Bohnert adds that Carnap's development of this distinction came in two stages—one syntactical, one semantical.

The first stage, Bohnert explains, was comprised by the attempt to analyze analyticity by means of reference to an uninterpreted language or formal calculus. Bohnert indicates that it had become possible to represent inferences in a way that made it clear that they depended on logical structure rather than meaning, and that this, plus the increase in rigor a formal approach made possible, motivated Carnap to develop his syntactic strategy, as did the goal of avoiding all empirical content and reference. Also important, Bohnert adds, was the refutation of Ludwig Wittgenstein's allegation that discourse about language involved one in an effort to say what could not be said; in sharp contrast to the Wittgenstein view in the *Tractatus Logico-Philosophicus*, Carnap desired to show that any philosophically significant metalinguistic claim could be so cast as to be at least as precise as sentences in the corresponding object language.

The core of the syntactic notion of analyticity, Bohnert tells us, is provability; while the feature of *being self-evident* is rejected as requisite for analyticity, *being provable by means available to human minds* is retained. Unfortunately, Bohnert continues, this approach faced problems of a purely syntactical sort, as Kurt Gödel proved that formal systems possessed of sufficient resources to contain number theory also contained sentences which, while purely formal, were neither provable nor refutable within the system by any finite process of proof. Some such sentences would be true but unprovable so long as the law of the excluded middle (the principle that every constructible or well-formed sentence is true, or else false) is not abandoned.

Some even suggested, Bohnert notes, that this law be regarded as synthetic *a priori*—that is, as both nonanalytic and yet knowable without appeal to empirical evidence. (This is not an alternative Carnap could cheerfully embrace, since empiricism apparently requires that analytic sentences be *a priori* and nonanalytic statements be *non-a priori* (*a posteriori*). Carnap, Bohnert continues, endeavored to expand the notion of provability so that deductions based on infinite classes of premises could count as proofs, but he did so at the price of there being some describable, finite, general method of proof by which "provability" could be characterized. Bohnert adds that, even with this expanded concept of provability, not every sentence one would wish to label "analytic" is provable in some system thus far constructed, and some at least have doubted that this approach actually remains within the limits proscribed by linking *being analytic* and *being provable by means available to human minds*. Whatever its final status, Bohnert contends, Carnap's efforts at developing a syntactical version of analyticity was instrumental in uncovering metalogic's potential.

In any case, Bohnert reports, Alfred Tarski's work persuaded Carnap that analyticity had a semantic aspect not covered by his own purely syntactical approach; he thus came to hold that an analytic sentence is such by virtue of being true, not merely in terms of its logical structure, but by the meanings of its terms. Thus, Bohnert indicates, Carnap became interested, not in languages conceived as mere formal structures, but conceived as syntactically constructed calculi which contain terms which designate nonlinguistic objects and sentences which, if true, correspond to nonlinguistic facts.

The core of the semantic conception of analyticity, Bohnert informs us, is *having null content*, or *having zero strength*, or *conveying no information*. Making use of concepts not unlike the class-of-all-possible-worlds notion of Leibnizian fame to define such quantitative notions as the strength of a sentence, Bohnert explains, Carnap correlates the degree of strength a sentence possesses to the amount of information it contains. The result is that one can show that analytic sentences have no strength, and so convey no information. And, Bohnert adds, Carnap has proposed languages in which modal concepts necessity, possibility, contingency) become expressible in such a way that every state of affairs expressed by an analytic sentence is a necessary one.

Given this characterization of Carnap's effort to develop a semantic conception of analyticity, Bohnert devotes a substantial and technical discussion to articulating it further and defending it against Quine's influential criticisms of the analytic-synthetic distinction.—*K.E.Y.*

ADDITIONAL RECOMMENDED READING
Ayer, A. J., ed. *Logical Positivism*. New York: Free Press, 1959. A collection
   of essays by various logical positivists, including three by Carnap.
Carnap, Rudolf. *The Logical Structure of the World* [and] *Pseudo-problems*

in Philosophy. Berkeley: University of California Press, 1967. A republication of two of Carnap's works, with a preface by their author.

Copi, Irving M. and James A. Gould, eds. *Contemporary Readings in Logical Theory*. New York: Macmillan Publishing Company, 1967. An excellent collection of essays on contemporary logic, including a paper by, and many references to, Carnap.

Kneale, William and Martha Kneale. *The Development of Logic*. Oxford: Clarendon Press, 1962. A comprehensive history of logic, with several references to Carnap.

Rorty, Richard, ed. *The Linguistic Turn: Recent Essays in Philosophical Method*. Chicago: University of Chicago Press, 1967. Contains two papers by Carnap and a good bibliography.

Weinberg, J. R. *An Examination of Logical Positivism*. London: Kegan Paul, Trench, Trubner & Company, 1936. A splendid discussion of logical positivism.

REASON AND EXISTENZ

Author: Karl Jaspers (1883-1969)
Type of work: Existential metaphysics
First published: 1935

PRINCIPAL IDEAS ADVANCED

No description of Existenz *is possible;* Existenz *can be clarified only by reference to concrete situations.*

Existenz *is the freedom of an individual, the possibility of decision; because man exists in this special sense, he is that which he can become in his freedom.*

The Encompassing is that which man encounters; considered as Being-in-itself, the Encompassing appears only in and through the Being-which-we-are. (We know what confronts us only in terms of what we are because of it.)

Reason and Existenz *develop mutually and are interdependent.*

In existential communication the self first comes to full consciousness of itself as a being qualified by historicity (determination in time), uniqueness, freedom, and communality.

The five lectures which comprise *Reason and Existenz* were delivered at the University of Groningen, Holland, in the spring of 1935. In these lectures the author knits together with a remarkable facility the various themes which are elaborated in his multi-volumed philosophical writings. *Reason and Existenz* is thus both a helpful summary and an excellent introduction to the author's philosophy.

Jaspers defines philosophy as the elucidation of *Existenz (Existenzerhellung)*. (We retain the term "Existenz" since the English "existence" is not the equivalent.) This elucidation of *Existenz* needs to be sharply contrasted with any attempt at a *conceptualization* of *Existenz* through objectively valid and logically compelling categories. Jaspers denies that a unifying perspective of the content of existential reality is possible. Nevertheless, a clarification of or elucidation of *Existenz* as it expresses itself in concrete situations can be productively undertaken. According to Jaspers the philosopher is the one who strives for such clarification.

Jaspers finds in the concrete philosophizing of Kierkegaard and Nietzsche a profound exemplification of the philosophical attitude. Both, in their interest to understand existential reality from within, had serious reservations about any program which intended to bring thought into a single and complete system, derived from self-evident principles. Any claim for a completed existential system affords nothing more than an instance of philosophical pretension. *Existenz* has no final content; it is always "on the way," subject to the contingencies of a constant becoming. Kierkegaard and Nietzsche in grasping this fundamental insight uncovered the existential irrelevancy of Hegel's system of logic. It was particularly Kierkegaard, in his attack on speculative thought, who brought to light the comic neglect of *Existenz* in the essentialism and rationalism of Hegel. Kierkegaard and Nietzsche further laid the foundations for a redefinition of philosophy as an elucidation of *Existenz* through their emphasis on the attitudinal, as contrasted with the doctrinal, character of philosophy. They set forth a new intellectual attitude toward life's problems. They developed no fixed doctrines which can be abstracted from their thinking as independent and permanent formulations. They were both suspicious of scientific men who sought to reduce all knowledge to simple and quantifiable data. They were passionately interested in the achievements of self-knowledge. Both taught that self-reflection is the way to truth. Reality is disclosed through a penetration to the depths of the self. Both realized the need for indirect communication and saw clearly the resultant falsifications in objectivized modes of discourse. Both were exceptions—in no sense models for followers. They defy classification under any particular type and shatter all efforts at imitation. What they did was possible only once. Thus the problem for us is to philosophize without being exceptions, but with our eyes on the exception.

At the center of Jaspers' philosophizing we find the notion of the *Umgreifende*. Some have translated this basic notion of Jaspers as the "Comprehensive"; others have found the English term, the "Encompassing," to be a more accurate rendition of the original German. The Encompassing lies beyond all horizons of determinate being, and thus never makes its appearance as a determinable object of knowledge. Like Kant's noumenal realm, it remains hidden behind the phenomena. Jaspers readily agrees with Kant that the Encompassing as a designation for ultimate reality is objectively unknowable. It escapes every determinate objectivity, emerges neither as a particular object nor as the totality of objects. As such it sets the limits to the horizon of man's conceptual categories. In thought there always arises that which passes beyond thought itself. Man encounters the Encompassing not within a conceptual scheme but in existential decision and philosophical faith. This Encompassing appears and disappears for us only in its modal differentiations. The two fundamental modes of the Encompassing are the "Encompassing as Being-in-itself" and the "Encompassing which-we-are." Both of these modes have their ground and animation in *Existenz*.

Jaspers' concern for a clarification of the meaning and forms of Being assuredly links him with the great metaphysicians of the Western tradition, and he is ready to acknowledge his debt to Plato, Aristotle, Spinoza, Hegel, and Schelling. However, he differs from the classical metaphysicians in his relocation of the starting point for philosophical inquiry. Classical metaphysics has taken as its point of departure Being-in-itself, conceived either as Nature, the World, or God. Jaspers approaches his program of clarification from the Being-which-we-are. This approach was already opened up by the critical philosophy of Kant, which remains for Jaspers the valid starting point for philosophical elucidation.

The Encompassing as Being-which-we-are passes into further internally articulated structural modes. Here empirical existence (*Dasein*), consciousness as such (*Bewusstsein überhaupt*), and spirit (*Geist*) make their appearance. Empirical existence indicates myself as object, by virtue of which I become a datum for examination by the various scientific disciplines such as biology, psychology, anthropology, and sociology. In this mode of being man apprehends himself simply as an object among other objects, subject to various conditioning factors. Man is not yet properly known as human. His distinctive existential freedom has not yet been disclosed. He is simply an item particularized by the biological and social sciences for empirical investigation. The second structural mode of the Being-which-we-are is consciousness as such. Consciousness has two meanings. In one of its meanings it is still bound to empirical reality. It is a simple principle of empirical life which indicates the particularized living consciousness in its temporal process. However, we are not only particularized consciousnesses which are isolated one from another, we are in some sense similar to one another, by dint of which we are disclosed as consciousness as such. Through this movement of consciousness as such man is able to understand himself in terms of ideas and concepts which have universal validity. Empirical existence expresses a relationship of man to the empirical world. Consciousness as such expresses a relationship of man to the world of ideas. Ideas are permanent and timeless. Thus man can apprehend himself in his timeless permanence.

The influence of Plato upon the thought of Jaspers becomes clearly evident at this point. We participate in the Encompassing through the possibility of universally valid knowledge in which there is a union with timeless essences. As simple empirical consciousness we are split into a multiplicity of particular realities; as consciousness as such we are liberated from our confinement in a single consciousness and participate in the universal and timeless essence of humanity. Spirit constitutes the third modal expression of the Encompassing which-we-are. Spirit signifies the appetency towards totality, completeness, and wholeness. As such it is oriented toward the truth of consciousness. It is attracted by the timeless and universal ideas which bring everything into clarity and connection. It seeks a unification of particular existence in such a way that every particular would be a member of a totality.

There is indeed a sense in which spirit expresses the synthesis of empirical existence and consciousness as such. But this is a synthesis which is never completed. It is always on the way, an incessant striving which is never finished. It is at this point that Jaspers' understanding of spirit differs from that of Hegel. For Hegel spirit drives beyond itself to its own completion, but not so for Jaspers. On the one hand, spirit is oriented to the realm of ideas in which consciousness as such participates, and is differentiated from simple empirical existence; on the other hand spirit is contrasted with the abstraction of a timeless consciousness as such, and expresses kinship with empirical existence. This kinship with empirical existence is its ineradicable temporality. It is a process of constant striving and ceaseless activity, struggling with itself, reaching ever beyond that which it is and has. Yet, it differs from empirical existence in that empirical existence is unconsciously bound to its particularization in matter and life, by virtue of which it can become an object in a determinable horizon. As empirical existence we are split off from each other and become objects of scientific investigation. Spirit overflows every objectivization and remains empirically unknowable. It is not capable of being investigated as a natural object. Although it always points to its basis in empirical existence, it also points to a power or dynamism which provides the impetus for its struggle toward meaning and totality.

It is through the Encompassing which-we-are that one has an approach to the Encompassing as being-in-itself. Being-in-itself never emerges independently as a substantive and knowable entity. It appears only in and through the being-which-we-are. In this appearance it is disclosed as a limit expressing a twofold modification: (1) the world, and (2) transcendence. The being-which-we-are has one of its limits in the experience of the world. The world in Jaspers' philosophy signifies neither the totality of natural objects nor a spatiotemporal continuum in which these objects come to be. It signifies instead the horizon of inexhaustible appearances which present themselves to inquiry. This horizon is always receding and it manifests itself only indirectly in the appearances of particular and empirical existence. It is never fully disclosed in any one of its perspectives and remains indeterminate for all empirical investigation. The Encompassing which-we-are has its other limit in transcendence. Transcendence is that mode of being-in-itself which remains hidden from all phenomenal experience. It does not even manifest itself indirectly. It extends beyond the horizons of world orientation as such. It remains the completely unknowable and indefinable, existentially posited through a philosophical faith.

All the modes of the Encompassing have their original source in *Existenz*. *Existenz* is itself not a mode but carries the meaning of every mode. It is the animation and the ground of all modes of the Encompassing. It is thus only in turning our attention to *Existenz* that we reach the pivotal point in Jaspers' philosophizing. In *Existenz* we reach the abyss or the dark ground of selfhood. *Existenz* contains within itself an element of the irrational, and thus never becomes fully transparent to consciousness as such. Consciousness is always structurally related to the universal ideas, but *Existenz* can never be grasped through an idea. It never becomes fully intelligible because it is the object of no science. *Existenz* can only be approached through concrete elucidations—hence, Jaspers' program of *Existenz-erhellung*. *Existenz* is the possibility of decision, which has its origin in time and apprehends itself only within its temporality. It escapes from every idea of consciousness as well as from the attempt of spirit to render it into an expression of a totality or a part of a whole. *Existenz* is the individual as historicity. It determines the individual in his unique past and his unique future. Always moving into a future the individual, as *Existenz*, is burdened with the responsibilities of his decisions. This fact constitutes his historicity. *Existenz* is irreplaceable. The concrete movements within his historicity, which always call him to decision, disclose him in his unique individuality and personal idiosyncrasy. He is never a simple individual empirical existent that can be reduced to a specimen or an instance of a class; he is unique and irreplaceable. Finally, *Existenz* as it knows itself before transcendence, reveals itself as freedom. *Existenz* is possibility, which means freedom. Man is that which he can become in his freedom.

As the modes of the Encompassing have their roots in *Existenz*, so they have their bond in Reason. Reason is the bond which internally unites the modes and keeps them from falling into an unrelated plurality. Thus Reason and *Existenz* are the great poles of being, permeating all the modes but not coming to rest in any one of them. Jaspers cautions the reader against a possible falsification of the meaning of Reason as it is used in his elucidation of *Existenz*. Reason is not to be construed as simple, clear, objective thinking (*Verstand*). Understood in this sense, Reason would be indistinguishable from consciousness as such. Reason, as the term is used by Jaspers, is closer to the Kantian meaning of *Vernunft*. It is the preeminence of thought which includes more than mere thinking. It includes not only a grasp of what is universally valid (*ens rationis*), but touches upon and reveals the nonrational, bringing to light its existential significance. It always pushes toward unity, the universal, law, and order, but at the same time remains within the possibility of *Existenz*. Reason and *Existenz* are thus inseparable. Each disappears when the other disappears. Reason without *Existenz* is hollow and culminates in an empty intellectualism. *Existenz* without Reason is blind incessant impulse and irrational striving. Reason and *Existenz* are friends rather than enemies. Each is determined through the other. They mutually develop one another and through this development find both clarity and reality. In this interdependence of Reason and *Existenz* we see an expression of the polar union of the Apollonian and the Dionysian. The Apollonian, or the structural principle, dissolves into a simple intellectual movement of consciousness, a dialectical movement of spirit, when it loses the Dionysian or dynamic principle. Conversely, the Dionysian passes over into irrational passion which burns to its own destruction when it loses its bond with the Apollonian.

The reality of communication provides another dominant thesis in the philosophy of Jaspers. Philosophical truth, which discloses *Existenz* as the ground of the modes and Reason as their bond, can be grasped only in historical communication. The possibility of communication follows from the ineradicable communality of humanity. No man achieves his humanity in isolation.

He exists only in and through others, and comes to an apprehension of the truth of his *Existenz* through interdependent and mutual communal understanding. Truth cannot be separated from communicability. But the truth which is expressed in communication is not simple; there are as many senses of truth as there are modes of the Encompassing which-we-are. In the community of our empirical existence it is the pragmatic conception of truth which is valid. Empirical reality knows no absolutes which have a timeless validity. Truth in this mode is relative and changing, because empirical existence itself is in a constant process of change. That which is empirically true today may be empirically wrong tomorrow because of a new situation into which one will have passed. All empirical truth is dependent upon the context of the situation and one's own standpoint within the situation.

As the situation perpetually changes, so does truth. At every moment the truth of one's standpoint is in danger of being refuted by the very fact of process. The truth in the communication of consciousness as such is logical consistency and cogent evidence. By means of logical categories one affirms and denies that which is valid for everyone. Whereas in empirical reality truth is relative and changing because of the multiple fractures of particulars with one another in their time-bound existence, in consciousness as such there is a self-identical consciousness which provides the condition for universally valid truths. The communication of spirit demands participation in a communal substance. Spirit has meaning only in relation to the whole of which it is a part. Communication is thus the communication of a member with its organism. Although each spirit differs from every other spirit there is a common agreement as concerns the order which comprehends them. Communication occurs only through the acknowledgment of their common commitment to this order. Truth in the community of spirit is thus total commitment or full conviction. Pragmatic meaning, logical intelligibility, and full conviction are the three senses of truth expressed in the Encompassing which-we-are.

But there is also the will to communicate Reason and *Existenz*. The communication of *Existenz* never proceeds independently of the communication in the three modes of the Encompassing which-we-are. *Existenz* retains its membership in the mode of empirical existence, consciousness as such, and spirit; but it passes beyond them in a "loving struggle" (*liebender Kampf*) to communicate the innermost meaning of its being. The communication of *Existenz* is not that of relative and changing particulars, nor is it that of an identical and replaceable consciousness. Existential communication is communication between irreplaceable persons. The community of *Existenz* is also contrasted with the spiritual community. Spirit seeks security in a comprehensive group substance. *Existenz* recognizes the irremovable fracture in being, accepts the inevitability of struggle, and strives to open itself for transcendence. Only through these movements does *Existenz* apprehend its irreplaceable and essentially unrepeatable selfhood, and bind itself to the historical community of selves who share the same irreplaceable determinants. It is in existential communication that the self first comes to a full consciousness of itself as a being qualified by historicity, uniqueness, freedom, and communality.

Reason plays a most important role in existential communication. Reason as the bond of the various modes of the Encompassing strives for a unity in communication. But its function is primarily negative. It discloses the limits of communication in each of the modes and checks the absolutization of any particular mode as the full expression of Being. When empirical existence is absolutized the essence of man is lost; he is reduced to an instance of matter and biological life, and his essence becomes identified with knowable regularities. He is comprehended not in his humanity, but in his simple animality. The absolutization of consciousness as such results in an empty intellectualism. Man's empirical reality is dissolved into timeless truths, and the life of the spirit remains unacknowledged. When spirit becomes a self-sufficient mode the result is a wooden culture in which all intellection and creativity are sacrificed to a communal substance. None of the modes are sufficient by themselves. Each demands the other. Reason provides the internal bond through which their mutual dependence can be harmoniously maintained.

For Jaspers, the truth of Reason is philosophical logic; the truth of *Existenz* is philosophical faith. Philosophical logic and philosophical faith interpenetrate as do Reason and *Existenz* themselves. Logic takes its impulse from *Existenz* which it seeks to clarify. Philosophical logic is limited neither to traditional formal logic nor to mere methodology; it prevents any reduction of man to mere empirical existence or to a universal consciousness. Philosophical logic is negative in that it provides no new contents, but it is positive in establishing the conditions for every possible content. Philosophical faith, the truth of *Existenz*, confronts man with transcendence and discloses his freedom. Philosophical faith is contrasted with religious faith in that it acknowledges no absolute or final revelation in time. Transcendence discloses a constant openness in which man apprehends himself as an "inner act," more precisely, an act of freedom. Faith is an acknowledgment of transcendence as the source of man's freedom. The highest freedom which man can experience is that freedom which has its condition in a source outside of itself.— *C.O.S.*

PERTINENT LITERATURE

Samay, Sebastian. *Reason Revisited: The Philosophy of Karl Jaspers*. Notre Dame, Indiana: University of Notre Dame Press, 1971.

Karl Jaspers was a philosophical outsider who took his degree in medicine and taught psychiatry. While writing a book, *The Psychology of World Views* (1919), he became interested in philosophy. But it was to remain characteristic that, when he took up a philosophical question, he kept in mind the questioner along with the question. As Sebastian Samay puts it, for Jaspers metaphysics and philosophical anthropology are dialectically intertwined. The question "What is Being?" is at the same time the question "What is man's place in the hierarchy of Being?" Similarly, the epistemological question "How can I think about Being?" works the questioner into the question, as appears from the title of his book *Reason and Existenz*. Jaspers tries, says Samay, to harmonize the clarity of reason with the urgency of existence without allowing either to dominate the other, so that it is no more proper to classify him as an existentialist than as a rationalist.

In *Reason Revisited*, Samay is concerned less directly with the problem of Being than with the problem of knowledge. A well-rounded study, it deals in Part I with the subject-object bifurcation and with the Enveloping (*das Umgreifende*), and in Part II it deals with the role of reason in science, prior to arriving at the main subject in Part III, reason and philosophy. The task here, says Samay, is to show how philosophical reason transforms the objective findings of science into an intuitive grasp of being as such.

Samay points out that Jaspers approached this question in two different ways: in *Philosophy* (1933), he was concerned with elucidating the existential consciousness of being; but in *Reason and Existenz*, he turned his attention to the clarification of philosophical self-awareness. The former study emphasized the human conditions of philosophizing; the latter explored the structure of philosophical logic.

Samay's chapter "Cipher Reading" is central to his exposition of Jaspers' doctrine of elucidation. Here he shows that, although Jaspers has no proofs for the existence of God—that is, no demonstration of Transcendent Being—he does show that the certitude of transcendence is implicated in the certitude of Existenz. For example, the statement "I have not created myself," while it does not lead to proof, does provide, when taken in a symbolic sense, a basis for philosophical faith. Metaphysical terms such as those which designate God as cause, love, or goodness, serve to dissolve the objective character of Being and make it transparent to Existenz. As such they belong to the class of symbols which we call ciphers. Where other symbols are interpretable by reference to objects, ciphers are interpretable only in terms of other symbols. In Samay's words, ciphers are merely evocative; they have no semantic function; they are intuitive and not interpretable.

If Jaspers' elucidation of Existenz may be called the way of symbols, his second approach to the problem of transcendental knowledge may be called the way of paradox. The problem is that thinking, which has its locus in general consciousness (consciousness-as-such), is called upon in philosophical reflection to affirm the limits of that consciousness. In a word, thought tries to transcend itself, and in doing so gives rise to "rational a-logic." "Through Reason," says Jaspers, "I catch sight of something which is communicable only in the form of contradiction and paradox."

"A-logic" is a technical term. In exploiting it, Jaspers is seeking to avoid the necessity of choosing between narrow forms of rational and ever-popular forms of irrationalism. That rational systems are necessarily incomplete is now recognized. Jaspers' point is that even though man knows this he is compelled to keep on trying. Jaspers' example is Immanuel Kant's statement that categories such as unity and plurality are derived from the original unity of the thinking consciousness. According to Samay, Jaspers is quite right in comparing Kant's predicament to the paradox of the liar, and in going on to say that we find "such circles and contradictions at the decisive point" in all genuine philosophies.

Kant, of course, was aware of these difficulties; and Samay says that, in the main lines of his thought, Jaspers was a Kantian. But whereas Kant was content to rule theoretical reason out of bounds and to affirm its authority only in the practical realm, Jaspers conceived of existential reason as joining the two. He regarded the tendency of reason toward comprehensive unity as being just as fundamental as its tendency toward clarity and consistency; and he saw this tendency as being grounded in self-conscious Existenz, with its infinite appetite for all the modes of the Encompassing.

This line of thought, given full rein, could easily turn into some kind of absolute knowledge. In fact, Jaspers speaks of it as absolute consciousness, the self-awareness of reason, the knowing of knowing, the philosophy of philosophy—expressions which suggest that Jaspers had real affinities with Georg Wilhelm Friedrich Hegel. But, as Samay reminds us, Jaspers intended no break between the theme of philosophical logic and the theme of existential elucidation developed earlier. All philosophical utterances, including those of a-logic, are ciphers. They express recognition, not cognition; they are not scientific statements about reality; rather they are interpretative explanations which, in Jaspers' words, "silently bring forth an unconcealment and transformation in the inmost being of man."

Samay refuses to be bemused by this kind of talk. While opening new perspectives, he says, Jaspers does not satisfactorily settle the question of Reason. Still, in stirring up a greater awareness of Reason and of Existenz he has done much.

Knauss, Gerhard. "The Concept of the 'Encompassing' in Jaspers' Philosophy," in *The Philosophy of Karl Jaspers* (The Library of Living Philosophers). Edited by Paul A. Schilpp. New York: Tudor Publishing Company, 1957, pp. 141-175.

Although "the Encompassing" (*das Umgreifende*) strikes us as a neologism, the term is a modern equivalent to the Greek *to periechein*, used by Anaximander in speaking of the Infinite and by Plato in speaking of the Whole.

With the pre-Socratics, the concept of an encompassing something was prior to their speculation as to its nature. And when their materialistic theories proved vulnerable to logic, Plato raised the notion to the ideal plane. It was in studying Immanuel Kant, however, that Karl Jaspers first gave serious thought to the concept. In an appendix to the second edition of his *Psychology* (1920), he called attention to Kant's theory of Ideas and argued that the critical philosophy, with its subject-object division, its assumption of the common source of sensation and understanding, and its deduction of the unity between nature and freedom, points to an unconditioned totality which, although it transcends intellection and is apprehended intuitively, is nevertheless encompassed by concepts. Because Kant continued, in the Platonic manner, to think of philosophy as a science, he was unable to carry his insights to fruition. That became possible only after Søren Kierkegaard had undermined philosophy's claim to objectivity. He, and later Friedrich Wilhelm Nietzsche, made it clear that philosophy's reverse side—namely, human *Existenz*—can give the lie to what appears on the front side. After Kierkegaard, says Gerhard Knauss, truth must be understood as encompassing both the subjective and the objective.

The idea developed by Jaspers was, says Knauss, one whose time had come, and it was in fact shared by his contemporaries. For example, both he and Martin Heidegger began by observing the differences between Being-in-itself and the manner in which Being becomes an object for us. But whereas Heidegger, in the tradition of ontology, renounced all objective being and surrendered prematurely to one mode of knowledge, Jaspers, like Plato and Kant, followed the tradition of periechontology, and used objective being as a means of arriving at philosophical faith.

Knauss develops Jaspers' thought in connection with the subject-object division. Whenever we think, we think of objects; nevertheless, there is something which we never find among the objects: namely, the subject. Kant taught us that Being as object is Being for a subject and that one of the conditions of knowledge is that what is known "appears" in forms supplied by the subject. But to be conscious of the subject's contribution to knowledge leads to the awareness that the Being in which we exist cannot be grasped as object. Thus, thinking takes on a new dimension, arising from immediate conviction to its encompassing horizons. Such thinking is dialectical in the broad sense that it turns against itself and revokes itself; but it is not discursive-progressive, because that method of advancing knowledge is conditioned on object-knowledge, whereas thinking of Being involves a countermovement in which object-knowledge is left behind. Jaspers calls the latter "fundamental knowledge," "self-awareness," or "philosophical faith."

The reader who wants to explore further Jaspers' modes of the Encompassing will find Knauss's account helpful. We shall note only what he has to say about the relation between the world and transcendence. Knauss sums it up in two statements: the world is the boundary we meet when we transcend Existenz outwardly; transcendence is the boundary we meet when we transcend Existenz inwardly. The world, which is an idea and not a perceptible object, is the Encompassing that we are not, because even though we are part of it, the world is not the cause of our Being. Thus, at the external limit of ourselves, we know that we are "different" from the world, and we know this by virtue of our freedom. When we experience ourselves as acting freely we experience our origin in something else than the world, and this "else" is transcendence. In Knauss's words, it is "the concealment of God, the consciousness of dependence, the concept of being created as a creature in the act of creation."

In assessing the significance of Jaspers, Knauss returns to the difference between ontology and periechontology: the former asks the question "What is Being?" and expects a precise answer because it thinks of Being as a thing; the latter asks "How can Being-in-itself become appearance to us?" and, having to look in two directions for its answer, ceases to expect precision. Ontology retains the orientation of a particular science, whereas thinking in the Encompassing reorients the search, exploring all possible ways in which we encounter what is.

Knauss insists that, whereas philosophy that is cast in the ontological mode tends to denigrate the sciences, Jaspers' philosophy respects the findings of the sciences, holding that without these philosophy itself would become a "mystical eccentricity." Indeed, according to Knauss, Jaspers shows us how to put an end to the dispute between positivism and realism which sets scientists against each other today. Kant saw it as the mission of philosophy in his time to clear up the scandal raised by those who denied the reality of the outer world and tried to fulfill this mission by showing that reality has different meanings for the scientist and for the metaphysician. Similarly, says Knauss, philosophy today has the mission to shore up the validity of scientific truth by showing where objective knowledge holds and where it fails. This is not the same as setting a new truth over the truth of the sciences, for what troubles the modern mind is the coexistence of many truths. "The task rather," says Knauss, "is to transform the scientific consciousness by a new ascertainment of Being."—*J.F.*

ADDITIONAL RECOMMENDED READING

Collins, James. "Jaspers' Quest of Transcendence," in *The Existentialists*. Chicago: Henry Regnery Company, 1952, pp. 88-127. Criticizes Jaspers from the Thomistic standpoint.

Heinemann, F. H. "The Philosophy of Detachment," in *Existentialism and the Modern Predicament*. New York: Harper & Row Publishers, 1958, pp. 59-83. An erstwhile existentialist finds himself disappointed in the way the movement worked out.

Schilpp, Paul A., ed. *The Philosophy of Karl Jaspers* (The Library of Living Philosophers). New York: Tudor Publishing Company, 1957. Jaspers' "Philosophical Autobiography" is of particular interest, disclosing what it meant to exist as a philosopher in Germany from 1914 to 1947.

Schrag, Oswald O. *An Introduction to Existence, Existenz, and Transcendence: The Philosophy of Karl Jaspers*. Pittsburgh: Duquesne University Press, 1971. One of many recent books seeking to give an overview of Jaspers' thought. This one is unpretentious and stays close to the themes announced in the title.

Wallraff, Charles F. *Karl Jaspers: An Introduction to His Philosophy*. Princeton, New Jersey: Princeton University Press, 1970. Another commendable attempt to summarize Jaspers' philosophy.

LANGUAGE, TRUTH AND LOGIC

Author: Alfred Jules Ayer (1910-   )
Type of work: Philosophy of philosophy, epistemology
First published: 1936

PRINCIPAL IDEAS ADVANCED

Metaphysics is impossible because metaphysical statements are meaningless.

A sentence is factually significant if and only if there is a method of verification an observer could adopt to determine the truth or falsity of the sentence; when experience cannot settle an issue, the issue has no factual meaning.

The propositions of philosophy are not factual, but linguistic; they are not factual reports, but either definitions of words in use or expressions of the logical implications of such definitions.

Value statements and statements declaring duties are neither true nor false; they express the feelings of the speaker.

Alfred Jules Ayer presents here a modified version of logical positivism that he prefers to call "logical empiricism." However, the doctrines, particularly their implications for philosophy, are largely those of logical positivism, and the work serves to bring these together succinctly and vigorously. Therefore, the book has had great importance in the twentieth century, both as a positivistic document and as a center of controversy about positivistic tenets. In it, Ayer offers to solve the problems of reality, perception, induction, knowledge, meaning, truth, value, and other minds. He presents no great new idea; rather, his are solutions others have proposed, but which Ayer has modified and brought into logical consistency. A second edition (1946) enabled Ayer, in a new introduction, to reply to his critics. He provided a further explication and changed a few beliefs, but essentially his position remained unchanged. The reader of *Language, Truth and Logic* who is unfamiliar with the field probably would prefer to reserve reading the new introduction until after examining the text itself.

Ayer attacks the possibility of metaphysics, saying that he will deduce the fruitlessness of attempting knowledge that transcends the limits of experience from the "rule which determines the literal significance of language." The sentences of metaphysics, failing to meet this rule, are meaningless.

The criterion of meaning Ayer finds in the *verification principle.* "We say that a sentence is factually significant to any given person, if, and only if, he knows how to verify the proposition which it purports to express—that is, if he knows what observations would lead him, under certain conditions, to accept the proposition as being true, or reject it as being false." Another possible kind of meaningful sentence is the tautology. But any sentence which is neither a tautology nor a verifiable proposition (by this criterion) is a mere pseudo-proposition, a meaningless sentence.

Certain provisions qualify this tenet. Ayer distinguished practical verifiability and verifiability in principle. Some sentences are not practically verifiable, because of inconvenience or the present state of science and culture.
If one could know what observations would decide such a matter if he were
in a position to make them, the proposition is verifiable in principle. A further
distinction is that between "strong" verifiability and "weak" verifiability. According to the "strong" theory, advanced by the Vienna Circle of logical
positivists, a sentence is meaningful only if it is conclusively verifiable empirically; according to the "weak" theory, it is meaningful if experience may
render it probable. Ayer chooses the "weak" theory, on the basis that since
no empirical demonstration is ever one hundred percent conclusive, the
"strong" theory leaves no empirical statement meaningful. By using the
"weak" theory, Ayer believes he allows meaning to general propositions of
science and to propositions about the past, two types which had given difficulty
to previous positivistic writers. The proposed principle rules out such assertions as the statement that the world of sense is unreal, and such questions
as whether reality is one substance or many. No experience could decide these
issues, so they have no literal significance. The metaphysician has usually
been misled by the grammar of his language, so that he posits an entity
("substance," "Being") where grammar requires a noun as the subject of a
sentence, even though thought may exert no such requirement.

By the abandonment of metaphysics, the philosopher is freed from the
function of constructing a deductive system of the universe from first principles. For first principles cannot come from experience, whose propositions
are hypotheses only and never certain. But if they are taken *a priori*, they
are only tautologies, which cannot apply to the universe as factual knowledge.

The problem of induction can be set aside as unreal. It is the attempt to
prove that certain empirical generalizations derived from past experience will
hold good also in the future. It must have either an *a priori* or an empirical
solution. But in the first case it is improper to apply tautologies to experience,
for they cannot apply to matters of fact; and in the second, we simply assume
what we set out to prove. Since Ayer can conceive no test that would solve
the "problem" through experience, he concludes that it is not a genuine
problem. In actuality, we place our faith in such scientific generalizations as
enable us to predict future experience and thus control our environment;
there is no general logical problem about this practice.

A common mistake is to assert that without a satisfactory analysis of perception, we are not entitled to believe in the existence of material things.
Rather, the right to believe in their existence comes simply from the fact that
one has certain sensations, for to say the thing exists is equivalent to saying
the sensations are obtainable. It is the philosopher's business to give a correct
definition of material things in terms of sensations. He is not concerned with

properties of things in the world, but only with our way of speaking of them. The propositions of philosophy are not factual, but linguistic in character— "that is, they do not describe the behavior of physical, or even mental, objects; they express definitions, or the formal consequences of definitions." Philosophy is a department of logic. It is independent of any empirical, not to say metaphysical, assumptions. Often propositions which are really linguistic are so expressed as to appear to be factual. "A material thing cannot be in two places at once" is actually linguistic, recording "the fact that, as the result of certain verbal conventions, the proposition that two sense-contents occur in the same visual or tactual sense-field is incompatible with the proposition that they belong to the same material thing." The question, "What is the nature of x?" asks for a definition, which is always a linguistic statement.

Philosophical analysis essentially provides definitions. But they are not the most frequently occurring kind; that is, *explicit* or synonymous definitions giving an alternate symbol or symbolic expression for the term to be defined. Rather, they are a special sort, *definitions in use*, which are made by showing how a sentence in which the definiendum occurs can be translated into equivalent sentences which do not contain the definiendum or any of its synonyms. An example taken from Bertrand Russell defines "author" in the sentence, "The author of *Waverley* was Scott," by providing the equivalent, "One person, and one person only, wrote *Waverley*, and that person was Scott." Such definitions clarify sentences both where no synonym for the definiendum exists, and also where available synonyms are unclear in the same fashion as the symbol needing clarification. A complete philosophical clarification of a language would first enumerate the types of sentence significant in that language, then display the relations of equivalence that hold between sentences of various types. Such a set of definitions would reveal the structure of the language examined; and any truly philosophical theory would hence apply to a given language.

Some of our symbols denote simple sense-contents, and others logical constructions, the latter enabling us to state complicated propositions about the elements of the logical constructions in a relatively simple form. But logical constructions are not inherently fictions. Rather, material things are among such logical constructions. The definition-in-use will restate the definiendum naming a material thing by translating it into symbols that refer to sense-contents that are elements of the material thing. In other words, roughly, to say something about a table is always to say something about sense-contents. The problem of the "reduction" of material things into sense-contents, long a chief part of the problem of perception, is a linguistic problem readily solved by providing definitions-in-use. To accomplish this reduction, Ayer stipulates that two sense-contents *resemble* each other *directly* when either there is no difference, or only an infinitesimal difference, between them; and *indirectly*, when they are linked by a series of direct resemblances amounting to an appreciable difference. He stipulates further that two sense-contents are *directly continuous* when within successive sense-fields there is no difference, or only an infinitesimal difference, between them, with respect to the position of each in its own sense-field; and *indirectly continuous* when related by an actual, or possible, series of direct continuities. Any two of one's sense-contents, then, are elements of the same material thing when they are related to each other by direct or indirect resemblance and by direct or indirect continuity.

Ayer assumes that the object of a theory of truth is to show how propositions are validated. Like all questions of similar pattern, the question "What is truth?" calls for a definition. Consequently, no factual theory is needed to answer it. The real question discussed most of the time in "theories of truth" is "What makes a proposition true or false?"

Ayer adopts the distinction between analytic and synthetic propositions. Each has its own validation. "A proposition is analytic when its validity depends solely on the definitions of the symbols it contains, and synthetic when its validity is determined by the facts of experience." While "Either some ants are parasitic or none are," an analytic proposition, is undubitably and necessarily true, it provides no actual information about ants. As a tautology, it has no factual content and serves only to help us understand matters of language. The valid propositions of logic are true by tautology and are useful and surprising in revealing hidden implications in our sentences. They can help us gain empirical knowledge, but it is not the tautologies which render empirical knowledge valid. Whether a geometry actually can be applied to physical space is an empirical question which falls outside the scope of the geometry itself. There is thus no paradox about the applicability of the analytic propositions of logic and mathematics to the world.

Synthetic propositions, Ayer affirms, are validated by experience. Experience is given in the form of sensations. Sensations are neither true nor false; they simply occur. Propositions about them are not logically determined by them in one way or another; hence, while these are perhaps largely dependable, they may be doubted. Similarly, they may be confirmed by additional experience. In other words, "Empirical propositions are one and all hypotheses." And, in fact, whenever a verification is carried out, it is applied to an entire system of hypotheses—a principal one, together with supplementary hypotheses which often are adjusted by the verification rather than by the principal hypothesis. Therefore, the "facts of experience" can never *per se* oblige us to abandon a particular hypothesis, since we may ever continue without contradiction to explain invalidating instances in various ways while retaining the principal hypothesis. We must of course retain a willingness to abandon it under certain circumstances because of experience, or else we make of it not a hypothesis but a definition. It must be granted that we are not always rational in arriving at belief—that is, we do not always employ a self-consistent accredited procedure in the formation of our beliefs. That a hypothesis increases in probability is equivalent to saying that observation increases the degree of confidence with which it is rational to entertain the hypothesis.

The exposition of synthetic propositions, every one of which is a rule for the anticipation of our future experience, constitutes Ayer's validation of the verification principle, for it comes to just what the verification principle states, that the literal significance of an empirical proposition is the anticipated sense-contents entailed in it.

To account consistently for statements of value with empirical principles, Ayer holds that descriptive ethical sentences are empirical statements and that normative ethical sentences are "absolute" or "intrinsic," not empirically calculable, and indefinable in factual terms. The normative symbols in a sentence name no concepts, add nothing to the factual content. Thus, normative sentences are not capable of being true or false. They simply express certain feelings of the speaker. They are not even *assertions* that the speaker has a certain feeling, for such assertions would be empirical and subject to doubt. Thus we remove the question of their having any validity at all.

But how, then, can we dispute about value? Ayer maintains that actually we never dispute about questions of value, but only about questions of fact. The pattern usual in such a dispute is to exhibit to our opponent what we believe to be the facts, assuming a common framework of value statements, and attempt thus to bring him to our way of seeing the facts.

As to religious knowledge, we cannot appeal to tautologies for factual truth about God, for these are mere stipulations of our own. Nor can we have empirical propositions about God, for we can conceive of no experience which would bring us different sense-contents if God exists than if he does not. Hence, the notion is metaphysical and meaningless.

Ayer applies a complete phenomenalism to the traditional problems of the self and knowledge of the world. He denies that the given needs a logical rather than sensory justification. Further, he rejects the pattern of subject-act-object as an account of perception. He defines a sense-content not as the object, but as a part of sense-experience, so that the existence of a sense-content always entails the existence of a sense-experience. Hence, the question of whether sense-contents are mental or physical is inapplicable. Such a distinction can apply only to the logical constructions which are derived from them. The difference between mental and physical objects lies in differences between the sense-contents, or in the different relations of sense-contents that constitute objects.

The self may be explained in similar terms. "It is, in fact, a logical construction out of the sense-experiences which constitute the actual and possible sense-history of a self." To ask its nature is to ask what relationship obtains between sense-experiences for them to belong to the sense-history of the same self. Rather than retain the metaphysical notion of a substantive ego, we can identify personal identity simply in terms of bodily identity, and that in turn is to be defined in terms of the resemblance and continuity of sense-contents. To say anything about the self is always to say something about sense-contents. I know other selves empirically, just as I know physical things and my own self empirically.

Ayer urges the unity of philosophy with the sciences. Rather than actually validating scientific theory, the philosopher's function is to elucidate the symbols occurring in it. It is essential to the task that he should understand science. Philosophy must develop into the logic of science.

As well as providing further exposition, Ayer's introduction to the second edition contains some modifications of doctrine which deserve notice. In the interim between editions, he came to accept a belief of the logical positivists, which he opposed in the first edition, that some empirical statements may be considered conclusively verified. These are "basic statements," referring to the sense-content of a single experience, and their conclusive verification is the immediate occurrence of the experience to which they refer. As long as these merely record what is experienced and say nothing else, they cannot be factually mistaken, for they make no claim that any further fact could confute. But this change makes little difference to the chief doctrine, Ayer maintains, for the vast majority of propositions are not of this sort.

Ayer introduces the term "observation-statement," to designate any statement "which records an actual or possible observation." To remove the objection that, as originally stated, the principle allows any indicative statement whatever to have significance, Ayer amends its expression to say that the principle of verification requires of a literally meaningful, nonanalytic statement that it should be either directly or indirectly verifiable. For it to be directly verifiable it must be an observation-statement or, in conjunction with one or more observation-statements, must entail at least one other observation-statement not entailed by the other observation statements alone. To be indirectly verifiable, first, in conjunction with certain other premises, a statement must entail one or more directly verifiable statements not deducible from the other premises alone and, second, the other premises must include no statement that is not either analytic, or directly verifiable, or indirectly verifiable independently.

Ayer gives up the position that *a priori* propositions are linguistic rules, for they can properly be said to be both true and necessary, while linguistic rules cannot be called true and are arbitrary. Descriptive linguistic statements of contingent empirical fact of language usage are, however, the basis for statements of logical relationships—which are necessary truths. Ayer admits doubts as to whether his account of the experiences of others is correct, yet says, "I am not convinced that it is not." He confesses error in assuming that philosophical analysis consists mainly in providing "definitions in use." Such a result is the exception rather than the rule; and in fact, for statements about material things such definition becomes impossible, since "no finite set of observation-statements is ever equivalent to a statement about a material thing."

Finally, rather than classify philosophical statements alongside scientific statements, Ayer states that "it is incorrect to say that there are no philosophical propositions. For, whether they are true or false, the propositions that are expressed in such a book as this do fall into a special category . . . asserted or denied by philosophers. . . ." The lexicographer is concerned with the use of particular expressions, but the philosopher, with classes of expressions; and his statements, if true, are usually analytic.—*J.T.G.*

PERTINENT LITERATURE

Evans, J. L. "On Meaning and Verification," in *Mind*. LXII, no. 245 (January, 1953), pp. 1-19.

Logical positivism was developed in the 1920's and 1930's by the philosophers (and scientists) who formed the Vienna Circle. The positivists' aim was to find a way to draw a distinction between science and metaphysics such that science would remain as *the* legitimate field of human knowledge while metaphysics (that is, most of traditional philosophy) would be ruled out as a pseudodiscipline. The weapon they devised to achieve that aim was the verification principle.

The verification principle was intended to be a test (criterion) to determine whether any given sentence is meaningful. Excluding sentences which express analytic (trivial) propositions (for example, "A red house is red"), the verification principle says that a sentence is meaningful if and only if the proposition it expresses is verifiable. That is, a sentence which expresses a nonverifiable proposition is literally meaningless, literally nonsense. (The positivists often went further and gave not only a criterion of meaningfulness but also a specification of what the meaning of a sentence is. Thus it was often said that "The meaning of a sentence is its method of verification.")

This principle, at least when "verification" was interpreted as "verifiable in sense experience" (and that was the interpretation implicitly accepted by friends and foes alike), was intended to be a tool which would reveal metaphysics to be nothing but nonsense. What is the view of philosophers today about the verification principle? To put it bluntly, no one accepts it. What were the reasons that produced this unanimity in opposition to verifiability? Surprisingly, there is no one work which systematically presents the case against the verification principle. A good account of the criticisms behind the current rejection of the principle can be found in the essay by J. L. Evans.

It is helpful to make a distinction between criticisms which the positivists could respond to by altering the principle and those which could not be accommodated by a new version of the principle. (There is, of course, no sharp distinction between those types of criticism; moreover, too much patching, even if each single patch seems successful, tends to undermine any thesis.) For example, if a proposition must be verifiable to be meaningful, there are even questions about whether scientific propositions are really meaningful. We cannot check, verify, every individual crow to determine whether it is black, so how can we verify "All crows are black"? Consequently, the positivists had to reformulate the principle to say that it did not require "complete verification." To see similar modifications in response to criticisms, see the reference to Carl G. Hempel in the bibliography following these essays.

There are other criticisms which are much harder to take into account by modifying the principle; for example, is the verification principle verifiable? If not, it is either analytic (trivial, uninformative), which no positivist would accept, or meaningless, which would be disastrous. So it must be verifiable. But then, by the positivists' own account, it cannot be more than a hypothesis; that is, it cannot be fully verifiable. Any ways around this criticism (and there are ways to remove its sting) inevitably seem *ad hoc*, invented to save the principle, and so are unsatisfying.

Probably the most decisive criticism has been the realization that there are many kinds of meaningful sentences which are quite unrelated to any issue of verification. "Pass the salt" and "How are you?" are sentences and meaningful, but talk of verifying them is completely beside the point. It becomes clear from this that verification is not a general criterion of meaning. In fact, at its best the verification principle tells us (something about) what is to count as an empirical proposition. And that means that metaphysical propositions, which do not purport to be empirical, escape from the positivists' way of condemning them.

Achinstein, Peter and Stephen F. Barker, eds. *The Legacy of Logical Positivism*. Baltimore: The Johns Hopkins University Press, 1969.

It was the aim of the logical positivists to reject metaphysics and to retain science. One of the most obvious features of the positivists' work was their extensive knowledge of and extreme regard for natural science. (A. J. Ayer is something of a rebel in this respect—there is far less of a "scientific" atmosphere in *Language, Truth and Logic* than in any of the other major positivist writings.) It is worth asking, in view of their intellectual allegiances, how their view of the nature of science has stood the tests of time and criticism.

The book under review addresses itself to this question. The papers by various philosophers which are collected in this volume are, with two exceptions, attempts to appraise the positivists' thought about the role of theories in science, about their views on the behavioral sciences, and about their contribution to the philosophy of mathematics. One of the exceptions should be noticed first. The introductory essay by Herbert Feigl, a member of the Vienna Circle, is a clear discussion of the beginnings and "spirit" of logical positivism and is well worth reading.

Before considering some of the papers specifically, there are a few general points to be noticed. All the authors agree that it is legitimate to talk about the *legacy* of positivism; that is, they agree that there are no more logical positivists. Even the former adherents, Feigl, Carl G. Hempel, and Ayer, are no longer philosophically committed to the positivists' program (no matter how much their present views are deeply shaped by those earlier ideas.) Again, all the authors represented here agree that positivism had a beneficial effect on philosophy. There is disagreement, however, on the further question of what that beneficial effect consists of. This lack of agreement appears most clearly in the papers by Hempel and Michael Scriven. Hempel, a former positivist, holds (in the conclusion to his paper) that the value to current philosophy of positivist thought resides in the detailed work done by the positivists and not in the sweeping general theories (for example, the verification principle) they offered. Scriven, on the other hand, is more representative of the other authors in that he claims that it was precisely in those broad slogans, which have turned out to be misguided, that positivism has had a good effect on philosophy. For it was these striking general views which made other philosophers rethink their fundamental views.

Of the papers on the nature of theory in science, the one most accessible to the beginner is Norbert Hanson's. The main theme of it and the others on this topic is the same: the positivists made a sharp distinction between theory and observation in science; the present authors agree that no such radical distinction between a formal structure of theory and the factual content of a science can be made. (They disagree, however, on how much of a distinction there is between theory and observation or interpretation.)

On the topic of the positivists' contribution to philosophical questions about the social sciences, the paper to start with is Scriven's. He considers several topics very critically, yet sympathetically: the positivists' doctrine of operationalism, their defense of value-free social science (Scriven's analysis and criticism of this is particularly good), and the positivist opposition to *Verstehen* theory (the idea that there is a special technique of "understanding" available to social scientists which is not available to physical scientists).

Stephen F. Barker's paper on the positivists and their philosophy is clear and helpful, even to those not well versed in such issues. And last, the piece by Stephen Toulmin, while idiosyncratic (it is really about Ludwig Wittgenstein and Toulmin), is nevertheless very instructive about the development of twentieth century philosophy, including the role of the logical positivists.

Urmson, J. O. *The Emotive Theory of Ethics*. New York: Oxford University Press, 1969.

One of the consequences of using the weapon of verifiability was that fields of human thought other than the intended target—namely, metaphysics—were also in the line of fire. Religious propositions, for example, were regarded as not empirically verifiable and so were relegated to nonsense. Although that particular outcome probably did not distress the positivists deeply, it turned out that, according to their view, moral propositions also were not empirically verifiable and so should be regarded as literally nonsensical. But that was a shocking conclusion; and so that morality should be meaningless seemed an important objection to the verification principle. Hence it was important to the positivists' program to find an account of moral propositions which would show them not to be nonsense, without surrendering the verification principle. The result was the emotive theory of ethics.

But are ethical claims unverifiable by observation? It is clear, as J. O. Urmson shows in this excellent book, that, given the intellectual situation in the 1930's, the positivists had to conclude that moral claims are not capable of verification. G. E. Moore presumably had shown that "good" did not name any *natural* property; that is, any property discoverable by the senses. That meant that moral propositions were not verifiable since "good" is essential in moral discourse. On the other hand, positivistic empiricists could not accept Moore's alternative view: namely, that "good" names a *non-natural* property. Such a view requires a doctrine of intuition, a notion repugnant to empiricists.

Although A. J. Ayer was not the first to formulate the emotive theory (Urmson gives the history of the notion), his account in *Language, Truth and Logic* is still the best short account, as well as having been influential at the time. According to Ayer, the problem is solved by holding that "good" and other terms *do not name* any property at all; hence, propositions containing the word "good" are not really propositions and so, of course, are not verifiable. But sentences containing "good" *do* have a function in discourse—they *express* feelings and stimulate actions. What look like propositions are really forms of command along with expressions of emotions.

Urmson is especially good at showing how the emotivist theory had roots other than those demanded by the positivists' program. One striking thing about Ayer's development of the theory was that it derived solely from considerations about sensible discourse and not from any thought about moral language itself. On the other hand, Charles Stevenson came to formulate an emotivist theory shortly after Ayer and came to do so by way of a consideration of the workings of moral language. (See Ayer's approval of Stevenson's more detailed work in a footnote to the Preface of the second edition of Urmson's book.) In fact, Stevenson turns out to be the hero of Urmson's study.

How stands the emotive theory today? Much of Urmson's criticism deals with details of formulation. But he also clearly argues that the emotivist's belief that moral sayings are neither true nor false and so are not subject to rational discourse is not acceptable. Moreover, the easy assumption that all evaluational language, including moral, aesthetic, political, and other, is to be given the same kind of account is cogently objected to by Urmson. Lastly, while the emotivists thought they were giving an analysis of the meaning of "good," Urmson argues that contemporary speech-act theory shows that they confused questions of meaning and act/use. Still, Urmson is very careful to point out that it was precisely the emotivists' realization that moral language does something other than state facts which led to the modern theory which is now being used to criticize its ancestor.—*M.R.*

ADDITIONAL RECOMMENDED READING

Ayer, A. J. *Part of My Life: The Memoirs of a Philosopher.* New York: Harcourt Brace Jovanovich, 1977. A fairly rare type of work; very informative.

——————— ., ed. *Logical Positivism.* New York: Free Press, 1959. The best anthology of positivist writings with a good introduction by Ayer and an especially large bibliography.

Hempel, Carl G. *Aspects of Scientific Explanation.* New York: Free Press, 1965. Includes the important paper "Empiricist Criteria of Cognitive Significance: Problems and Changes."

Kraft, Viktor. *The Vienna Circle: The Origin of Neo-Positivism.* Westport, Connecticut: Greenwood Press, 1969. An excellent account.

PERSONAL REALISM

Author: James Bissett Pratt (1875-1944)
Type of work: Epistemology
First published: 1937

PRINCIPAL IDEAS ADVANCED

Images and symbols are not the objects they refer to; objects exist independently of symbols, and symbols have meanings only because selves endow them with meanings.

In conceiving individual things we may be led, by our knowledge of the respects in which they are similar, to use the same concept for them; Platonism and nominalism are indefensible extreme positions.

Rationalism concerns itself with the characters of things at the expense of the independent existence of things.

A true judgment corresponds to objects in the sense that the objects may be as the judgment describes them as being.

Causation is an objective relation; there are substantial, physical objects which are causal factors in the order of nature.

New realism—realism without dualism—has difficulty accounting for illusions and memory; critical realism, which asserts the independent existence of ontological objects distinct from the epistemological objects by which the former are known, is preferable.

This book is an expression and a defense of Pratt's mature thought on the nature of human knowing and the status of self in the world. He was very much concerned with human personality and its moral and religious standing in the nature of things. Pratt was a student of the psychological aspects of religion and well versed in both Eastern and Western religions. Thus, he had a wide perspective and many interests. *Personal Realism* is concerned with the clarification of his ideas on basic themes in contemporary thought. His purpose was to defend critical realism, with emphasis on dualism and transcendence.

Pratt begins by drawing a contrast between rationalism and empiricism, much after the manner of A. K. Rogers. While rationalism stresses the logical coherence of thought and tends to identify thought and existence, empiricism devotes itself to the world of empirical facts, to existence and the various kinds of existent things. Rationalism tends to be abstract and *a priori* in its outlook, while empiricism dwells on concrete experience and beliefs. The influence of his teacher, William James, is shown here in Pratt's thought. He was willing to learn from rationalism all he could but sought empirical probability about basic questions. He argues that philosophy has something to add to the special sciences. It asks unavoidable questions about the general nature of human knowing, about causation, and about the relation of mind to matter, questions which the sciences do not quite broach.

In his discussion of the term "meaning," Pratt refers to the wide extension of the use of the term but chooses two examples apparent in everyday experience as central, namely, pointing, or reference, and the significance of symbols, such as words. The first of these two meanings of "meaning" comes out in the sentence: "No, I do not mean Rome, N. Y., but Rome, Italy." The proper name denotes, selects, points to an object. The second meaning of "meaning" is apparent when a synonym of a word or phrase is given, as in a definition: "'Dog' means the animal that barks." While a person can *mean* in the sense of referring to something, a symbol acquires meaning through linkage in experience.

There are, of course, several interesting philosophical points involved. Proper names must be distinguished from general names and both from abstract terms. These items are taken up in logic and are under considerable discussion today. What Professor Pratt chose to stress, as an empiricist, is the point that while symbols have meaning or significance, their objects are only what they are. Objects are independent of symbols; what we seek to do is to characterize objects. This reference to objects and their characterization has been too much neglected by psychologists. It is at this point that Pratt introduces the question of transcendence. The image or symbol used is not the object referred to. It is in terms of this contrast that Pratt defends critical realism against idealism and various forms of the "new realism." The note of personal realism is struck in the assertion that it is a self which puts meaning into symbols. Pratt argues—against the logical positivism of the time—that statements have meaning apart from their verification. Verification and its methods concern knowledge and truth.

Pratt deals with the perennial topics of terms and relations, universals and existence. He regards relations as internal but not wholly constitutive of their terms. This is a natural, empirical view. Again, qualitative data are not analyzable into relations. On the other hand, acquired properties do involve relations: a person could hardly be a father apart from paternity. Turning now to universals, Pratt seeks to avoid both Platonism, which tends to reify them, and extreme nominalism, which denies them altogether. We discover character with individuals. In conceiving individuals, we may be led to use the same term for them. Then we have a class and speak of a common connotation. We are also likely to speak of the members of a class as similar, similar with respect to some characteristic. After all, we are thinking about objects, not intuiting them.

This fits in with critical, referential realism. Language and communication support "free ideas" or concepts. We speak both of concepts and of conceiving, just as we speak of percepts and perceiving. We must be careful here and not make unnecessary entities. What do we *grasp* in conceiving? It would seem to be the general properties of things. In grasping these general properties, we have knowledge about the things. But the danger to avoid is that of making entities out of them. To call concepts universals encourages this tendency. Even to speak of *universalia in re* gives them something of this status. Nominalism has wanted to stress individuals and their similarity. Here, it would seem, we have the job of adjusting the mechanism of human knowing with its use of concepts to the ontological situation. So-called psychological nominalism with its stress on sensations and images could not quite do justice to transcendent knowing. We know through and by means of concepts. It might be said that the term universal is tied in with the *function of cognition*. For example, we know that *this* thing is square, and also that *that* thing is square.

Pratt makes much of existence as contrasted with essences or concepts. Here he is arguing against objective rationalism of the Blanshard variety, which is also to be found in Royce and Joachim. He writes that rationalism rules out change, duration, and individuality. He argues that, after all the qualities of things are abstracted, there remains a residue which is not identical with them. Here lies the *that* as distinct from the *what*. As an empiricist, Pratt regarded this distinction as basic.

Inevitably, Pratt was led to defend the correspondence theory of truth, just as the rationalist supports the coherence theory. He argues that since the judgment in an individual mind can refer to objects outside itself, the judgment may correspond to these objects in the sense that as referents they are what the judgment asserts them to be. He claims that the pragmatic theory of truth is not so different from the coherence theory as is usually supposed. He argues that the principles of logic apply to the world, for without them, we could not investigate it.

Professor Pratt uses solipsism as a sort of test. In a way, George Santayana did the same and got animal faith. Pratt, on the other hand, stresses transcendence and communication. Communication, he argues, works through the body and the use of symbols. A letter sent to China is read by the recipient and understood. The panpsychist is a realist of sorts who wants to interpret the material world as ultimately mental in nature. The pragmatist seeks to read everything in terms of an "if-then" relation; observability is substituted for enduring things. Such endurance is considered by the pragmatist as unverified, unnecessary, improbable, and really meaningless. In Pratt's opinion, pragmatism is nearer to solipsism than it admits. We have already noted that Pratt, like A. K. Rogers, found objective idealism or objective rationalism very ambiguous in its claims; such theories confused thought and things.

As one would expect, Pratt takes causation to be an objective relation. It must be distinguished from general causal laws and from mere invariability. Time flow, important for causality, makes it different from logical implication.

In his discussion of the general, realistic hypothesis, Pratt defends the belief in substance and in physical things as factors in the executive order of nature. Later, as we shall see, he supplements it with an appeal to theistic purposiveness. This is prepared for by his dualism and his idea of the self.

Pratt then proceeds to consider the "new realism" or, as he calls it, realism without dualism. He rightly points out that realism had once ruled almost unquestioned but that it was nearly driven from the field by various schools of idealism—Berkeleian, Kantian, neo-Kantian, and positivist. As he remarks, in the last part of the nineteenth century it was about all that a philosopher's reputation was worth to suggest there was anything in realism. In the United States, pragmatism undoubtedly operated as a transition movement. The campaign of logical positivism had much the same context. That is probably why it and pragmatism got along so well together. One could do without epistemology and ontology if one had colorful slogans praising the unity of science, together with a sufficiency of logical and linguistic puzzles. Often this is the way in which advance is made in philosophy.

Since Pratt lived through this era, it is interesting to note his reactions. The first step was to regard mind as pure activity, a sort of transparent awareness. This gave a form of naïve realism: mind contemplates the nonmental—which may consist of what were called sense-data. British neorealism tended to take this form, while American new realism followed suggestions in William James and ended in a panobjectivism which sought to eliminate "mental awareness" and ally itself with behaviorism. But how deal with illusions and with memory? Pratt expresses the belief that the role of ideas in knowing cannot be avoided and that "ideas" were in some measure invented to supplement naïve realism.

American new realism, or epistemological monism as it was often called, identified thing and idea. The tulip one sees and *one's idea* of the tulip are identical. But it is hard to carry out this new concept in detail. What was called objective relativism was an attempt to keep presentational, or naïve, realism by introducing relations of percipient organisms as part of the quality of the object. Whitehead explored this scheme. Pratt holds that it simply will not do.

He then gives his version of critical realism, reminiscent of his contributions to *Essays in Critical Realism* (1920). It is interesting to note that he resorts to Broad's distinction between an epistemological object and an ontological object: the mind does not literally include the objects it knows; and two minds can concern themselves with an identical object. The job, evidently, is to understand what human knowing involves. Pratt's dualism favored his adoption of Broad's terminology, but he had difficulty connecting the epistemological object with the ontological one. Quite rightly, Pratt appeals to psychology against the new realism and quotes Aristotle and C. A. Strong.

The adoption of a mind-body dualism makes *transcendence* something of a mystery. This is the case with Arthur O. Lovejoy as well as with Pratt. But if we can break down transcendence into a reference connected with response and the evidential value of sensory data under the control of external things, transcendence becomes an achievement resting on the "form and to" structure of perceiving. It is the chair, itself, which we are looking at, referring to, and characterizing.

Materialism, parallelism, and interaction remain to be considered. According to Pratt, traditional materialism tended to epiphenomenalism; and it is hard to see how logical implication could be given a base in physical, causal necessity. Pratt agrees with Paulsen that we *mean* different things by the physical and the psychical. But all this may signify that traditional thinking was dominated by wrong assumptions. Pratt is open-minded enough to consider an identity theory along the lines of emergence and double knowledge. His chief objection seems to be that it does not do justice to the self.

Pratt's basic objection to the double-knowledge view would seem to be logical. The "essence," the brain as a structural and moving system, is not identical with the "essence," pain. De Witt Parker seems to have had much the same logical objection. However, the advocate of the double-knowledge view might well reply that he is not asserting the identity of these two meanings, only that the type of knowledge given in the one, which is knowledge about, does not reach participation in cerebral activity and that, in consciousness, the agent is on the inside of this activity. Pratt recognizes the subtlety of this theory but keeps to his dualism. Certainly, such an enlarged materialism must explore the status and function of awareness and consciousness.

Pratt then proceeds to defend interactionism with dualism of process because of his conviction that complete parallelism would involve an extraordinary series of coincidences.

In introducing the theory of interaction, the author notes that the meaning of mind which identifies it with a stream of consciousness does not do justice to all we actually mean by mind. Consciousness is fragmentary and does not have the substantive unity which reasoning and decision imply. More is needed: there must be agency. The self is such an agent; and it is the self which interacts with the body. Such a self is organic to the body or embodied. The self is the mind as perceiving, conceiving, and willing. Because its unity with the body is so intimate I feel that whoever does things is *I*. Yet the body is not a part of the self. It is, rather, the self's closest environment or, as W. E. Hocking puts it, a "piece of property," of the self. In perceiving, for instance, the self and the brain act jointly, making up a unitary whole. Pratt is inclined to adopt the theory that the self has the capacity of producing sensations and meanings in response to sensory processes of the brain. This is the logic of animism. Perhaps only an enlarged, evolutionary materialism with a clear epistemology can meet animism.

In the chapter on "Knowledge and the Self," a strong argument is put forward for the purposive and unifying role of the self as a subject. Associationism and even *Gestalt* theories are rejected as not doing justice to activity and organizational power. Thinking, judging, and planning do not terminate in sensations and images. It is the self which refers beyond the given to what is meant. Arguments from Descartes, Kant, Rudolf Lotze, and Franz Brentano are used. There still remains the question of just what the *subject* is. It is not the *I* of self-consciousness with its social overtones, but is presupposed by it. Feelings as subjective point to the self.

The self, then, is a concrete substance exercising capacities. It is an agent and has inherent unity. It maintains itself in and through its experiences. In some sense, it endures through time, but it also changes in it. The question of the nature of self-consciousness has been an important one from the time of the ancient Indian thinkers to Hume. We have knowledge about the self. Do we have also some sort of direct acquaintance with it? Pratt finally takes his stand on a kind of intuition of the self as subject.

In his treatment of the will and its freedom, Pratt rejects indeterminism and supports self-determination. Here, again, the stress is upon activity.

In what sense can there be a science of man? Can psychology formulate laws like those of physics and chemistry? Pratt doubts it. We can have statistical generalizations and types, but it is unlikely that we can make deductive predictions of the sort the inorganic sciences achieve. For Pratt, the nature of the self must be considered. Laws connect events, but selves make decisions.

Pratt's speculations are along teleological and theistic lines. A purpose must be a cause if it is to have an effect. Is there evidence of purpose in nature as a whole? Pratt suggests a kind of immanent teleology in the long development of living things. The analogy between the self and the body is usable for theism. God may act as a musician who improvises on an instrument, but perhaps not all things are under his control. Pratt does not believe in special providences of the popular religious kind; he admits that we are here in the realm of overbeliefs, of speculation.—*R.W.S.*

PERTINENT LITERATURE

Blanshard, Brand. "Critical Realism: Essences Replace Ideas," in *The Nature of Thought*. Vol. 1. New York: Macmillan Publishing Company, 1935.

In 1920, *Essays in Critical Realism* (London: Macmillan and Company) appeared, the joint product of seven American philosophers. Six were Professors Durant Drake, Arthur O. Lovejoy, A. K. Rogers, George Santayana, Roy Wood Sellars, and C. A. Strong; the seventh was James Bissett Pratt. Probably America's most influential twentieth-century idealist has been Brand Blanshard, who discusses the overall perspective of critical realism and makes particular reference to Pratt's views. He begins with exposition and continues by offering an extended critique.

Critical realism, Blanshard tells us, is a compromise position. It rejects a realism which contends that everything that can be thought of is also something that exists, for while we can think about pink rats and hobgoblins, there are none. It also, Blanshard continues, rejects idealism, maintaining that there are physical things and that a physical thing is never part of a mental state. Thus, Blanshard explains, the critical realist recognizes both mental states and physical things and, since critical realists suppose that we have empirical knowledge, endeavors to offer an account of how such knowledge is possible. This account, Blanshard continues, does not include our being directly and noninferentially aware of physical things.

Critical realists distinguish, Blanshard tells us, between the *what* and the *that* of a physical thing; what we are directly aware of in cases of empirical knowledge is not the *that*, but the *what* of the things we know. Blanshard adds that the *what* of a thing is the *set of properties* which *make* it the sort of thing it is; the *that* of a thing is its actual spatiotemporal existence. An image of an orange and a real orange can share a *what*, but only the real orange has a *that*. (The critical realist's term for "what" is "essence.")

The critical realist's account of empirical knowledge, Blanshard notes, involves there being a direct and an indirect object of such knowledge. Its direct object is the essence of the thing known; its indirect object is the existence of the thing known. Thus, Blanshard says in explication of the critical realist's account of knowledge, the *that* (actual existence) of a thing is known through its *what* (essence).

The essence of a thing is not, Blanshard adds, located at the time or place at which the thing whose essence it is is located. Indeed, an essence is not created by there coming to be a thing which embodies it, nor does it cease to be by the demise of something which embodies it; an essence is aspatial, atemporal, and nonmaterial.

All this, Blanshard explains, provides the clue to the critical realist's account of perception and judgment. The critical realist finds these essentially to be identical. To perceive something *A* is to (directly) experience the essence of *A*, which the perceiver takes or judges to be the essence of a spatiotemporal *A*. This much, Blanshard suggests, is common ground between the various critical realists.

To this shared account, Blanshard indicates, some critical realists, Pratt included, add the view that essences are discovered, not in perceptual or sensory data *per se*, but in the meaning such data is judged to have. Thus Blanshard quotes Pratt to the effect that, whereas no two persons will have the same set of images and sensations, they may nevertheless attribute—or, more accurately, discover—the same meaning in their diverse data; they may proffer the same judgment although their sensory contents differ.

Blanshard is not persuaded, however, that this account of perception does in fact correctly analyze, or even allow for the possibility of, empirical knowledge. The meanings "given to thought and affirmed in judgment," he allows, may be considerably more constant from one perceiver to another than is their sensory data or perceptual content. Nevertheless, he continues, these meanings and judgments do vary considerably from one person to another, over a lifetime of an individual from childhood to maturity, and from one historical era to another.

The character of physical things, Blanshard maintains, does not vary and change in this fashion. Hence, he concludes, knowledge of a relatively stable physical world will not be accounted for, or even allowed, by a theory which grounds it on our acquaintance with items as varying and unstable as meanings of the sort Pratt and some of the other critical realists proffer. Nor, Blanshard continues, will it do to argue in reply that our knowledge of physical reality is after all radically imperfect and inexact. For while this may be true, it was from just such a situation as that of our empirical knowledge being in this sad state that critical realism was intended to set us free.

Another feature, Blanshard notes, of the critical realist's doctrine is that when one makes a true perceptual judgment or possesses a piece of empirical knowleldge, one is acquainted with the *what* or essence of the object about which the judgment is made. If, for example, one judges truly that Caesar's face had a particular contour, then, on the critical realist's view, one is directly acquainted with the *what* or essence of Caesar's face, although of course not with the *that* or existence of his face, since that face no longer exists and since the existence of any physical item is for the critical realist never an object of direct acquaintance. Blanshard suggests that this view of our relation to essence is strikingly similar to the neorealism which critical realism rejected, and he notes that some of the critical realists were uneasy with it.

It is clear that Blanshard rejects critical realism; he concludes his discussion by offering five objections to it, and he does not think it can provide effective answers to these objections. Only two of them will be described here.

One consequence of critical realism, Blanshard contends, is that essences are the only (direct) data of experience, and essences are eternal and universal rather than temporal and particular. It follows, Blanshard concludes, that sensory or perceptual data have two surprising features: they are eternal and universal. If one feels tired, then, what one is directly and noninferentially feeling is something which has somehow "been in being from all eternity." Blanshard suggests, however, that the positing of such an item as an eternal essence of tiredness seems to be just the sort of entity Occam's razor ("Do not multiply entities beyond necessity") was intended to shave away. (Nor can the critical realists complain that they reject Occam's razor, for they have made substantial use of it in their criticism of opposing views.)

Another problem with critical realism, Blanshard finds, concerns how it is possible to experience essences. Perhaps one can state Blanshard's view in this way. One aspect of the problem, in effect, concerns the difficulty of an atemporal item's being a cause (or an effect) or otherwise participating in any temporal process (including perception). Another part of the problem is that while essences are changeless (since they are eternal), anything that is an effect is such that its character or nature depends to at least some degree on its cause. Then, however, if the content of a perception has a cause, that content cannot be an essence, since the alleged essence will have had its particular changeless character long before the cause of a particular perceptual experience occurred. Finally, essences are abstract entities, and, Blanshard contends, "effects, like causes, are always concrete."

These are some of Blanshard's reasons for rejecting critical realism. He nevertheless confesses that without a great amount of amendment he could accept the theory (although the amendments, of course, would have the effect of making the view identical with Blanshard's form of idealism).

Sellars, Roy Wood. "American Realism: Perspective and Framework," in *Self, Religion, and Metaphysics.* Edited by Gerald E. Myers. New York: Macmillan Publishing Company, 1961.

Professor Roy Wood Sellars (himself—along with James Bissett Pratt, Arthur O. Lovejoy, and others—one of the American Critical Realists), in this contribution to a volume published in memory of Professor Pratt, reflects on the rationale behind critical realism in general and on Pratt's contribution to critical realism in particular. (He also considers his own development of that realistic perspective; but this review will focus on Sellars' discussion of the movement and on Pratt's contributions.)

Pratt, A. K. Rogers, and Lovejoy, Sellars reports, were critical realists who were mind-body dualists, holding minds to be one kind of thing and bodies to be a quite different kind of thing. A mind, they held, was able to know proportions concerning the existence and properties of physical things by means of having intentional perceptual states. An intentional perceptual state is one which is of an observable object, in a perhaps *sui generis* sense of "of."

Sellars notes that Pratt and the others held that mind, by virtue of having such states, was able to transcend or "get outside" itself and to "get to objects." Sellars indicates that they took such transcendence as unanalyzable or primitive, and they (in his opinion, mistakenly) failed to seek out a natural or physiological mechanism which made perceptual knowledge possible.

Pratt, Sellars adds, shared with the other critical realists the position of neorealism, which, he indicates, made consciousness a sort of cognitive searchlight which fell upon physical objects, thereby making them known. (Nonmetaphorically, they rejected the neorealistic claim that physical objects are directly and noninferentially perceived.) Also shared, Sellars continues, was a rejection of "the Lockean gambit" of inferring the existence and properties of physical things from ideas, where an idea was conceived of as private to each perceiver and as the *terminus*, or only direct object, of perception. This

Lockean view required that one infer from private or individual perceptions to public objects, and the critical realists found such inference neither necessary nor successful. Pratt, in particular, not only dubbed the Lockean view false but also blamed it for "many hopeless vagaries in epistemology."

Pratt's version of critical realism, Sellars indicates, relied on an introspective knowledge of mind and its states. It rested its hopes of accounting for empirical knowledge essentially in the structure it claimed to discover in mental, and particularly in perceptual, states—an "outer-directedness" reflected in the intentionality (Franz Brentano's term), of *being-of-some-object* character, of such states.

Further, Sellars remarks, Pratt (among other realists) rejected pragmatism, idealism, and mechanism. At various places, Sellars suggests the following as among the reasons why they did so. Pragmatism underemphasized the cognitive, correspondence-type claims we make to empirical knowledge. Idealism substituted coherence among propositions for correspondence of concept to object (or proposition to fact). Mechanism ruled out teleology, and teleological propositions are necessary if we are to describe properly and understand mental states and the ability of minds or persons to interact with bodies in such a manner as to alter what would otherwise have been the outcome of mechanistic processes. Thus, Sellars informs us, Pratt held to a dualism of kinds of processes.

To this perspective, Sellars opposes one which is not dualistic but materialistic, seeking the sources of intentionality in some neural process in the brain and viewing references to the mind as disguised references to bodily capacities to behave in various linguistic and nonlinguistic ways. Such dualisms as Pratt's, Sellars in effect suggests, do not fit nicely into a purely evolutionary framework for interpreting nature, and this, in Sellars' view, is a defect in dualism rather than a defect (as Pratt might suggest) in a purely evolutionary perspective.—*K.E.Y.*

ADDITIONAL RECOMMENDED READING

Blau, Joseph L. *Men and Movements in American Philosophy*. Englewood Cliffs, New Jersey: Prentice-Hall, 1952. A discussion of American philosophy, with references to Pratt.

Macintosh, D. C. *The Problem of Religious Knowledge*. New York: Harper & Brothers, 1940. A discussion of idealisms and realisms in religious thought, with references to Pratt.

Pratt, J. B. *Adventures in Philosophy and Religion*. New York: Macmillan Publishing Company, 1931. A further presentation of Pratt's views.

_____ . *What Is Pragmatism?* New York: Macmillan Publishing Company, 1909. A discussion of pragmatism by Pratt.

Schneider, Herbert W. *A History of American Philosophy*. New York: Columbia University Press, 1946. A good general history of American philosophy.

_____ . *Sources of Contemporary Philosophical Realism in America.* Indianapolis: Bobbs-Merrill, 1964. An anthology of American Realism, giving some of Pratt's intellectual context.

NATURE AND MIND

Author: Frederick James E. Woodbridge (1867-1940)
Type of work: Metaphysics, epistemology
First published: 1937

PRINCIPAL IDEAS ADVANCED

Pragmatism is important because of its emphasis on contexts and operations; the pragmatic method is useful for the clarification of ideas.

Despite pragmatism's usefulness as a method of clarification, it errs in rejecting objects antecedent to knowledge to which an idea must conform if it is to be true.

The alternative to a theory of perception which makes ideas the objects of perception is an operational realism, a theory which rejects sensations as myths and which understands perception as a sense operation directed at objects.

A cooperative working of naturalism and humanism, of science and art, is the natural outcome of a theory in which the antithesis between science and metaphysics is regarded as unfortunate.

This collection of essays by Professor Woodbridge was presented to the author on the occasion of his seventieth birthday by Amherst College, the University of Minnesota, and Columbia University, institutions with which he had been associated. He was a graduate of Amherst where his interest in philosophy had been stimulated by a famous teacher of the subject, Professor Garman; and he had taught at both Minnesota and Columbia. The essays were carefully selected to bring out in a unified way Woodbridge's position and its development. Its priority to the work of G. E. Moore and Bertrand Russell is worth noting.

The collection begins with the essay "Confessions," which Woodbridge contributed to the project, *Contemporary American Philosophy*. After this conscientious review of his thought come sections on metaphysics, logic, consciousness, and cognition. The conclusion consists of addresses on various occasions. Taken together, the material gives a clear picture of the man and his work; and anyone who reads these essays carefully is put into touch with philosophy as it was developing in the United States in the first part of the twentieth century.

Woodbridge's reaction to pragmatism is particularly interesting. It was similar to that of the new realists and the critical realists. It is clear that he wanted cognition to be direct, and he was fearful of a subjective consciousness engrossed with "ideas."

Woodbridge had a keen interest in the history of philosophy and a sense for its currents. Of equal importance was his interest in the growth of the positive sciences. In a broad sense he was a realist, as much one of attitude as of specific doctrine. it is said that he was fond of quoting from Matthew Arnold the saying: "Things are what they are and the consequences of them will be what they will be; why then should we wish to be deceived?"

Professor Sterling Lamprecht, one of Woodbridge's students who later taught at Amherst, sums up his teacher's perspective in these words: "This kind of attitude was bound to generate doctrines when it was firmly sustained through a course of philosophic reflections. It was bound to generate metaphysical doctrines." The metaphysical view resulting was analytic in character, and was concerned with nature and man's inclusion in it. There was nothing about this metaphysics of that transcendental import which current positivism has in mind when it rejects metaphysics. Perhaps the term ontology is less misleading. In any case, the Viennese positivists were contending with German idealists and existentialists and had little knowledge of American philosophy.

Both American pragmatism and American realism were, in the main, naturalistic in perspective. While British empiricism tended to link up with Hume, such was not so much the case in American thought. Woodbridge tended to wrestle more with Locke than with Hume. He kept up an interest in Aristotle and sought to revise the ancient categories. It is evident that the parochialism of "Cambridge talking to Oxford" did not dominate his thought. Philosophers who get engrossed in minor technicalities are sometimes led to affirm the incredible, and Woodbridge sensed this danger in connection with traditional idealism. Surely, the world is not mind-dependent. The cure he advocated was ever fresh contact with concrete realities: confront the abstract with the factual, take second thoughts.

In his "Confessions," Woodbridge indicates that Aristotle, Spinoza, and Locke were the philosophers in whom he was most interested. Perhaps Hobbes should be added. When Santayana's *Life of Reason* came out in 1905 Woodbridge reviewed it; it seemed to him a matchless commentary on human thinking, for it exhibited the passage from the natural to the ideal, from common sense to reason. The continued interest in Santayana at Columbia as against his neglect at Harvard perhaps stems from this enthusiasm.

Woodbridge was seeking to revise Aristotle's categories of prime matter and form, in order to substitute structure, behavior, and a natural teleology of sequence. These general characteristics of the world he thought of as metaphysically fundamental. One can note a certain impatience with epistemology, as was the case with Dewey. There was frustration, the feeling that philosophy had become so immersed in the operation of knowing that it had made states of mind their own objects. But was epistemology to blame here? Is not the concentration on states of mind a bad foundation for epistemology? After all, can we have knowledge about our world without cognitive operations? The struggle between pragmatism, new realism, and critical realism in American philosophy was to concern itself with the need for a reorientation in epistemology. Pragmatism, under Dewey, took the path of a logic of inquiry, but Woodbridge wanted to keep ideas and things somehow together. Consciousness, he held, was relational. It seems that he meant by consciousness, cognition or consciousness *of* something. The term is, unfortunately, ambiguous. A stream of consciousness—to use James's expression—is one thing, and an act of cognition, or directed knowledge-claim, is another.

While a little impatient with the *vanities* of epistemology, Woodbridge faced up to unavoidable problems. Somehow, ideas, mind, and the order of things had to be brought together. While Locke stressed ideas, Spinoza emphasized logic and discourse and substance. Here was kinship with Aristotle. In this setting, Woodbridge worked out his analytic metaphysics of structure and behavior and his notion of natural teleology. To Aristotle, he owed his recognition of the importance of language. Truth is not a matter of nature; the *saying* of things is.

Such retrospection enables us to comprehend Woodbridge's intellectual Odyssey. It is clear that he had early rejected subjectivism and idealism because they involved wrong perspectives. But the job was to connect cognition with the natural order of things. What he was after was a *direct realism*. As with the new realists who were becoming vocal at the time, this was taken to involve presentationalism or the givenness of the object. Woodbridge struggled with *sensations* in this connection. Can they be given up and be translated into *sensings*? Dewey faced the same problem in a similar attempt to escape the subjective and the intra-cortical. But cannot we have a direct realism while regarding sensations as guiding perceiving when perceiving is regarded as a referential act concerned with external things? The emphasis, then, is upon cognizing as a mediated achievement.

A good place to begin, if one wants to appreciate Woodbridge's setting in American thought, is with the essays "The Promise of Pragmatism" and "Experience and Dialectic."

Woodbridge believed that the value of pragmatism lay in its stress upon the clarification of meanings, and that the shift to the problem of truth was, in many ways, unfortunate. "When it was claimed that an idea is true because it works, the rejoinder was ready and well-nigh inevitable that an idea works because it is true." As a good Aristotelian, Woodbridge probably took agreement with existence to be the criterion of truth.

The valuable feature of pragmatism was, then, its stress upon context and upon operations. One can understand otherwise cryptic remarks if one focuses on their contexts. Woodbridge's remarks on Whitehead and Sir Arthur Eddington in this connection show robust common sense. What does one mean by society? How could one send out a message tomorrow and receive it today? To answer such questions, any shift in vocabulary should be indicated; what *is* the context of one's remarks? The dogma which denies that ideas could possibly represent, stand for, or duplicate objects might well submit itself to pragmatic analysis.

In the second essay mentioned above, Woodbridge queries Dewey's proneness to dialectical discourse. While granting Dewey's starting point, the need to exercise intelligence in reflective thinking on problems, Woodbridge does not admit that it involves a rejection of objects antecedent to knowledge to which knowledge must conform to be successful. He asks whether Dewey's rejection of antecedent objects follows from his emphasis upon inquiry. He claims that Dewey's statement to the effect that only the *conclusions* of reflective inquiry are *known* begs the question. Really, do what things are and the way they operate depend on the outcome of inquiry? Is there not a touch of anthropomorphism in Dewey's position? Man is a sample of nature but there are many other samples. Dewey seems to argue them into illegitimacy. He expresses a preference for the precarious and incompleted. The outcome is a dialectical playing off of the permanent and the changing in a conceptual way against one another. Dialectic is put in the place of the kind of metaphysics that fits in analytically with investigation. Why did Dewey think in this fashion? One answer is that he associated permanence with the timeless and eternal of objective idealism. Woodbridge is restrained in his criticisms but they have point. It is unfortunate that so many American philosophers think that they have to choose between Russell's philosophy as inspired by Hume and vitalized by mathematical logic, and Dewey's instrumentalism. Woodbridge was seeking a realistic alternative.

In his criticism of epistemology, Woodbridge had in mind the Lockian interposition of *ideas* as cognitively terminal. He had learned the lesson of Locke's unperceived things and its support for idealism, and thus he thought of epistemology *contextually*.

In his theory of perception, Dewey was motivated, much as Woodbridge was, by the fear of a subjective mind. It would be absurd to end up with cognition terminating on, and concerned only with, mental states *in* the brain. One must firmly reject this cortical and subcutaneous view of the status of mind. What is an alternative? Presentational realism. Things are as they are experienced. It is an affair of behavioral transactions. In many ways, Woodbridge's answer is similar to Dewey's. Eyes and ears are for *sensing* what is out there to be sensed. Sensing is a form of cognition and does not require those peculiar entities which psychologists call sensations.

The interesting fact is that Woodbridge returned to this question again and again. He had a marked feeling for the realities of the situation. Nothing G. E. Moore wrote is superior to Woodbridge's little essay in this book entitled "The Deception of the Senses." As he puts it, our proper question is not "What is the thing?" but "Why does it appear different?" Why does the straight stick in water appear bent? His answer is that the stick must appear bent under these conditions. Science has its explanation in terms of optics. Railroad tracks should look *as though* they converged.

In *Nature and Mind*, Woodbridge does not once refer to Moore. There were at this time two centers of thought in the English-speaking world. The British group gradually edged away from the Americans; and the era of Moore, Russell, and Wittgenstein began. Oxford talked with Cambridge and Americans began to listen in. The whole development is complex, and it must not be oversimplified.

Is there not another alternative to subjectivism? The whole question of the mechanism of perceiving comes up for consideration. May not sensations guide response and be information-carrying? What we really do in perceiving is to refer selectively to the things around us and to characterize them. We develop concepts in touch with the information-carrying sensations, but the import of the concepts is objective and concerns what we are referring to. The unit on which all this is founded is sensorimotor. The brain is not primarily concerned with itself; it is an organ of adjustment.

Having taken the alternative of sensing things and not having sensations and appearances to be used in cognition of a referential sort, Woodbridge argued that consciousness must be relational. Consciousness *of* something is cognitional and makes no difference to things.

Woodbridge argues that sensations, as traditionally conceived, are myths. Gilbert Ryle, in *The Concept of Mind* (1949), has sought to do the same in terms of linguistic behaviorism. What Woodbridge puts in the place of sensations are sensings, operations directed at objects. The operations are the same; it is the objects that differ.

Thus, both Dewey and Woodbridge returned to naïve, or presentational, realism in order to escape subjectivism. Things are as they are sensed, though sensing has it complex, external conditions, as in the case of the stick that looks bent in the water or the case of converging railroad tracks. But could we not equally say that we perceive *through* our sensations, thus conditioned, the things we are looking at? We use the evidence of our senses, a locution which is well founded. In this manner, also, we can escape the influence of the introspective tradition combined, as this was, with the limited, causal approach which neglected response. Sensations are not cognitively terminal, but they are aids in perceiving. It was this line that the critical realists began to explore. So far as cognition is concerned, it is also a form of objective realism; that is, it is the external thing to which we are responding and to which we are referring.

Curiously enough, while the United States has been conventionally a religious area, its social science and philosophy have been dominantly naturalistic, as is recognized abroad. None of the four existentialist theologians, Maritain, Berdyaev, Buber, and Tillich, of whom we hear so much these days, is an American thinker.

Woodbridge, of course, antedated existentialism. He was concerned to qualify traditional naturalism by including man in nature and spelling out a natural teleology. In his view, everything is somehow real and must be taken account of. Perhaps the positive sciences have been too much under the spell of the mechanical, and literary humanism has tended to look backward and exalt the past. But the present alone is actual and creative. It is well to have a long vista, but it should lead up to the situation of the time. Thus the cooperative working of naturalism and humanism, of science and art, is the thing to be desired.

The antithesis between science and metaphysics is unfortunate, Woodbridge believed. While Aristotle had a cosmology which has been outgrown, his metaphysics is concerned with first principles: it emphasizes categories or the general features of being, and it is quite prepared to apply these in the special sciences. In his reformulation of Aristotelianism, Woodbridge wanted to avoid *materia prima* and form and put, in their place, structure and behavior. Nature *is* structure. As a believer in substance, Woodbridge was opposed to an analysis in terms of events alone.

Woodbridge's addresses reveal the man and his outlook. They are sane and robust. In the "Enterprise of Learning" the emphasis is upon knowledge and the "inquisition of truth"—Bacon's phrase. Let us keep the imagination awake and creative, Woodbridge urged; the life of reason is unquestionably the best life for man. Santayana is here allied with Aristotle against any popular form of pragmatism.

In "The Discovery of the Mind" Woodbridge deliberately propounds the belief that the university is the most important of human institutions. It is well to have such a thing said in these days of giant corporations and organizational men. It marks the distinction between pure and applied science. How are these to be ordered?

The lecture on "The Practice of Philosophy" has an amusing remark on confessing to other people that one's profession is that of being a philosopher. There is, Woodbridge notes, always surprise. But one is left wondering whether there are not, in addition, disbelief, amusement, and a sense of deep waters.—*R.W.S.*

PERTINENT LITERATURE

Costello, Harry T. "The Naturalism of Frederick Woodbridge," in *Naturalism and the Human Spirit*. Edited by Y. H. Krikorian. New York: Columbia University Press, 1944.

Frederick Woodbridge, Harry T. Costello notes, was a "naturalistic" philosopher, holding nature, rather than God or the Absolute or anything else, to be ultimate; that is, not dependent on anything else for its existence. For such philosophers, Costello suggests, the term "Nature" tends to connote something "very solid and real, an emotional unification of all things." Thus "nature" designates not only the orderly physical universe but also an object of "natural piety" or religious feeling. While not himself sharing this feeling, Costello reports, he declares that Woodbridge's feelings toward nature included no element of pride in disillusionment. Rather, he viewed nature as neither overly solicitous nor overly alien to human life and purpose.

Part of Woodbridge's naturalism, Costello reminds us, is his characterization of mind in behavioral terms. Woodbridge's view (although Costello reports that Woodbridge sometimes qualifies and "even reverses" these remarks) is that there is no mind above and beyond behavior. The body walks, and the body thinks. Walking is one sort of behavior, thinking another. Costello appears to have doubts about this sort of naturalistic analysis of mind. Walking, he says, involves simply the coordination of bones and muscles in the present. But thinking, if bodily behavior it be, is "directed toward things remote, in the past, perhaps imaginary, perhaps abstract." *Part* of Costello's point seems to be concerned with what Brentano called "intentionality"—that thought generally has an "intentional object," something toward which it is directed, although that object need not now exist, and indeed may never exist. Part of Costello's point seems to be that thought has, and behavior has not, this feature of intentionality. In any case, Costello raises the question as to whether thought may not be so different from (allegedly) other bodily behavior as in fact not to be bodily behavior at all.

Woodbridge, Costello continues, granted that each person has his or her own inner life of thought, perceptions, and images, and he suggested that this difference was to be explained in terms of our having (or being) different bodies. Here, too, Costello expresses his reservations, allowing that it is the case that individual minds are associated with individual bodies; but he is not convinced that the separateness of minds is, or at any rate is simply, a function of the separateness of bodies. Rather, taking his cue from Immanuel Kant's remarks concerning a transcendental unity of apperception, Costello (in effect) contends that what distinguishes one mind from another is the experiences it has, that for an experience to "belong" to a mind requires that the mind synthesize that experience into an autobiographical unity with other experiences which occurred at different times, and that this sort of synthesizing, necessary to the structure of mind, is not reducible to, or a sheer function of, the brain or the body as a whole.

Woodbridge, Costello reports, was not at all inclined to reduce thinking to the having of images. Rather, upon once being asked whether imageless thought occurred, Costello tells us, Woodbridge responded by saying that the real question was whether any thought ever occurs which is not imageless—that is, whether anything that does involve having images is properly called "thought."

In another departure, perhaps, from the usual naturalistic stance, Woodbridge refused to ban teleological descriptions and explanations of natural phenomena. Thus, Costello explains, while refusing to view nature as in any respect whatsoever created or planned or sustained by a Divine Mind, Woodbridge felt that the language of the adaptation of means to ends in natural processes was as appropriate and accurate as the language of nonteleological, mechanistic causation. Nor was he inclined to replace systematically the former by the latter.

In what is doubtless the most difficult (or obscure) of the Woodbridgean themes he expounds, Costello indicates that Woodbridge, perhaps impressed by what he thought to be an element of truth in objective idealism, spoke of "objective mind," which Costello describes as "the realms of truths and their implications." Expressing doubts as to where Woodbridge's thoughts end and his own begin, Costello expounds Woodbridge's notion of a realm of objective mind by use of the term (which he himself says is ambiguous) "structure."

The general idea, apparently, is that nature is knowable only if its events follow certain (repeated) patterns or structures. (This concept provides for the possibility of there being laws of science.) Further, nature is knowable only if we can apply mathematics to natural phenomena in such a way as to yield general truths concerning (so to say) nature's behavior. ("Structure," then, sometimes refers to recurrent patterns in nature, sometimes to characteristics of systems of mathematics.)

One view about the exact sciences, such as formal logic and mathematics, Costello reminds us, is that their subject matter is as much a product of human invention as are the particular symbols that happen to be used to express that subject matter. Costello indicates that John Dewey held this view. Costello finds this view attractive, but is also impressed not only by the great precision but also by the nonarbitrary character of mathematical and logical reasoning. He says that the endeavor to attain precision of expression and rigor of proof in such areas is a "genuine search." Further, the pragmatic utility of the formal sciences, he suggests, is due to the fact that the formal sciences "reveal systematic connections not made by human fiat."

Costello reveals that Woodbridge was not much interested in symbolic logic and did not tend to seek philosophic counsel with the symbolic logicians on his faculty. But the views that fall under Woodbridge's doctrine of "objective mind," Costello suggests, include two assertions, or, perhaps, assumptions. One is that the "structures" of the natural sciences and the "structures" of the formal sciences are somehow continuous, somehow "the same sort of thing." The other is that at least a significant part of the researches that fall within the formal sciences are genuine discoveries of mind—phenomena independent of mind—independent, abstract "structures." The second assumption is motivated in part by the precision, rigor, and freedom from arbitrariness that the formal sciences frequently possess. It is also motivated in part by the first assumption (along with a realistic view of science—a view of science on which its objects are themselves mind-independent denizens of the natural world). This, perhaps, captures what Costello means when, expounding Woodbridge (with whom he here seems to agree), he says that "there is a realm that symbols mean."

Delaney, C. F. *Mind and Nature: A Study of the Naturalistic Philosophies of Cohen, Woodbridge, and Sellars.* Notre Dame, Indiana: University of Notre Dame Press, 1969.

Frederick Woodbridge, C. F. Delaney informs us, is a naturalistic metaphysician. Delaney's essay explains in some detail what this amounts to; fundamentally, it involves Woodbridge's developing a nontheistic theory of nature which includes within its scope a theory of mind. Delaney begins with the theory of mind.

As Delaney explains Woodbridge's theory of mind, the theory is developed in conscious contrast to competing views which he thought inadequate. Woodbridge, Delaney explains, does not think that minds are ever "immediately given" as objects of knowledge; he denies that anyone is ever directly and noninferentially aware of his or her own (or any other) mind. Were persons so aware, while questions might arise as to the nature of mind, there would be no question as to whether minds exist. But, Delaney continues, Woodbridge (with reference to René Descartes and David Hume) finds that there are disagreements about even the existence of (substantival) minds.

Woodbridge, Delaney notes, compares the claim that there are minds to the claim that there are gravitational forces; both claims, he contends, provide a mixture of theoretical claim and descriptive report. Woodbridge's view, Delaney indicates, can be expressed by saying that for him the existence of minds is implied or presupposed by, rather than found in, experience. The experience which implies or presupposes the existence of mind is human thinking.

Delaney remarks that Woodbridge makes a distinction not between mental substances and physical substances but between behavior which is mental and behavior which is physical. Walking and breathing provide examples of physical behavior; perceiving and imagining provide examples of mental behavior.

As Delaney emphasizes, this is a distinction between activities, not entities; it says something about what entities do, not about what entities are. True, language uses the substantives "mind" and "body," but, as Delaney presents Woodbridge's account, this is a matter of using nouns to refer to behavior, although such terms seem to stand for something of another sort.

"Body," Delaney adds, stands, on Woodbridge's view, for physical behavior, and also for "spatial and temporal bulks" (so that "body," but not "mind," turns out for Woodbridge to refer to entities or objects). In this latter sense—that in which "body" designates, not a type of behavior, but a "spatial bulk"—space contains a great many bodies which together constitute nature, or the world.

Delaney notes that the natural sciences—those sciences which study spatio-temporal bulks—endeavor to provide complete knowledge about their objects of investigation without even the most laconic reference to mental behavior or activity. Yet ordinary, everyday experience suggests that a wide range of mental behavior occurs. Here, Delaney says, Woodbridge finds a philosophical problem. How are we to relate the results of the natural sciences to the deliverances of everyday experience?

Woodbridge, Delaney continues, describes the traditional approach to this problem as involving the thesis that there is a mental agent which acts in the world through the mediation of the agent's body. This view (which Woodbridge associates with Descartes and John Locke) seems to Woodbridge to involve both an incorrect account of mind and a very implausible doctrine of nature.

Delaney's account of Woodbridge's objections to the agency view can be put briefly as follows. Woodbridge claims that the agency view entails that what we are aware of—what we experience—is not physical objects or physical states but our own perceptions or ideas. We then, in effect, have "two worlds"—one of physical objects and one of ideas. Then we have the difficult if not insuperable problem of how to relate these two worlds, or sorts of items.

Woodbridge's own alternative, Delaney says, runs along these lines. The traditional view makes the qualities we suppose physical objects to possess, and to be perceived as possessing, into mind-dependent qualities, leaving only quantitative motions existing in the world independent of thought. Further, Delaney suggests, Woodbridge is not confident that the traditional view can escape having to *infer* the existence of a material world, or even stop short of an idealism for which objects are simply sets of (mind-dependent) perceptions.

Following his own naturalistic interpretation of Aristotle, Delaney tells us, Woodbridge develops a theory in which "mind" has an ambiguous reference, designating on the one hand the existence of structures in nature which render nature intelligible and on the other hand (as we have seen) certain behaviors or activities on the part of some "spatial bulks." In the latter sense, there are many minds; more carefully, many bodies come in the course of their development to be able to perceive, think, and imagine, and thus, in Woodbridge's view, become minds without ceasing to be bodies. In sum, for Woodbridge, a mind, essentially, just is a body which is able to perceive, think, and imagine. Or, to revert to "mind" as a term referring to various activities, a body "has a mind" only insofar as it is capable of performing mental functions. Delaney adds that Woodbridge regards the ability (or set of abilities) to perform mental functions as being itself a function of the organization and complexity of those physical organisms which possess it.

"Mind" in this sense, Delaney informs us, is for Woodbridge secondary;

what is for him the primary sense of "mind" is that in which it designates that set of structures which renders nature intelligible or knowable. (This seems, in fact, to be a technical use of "mind" which occurs often in Woodbridge's technical term, "objective mind.") Briefly, Delaney's exposition of Woodbridge's doctrine of structures suggests that (1) whatever is knowable is so by virtue of having some structure (roughly, order or pattern) or other; (2) structures are mind-independent; they are discovered, not invented; (3) there are (increasingly abstract) levels of structures; (4) structures are taken to be "given," not explicable or in need of explanation; and (5) a structure is not physical but "logical." (Woodbridge finds the existence of such a realm of structures a presupposition of thought.)

Delaney presents Woodbridge as a naturalistic metaphysician who argues for two senses of "body" and two meanings of "mind," and accordingly develops a theory of nature in which nature is comprised of the referents of these terms, only one of which is taken to refer to substantival entities. The intent, Delaney reports, is to develop an account of nature in which human beings are both the highest representatives of natural processes and the best clue or model for understanding nature as a whole.—*K.E.Y.*

ADDITIONAL RECOMMENDED READING

Blau, Joseph L. *Men and Movements in American Philosophy*. New York: Prentice-Hall, 1952. A history of American philosophy from colonial times through Dewey, with references to Woodbridge.

Lamprecht, Sterling P. "Woodbridge, Frederick James Eugene," in *The Encyclopedia of Philosophy*. Edited by Paul Edwards. New York: Macmillan Publishing Company and Free Press, 1967. A brief description of Woodbridge's views, plus a short bibliography.

Muelder, Walter G., Lurence Sears, and Anne V. Schlabach, eds. *The Development of American Philosophy*. Boston: Houghton Mifflin Company, 1940. A rich selection of essays from a wide variety of American philosophers, including Woodbridge on "Natural Teleology."

Persons, Stow. *American Minds*. New York: Henry Holt and Company, 1958. A history of ideas in America, historically rather than philosophically oriented.

Peterfreund, Sheldon P. *An Introduction to American Philosophy*. New York: The Odyssey Press, 1959. Selections, interspersed with commentary, from Peirce, James, Royce, Santayana, and Dewey, with a summary of Woodbridge's views.

Schneider, Herbert W. *Sources of Contemporary Philosophical Realism in America*. Indianapolis: Bobbs-Merrill, 1964. A selection of essays by American philosophers, containing an essay on the problem of time by Woodbridge.

THE KNOWLEDGE OF GOD AND THE SERVICE OF GOD

Author: Karl Barth (1886-1968)
Type of work: Theology
First published: 1938

PRINCIPAL IDEAS ADVANCED

Christian theology must be Church theology, and it must be centered in Christ; natural theology rests on an error.

The paradox of revelation is that although God reveals himself, he is forever the Hidden God.

History has had two significant phases: the history of Israel, of God's faithfulness despite man's unfaithfulness, and the history of the promise fulfilled, of God's becoming one with man.

Christian truth rests entirely on the fact of the resurrection of Christ.

In the service of God man is saved by Christ from having to justify himself before the law; but he is therefore bound by gratitude and love.

The current renaissance of Protestant theology, after nearly a century of theological deemphasis and cultural accommodation, has as its founder Karl Barth and as its date of birth 1918. After Immanuel Kant's destructive interpretation of the Theistic proofs, Protestant theologians concerned with a defense of Christianity against its "cultured despisers" followed the lead of Friedrich Schleiermacher (1768-1834), understanding revelation in terms of a unique, universal experience called "God-consciousness" or "absolute dependence." This "liberal" tradition, continuing through a diverse line from Adolph Harnack to Paul Tillich, led in its extreme "modernist" forms to teaching, as H. Richard Niebuhr says, that "a God without wrath brought men without sin into a kingdom without judgment through the ministrations of a Christ without a cross." Above all, the unique centrality of Jesus Christ as the incarnate God-man, the impotence of the human will, the centrality of both Cross and Resurrection, tended to give way to a highly optimistic doctrine of man, revelation as universal religious experience, a religion of morality, and Jesus as perfect man. Differences between religions were understood primarily in terms of degree, Christianity being the most morally pure. Increasingly, Christianity was becoming a cultural phenomenon of Western culture.

Into this liberal milieu came Barth, pastor of a small Swiss church and theological advocate of Schleiermacher. As he tells it, with the German guns of the approaching war as threatening background, the weekly ritual of sharing religious experiences became manifestly meaningless. Unless the Divine God of Creation stands in damning judgment over the follies of prideful men, Christianity is simply irrelevant; but if man's rebellion and God's judgment establish as fact Kierkegaard's unheeded "qualitative distinction between time and eternity," God and man, then the message of Christ as Incarnate Mediator becomes the one relevant proclamation.

In exploring the theological profundities of orthodox Christianity from this now existential human predicament, Barth not only began the theological revival termed "neo-orthodox" or "neo-Reformation," but effected a fresh reexamination of Pauline theology and the thought of Søren Kierkegaard (1813-1855). These three elements converged in 1918 in Barth's theological bombshell entitled *The Epistle to the Romans*. Although the various editions of that volume show increasing movement away from "liberal" tenets, this work from the first was a fresh consideration of St. Paul's doctrine of man from the perspective of Kierkegaard's understanding of despair, original sin, and the absolute centrality of God's unique act in Christ. The theological world was ripe for such a pronouncement of judgment, not only on mankind but also on the Protestant capitulation to culture. Barth likens his effort to that of climbing a belfry at night and, while grasping for support, finding that he has pulled the bellrope and awakened a sleeping city. Barth's "fame" was almost immediate; overnight he found himself in the midst of a wide and vigorous theological debate extending undiminished into the present.

This first major work by Barth was not so much an exegesis of St. Paul as it was a violent challenge to the fundamental tenets of liberal theology, especially those concerning revelation and man's finite condition. Barth's statements were extreme and his judgments uncompromising. The most famous debate to result was that with his early sympathizer, Emil Brunner. In the volume *Natural Theology*, Brunner tried to remain loyal to Barth's basic position while still making contact with the dictates of reason; only by establishing a natural human point of contact upon which Divine Grace may act, Brunner insisted, can there be any truly human response, any answer to revelation which is not simply God's self-answer. Barth's reply was emphatic: "Nein!" God is Subject, never Object; if he is to be known, it can be only when the Divine Subject reveals himself and wills a human response.

From this point the theological vocation of Barth emerged. At first he had understood this central Christian revelation in largely negative terms. He likened revelation to a crater left by a meteor—not the object itself but only the result of the impact was visible. The impact of divine judgment on history was indelible, but God himself remained forever hidden. Gradually Barth's understanding of revelation changed. He remained consistent in his total rejection of the *analogia entis* maintained by Roman Catholics and liberals, for there is no visible analogy between the natural and the supernatural realms. God is "totally other." But Barth came to see an *analogia fidei* (analogy of faith) which gives valid content to revelation, for in Christ the Divine Subject has become Object. For men of faith, operating in the Community of the Holy Spirit, valid communication concerning the divine is possible.

Consequently, Christian theology must have two basic features. It must be *Church* theology—the internal dialogue of the fellowship of believers—and it must be completely Christocentric; every Christian affirmation must have the God-man as both content and norm. The result has been Barth's monumental *Church Dogmatics* (*Kirchle Dogmatik*). Those volumes of that work which were finished have already placed Barth in the company of Luther and Calvin as the great theologians of Protestantism.

The best single volume for understanding Barth's position, especially in regard to philosophical inquiry, is his Gifford Lectures of 1937 and 1938, entitled *The Knowledge of God and the Service of God According to the Teaching of the Reformation*. Barth's appearance as a Gifford Lecturer was an oddity requiring justification. The will of Lord Gifford declared that the subject must be "natural theology," that science of God, his relation to the world, and human morality resulting from such knowledge, which is constructed by human reason in independence of special, supernatural revelation. Barth's answer to this stipulation is one of the most uncompromising in the history of Christianity—"I certainly see—with astonishment—that such a science as Lord Gifford had in mind does exist. . . . I am convinced that so far as it has existed and still exists, it owes its existence to a radical error." It is Barth's central insistence that any theologian of the Reformation, basing his faith, as he must, wholly upon God's revelation in Jesus Christ, is implicitly and explicitly opposed to all forms of natural theology. His Gifford Lectures are the attempt to clarify natural theology by exhibiting what he regards as its strongest and most vehement opponent—the theology of the Reformation. For this purpose Barth uses John Knox's Scottish Confession of 1560 as a systematic summary of Reformed theology.

But Barth's lectures have a second intent as well; not only is natural theology opposed, but the Church's compromising betrayal of its own foundations must be challenged. Judged by its ancient creeds, Prostestantism must be driven back to Scripture as its sole authority.

For Barth, God can be known only when the distinction between Creator and creature is drawn. But since man in his self-righteousness universally makes himself or his works "god," such a distinction is acknowledged only when God *makes himself visible*, thereby drawing the bounds of creatureliness and smashing man's petty absolutes into the realm of the relative. Thus the *only* knowledge of God is faith, but it is unique knowledge, for it binds and commits one totally. Its objectivity comes not from human vindication, but only from its own universal validity in the life of the believer. Yet *the* revelation is not the elimination of mystery, for the one revealed is the Hidden God— God remains always above man's concepts and potentialities. In fact, for Barth, this is the paradox of revelation—the Hidden God of Majesty *is with us*—this is to call him "Father." Such a thing simply cannot be known by reason, for it is so only if one is personally addressed as "son." This relation rests not in necessity, but in divine decision; he who decides can be the only revealer of the decision.

The God-man revelation which is Jesus Christ reveals that God takes man seriously; although God does not need his creation, he wills it to be a reflection of his glory. All creation is indebted to God, for all exists by him (as Creator), through him (as Sustainer), and for him (as Redeemer). But Christ separates man from the rest of creation, for He reveals that *"man has been called to present to the Creator the gratitude of the creation."* This is the meaning of man as the "image of God"—not that man possesses something, but that his destiny is to image God's glory through gratitude. It is on the basis of this broad cosmic context that Barth's position is so uncompromising. We know absolutely nothing about God, the world, or man outside of Jesus Christ; without his revelation of the creating, sustaining, and governing of the world, of God's glory and man's, everything is "confused myth and wild metaphysic."

There is likewise no anthropology except from the perspective of Christ; therein the validity of "original sin" is seen. In the light of man's intended vocation, man's existence in ingratitude and self-centeredness is seen as a "defacement of God's image of man." Because this is a matter not simply of acting against God but also of *being* against him, it can be undone by God alone. Here is where Barth takes fundamental exception to existentialist Christians such as Tillich. For Tillich, man's awareness of the human dilemma drives one *to* revelation. Barth's Christocentricity operates even here: since man's dilemma is known only through Christ, "if we know that we cannot save ourselves, we know already that we are *saved* by God." This is the tension which is redemption—humiliation for the sake of exaltation.

Since history is the plane of relation between God and man, its meaning comes from Christ as its center. Through him history assumes two parts. The first is the history of Israel—the history of God's faithfulness despite man's unfaithfulness. Israelites are chosen people, sought, judged, sustained by faith in God's promise of a deliverer. The second history is that of the promise fulfilled—the Church as the history of "God's becoming one with man." These histories repeat themselves in the sense that Adam's act is repeated throughout history, and the Church is sustained by the One who has come and will come again. The continuity of history is that of those who emerge while man again and again is unfaithful and is judged. Since the emerging ones are as guilty as all others, continuity is a miracle which rests in the fact that these saving few admit their guilt. The true Church through history is the few who live in the promise of God while knowing themselves unworthy. Although Christ appeared at one point in history, he is the savior of all believers in all times for they are saved through their faith in the promise of which he is the fulfillment.

In all this Barth is attempting to restore the orthodox belief of early and Reformation Christianity. But there is one important difference which distinguishes him from both "fundamentalists" and "liberals." Against the former he insists that the Bible is a *human* document requiring critical analysis for its proper understanding. Against the liberals, Barth insists that such biblical criticism cannot prove or disprove the revelation itself. The revelation is not the Scripture but God's act in Christ. The former is simply the human account of the latter. The Holy Spirit witnesses to the revelation *through* the Scripture, and without such a witness revelation can never be known.

One of the most intriguing aspects of Barth's work is his attempt to untangle perennial theological knots by understanding them from his consistent Christocentric perspective. Central is the problem of predestination. For Barth, Calvin's doctrine is totally unacceptable, for he distinguished between God's eternal decree and the existence of Christ, understanding the former in terms of an alien philosophical system. But when Christ alone is taken as presupposition, the problem is answered by seeing that God's eternal decree *is* Jesus Christ. It is Christ who is the only cursed man and the only elected man. In electing Christ, God takes all the incapacities of man upon himself; he who judges endures the judgment. Since it is through Christ that God regards man, it is only in Christ that man can understand himself—so to understand is to be as Christ.

In consistency, this means for Barth that in Christ man is not simply restored; instead, he is made a new creature, higher than at Creation. This elevation comes from man's absolution in the Crucifixion and his affirmation as righteous in the Resurrection. In the face of man's rebellion, God in justice must be against man; yet in Christ he has decided for fellowship. The problem is that God alone can forgive, for Sin is against him; man alone can seek atonement, for he is responsible. It is in Christ that justice and mercy are brought together—in Christ, man is what he ought to be and is not; in Christ, God is what he is from eternity. In regarding man through Christ's perfect humanity, God's fellowship with man is proper; from the side of man, this "yea" spoken to sinful men appears as free mercy. Above all, Christ alone endured God's punishment, the realization of sin and death. This completeness of humiliation and self-sacrifice occurred not only in time; as God's very act it occurred also in eternity. Only because he is God can his infinite sacrifice and humiliation have infinite significance.

But this forgiveness can be consummated only in the Resurrection, the guarantee, as Barth says, that the Author of life is victorious over the Author of death. Since man's acquittal brings everlasting life, the fact that Christ has the power to forgive sin needs as thoroughgoing proof as the fact of his death. It is here that Barth's severance with liberalism is complete: "For if Jesus Christ has not risen . . . as man, and therefore visibly and corporally risen from the dead, then He has not revealed Himself as the Son of God, then we know nothing about His having been so, nor do we know anything of the infinite value of His sacrifice. In that case we would have no knowledge of the forgiveness of our sin or of our election or of God's gracious decision in our favour. In that case the whole Christian church is based on an illusion and the whole of what is called Christianity is one huge piece of moral sentimentalism. . . ." This is the core of Barth's wholesale rejection of natural theology in all forms—"our knowledge that this is no dream but the truth, and the fact that we have received that knowledge, rest entirely on the Easter message literally understood."

Redemption does not mean that the believer is visibly changed; the change is in Christ, and thus only by faith is it in man. The change is that all things, man's hopes, direction, future, are made to rest upon Christ. These are unknown, yet fully known, for they rest in the hands of One who cannot fail. This, for Barth, is faith, this is trust, this is perfect assurance, this is salvation. It is in this sense that the future is founded upon the past, and the future transforms the present.

What looms large in Barth's theology is the question of man's freedom, for "man's salvation is the work of God *exclusively*." This problem has to be balanced with Barth's view of salvation, which comes close to universalism— God is the one "who wills that all men be succoured and who acknowledges our sin only as forgiven sin. . . ." Now, faith can proceed only from the inspiration of the Holy Spirit. But, Barth affirms, it is *only* the man of faith who knows his incapacity to prepare for, persevere in, or perfect faith; only he can view the unfaith of the unbeliever as inevitable.

Yet, Barth affirms, everyone comes to faith who in his freedom does not evade the action of God in Jesus Christ appointed *for him*. To the unbeliever this freedom comes as a challenge *to decide*; from the perspective of the decision made, one can only confess that the decision itself was a Divine gift. This does not mean that man is passive or that reason has been sacrificed. For Barth, the Holy Spirit operates *through* the human spirit; faith occurs in "a perfectly human way." Thus the decision for faith is made in the same way as all other decisions, yet the fact that one *does* decide is the doing of the Holy Spirit.

In effect, what Barth is doing is insisting that such problems as predestination and freedom are made insoluble when systematized by logic; rather, they must be seen as soteriological inferences, as confessions of faith, not philosophical statements. Faith confesses election as a personal fact; reason insists on freedom as a universal fact. The believer can hold these in tension, for he has experienced as fact both responsibility for sin and Christ as the source of salvation. Barth's insights here have brought together aspects of liberalism and orthodoxy in such a way that St. Paul's theology and theological method have been reopened for fresh consideration.

Barth's understanding of man's proper service to God follows quite consistently. Once again, his understanding is in radical opposition to natural theology and to the Roman Catholic position. Although there are natural laws, there can be no distinction between the natural and divine ends of man. God's law demands unconditional obedience; no distinction of degree is possible. But in Christ we know that the one man who stands before the law is Christ; thus no man need justify himself before the law. Jesus Christ is both the law and its fulfillment. Salvation means simply this—that Christ's obedience, thankfulness, love, and service are imputed to man. As a result the believer is freed from what he cannot do, but yet made totally subject to a new law, the law of gratitude, and thus penitence and love to God and neighbor. Obedience now rests alone in holding to the fact of salvation in Christ; all things else, if not a reflection of this fact, are not righteousness but self-righteousness.

Evaluating Barth's position is as much an either/or as the theology he espouses. He does not address the philosopher and does not expect to be heeded by him. He is a Church theologian who claims nothing more. Yet the philosopher cannot escape him, for, as these Gifford Lectures indicate, part of his witness is to oppose philosophical theology unceasingly. This is done not by criticizing, arguing, or employing dialogue, but by proclaiming the teachings of the Reformation as the "exact opposite" of natural theology. Perhaps no other man has so exhibited to the philosophers the fundamental difference of kind between "rational knowledge of God" and the "religious life of faith." Perhaps, too—as many Protestant theologians firmly believe— it has been Barth more than any other man who has saved Protestant Christianity from slow death by innocuousness, extinction by amalgamation. Right or wrong, in stimulating in Protestants a passionate search for their fundamental *raison d'être*, Barth is contributing significantly to the great theological renaissance of modern times.—*W.P.J.*

Pertinent Literature

Bromiley, Geoffrey W. *Historical Theology: An Introduction*. Grand Rapids, Michigan: Eerdmans, 1978.

Whether or not the arguments are successful, it is the stuff of natural theology to argue from the existence of things that might not have been, from items that have causes, from things which behave in an orderly fashion, and from objects which are good although not perfectly so, to a being which cannot fail to exist, is an uncaused cause, is an intelligent cause of cosmic order, and is perfectly good. Such inferences do not contain premises or conclusions which require expression in the language of any one religious tradition; rather, such arguments are usually so stated as to focus attention on data common to all persons and to rely on inferences universally recognizable as valid. The idea is to remain on common ground—to stay within the limits of shared knowledge which does not rest on any particular religious foundations. The results of natural theology are often presented by their proponents as prolegomena to the details of their particular religious perspective. Given the view of knowledge of God that Karl Barth propounded, as described by Geoffrey W. Bromiley, it is clear that natural theology plays no role in Barth's thought.

Bromiley explains that according to Barth, knowledge of God is objective. God, in his triune life, is objective to himself; he possesses knowledge of himself as he is. God is, for Barth, also objective with respect to human beings insofar as he gives knowledge of himself to us; he is transcendant with respect to us, not dependent on us, and knowable by us only as he pleases. Nevertheless, Bromiley indicates that Barth believes that he gives knowledge of himself through other objects—objects not identical with himself or with us. Knowledge of God, then, is mediated knowledge, knowledge gained through some medium, some object, which God chooses to use as a means of making himself known to us. This medium, or object, according to Barth, is not chosen by us, and it is not possible for us to begin by reflecting on some object and end up with a knowledge of God. Barth, Bromiley notes, holds that God himself chooses the object which will mediate knowledge of himself as well as the occasion on which it will do so. The gift of such knowledge, Barth claims, does not presuppose our own ability to possess it or to be given it; God makes us able to receive this knowledge as well as giving the knowledge to us.

Bromiley recounts that in Barth's view the objective knowledge of God, given by him through the mediation of an object he has chosen, is knowledge of a divine subject, of one who is to be loved and feared. Fear, in this context, amounts to the recognition that, but for God's love and our freedom to return that love, there is nothing positive for us. Barth refuses to make the distinction, common in the history of philosophy and theology, between general knowledge and special knowledge of God, or between common knowledge and having knowledge. Knowledge of God, Bromiley adds, is for Barth knowledge of God as Subject who is loved and feared. It is both clear and mysterious: clear in that God has in fact given us understanding and certainty, mysterious in that such knowledge was available only by his gift and not through our efforts.

Barth holds, Bromiley indicates, that knowledge of God requires a readiness on our part to receive it; the readiness is given with the knowledge. Natural theologians assume that there is, in human beings, an ability, and at least at times a readiness, to receive at least some knowledge of God—an ability and readiness not created by a special manifestation of divine grace but rather present in human beings from creation. Barth rejects such perspective.

According to Bromiley, Barth interprets divine incomprehensibility not as a matter of our being unable to conceive of God but rather as a matter of our inability to bring about knowledge of God on our own. What we can know by our own efforts, he thinks, we resemble, we can master, and we can become one with. None of these things, Bromiley adds, is for Barth the case with respect to God. Hence, Barth contends, any knowledge of God that we come to possess will be ours through a process initiated, sustained, and completed by God.

Bromiley reminds us that in Barth's theology, divine incomprehensibility or hiddenness has, as its positive side, God's gracious revelation. Barth sees natural theology as a way of denying our dependence on God for knowledge of God, and hence as an inveterate enemy to the Christian Gospel. God's gracious revelation centers in Jesus Christ. Knowledge of God is mediated through Christ. The nature and purposes of God are to be interpreted and understood through Jesus Christ. Barth's conclusion, says Bromiley, is that since this is not the procedure of natural theology, natural theology is to be rejected.

Barth's perspective in this regard, Bromiley reports, is seen in the new ground he breaks in treating the doctrine of election. He refuses to find the basis or content for a doctrine of election in tradition, usefulness, experience, or a general notion of divine omnipotence. Election must have its source in Christ. The human race, in a process going from Adam through Abraham and the remnant of Israel, is narrowed down to this one man. The election is the election, primarily, of Christ himself, and of others (the community of Israel and the Church, and individual persons) only secondarily and in him. In so reasoning, Bromiley points out, Barth makes the doctrine of election part of the doctrine of God, something Bromiley sees as a most unusual procedure in the history of theology. Election is a matter of God's graciously determining to be God only in Jesus Christ; in these terms, he is Lord of Israel and of the Church, and is Creator, Reconciler, and Redeemer. So, for Barth, creation, redemption, judgment, revelation, and so on through every basic Christian theological category, are to be treated and understood in a Christocentric manner.

For all his insights, Bromiley contends, Barth's views on these matters are not without their problems. He suggests that Barth's interpretation of Scripture consists more of meditation than exposition. Because he does not come to grips with natural or general revelation, the suspicion arises, Bromiley contends, that Barth's view requires that ignorance of God stems from one's being a creature rather than from one's having sinned. Further, Bromiley adds, it may be that his attempt to read all of the Bible Christocentrically reads more into the Old Testament than is really there.

Berkouwer, G. C. *General Revelation*. Grand Rapids, Michigan: Eerdmans, 1955.

In 1887 Lord Gifford, in the will that established the famous and distinguished Gifford Lectures, specified natural theology as their subject and stipulated that they should serve the "promoting, advancing, teaching, and diffusing" of the study of natural theology. G. C. Berkouwer explains that, as an unrelenting opponent of natural theology, which he viewed as owing its very existence to a radical error, Karl Barth felt that he could give a series of Gifford Lectures only by being unfaithful to his own understanding of Reformed theology, which of course he was quite unwilling to do, yet he gave the 1937-1938 Gifford Lectures. The rationale, Berkouwer tells us, was that natural theology exists only by contrast to another sort of theology; namely, revealed theology. Thus Barth would "promote, advance, teach, and diffuse" natural theology by utterly opposing it, by championing his version of Reformed theology, and explaining why that theology was incompatible with there being any genuine natural theology, and thereby mark out the nature of natural theology by way of sharp contrast.

In Berkouwer's view, it is not too much to say that Barth carried on an offensive against natural theology. For Barth, he notes, the Christian Church, and the salvation of the believer, rests only on the gracious revelation given by God in Jesus Christ, and that revelation is unique and exclusive. Natural theology presupposes that human beings have the capacity and prowess to inform themselves about God, human nature, and the world. This presupposition must be rejected by anyone who accepts the uniqueness and exlusiveness of the revelation in Christ. Thus, Berkouwer reminds us, for Barth, Roman Catholic and modern Protestant theologians, and to some degree even the Reformers, Martin Luther and John Calvin themselves, in their willingness to use natural theology in effect deny the core of Christian theology.

Berkouwer adds that Barth claimed that one must know Jesus Christ in order to know anything at all about revelation. The revelation in Christ contains something utterly new, completely unknown previously. Apart from the incarnation of God in Christ, one cannot, for Barth, speak of revelation at all.

Berkouwer makes it clear that in Barth's theology the Bible itself is not viewed as revelation, but as a sign or witness to revelation. The same applies to the words and deeds of Christ, the Virgin birth, the empty tomb, and the testimony of the Apostles. These serve for Barth as but pointers to what alone is revelation: Jesus Christ himself. This revelation is unrepeatable. Berkouwer describes Barth as holding that since revelation is comprised of something that took place as a result of the free activity of God himself, and that that something was (as it were) a doing and not a saying, revelation comes not in terms of propositions or statements, but as an event. Further, since the divine revelation which is God himself incarnate in Jesus Christ who comes in judgment and in grace, and since this revelation is the only revelation, and since revelation is the only source of knowledge of God, there is no general knowledge of God—apart from his saving activity on our behalf—and no knowledge of God present in those who are not dependent for that knowledge on the revelation which is Christ.

Berkouwer explains that, in Barth's view, the Old Testament serves as an "antiquity," and the New as a "recollection," of the Incarnation. In the one, Christ is expected; in the other, he is remembered. In Barth's view, while appreciative recognition of the beauty or power of nature may be a "creaturely revelation," it does not reveal God. God is not knowable apart from his grace, and his grace is not accessible apart from Christ. Natural theology is traditionally presented as a knowledge of God which is independent of any knowledge of his grace or mercy; in other terms, it is presented as giving knowledge about God which need not yet be a knowledge of God. Barth denies that there is any knowledge of God which is not a knowledge of his mercy and grace, or any knowledge about God which is not a knowledge of God. There is no such thing as knowing about God in advance, or of independence of revelation; and there is no revelation except in Christ.

Berkouwer remarks that Barth's position, quite intentionally, is radical. Barth thinks it necessary because he thinks that natural theology is an "assault on the Christian idea of God." Natural theology, he argues, depends on our being able to know the existence, the being, of God while knowing nothing of his mercy and grace. As Berkouwer says, this possibility, in turn, rests on an alleged analogy of being between God and creature.

Berkouwer investigates Barth's position on this issue along these lines. In order for such knowledge to be possible, Barth argues, the unity of God's nature must be sacrificed. One would have to be able to distinguish between God as Creator and God as Redeemer. Barth contends that God cannot be without being gracious; so he cannot be known to be without our knowing him to be gracious. Natural theology, Berkouwer presents Barth as holding, is but the attempt of the natural, or unredeemed, person to have knowledge of God without relying on God for that knowledge, without depending on God's grace. Further, the "God" that natural theology gives knowledge of is not the God who revealed himself in the Incarnation, but simply an Aristotelian Deity who is not merciful and gracious. If natural theology established the existence of its sort of deity, this, Barth argues, would be bad news. So the analogy of being doctrine, and the natural theology that goes with it, is properly said to be "the invention of the anti-Christ."

One basic question here, Berkouwer points out, concerns authority; Barth insists that the only authority we can have for claiming a knowledge of God is God himself in his revelation in Christ. Berkouwer suggests, then, that it is not surprising that Barth denies that the Bible teaches that God is knowable to human beings through a revelation which is "built into" the physical creation: for example, in Psalm 19 or the first two chapters of Romans. The "main line" of biblical teaching concerns God's revelation in Christ, and any other, lesser, line must be consistent with this main one. The Apostles and prophets testify to divine grace and judgment. For Barth, Berkouwer adds, any alleged revelation besides the revelation in Christ is not a real revelation, but a sort of echo of the real revelation. Any passage that seems to ascribe a higher status to anything must be read in the light of the Gospel: Paul in Romans speaks of the knowledge the pagan may have now that revelation in Christ has occurred, not of the knowledge the pagan can have been given of a general revelation built into the cosmos. It is clear, then, Berkouwer notes, that Barth is no more a friend of general revelation than he is of natural theology.—*K.E.Y.*

ADDITIONAL RECOMMENDED READING

Berkouwer, G. C. *The Triumph of Grace in the Theology of Karl Barth*. Grand Rapids, Michigan: Eerdmans, 1956. A sympathetic and explanatory account.

Bromiley, Geoffrey W. *Introduction to the Theology of Karl Barth*. Grand Rapids, Michigan: Eerdmans, 1979. A clear and useful introduction.

Casalis, Georges. *Portrait of Karl Barth*. Garden City, New York: Doubleday & Company, 1963. A clear summary account.

Clark, Gordon. *Karl Barth's Theological Method*. Philadelphia: Presbyterian and Reformed Publishing Company, 1963. Examines the relation of Barth's philosophical procedure to his views.

Mackintosh, H. R. *Types of Modern Theology*. New York: Charles Scribner's Sons, 1937. A general account that places Barth's thought in the context of modern theology.

Van Til, Cornelius. *The New Modernism*. Philadelphia: Presbyterian and Reformed Publishing Company, 1947. Focuses on what is distinctive in the modernist view.

LOGIC, THE THEORY OF INQUIRY

Author: John Dewey (1859-1952)
Type of work: Logic, epistemology
First published: 1938

PRINCIPAL IDEAS ADVANCED

Logic is inquiry given a theoretical formulation; logical theory is the comprehensive theory of how people solve problems through conducting inquiries.

The process of inquiry involves the following stages: (1) the indeterminate situation, a case of disturbed equilibrium between an organism and its environment; (2) the institution of a problem, the change of a situation from indeterminate to problematic as a result of the active interest of an inquirer; (3) the setting up of a hypothesis, an anticipation of the consequences of certain operations; (4) the deductive elaboration of the hypothesis, together with experimental testing; and (5) the termination of inquiry, the establishment of a settled outcome; the situation has become determinate.

Universal propositions which have existential import (which are about existing things) differ from those which do not have such import, but the difference is factual, not formal.

Since propositions are instruments used in the process of inquiry, it is proper to characterize them as effective or ineffective, rather than as true or false.

Logic, the Theory of Inquiry is John Dewey's third extensive statement of his views on logic. In 1903 he contributed five articles to the volume, *Studies in Logical Theory.* Thirteen years later, in 1916, he expanded these views in his book, *Essays in Experimental Logic. Logic, the Theory of Inquiry*, published in 1938, is the fullest and most recent statement of his position. (He wrote one other book on logic, *How We Think*, which appeared in 1910—a popular account rather than a technical, philosophical discussion.) These books, published over a period of thirty-five years, indicate that Dewey was concerned throughout his life with logical theory. He adopted a position quite early in his career, and retained it and elaborated on it as his own philosophical thinking developed and matured. The books also indicate the great importance Dewey attached to logical theory. It is no exaggeration to say that he regarded it as near the very center of his philosophical position. Inasmuch as Dewey is perhaps the most widely known and most influential philosopher America has produced, and since he regarded his logic as fundamental to his general philosophical orientation, it is clear that *Logic, the Theory of Inquiry*, his final word on the subject, is well worth study by anyone who wishes to understand the role Dewey has played in recent American philosophy.

Although the book is important, it is also forbidding. It is long, and it suffers from the defects found in almost all of Dewey's technical writing, namely, an odd technical vocabulary and a writing style that is tiring and hard to follow. The key points are not highlighted, but are almost buried in a text that is monotonously heavy. In spite of the many examples and illustrations Dewey gives, his writing remains abstract and colorless.

A great many questions are discussed in the book—too many, in fact, to be covered in a short review. But it is possible to give a brief résumé of the process of inquiry, as Dewey sees it, and to discuss a few of the more controversial elements in Dewey's theory.

The title of the book, *Logic, the Theory of Inquiry*, indicates the problem Dewey regarded as the chief one for logic. Logic is inquiry given a theoretical formulation; logical theory is the comprehensive theory of how people solve problems through conducting inquiries. Inquiry is *the* topic throughout the book, and it is Dewey's description of this process that gives the book its unique character as a study of logic.

Dewey, departing from the usual accounts of syllogism, immediate inference, and so on, discusses the role he feels they play in inquiry instead of treating them as kinds of formal patterns of deduction. It is appropriate, therefore, to begin by noting what Dewey means by "inquiry." He defines it as the "controlled or directed transformation of an indeterminate situation into one that is . . . determinate." The original "indeterminate" situation is replaced, through inquiry, by one that is "determinate" or "unified."

Part of what Dewey meant by speaking of an "indeterminate situation" as becoming "unified" emerges out of the discussion which begins the book and precedes the account of inquiry proper. The first hundred pages of the book are devoted to an account of the emergence of inquiry out of a matrix of antecedent biological and cultural conditions. Dewey apparently believed that his naturalism required of him that he show a continuity between the prior biological and cultural activities which do not illustrate the peculiar characteristics of inquiry and the more specific activities which do. His point is that inquiry develops naturally out of behavior which is not inquiry. According to Dewey, the general pattern of life behavior out of which inquiry emerges is, of course, the pattern of adjustment between living organisms and their environment. Generally, organisms find themselves at times out of adjustment with the environment, and this forces them to take steps to restore the balance or harmony of a satisfactory adjustment. Inquiry is one specific technique—a most important technique—by means of which certain organisms (human beings) can sometimes restore a satisfactory adjustment between themselves and the environment. There is nothing mysterious about logical behavior to Dewey, then. It is a specific kind of human behavior that is properly subsumed under the general behavior of organisms as they seek to restore proper adjustment between themselves and the environment. An "indeterminate situation" is one in which the human organism is out of adjustment with the environment; when proper adjustment is restored, the situation is "unified" again.

There is another sense in which inquiry (logic) is not mysterious to Dewey. He spends a considerable amount of time arguing that the problem-solving in which all of us engage on the level of common sense and the problem-solving in which the technical expert engages are in their essentials identical. He proposes his theory of inquiry as an empirically derived and validated account of how people do, in fact, think. It is an attempt to explain how scientists, philosophers, machinists, housewives, and others proceed in trying to solve the problems they face in their lives. In all these cases, Dewey feels, people find themselves in indeterminate situations, and adopt as the intended outcome or consequence of action the desired resolution of these situations. Inquiry is thus a process of instituting means to reach desired ends, and logic is the general empirical theory of this process. The fundamental character of this means-consequence relation which logic seeks to describe and explain is qualitatively the same for common sense as it is for the most sophisticated scientific investigation.

The denial that there is any significant difference between commonsense inquiry and the inquiries of the technical experts is related to Dewey's rejection of the position that logic is a formal science. He rejects the view that logic is the study of the formal conditions which justify valid inference. He believes that such formalistic logical theories are really derived from metaphysical and epistemological theories that are either out of date or mistaken. He calls such theories "spectator" theories which declare that the logician should spend his time investigating "the eternal nature of thought and its eternal validity in relation to an eternal reality." Dewey wanted nothing to do with "the eternal." In opposition to such views, Dewey thought that the emphasis should be on what he calls the "evolutionary method" of the "natural history of thought," and this, in turn, requires that commonsense problem-solving be taken into account just as fully as scientific reasoning.

Dewey divides the process of inquiry proper into a series of steps or stages. These stages are (1) the indeterminate situation, (2) institution of a problem, (3) determination of a problem-solution: hypotheses, (4) reasoning, and (5) the construction of judgment. Each of these steps will now be described.

(1) *The Indeterminate Situation.* The process of inquiry is initiated in what Dewey calls the "indeterminate situation." He states that the indeterminate situation is "by its very nature" questionable, uncertain, unsettled, disturbed, troubled, confused, full of conflicting tendencies. These conditions, it should be noted, pervade the given materials of the particular situation which initiates inquiry. It is the situation itself which is marked by these characteristics; not merely the inquirer. The situation itself is a specific case of disturbed equilibrium between an organism and the environment; and this disturbed, indeterminate situation produces a need to restore equilibrium. It is out of this

situation that inquiry grows.

(2) *Institution of a Problem.* The second stage of inquiry is reached when the inquirer becomes aware of the indeterminateness of the situation in which he finds himself. He then begins to look for a way out of this uncomfortable situation, and when this happens the situation changes from an "indeterminate" to a "problematic" one. If Dewey is emphatic in saying that the indeterminateness of the initial situation is not merely in the mind of the inquirer, we may be just as emphatic in saying that a situation cannot become problematic unless the inquirer is himself mentally involved. When the doubt, confusion, and the rest do come to the attention of the inquirer—in a sense, when they are located in the mind of the inquirer—then the situation as a whole becomes problematic rather than indeterminate.

This movement from the indeterminate to the problematic involves two activities which really advance the inquiry. It involves both (a) seeing certain facts—the elements of the total situation which are or are not out of adjustment—and also (b) seeing just what the problem is. Problems always grow out of actual situations. Furthermore, to mistake the problem involved is to embark on a wrongheaded effort to resolve the disequilibrium. Thus the situation becomes problematic when the inquirer notes the facts and identifies the problem which he must solve to restore adjustment.

(3) *Determination of a Problem-Solution: Hypotheses.* In the third stage of inquiry the person involved must again take account of the facts of the situation and the problem with which he is faced, but now he must add to these a suggestion about how the problem can be solved. This fact indicates that, in contrast to the preceding steps, the third step is not a mere reading off of something concrete and actual; instead, it is an anticipation of future consequences—a possibility—which Dewey calls an "idea." The terms of the problem, the facts, are obtained by observation; the hypothesis or idea is an anticipation of what will happen when certain operations are performed on the materials of the problem. And this fact, that the hypothesis has future reference, that it is an anticipation, means that the hypothesis must be expressed in symbols. It is this that introduces the conceptual element into the procedure of inquiry.

(4) *Reasoning.* There are two related kinds of activity that are involved in the fourth step in the process of inquiry. The complex act of reasoning includes as one aspect what usually comes to mind when a logician mentions "reasoning"; namely, the deductive elaboration of the hypothesis. But it also includes the experimental testing of the deductive consequences of the hypothesis. Dewey's "reasoning," then, includes both the deductive elaboration of the hypothesis and its experimental testing. The two activities are said, by Dewey, to be "conjugate." That is to say, in inquiry the two go hand in hand; both are essential to the successful prosecution of an inquiry, and the one illuminates and sustains the other. This is characteristic of Dewey's position

as a whole; he consistently relates conceptual elaboration to existential development, and he insists that failure to realize that these two activities go hand in hand is responsible for many of the inadequacies of other logical theories. (We shall return again to this aspect of Dewey's view.)

(5) *The Construction of Judgment.* The outcome of inquiry is the resolution of the problem which initiated the inquiry. The indeterminate situation is transformed into a determinate one, the discordant elements are unified. Judgment, according to Dewey, is "the settled outcome of inquiry." It should be stressed here that Dewey is using the word "judgment" in a sense that differs from the usual one. Ordinarily, logicians mean by "judgment" the assertion of a proposition, but Dewey uses the word to refer to the settled outcome, the state of affairs that is established when an inquiry is successfully terminated. At the termination of the successful prosecution of the first four steps in inquiry a person is in a position to affirm a proposition which states the conclusion of the inquiry. Logicians often call this concluding proposition "final judgment," but Dewey prefers to call it a "warranted assertion" and reserve the word "judgment" for the settled situation which a warranted assertion describes.

Here again we see a correspondence between the conceptual elaboration and the existential development in inquiry. This is a persistent theme in Dewey's logical position, and it therefore merits a somewhat longer discussion.

A good way to begin the discussion of the parallelism between the conceptual and the existential is to restate Dewey's account of inquiry in other terms. Inquiry starts with discordance or lack of adjustment between the inquirer and his environment. It ends with the establishment of a settled relationship between the inquirer and the environment. Dewey's analysis consists of showing what takes place in the movement from the one situation to the other. The indeterminate situation is subjected to analysis and this gives rise to two parallel processes, one dealing with existential, material means (concrete, physical reality—"the facts"), which Dewey designates as "inference," and another dealing with conceptual, procedural means (possible future operations—conceptual meanings), which he calls "discourse" or "implication." The first products of analysis of the indeterminate situation are *data* (facts), on the one hand, and *meanings* (concepts), on the other. Data are material means which are used in inference and meanings are procedural means which are used in discourse or implication. These two initial products of analysis, data and meanings, are then elaborated by the parallel processes of experimental testing and deductive reasoning.

The relations between meanings or concepts permit the inquirer to formulate possible operations for settling the disturbed indeterminate situation. The relation of implication which joins meanings permits formulation in propositions, and these in turn can be elaborated and developed in conjunction with other propositions to reveal further implications of meanings. Such determination of implications between propositions discloses the possible future operations which may be engaged in to resolve the indeterminate situation.

Data, the existential or factual correlatives of meanings, are connected to one another by a relation called by Dewey "involvement." When data and their involvements are formulated in propositions they can be elaborated and developed in inference, a process which parallels discourse but which holds between propositions about (factual) data, while discourse applies to propositions about (conceptual) meanings. In both cases, inference and discourse (implication), the fact that the inquirer is working with propositions and verbal symbols enables him to relate involvements and implications to one another without performing concrete physical operations. This is the factor which makes it possible for the inquirer to anticipate and control the course of inquiry. The use of verbal symbols in propositions enables the inquirer, as Dewey puts it, to behave toward the absent as though it were present. Finally, propositions which formulate possible operations are brought together with propositions about data and the result is experimentally tested. Some of the possibilities become actualities, thus providing a concrete resolution of the problem; that is to say, these actualities give rise to judgment.

Consistent with this doctrine that inquiry involves the parallel processes of inference and discourse is Dewey's theory of propositions, one of the debated elements of his theory. The usual doctrine concerning propositions begins with the traditional Aristotelian schedule of propositions, the "A," "E," "I," and "O" propositions that are the units of the standard discussion of immediate inference and the syllogism in introductory logic texts. The usual treatment of these four forms includes the point held by the older logicians, that universal propositions, the "A" and "E" forms (All S is P, and No S is P), had existential import; that is, the subject terms of universal propositions ("All" or "No" statements) were held to denote classes which did have members. The usual account then goes on to point out that, in the modern interpretation of propositions, universal propositions lack existential import while particular propositions have existential import. The universal affirmative proposition "All men are mortal" is interpreted, from the modern point of view, as saying, "If anything is a man, then it is mortal," but this does not necessarily imply that there are any men. The particular affirmative proposition ("Some men are mortal"), in contrast, is interpreted as, "There is at least one thing which both is a man and is mortal," and here the "there is . . ." does imply that there are men. In the case of a universal proposition which does have existential import an additional assertion to the effect that there are men is conjoined to it to yield, "If anything is a man, then it is mortal, and there are men." The point which is pertinent here is that a universal proposition which lacks existential import can be distinguished from one which has existential import by noting the *forms* of the two propositions. If a universal proposition has existential import, it is conjoined with another proposition which asserts this existential import.

Dewey does not accept this analysis. He distinguishes universal propositions which have existential import from those which do not, but the difference is not for him one of form. He makes the distinction by reference to the role played in inquiry. Those universal propositions which play a role in discourse or implication (the realm of conceptual meanings) he calls "universal" propositions, while those universal propositions which play a role in inference (the realm of existential data or facts) he calls "generic" propositions. Here, then, is another instance of how Dewey rejects the formal logicians' positions on behalf of his own nonformalist, instrumentalist position. He regarded the difference between the two kinds of propositions as not a formal difference; but in this case he was mistaken. Formal logicians can distinguish those universal propositions which lack existential import from those which have it, and they can do so on formal grounds.

It has been mentioned that Dewey distinguishes universal and generic propositions on instrumental grounds; that is, by noting what kind of means they are in the means-consequence relationship which governs inquiry. This concern with the means-consequence character of inquiry led Dewey to diverge in another way from usual logical doctrine. The usual doctrine is that propositions are either true or false. Dewey rejected this view. For Dewey, "truth-falsity is not a property of propositions." Instead of taking truth value as the fundamental property of propositions, Dewey takes their function as *means* in the process of inquiry to be their distinctive feature; propositions are *means* promoting the passage from a problematic situation to a determinate one. Furthermore, Dewey states that if they are fundamentally means, then they are to be characterized as *effective* or *ineffective* rather than as true or false.

This, of course, is a radical departure from the usual account of propositions, and the question naturally arises as to why Dewey made this departure. His case rests on his definition of propositions as means for conducting an inquiry. Many things function as means to ends; hammers, for example, function as means in the building of a house. Yet hammers are not said to be true or false, nor are other means of the same sort (tools). Not all means, then, are either true or false. From this Dewey moves to the conclusion that propositions, since they, too, are means, are also neither true nor false.

Surely Dewey reasoned incorrectly in this case. What his argument amounts to is a generalization from "Some means are not true or false" to "No means are true or false." This is an illegitimate inference. It may be that propositions are neither true nor false, but Dewey's argument has not shown this to be the case.

There are many other topics included in *Logic, the Theory of Inquiry*; Dewey's range of learning was enormous. However, the points mentioned above indicate the underlying thesis of the book together with the implications, as Dewey sees them, of this thesis for some of the questions that make up the substance of logical theory. Dewey was concerned to write out a logical theory which was oriented toward problem-solving, toward what is often called the logic of discovery. He kept his attention focused on this purpose, and his book is very illuminating on a number of aspects of this problem. He tended to slight formal logic, and he failed to appreciate the contributions made by formal logic to the logic of exposition or justification. Nevertheless, Dewey's case is stated carefully and at length, and its implications are traced for many sub-areas within the larger domain of logic.

Dewey stands in the tradition of Bacon and Mill in logic, but surely he was more rigorous and relevant than either of them. His care and caution have made his book a notable advance over those of his predecessors in the tradition of empirical logic. He has avoided most of Bacon's and Mill's mistakes. Finally, Dewey's account has the merit of providing a bridge for better understanding between logicians and some of the other workers in the general province of knowledge. If logic is concerned with knowing, Dewey's account may help psychologists, biologists, and logicians to find some common ground for understanding their respective roles in determining the processes and conditions of knowing. This is a most valuable contribution for any scholar to make.
—R.E.L.

PERTINENT LITERATURE

Dicker, Georges. *Dewey's Theory of Knowing* (Philosophical Monographs). Philadelphia: University City Science Center, 1976.

John Dewey's criticism of traditional epistemology stems from his belief that all the traditional theories of knowledge are based upon an unexamined and mistaken conception of knowing. The underlying assumption of these theories is that knowing is a relation between a knower and a thing known in which the knower is conceived analogously as a viewer or passive spectator of the thing known. The label Dewey uses to designate collectively all theories which share that assumption is "The Spectator Theory of Knowledge." Georges Dicker, in a penetrating essay on *Logic, the Theory of Inquiry*, proceeds to examine Dewey's alternative to the mainstream theories of knowledge. Dicker's twofold approach is first to elucidate carefully Dewey's theory of inquiry, and second to demonstrate how that theory serves both as a critique of the Spectator Theory and as a viable alternative to it.

Dicker's study is divided into four chapters. Chapter One provides a relatively detailed exegesis of Dewey's theory of inquiry, the process by which intelligent organisms purposefully seek and acquire knowledge. Inquiry is defined by Dewey as the transformation of an "indeterminate" or "problematic" situation into a "determinate" or "resolved" situation. The inquiry process originates when an individual finds himself in an unsettling, troubling, uncertain, precarious, problematic situation, a situation of mental, psychological, or physiological imbalance. Only through manipulations and actual changes in the environment, changes in the relationships and interactions of the constituent elements of the problematic situation, can balance be restored. Inquiry thus implies activity and involvement on the part of the inquirer. The instruments for guiding the actions of the inquirer are facts and ideas formulated as hypotheses subject to experimental verification. By anticipating the consequences of what will happen when certain operations are executed, the individual is led to a choice of what he should do to resolve the problematic situation. The final stage of the inquiry process is the resolved situation which, for Dewey, is tantamount to the acquisition of knowledge.

In the second chapter Dicker focuses attention on the broad criticism of Dewey's epistemology that has been leveled by such notable critics as Arthur Murphy, A. O. Lovejoy, and Bertrand Russell, among others. The charge by these critics is that Dewey has confused epistemology with methodology and that his theory of inquiry, while providing an interesting account of the process of attaining knowledge or *coming-to-know*, does not render an account of *knowing*. Hence, it is argued, Dewey's theory neither undermines nor provides a genuine alternative to the Spectator Theory. Dicker sets the stage for answering this criticism by showing that (1) the Spectator Theory does imply an account of coming-to-know, an account based on the analogy of seeing an object, over against which Dewey's doctrine of inquiry certainly is an alternative explanation and (2) since the outcome of inquiry is indeed knowledge, Dewey's theory of inquiry does provide an account of knowing— that is, of what it means to have knowledge. In short, Dicker clearly explains how Dewey's theory of inquiry pertains to both the *process* of coming-to-know and *having knowledge* (as a product).

The third chapter provides an explication and defense of Dewey's implicit account of knowing (as a product). Briefly stated, Dewey's definition of knowledge could be expressed as *"the ability to anticipate the consequences of putting things through various changes."* Knowing, for Dewey, is best understood as a capacity or disposition, not some conscious state or episode as presumed by the Spectator Theory. Being the culmination of the inquiry process, knowledge is what renders an individual's actions intelligent, what enables the individual to effect those changes in the environment which transform a problematic situation into a resolved situation. Dicker also notes that in Dewey's view there is a continuity between the *acquiring* of knowledge, the *having* of knowledge, and the *using* of knowledge; after all, once a certain knowledge is achieved, this knowledge can then be used by the individual to fulfill some new purpose and serve as a basis for new hypotheses or ideas in a new inquiry.

Dicker's last chapter addresses Dewey's "constructionalistic" statements about the object of knowledge. Dewey's terminology often suggests that through the process of inquiry the knower literally makes or constructs the object of knowledge. Dicker argues that although Dewey does not clearly distinguish between "the object of knowledge" and "knowledge of the object," a careful reading reveals that his theory of inquiry is fully compatible with commonsense realism regarding the independent ontological status of objects of knowledge. In asserting that the object of knowledge is not an "antecedent reality" but is something brought into being by the process of inquiry, Dewey does not wish to deny the independent existence of material objects; instead, his main point, in the context of his attack against the Spectator Theory, is that knowledge is not acquired by an instantaneous and passive apprehension of reality, but is the outcome of a temporal process involving experimental operations by the knower. More than anything else, Dewey is stressing the extent to which "knowing" implies an ongoing dynamic process of interaction between an organism and its environment, or, translated into epistemological terms, between the knower and the object known.

Nissen, Lowell. *John Dewey's Theory of Inquiry and Truth.* Vol. V. The Hague, The Netherlands: Mouton & Company, 1966.

Upon critically evaluating John Dewey's closely connected theories of inquiry and truth, Lowell Nissen concludes that both doctrines should be rejected, because both essentially consist of statements which are either outright mistaken or so broad as to be at best only trivially true.

Nissen maintains that Dewey's definition of "inquiry" as the transformation of an indeterminate situation into a determinate one is much too broad, fitting many examples which no one, including Dewey himself, would consider as inquiry. Furthermore, Dewey does not consistently keep to his own definition: at times he writes as if when an inquiry were not successful—if the given problematic situation were not resolved—it should not properly be called an "inquiry"; yet the purpose of his *Logic, the Theory of Inquiry* is to set forth the methods of successful as against unsuccessful inquiry.

At the heart of Dewey's account of inquiry is his concept of a situation, a concept which Nissen contends is marred by serious faults. Dewey states that a situation is "*not* a single object or event or set of objects or events." Does he mean that objects and events may be a part of a situation but that a situation is more than these? If so, what more is there? Or does he mean that objects and events are not even parts of a situation? He sometimes equates "situation" with "contextual whole," implying that all inquiries occur within an experiential context. A context ordinarily is conceived of as a background of some sort, yet inquiry supposedly focuses on what the center of attention is, more or less ignoring the rest. Thus defining "situation" in terms of a context seems incompatible with how Dewey views the role of a situation in any inquiry. At still other times Dewey elucidates the concept of a situation in terms of human experience and the interaction of organisms with their environment. Even then it is unclear whether a situation *is* an experience or whether it refers to the interacting elements of the experience.

Nissen articulates similar apparent defects associated with other key concepts in Dewey's theory of inquiry. The notion of an "indeterminate situation" is hazy; Dewey's description of how an organism formulates and solves problems is muddled; his conception of "ideas" as hypotheses, or "anticipated consequences of what will happen when certain operations are executed under and with respect to observed conditions," is puzzling and confusing; and in his explanation of "judgment" as the terminus of the inquiry process he vacillates between holding that a judgment is a grounded proposition (what he refers to as "warranted assertibility") and holding that it is a change in the world—namely, a resolution of some problematic situation.

When it comes to Dewey's theory of truth, Nissen's appraisal is equally negative. Borrowing from Charles Sanders Peirce's definition of truth, Dewey calls truth the opinion which would ultimately be agreed upon by all who would complete a serious (scientific) inquiry on a given matter. Such a description, Nissen argues, is loaded with problems. In an ironic way, since what is required is only that there *would be* unanimous agreement if inquiries were carried out, truth is thus viewed as independent of any inquiry, yet very much dependent, if an inquiry is performed, on its having a certain result. To determine any particular truth would necessitate a poll of opinions arrived at by all persons who ever investigated a given subject, as well as all persons who ever will or ever could—which obviously is impossible. Do all opinions deserve equal weight? If not, how do we make appropriate distinctions? If one person holds a differing opinion from everyone else after conducting a thorough investigation, does that categorically rule out that the others' opinions are thereby not true? Nissen's list of critical remarks continues on and on. He even considers Dewey's widely proclaimed declaration that "truth is determined by consequences," and he concludes that no matter how such a statement is interpreted, it cannot withstand the test of numerous counter-examples which can be imagined.

Nissen concludes that neither Dewey's theory of inquiry nor his doctrine of truth merits philosophical acceptance.

Thayer, H. S. *The Logic of Pragmatism: An Examination of John Dewey's Logic*. New York: Humanities Press, 1952.

The words "experience," "nature," and "intelligence" designate three crucial themes in John Dewey's philosophy. The focus of H. S. Thayer's critical study on *Logic, the Theory of Inquiry* is that part of Dewey's philosophy is concerned with human intelligence—to be specific, with Dewey's so-called logic, or theory of inquiry, the process by which problems are investigated deliberately and methodically and warranted solutions are arrived at.

Because the development of human intelligence is so intimately connected with experience and nature, in the first part of his book Thayer explores in a general way what Dewey means by those latter two notions. Experience and nature constitute an organic continuum, according to Dewey, experience being an ongoing affair *in* nature and *of* nature. Because experience provides the only intelligible access to nature, experience is conceived by Dewey as the starting point of all inquiry and the ultimate basis of all knowledge. Indeed, experience presents itself as a method for penetrating nature and disclosing nature's secrets. Dewey's logic is essentially a detailed description of what he takes to be *the* method of experience, the empirical method.

Thayer's exposition of Dewey's theory of inquiry is clear, straightforward, and generally accurate. From a philosophical standpoint, however, Thayer's most valuable contribution lies in his effort to improve upon Dewey's theory by overcoming what he regards as three important weaknesses or flaws in Dewey's analysis. The bulk of his book centers on these three points.

The first major problem Thayer sees is that Dewey's description and account of an "indeterminate situation" is empirically inadequate. Thayer remedies the difficulty by defining an indeterminate situation as one constituted by certain *behavioral* characteristics (specified by such behavioral terms as "doubt," "troubled," and "confused") and *physical* characteristics (specified by such physical terms as "unsettled," "unbalanced," and "open"). He then defines a determinate situation as having the opposite behavioral and physical characteristics. Once the requisite behavioral and physical terms are operationally defined, it becomes empirically feasible to answer the question: Is such and such a situation indeterminate or determinate? It is simply a matter of applying the appropriate procedures of observation and measurement.

The middle phase in the process of inquiry involves the formation of hypotheses as initial plans of action for resolving a given problem. The meaning content of hypotheses Dewey refers to as *propositions*. Contrary to tradition, Dewey maintains that propositions are neither true nor false; truth and falsehood he reserves as properties of what he calls *judgments*, which are equivalent to the settled outcomes of inquiries. As a second major point of contention, Thayer presents a strong critique of Dewey's general theory of propositions. He demonstrates the desirability of holding that propositions are either true or false, then shows how his proposed revision actually reinforces Dewey's overall theory of inquiry. Just as inquiry is conceived of informally as a transformation from an indeterminate to a determinate situation, from a more formal standpoint the same process can be stated as the facing of a problem, the construction of a set of propositions as possible solutions, their subsequent testing, and the confirmation of one of the propositions as a conclusion warranted by virtue of the intermediate operations which have produced it.

Finally, Thayer questions Dewey's claim that inquiry effects an existential transformation, that a modification of existential conditions actually occurs as a result of an inquiry process being brought to completion. Thayer gives a number of examples of apparent inquiries which, upon completion, do not seem to result in any real transformation of a situation—except perhaps in some subjective or psychological manner inherently incapable of being publicly verified. What does occur, Thayer emphasizes, is that on the basis of what is revealed through acts of verification a given proposition is judged true or false. The completion of an inquiry corresponds to a situation in which an assertion is warranted that "such and such a proposition is true (or false)." Therefore Dewey is correct, according to Thayer, in his view that the terminus of any inquiry is "warranted assertibility," but mistaken in his belief that through inquiry the existential conditions of a situation are necessarily altered.

Regardless of these three shortcomings, Thayer praises Dewey for putting forth the finest and most extensive original description of the empirical method, the procedures governing investigations, and, what amounts to the same thing, the patterns in the development and implementation of human intelligence.—*R.A.S.*

ADDITIONAL RECOMMENDED READING

Geiger, George R. *John Dewey in Perspective*. New York: Oxford University Press, 1958. This book provides a lucid and intelligible articulation of the key elements which make up Dewey's philosophy as a whole. The author shows how Dewey's epistemology, his value theory, his pragmatism or instrumentalism, as well as his views on science, politics, and education are all grounded in his affirmation of human experience as an ongoing transactional process in and of nature.

Hook, Sidney. *John Dewey: An Intellectual Portrait*. New York: John Day Company, 1939. A clear and nontechnical introduction to the central ideas in Dewey's philosophy. Included in the book are chapters on "Truth," "Logic and Action," "Body, Mind, and Behavior," and "Nature and Man." Hook's fine reputation as a philosopher and commentator is widely recognized.

Kestenbaum, Victor. *The Phenomenological Sense of John Dewey: Habit and Meaning*. Atlantic Highlands, New Jersey: Humanities Press, 1977. A thought-provoking study aimed at clarifying and expanding Dewey's concept of habit from an existential phenomenological point of view. The author argues that Dewey's logical theory and epistemology, his value theory and philosophy of education, as well as his more general conception of experience and nature, are all grounded in a doctrine of prereflective, habitual meaning. By making explicit the phenomenological undertones in Dewey's work, Kestenbaum paves the way for a more comprehensive understanding of Dewey's philosophy as a whole.

Pollock, Robert C. "Process and Experience," in *John Dewey: His Thought and Influence*. Edited by John Blewett. The Orestes Brownson Series on Contemporary Thought and Affairs. No. 2. New York: Fordham University

Press, 1960, pp. 161-197. An outstanding original essay on the substance and historical significance of Dewey's organistic theory of nature and human experience. Pollock brilliantly illustrates the depth and power of Dewey's conception of the universe and of the unfolding drama of man's ongoing interaction with the natural environment.

Schilpp, Paul A., ed. *The Philosophy of John Dewey* (The Library of Living Philosophers). New York: Tudor Publishing Company, 1951. In accordance with the general aim of the Library of Living Philosophers series, this book brings together a set of interpretative and critical essays by some of Dewey's scholarly contemporaries. Among the many facets of Dewey's philosophy which are discussed, in particular there are essays on his logical theory, his epistemology and naturalistic metaphysics, and his philosophy of science. Also included is a reply by Dewey to his critics, an intellectual autobiography, plus a complete bibliography of his writings.

THE NATURE OF THOUGHT

Author: Brand Blanshard (1892-   )
Type of work: Philosophy of mind
First published: 1939

PRINCIPAL IDEAS ADVANCED

Thought aims at truth.

The activity of thinking and the object of thinking cannot be considered separately.

The test of truth, the nature of truth, and reality itself can all be understood by reference to coherence.

Reality is the coherent perfection of partially realized thoughts in finite minds.

Blanshard is a happy example of a philosopher who, early in his career, staked out a position sufficiently promising for him to devote his academic lifetime to its exploration and defense. The view that mind is an autonomous realm and that thought has no other goal than truth impressed itself on him before he knew that this lay in the great tradition of Plato and Hegel, and that it had been fully worked out by Bradley, Bosanquet, and Royce. *The Nature of Thought* is a protracted exposition of this thesis, composed over a period of fifteen years. Blanshard took time to study carefully all serious alternatives to his position, and the bulk of the work is the result of the painstaking care with which he has restated and assessed these alternatives.

In Hegelian fashion, Blanshard has tried to find some truth in every point of view. Making no great claims to originality, he has developed his thesis largely in terms of other men's statements. But he is no mere eclectic. From the opening sentence his thesis is clear and emphatic: "Thought is that activity of the mind which aims directly at truth." And the exposition, while ample and gracious, is straightforward and direct, reflecting the author's resolution to bring down to earth and make practical a mode of thinking which renowned philosophers have often been content to leave at Olympian heights.

There is a deliberate ambiguity in the book's title. Does the author mean to discuss the activity of thinking, or that which thinking has for its object? Both are called "thought." Blanshard deals with both, alternating between one and the other. In fact, his main contention is that they cannot be taken separately.

This brings him into sharp opposition to many contemporary philosophers. Students of logic, epistemology, ethics, and religion have in recent years declared that no light is shed on the objects of thought by considering its subjective conditions. They have seen a danger to free inquiry, and indeed to all meaningful human activity, in philosophical systems, whether idealistic or naturalistic, and have declared their independence not only of metaphysics, but also of historicism, which professes to explain everything in terms of historical development, and of psychologism, which makes a corresponding claim for the study of the human mind. Blanshard was certainly aware of these dangers. But he maintained that there is even greater danger in the fragmentization that characterizes the modern approach. In his view, to study logic or ethics apart from their grounds in thought and in reality can lead only to skepticism or irrationalism.

Blanshard states the problem by outlining the views of psychologist E. B. Titchener, who, in the interests of delimiting his science to include only intelligible matter, had insisted that it must exclude mind from its purview. Titchener had taught that it is possible to draw a line between man's sensitive life and the realm of meaning which attaches to it, and he had held that if psychology is to remain a distinct field of inquiry, it must not be drawn into discussions about ethics and logic. With this recommendation, however, Blanshard disagrees. Long connected with the University of Michigan, both as a student and as a professor, he echoes an idealist tradition which goes back to the days when John Dewey, then a disciple of Hegel, taught there. In a book called *Psychology* (1886), Dewey argued that psychology is a central science which, because it includes knowledge, includes every other science. Blanshard agrees with the early Dewey that knowledge implies a reference to mind and cannot be understood apart from psychological processes, and that as a result anyone who wants to know the nature of the world must study the nature of thought. In other words, a philosopher must not neglect psychology.

A difficulty is that, in recent times, psychology has sought to get free from philosophy and establish itself as an empirical science. Sometimes, as in the case of American behaviorism, it has only brought back a discredited philosophy—mechanistic materialism—in a new form; and Blanshard turns aside to devote a chapter to exposing this movement, which he regards as impossibly naïve. But other psychologists, by restricting themselves to description and analysis, have, in his opinion, let the fetish of method stand between them and an adequate account of our mental activities. Dewey's functionalism, according to Blanshard, was nearer the truth because it let no presuppositions obscure the teleological character of thinking. Blanshard was not attracted to Dewey's pragmatism, which, with its strong biological bias, makes thought subservient to organic impulses; but very often his own psychology echoes the language of the pragmatists (both William James and Dewey). The explanation is found in his sympathy with their contention that the mind never works except when motivated by some purpose.

For pragmatism, an idea is an incipient act; but for Blanshard it is an incipient object. According to his view, the intellect does not merely serve the needs of the body: it has its own goal which it seeks to realize; namely, perfect union between mind and being. Common sense has grasped this fact and tried to express it by saying that the idea resembles its object. But the dualism which such an explanation creates between the two orders of being, mental and physical, is philosophically unsound—there being no intelligible way of explaining the sense in which the idea and its object are the same. Blanshard believes that the truth of common sense is preserved and the philosophical difficulty overcome by his theory. It agrees with common sense that ideas are not in fact identical with their objects; but it overcomes the qualitative dualism between them by maintaining that ideas are potentially what they represent. Their stand in relation to things is much like that in which acorns stand to oak trees: ideas are the same, and not the same, as things. They are halfway houses on the road to reality, to use an expression of Blanshard.

For Blanshard, as for the pragmatists, thinking is problem-solving. He speaks of the activity as analogous to building a bridge from the mainland to an island. The mainland is the body of understanding which a person already possesses, and the island is some factual knowledge that is as yet unassimilated by the mind. The aim of thought is to bring the new into intelligible relations with the old. We may want to know the cause of a thing, or the end which it serves, or its definition in terms of a familiar scheme of classification. Blanshard does not shirk the psychological questions here involved; for example, whether thoughts leave traces or dispositions which enable us to bring the past to bear upon the future; or, again, whether there is a subconscious activity of the mind involved in all creation and invention. But these questions are incidental to his main inquiry, which has to do with the mind's goal and fulfillment in truth.

Blanshard tries always to keep in view the two ways of viewing the movement of thought. When engaged in thinking, a person seems, on the one hand, to be seeking his own fulfillment as a rational being, exorcising the ignorance and doubt which limit his freedom. On the other hand, he seems to be trying to reach beyond himself and embrace something entirely transcendent to thought; namely, the nature of things as they are. In modern philosophy, according to Blanshard, critical realism and neorealism have divided these two aspects between them. The former emphasizes the role played in knowledge by ideas, or contents of the mind, and sees thought mainly as an effort to bring these into consistent and orderly relations; but it loses sight of the transcendent end of knowledge. The latter emphasizes the direct acquaintance which thought has with objects, but it denies that specifically mental contents even exist. The one loses the world; the other loses its own soul. But Blanshard thinks that such half-views are unnecessary. The merit of his theory is that it saves both thought and its object, without permitting one to encroach on the other. The two are never in fact identical, for reality is the perfection and fullness of being which is but imperfectly and partially realized in the finite mind. But the transcendence of the end over its immanent realization in thought is merely one of degree.

Blanshard's view leans hard on the coherence theory of truth. On the one hand, thought strives for coherence; on the other, reality possesses coherence: all that distinguishes them from each other is the difference in degree. Common sense, which thinks of truth as an agreement between the mind and the world it seeks to know, falls short of comprehending what knowledge actually involves. Suppose someone says, "That is a cardinal singing in the bush." It is naïve to think, with the man on the street, that the way to confirm the judgment is to inquire whether the fact agrees with our thoughts; for any new observation which we make will necessarily have the same problematic character as the one we are seeking to verify. What we finally affirm to be the truth is the state of affairs which renders the several aspects of experience coherent with each other and with our previous knowledge. Blanshard gives separate consideration to three related questions: What is the test of truth? What is the nature of truth? What is reality? But his answer in each case is the same, namely, "coherence." "Coherence is a pertinacious concept and, like the well-known camel, if one lets it get its nose under the edge of the tent, it will shortly walk off with the whole."

Blanshard admits that there is no proof that reality is coherent, much less that coherence exhausts the nature of being. His contention, however, is that only such a view of the world accounts for the accuracy, dependability, improvability, and scope which our thought possesses. Thought seeks understanding, and in the measure that we understand anything we see the necessity for it. Blanshard, therefore, devotes a major portion of his book to exploring the kinds of necessity in order to see which is adequate to account for knowledge.

Empirical philosophy has, in his opinion, totally failed to account for necessity. Mistakenly supposing that the contents of the mind are atomic sense impressions, each inherently independent of every other, it has tried to explain the order and connection that come to govern a man's thinking as having no other basis than habit, whether that of the individual (John Stuart Mill) or of the race (Herbert Spencer). Blanshard believes that this contention can be disproved at the psychological level because the laws of association by which the connections are allegedly explained do not describe the way learning actually takes place. But his chief line of argument is that the theory leads to skepticism and, if consistently applied, precludes our ever understanding anything, even how the mind works. Mill's account of syllogistic reasoning, for example, makes inference impossible to confide in because each step in the proof is held to be determined entirely by psychological laws.

Logical positivists have sought to save empiricism by locating intelligibility in language and in the conventions of formal logic. Thus, pushing empiricism to the limit, they deny that there is any necessary connection between being a man and being mortal; but they allow that there is a kind of necessity governing the use of the terms "man" and "mortal," once we have agreed to relate them in a certain way. In their view, all inference is but an expanded tautology: it tells us nothing at all about matters of fact. Blanshard's criticism of formalism goes deep. Like the Hegelians, he objects to the principles of abstraction which underlie even traditional logic. There is a radical difference, according to Blanshard, between the concrete universal with which the mind actually advances toward knowledge of the world and the empty counters of the formal logician. "Man" is an example of the former: it is general but not abstract, a richly intensional term which the mind forms by moving from particular ideas to a more general one that embraces them. Contrast it with the abstract, purely extensional notion employed by the formal logician; for example, "the class of rational bipeds past, present, and future." Actual thought operates with terms like "man" and is concerned with following out relations which are actually given in experience. Thus, says Blanshard, when we affirm that being human implies being mortal, "we mean, foggily without doubt, and if you will, unjustifiably, but still beyond all question, that the *character* of being human has some special and intimate connection with liability to die." And he denies that the formal logician has shed any light on the necessity here uncovered when he points out that, by the rules of the syllogism or by the truth tables, the conjunction of the propositions "All men are mortal" and "Socrates is a man" implies the proposition "Socrates is mortal." On the contrary, we are plunged into deeper darkness. In their efforts to escape from the imperialism of metaphysics and psychologism and historicism, logicians have set up a dictatorship. In the language of A. J. Ayer, "Philosophy is a department of logic."

The scientific account of the world leads, in Blanshard's opinion, to a sounder view of things. In the first place, it takes for granted a course of nature in which every event is causally related, either directly or indirectly, to every other event; in the second place, it is committed to the belief that man's mind is capable of understanding these relations. If we hold fast to both of those principles, Blanshard says, we must come in the end to the view that events are constituted by their relations to all other aspects of reality. This is the theory of "internal relations" for which modern idealism has contended. A rival view, which has found favor with empirical philosophers, including such men as Ernst Mach and Bertrand Russell, is that no event really influences any other and that our knowledge of nature is limited to observing regular sequences between events. But Blanshard argues that when we state that water extinguishes fire, we affirm something more than the mere regularity with which the phenomenon occurs; namely, some connection between the natures of water and of fire. In his view, the meaning of water includes its relations to fire, as well as to other things such as soap and dirt. To understand anything, according to idealism, is to grasp the system of relations in which it is found. If the system is incomplete, we try to piece it out or if necessary modify it until the missing connections are found. Thus, we explain why water extinguishes fire by making use of hypotheses about temperature and oxidation. Scientific theories such as these provide a larger area of coherence and present a higher level of truth than is available to our native experience; and, even though we do not claim, as common sense is prone to do, that our theories reproduce the actual structure of the world of things, still, the confidence which we repose in them would be without foundation if reality were itself without coherence.

Blanshard writes with a marked sense of mission. Like the commonsense philosophers of an earlier day, who battled skepticism and agnosticism, he is vexed that in an age of unprecedented intellectual achievement philosophers can find nothing better to do than to raise doubts as to whether knowledge is possible. He is sure that their misgivings are the result of mistaken theories and that a sound analysis not only permits but demands that we take a thoroughly rationalistic view of the world. At this point, his inquiry opens out onto the problems of metaphysics, which he does not venture to discuss. But he does admit his allegiance to that *perennial philosophy* which through the centuries has maintained "the doctrine that through different minds one intelligible world is in the course of construction or reconstruction . . . [and] that the secret of sound thinking is the surrender of individual will to an immanent and common reason." Concluding his work on the eve of World War II, he lamented the passing of a time when educated men recognized a common standard of judgment and obligation; but he refused to believe that the defeat of reason and truth was more than temporary, and ventured to think that his own "insistent and reiterated emphasis . . . on the membership of minds in one intelligible order [might] serve, however minutely, to confirm the belief in a common reason and the hope and faith that in the end it will prevail."—*M.E.*

PERTINENT LITERATURE

Nagel, Ernest. "Sovereign Reason," in *Freedom and Experience, Essays Presented to Horace M. Kallen.* Edited by Sidney Hook and Milton R. Konvitz. Ithaca, New York: Cornell University Press, 1947, pp. 260-288.

Ernest Nagel is a distinguished philosopher of science, an exponent of scientific naturalism and logical empiricism. His philosophical perspective is almost absolutely antithetical to that of Brand Blanshard, a rationalist deeply indebted to the Hegelian tradition. Nagel's essay is a trenchant critique of Blanshard's theory of reason. Blanshard had portrayed the goal of reason to be an intelligible system of knowledge, a fully coherent whole in which every judgment entails and is entailed by every other, and which, moreover, becomes one with the objective order of reality construed as a comprehensive system of internally related parts. Nagel finds Blanshard's vision of reason as sovereign in thought and reality to be logically indefensible.

Nagel locates the crux of Blanshard's theory of reason in the doctrine of internal relations. A relation is internal to the terms it relates if it determines the nature of the term so that the removal of the relation alters the term's nature. The doctrine of internal relations holds that all relations are internal. In this context Nagel finds the concept "nature" ambiguous, and after distinguishing several meanings, he argues that Blanshard identifies the nature of a term with the term itself and considers the term to be the totality of its properties. Blanshard, then, makes no distinction between the essential and the accidental properties of the term, all the properties being on an equal footing.

Next Nagel examines Blanshard's arguments for the doctrine of internal relations. First to be considered is Blanshard's claim that all things are related to one another. This claim depends on the conception of difference as a relation, and therefore as an internal relation. For, at the very least, one thing differs from another, and if difference is an internal relation, then it is internally related to the thing from which it differs. From the internal relatedness of all things, two implications follow: (1) there is only one individual thing—the whole which absorbs all lesser things as parts of its nature, and (2) every true statement about it is analytic in that it simply explicates what the whole contains.

Turning from things, Nagel takes up the thesis that universals are internally related. He distinguishes two versions of this claim: (1) that internal relations hold between some universals, and (2) that every universal is internally related to all other universals. Blanshard upholds the second version. Nagel refutes Blanshard by maintaining that some universals—number—are independent of other universals, their natures unaffected by any relations into which they may enter with these other universals.

Nagel also scrutinizes Blanshard's causal argument for the doctrine of internal relations. The argument has two parts: (1) that all things are causally connected, and (2) that causal connections involve logical necessity. Nagel concentrates on the second part, on the grounds that if it is false, then all things, although causally connected, are not related by logical necessity, so that the doctrine of internal relations falls. In particular, Nagel focuses on the psychological process of reasoning, which Blanshard cites as a sequential process of judgments in which the concluding judgment is necessitated by the antecedent judgments functioning as premises. Nagel disputes the core of the argument. He distinguishes propositions from judgments, and while allowing that logical connections of necessity may hold between propositions, he denies that they hold between judgments, which are psychological events.

From Nagel's perspective of scientific naturalism, Blanshard's theory of reason is misguided. Ambiguities and vagueness creep into Blanshard's arguments, undermining his program for reason. That everything in the world is logically connected becomes little more than a faith, and that reason, in satisfying its own impulses for rational necessity, reflects the nature of reality, is reduced to a fanciful hope. For Nagel, contingency is a pervasive characteristic of reality; it infects reasoning itself.

Rescher, Nicholas. "Blanshard and the Coherence Theory of Truth," in *The Philosophy of Brand Blanshard* (The Library of Living Philosophers). Edited by Paul A. Schilpp. La Salle, Illinois: Open Court, 1980, pp. 574-588.

Nicholas Rescher has undertaken in his book *The Coherence Theory of Truth* (Oxford, 1973) to refine and reformulate the theses of objective idealism by translating them into the contemporary philosophical idiom of symbolic calculi. In this essay he concentrates on Brand Blanshard's coherence theory of truth. Blanshard had maintained that coherence is not only the test for truth, but that it is the nature of truth as well. Rescher condemns Blanshard's theory for failing to render intelligible the relation of truth to reality. He borrows a passage from Bertrand Russell, who rejected the coherence theory of truth because a system of statements may be coherent—as, for example, a novel—and yet not be true. For the nature of truth requires that the statements relate not merely to one another but to reality. Hence correspondence serves better than coherence as the nature of truth. Rescher therefore denies that coherence is the nature of truth, but he accepts coherence as the test of truth.

Blanshard argues from coherence as the test for truth to coherence as the nature of truth; he holds that a discrepancy between the test and the nature of truth would be incoherent, and hence would fail the test of truth. Rescher examines Blanshard's argument and finds it defective. It holds that the test of truth is the failproof guarantee of truth. And Rescher is distrustful of a failproof guarantee of truth. He prefers a test of truth which may authorize us to claim that a proposition that passes it is true. As an authorizing criterion, coherence as the test for truth is regulative. Propositions that pass the test are warrantedly classed as true. This allows, of course, that a proposition may be true without in fact being subject to, or passing, the test, and, further, that a proposition may pass the test without in fact being true. Rescher finds this latitude preferable to Blanshard's tight connection between the test and the nature of truth. For, according to Blanshard, if a proposition passes the coherence test of truth, then it must be true.

Rescher probes Blanshard's conception of coherence. While Blanshard defines truth as coherence, he allegedly fails to provide a satisfactory definition of coherence. In regard to the nature of coherence, Blanshard deems a system of knowledge coherent if every judgment it contains entails and is entailed by the rest of the system. Rescher charges that this conception of coherence implies that every judgment is redundant, since it is already contained in the rest of the system. Next Rescher considers the sort of things that cohere, and in this regard he finds Blanshard's views ambiguous. He rejects the suggestion that it is beliefs that cohere, on the grounds that no one would want to hold that only those propositions we believe can possibly be true. He also denies that it can be the widest system of propositions, embracing the possible as well as the real, that coheres and hence passes as true, because such a system, making no distinction between the actually real and the merely possible, would be insecurely related to reality. Nor does Rescher find that for Blanshard experience can function as that with which propositions must cohere, for the conception of experience is vague.

Rescher contrasts Blanshard's coherence theory of truth with Francis Herbert Bradley's and maintains that Bradley's theory is superior. Bradley, according to Rescher, accepted coherence as the test for truth and correspondence as the nature of truth. Bradley also defined his criteriological conception of coherence to consist in the claim of system to be an arbiter of those propositions competing to be considered true.

Blanshard's incisive, detailed reply follows Rescher's essay in almost equal length.

Rorty, Richard. "Idealism, Holism, and 'The Paradox of Knowledge,'" in *The Philosophy of Brand Blanshard* (The Library of Living Philosophers). Edited by Paul A. Schilpp. La Salle, Illinois: Open Court, 1980, pp. 742-755.

In 1963, Richard Rorty, a former student of Brand Blanshard, reviewed his mentor's *Reason and Analysis* for *The Journal of Philosophy*, LX (1963), pp. 551-557. This densely packed essay amplifies themes iterated in the review, while it widens the compass to include Blanshard's *The Nature of Thought*. Rorty professes to be a holist, an appellation he also applies to Blanshard. Holism is the doctrine that wholes are more real or more valuable than the sum of their parts. Rorty's profession of holism is remarkable in that, although schooled in the history of philosophy, he subscribed to contemporary philosophical analysis when he wrote this essay, and analysis concentrates on parts. Upon reexamining Blanshard's *The Nature of Thought*, Rorty is struck by two things. First, many of the points Blanshard scores against sense-data theories, logical positivism, and reductionistic theories of meaning are similar to those made by such analytic philosophers as Ludwig Wittgenstein, W. V. O. Quine, J. L. Austin, and Roy Wood Sellars. Second, Blanshard's project is remote from the preoccupations of these contemporary analytic philosophers.

To indicate common features despite differences of idiom between Blanshard's thought and later analytic philosophy, Rorty shows how both converge on denying that atomic sense data can serve as the foundations of knowledge. Additional topics explored by Rorty pertain to the analytic-synthetic distinction, with its corollary dichotomy of logical necessity and empirical contingency, and also to the relation between universals and particulars.

On analyticity and necessity, Rorty compares Blanshard with Quine. He reports Blanshard as representing the doctrine of degrees of necessity and as affirming that every judgment partakes of its appropriate degree of necessity. He relates that Quine denies the validity of the analytic-synthetic distinction on the grounds that analyticity cannot be defined. Since for analytic philosophy, necessity is customarily defined in terms of analyticity, Quine seems to undermine necessity, just as Blanshard rejects contingency. However, these two apparently opposite philosophial directions, in Rorty's interpretation, actually meet. For necessity (and analyticity), on the one hand, and contingency (and syntheticity), on the other, are contrasting terms, neither of which is meaningful without the other, and Blanshard and Quine concur in replacing black and white with shades of gray.

On particulars and universals, Rorty compares Blanshard with Wilfrid Sellars. Blanshard is the proponent of the doctrine of the concrete universal and of the doctrine that the only true particular is the Absolute. What are miscalled "sensed particulars" by run-of-the-mill empiricists, Blanshard calls "specific universals." Hence, a particular thing is tantamount to a congeries of specific universals. By contrast, Sellars is a nominalist. While he agrees that knowledge is not based upon sensed particulars, he nevertheless insists that what we know are facts, and facts are about these particulars. Thus for Sellars particulars are real. To the question whether Blanshard or Sellars is right, Rorty's answer is that, since universals and particulars are contrasting terms, the two opposed philosophers are closer to each other than their different idioms reflect.

Rorty finds that what separates Blanshard from contemporary analytic philosophy is his overall project. Whereas the later analysts discard the traditional quest for epistemological foundations, not only in regard to sense experience, but also in regard to thought, Blanshard clings to reason, to thought, to what Quine has caustically dubbed "the idea idea." Blanshard's allegiance is traced back beyond Hegelianism to the seventeenth century. According to Rorty, during the seventeenth century, with the rise of modern science, philosophers succumbed to the paradox of knowledge. They came to believe that all they could know reduced to ideas locked up in their own minds. Thus skepticism burst forth. Unlike the recent analytic philosophers, Blanshard remains entangled in the seventeenth century philosophical problematic.

Although the implication of Rorty's essay is that the later analytic philosophers have rightly won the day, he expressly offers his commentary as a reconciliatory and mediating way of looking at seemingly opposed points of view. Blanshard's cogent response follows in an essay longer than Rorty's. He concludes with his expression of gratitude to Rorty "for having brought to light some areas of coincidence" between the thought of the analytic philosophers and his own.—*A.J.R.*

ADDITIONAL RECOMMENDED READING

Bertocci, Peter. "Does Blanshard Escape Epistemic Dualism?," in *The Philosophy of Brand Blanshard* (The Library of Living Philosophers). Edited by Paul A. Schilpp. La Salle, Illinois: Open Court, 1980, pp. 601-617. A sympathetic critique of Blanshard's epistemology by the leading living personalist.

Caws, Peter. "Coherence, System, and Structure," in *Idealistic Studies*. IV, no. 1 (January, 1974), pp. 2-17. A comparative critical study of Blanshard's philosophy and structuralism.

Harris, Errol E. "Blanshard on Perception and Free Ideas," in *The Philosophy of Brand Blanshard* (The Library of Living Philosophers). Edited by Paul A. Schilpp. La Salle, Illinois: Open Court, 1980, pp. 480-509. A penetrating criticism which, among other things, underscores the difficulty in Blanshard's early thesis that the idea is its object potentially, a thesis which Blanshard yields in his replies to Harris, Reck, and Bertocci in this volume.

Landesman, Charles. "Specific and Abstract Universals," in *Idealistic Studies*. IV (January, 1974), pp. 89-105. A probing analysis of Blanshard's theory of universals.

Reck, Andrew J. *The New American Philosophers*. Baton Rouge: Louisiana State University Press, 1968. An appreciative exposition of Blanshard's idealism and rationalism in the framework of American philosophial thought since World War II.

Rome, Sydney and Beatrice Rome, eds. "Interrogation of Brand Blanshard conducted by Louis O. Mink," in *Philosophical Interrogations*. New York: Holt, Rinehart and Winston, 1964, pp. 201-257. Contains Blanshard's reply to Nagel.

AN ESSAY ON METAPHYSICS

Author: Robin George Collingwood (1889-1943)
Type of work: Philosophy of metaphysics
First published: 1940

PRINCIPAL IDEAS ADVANCED

Any intelligible statement finally rests upon certain absolute presuppositions.

Ordinary presuppositions are either true or false; but absolute presuppositions are neither true nor false, for they are not factual.

Although it is a mistake to treat absolute presuppositions (such as the belief in the uniformity of nature) as if they were factual propositions to be confirmed by sense experience, it is also a mistake to suppose metaphysics impossible and to narrow rational investigation to empirical inquiry.

The metaphysician is a kind of historian whose task it is to discover absolute presuppositions in the thought of others.

In designating his philosophical books "essays," Collingwood, who preserved a keen sense for etymologies, meant to imply that they were not general "treatises," and he made no claim either to comprehensiveness or system. On the contrary, they were written, each one, to make a special point.

These remarks apply to the work in hand, both to its outline and to its texture. It is far from being a "metaphysical" book, in the usual sense of that word. Instead of propounding the author's metaphysics, it is a lively statement of the importance of metaphysics, sharpened by a polemic against certain antimetaphysical tendencies, and it is enforced by three extended illustrations (which make up half of the volume).

Collingwood argued that any intelligible statement, if fully fathomed, rests upon a series of presuppositions which terminate in one or more absolute presuppositions. And this is not a mere matter of fact that happens to be the case but a consequence of the nature of the understanding itself. Not merely philosophy, but everything that is included under science (taken in the sense of systematic thought about a determinate subject matter) involves logical or *a priori* elements.

Writing on board a freighter, Collingwood took as an example a cord which the crew had stretched above the deck. He recognized it as being a clothesline. But this supposition presupposes another thought; namely, that the line was put there on purpose. Had this assumption not been made, the thought which identified it as a clothesline would never have occurred. In other words, every thought which we can put into words is the answer to some question and can be understood only if the question is sensible. But a sensible question rests upon other thoughts which, if put into words, are likewise answers to questions—and so on, until we finally come to a thought which is not the answer to any question. It is an absolute presupposition.

R. G. Collingwood is almost as well known as a historian (Roman Britain) as he is as a philosopher. And the circumstance is relevant to understanding his views on metaphysics. (See *An Autobiography*, 1939.) As an excavator he formulated and was instrumental in giving currency to the methodological principle: never dig except to find the answer to a question. As a historian, he brought to new clarity the concept that the only subject matter of history is the thoughts of men who lived in the past. "Why did Caesar invade Britain? Did he achieve his purpose? If not, what determined him to conclude the campaign?" Armed with questions of this sort, the archaeologist becomes something more than an antiquarian and the historian something more than an editor of texts: they become scientists. They increase our store of relevant knowledge. And they do this by following Bacon's advice about interrogating nature.

Collingwood relates that it was this kind of intellectual discipline which overthrew in his mind the claims of the Oxford realists under whom he had studied philosophy. He abandoned their claim that knowledge is made up of simple truths which are independent of each other and immediately knowable; he maintained, to the contrary, that a fact is meaningful only as it fits into an inquiry. Moreover, he argued, a particular inquiry is always part of a more comprehensive undertaking—civilization itself—which gives it backing and direction, for at any given moment, men of a living culture are engaged in solving the problems of human existence, starting from certain beliefs and commitments. But these are the considerations that are commonly called metaphysics, after the treatise by Aristotle in which they were first systematically dealt with.

In Aristotle, according to Collingwood, two quite different inquiries are confused. Aristotle perfected the logic of classification by genus and species. He saw that at the bottom of the table there must be *infimae species* which are fully differentiated and that, by the same logic, there must be at the top a *summum genus*, which because completely undifferentiated may be designated by the term Pure Being. In a different context, Aristotle dealt with the structure of the sciences. Much better than Plato, he understood the necessity of delimiting a particular subject matter and defining the presuppositions which it involved; and he saw that this task was a distinct one which required a new science to deal with it, which he called first philosophy, wisdom, or theology. So far, so good. But Aristotle made a mistake. Influenced too much by the ontological tradition from Parmenides to Plato, he allowed himself to suppose that the first principles of the sciences could be identified with the Pure Being of his logic of classification. And metaphysics, in the history of Western philosophy, has ever since had great difficulty in extricating itself from this confusion. In Collingwood's view, Kant's *Critique of Pure Reason* is a notable attempt to set it free. The Transcendental Aesthetic and the Analytic pursue the proper task of metaphysics—seeking for absolute presuppositions; and the Transcendental Dialectic exposes the fallacies of pseudometaphysics, which seeks to fit these absolute matters into a conditional scheme of things.

There is a significant agreement, at this point, between Collingwood and various antimetaphysical groups in our own time. He insists that much of what is traditionally called metaphysics is bad science because it seeks to treat transcendental issues as matters of fact. Ordinary presuppositions are factual: they can be stated as propositions, and are either true or false. But absolute presuppositions are not factual: they do not answer any question and are neither true nor false. Properly speaking, they are not propositions at all.

But if Collingwood agrees with the realists and positivists in assailing the claims of ordinary metaphysics, his emphasis on the importance of absolute presuppositions represents a significant protest against this group. In his opinion, their radical empiricism is a species of anti-intellectualism. Such empiricism accounts for truths such as: "This is the back of my hand"; but it breaks down when called upon to account for complex truths which make up natural science, not to speak of ethics and politics. He sees it as part of a dangerous tendency in the contemporary world which he broadly designates as irrationalism and, in its philosophical expression, as antimetaphysics.

The second part of *An Essay on Metaphysics* is given over to the discussion of two characteristic expressions of this antimetaphysical tendency. The first is pseudopsychology. Collingwood has no quarrel with psychology so long as it sticks to its subject. It began as a distinct science when modern (sixteenth century) thought began to insist on a sharp distinction between mental (logical) and physiological (mechanical) explanations of human conduct. Emotion or feeling did not seem to fit in either of these realms; therefore, psychology arose to take account of this third realm. Properly it deals with problems of motivation which cannot be accounted for either by mechanical or by rational means. And there are such problems. But the problems of ethics, aesthetics, and religion are not among them. These are rational pursuits, each with its own logic and presuppositions. They are mental sciences which fall outside the province of psychology. But it is part of the irrational tendency of the past century (Collingwood can only reckon it as analogous to a disease, "a kind of epidemic withering of belief in the importance of truth") that we have suffered psychology to extend its principles of explanation to include these rational pursuits. Freud's *Totem and Taboo* (1913) is cited as an example of the errors and confusions which come when a great psychologist tries to apply to significant activity categories which are legitimately used to understand aberrant behavior. If the presumptions of psychology are not turned back, science itself is doomed. Citing at length three instances of careless thinking to be found in standard psychology books, Collingwood affects to think that psychology is a deliberate conspiracy to undermine our scientific habits.

The other characteristic expression of antimetaphysics is positivism. Collingwood admits that it has greater respect than does psychology for the autonomy of man's rational activity; but in maintaining that science is made up entirely of empirical truths, it is a victim of the same irrationalist infection. John Stuart Mill set the pattern when he maintained that the principle of uniformity in nature is an inductive inference, whereas it is the absolute presupposition on which induction depends. Bradley, according to Collingwood, disclosed his own positivist affinities when he defined metaphysics as "the finding of bad reasons for what we believe on instinct." Mill saw rightly enough that the science of his day presupposed belief in the uniformity of nature: but he introduced radical incoherence when he treated it as a proposition which must be verified by experience.

The irrationalist propensities of positivism become most clear, however, in the dictum of the logical positivists that any proposition which cannot be verified by appeal to observed facts is nonsensical. That is to say, because they cannot be treated as factual statements, the absolute presuppositions of science, ethics, and politics are subrational. Collingwood agrees with Ayer's strictures on pseudometaphysics; that is, a science which would treat absolute presuppositions as if they were facts; but he blames Ayer for what seems to him to be merely a petulant attack arising from the lunatic fear that in some way metaphysics is a threat to science. The threat which Collingwood sees is the habit of mind which narrows rational investigation to the limits of sense verification.

The remainder of the book is given to three examples which illustrate the thesis that metaphysics is the science of absolute presuppositions. The first is an illuminating account of the role theology has played in Western intellectual history. One of the names which Aristotle gave to the science of first principles was "theology." And, according to Collingwood, the classic concern of Greek philosophy was to formulate the new convictions which had replaced the older Homeric beliefs. Thales is important because he gave expression to the new belief that the multiform spheres of nature are at bottom one; Heraclitus, because he saw that all change is according to law. These, according to Aristotle, are *divine* matters. And far from being hostile to art, ethics, and knowledge, they were the foundations upon which Greek achievement rested. They were also the measure of its limitations. The failure of the Greek polis and the later collapse of the Roman empire are traced by Collingwood to metaphysical causes; that is, to inadequacies in the fundamental axioms of the Hellenic mind. Men could not overcome the impression that the world falls into irreconcilable parts: necessity and contingency, or eternity and time, or virtue and fortune. And it was the sense of the contradictions in human existence which this world view entailed that left them unnerved in the face of the progressively greater challenges to which their own achievements gave rise.

Then came Christianity. Of the host of religions that crowded the shores of the Mediterranean Sea during imperial times, it alone offered an improved metaphysics. Athanasius and Augustine are only the best known of a number of first-rank intellects who would have been drowned in a sea of trivialities if they had not been able to extract from the Gospel the basis for a new science. The trinitarian statements are properly understood as a highly fruitful solution to the metaphysical problem which had defeated the Greeks. In this connection, Collingwood chides Gibbon for obscuring an important truth in order to be clever. Gibbon said that the doctrine of the Logos was taught in the school of Alexandria in 300 B.C. and revealed to the Apostle John in A.D. 97. As Collingwood points out, Gibbon took this fact from Augustine, but he omitted the point which Augustine went on to make and which proved the key to Christianity's success; namely, that the Christians for the first time bridged the chasm between time and eternity, inasmuch as the Logos was made flesh. One must, Collingwood says, "regret the slipshod way in which Gibbon speaks of Plato as having 'marvelously anticipated one of the most surprising discoveries of the Christian revelation.'"

Collingwood maintains that Christian theology provided not merely a rallying point for good minds during the decline and fall of Rome, but that it also furnished the fundamental assumptions which enabled European science to make such advance over that of the Greeks. In part, Aristotle's presuppositions agree with those of modern man—that there is one God, and that there are many modes of God's activities—but in part they disagree, notably on the question as to the origin of motion, which Aristotle tried to explain but which modern science takes as a presupposition. In this connection, Collingwood analyzes the trinitarian confession. The "I believe" indicates from the very first that we are dealing not with propositions but with presuppositions. The doctrine of One God, in whom, however, are contained not merely the principle of Being but also those of Order and of Motion, places all these severally and together on the plane of absolute presuppositions. This doctrine, and not the metaphysics of Pythagoras, Plato, Aristotle, or Plotinus, provided the indispensable foundation upon which Galileo and Newton founded modern science.

We cannot deal at any length with Collingwood's further examples. They are "The Metaphysics of Kant," to which we have briefly alluded, and "Causation," a suggestive account of the perplexities involved in that essentially anthropomorphic concept. Collingwood reports that Western science has made varying assumptions about causation: Newton held that some events have causes and others not; Kant, that all events have causes; and modern physics, that no events have causes. And here we observe an important feature of the subject that has not hitherto been mentioned. Collingwood talks about absolute presuppositions; but he means no more than that they are taken as absolute by the person (or society) which makes use of them. They change unaccountably, as in the instance of causation. And they may change for the better or for the worse. But their change can never be a matter of indifference; rather, the whole well-being of a civilization is dependent upon them. For a civilization, Collingwood insists, is at bottom a way people live; and if the way turns out to be impracticable, the problem is not to save the old civilization, but to save the people by inducing them to live in a different way. The new way will be based upon different absolute presuppositions, and in time it will produce a new science and a new culture.

Now it is no task of the metaphysician to say what absolute presuppositions one should or should not hold. His business is merely to discover them. And he is most likely to find them, not in the writings of philosophers, but in those of constructive workers in the various fields of human interest; that is, in physics or law. Essentially, he is a historian. For it makes no difference whether he investigates the "so-called past" or the "so-called present." In either case, he has to do first-hand historical work, and the things he studies—namely, absolute presuppositions—are historical facts. It is thus that metaphysics takes its place among the sciences. For, as Collingwood has insisted, an absolute presupposition, taken in relation to the truths that are based upon it, is not a truth. But, viewed historically, it is. In order to preserve the distinction, Collingwood provides us with a special rubric to be applied to every metaphysical proposition: "In such and such a phase of scientific thought it is (or was) absolutely presupposed that. . . ." The statement as a whole is a proposition which may be true or false.

Taken in this way, metaphysics has the same importance as any other kind of history; namely, helping us understand the human enterprise. When it studies the so-called present, it has the special utility of disarming reactionary thinkers who, because of inattention to historical tensions, remain wedded to the errors of the past. We expect to find such reactionaries among pseudometaphysicians, with their commitment to eternal truths and deductive proofs. But there are just as many among antimetaphysicians who, in their ignorance of the role played by absolute presuppositions, perpetuate outmoded assumptions under the guise of intuitions or inferences. Collingwood cites examples of new realists and analysts who continue to affirm the "law of causation." For instance, John Wisdom: "I do not know *how* we know that things are as they are because they were as they were. But *we* do know it." The "we," says Collingwood, can only be a group or society of persons whose reverence for the past has blinded them to the developments of twentieth century science. The group does not include contemporary natural scientists or those philosophers who understand what the natural scientists are doing. He quotes Russell: "The law of causality, I believe, like much that passes muster among philosophers, is a relic of a bygone age, surviving, like the monarchy, only because it is erroneously supposed to do no harm."

In Collingwood's opinion, the sciences (both natural and historical) are in flourishing condition, and prospects for their growth were never more promising—if the anti-intellectual threat does not overpower them. He sees two great danger spots: a political order in which reason is replaced by emotion and an academic atmosphere in which pseudosciences are nurtured alongside the true. Like the geese that saved the Capitol, Collingwood must warn men of the peril. "I am only a professorial goose, consecrated with a cap and gown and fed at a college table; but cackling is my job, and cackle I will."—*J.F.*

PERTINENT LITERATURE

Mink, Louis O. *Mind, History, and Dialectic: The Philosophy of R. G. Collingwood.* Bloomington: Indiana University Press, 1969.

Going against the interpretations of T. M. Knox, Robin George Collingwood's student, friend, and chief editor, and Alan Donagan, a respected Collingwood scholar, both of whom maintain that Collingwood's major philosophical writings fall into two or three distinctive classifications as reflected by radical shifts in his views, Louis Mink argues convincingly that the entire corpus of Collingwood's work should be understood as a continuous examination of the possibility and nature of dialectical thinking. A similar position is taken by Lionel Rubinoff in *Collingwood and the Reform of Metaphysics: A Study in the Philosophy of Mind* (Toronto: University of Toronto Press, 1970).

Mink's book is divided into two parts, corresponding to what he conceives as the form and the content of Collingwood's philosophy—the form being the idea of dialectic, the content consisting of Collingwood's particular theories. Part I is a careful exposition of Collingwood's notion of dialectic as developed in his writings. In Part II Mink shows how this notion of dialectic bears on the meaning of Collingwood's logic of question and answer, his doctrine of absolute presuppositions, his theory of art as imagination, and his famous theory of history as a science of mind.

Collingwood's concept of dialectic is not to be confused with any popular meanings of the term. By dialectical thinking he means something other than a Socratic style of dialogue or a special method of reasoning. Dialectic, for Collingwood, is not tied to a process of development through stages of thesis, antithesis, and synthesis, as in the absolute idealism of Georg Wilhelm Friedrich Hegel or the dialectical materialism of Karl Marx. Nor does Collingwood wish to postulate any dialectical laws of nature or of history. According to Mink, dialectic in Collingwood connotes an experiential process through which the *implicit* becomes *explicit*. The book is an attempt to clarify and expand upon this claim.

Collingwood identifies five fundamental types of experience, or modes of knowledge: art, religion, science, history, and philosophy. In his writings he attempts to elucidate the concepts and conceptual schemes implicit in the different forms of experience. By so doing, he shows how these forms relate to one another and how each succeeding form serves to make explicit what in the previous form was only implicit. To say that an element is "implicit" in experience is to say that it is there in a relatively amorphous way, yet capable of becoming crystallized when attended to from a different perspective, or level of consciousness.

The phenomenology of experience present in Collingwood's pentateuch of forms may be described roughly as follows. Explicitly, aesthetic consciousness is intuitive—that is, immediate and unreflective; implicitly, however, it is self-reflective and grounded in the conceptual structures of language. The fundamental and implicit underlying feature of religion is the fact that the direct objects of religious experience are symbolic, pointing to meanings which they do not contain in and of themselves. Whereas scientific knowledge can be formulated explicitly as a set of answers, implicitly no scientific proposition can be separated from the question it is meant to answer. The implicit element in all historical thinking is the selective, constructive, critical activity of the historian as he tries imaginatively to re-create the past. Finally, philosophical thought, while ostensibly directed toward some subject such as art, religion, science, or history, implicitly has as its genuine object thinking itself and the dimensions of concrete human experience. Philosophical knowledge alone, therefore, can properly be called *self*-knowledge.

By pursuing the theme of dialectic, Mink develops a cogent and illuminating interpretation of what is perhaps the single most important component of Collingwood's philosophy: the doctrine of absolute presuppositions. Absolute presuppositions, in Mink's view, are implicit conceptual schemes which determine the formal features of human experience. Absolute presuppositions provide the conceptual underpinning for scientific inquiry. They function much like Immanuel Kant's *a priori* categories of the understanding, in the sense that they constitute necessary conditions for the possibility of experience in general. The task for metaphysics, states Collingwood, is the articulation and codification of the absolute presuppositions foundational to man's knowledge as it has developed and changed over time.

Some examples of absolute presuppositions include: (1) the principle of causation (that every event has a cause), which is part of the conceptual framework of Newtonian science; (2) the principle of continuity: namely, that between any two terms in a series there always is a third term; (3) the principle of the permanence or indestructibility of substance, illustrated by a person who hits a golf ball into the rough and cannot find it but goes on searching for it under the supposition that "It must be somewhere hereabouts"; (4) the principle of the uniformity of nature, or that the universe is governed by general laws, which is basic to all scientific inquiry; (5) the idea of motion, which helps shape and give meaning to sense perception; and (6) the notion of freedom, without which most of the social sciences would make little sense. Mink notes how much Collingwood emphasizes that absolute presuppositions are not timeless entities, but are subject to change during the course of history. Thus Newtonian physics, for example, is based on an entirely different set of absolute presuppositions from that involved in Albert Einstein's theory of relativity.

All in all, Mink's study is one of the most readable, informative, and instrumental commentaries available on the philosophy of R. G. Collingwood.

Post, John Frederic. "A Defense of Collingwood's Theory of Presuppositions," in *Inquiry*. VIII, no. 4 (Winter, 1965), pp. 332-354.

Post devises an elaborate defense of Collingwood's theory of absolute presuppositions by reconstructing it in terms of a formal language. In so doing he attempts to overcome three apparent weaknesses in Collingwood's doctrine. The result is a detailed formulation of a model of systematic inquiry implicit in Collingwood's account.

The first weakness of Collingwood's theory as presented in *An Essay on Metaphysics* is the apparent psychologism of what purports to be a purely logical investigation. Supposedly Collingwood's purpose is to diagram the logical relationships between answers, questions, and their presuppositions. Yet his language often suggests that he is concerned with psychological relationships, as when he claims that "whenever anybody states a thought in words, there are a great many more thoughts in his mind than are expressed in his statement"; or when he says that the "logical efficacy" of a presupposition is that it "causes" questions to arise in one's mind, and that presuppositions must be "supposed by someone" to give rise to particular questions. Such statements give the impression that presupposing, for Collingwood, is an act of thinking, and that the relationship between statements, questions, and presuppositions is in part at least psychological, not purely logical. Post shows how this unhappy psychologism can be avoided.

A second often-noted criticism concerns Collingwood's imprecise and misleading terminology. He maintains that every question arises logically from a direct presupposition. The direct presupposition of the question "Has he stopped beating his wife?" is presumably "He has been in the habit of beating his wife." But the idea of a "direct presupposition" is extremely vague if applied to many common, everyday questions. Using Post's example, it is totally unclear what the direct presupposition is for the question "Do unicorns exist?" In the question "What color is his coat?" is the direct presupposition "He has a coat," or is it "His coat is colored"? How does a "direct" presupposition differ from an "indirect" one? And how do *absolute* presuppositions differ from *relative* presuppositions? By using a formal language to define the basic terms of Collingwood's theory, Post achieves greater clarity and precision.

The third weakness Post addresses is the dilemma created by the central proposition that "Every statement that anybody ever makes is made in answer to a question." The proposition seems either trivially true or plainly false. It is surely true that for any given statement it is possible to construct a question to which the statement is an answer, simply by changing the statement's mood from declarative to interrogative and adding a question mark. But that cannot be all Collingwood means. However, if the claim is intended as a description of what goes on in a person's mind whenever he makes a statement, it is simply false. People's statements are not always (in fact, not usually) preceded by an utterance or thought of a question.

Post's defense begins by declaring that Collingwood's theory should be interpreted as a theory of systematic inquiry. Next, he stipulates that the theory be treated not as a *description* of how all inquiries *actually* proceed, but as a *prescription* of how they *should* proceed. Just as any valid argument should exhibit a proper argument form, so, too, should a well-conceived inquiry follow a proper pattern. Post then goes on to use a formal language (L) to describe what this proper model of inquiry looks like in Collingwood's view.

A sample of Post's approach is illustrated by his syntactical definitions of "question," "systematic inquiry," "initial presupposition," and "subsequent presupposition." (He uses the terms "initial" and "subsequent presupposition" in hopes of avoiding Collingwood's misleading adjectives "absolute" and "relative.") A question of L is an interrogative sentence (IS) of L. A systematic inquiry (SI) is a finite sequence of sentences of L, beginning and ending with a non-IS, such that each non-IS (except the first) is an answer to an IS on the preceding line, and each IS has on the line preceding it a non-IS with 'SP' (subsequent presupposition) written in front of its line number if the line is not the first. The non-IS on the first line has 'IP' (initial presupposition) written in front of its line number. The last line of an SI is the conclusion (C) of that SI.

The semantical machinery in Post's presentation becomes somewhat complex, but for those who can follow it, the account suggests a framework for better understanding Collingwood and for developing a more comprehensive model of inquiry.

Ritchie, A. D. "The Logic of Question and Answer," in *Mind*. LII, no. 205 (January, 1943), pp. 24-38.

A. D. Ritchie provides a clear, understandable interpretation of Robin George Collingwood's so-called "logic of question and answer." He recognizes that far from proposing a "new logic" to supersede the principles of traditional Aristotelian logic, Collingwood is laying the foundation for a formalized theory of inquiry. Challenging the doctrine that knowledge consists of atomic intuitions, atomic truths, or atomic propositions, assertions, or judgments, Collingwood seeks to demonstrate that knowledge is a complex unity composed of specific answers to specific questions. In fact, Collingwood goes so far as to claim that the meaning of a proposition is relative to the question it is intended to answer.

Collingwood's theory may be summarized roughly as follows. Every proposition which conveys knowledge must be conceived as an answer to a question. If the question had not been asked (consciously or otherwise), the answer would not have been obtained. No question ever arises *in vacuo*, but stems from something either known already or taken for granted. Using Collingwood's hackneyed example, the question "Has the man stopped beating his wife?" appropriately arises only insofar as it is either known or taken for granted that the man has been in the habit of beating his wife. Thus every question is grounded in a set of presuppositions. Furthermore, the answer to any question presupposes whatever the question presupposes. Any body of knowledge, therefore, is an interrelated system of answers, questions, and presuppositions.

More than anything else, Collingwood is trying to show how empirical knowledge is tied essentially to systematic inquiry through the explicit asking and answering of questions. The paradigm of the scientific method is reflected in Francis Bacon's memorable exhortation to "put Nature to the question." In seeking knowledge about nature, the scientist does not merely sit back and wait respectfully upon nature's utterances. By no means; the scientist pursues the inquiry by formulating questions and then devising tortures as means of compelling nature to answer. In a court of law, inquiry proceeds by way of questioning the witnesses, in hopes of finding certain answers. Likewise, historical inquiry develops according to this same model of question and answer.

Ritchie explains how Collingwood's view is appreciably similar to the traditional theory of hypothesis and verification. To the extent that a hypothesis is regarded as something suggested and awaiting verification or falsification, it may be understood as a question to which the answer Yes or No can be given under suitable conditions. In addition, part of the value of a hypothesis is in determining the actual method of empirical investigation. For example, if the question is how many black marbles are in the bag, that will lead to one method of inspection, whereas if the question is how many poisonous snakes are in the bag, that will necessitate a much different approach. The point here is that scientific empirical knowledge is the fruit of a systematic process of inquiry, a process set into motion and guided by specific questions or hypotheses.

Although Ritchie acknowledges agreement with Collingwood's analysis as it applies to precise and scientific knowledge sought out deliberately by inquisitive thinkers, he disputes whether *all* genuine knowledge is modeled on question and answer. What might be classified as "primitive knowledge," he states, simply emerges willy-nilly with a minimum of questioning and answering. Walking outside during a winter blizzard, one just knows that "It's cold out there!"—without any asking of specific questions.

It would be a mistake, however, to attribute to Collingwood the view that all knowledge is based on explicit questioning and answering, for he himself distinguishes between the low-grade, casual, haphazard thinking of everyday experience, which yields only low-grade knowledge, and the high-grade thinking of scientific inquiry, which produces high-grade knowledge. The point that Collingwood wishes to emphasize—and here Ritchie is perfectly right—is that scientific knowledge, in the proper sense of the term, originates and develops through an inquiry process of question and answer.—*R.A.S.*

ADDITIONAL RECOMMENDED READING

Donagan, Alan. *The Later Philosophy of R. G. Collingwood*. Oxford: Clarendon Press, 1962. A critical study of Collingwood's philosophical work from 1933 to his death in 1943. The author is not hesitant to debate Collingwood openly when he thinks Collingwood is mistaken. The book's value can be measured in part by the controversy and argumentation to which it has given rise regarding the interpretation of Collingwood's ideas.

Krausz, Michael, ed. *Critical Essays on the Philosophy of R. G. Collingwood*. Oxford: Clarendon Press, 1972. This fine collection of essays by some of the most respected Collingwood scholars provides discussion covering a wide range of his thought. Topics include his philosophical method, his philosophy of mind, his doctrine of absolute presuppositions, and his ideas on art, religion, history, education, ethics, and politics. The essays are all original, being commissioned especially for this book.

Llewelyn, John E. "Collingwood's Doctrine of Absolute Presuppositions," in *The Philosophical Quarterly*. XI, no. 42 (January, 1961), pp. 49-60. An important essay which criticizes Collingwood's theory of absolute presuppositions. Llewelyn briefly outlines the theory, warns the reader of three possible misinterpretations, then presents in detail a number of what he considers to be basic flaws in Collingwood's doctrine.

Mackay, Donald S. "On Supposing and Presupposing," in *The Review of Metaphysics*. II, no. 5 (September, 1948), pp. 1-20. This paper continues to demand the attention of those interested in understanding Collingwood's notion of an absolute presupposition. The author nicely illustrates the distinction between ordinary *suppositions*, including definitions, assumptions, axioms, postulates, theorems, hypotheses, and the like, which originate through mental acts of stipulation, and absolute *presuppositions*, which constitute necessary and limiting conditions for the very possibility of scientific or philosophical inquiry. Mackay suggests that absolute presuppositions exhibit neither a temporal nor a logical priority, but rather a "heuristic priority," in the sense of being the underlying first principles at the base of any investigation.

Rubinoff, Lionel. *Collingwood and the Reform of Metaphysics: A Study in the Philosophy of Mind.* Toronto: University of Toronto Press, 1970. A comprehensive reconstruction of Collingwood's philosophy into a system, using as the central theme Collingwood's aim toward a *rapprochement* between philosophy and history. The author argues against the view that Collingwood's "later philosophy" reflects a dramatic shift away from his earlier idealism to a radical historicism.

Rynin, David. "Donagan on Collingwood: Absolute Presuppositions, Truth and Metaphysics," in *The Review of Metaphysics.* XVIII, no. 2 (December, 1964), pp. 301-333. A brilliant defense against Alan Donagan's attack on Collingwood's theory of absolute presuppositions. By interpreting absolute presuppositions as conceptual commitments undergirding all systematic thinking, Rynin makes sense of Collingwood, while at the same time demonstrating the inadequacy and shortsightedness of Donagan's criticisms.

AN INQUIRY INTO MEANING AND TRUTH

Author: Bertrand Russell (1872-1970)
Type of work: Epistemology
First published: 1940

PRINCIPAL IDEAS ADVANCED

Empirical knowledge has its basis in percepts (sense experiences); from basic propositions about percepts empirical knowledge is constructed.

Although basic propositions are not indubitably true, as propositions of the utmost particularity, referring to percepts, they are the most dependable propositions of empirical inquiry.

Empirical knowledge requires provision for general statements, for stating logical relationships, and for modes of inference.

Propositions are both objective and subjective; they are objective in that they indicate factually, and they are subjective in that they express the state of mind of the speaker (belief, denial, or doubt).

Sentences are true if what they indicate is the case; to know a sentence to be true one must perceive its verifier (the event the sentence indicates).

The phrase "theory of knowledge," Russell says, has two meanings. One kind of theory, the lesser, accepts whatever knowledge science presents, and seeks to account for it. Russell's concern is with the wider kind, which embraces all problems of establishing the nature and validity of all knowledge. Confining his attention in this work to empirical knowledge, he undertakes to discover two things, principally: (1) What is meant by "empirical evidence for the truth of a proposition"? (2) What can be inferred from the fact that there sometimes is such evidence?

Russell brings to the problem of a theory of empirical knowledge the full force of its counterpart, logical knowledge, to whose modern development he is a foremost contributor. He attacks the problems of his general task by translating their elements into formal logical symbols, so as to achieve a precision lacking in the language in which the problems are usually couched. Yet the book does not consider problems of logic as such, except when they are relevant to epistemology.

To talk about epistemological matters, Russell sets up a modern linguistic apparatus. He conceives a hierarchy of languages, at whose base is the object-language or primary language. Terms in the object-language include subjects and predicates. While ordinary language may provide a beginning, we should transform every subject of the object-language into a unique proper *name*, making use of coordinates in the visual field and of measures of time for discriminating the object named. The name will apply to a complex; and sometimes we must give names to complex wholes without knowing what their constituents are. We learn the names of things ostensively, and only of those things we actually perceive while hearing or coining their names. The names are employed as subjects in propositions of the simplest sort, called *atomic* propositions. We may designate their predicates *relations*. Letting R stand for the relation "above," the proposition "A R B" consists of the relation R and the names A and B, and asserts that A is above B. This is a dyadic relation. Predicates may take any number of terms. The predicate of a single name is a monadic relation: "$f(A)$" states that a characteristic f is an attribute of A.

The secondary language consists of statements about the primary language (thus it must include the primary language within it). Therefore all words for logical conceptions, such as "is true," "is false," "or," "if," belong to the secondary language. All logical truths, since they depend for their truth on rules of syntax, are at least on this level, if not higher. An important group of propositions of the secondary language are those stating *propositional attitudes*, such as "A believes proposition p."

The distinctive feature of empirical rather than logical truth is, of course, its basis in percepts, the sense images by which perception is possible. Russell adapts A. J. Ayer's phrase "basic propositions" to designate those propositions arising as immediately as possible from percepts. A basic proposition "is a proposition which arises on occasion of a perception, which is the evidence for its truth, and it has a form such that no two propositions having this form can be mutually inconsistent if derived from different percepts." Examples in ordinary language are "I am hot," "That is red." Many basic propositions may arise describing a single percept, for we perceive a sensory whole combining the entire fields of vision, touch, and so on; and within this field we identify smaller wholes of sensory complexes—the individual objects of the world. Basic propositions need not be atomic propositions. An important group includes some propositions stating propositional attitudes— "I believe proposition p"—and thus basic propositions may occur in the secondary language as well as in the primary.

Unlike most prior writers, Russell does not affirm that basic propositions are indubitably true. He is quite willing to doubt them, particularly those involving the memory of percepts. But what distinguishes basic propositions from others is their immediacy, whereas other propositions rest to some degree on inference. The evidence for a basic proposition is the momentary percept which causes it, and nothing can ever make a percept more or less certain than it is at the moment of its occurrence. It is from basic propositions that Russell proceeds to erect the structure of empirical knowledge. Since basic propositions are based on the least questionable objects of experience, they are the most dependable propositions in empirical inquiry. Thus, empirical knowledge is founded on propositions of the utmost particularity. Russell criticizes other writers for failing to screen out all traces of inference in the propositions they have regarded as basic.

A pure empiricism, depending only upon percepts for validation, would be self-refuting. It must contain some general proposition, which cannot be a basic proposition, about the dependence of knowledge upon experience; and the consequence is that such a proposition could not itself be known. Empirical knowledge requires certain additional elements besides basic propositions. These include provisions for making general statements and for stating logical relationships. Empirical knowledge, in other words, needs some epistemological premises as well as factual premises. Modes of inference are also required. These modes include the usual logical operations of deduction. More important in empirical knowledge, however, are nonlogical patterns of inference; namely, reasoning by analogy and by induction. As an example: Russell throughout assumes that things perceived *cause* perceptions, and that perceptions *cause* propositions. His notion of cause is that it is a convenient device for collecting together propositions of certain percepts; it is something that we can arrive at inductively from appropriate combinations of percepts. Without some such organizing scheme for relating percepts, we would have nothing resembling empirical science. Yet neither causality nor induction is perceived, nor are they validated by logical syntax.

An innovation, no doubt startling to logicians, which Russell finds necessary to epistemology is to supply substantial meaning rather than merely formal meaning to logical terms. He finds these in psychological fact. "Or" rises from a hesitation, a conflict between two motor impulses when the organism is suspended between two courses of action. "Not" expresses a state of mind in which an impulse to action exists but is inhibited. "True" has its psychological ground in an expectation that is fulfilled; "false" in the surprise when an expectation is defeated. Such interpretations as these become possible when we accept into epistemology not only logic but psychology and physical science, as we must in order to account for empirical rather than purely logical knowledge.

Russell is now able to develop a theory of significance. Regarded epistemologically, a proposition has two sides, objective and subjective. The objective side is what it *indicates* factually. The subjective side is what it *expresses* about the state of mind of its originator; and this is called its *significance*. What it expresses may be belief, denial, or doubt. These distinctions, not needed in logic, solve many puzzles of epistemology. The points concerning significance are independent of truth or falsity of the proposition; truth and falsity come into the relation of the proposition to what it indicates. A proposition does not necessarily consist of words; it is psychological, of the stuff of belief, not language. But words may always be found to state the belief which, as a proposition, may underlie the many possible ways of saying it, in one or in various languages. Russell provides a sample language to show that the psychological conditions of significance can be translated into precise syntactical rules.

Logical sentence-patterns can start from particular propositions recording percepts and extend our thought over material that we have not experienced, and in this way we can expand our body of statement. If we know "Socrates is mortal" we can think "Something is mortal," or "Everything is mortal," and so on. Then further inquiry so as to have new percepts may test whether the new statements should be added to belief. Simple statements of immediate percepts may be expressed with constants—particular names—and predicates. But any statement covering a percept one has not actually had must contain a variable term in place of a constant, for one can neither give nor learn a name (in Russell's sense) for an object one has not perceived. An epistemological language will need names, whereas a logical language does not deal with particulars and has no use for names. By the use of variables rather than names, it is possible to have propositions transcending one's experience. This is in fact what happens whenever one receives information from another person.

Thus far Russell has investigated meaning. In effect, he has constructed an epistemological language, so that one can know what kinds of sentences are possible as statements of percepts and their relationships. It remains to examine the relationship between meaning and truth, between language and the world.

Among the many possible theories of truth, Russell adheres firmly to a correspondence theory. Truth is defined by events, not percepts, although it becomes known by percepts. Truth is thus a broader concept than knowledge. The truth of a proposition is established by perception of its *verifier*. The sort of sentence which provides the model for truth is a spontaneous sentence that expresses what it indicates—that is, in which the subjective and the objective content coincide. Such a sentence is "I am hot!" Provided the sentence is stimulated by the immediate circumstances of the moment, there is no reason to doubt it. The verifier of a true sentence is what the sentence *indicates*; in other words, what makes that sentence true is that I was hot when I said it. Similarly, the verifier of a sentence about the future is the occurrence of what it indicates, and when that occurrence is perceived, the sentence is verified. A false sentence has no verifier, and it indicates nothing. Obviously, some verifiers may never be perceived, and there are some sentences whose truth or falsity we never know. Sentences are true if their verifiers occur, but when verifiers are not perceived the sentences cannot be said to be known. The presence of an observer, Russell affirms, is no requisite of verifiers occurring.

The verifier of a basic proposition is a single occurrence at a moment of time. As to sentences containing variables, there is (usually) not just one but a collection of verifiers for them. The actual verification of such sentences depends on what is said. "All men are mortal" says "For any x, if x is a man then x is mortal." This can never be verified by empirical knowledge because it would be impossible to examine all values of the variable—all men. "Some men live in Los Angeles" says "There is an x such that x is a man and x lives in Los Angeles." This can be verified by one of a very large number of verifiers, since any individual man living in Los Angeles can be the assigned value of the variable. In this fashion, propositions which are not basic, but which, rather, by the use of variables indicate occurrences beyond the speaker's experience, may be verified. We can give in advance a description of the occurrence which would make the proposition true, but we cannot name the occurrence. The relation between a sentence and its verifier is often much more remote than the explanation of simple cases would suggest.

Russell denies that either the verification or the verifier of a sentence constitutes its meaning. The verifier, as what the sentence indicates, relates to its truth; but we must know what the proposition means before we can know either its significance or its verifier; that is, before we can know either what it expresses or what it indicates. This knowledge is based ultimately on our ostensive learning of object-words.

Known error arises in the experience of surprise upon a disappointed expectation. Its simplest case requires a combination of expectation, perception, and memory, in which either the expectation or perception must be negative, the others being positive. This combination accounts for our perceptions which seem to be negative perceptions, such as in "There is no cheese in this cupboard." We examine every object in the cupboard having a size which might result in a percept of cheese, but in every such case the expectation is disappointed.

The relation of empirical knowledge to experience is explained by Russell as follows: I must depend completely upon my own experience for all beliefs whose verbal expression has no variables; these include only basic propositions of immediate experience and memory. Though not indubitable, they are highly trustworthy. All my knowledge of what transcends *my* experience, including everything I learn from others, includes variables. When someone tells me, "A is red," using a proper name for something I have not experienced, if I believe him, what I believe is not "A is red" since I am not immediately acquainted with A, but "There is an x such that x is red." (Future experience giving me a percept of A together with a percept of the name "A" may later entitle me to believe "A is red.") Such a view of the nature of empirical knowledge would commit us either to depleting the body of knowledge to an intolerably small set of beliefs, or else to relaxing our insistence that only the belief in true statements may be called knowledge. In order to admit the statements one believes on testimony, statements of things ever experienced anywhere by other human beings, and statements assumed in physical science, we should have to do the latter. In fact, upon examining the limitations of pure empiricism, Russell concludes there are no true empiricists.

Certain principles of logic make difficulties in our epistemological language when we attempt to apply nonsyntactic criteria of truth. They are the principles of extensionality and atomicity. Loosely, the principle of extensionality allows us to insert any atomic proposition in the place of a given atomic proposition in a sentence in the secondary language. But this will obviously not do for sentences stating propositional attitudes. "A believes *p*" should not entitle us to say, by substitution, that A believes any or all propositions whatever. The principle of atomicity in effect requires us to reduce the complex parts of any proposition on a higher language level to their components on the atomic level, then be governed in assessing the truth of the whole by the relationships thus exhibited. Difficulties which these two principles raise in logic have been attacked by Wittgenstein and others by distinguishing between the assertion of a proposition and the mere consideration of a proposition. Russell affirms, however, that the appropriate distinction to be made is between indication and significance. The principle of extensionality will be found to apply to all occurrences of a proposition within a larger proposition when its indication is what is relevant, but not when only its significance is relevant, as is the case with sentences of propositional attitudes. Russell is less sure whether atomicity must be accepted or denied; upon considering the immediacy of perception and, in contrast, the elaborateness of inference involved in applying the principle of atomicity, he is inclined to believe that its application is irrelevant to the theoretical construction of empirical knowledge.

Another matter arising in logic is the challenge to the law of the excluded middle (which says that a proposition must be either true or false, not a third thing). It has been suggested that sentences as yet unverified should not be called either true or false. But Russell clings to a realism, and a correspondence theory of truth, declaring that a sentence is true if its verifier occurs, even though its perception may not be part of anyone's experience. This outlook is extremely helpful in framing hypotheses, he says, and we should not attempt to do without it.

A continually recurring question in any investigation involving logical and nonlogical knowledge is whether anything about the structure of the world can be inferred from the structure of language. Since words are sensible objects, Russell believes that such inference is possible. While we confine the investigation to names and their objects, we have no reason to attempt such inference. But on examining sentences, we find that those like "A is to the left of B" cannot be explained without raising the question of universals. There is no escape from admitting relations as part of the nonlinguistic constitution. A universal is the meaning of a relation-word. "Above" and "before," just as truly as proper names, mean something in perception. Thus, in a logical language there will be some distinctions of parts of speech which correspond to objective distinctions. Again, when we ask whether the word "similar" in recurring instances means the same thing or only similar things, there is no logical escape from granting that it means the same thing, thus establishing the universal "similar." Russell concludes, although with admitted hesitation, that there are universals, and not merely general words. Knowledge must then be not of words alone but of the nonlinguistic world also. One who denies this fact must deny that he even knows when he is using a word; a complete agnosticism is not compatible with the maintenance of linguistic propositions. Hence, Russell believes that the study of syntax can assist us to considerable knowledge of the structure of the world.

With this work, given as the William James Lectures at Harvard University in 1940, Russell has performed at least three worthy services for modern epistemology. By asserting that more than one thing can be known from one experience, that there is more than a single kind of knowledge, and that the mind can attain negative knowledge through perception, he has assigned to the mind a fuller role in shaping its life than that accorded it by positivists and reductionistic philosophers. He has pointed out the necessity for a metaphysic, if only a very simple one, and in doing so has given strength to the counterclaim against logical positivism that logical positivism is itself a metaphysic. Most important, his penetrating criticism has shown the importance of the limitations upon empirical knowledge that its advocates, in their consciousness of the limitations of other kinds of knowledge, are prone to overlook.—*J.T.G.*

PERTINENT LITERATURE

Einstein, Albert. "Remarks on Bertrand Russell's Theory of Knowledge," in *The Philosophy of Bertrand Russell* (The Library of Living Philosophers). Vol. V. Edited by Paul A. Schilpp. Evanston, Illinois: The Library of Living Philosophers, 1946, pp. 277-291.

Albert Einstein used the opportunity afforded by his being asked to contribute to The Library of Living Philosophers' volume on the work of Bertrand Russell to say something about Russell's attempt to resolve the problem concerning the relation of what Einstein calls "sense-impressions" to knowledge. Although Einstein is critical of Russell's reply to that question, it is evident that the great physicist was most of all concerned to generate inquiry concerning the question as to whether "pure thought," as he puts it, can contribute to knowledge—presumably to knowledge of the physical world. (One supposes Einstein must sometimes have wondered how much of what he suggested about the physical world was based on sense experience and how much was the product of his creative intelligence operating independently of any reference to sense-impressions.)

It would be a mistake to think that since Einstein was a physicist he was not therefore a philosopher. As he himself indicates in his essay, "The present difficulties of his science force the physicist to come to grips with philosophical problems to a greater degree than was the case with earlier generations." Not only was Einstein stimulated to be philosophical, but he also shows a remarkable ability to say significant and provocative things in short order.

Einstein begins his critique of Russell with a quotation from *An Inquiry into Meaning and Truth* in which Russell makes the point that we are all naïve realists in childhood but that modern science forces us to realize that the relationship between physical things and the subjective responses to them are very complex and puzzling. If what an observer observes are the effects of things on himself, then knowledge appears to stem from the subjective. Russell concludes: "Naïve realism leads to physics, and physics, if true, shows that naïve realism is false. Therefore, naïve realism, if true, is false; therefore, it is false." (By "naïve realism" Russell means the uncritical belief that "things are what they seem"; he does not explain, however, what it is to believe that things are what they seem. It is nevertheless clear that they do not, at least to a child, seem to be what later on the child learns physics says they are.)

The empirical procedure, the method of acquiring knowledge about physical things through "a working-over of the raw-material furnished by the senses" (as Einstein puts it), has worked and is generally accepted, he writes. But this success in no way implies the impossibility of acquiring knowledge of "reality" by pure speculation.

Einstein describes David Hume as having made the point that essential concepts—such as that of causality—cannot be derived from sense-impressions. That revolutionary point, Einstein claims, has influenced the *best* of the philosophers ever since—Russell included. If whatever we know empirically is not certain, one would be crushed were it not for Immanuel Kant, who maintained (although for the wrong reasons) that if any knowledge is certain, it is grounded in reason itself.

Einstein then comments that although most persons now agree that the concepts Kant thought certain are not certain, there is something correct in what Kant said—namely, that "in thinking we use, with a certain 'right,' concepts to which there is no access from the materials of sensory experience, if the situation is viewed from the logical point of view."

Einstein then goes further. He calls the concepts that make knowledge possible, concepts not derived from sense experience, "free creations of thought which cannot inductively be gained from sense-experiences." He gives as an example the series of integers, and he argues that it would be a mistake to abandon useful concepts and propositions not inductively demonstrable on the ground that they are "metaphysical." All that is required is that the concepts and propositions be such as to make the conceptual system a unified and parsimonious one.

Hence, Einstein concludes, despite Hume's skepticism the only thing to fear is the "fear of metaphysics" itself. Such fear, leading to the rejection of useful concepts that cannot inductively be established, is, he writes, a "malady" just as bad as the early philosophical practice of "philosophizing in the clouds."

The bearing of all this on Russell is that Einstein attributes Russell's conception of things as bundles of sense-qualities to be a consequence of his giving way to the fear of metaphysics. Einstein sees no reason why the "thing," as conceived by physics, cannot function as an independent concept "together with the proper spatio-temporal structure."

(In his reply, also given in the Paul A. Schilpp volume, Russell argues that we are stimulated by experience to count—our having ten fingers led to the decimal system. He contends that it is doubtful that concepts arise independently of sense experience. And he defends his reducing things to bundles of qualities by appealing to Ockham's razor.)

Jager, Ronald. *The Development of Bertrand Russell's Philosophy*. New York: Humanities Press, 1972.

Ronald Jager's study of Bertrand Russell's philosophical development was published in the centenary year of Russell's birth in the Muirhead Library of Philosophy Series. Jager's book is ambitious and rewarding. It attempts to provide a comprehensive account of Russell's intellectual development, and although it could hardly be expected that this work would remark on everything significant accomplished by Russell, it ably surveys the basic stages of Russell's intellectual pilgrimage.

Beginning with an overview of Russell and his work, Jager proceeds to discuss Russell's early metaphysics, his theory of logic, his philosophy of mathematics, logical atomism (including theories of language and theories of knowledge), neutral monism (mind and matter, and the private and public world), politics and education, and ethics and religion. The study concludes with an account of Russell's views concerning the relations of religion and philosophy.

The study of any work by Russell profits from some acquaintance with ideas developed in other works. Hence, although Jager has little to say about *An Inquiry into Meaning and Truth*, he has enough to say about the views presented there but expressed and defended in other works to make the reading of this study all the more rewarding. The sections on truth of propositions, sense-data and constructions, the neutrality of sensations, perception and the external world, perspectival privacy and egocentricity, and structure and knowledge are especially helpful. Of the chapters "Atomism: Theory of Language," "Atomism: Theories of Knowledge," "Neutral Monism: Mind and Matter," and (especially—for here a criticism of the work figures prominently) "Neutral Monism: The Private and the Public World" are the most helpful for one studying *An Inquiry into Meaning and Truth*.

In his Introduction to Russell's philosophy Jager identifies three phases of his thought: the realist phase, the atomist phase, and the neutral monist phase. The realist phase, according to Jager, was concerned with the metaphysical doctrine of external relations; the atomist phase with logical considerations; and the neutral monist phase with the ideals of science. Jager then identifies two dominant themes in Russell's work—the idea that philosophy must begin with logical analysis and then proceed to synthesis, and the idea that technical devices (of logic and mathematics) have their counterparts in general philosophy, and *vice versa*. Jager's study is a critical examination of Russell; the attempt is made not only to explicate Russell's work but also to point out its weaknesses and strengths. The result is a very helpful and substantial work of philosophical review.

Chisholm, Roderick M. "Russell on the Foundations of Empirical Knowledge," in *The Philosophy of Bertrand Russell* (The Library of Living Philosophers). Vol. V. Edited by Paul A. Schilpp. Evanston, Illinois: The Library of Living Philosophers, 1946, pp. 419-444.

Roderick M. Chisholm, of Brown University, presents a searching and detailed examination of Bertrand Russell's account of epistemological order. It is an account which distinguishes between primitive knowledge, consisting in the knowledge of the truth of certain basic "psychological premises," and derivative knowledge based on the former. The focus is on the idea of basic propositions since a psychological premise is defined as a proposition "expressing a belief not derived from any other belief."

Chisholm not only considers what Russell said—an effort that requires speculation on Chisholm's part—but also what Russell might have said; that is, other possibilities that bear on the problem of epistemological order. The analysis throughout is careful and rewarding, and Russell wrote an extended reply (also included in the Paul A. Schilpp volume).

The problem Chisholm considers is that of giving an account of basic propositions such that they can be seen to be indeed basic—not dependent for their understanding or their truth on anything beyond what is given; the evidence for such a proposition was presumed by Russell to be a "perceptive occurrence" which is its cause. Such a proposition must be synthetic, known to be true independently of other propositions, and determinable by analysis as given ("postanalytically" given, as Chisholm puts it). The difficulty in giving such an account is that of formulating immediate knowledge so as to generate epistemological premises that are synthetic, do not refer beyond given sense-data, and can be logically related to the propositions of science.

Chisholm finds difficulties in Russell's suggestion in *An Inquiry into Meaning and Truth* that a basic proposition (reporting a red "patch" as given) of the form "This is red" is better expressed in the form "Redness is here"; the term "red" is a name, not a predicate, and what it names is the quality "red" itself. Such a proposition, Russell argued in his work, does not describe a substance as being red; it refers to a quality as "here-now": "There is something that is redness here-now."

Chisholm reports Russell's view as that of maintaining that in the perceptual situation we are confronted by the universal ("redness") and not by a particular or instance of the universal. Moreover, in this formulation "a more perplexing problem" arises, Chisholm argues—that of avoiding "ego-centric words" in the formulation of basic propositions. ("Ego-centric words" are such words as "this," "that," "here," "now," "I," "me," and so forth, according to Russell in *An Inquiry into Meaning and Truth*.)

As Chisholm reads Russell, Russell attempts to solve the problem of eliminating egocentric particulars by regarding the quality referred to in a basic proposition as part of a "bundle" of qualities; the bundle of qualities is the subject of the proposition, specified by a "name" (such as "this" as in "This is hot," the term "hot" naming the quality); and the judgment of perception, although a "judgment of analysis" (report of analysis) is "not an analytic judgment" (judgment by definition) because we can refer to the bundle by a name without knowing what qualities constitute the bundle.

Chisholm dismisses Russell's theory as having no plausibility. He argues that Russell appears to reintroduce the notion of substance in talking about the unexperienced parts of a whole. Chisholm also argues that not all judgments of perception are judgments of analysis and, finally, that if the "bundles" are bundles of qualities, it would be possible for such a bundle to recur (and hence the presumed basic proposition would not be concerned with a unique fact of the kind that could serve as the foundation of empirical knowledge).

Chisholm suggests, as an alternative solution to the problem of egocentric particulars, the introduction of "time-qualia," on the assumption that *times*, like colors, sounds, and so on, can be experienced immediately; the reference to a time of a quality would thus be specific without the use of an egocentric word.

In his reply to Chisholm, Russell spends more than half of the space defending the claim that there is an epistemological order. He states his agreement with most of what Chisholm writes. He denies, however, that he asserted or believes that a quality is a universal; it is a particular. He reaffirms his belief and hope that every judgment of perception is a partial analysis of a whole that is a bundle of qualities. He argues that although we can always experience the parts of such a bundle if we attend to them, it is also possible that we can identify a whole without attending to each and every one of its parts. The possibility of recurrence Russell regards as "a merit." Finally, he rejects the "time-qualia" proposal as "not . . . plausible" for two reasons: he can find no sense qualia in his experience, and the theory makes time absolute instead of relational.

ADDITIONAL RECOMMENDED READING

Pears, D. F., ed. *Bertrand Russell: A Collection of Critical Essays*. Garden City, New York: Anchor Books, 1972. An excellent anthology of critical articles by eminent philosophers: W. V. O. Quine, A. J. Ayer, D. F. Pears, Jaakko Hintikka, Anthony Quinton, Grover Maxwell, Charles A. Fritz, Jr., G. Kreisel, Rudolf Carnap, Kurt Gödel, David Kaplan, Charles S. Chihara, Jules Vuillemin, and D. H. Munro. Harru Ruja provides an excellent bibliography of works by and about Russell.

Schilpp, Paul A., ed. *The Philosophy of Bertrand Russell* (The Library of Living Philosophers). Vol. V. Evanston, Illinois: The Library of Living Philosophers, 1946. An invaluable collection of critical articles, plus Russell's autobiographical account, replies to his critics, and a bibliography of his writings to 1944. Includes material by Hans Reichenbach, Morris Weitz, Kurt Gödel, James Feibleman, G. E. Moore, Max Black, Philip P. Wiener, Albert Einstein, John Laird, Ernest Nagel, W. T. Stace, Andrew Paul Ushenko, Roderick M. Chisholm, Harold Chapman Brown, John Elof Boodin, Justus Buchler, Edgar Sheffield Brightman, Eduard C. Lindeman, Boyd H. Bode, and Sidney Hook.

REVELATION AND REASON

Author: Heinrich Emil Brunner (1889-1966)
Type of work: Theology, epistemology
First published: 1941

PRINCIPAL IDEAS ADVANCED

Divine revelation alone must be the ground, norm, and content of the Church's proclamation; for a believing Church, inquiry begins with revelation and works toward reason.

Revelation is Jesus Christ; and faith is not belief in doctrine, but knowledge through personal encounter.

Since God is Absolute Subject, there is no knowledge of God except by God's own action.

God known through reason is an abstraction; God known through revelation is a living person.

Reason is not a thing-in-itself, but a relation which is what it is because of the original revelation in Creation; man, the sinner, retains his rational nature, but what he has lost is the right attitude of reason.

Emil Brunner is one of the best-known spokesmen for the neo-orthodox movement in contemporary Protestant theology. Its leading representative is certainly Karl Barth, but Brunner has been more widely read in this country. The reason for this is threefold. First, Brunner's style is far more readable, and therefore his books have been translated into English sooner than Barth's primary works; second, Brunner has been the more systematic of the two; third, and most important, Brunner is not as extreme and uncompromising as Barth. Brunner's mediating attempt is more amenable to the Anglo-American temperament. While Barth takes the extreme Christianity-against-culture approach, thoroughly unsympathetic to all philosophical approaches to theism, and others such as Paul Tillich stand at the opposite pole, Brunner attempts to bridge these extremes, bringing the truths of revelation into meaningful dialogue with the truths of reason.

Yet, in assuming such a mediating role, it is necessary for a theologian to make one end of the spectrum the foundation of his dialogue. In this Brunner clearly exhibits himself as belonging to the Barthian predilection. *Revelation and Reason* is one of his best and most representative works in this regard. Here he makes his point of departure quite clear. "It is no accident that there are plenty of books with the title *Reason and Revelation*, but that there is none with the title *Revelation and Reason*. The usual order, 'Reason and Revelation,' is derived from the medieval-Catholic doctrinal tradition. . . . The reversal of this order, suggested by the title of this book, is the necessary consequence of a theological outlook which understands even the man who has not been gripped by the Christian message—and his reason—from the standpoint of the Word of God. . . . We do not begin our inquiry with reason and then work up to revelation, but, as a believing Church, we begin our inquiry with revelation and then work outwards to reason." Brunner and Barth begin together, and are in fundamental agreement, but Brunner moves farther out beyond the confines of the Church.

This difference began early in Brunner's career and caused a split between the two men. The argument began over the problem of the *imago Dei*, the image of God. In Genesis 1:27 it is recorded that "God created man in His own image, in the image of God He created him." From the inception of Christian theology the problem which has emerged is this—what is this image in man, and what is its condition consequent to man's fall? While theologians such as St. Augustine, Luther, and Calvin speak vehemently of this image being "lost," "corrupted," or "thoroughly maimed," other theologians have regarded man's plight in a more optimistic light.

Saint Thomas Aquinas and consequently Roman Catholics in general translate the passage to read, "God created man in His image, in His likeness created He him." The distinction is thus made between "image" and "likeness." The image, characterized by reason, is not lost but was preserved after the fall in essential integrity. Man's reason, even outside the purgative affects of grace, can function correctly and permit man to know and fulfill the natural end of man, characterized by the natural virtues of justice, prudence, temperance, and fortitude. Further, natural (unaided) reason can know God's existence and some of his attributes. In other words, reason is a powerful aid in bringing man to faith, and thus is the natural ally of the Church. It is the "likeness" of God in man which was lost in the fall. This likeness, those qualities which render man God-like, are characterized by the virtues of faith, hope, and love; the attainment of these is the theological end of man, for which divine grace, mediated through the sacraments of the Church, is indispensable.

During the Protestant Reformation this problem of the divine image became central. Man cannot "earn" salvation, Luther insisted; man can neither know nor follow God unless grace transforms the individual—"*all* man's righteousness is as filthy rags." Following St. Augustine, the Reformers insisted that it is the will, not reason, that is central in man; until the will is reoriented in love to God through grace, all acts, reasoning, and thoughts are sinful, for they have the self as center. The image in man is totally disoriented, and thus depraved; reason is not the agent of truth, but simply the act of rationalizing for the human *status quo*. Faith and faith alone justifies, and faith is God's doing and God's alone.

During the period of liberalism in Protestantism, the Reformation doctrine of man was largely lost; the chasm between reason and grace was glossed over, and revelation was judged before the bar of reason. With the theological renaissance in contemporary Protestantism, however, what was rediscovered (meriting for the movement the title "neo-orthodox" or "neo-Reformation") was this very matter of the Reformation doctrine of man. Taking their lead from Luther, and consequently St. Augustine and St. Paul, theologians like Brunner and Barth insisted upon the impotence of the divine image in man. Barth, the father of this movement, was most uncompromising at this point; it is here, he insisted, that Roman Catholics and Protestants are forever divided. God is known only when the Eternal Subject acts toward men; this was done at one point in history. Since God is subject, all attempts of reason to know him are doomed to failure and perversion, for of necessity they make the Subject into an object.

With this Brunner agreed, but he saw clearly the difficulty involved in Barth's insistence. If the image is utterly lost, in what respect is man still man? Unless something of man's essential nature remains, two consequences are inevitable. First, the Christian theodicy collapses, for man can no longer be regarded responsible for his own actions and, consequently, for the continuation of the effects of the fall; second, if salvation is totally God's doing, in which man is the unconscious pawn, how can one say that it is man who is saved? Without freedom in some regard, salvation is simply God's answer to his own call. Brunner's fundamental difficulty is thus explained by this question: How can man be placed in true dialogue with the God of grace, responsible for his sin as well as capable of response, and still be regarded as impotent without divine grace?

Brunner's basic insistence is that, despite the present glorification of scientific method, divine revelation alone must be the ground, norm, and content of the Church's proclamation. The past error of the Church has been in mistaking Scripture or dogma for revelation. For Brunner, revelation *is* Jesus Christ, "God Himself in His self-manifestation within history." Revelation is event, and Scripture simply witnesses to it. Correlatively, faith is not belief in doctrine, but knowledge through personal encounter which creates obedient trust. Roman Catholicism and Protestantism have tended to forget this, the former absolutizing the Church, the latter absolutizing Scripture.

Science and biblical criticism have destroyed the idea of biblical infallibility and are making possible a correct understanding of revelation. What needs to be done now, Brunner holds, is to show that faith does not suppress any legitimate claim of reason; rather, "the true interest of reason is only rightly preserved and maintained in faith." Because revelation illumines the mind *through* man's acts of understanding and will, faith must be dialectical—God *and man* in dialogue. The theologian is thus characterized not by greater faith, but by "greater power of thought in the service of faith." Natural and revealed knowledge are poles apart, but without the former, the latter remains unexpressed and vaguely understood.

Brunner's fundamental insistence is that since God is "Absolute Subject," there is no true knowledge of God except that which is given by God's own action. This fact indicates human sin, for it implies man's separation from God; in the beginning there was an original revelation from which man turned. The aim of the second revelation, Jesus Christ, is not simply the communication of knowledge but human restoration, the creation of the community of love. This occurs when revelation effects the disclosure of the neighbor as a "Thou" because God replaces the "I" as center. It is for this reason that the history of revelation *is* the history of salvation.

Revelation is always unexpected, for man has no right to expect forgiveness. The most critical revelation is the sacrificial death of Jesus Christ, for on it alone divine forgiveness depends. But this revelation must not be separated from its reception—the subjective process is an integral part. Revelation is both fact and illumination. This total act of faith is *sui generis*, for it belongs totally in the "I-Thou" dimension, not that of "objective" knowledge. Faith is a subject-subject relation with Christ which *is itself* justifying; theology is reflection upon this faith.

Faith is supernatural in the sense that its origin is God. But, Brunner maintains, it is also natural, for it enables man to become that for which he was created. Man can love unselfishly only when he has first been loved; he can give himself unconditionally only because God so gave himself in Jesus Christ. Without this event, every human attempt makes God a means to an end, one relation among many.

Consequently, Brunner insists, the mode of "knowing" God affects completely the nature of the "God" known. The "God" known through reason is an object, an absolute, an abstraction. The God of Christian revelation, however, is a living person. In believing on faith, God is not first known as Creator, but in knowing God as Lord he is then known as Creator *ex nihilo*. Likewise, God is "wholly other," knowing wrath against human sin; still he reveals himself as willing to love the sinner. Such a paradox, resting in God's *decision*, cannot be known through reason—"this idea of God bursts through and destroys all fundamental categories of thought." Further, in Christ God is revealed as Triune—God throughout history is he "who is to be revealed, who reveals, and who is being revealed: Father, Son, and Spirit." Herein the Incarnation is revealed as at the heart of God's eternal plan.

Revelation, however, is not only of God but of man. It is through Christ that man truly knows himself as sinner, as disobedient to the original revelation. If Christianity does not affirm this critical revelation, Brunner insists, it must affirm man as *essentially* sinful. But for Brunner, man's freedom is primary, and man is distinguished from other creatures by his ability to sin. It is this original revelation which makes man a responsible being.

Here we come to the heart of Brunner's understanding of reason. Reason is not a "thing-in-itself," but a relation, for it comes from perception. When the philosopher says that the core of reason is transcendental, he is pointing to what Christianity identifies as reason's essential relation to God. Every use of reason, Brunner insists, implies this relation which is the general revelation; for example, multiplication implies the presupposition of infinite number, verification implies the standard of "absolute Truth." But not only is reason what it is because of the general revelation, but therein is contained the cause of its unrest—it is "derived from God and has been made for God." Thus, for Brunner, reason is not ignored in faith, but fulfilled, restored to its created relation. Man is nothing in himself; the same is true of reason.

This original or general revelation is revelation in Creation. It is further witnessed to in conscience. Man knows within himself what is commanded and forbidden, but not why or by whom. Barth mistakenly denies this revelation; Brunner affirms, because he sees it as competing with particular revelation. But for Brunner the former is the presupposition of the latter. Yet Brunner rejects "natural theology," for because of the fall only one "whose eyes have been opened by Jesus Christ" is in a position to recognize the general revelation which is given to all men. For the sinner, general revelation has no "saving significance," for in it God does not meet man personally. In both kinds of revelation the same Triune God is revealer; only the form differs. In this rests the significance of the Crucifixion: man is not simply ignorant but guilty in his ignorance, for he does not know because he *does not want to know*. Man retains the *imago Dei*, his rational nature, but what is lost is the right attitude of reason. Thus, for Brunner, general revelation is the basis for human responsibility, being the point of contact for the "call to repentance." This, Brunner insists, is the truth of Scripture which Barth refuses to admit because he does not clearly distinguish between "knowing" and "being."

In the Old Testament, God reveals *who* he is—herein rests the importance of God's name. In the New Testament, God reveals *what* he is—thus the importance of God's Word. Through revelation of his name God's presence is established as the "Thou," but, for Brunner, God is still not personally present—he is revealed as promise. The Old Testament prophecy of the "suffering servant" is the climax, for it is the supreme promise of the divine act fulfilled in Jesus Christ. Christ could come only to people prepared by God's promise. In Christ, God's being and will are "finally and completely revealed." As a teacher Jesus is simply one among many. His uniqueness is that his message and person are identical, for revelation and atonement are one. Brunner's Christology is as "high" as any in contemporary theology— Jesus Christ "is God Himself. When He speaks, God Himself speaks; when He acts, God Himself acts; in His personal presence the personal presence of God has become real." All intellectual Trinitarian and Christological affirmations Brunner holds to be simply attempts to express this fact.

Scripture is necessary, but it belongs to the Old Testament revelation, for it is not itself the personal confrontation. Yet through it the confrontation occurs. And since reception is part of revelation, the apostolic response is an indispensable part of the divine act itself. The Scriptures are divinely inspired, but, for Brunner, this inspiration is far from "verbal" or literal. They are human testimonies under the guidance of the Spirit.

Man cannot be redeemed without the Scripture, yet the Scripture is not sufficient; each man must be addressed where he is. This is the task of the Church. Although its doctrine is not revelation, Christ is present only "through definite ideas." Thus, for Brunner, theology and preaching must remain in constant dialogue, both being confessional, and the temptation of a closed theological system must be totally dismissed.

Certainty of the Christian revelation is derived in only one way—one believes only when the Holy Spirit permits the Scriptural witness to dawn on one as Truth. In this manner the believer "knows" Jesus as the Christ in the identical manner as the first disciples. To so know is to be redeemed. But faith is always imperfect, for it is always a process of "*becoming* sure." The world contradicts the victory which the Resurrection promises. Consequently, in this life one lives by faith, not by "sight"—risk, doubt, uncertainty are always present. This wrestling with unfaith is man's continual temptation to sin, springing not from intellectual honesty but from the intellectual arrogance of making human reason the measure of all things. The Church's disastrous response was the attempt to provide "proof." The necessary weakness of all such attempts, Brunner contends, has greatly weakened contemporary Christianity. It is only to a man whose belief in the autonomy of reason has been shattered that it can be shown that revelation possesses its own logic and facts. God must not be given a place within reason, but the reverse. It is only when this reversal does not occur, Brunner claims, that revelation and reason are at odds.

Brunner attempts to bring this contention to play on some crucial relations between Christianity and other areas. First, in regard to other religions, Christianity must not assume itself to have a monopoly on revelation but other revelations are given only the preparatory and prophetic function which belongs to the Old Testament. In all religions there are distorted "relics" of the original revelation, but only in Christianity, Brunner insists, has the Word become flesh. Second, in regard to "naturalistic" philosophy of religion, he is uncompromising—"A man is *either* a believing Christian *or* a religious man in the sense of Schleiermacher or Kant; but he cannot be both." Third, in regard to science, revelation provides no knowledge at all concerning the scientific structure of things. Biblical "science" is prescientific and must be rejected as extraneous. Science can understand miracles in a perfectly natural way, and this does not destroy revelation. Faith is not dependent on miracles, for a miracle is seen to be such only through the eyes of faith. A miracle declares nothing more than God's freedom from the limitations of the world. Jesus Christ is the only indispensable miracle. The scientist, Brunner claims, who is cognizant of the "miracle" of life and mind cannot be antagonistic to the Christian claim. The tension between Christianity and science arises only when either leaves its own sphere. And last, philosophy witnesses to revelation through its presuppositions. In the moral realm it points to the human condition with its bludgeoning "ought." The convincing power and content of the theistic arguments depend on their support by the Christian tradition, without which they are tentative and misleading.

What Brunner is attempting to do throughout is to restore the Augustinian understanding of faith and reason. For St. Augustine, they belong together. The correct relation is "faith seeking understanding." An autonomous philosophy is impossible. The reversal of St. Thomas Aquinas, understanding seeking faith, permitted the wedge which eventually ended in the contemporary autonomy of both spheres. While Barth has attempted to restore faith through the total rejection of autonomous philosophy, Brunner attempts the same restoration by bringing reason back to its former Augustinian relation. As Brunner says, the difference between the Christian theologian and the Christian philosopher is one of subject, not of method. The problem of Christian philosophy is that of penetrating every sphere of life with the Christian spirit—"Christ conquers the reason and in so doing makes it free to serve." —*W.P.J.*

PERTINENT LITERATURE

Hordern, William. *A Layman's Guide to Protestant Theology*. New York: Macmillan Publishing Company, 1968.

Heinrich Emil Brunner was an early supporter of much of the new theological perspective introduced by Karl Barth. Nevertheless, he strongly disagreed with Barth regarding what Brunner in a 1929 article called "The Other Task of Theology." Brunner argued that alongside dogmatic theology, which expounds the content of Christian doctrine, should be apologetic theology, which would relate dogmatic theology to current intellectual issues and problems: Brunner called this sort of theology "eristic" ("eris" meaning "dispute") and "missionary" in view of its endeavor to relate Christianity to contemporary thought.

The core of apologetic theology, or apologetics, according to Brunner, is not proving to nonbelievers that Christian doctrines are true, but is rather a matter of exposing and challenging the presuppositions or assumptions of non-Christian thought as well as relating dogmatic theology to the issues of the day. Not to engage in this effort, he claimed, is an exercise in Chinese-wall-building. Without apologetics, dogmatics is in isolation from the world of thought to whose inhabitants the Christian message is directed. Brunner wrote much in the area of apologetics or eristic theology; *Revelation and Reason* is one of his contributions to it. William Hordern discusses Brunner's notion of "truth as encounter" and the concepts most closely connected with it.

We distinguish, Hordern notes, between the subject, or one who thinks, and the object, or what is thought about. He adds that it is easy to go on to distinguish objective thinking, in which one lets the facts speak for themselves irrespective of one's desires, and subjective thinking, in which one lets one's desires determine what the facts are taken to be; a further step is to assume that all thinking whatever is either objective or subjective. Brunner, Hordern points out, was not willing to make this assumption.

If one applies this dichotomy to theology, Hordern claims, one has the alternatives of trying to base theology on each person's inner experience or of resting it on statements found in the Bible. He reports that Brunner rejects the former because the net result is innumerable appeals to individual authority on behalf of incompatible views—in short, subjective chaos. The latter, he says, Brunner rejects because it supposes that revelation lies ready to hand within the covers of a book, and such a view, he holds, is inconsistent with the fact that revelation requires an encounter which God Himself initiates.

Hordern specifies various sources of Brunner's thought. One source of Brunner's emphasis is the doctrine of the Reformers that the Holy Spirit speaks to the believer through the Bible, so that there is both external and internal witness. Another is the biblical record itself to the effect that rather than human beings seeking God, God seeks human beings, and if a creature does seek the Creator, it is on the Creator's initiative. Still another is the distinction Brunner accepts from Søren Kierkegaard and Martin Buber between I-it and I-thou relationships, and the corresponding distinction between it-knowledge and thou-knowledge.

According to Hordern, Brunner proposes that the best analogy for understanding the knowledge of God is the knowledge one person has of another when they know each other as persons—when their knowledge of the properties and traits of each other is mingled with mutual affection and concern. For Brunner, Hordern explains, such knowledge is objective in the sense of involving awareness of things that are true independent of whether one wants them to be true, but it is not disinterested and detached. It is subjective in the sense of including personal involvement, desires, and hopes, but not in the sense of being necessarily unrelated to, or unconcerned with, the facts of the matter. In Brunner's view, Hordern emphasizes, it fits neither the model of the purely subjective nor the model of the purely objective, and yet it is of great importance to us.

Hordern indicates that Brunner follows up this analogy, proposing that knowledge of God is a matter of God's encountering human beings, causing them to have an experience of which he is the object, but in which they do not and cannot remain possible observers; in such experience, we have a sort of knowledge which perfectly fits neither the objective nor the subjective pattern, but which contains elements of both.

Jewett, Paul K. *Emil Brunner's Concept of Revelation.* London: James Clarke and Company, 1954.

Paul K. Jewett tells us that while Søren Kierkegaard had said that faith is the "cross of speculation" on which reflection is crucified, Heinrich Emil Brunner both refined and mitigated his polemic against reason. It is for him not revelation *or* reason, but revelation *and* reason. Reason, the capacity for logically consistent reflection, is for Brunner God's good gift. Yet, Jewett notes, Brunner also speaks favorably of paradoxes. Understanding why he not only insists the light of reason in human beings is God's "highest and most glorious creation" but also favors the use of paradox in theology will bring with it an understanding of Brunner's view of the relationship between revelation and reason.

Jewett remarks that Brunner distinguishes between two kinds of truth, which he describes variously as objective, subjective, rational, personal, abstract, truth which is communicated, God truth, world truth, it-truth, and thou-truth. Translated into distinctions between kinds of knowledge, one gets the knowledge of address and the knowledge of reflection, or natural knowledge and revelational knowledge.

These distinctions, Jewett suggests, come to much the same thing. "It-truth" is truth accessible to human beings by their own effort. While all truth is God's truth, there are truths we can come to know on our own, given the capacities God has given us and the intelligible nature of the world God created. Jewett says that, for Brunner, such truth concerns not God but the world, and the basic criterion for such truth is coherence, or absense of contradiction in a system or network of propositions. Brunner thinks that our temptation is to suppose that all truth is it-truth.

Jewett explains that if one yields to this temptation, then, according to Brunner, one's knowledge of "God" will be knowledge of an uncaused cause which is conceived of more as an abstract principle than as a person and is more properly called "The Absolute" than "God." One will attempt to explain and interpret everything in statements expressing only it-truth and learned autonomously. Brunner, taking a cue from Immanuel Kant, maintains that such attempts at full explanation and interpretation inherently end in antinomies. Hence they inherently fail.

Jewett adds that correspondingly, for Brunner, practical reason, reason concerned with conduct, both shows what duty demands and reveals that one has not met this demand; therefore, a sense of guilt arises; for one knows that he has done what ought not to have been done and left undone what ought to have been done—and so faces an antinomy of sorts between what one is and what one ought to be. The temptation here is to assume that one can bridge the gap by one's effort alone. Jewett writes that Brunner holds that the moral gap between what we are and what we ought to be is our fault, created by our wrong choices, freely made, although he also holds that, once created, the gap is something we cannot bridge. The presence of antinomies in explanations and interpretations which stick to it-truth alone is, in Brunner's view, inherent; we are at fault here, in his opinion, only by virtue of failing to recognize this inherent limitation.

Brunner, Jewett finds, sometimes goes so far as to condemn reason, or our rational capacity, itself for the antinomies, and even to place the moral blame on the finitude rather than the fallenness of humankind. But these, Jewett contends, are not the central and sustaining features of his thought.

Jewett remarks that, for Brunner, it-truth must be joined by thou-truth if the presence of antinomies is to be eliminated. Thou-truth is truth about God which is not acccessible to us by our efforts, but comes only from God's activity on our behalf. One who accepts revelation, Brunner contends, gives up the claim to accepting only truth that he or she has ferreted out autonomously. Analogously, in Brunner's view, repentance and acceptance of God's forgiveness because of what Christ did for us obviates any pretense of complete autonomy concerning the gap between what we are and what we ought to be.

Jewett reminds us that according to Brunner revelation involves things which are "inconceivable": that God created the world from nothing, and that God the Creator became one of us to redeem us from our sins. These truths, Brunner claims, do not and need not meet the criterion of systematic coherence or absence of contradiction. Thou-truth is "seen" in the act of decision of accepting it; it is grasped when one is involved in the divinely initiated encounter with God which comprises revelation. When we *speak* about revelation, it is no longer *revelation* that we speak about.

As the emphasis of this last sentence indicates, Brunner uses paradox to deal with the alleged ineffability of revelation. Brunner, then, Jewett points out, ascribes to reason the range of it-truth, and to revelation the range of thou-truth. So long as each observes its "proper boundaries," Brunner holds, no conflicts can arise. For example, any conflict between science and faith is really between pseudoscience and faith or pseudofaith and science.

Still, Brunner insists that the same rational capacities which make the seeking and finding of it-truth a possibility is involved in grasping revelation in a divine-human encounter, although it may not be clear how this happens or clear how it *can* happen. Repentance, for example, is a condition of faith and involves a change of thought about oneself and God; but a change of thought is thought, and thought is the exercise of our rational capacities. So, Jewett emphasizes, for Brunner, the exercise of reason is an essential component in the exercise of faith. The God who created the world as the locus of it-truth is himself the locus of thou-truth.

Jewett adds that Brunner denies that it is possible to give an exact account of the spheres proper to reason and to revelation. What can be said about this involves the law of contiguity which is usually expressed in terms of a series of concentric circles around a center.

Jewett expounds Brunner's notion as follows: The center represents "the dimension of the personal." The circles represent "the dimension of the non-personal." Logic and mathematics fall within the most exterior circle. Theology falls within the circle nearest the center. Other disciplines fall in the circles in between. Psychology will probably be closer to the center than chemistry, which will thus be nearer to mathematics and logic than is psychology. The degree of competency that reason possesses in a discipline, according to Brunner, is a function of how closely that discipline approaches to the "sphere of the personal." The closer the approach, the less the competence. But no fully adequate statement of the relationship between reason and revelation is possible.

Jewett indicates that Brunner talks of the disturbance of rational knowledge brought about by sin and of the corrective role of faith. Because of sin, when as sinners we reason concerning what is personal, we deal with it in abstract terms. Reason, uncorrected by revelation, treats persons as objects, or replaces thou-truth by it-truth. Even in theology, Brunner claims, one finds a tendency to treat God as an impersonal principle. Further, Jewett notes, while he grants that theology requires the use of concepts, the truly biblical theologian, according to Brunner, will not regard any system of theology as fixed or final.

Beyond this, however, Jewett emphasizes, is Brunner's radical theory of statements which express revelation as paradoxical—not merely apparently but really contradictory. For Brunner, the revelation, God's Word, is expressed in human words, and the human words express a paradox or contradiction. Is God's Word, the revelation itself, then also contradictory? Brunner's answer is negative. Although the connection between the Word and (human) words is sacramental and indissoluble, still the words are but a sign pointing to the Word. Jewett points out, however, that in fact contradictory statements point nowhere, or anywhere one pleases, and a revelation expressed in contradictions leaves us without a revelation. Further, Jewett insists, in Brunner's view we are left with no criterion for deciding between competing alleged revelations. What begins as an appeal to the final authority of a word from God ends in subjectivism.—*K.E.Y.*

ADDITIONAL RECOMMENDED READING

Allen, Edgar L. *Creation and Grace: A Guide to the Thought of Emil Brunner*. London: Hodder and Stoughton, 1950. A discussion of Brunner's thought through some of its key concepts.
Henry, Carl F. H. *God, Revelation and Authority*. Waco, Texas: Word Books,

1976. A detailed statement of orthodox Protestant theology, including its relation to Brunner's thought.

Humphrey, James Edward. *Emil Brunner*. Waco, Texas: Word Books, 1976. An introduction to Brunner's theology.

Jewett, Paul K. *Emil Brunner*. Chicago: Inter-Varsity Press, 1961. A short and useful introduction to the man and his thought.

Kegley, Charles W., ed. *The Living Theology of Emil Brunner*. New York: Macmillan Publishing Company, 1962. An excellent collection of essays on Brunner's work.

THE NATURE AND DESTINY OF MAN

Author: Reinhold Niebuhr (1892-1971)
Type of work: Theology
First published: 1941-1943

PRINCIPAL IDEAS ADVANCED

Man is both a child of nature and a spirit who stands outside nature.

Man has the capacity for self-transcendence; he can view himself as an object, thereby making himself a moral creature, subject to conscience.

Man's state of anxiety supplies him with the creative energy to transform the natural through the love of God.

The alternative to faith, made possible by man's freedom, is sin; and sin is an act of will whereby the self, rather than God, becomes the center of human concern.

God is agape, *self-giving love, and such love is not possible in this life; but by commitment to such love man transcends himself and in the knowledge of God's forgiveness accepts judgment without despair.*

Reinhold Niebuhr is perhaps more responsible for the contemporary renaissance of theology in America than any other single man. With the possible exceptions of Jonathan Edwards and Horace Bushnell, America has been rather unsuccessful in making unique contributions to Christian theology. Rather, the American contribution to religion, especially since the latter part of the nineteenth century, has been a unique social fervor, an ethical "activism," which is often absent in Continental Christianity.

This social passion grew during the last century into the movement known as the "social gospel," fathered by Washington Gladden. Although it is dangerous to generalize concerning this diverse group, the social gospel became characterized by an accent on human capacity, the ethical side of religion, the "simple teachings of Jesus," and a rather wholesale de-emphasis of theology and dogma. Walter Rauschenbusch was the most moderate and profound representative of this movement. Niebuhr has called him not only the real founder of social Christianity but "its most brilliant and generally satisfying exponent to the present day."

As a young devotee of Rauschenbusch, Niebuhr entered a Detroit labor parish in 1915, prepared to establish social justice through the nurturing of human love. In the crucible of social conflict, Niebuhr discovered that the key problem was not one of personal ethics but of social structure and strategy. Detroit industrialists were no less moral in their personal relations than the average laborer, but in a system of competitive capitalism, operating by the impersonal laws of market, profit, supply, and demand, direct application of the "simple teachings of Jesus" to the social sphere was impossible. As a result of this practical conviction, Niebuhr wrote a volume in 1933 which shook the American theological scene as strongly as did Barth's *The Epistle to the Romans* on the Continent in 1918. While strongly tempered by liberal theology, Niebuhr's *Moral Man and Immoral Society* marked the beginning of social realism in contemporary American Christianity. Gone was the idealism of the liberal period; the Kingdom of God was not man's to build, not simply in this generation but in any generation. The Kingdom was the "impossible possibility" standing over against man eternally, the ideal perfect community of mutual love, judging all man's attempts to emulate it. The only possible possibilities were transient and imperfect forms of justice.

Accompanying these insights came Niebuhr's rejection of absolutism in ethics: there are no absolute goods and evils. The problem of ethics is the never-ending task of finding "proximate solutions for insoluble problems." Accompanying this position, classically formulated in Niebuhr's *An Interpretation of Christian Ethics*, was a growing shift in emphasis from the liberal stress on society as the molder of man, to the nature of man as the key to the nature and problems of society. The orthodox doctrine of original sin became increasingly more relevant for Niebuhr in understanding the problems of culture. Man is essentially self-centered, seeking self-aggrandizement and domination over others. While this tendency can be checked to a large degree on the personal level within the small confines of the interdependent family, in the larger dimensions of community, group, nation, and hemisphere, personal pride is compounded into impersonal, immoral, irresponsible pressure groups seeking their own untempered ends in hypocritical self-righteousness.

This understanding early led Niebuhr to sympathy with the Marxist analysis of social forces, but he saw that the Marxist realism about the present was naïvely undermined by an unfounded optimism about human capacity in the proletarian future. In 1944 these thoughts coalesced in a brilliant vindication of democracy, *The Children of Light and the Children of Darkness*. Here was combined Niebuhr's political movement to the "left" with his theological movement toward the "right." All previous apologies for democracy, he declared, were wrongly grounded on an optimistic doctrine of man, defending it as the only form of government which respected human capacity. Such a defense, Niebuhr insisted, can lead only to catastrophe; Locke must be tempered with Hobbes, as well as the reverse.

Man is capable of self-transcendence, but he is likewise motivated by an even stronger desire for domination. Socialism controls man, but in a manner which undercuts the creativity that emerges from self-transcendence; further, those tendencies which make control necessary undermine the integrity of those given the power to control. On the other hand, laissez faire democracy so liberates man that his selfish propensities, compounded by monopoly, by cartels, and by simple numbers, destroy the integrity of the less organized and less privileged, using them as tools for maintaining their competitive place in society. The plight of the worker several decades ago, exploited by the industrialist not out of vindictiveness but out of the necessity of competing in an uncontrolled business world, is Niebuhr's favorite case in point.

The only realistic answer for this dilemma Niebuhr sees in democracy. The only structure for social justice is that of competing pressure groups, deadlocked by their conflicting self-interests and thereby forced into self-transcendence for the mutual good. Since group power is never constant but changed by the circumstances of each new situation, democracy has two unique advantages. Its carefully designed system of internal checks and balances is alone in a position to prevent excessive governmental control, while its representative legislation can delegate power to the underprivileged and restrain the irresponsible. This system requires constant change and vigilance, for today's justice may be tomorrow's greatest injustice. To summarize with one of Niebuhr's most famous statements, "man's capacity for justice makes democracy possible; but man's inclination to injustice makes democracy necessary."

This is the basic understanding which runs throughout Niebuhr's prolific writings on economics, political theory, international relations, and the like. His writing career, however, was climaxed in 1939 with his two Gifford Lecture series, combined in a large volume entitled *The Nature and Destiny of Man: A Christian Interpretation*. It is indicative of the contemporary theological scene that a social ethicist, confessedly a minister and not a scholar, should have produced such a theological classic. Niebuhr's lifetime of practical thinking is here placed in a carefully created intellectual dialogue attempting to bring the various aspects of his thought into a systematic structure.

One appraisal of Niebuhr's general theological position may be helpful. Although he is often placed in the general school of "neo-orthodoxy" (see the article on Karl Barth's *The Knowledge of God and the Service of God*), this label is misleading. Niebuhr remains in essential agreement with Rauschenbusch on such theological matters as Christology, redemption, and eschatology, with one fundamental difference: his doctrine of man is far more "orthodox." But even here there are differences. It appears that the combination of a negative doctrine of man with an essentially "liberal" understanding of the remaining tenets of Christianity is the reason for much of the ambiguity in Niebuhr's thought. *The Nature and Destiny of Man* is Niebuhr's most conscientious attempt to reconcile these elements, but it remains an imperfect attempt. As a result, it is the first series of the lectures dealing with the nature of man, that is Niebuhr's best work; it is without doubt a unique and lasting contribution to American theology.

"Man has always been his own most vexing problem." Thus Niebuhr begins, analyzing rationalism, romanticism, Marxism, idealism, and naturalism as alternative attempts of Western thought to come to terms with the curious contradictions constituting the enigma which is man. For Niebuhr, anthro-

pology is *the* problem from which all others follow, and theological anthropology alone is capable of dealing with the whole man. He systematically
undermines every attempt to establish man as a simplex being, whether in
terms of reason, animality, or the like.

For Niebuhr, every human contradiction points to two paradoxical facts
about man. First, "man is a child of nature, subject to its vicissitudes, compelled by its necessities, driven by its impulses. . . ." Second, man is a "spirit
who stands outside of nature, life, himself, his reason and the world." It is
only the Christian view which succeeds in holding these two aspects together.
Not to do this is to overestimate or underestimate man, both of which actions
bring tragic practical consequences, whether they be the tyranny of totalitarianism or the exploitation by laissez-faire captialism.

For the Christian, man is created in the "image of God," and in this rests
his transcendence over nature. As Niebuhr understands this, the *imago* refers
to man's capacity for self-transcendence, to make an object of himself, to
stand continually outside himself in an indefinite regression. This is the root
of "conscience," for it gives to man a capacity for objectivity about himself,
viewing himself as an object, appraising the degree to which this "object" acts
as he would want to be acted toward. This ability and this inborn "golden
rule," similar to Kant's ethic of rational consistency, is the source of morality
for Niebuhr. Man is not only "spirit" but he is also "natural"; he is a finite
creature. Finitude does not mean evil, but dependency, creatureliness. This
polarity means that man is at the intersection of time and eternity, or finitude
and infinity, or nature and spirit.

The law of man's nature is love, pointed to by man's self-transcendence
but clearly revealed in the Christian revelation. God's intent was that man
should have faith, trust, in the Creator, loving him for the gift of existence,
and in gratitude loving his neighbor as he had been loved. Being at the
intersection of nature (under the necessity of instinct, need, and drive) and
spirit (under the freedom of infinite possibility), the inevitable condition of
man is anxiety. If man trusts in God, he knows his anxious state to be God-
intended, and anxiety therefore becomes the energy of creativity—infinite
possibilities come as challenges, as leaven for humble achievement in service
to God and man. The spirit transforms the natural by bringing it to fulfillment—this is to become a self. This was God's plan in creating the world.

Because of man's freedom, another option is open. This possibility Niebuhr
finds classically portrayed in Genesis in terms of the Garden of Eden. This
story, he insists, is not history but myth—myth, however, not in the sense of
"falsehood," but in the Platonic sense or the sense in which it is used in
literature. Myth is the vehicle for communicating truths which are beyond the
capacity of concept to communicate. Adam, then, is not simply "first man,"
but *every* man. What Adam did, all men do, not because he did it but because
man is what he is. It is at this point that Niebuhr's difficult distinction arises—

the fall of each man is "inevitable" but not "necessary." Reminiscent of Kierkegaard, from whom Niebuhr drew much of his analysis, the fall is a personal affair, something which cannot be universally understood, but something which *I* do, for which I know *myself* responsible, and which I understand *in myself*. The feeling of guilt attending all actions is the guarantee of responsibility despite inevitability.

This alternative is the way of sin, as opposed to the way of faith. Anxiety is its psychological condition, but it is not the cause—the cause is the will. If the self does not *accept* anxiety as God-given for creativity, he has no option but to try to eliminate it. This is sin, for it stems from disbelief, lack of trust—it is the substitution of the self and its own strength for God as center. This "elimination" of anxiety can be attempted in two ways, for anxiety, being the product of an intersection, can be denied by denying either dimension of the human polarity.

The first way, by far the most universal, is that of "pride." This is the denial of one's natural aspect, to reject one's limitations by deliberately mistaking one's self-transcendence for achievement. Man, with the capacity to envisage the whole, is tempted to imagine himself as the whole. This is not a matter of ignorance, but of willed self-deception. There are four basic types of pride: pride of power (glorification in personal and group superiority, false or real), pride of knowledge (especially apparent in conflicting ideologies), pride of virtue (best exemplified by moral self-righteousness), and pride of spirit (religious fanaticism). These are all rooted in insecurity, tempting one to self-deception by deceiving others in a façade of word and deed. In effect, pride is the elevation of the relative to the Absolute.

The second way is that of sensuality. Anxiety is "eliminated" by denying one's freedom, one's capacity for self-transcendence, and one's responsibility, affirming animality as man's essential nature. This may be done either to assert the self or to escape the self. In reality sensuality is a result of pride, for one's own pleasure is made the only center. In whatever form it takes, sin is best understood as the attempt to hide contingency, to seek security at the expense of others. The continuity of sin rests in the fact that while anxiety tempts one to sin, the sin only compounds the insecurity in a vicious circle.

The fact that self-deception, rationalization, is involved in all sin is the living refutation, for Niebuhr, of the doctrine of total depravity; unless the will is successful in disguising its actions it cannot bring itself to do them. Thus there are no personal acts which are purely evil, and yet it must be affirmed that pride infects every human action, to a lesser or greater degree. But since the self, never deserving unconditional devotion, cannot ever fully convince itself, it craves allies to strengthen the deception. Herein lie the demonic proportions of group pride, formed by the attempt of individuals to escape insecurity in a blind, absolute devotion to race, religion, institution, nation, or party. Such idolatry is ruthless, for it possesses the instruments for power. There is no group which escapes "sinful pride and idolatrous pretensions." This means that all judgments and distinctions are relative, and always a matter of degree; they cannot be made previous to the occasion. A "Christian" group or nation is characterized not in its achievement but in its willingness to hear judgment. Since a nation has no collective capacity for self-transcendence, its hope rests in a creative minority, heard because of the tension of competitive forces.

Man, though "fallen," has a "vision of health," an awareness of the law of love as the "ought" of which he is incapable. This awareness is the "point of contact" for the Christian revelation. It is here that Niebuhr's liberal theology is apparent. Although Niebuhr is willing to use much of the traditional terminology concerning Jesus Christ, he makes it clear, as does Tillich, who greatly influenced him, that they have only symbolic meaning. Jesus is the fulfillment of prophetic religion, making vicarious suffering the final revelation of the meaning of history; for Niebuhr this means that God takes the sins of the world on himself in the sense that divine forgiveness is the reverse side of divine judgment. This forgiveness cannot be effective until man takes sin seriously, knowing that sin causes God to suffer—this is the message of the Crucifixion which brings man to contrition. Without such contrition divine forgiveness could not be appropriated. To the degree that man has faith in this fact as the truth of history, to that degree can anxiety become creative.

Niebuhr rejects the Chalcedonian and Nicene formulations of a two-nature Christology, declaring that although "it is possible for a character . . . to point symbolically beyond history and to become a source of disclosure of an eternal meaning, purpose and power which bears history," it is "not possible for any person to be historical and unconditioned at the same time." Through Jesus, love is established as the center of life, but only in principle, not in fact. In this life, love is suffering, not triumphant. The Kingdom of God is not in history nor ever will be—it is the hope which keeps man from the despair of the moment through his faith that the divine power cannot be overcome.

Through Jesus Christ it is known that God is *agape*, self-giving love, and that a life so lived can only end tragically, for it refuses "to participate in the claims and counterclaims of historical existence." Thus love as taught by Jesus is impossible, for to exist is to participate in the balance of competing wills which *is* the structure of this life. Such love transcends history; but to the degree that man is capable of self-transcendence, to that degree does this "impossibility" become "possible," not in the sense of being attainable but of being relevant—it judges every human attempt, revealing possibilities not realized or seen. Yet since this awareness of infinite possibility is that which tempts man to pride or sensuality, it is only in awareness of divine forgiveness that man can accept judgment without despair. This is the Christian answer for Niebuhr.

Such an understanding means that, for Niebuhr, there is no progress in history. This does not mean that there is no achievement, but since man's duality is never overcome, every greater possibility for good brings with it in direct proportion a greater possibility for evil. For example, atomic research brings the possibility of unlimited industrial energy, but also the possibility of total cosmic disaster. Mankind always walks the tightrope between antithetical possibilities, for each will walks the tightrope between the will-to-realization and the will-to-power.

What remains as an enigma in Niebuhr's position is the combination of a negative doctrine of man with a liberal Christology. In liberal theology, the optimism concerning the former is the respective "weakness" of the latter. But while Niebuhr's anthropology became more negative, his Christology and understanding of redemption did not change accordingly. It is for this reason that Niebuhr's ethic makes no fundamental distinction between the "redeemed" and "unredeemed" man. For him, social ethics and Christian ethics are identical, and what he calls "personal ethics" is totally unrelated to the former. Yet whatever other implications are involved here, it cannot be denied that, on the one hand, Niebuhr's doctrine of man has proved a powerful stimulus to the renaissance in American theology, and that, on the other, it has made ready contact with secular thinking in almost every area of group relations.—*W.P.J.*

PERTINENT LITERATURE

Wolf, William John. "Reinhold Niebuhr's Doctrine of Man," in *Reinhold Niebuhr: His Religious, Social, and Political Thought.* Edited by Charles W. Kegley and Robert W. Bretall. New York: Macmillan Publishing Company, 1956.

William John Wolf's essay serves as an excellent guide to Reinhold Niebuhr's use of dialectic in expounding his doctrine of man. As opposed to those who absolutize the logical principles of consistency and coherence, Niebuhr takes the position that most important truths about reality, including those concerning man and history, must be set forth in order to make room for insights that contradict, or seem to contradict, one another. At once exemplary of Niebuhr's dialectical (Wolf prefers to say "relational") thinking and indicative of his method as a whole is his integration of analysis of the human situation with the insights of Christian revelation. Here experience confronts faith, and the two interpenetrate each other on every level of Niebuhr's thought.

On the one hand there is historical and introspective evidence to show that, contrary to idealist, romantic, or even naturalist assumptions, human dignity is not to be correlated with virtue but with the radical character of human freedom, so that, paradoxically, as Niebuhr writes "both the majesty and the tragedy of human life exceed the dimension with which modern culture seeks to comprehend human existence." On the other hand, to the eyes of faith, revelation through Hebrew prophecy prepares the way for the Christ in whom man's essential nature is definitively revealed. Here general revelation, which is universally accessible to persons through the relation in which they always stand to God, and special revelation, which is given by way of the salvation-history of the people of God, are related dialectically. The former requires the latter to free it from caprice, and the latter requires the former to ground it and make it credible.

In general revelation, what is recognized philosophically as man's capacity for self-transcendence—memory, imagination, self-criticism—is lifted into a religious context. Man is shown to possess (1) a sense of reverence for majesty and of dependence upon an ultimate source of being, (2) a sense of moral obligations laid upon him from beyond himself, and (3) a longing for forgiveness. These are organized hierarchically and are more clearly defined by the social-historical revelation in the Bible of God as creator, judge, and redeemer. That revelation in turn opens out on a still more crucial dialectic. For the revelation of Christ is itself twofold. As "Adam," as man unfallen, Christ reveals the essential nature of man as created in and for love. As the "Second Adam" Christ reveals on the cross that all men actually contradict their own essential nature even as he also discloses that only the revelation given in himself can lay bare the radical character of that self-contradiction. Niebuhr's Christology depicts God the redeemer as reenforcing God as judge even as it shows that God's mercy can always absorb the consequences of a divine justice that perceives corruption in man's highest moral and cultural achievements.

Wolf is least able to follow and comprehend Niebuhr's dialectic when he considers his doctrine of sin, with its endeavor to portray inescapability and responsibility at once. What does it mean to say that sin is "inevitable but not necessary," and then to juxtapose to this the assertion that man is responsible for his sin, although not always in the sense of having made a conscious choice? In order to emphasize that historical guilt rather than ontological fate underlies the alienation of man from God, Niebuhr insists that among men there is an "equality of sin" that also allows for an "inequality of guilt." This introduces more problems than it solves. Finally, man sins, Niebuhr says, out of unwillingness to accept his finiteness, which is rooted in unbelief. But if unbelief is really more basic than pride, then Niebuhr should let it account also for weak irresponsibility and irresolution, perversities which have little to do with defiance of one's creaturely status. Wolf does find, on the other hand, that Niebuhr's trenchant analysis of man as living precariously on the boundary dividing nature and spirit lays the groundwork for a far more adequate view of the Fall than does either the Protestant doctrine of total depravity or the more optimistic Roman Catholic theory involving the mere loss of "superadded gifts."

Niebuhr is sometimes branded a pessimist by those who accuse him of overlooking sanctification and redeeming love in overstressing justification and forgiveness. Wolf grants that Niebuhr's faulty assertion that "sin is overcome in principle but not in fact" partially warrants such criticism, but critics here betray an inability to understand Niebuhr's dialectic. Niebuhr's real intention, Wolf maintains, is to return to the New Testament doctrine of two-dimensional grace, and this is demonstrated by his exegesis of Galatians 2:20: "I am crucified with Christ, yet nevertheless I live—yet not I but Christ liveth in me." There grace is seen to be (1) *forgiveness*, which, through repentance, constantly empowers man for new fulfillments and (2) *power*, which, impinging on still sinful man, must partake of forgiveness in order to counter his unwarranted claims to excell in righteousness.

Wolf believes that Niebuhr brings new relevance to the belief in Resurrection of the Body, which for him symbolizes man as a unitary creature partaking equally of nature and spirit. He also finds Niebuhr moving well beyond both Reformation and Counter-Reformation theology in showing the relevance to culture generally of Christian redemption. Wolf, however, finds Niebuhr's doctrine of the Church inadequate. Although Niebuhr is justifiably critical of the obscurantism and sentimentality, the tyranny and self-righteousness that have characterized the churches throughout history, and although it may be right to see what Wolf calls the "hidden churches" of secularism as delivering man from ecclesiastical evils, nevertheless the churches of Christendom clearly have internalized a dialectic of their own, and have consequently borne and still bear in themselves a genuine revelation of Christ which always witnesses against the existing institution.

It is, however, for his steady adherence to the biblical view of man, centered in history, that Niebuhr deserves the highest commendation. It seems clear that Wolf's considerable approbation rests on the belief that Niebuhr's dialectic is generally true to the spirit of Saint Paul.

Bennett, John C. "Reinhold Niebuhr's Contribution to Christian Social Ethics," in *Reinhold Niebuhr: A Prophetic Voice in Our Time.* Edited by Harold R. Landon. Greenwich, Connecticut: The Seabury Press, 1962.

Scarcely anyone is more qualified to discuss *The Nature and Destiny of Man* than John C. Bennett, who was in constant touch with Reinhold Niebuhr for decades as his student and colleague, although Bennett's own liberal theological position sometimes makes it difficult for him to appreciate the genuine biblical grounding and evangelical strain in Niebuhr's thought. Bennett observes that Niebuhr in his social ethics never lays claim to any method. He simply thinks. His thought changes in emphasis according to the issues which challenge him. Since his living dialectic grows out of polemics, he tends to be more clear when he is pointing out the flaws in others' thinking than when elaborating his own position. Much of that position we can only infer from the criticism he makes of a wide range of orientations from Catholicism through Protestant sectarianism to Marxism and secular rationalism. Never does Niebuhr advocate theological authoritarianism. Only those who do not understand him label him as orthodox, Biblicist, or irrationalist. He never lost touch with Protestant liberalism, and he criticized rationalist systems only in the name of a broad empiricism. Most of his famous paradoxes are homiletic—intended to underscore a point. The few that are meant to be descriptive of reality, such as grace *versus* freedom, spring not from irrationalism but from his openness to all the complexities of experience.

Although Niebuhr sees Christ as the ultimate criterion for all manifestations of God to man, he is never a theological or an ecclesiastical monopolist. With Paul Tillich, he believes in grace mediated apart from conscious acceptance of Christ. For all men universally the key to overcoming the basic anxieties that drive toward destruction and self-centeredness is the acknowledgment through faith, understood very broadly, of God's forgiveness. Bennett singles out three central teachings in Niebuhr's doctrine of man that come near to negating the distinction between world and church and so play into this theme of "common grace." They all bear on the single question as to the limits of moral achievement due to man's sin:

1. Egocentricity and sinful pride are found on all levels of personal development, of cultural achievement, and of religious pretension. All men and communities—the Church in particular—are vulnerable to the temptation to abuse power.

2. Fatalism and pessimism are to be shunned. Specific problems should be confronted with a "hopeful openness." No specific limits are set for the achievement of more perfect and inclusive human relations.

3. It can be better not to know of justification by faith than to use it as a cushion for perverse complacency.

Each of these precepts qualifies the other two, so that no neat answer to the question of what is possible can be found. Each is a warning against a different error. Which of the three is to be stressed at any particular time depends on which error is most tempting.

This kind of flexibility in relation to concrete circumstances characterizes Niebuhr's entire thought. There is a pragmatism in his ethics which is born of the fear that a principle or value may become an absolute and so occasion casuistry. His own only absolute is love, which he relates to concrete situations through a set of values which are continually having to be repositioned to be kept in balance.

Niebuhr exhibits a perfectionist tendency, Bennett thinks, in referring to pure love as "an impossible possibility." And yet he counters this tendency in himself by insisting that without some real component of sacrificial love or *agape* the mutual love that men can and do know would disintegrate.

Justice, in turn, is an extension of mutual love. Niebuhr's repudiation of the way Martin Luther separates the two realms of love and justice is a key to the understanding of his own position. The two realms must interact if only because love is no substitute for justice. Given the illusions of paternalistic love and the ubiquity of self-interest, structures of justice are necessary in order to leave open always the possibility of defense precisely against the loving. On the other hand, love seeks constantly to transform the structures of justice for the sake of the weak and the exploited. Love acts here through the principle of equality so as to bring to light the corruption that besets the powerful under every existing structure of justice. Niebuhr's criticism of the many types of male dominance in church and society is one of the best examples of his application of this principle.

Any form of complete moral relativism is anathema to Niebuhr. Concrete decisions do involve considerable relativism, but decisions should be made under the judgment of love. The application of love in concrete decisions must be governed by attention to justice and freedom with respect to every person, every neighbor affected. The relating of this criterion to concrete, unforeseeable circumstances lends an inescapable relativism to every decision.

Bennett closes with a mention of several unsolved problems in Niebuhr's thought:

1. Is there no message for a generation that has not experienced the optimistic illusions which Niebuhr so effectively combated? The very fact that Niebuhr's polemics have been so successful creates a need for hope among people tempted to despair.

2. What is to be said to those men and societies that seek justice through economic and social revolution and that do not share Niebuhr's more purely political concerns?

3. To what extent can there be an area of moral freedom in the years ahead as we confront the nuclear dilemma? Perhaps the old correctives for idealistic illusions should relinquish their place to correctives for the new illusions of political realism.

Gilkey, Langdon. "Reinold Niebuhr's Theology of History," in *The Legacy of Reinhold Niebuhr*. Edited by Nathan A. Scott, Jr. Chicago: University of Chicago Press, 1975.

Recent leftist theology, both Catholic and Protestant, has attacked Reinhold Niebuhr for blessing the status quo instead of offering a challenge to it. It has seen him as too pragmatic and therefore too compromising in his anti-utopianism, as hiddenly conservative in his "liberalism," as too "realistic" to bring judgment on social evils, and as too oriented toward personal reconciliation to be interested in social change, whether revolutionary or reformist. Langdon Gilkey contrasts Niebuhr's theology with the new eschatological theories of liberation and suggests that his views are more relevant than the new theology to the present historical and political situation.

If the basic dialectic in eschatological theology is temporal, setting a past and present marked by sin and suffering over against the new future of an encroaching God, Niebuhr's is one that juxtaposes transcendence and creatureliness, eternity and time, God and the world. Thus for Niebuhr there can be a religious challenge to all political structures, past and future, only because man, in his vertical ascent—in his relating to God's will—transcends all structures, and not because he finds them "questionable" through this "transcendence" simply into a new historical future.

Niebuhr believes that man's essential nature is always the same and always paradoxical. Man is simultaneously finite and self-transcendent, creature and *imago dei*; he is both vitality and form, nature and spirit; at once individual and communal, he lives under natural necessity yet is free; he is fraught with incompleteness while open inevitably to indeterminate possibilities. Human creativity is founded on the search to resolve these tensions. Man is forever open to the future. Because there are indeterminable possibilities for higher levels of human achievement and no discernible limits, and also because there is always the possibility of a fall, a "final" or a "finally redeemed" society such as liberationists envision, within the confines of history, is inconceivable.

For Niebuhr, because man is both finite and self-transcendent he is tempted by anxiety concerning the future so that, losing trust in God, he falls. Sin does not arise from man's animal or cultural past or from some particular social structure so that it might at last be swept away from historical life by a God who acts eschatologically from out of the future. Rather, sin as involving an absolutizing of the finite is a permanent possibility wherever there is freedom. The power of sinful persons to make use of the structures of communal justice for their own ends threatens the stability and the benevolence of every social order. All advances in social structure are accompanied by new possibilities for evil as well as for good. Thus, contrary to liberationist hopes, all human communities, no matter how just, can only approximate love, even though a kingdom of genuine love always retains its relevance as a judgment and a lure against every actual approximation of justice.

Niebuhr rejects the eschatologist's messianic hope for a qualitatively new future in which there will be a final historical victory of the righteous over the unrighteous. For him, "'*all* are unrighteous.'" Even the "good" are sinners and would be tempted to be sinners all the more if they presumed to claim and wield a completely righteous power. The Gospel for Niebuhr resolves the problem of history and discloses its meaning not through God's power as an overmastering sovereignty confronting evil men and their evil works but through God's forgiving love that comes as mercy upon such men and all they do.

The center of the Gospel for Niebuhr is atonement, in which divine love takes the evil of history onto itself through the suffering of Jesus, making new life possible for sinful men. Only by working in and through human freedom does divine grace accomplish transformation, turning man's spiritual creativity away from destructiveness and bestowing upon it the possibility of continually being renewed. Renewal can never be complete because history achieves meaning only provisionally. It is this renewal, however, that is the principle of hope in history rather than the total eschatological fulfillment of the liberationists, because if history is to continue as *history*, God's providence and mercy must continue in any future. It is doubtful, on the other hand, whether for the liberationists there is any freedom, since for them all is determined by God from the future.

Niebuhr put forth a theology of atonement, justification, and reconciliation rather than a "messianic" one because he believed it was a better *political* theology. In it he aimed to provide the most fruitful ground possible for political action. He knew that only when belief in a cause is qualified by a humble awareness of both its relativity and its ambiguity can it be free of pride and thus saved from cruelty and self-destruction. It was not the eradication of hope that he sought but rather the eradication of the nemesis of fanaticisms that result in self-destruction and despair. Niebuhr believed that political structures which are relatively unjust need to be criticized and reordered from inside or resisted if they are threatened from outside. Since, in speaking of the "equality of sin and the inequality of guilt," Niebuhr equated guilt with the injurious consequences of sin, he never doubted that the principle most basic to guilt, defined in his way, was power. Thus even if sin must still remain in the future, a correction of the unjust distribution of power would necessarily reduce "guilt" and therefore suffering.

In Niebuhr's eschatology future history precisely is *not* the liberationists' "locus for divine fulfillment." In tandem with creation, eschatology provides the symbolic horizon that allows history to be understood as it actually is. All historical attainments, including future ones, are partial only. History stands under a judgment and points to a fulfillment *beyond* history, since history's final meaning *transcends* history. That meaning—seen as the transcendent kingdom that both judges and attracts men toward social achieving—would have to be lost if it were considered as an ingredient of history. For then it would be either impotent as something incredible, or demonic as something believed.—*C.W.L.*

Additional Recommended Reading

Brown, Delwin. "Hope for the Human Future: Niebuhr, Whitehead, and Utopian Expectation," in *Iliff Review*. XXXII (Fall, 1975), pp. 3-18. An excellent contrasting of Niebuhr's dialectical theology with the process orientation of Alfred North Whitehead.

Carnell, Edward John. *The Theology of Reinhold Niebuhr.* Grand Rapids,

Michigan: Eerdmans, 1960. An appraisal of Niebuhr's thought from the vantage point of early Reformation theology with a focus on his dialectical view of time and eternity.

Harland, Gordon. *The Thought of Reinhold Niebuhr.* New York: Oxford University Press, 1960. An excellent survey of Niebuhr's social ethics followed by an overview of his application of his thought to the political and social problems of his day.

Link, Michael. *The Social Philosophy of Reinhold Niebuhr: An Historical Introduction.* Chicago: Adams Press, 1975. A very readable and up-to-date assessment of Niebuhr's thought as a whole.

Raines, J. C. "Sin as Pride and Sin as Sloth: Reinhold Niebuhr and Karl Marx on the Predicament of Man," in *Christianity and Crisis.* XXIX (February 3, 1969), pp. 4-8. Niebuhr *versus* Marx on the issue of human nature.

Ramsey, Paul. "Love and Law," in *Reinhold Niebuhr: His Religious, Social, and Political Thought.* Edited by Charles W. Kegley and Robert W. Bretall. New York: Macmillan Publishing Company, 1956, pp. 79-123. Perceptively analyzes what Ramsey considers to be a partial reinstatement of natural law theory in Niebuhr's equating of Christian love with natural or essential law.

Scott, Nathan A. *Reinhold Niebuhr.* Minneapolis: University of Minnesota Press, 1963. A classic survey of Niebuhr's thought which establishes *The Nature and Destiny of Man* as his masterpiece.

EXPERIENCE AND SUBSTANCE

Author: De Witt Henry Parker (1885-1949)
Type of work: Metaphysics, value theory
First published: 1941

PRINCIPAL IDEAS ADVANCED

Experience, as something concrete and given, is existentially ultimate; in the experience of the self we have an illuminating sample of reality.

What we regard as physical objects quite different from our sensations are actually constructions integrating sensory data and meanings.

The generic concepts of being derive their sense from the given characteristics of experience.

Hume's analysis of causation is inadequate for it fails to take into account the critical role of volition in influencing action.

Substances cannot be reduced to their characteristics; they are relatively independent, have causal efficacy, and endure through change.

Space is a manifold of actual and possible relations; time is a term for events and their coming into being and ceasing to be; the self is best understood as present in the focal self, and as having come out of the matrix self.

Experience and Substance is characterized by its author as belonging to the tradition initiated by Plato, Aristotle, and Plotinus, recast by Berkeley, Leibniz, and Fichte, and enriched in our own day by the insights of Bergson, James, and Whitehead. Its argument is along the lines of what is called speculative empiricism in which an empirical base is a point of departure for suggestions and inferences. The resultant point of view is labeled idealist, finitist, and monadistic. Quite naturally, there is a running polemic against materialism in its various forms, old and new. This polemic is of special interest since it brings out in a sharpened way Parker's own principles. When we get these clearly before us, we soon realize how logical the development of his thought is.

Essentially, Parker's thesis is that *experience*, as something concrete and given, is existentially ultimate; in the experience of the self we have an illuminating sample of reality. He denies that the verb "exists" has application in any meaningful way to anything other than ingredients of experience, such as sensa (the given elements of sensation), thoughts, desires, satisfactions, and frustrations, within the circuit of selves or monads. On this foundation the author builds the framework of what he calls an Omega System having eternal status. The analogy with the theses of Whitehead is evident, though Parker is opposed to the Platonic base in the latter's position, being himself more Aristotelian. Both, however, are theists and opposed to what is currently called naturalistic humanism.

Experience and Substance is a careful discussion of related topics, beginning with a definition of subject matter and taking up generic problems in succession.

The book is delightfully written. The style is vivid and concrete and technicalities are translated, as much as possible, into their empirical bases. Parker's training in aesthetics and his wide culture are drawn upon to illuminate his more abstract arguments. Realists and materialists will find in this book analyses which they cannot ignore. There is competent familiarity with modern logic and mathematics as well as with physics, biology, and psychology. Parker was a graduate of Harvard University in the days of its outstanding teachers in philosophy, and one observes something of the range and spirit of Josiah Royce. This is a mature book reflecting years of careful thought and decision.

There are few philosophical issues which are not explored in this volume. The examination of time, relations, and causality is, perhaps, particularly outstanding. As an unashamed metaphysician, Parker was concerned with the eternal and its relation to time and change. This framework is somewhat similar to that of Whitehead; both were opposed to positivism. Wrote Parker: "The traditional conception of the province of metaphysics was defined once and for all by Aristotle as the study of being as being." Ontology is a transcription of that dictum. It is worth nothing that Parker differs from Whitehead and Russell in seeking to reform the category of substance.

Parker believed that metaphysics is maligned when it is associated with the transcendental or quasi-unknowable. It consists of necessary or foundational beliefs. It involves a catharsis of prejudices and analyzes what people often consider obvious, the nature of physical things and of other minds. As a matter of fact, Parker, like Berkeley, considered the things of common sense and science to be phenomenal constructions. He was well aware of the role played in modern thought by theory of knowledge, and he moved in the ambit of British empiricism and Kant. He mentions critical realism, but does not consider it critical enough.

In his account Parker regards sensations as being at once in the mind of the percipient and external to the mind as control, thus constituting a sort of boundary between monads. Contrary to Leibniz, Parker argues that monads are causally related. The result is somewhat akin to naïve, or presentational, realism. In fact, Parker makes much of the inseparability of so-called primary and secondary qualities as features of experienced *qualia*, in this resembling Berkeley and Whitehead. But the question is, of course, whether the properties we ascribe to things are mere transcripts of sensory qualia. Parker's view takes things to be constructions integrating sensory data and meanings.

For Parker, idea and object are capable of literal confrontation, both being experienced. Concepts apply to sensory data which demand interpretation. And some datum is always at the base of a concept. In fact, Parker's theory of universals is to the effect that they concern the generic features of the given. This position is in accordance with the traditions of British empiricism.

In Parker's empirical metaphysics the connection of all discourse with the *given* in experience is made explicit. However, the emphasis is upon those generic concepts which grasp the most fundamental stratum of being. These are called categories, and concern the basic characteristics of whatever exists, such as space, time, relations, and causality. In all this Parker was opposed to what we may call *a priori rationalism*; he wanted to check up on all assumptions. There are many insights in his speculative enlargement of empiricism. Perhaps realistic corporealism could profit from them. Certainly, one may find much that is admirable in Parker's suggestions about the generic characteristics of the cosmos. Concepts are responsible to the evidence of the senses and to the indications of life as lived.

Following Bradley, Parker speaks of centers of experience. These are his monads. In a way, *to be* is to experience. This approach fits in logically with Bradley's denial that anything but idea is thinkable and with Whitehead's rejection of *vacuous*; that is, nonsensuous, actualities.

The centricity of centers rests on activities such as symbolism, conception, and volition. In his treatment of these activities, Parker supplements Hume and Berkeley with Brentano. Here the Aristotelian tradition again enters. Much is made of symbols and meanings as additional to sensations. But Berkeley's framework is retained. Conception is an activity of the self which finds expression in belief and in description. Volition is the guidance of experience from within. In criticizing Hume's treatment of causation, Parker made much of volitional control: we can control our actions and affect other persons. He suggests that Hume was still influenced by Cartesian dualism in his rejection of volition as a true cause of movements.

Volition is the guidance of experience from within. Symbolizing, conceiving, and volition are integrated, although any one may be dominant for a time. A sensation is an event rather than an activity. Here Parker diverges from Brentano, on the one hand, and from G. E. Moore, on the other. At one time, at least, Moore described the consciousness as able to be directly aware of nonmental data. Parker regarded this as mythical, and interpreted sensations as mental events encompassed by activities. And he argues that Brentano overdid the emphasis on reference as a mark of the psychical. He refers to the serial dimension of sensory qualia as a mark against the polarities of conception and volition, such as acceptance and rejection.

To avoid the pitfall of a shut-in mind, the author appeals to the thesis that sensations are on the boundary between minds and nature. Here we *intuit* control and countercontrol. At the human level, one presses another's hand in greeting and the pressure is returned. Such communication is more basic than the argument from analogy. Language develops within this context of intercourse.

The strength of the Aristotelian tradition in Parker has already been mentioned. It now appears in his defense of the category of substance. His *empirical recasting* does not go as far as either Russell and Whitehead went, or the logical positivists. What he does is to modify the logic of Leibniz by developing relational statements; his monads have causal windows.

There are, he argues, four important features in the concept of substance. The first is to the effect that nothing can be reduced to its characteristics. The second concerns relative independence. The third bears on causal efficacy, while the fourth calls attention to conservation, or endurance, through change.

A polemical note of some interest enters. Parker argues that the materialist who identifies the mind with the brain must hold that experience is a predicate of the brain. It is evident that there are linguistic traps here. People do say that a man has a good brain much as they say that he has a good mind. But how does this functional goodness manifest itself? Parker argues, first, that materialism involves an enlargement of the notion of matter. "It is so enriched that it no longer means matter." But that is an appeal to definition. Parker treats the notion of emergence and levels with respect; his treatment of levels of causality is excellent.

As against pragmatism, Parker accepts a picturing notion of truth, a kind of correspondence theory. The pertinent question is whether meaningful statements have sensory data as their objects or refer to something beyond the data which is controlling them. It appears likely that Parker had the latter notion in mind for he was very much interested in other selves. His phenomenalism covers ontological panpsychism. It appears that he rejected C. I. Lewis's two types of knowledge—that which terminates on sensory data and that which is more open and nonterminating—as insufficient. To this extent, Parker was a realist. But he was not a physical realist. Material things are constructions, he argues; the Berkeleian view of perception was essentially held.

In considering the generic, or fundamental, categories, Parker had many valuable insights. Newtonian space is rejected, and space is thought of as a manifold of actual and possible relations and positions. Mathematical points should not be reified. Time is a term for events and their coming into being and their ceasing to be. Duration is a relational term pointing to parallel series of events. Even the matrix self has duration in time only in this sense. The author gives no analysis of the distinction between the occurent and the continuant, but there is something analogous in his distinction between the focal self and the matrix self. According to Parker, memory depends on traces, or echoes, of the past. This is the basis of his doctrine of historical truth as eternal. It leads him to a matrix self of the universe, which is eternal, and to creation. The resemblance to Whitehead's theism is evident.

The treatment of relations finds a middle ground between Russell and

Bradley. Symbols must not be allowed to get in the way of thought. Ropes or brackets may be better symbols than words. Parker distinguishes between static and dynamic relations and between original and acquired properties. His stress on acquired properties represents his break with Leibniz and his recognition of time in an evolutionary sense.

As against Hume, Parker defends the objectivity of causality. Decisions and tendencies are at the foundation of causal sequences. Successful wagering rests on forces in nature itself. Thus Parker provides a metaphysical basis for induction which is in accord with the idea of initial probability. The treatment of levels of causality is quite in line with theories of emergence.

The summary of value theory in this book condenses what Parker worked out elsewhere in detail. Volition and satisfaction are the bases of value as an experience. In this way Parker links value and existence much as did Bosanquet. He is critical of Perry's formula to the effect that value is any object of any interest.

The concluding chapters are devoted to the consideration of the eternal. Passing by essences, or universals, as timeless, Parker develops the thesis that there is an ultimate level which is permanent and really highest; he calls this the Omega System. Roy Wood Sellars once called it the "floor of being." As a theist Parker exalts it. He argues that the whole must be more *complex* than any part.

Some interesting remarks are made on constants in nature such as the gravitational constant and Planck's h. These would be, in a sense, *a priori*, though in a non-Kantian sense. It may be recalled that Sir Arthur Eddington was seeking such factors in a rationalistic way. Science is often more ontologically inclined than positivists admit.

The topic now shifts to the meaning of the term "existence." Parker regards it as involved with the given. To say that *this* sense-datum exists is tautological. Perhaps "existence" arises as a term in connection with the application of concepts. "There are lions" or "Lions exist" concerns the applicability of a concept to an observable world. The statement involves a terminal statement of the form *"This* is a lion."

In this book Parker argues for theism. The mystic may be right in his feeling that he is in communication with the Eternal. There is a touch here of Hocking's approach. What Parker argues for is the initial probability of the religious view of the world, and he supplements his argument with a pragmatic defense.

While sympathetic to the arguments of the Neosupernaturalists such as Tillich and Barth, Parker was not impressed by them; they are supports of a tradition.

In the last analysis, Parker turns to Plotinus and emanation. God created the universe because of his need for companionship. Parker is frank enough to say that the scientific view of the world is an alternative, but holds that it lacks the recognition of the ultimacy of experience.

There are other points which could be examined, for *Experience and Substance* is a mature book. It is a systematic development of a point of view. It is delightfully written and reflects intimate acquaintance with the relevant literature. It was meant as a conscious challenge to naturalism and materialism. Such debates give vitality to philosophy.—*R.W.S.*

PERTINENT LITERATURE

Reck, Andrew J. *Recent American Philosophy*. New York: Pantheon Books, 1964.

Although the author acknowledges that De Witt Henry Parker's contributions to metaphysics never received from his contemporaries the critical attention and appreciation they deserve, Andrew J. Reck esteems Parker to have been one of ten representative American thinkers who flourished during the first half of the twentieth century and who enhanced the luster of the golden age of American philosophy. The other philosophers in Parker's company reported in this book are Ralph Barton Perry, William Ernest Hocking, George Herbert Mead, John Elof Boodin, Wilbur Marshall Urban, Roy Wood Sellars, Arthur O. Lovejoy, Elijah Jordan, and Edgar Sheffield Brightman. The author devotes Chapter Six to an exploration of Parker's metaphysics of values. Central to this study is Parker's *Experience and Substance*.

Parker is best known for his theory of values. He located values in the inner world of mind, describing them as satisfactions of desire governable by norms; and at the same time he upheld their existence, underscoring the unity of value and existence. He sketched and classified the forms of value in life, moral and aesthetic, and he uncovered the noncognitive aspects of value expressions without surrendering completely to noncognitivism. He undertook to erect his theory of values on metaphysical foundations, to which *Experience and Substance* is the centerpiece.

Parker's metaphysics is a kind of voluntaristic idealism. He considered mind—in particular, will—to be the key to ultimate reality. His method in metaphysics is the appeal to experience, so that his metaphysics is empirical through and through. To *be* is to experience or to be experienced. He reinterpreted and reformed the fundamental categories of experience—substance, space, time, and causality.

In examining Parker's metaphysics, Reck focuses on substance, the self, and the Omega system. He shows how Parker translated the four Aristotelian criteria for substance—being a subject but never a predicate, independence, causal efficacy, and constancy through change—into the terms of experience. That substance is a subject signifies that it is unique, an ultimately indescribable center of experience, such as a monadic self is. The independence of substance means that the substantial subject is not grounded in any being other than itself, although Parker allowed that it was causally interconnected with other beings. The causal interconnection of monadic substances is linked directly with their causal efficacy, while the constancy of substance, its capacity to preserve itself or to endure through change, is manifest not in a putative eternity but rather in its temporal persistence within the stream of experience.

Parker's analysis of the self distinguishes two aspects: the focal self and the matrix self. Reck stresses that these are not two selves but two aspects of the same self. Perceiving, conceiving, and willing are activities going on in experience which indicate centers, substantial selves that are subjects—independent, causally efficacious, and constant. As an event, coming and going, flashing into and out of existence, consisting in the activity going on now, the self is focal. However, the focal self does not emerge in a vacuum; it appears against a background, a stable layer of deeper significance, discoverable in the life plan that organizes the fundamental values which the focal self and all its precedent and successive focal selves adhere to and/or realize. This is the deeper self, or matrix self, although it cannot exist unless there is a focal activity to carry it on.

The Omega system is to all experience and its interconnection, to all monadic selves, what in the individual the matrix self is to the focal selves; it is the ultimate ground of Will, value, and existence. It is eternal and expressive as a single Will in the entire cosmos. Hence Reck interprets the Omega system as Parker's cosmological equivalent of God. It supports Parker's theory of values because it is presented as an immanent God committed to the same ideals that we have.

Sellars, Roy Wood. "Reformed Materialism and Intrinsic Endurance," in *The Philosophical Review*. LIII, no. 4 (July, 1944), pp. 359-382.

Roy Wood Sellars was De Witt Henry Parker's longtime colleague at the University of Michigan. Close friends, yet mutually respecting and respected philosophical adversaries, they bestrode the main fields and major types of philosophy in their times. Parker concentrated on values, authoring significant and influential treatises in aesthetics and moral philosophy; he was an empiricist in epistemology and an idealist in metaphysics. Sellars leaned heavily upon the natural sciences, drawing upon evolution, physics, and psychology in order to formulate his own philosophy; he was a pioneering critical realist in epistemology and a materialist in ontology. Sellars' materialism was inconsistent with any form of theism, and he was bold enough to assert his atheism.

In this article Sellars presented his materialistic ontology, his critical gaze fixed upon Aristotelian and neo-Thomistic forms of theism. At the same time he occasionally shifted his critical eye upon the theistic philosophies of Alfred North Whitehead and Parker. Respecting the philosophical achievement of

Parker, Sellars nevertheless rejected the type of philosophy which his colleague's work represents. This article in its asides constitutes the most fundamental criticism of Parker's metaphysics to appear in print.

Sellars' reformed materialism consists of four basic principles: (1) stuff or material, (2) dynamic connections and organization, (3) intrinsic endurance, and (4) integrative levels involving efficient causality.

The first principle finds Parker and Sellars in agreement to the extent that both thinkers considered the category of substance to be indispensable. In retaining the category of substance, both Sellars and Parker rejected the tendency of contemporary thinkers to uphold what Sellars called "eventism." This is the theory that reality is composed wholly of events, construed as dynamic patterns of qualities devoid of anything to which they belong or which supports them. In addition, Sellars as a critical realist had no use for the phenomenalist view that reduced things to classes of sensed qualities. However, Sellars and Parker parted company in their conceptions of what substance is—Parker having opted for mind or spirit, Sellars for matter. The crux of their opposition is manifest in Parker's reaction to Sellars' second principle.

The second principle maintains that matter consists in activity with structure. From Parker's point of view this is Sellars' most radical principle. While Parker, who, like all idealists, identified activity with mind, insisted that this principle, if accepted, would destroy the historic difference between idealism and materialism, Sellars on his side was emphatic that, in light of the discoveries of modern physics, it offers the only proper way to interpret matter. Classical materialism was mistaken in defining matter as static and passive.

The third principle, taken up in the title of the essay, sharpens Sellars' rejection of theism. By "intrinsic endurance" he meant to deny that the physical world is contingent and to affirm that the cosmos is material in nature and exists in its own right. From Sellars' point of view the doctrine of intrinsic endurance negates theism, which regards the physical world as dependent and derivative from a higher form of spiritual being. Hence materialism, in disposing of any need of God or gods, is tantamount to naturalism. The intrinsic endurance of matter simply guarantees that the physical universe is independent being in its own right, totally without need of any other being which allegedly creates it or from which it supposedly emanates.

All four principles are interwoven in Sellars' thought. The fourth principle articulates the dynamic and structural aspects of substantial matter. It represents the fact that active material substances, causally interacting with each other, unfold a material cosmos in which composite material substances are structurally and dynamically interrelated. At the base of the structure, the levels of which display evolutionary development, is matter. In Sellars' scheme appeal to theistic creation is unnecessary, since not only does the physical world contain intrinsic endurance but also by means of integrative causality it gives rise to the emergence of novel levels of existence.

Sellars contrasted his materialism with theism, observing that there are many subtle variations of the theistic hypothesis. As he remarked, "A brilliant recent development of emanation is Parker's Omega System which makes what I call the floor of being higher in quality than the monads which are maintained by it."

Hartshorne, Charles. Review of De Witt Henry Parker's *Experience and Substance*, in *The Philosophical Review*. LI, no. 5 (September, 1942), pp. 523-526.

Charles Hartshorne is today the dean of process philosophers. When he wrote this review of De Witt Henry Parker's metaphysics, he was a young man known mainly for his work on C. S. Peirce and for his espousal of a process theology that was indebted to Alfred North Whitehead. Although his logical formulation of this type of theism had not yet been fully accomplished, it had already become visible. The issue of *The Philosophical Review* that contains Hartshorne's review of Parker's masterpiece also contains a review of Hartshorne's *Man's Vision of God* (1941). Hartshorne's review is noteworthy not only because it displays the high regard of a promising younger philosopher for the consummatory work an older philosopher harvested near the end of his career, but also because, despite its brevity, it endures as an exemplary philosophical criticism and interpretation.

Hartshorne's praise for Parker's masterpiece is unequivocal. In the first sentence he describes the book as "one of the best metaphysical essays of recent decades"; and in the last paragraph he urges "every philosopher to read this book." He mentions, in particular, the chapters on matter, relations, and causality, and he attributes to Parker credit for showing, more simply than Whitehead does, the meaninglessness of the idea of matter when it is considered to be something existing independently of the monads, as well as the meaninglessness of the idea of causality unless it is conceived in psychosocial terms.

Hartshorne points out that Parker's metaphysics pursues the generic features of existence to discover necessary beliefs, and that it proceeds, not by endeavoring to go beyond experience, but by finding these generic features within experience, beginning with our own human experience. The resultant system of metaphysics is idealist, finitist, and monadistic, and belongs to an ancient tradition conspicuously enriched in the present century by the contributions of Henri Bergson, William James, and Whitehead.

According to Hartshorne, the two basic principles of Parker's metaphysics are: (1) that all existence is social, and (2) that all existence is finite.

On the sociality of existence Hartshorne cites Parker's expressed attitude that the love of truth is tantamount to the love of company; it impels one to transcend oneself, to acknowledge a reality beyond oneself. Other themes mentioned in Hartshorne's succinct review are pertinent to the sociality of existence, such as the nature of causality, which involves control and countercontrol from different monads as centers of experience and which consequently connects them in systems.

The principle of finitude, Hartshorne remarks, is "perhaps less orthodox" than the principle of the sociality of existence. By means of the principle of finitude Parker denied that any actual collection could be infinite in number. By parity of reasoning, he denied that there could be an infinite series of past events. Hence he concluded that there must have been a first event. This first event, Parker surmised, sprang out of an activity which Hartshorne characterizes as "the creative activity of God."

Hartshorne examines Parker's conception of God, pointing out, on the one hand, that God is limited by the creative activities of others and so is not responsible for the existence of evil, and, on the other hand, that God is omnipotent in the sense that there are no limits imposed externally upon him. God is all-good; he chooses a cosmos in which existence is social, and he suffers all the misery of his creatures.

Hartshorne cites two respects in which he finds Parker unconvincing. He does not think that Parker's objections to Whitehead's doctrine of the immortality of the past would survive criticism. Nor does he accept Parker's reasons for denying that subjects can embrace each other's feelings—that, in other words, their experiences overlap.—*A.J.R.*

Additional Recommended Reading

Parker, De Witt Henry. "Basic Categories and Attitudes of the Value Situations," in *The Review of Metaphysics*. XIII, no. 4 (June, 1960), pp. 555-596. Posthumously published first chapter of the manuscript left by Parker at his death and edited by William K. Frankena for publication in *The Philosophy of Values* (Ann Arbor: University of Michigan Press, 1957), from which it was omitted, this article contains Parker's last statement on the metaphysics of value.

_____ ."Some Comments on 'Reformed Materialism and Intrinsic Endurance,'" in *The Philosophical Review*. LIII, no. 4 (July, 1944), pp. 383-391. Parker's critical discussion of Sellars' metaphysics and defense of his own.

Reck, Andrew J. "Comments on Dewey, Randall, and Parker Concerning Experience and Substance," in *The Journal of Philosophy*. LVIII, no. 6 (March 16, 1961), pp. 162-166. A critical comparative study.

_____ . "Substance and Experience," in *Tulane Studies in Philosophy*. XV (1966), pp. 31-45. A speculative essay that takes off from Parker's metaphysics.

Walsh, Dorothy. "Fact and Value," in *The Review of Metaphysics*. XI, no. 2

(December, 1957), pp. 256-264. A critical study of Parker's philosophy of values.

Weiss, Paul. Review of De Witt Henry Parker's *Experience and Substance*, in *Ethics*. LI, no. 4 (July, 1941), pp. 487-488. A critical notice of Parker's masterpiece by a famous metaphysician.

INTRODUCTION TO SEMANTICS

Author: Rudolf Carnap (1891-1970)
Type of work: Philosophy of semantics
First published: 1942

PRINCIPAL IDEAS ADVANCED
To study any language a metalanguage is needed—a language about language.

Semantics is the study of linguistic expressions insofar as they serve to designate.

A semantical system is a system of rules, formulated in a metalanguage, for determining the truth-conditions of sentences in a language.

Sentences are logically true when they are true because of semantical rules.

Carnap is known as a logical empiricist with roots in the Vienna Circle of logical positivists, and as a prolific logician. Whereas other students of semantics have largely been interested in relating the use of language to the empirical world, Carnap is interested in pure semantics; that is, in discovering what languages are in and of themselves. *Introduction to Semantics* sets forth the chief principles of semantics upon which more specialized theory may be expected to depend.

In order to investigate a language, another language is needed in which the first may be discussed and described. The language investigated is called the *object language*; the other, the *metalanguage*. When the metalanguage is discussed, this is done in the metametalanguage, and so on. A metalanguage includes the object language, since that must be reproduced in the discussion of itself.

Carnap adopts the diversions of linguistic study suggested by C. W. Morris. If the investigation includes the user of a language, "we assign it to the field of **pragmatics**. . . . If we abstract from the user of the language and analyze only the expressions and their designata, we are in the field of **semantics**. And if, finally, we abstract from the designata also and analyze only the relations between the expressions, we are in (logical) **syntax**. The whole science . . . is called **semiotic**." *Descriptive semantics* is the study of historical languages; *pure semantics* is the construction and analysis of semantic systems. *Pure syntax* deals similarly with syntactical systems. Carnap's study is concerned with pure semantics and pure syntax; further, it is limited to declarative statements. His four chapters beyond the introductory one are addressed to the construction of semantical systems, the consideration of the semantics of logical truth, pure syntax, and finally the relation of semantics and syntax. After describing aims and principles within each section, Carnap usually gives precise definitions in the notation of formal logic and develops theorems from these. This material, impossible to reproduce in a brief review, comprises much of the wealth of the work. It may be remarked that while the work is an original contribution and not a textbook, it should be beneficial collateral reading for the beginning student of formal logic. The separation of semantical problems from logical ones enables one to deal precisely with questions concerning the foundations of logic.

The definition Carnap offers for "semantical system" stems from logical positivism. "By a **semantical system** (or interpreted system) we understand a system of rules, formulated in a metalanguage and referring to an object language, of such a kind that the rules determine a **truth-condition** for every sentence of the object language, i.e. a sufficient and necessary condition for its truth. In this way the sentences are *interpreted* by the rules, i.e. made understandable, because to understand a sentence, to know what is asserted by it, is the same as to know under what conditions it would be true. To formulate it in still another way: the rules determine the *meaning* or *sense* of the sentences." As a consequence of such a presupposition, the theory of truth and the theory of logical deduction depend on semantic considerations and belong to semantics.

To construct a semantical system, first a classification of its signs is given; then follow rules for the formation of its sentences, rules of designation, and finally rules of truth. Carnap offers several examples of semantical systems so constructed. The chief aim of each is the definition of what "true" means in the particular system; the rules are steps toward this result. The word "true" is used in the "semantical" sense described by the logician Tarski. That is, to assert that a sentence is true means the same thing as to assert the sentence itself. In pragmatics the two assertions may have different intents, emphasis, or effects, but in semantics such considerations are unnecessary. Rather, it is convenient to adopt the semantic conception of truth to enable ready passage from level to level, for example from metalanguage to object language. The semantic "definition" is not a definition of truth, but a criterion of the *adequacy* (accord with our intentions) of a predicate for the concept of truth within a given system. "True" thus becomes a predicate applicable by the rules of a system to sentences of the system. While practical considerations usually govern even the arbitrary language we devise, as well as the natural languages, the view of truth is divorced from that of verifiable belief. In pure semantics the conditions of the truth of sentences in a system need not be found outside the system but must be provided within it. The truth-tables often used in calculi to show the relations among sentences are semantical rules stipulating truth-conditions. From the radical concept of truth other usual radical concepts may be defined: "false," "implicate," "equivalent," and so on. Some concepts which are "absolute"—that is, not dependent on language—can then be introduced by showing to what kind of formations they correctly apply. In systems containing variables, rules of determination are required, to show which entities are determined by expressions with free variables and which attributes are determined by sentential functions.

Designation is a relation between an expression and another object; when the expression is a sentence and is true, it designates a proposition determined by the sentence. The terms of the sentence may be said to designate individuals, attributes, or relations. This conception of designation is made for convenience to extend the usual understanding of the word.

Carnap devotes a chapter to problems of logical truth. This branch of the inquiry he terms "L-semantics"; for example, logical truth is called "L-truth." The L-concepts are contrasted with the C-concepts, those pertaining to a calculus, and the F-concepts, those pertaining to empirical fact. The L-terms apply whenever the corresponding radical term applies for solely logical rather than factual reasons. For example, a sentence is L-true if it is true by reason of being a tautology—that is, true because of its logical structure as determined by semantical rules. The full meaning of the L-concepts is contained only in definitions of them. Carnap sets up a set of postulates and their derived theorems in order to lay grounds for the desired definitions. The need for this system is provisional, however, and the system is replaced later by a method of developing the definitions in which postulates are not necessary. That the term for L-truth will apply when for logical reasons the radical term applied is at first seen as following from the semantical rules of the system in question. This understanding may be broadened, taking the metalanguage into account, by adding that a predicate for L-truth is adequate when it applies to a sentence in an object language and when the sentence in the metalanguage stating that it is true is itself L-true. To define a concept of L-truth with adequacy for general semantics rather than for a particular system remains still to be accomplished.

Concepts which do not depend upon reference to semantical systems are absolute concepts. The terms for them may be applied to the designata of expressions (rather than to the expressions, in which case the terms are L-terms). The designata of sentences are propositions. Carnap recognizes that the nature of propositions is controversial. There are two general usages: (1) a proposition is simply a declarative sentence; (2) a proposition is that which is expressed by a declarative sentence. Although in "Foundations of Logic and Mathematics" (1939), Carnap had used the first sense, in *Introduction to Semantics* he confines himself to the second. However, even upon eliminating the first sense there remains some controversy as to what propositions are and whether they are the "meanings" of sentences. Carnap makes a beginning of a general theory of propositions, and to do so he introduces the important ideas of L-state and L-range. An L-state with respect to a given semantical system is a possible state of affairs dealt with in that system with respect to all properties and relations dealt with in the system. Thus, an L-state is a proposition, something designated by a sentence (or a collection of propositions designated by one or a collection of sentences). The class of possible L-states admitted by a given sentence in the system is the L-range of that sentence. The basic premise mentioned earlier is seen again here. If we understand a sentence, we know what possible cases it admits; hence, semantical rules determine under what conditions the sentence is true, and factual knowledge is not required.

The concept of L-state may be broadened to include sentential classes as well as single sentences. Carnap develops methods for definite L-range in nonextensional systems and analogous concepts for systems with an extensional metalanguage.

Having expounded in detail the concepts of L-range and L-state, Carnap proceeds to develop from them, without the use of postulates, a general semantical system. First using as the primitive term the L-range of a sentence, he defines the universal L-range and the null L-range. Through these, respectively, he defines L-truth and L-falsity, as well as L-equivalence, L-disjunction, L-exclusion, and L-nonequivalence. Then, upon introducing the second primitive, the real L-state, he develops definitions of the radical concepts of truth, falsity, implication, equivalence, disjunction, and exclusion.

Not all sentences are tautologous; that is, L-true or the opposite. Those to which the radical term ("true" or "false") but not the L-term ("L-true" or "L-false") apply are *factual* sentences (traditionally, synthetic as opposed to analytic). To determine their truth-value, factual knowledge is needed. To these we may apply F-terms, standing for F-concepts, generated from the pertinent radical concepts.

A final L-concept is that of L-content. When Carnap analyzes the concept *content* of a sentence as meaning "something like the strength or assertive power of a sentence," he notes that we commonly say that the content of one sentence is included within that of another. He expresses this in two postulates linking the content of such sentences with the relation of L-implication. It becomes evident that the relation of inclusion among L-contents is always inverse to that among L-ranges. That is, the L-content of a sentence is all that is dealt with by a system but excluded by that sentence. The assertive power of sentences resides in the power of a sentence to exclude cases, leaving a much narrower set of cases (its L-range) which may actually obtain.

Syntax, which Carnap finds in this volume to be founded on semantics, is the theory of syntactical systems or calculi. To construct a calculus, there are required a classification of the signs, rules of formation of sentences, and rules of deduction consisting, first, of a collection of primitive sentences and, second, of rules of inference. The calculus may optionally contain rules of refutation, and definitions. Carnap provides some sample calculi, together with descriptions in the metalanguage of their relations to one another and ways of passing back and forth among calculi. Definitions in *general syntax* of the terms "proof in a given calculus" and "derivation in a given calculus" give the explanations of the procedures of calculi of ordinary kinds. C-concepts and C-terms are elicited from the radical terms in a manner considerably analogous to that for the L-concepts and L-terms. In an appendix, Carnap comments on differences in the discussions of syntax in this book and in his earlier work, *The Logical Syntax of Language* (1934), differences arising out of the fact that in the later work he came to assign the foundation of syntax to semantics, whereas previously he had regarded it as complete in itself. The field of theoretical philosophy may even extend to pragmatics, he suggests.

A semantical system which contains all the sentences of a calculus is an *interpretation* of that calculus, and through its truth-conditions the sentences of the calculus may be interpreted. If, furthermore, all the C-concepts of the calculus are in agreement with the radical concepts of the semantic system, then that system is a *true* interpretation of the calculus; otherwise it is a *false* interpretation. Again, if the radical concepts apply correspondingly to the C-concepts by reason of logic alone, not fact, the semantical system is an *L-true* interpretation. Conversely, when a system is a true interpretation for a calculus, the calculus is said to be *in accordance with* the system; and when C-concepts coincide with the radical concepts (or the L-concepts) of the semantical system, the calculus is said to be an *exhaustive* calculus for (or an L-exhaustive calculus for) that system.

Two reservations must be held in mind in treating *Introduction to Semantics* as a contribution to philosophy. One is that it is a first volume of a series, providing the beginning points but not the complete developments of theories which have been projected for later volumes of the series. The second is that the author himself draws our attention to the fact that the book is a first attempt at setting forth the semantical principles required by logic and science; he often identifies for us problems for which satisfactory solutions are not yet completed. For example, the problems of defining L-truth and the other L-concepts for systems in general rather than particular systems, and of defining logical and descriptive signs distinctively, are yet unsolved. And in addition, some of the author's methods or assertions are under challenge; for instance, the question has been raised as to whether propositions are the designata of sentences, or whether sense or connotation are to be considered necessary concepts of semantics. *Introduction to Semantics* is, nevertheless, a central book in the field of semantics because the claims it makes are both so broad and so novel that their potential fruitfulness is not readily evident; and it deserves a long period of trial and consideration.—*J. T. G.*

PERTINENT LITERATURE
Black, Max. *Problems of Analysis*. Ithaca, New York: Cornell University Press, 1954.

Pure semantics, Max Black notes in Chapter 14, "Carnap on Semantics and

Logic," lacks empirical reference. The objects under discussion in a pure semantic system will be whatever items satisfy the axioms of the system; but pure semantics, he suggests, is not, in contrast to pure mathematics, of sufficient interest to be much pursued on its own. Rather, he adds, the interest of semantics is closely tied to its alleged fundamental philosophical importance, and presumably this importance is ascribed to impure or descriptive semantics. Descriptive semantics, in turn, is to some significant degree an empirical discipline and is to be assessed in terms of the adequacy of its primitive concepts, and the fruitfulness of its procedures, in coming to terms with those problems which fall within its scope.

Black then proposes to consider the degree of success descriptive semantics has relative to solving its problems, and asks what these problems are. Basic among them, Black believes, is the problem that has faced past varieties of empiricism—namely, how to account for such "necessary" truths as appear in mathematics, logic, or philosophy. For it is empiricism's hallmark to pledge exclusive epistemic reliance on experience, from which no justification of necessary truths is forthcoming. Thus, commenting on a commendation of semantics by Robert Hofstadter ("On Semantic Problems," in *The Journal of Philosophy*, XXXV, 1938, p. 232) to the effect that it is a "new scientific discipline" which faces problems an older empiricism could not adequately handle and puts them "in the way of receiving definite treatment," Black asks how this treatment handles "necessary" truths. The gist of semantical treatment, apparently, is to give such truths a "linguistic interpretation." Here Black finds his first real difficulty: namely, that a really clear statement and defense of the view that logic can be fully subsumed under semantics "is impossible to find." To deal with this difficulty, Black considers various relevant statements by Rudolf Carnap which involve the identification of logic with either syntax or semantics, from which he is able to produce a clear statement of the thesis. These statements come from *The Logical Syntax of Language*, but the perspectives of "Foundations of Logic and Mathematics" and *Introduction to Semantics* are also considered.

Carnap, Black finds, proposes two (not incompatible) theses. One reduces logic to syntax, the other reduces logic to semantics, and they share the denial that logical theorems possess "factual content." Of course, Black insists, what is meant by "logic" in the suggestion that "Logic is reducible to syntax (or: to semantics)" should be what is generally meant by that word if Carnap's thesis is to have philosophical interest and express Carnap's intent. Yet, Black contends, what Carnap ends up calling "logic" as he carries through his argument turns out to be quite different from what the term generally means.

In order to test Carnap's thesis, Black notes, he needs a simple statement which expresses a necessary truth. He chooses this example: (1) *Smith cannot be in New York without necessarily being either in Paris or New York*. One advantage of this example, Black notes, is that it has a simple morphological structure. This structure can be brought out as follows. Let "N" be the sentence "Smith is in New York" and "P" be the sentence "Smith is in Paris." "P or N" will then be "Smith is in Paris or (Smith is in) New York," and we can express (1) as: *N cannot be true without it necessarily being true that P or N is true.* More simply, and in line with Carnap's proposal to reduce logic to syntax or semantics, Black notes, we can express (1) in terms of: (2) *P or N is a consequence of N.* Exactly what "consequence" means will require explication.

This explication comes, Black explains, by noting that Carnap defines "consequence" only in relation to some language or calculus. Thus (2) is replaced by: (2a) *P or N is a consequence of N, in the calculus K.* In turn, Black emphasizes, the reference of "K" now needs to be specified, after which we shall need to be told what "consequence" means in *K*. This specification, Black continues, can be in terms of some calculus or language whose elements and rules for combining elements are simply made up by us; this is the first possibility. Alternatively, he adds, as a second possibility, the specification can be in terms of some actual, albeit idealized and formalized, language.

Black summarily rejects the first way of providing reference to "K," since were it adopted, (1) or (2) would be replaced by some items as: (3) "Some *X* has a certain relation to some *Y* (*X* and *Y* being variables)" or (4) "In accordance with certain conventions defining 'consequence,' any *X* satisfying a particular condition *A* will be in the relation *consequence of* to some *Y* which satisfies another condition *B*." Plainly neither (3) nor (4), nor anything similar, will be adequate as an analysis of (1) or of (2). Still, Black explains, since so much of the work of Carnap (and others) has been in the sort of pure semantics instanced by the specification of "K"'s reference in terms of the first aforementioned possibility or alternative, some philosophers have mistakenly thought researches into pure syntax might give a direct and satisfactory analysis of necessary statements.

Along the lines of the second possibility, Black suggests, let the reference of "K" be specified within descriptive (rather than pure) semantics and construed to be (an axiomatized and clarified) English. Then (2) will be replaced by, or regarded as translated into: (2b) *P or N is a consequence of N, in the language E.* Thus construed, Black indicates, *E* will contain a vocabulary, rules for the appropriate or meaningful combination of vocabulary into expressions, and rules for transforming one admissible expression to another. In particular, "N" and "P or N" continue to have the sense previously assigned to them.

Black turns, then, to the meaning of "consequence" in (2b), although the characterization will remain general since only a general meaning is available unless *E* is further specified. For one thing, the consequence relation is formal, Black notes, being grounded not in the meaning of the relevant sentences but on the order of occurrence and the kinds of symbols which comprise them. Examples of formal relations among symbols, Black notes, are these: that one English word contains more syllables than another; that two sentences have a word in common; that one sentence is part of another. *P-or-N* and *N*, Black points out, are indeed connected by a certain formal relation—that which holds between sentences *1* and *2* when sentence *1* is a compound sentence formed of any sentence whatever plus *or* plus *2*. Black suggests that we call this last formal relation "Typographical alternation"; whether one of two sentences bears this relation to the other can be discerned by examining not their meanings, but their symbolic placement. One way, then, of defining "consequence" in (2b) is in terms of typographical alternation. While this would illustrate a purely formal definition of "consequence," there would be plenty of cases of implication which it did not cover, and so it would not be a satisfactory definition.

Black then makes several objections to this (or any other) purely syntactical interpretation of statements involving logical implication. One is that some statements—for example, "My pencil cannot be red unless it is colored"— involve implication but seem to have no syntactical correlates in terms of which this implication is capturable. Another objection is that two sentences may stand in a great many purely formal relations to one another even though neither proposition expressed by these sentences implies the other; thus implication must be some special sort of formal relation or set of formal relations. Black contends, however, that there is no way of appropriately marking out that sort or set. Still another objection is that while the validity of a syntactical or linguistic interpretation of logic depends on the degree to which it reflects actual testing procedures for establishing that statements in logic are true, the linguistic interpretation fails to reflect these procedures. The gist of this last criticism is that logical connections *are not*, and linguistic connections *are*, conventional.

Black concludes his essay by arguing against Carnap's efforts to offer a semantical, rather than syntactical, interpretation of logic.

Hall, Everett W. *Philosophical Systems: A Categorical Analysis*. Chicago: University of Chicago Press, 1960.

Everett W. Hall begins by noting that, like Ludwig Wittgenstein, Rudolf Carnap claims that, tautologies aside, every statement that is meaningful (either true or false) is scientific; hence, philosophy (as nonscientific) includes no knowledge of, hypothesis concerning, or even reference to, the world. How, then (if at all), Hall asks, does Carnap avoid basing this claim on one or another sort of metaphysical commitment, in particular that of logical positivism?

Hall notes that in his Introduction to *The Logical Syntax of Language*, Carnap announces that the antimetaphysical outlook and attitude of logical positivism will find no role in his own view, neither as assumption nor as thesis. Carnap contends that his inquiries are to be formal in nature and in no way rest on any philosophical doctrines. Hall describes this prediction as "hasty." His reason for so characterizing Carnap's prediction has to do with Carnap's program (as Hall describes it) of replacing philosophy by the logic of science; the logic of science, in turn, is interpreted as the syntax of the language of science. (Syntax is concerned not with the users of a language or with the connotations and denotations of a language's signs, but only with the signs themselves and the rules governing their combination and manipulation.) The point of this replacement, Hall explains, is to clarify the language of science by removing from it what Carnap regards as metaphysical and ethical pseudoconcepts.

Carnap must, and does, distinguish, Hall notes, between an expression, on the one hand, and what it designates, on the other. (This, Hall notes, involves Carnap, as he was later to realize, in semantics as well as syntax.) In any case, Hall explains, Carnap uses the distinction between an expression and what an expression designates as the basis for distinguishing between the material mode of speech and the formal mode of speech. The material mode, as Carnap conceives it, is ostensibly about extralinguistic items but in fact concerns syntax; it appears to be concerned with numbers, properties, experiences, facts, time, space, and other varieties of extralinguistic things, but in reality is about terms or signs (which designate numbers, properties, experiences, and so on) and their connections.

The formal mode of speech is comprised of syntactical sentences which are explicitly about linguistic expressions and language. Carnap's program involves translating sentences in the material mode of speech into sentences in the formal mode of speech, which process allegedly makes clear what was really being asserted, albeit unclearly, by the use of material mode sentences.

Hall notes some examples of this translation procedure. "The world is the totality of facts, not things" is translated into "Science is a system of sentences, not names." Again, "A fact is a combination of objects" is rerendered as "A sentence is a series of symbols." Sometimes, Hall notes, a single material mode sentence requires two formal mode replacements. Thus "There is indeed the expressible" is translated as "There are sentences which are not sentences" and "There are object-designations which are not object-designations." As a final illustration of Carnap's translations, Hall offers the move from "Propositions cannot express anything higher" to "The higher sentences are not sentences."

Hall finds the basic, and in his view ultimately unanswerable, question regarding Carnap's translations to be this: Why make them? Hall notes that it is not that Carnap is merely telling us that, should we happen to wish it, here is a way to eliminate metaphysics—although, of course, if we do not wish to do any such thing, then that is fine. Rather, Carnap distinctively favors the elimination of metaphysics and enters the lists on the side of those who try to do so, even to the point of providing a means for doing it. The necessity, and the solid rationale, for doing this escapes Hall, as it has escaped others who are not logical positivists.

Hall invites us, in particular, to look at the device of material-mode-to-formal-mode translation. This, he indicates, is essentially a matter of taking an expression which designates a word in the material mode of speech and finding a syntactical property for it that matches the syntactical property the material mode word has in its own sentential context. This occupation Hall finds "unexciting and unchallenging." The philosophical interest is in the claim that, having thus correlated a material mode term and a formal mode term, the latter is to replace the former. The rationale for this, Hall reminds us, is the claim that the material mode member of such a correlation "really is" the formal mode member, albeit in disguise. Thus, in Carnap's view, we in effect say something about space, or time, or experiences, really only in order to say something about the word "space" or the word "time" or the word "experiences."

In reply to this view, Hall suggests the tactic of turning the tables. He does so as follows. Carnap, he reminds us, wishes to say something about metaphysics without himself getting involved in metaphysics. Thus Carnap finds something to say about syntax which corresponds with what he wants to say about metaphysics. His syntactical "translations" are, albeit disguised, antimetaphysical assertions. Thus, Hall suggests, while Carnap wants to say that the world contains only those objects that science says it contains, he says instead something about syntax which is only correlated with what he wants to say about science and the world.

In effect, therefore, Hall finds Carnap's antimetaphysical stance to be without adequate rationale, and argues that one would be as reasonable (not more, but also not less) to translate from formal to material mode as to translate in Carnap-fashion from material to formal.—*K.E.Y.*

ADDITIONAL RECOMMENDED READING

Carnap, Rudolf. *Meaning and Necessity: A Study in Semantics and Modal Logic*. Chicago: University of Chicago Press, 1947. A mature presentation of Carnap's views, with an important supplement containing five articles by Carnap, including his reply to Church.

Church, Alonzo. "On Carnap's Analysis of Statements of Assertion and Belief," in *Analysis*. X, no. 5 (April, 1950), pp. 97-99. A critique of Carnap's efforts to replace commitment to propositions by commitment to sentences.

Kraft, Viktor. *The Vienna Circle*. New York: Philosophical Library, 1953. An account of the Vienna days of logical positivism by one who participated in them, with many references to Carnap.

Olshewsky, Thomas M. *Problems in the Philosophy of Language*. New York:

Holt, Rinehart and Winston, 1969. A substantial collection of essays in philosophy of language, including three by Carnap.

Pap, Arthur. *Semantics and Necessary Truth*. New Haven, Connecticut: Yale University Press, 1958. Contains extensive discussions of Carnap's views.

Quine, W. V. *The Ways of Paradox*. New York: Random House, 1966. Contains discussions of Carnap on various topics.

BEING AND NOTHINGNESS

Author: Jean-Paul Sartre (1905-1980)
Type of work: Existential metaphysics
First published: 1943

Principal Ideas Advanced

Being is never exhausted by any of its phenomenal aspects; no particular perspective reveals the entire character of being.

Being-in-itself (en-soi) *is fixed, complete, wholly given, absolutely contingent, with no reason for its being; it is roughly equivalent to the inert world of objects and things.*

Being-for-itself (pour-soi) *is incomplete, fluid, indeterminate; it corresponds to the being of human consciousness.*

Being-in-itself is prior to being-for-itself; the latter is dependent upon the former for its origin; being-for-itself is derived from being-in-itself by an act of nihilation, for being-for-itself is a nothingness in the heart of being.

Freedom is the nature of man; in anxiety man becomes aware of his freedom, knows himself responsible for his own being by commitment, seeks the impossible reunion with being-in-itself, and in despair knows himself forever at odds with the "others" who by their glances can threaten a man, turning him into a mere object.

The subtitle of *Being and Nothingness, An Essay on Phenomenological Ontology*, states clearly the central intention of the author. Jean-Paul Sartre is at one with Parmenides and Plato in his contention that the chief problem of philosophy is the problem of being. Significant differences, however, emerge in a comparison of the ontological investigations of the ancient Greeks with those of the contemporary Frenchman. The adjective, "phenomenological," in the subtitle of Sartre's classic, indicates one of these significant differences.

Sartre's ontology is an ontology that follows in the wake of Immanuel Kant's critical philosophy, Edmund Husserl's phenomenological reduction, and Martin Heidegger's ontology of *Dasein*. *Being and Nothingness* has all of the Kantian reservations about any philosophy which seeks to proceed beyond the limits of possible experience, draws heavily from the phenomenological investigations of Husserl, and exhibits basically the same form of analysis and description as was used in Heidegger's *Being and Time* (1927). Nevertheless, Kant, Husserl, and Heidegger intermittently throughout the work fall under some rather trenchant Sartrian criticism. Kant's chief mistake was his appeal to a "thing-in-itself" which somehow stands behind the phenomena. In Sartre's phenomenological ontology there is nothing concealed behind the phenomena or the appearances. The appearances embody full reality. They are indicative of themselves and refer to nothing but themselves. The Kantian dualism of phenomena and noumena, appearance and reality, is abolished, and being is made coextensive with phenomena. Husserl comes in for a similar criticism. His hypothesis of a transcendental ego is pronounced useless and disastrous. The fate of such a view, according to Sartre, is shipwreck on the "reef of solipsism." The faults of Heidegger are not as grievous as those of Kant and Husserl. As becomes apparent on every page of *Being and Nothingness*, Sartre's analysis is markedly informed by Heideggerian concepts. Yet Heidegger, argues the author, neglects the phenomenon of the lived body, has no explanation for the concrete relatedness of selves, and misinterprets the existential significance of death.

Being, in Sartre's analysis, evinces a *transphenomenal* character. Although there is no *noumena* and no *thing-in-itself* which lies concealed behind the phenomenal appearances of being, being is never exhausted in any of its particular phenomenal aspects. Being, in the totality of its aspects and manifestations, never becomes wholly translucent to consciousness. Everything which has being "overflows" whatever particular categories, designations, and descriptions human knowledge may attach to it. Being evinces relationships and qualities which escape any specific determination. Although being is reduced to the whole of its phenomenal manifestations, it is in no way exhausted by any *particular* perspective that man has of the phenomena. All phenomena overflow themselves, suggesting other phenomena yet to be disclosed. This primordial being, transphenomenal in character, expresses a fundamental rupture into "being-in-itself" (*en-soi*) and "being-for-itself" (*pour-soi*).

Being-in-itself designates being in the mode of fullness or plenitude. It is massive, fixed, complete in itself, totally and wholly given. It is devoid of potency and becoming, roughly equivalent to the inert world of objects and things. It has no inside and no outside. It expresses neither a relationship with itself nor a relationship to anything outside itself. It is further characterized by an absolute contingency. There is no reason for its being. It is superfluous (*de trop*). "Uncreated, without reason for being, without connection with any other being, being-in-itself is superfluous for all eternity."

Being-for-itself is fluid and vacuous rather than fixed and full. It is characterized by incompleteness, potency, and lack of determinate structure. As being-in-itself is roughly equivalent to the inert and solidified world of objectivized reality, so being-for-itself generally corresponds to the being of human consciousness. These two modes of being, however, are not granted an equal ontological status. Being-in-itself is both logically and ontologically prior to being-for-itself. The latter is dependent upon the former for its origin. Being-for-itself is inconceivable without being-in-itself and is derived from it through an original nihilation (*néantisation*). Being-for-itself thus constitutes a nihilation of being-in-itself. Being-for-itself makes its appearance as a nothingness which "lies coiled in the heart of being—like a worm." The being of the for-itself is a "borrowed" being which emerges from the in-itself by virtue of its power of negation. The source of the power of nothingness remains inexplicable and mysterious. The for-itself simply finds itself *there*, separated and at a distance from the absolute fullness of the in-itself. The for-itself emerges as an irreducible and ultimate datum.

One of the fateful consequences of the primordial rupture of the for-itself from the in-itself is the introduction of nothingness. Sartre makes it clear that it is through man or human consciousness that nothingness comes into the world. In his discussion on nothingness Sartre is intent upon rejecting the Hegelian dialectical approach and substituting for it a phenomenological account. For Hegel, being and nothingness are dialectical concepts which take their rise from the same ontological level of mediated reality. Sartre maintains in his phenomenological approach that nothingness is dependent upon being in a way that being is not dependent upon nothingness. Nothingness is not an abstract idea complementary to being, nor can it be conceived outside of being; it must be given at the heart of being. Nothingness demands a host, possessing the plenitude and full positivity of being, from which it borrows its power of nihilation. Thus, nothingness has only a borrowed or marginal being. Although Sartre never acknowledges his debt to Augustine on this point, his analysis seems to draw heavily from Augustinian sources. Augustine had already described evil as a tendency toward nothingness, the movement presupposing perfect being as a host in which evil exists as a privation of the good. It would indeed seem that in its basic outlines Sartre's analysis of nothingness is little more than a secularized Augustinianism. The introduction of nothingness raises the question of its relation to negative judgments.

As Heidegger had done before him, Sartre insists that nothingness is the origin and foundation of negative judgments, rather than vice versa. This foundation finds its clarification in the context of human expectations and projects. Sartre, as an example, tells of expecting to find a person (Pierre) in a café when in fact he is not present: my expectation of finding Pierre has caused the absence of Pierre to happen as a real event pertaining to the café. I discover his absence as an objective fact. I look for him and find that he is not there, thus disclosing a synthetic relation between Pierre and the setting in which I have expected him to be. There obtains a *real* relation between Pierre and the café, as distinct from the relation of *not-being* which characterizes the order of thought in simple negative judgments. To make the negative judgment that Pierre is not in the café has purely abstract meaning. It is without real or efficacious foundation.

We have observed that it is through man that nothingness comes into the world. The question then arises: what is it about the being of man that occasions nothingness? The answer is: freedom. The freedom which is here revealed should in no way be identified with a property or a quality which somehow attaches to man's original nature. Freedom *is* the "nature" of man. There is no difference between the being of man and his being-free. As becomes apparent later in *Being and Nothingness*, Sartre's ontology of man is a philosophy of radical and total freedom. This consciousness of freedom is disclosed in anxiety. "It is in anxiety that man gets the consciousness of his freedom, or if you prefer, anxiety is the mode of being of freedom as consciousness of being; it is in anxiety that freedom is, in its being, in question of itself." There is thus an internal connection among nothingness, freedom, and anxiety. These are interrelated structural determinants of the being of man.

Nothingness, freedom, and anxiety provide the conditions which make possible the movement of "bad faith" (*mauvaise foi*). Bad faith is a form of self-deception which in making use of freedom denies it. Bad faith is akin to lying, yet not identical with it. In lying one hides the truth from others. In bad faith one hides the truth from oneself. In the former there is a duality of deceiver and deceived; in the latter there is a unity of a single consciousness. Bad faith does not come from the outside. Consciousness affects itself with it. In describing the pattern of bad faith Sartre develops the example of a woman who consents to go out with an amorous suitor. She is fully aware of his intentions and knows that sooner or later she will have to make a decision. An immediate decision is demanded when he caresses her hand. If she leaves her hand there she encourages his advances; if she withdraws it she may well preclude any further relationship with the suitor. She must decide, but she seeks means for postponing the decision. It is at this point that bad faith comes into play. She leaves her hand in his, but does not notice that she is doing so. She becomes all intellect, divorces her soul from her body, and transforms her body into an object or thing—into the mode of "being-in-itself." Her hand becomes "a thing," neither consenting nor resisting. She objectivizes her body, and ultimately herself, as in-itself, and thus stages a flight or an escape from herself as for-itself. She loses her subjectivity, her freedom, and her responsibility for decision. She exists in bad faith.

The pursuit of being leads to an awareness of nothingness, nothingness to an awareness of freedom, freedom to bad faith, and bad faith to the being of consciousness which provides the condition for its possibility. We are thus led to an interrogation of the immediate structures of the for-itself as consciousness. The immediate consciousness in which the self experiences presence is what Sartre calls the nonpositional consciousness. This consciousness characterizes the level of primitive awareness, and is prior to the positional consciousness which is the reflective consciousness of the intentional action. Nonpositional consciousness is prereflective; therefore, Sartre describes it as a prereflective cogito (*cogito pre-reflexif*). This prereflective cogito quite clearly precedes the Cartesian cogito, which is a movement of reflection, and becomes the foundation for it. Positional consciousness, on the other hand, is reflective in character, directed toward some intentional object. Sartre has taken over Husserl's doctrine of intentionality and has made it central to his description of the positional consciousness. Positional consciousness is always consciousness *of* something. It is directed outward into a *world*. But the positional consciousness can also be directed reflexively upon itself. Consciousness can become conscious of itself as being conscious. It is in this way that the ego or the self is posited or derived. Both the world and the ego or self are posited by the projecting activity of the for-itself in its nonpositional freedom, and they become correlative phenomena inextricably bound up at their very source. Without the world there is no ego, and without the ego there is no world. Both the world and the ego are hypostatized through reflection as unifying, ideal limits.

One of the central structural elements of the for-itself is facticity. The for-itself apprehends itself as a lack or decompression of being. It is not its own foundation. It is a "hole" in the heart of being, infected with nothingness, abandoned to a world without justification. It discovers itself thrown into a situation, buffeted by brute contingencies, for the most part superfluous and "in the way." Facticity indicates the utter contingency and irrevocable situationality of the being of the for-itself. Without facticity consciousness could choose its attachments to the world—it would be absolute and unfettered freedom. But the freedom which the for-itself experiences is always restricted by the situation in which it is abandoned. Nevertheless, the freedom of the for-itself is a *real* freedom and even in its facticity the for-itself perpetually relates itself to itself in freedom. I do not become a bourgeois or a Frenchman until I *choose* to become such. Freedom is always present, translating facticity into possibility. In the final analysis the for-itself is totally responsible for its being.

Value and possibility provide two additional structures of the for-itself. Value is an expression of an impossible striving toward a coincidence of being. The for-itself perpetually strives to surpass itself toward reunion with the in-itself, thus achieving totality by healing the fundamental rupture in being. But this totality is an impossible synthesis. As soon as the for-itself would become coincident with the in-itself it would lose itself as for-itself. A final totality remains forever unattainable because it would combine the incompatible characteristics of the in-itself (positivity and plenitude) and the for-itself (negativity and lack). The impossible striving for reunion gives rise to the unhappy or alienated consciousness. The for-itself is "sick in its being" because it is haunted by a totality which it seeks to attain but never can without losing itself as for-itself. "The being of human reality is suffering because it emerges in being as perpetually haunted by a totality which it is without being able to be it, since it would not be able to attain the in-itself without losing itself as for-itself. Human reality therefore is by nature an unhappy consciousness, without the possibility of surpassing its unhappy state." Now possibility, as an immediate structure of the for-itself, provides further clarification of the meaning of the for-itself as lack. The possible is what the for-itself lacks in its drive for completeness and totality. It indicates the *not yet* of human reality, the openness of its constant striving.

The structures of the for-itself are ontologically rooted in temporality, which provides their unifying ground. This temporality is understood in Sartre's phenomenological analysis as a synthesis of structured moments. The "elements" or directions of time (past, present, and future) do not constitute an infinite series of nows, or collected "givens," in which some are no longer and others are not yet. If time is understood as an infinite series of discrete nows, then the whole series is annihilated. The past nows are no longer real, the future nows are not yet real, and the present now is always slipping away, functioning only as a limit of an infinite division. In such a view time evaporates and is dissolved into an infinite "dust of instants" which are ontologically anemic. A phenomenological analysis of the time of the immediate consciousness avoids this dissolution of temporality by describing the elements of time as "structured moments of an original synthesis."

Following Heidegger, Sartre speaks of time as an *ecstatic* unity in which the past is *still* existentially real, the future *already* existentially real, and in which past and future coalesce in the present. However, Sartre differs from Heidegger in refusing to ascribe ontological priority to the future. No ecstasis of time has any priority over any of the others; none can exist without the other two. If, indeed, one is to accent any ecstasis, Sartre maintains that it would be phenomenologically closer to the facts to accent the present rather than the future. The past remains an integral part of my being. It is not something which I had or possessed at one time; it is something of which I am aware here and now. The past is always bound to my present. Man is always related to his past, but he is at the same time separated from it insofar as he engages in a constant movement from himself as past to himself as future. The past tends to become solidified and thus takes on the quality of an in-itself. It is defined as a for-itself which has become an in-itself. It takes on a character of completeness and fixity, but it still remains mine, and as long as it remains a part of my consciousness it can be recovered in an act of choice. The past provides the ontological foundation for facticity. In a very real sense the past and facticity indicate one and the same thing. The past makes possible my experience of abandonment and situationality. In contrast to the past which has become an in-itself, the present remains a full-embodied for-itself. The author defines the present as a "perpetual flight in the face of being." It exhibits a flight from the being that it was and a flight towards the being that it will be. Strictly speaking, the for-itself as present has its being outside of itself—behind it and before it. It was its past and will be its future. The for-itself as present is not what it is (past) and is what it is not (future). The future is a mode of being which the for-itself must strive to be. As a mode of being it designates an existential quality which one *is*, rather than an abstract property which one *has*. The future is a lack which is constitutive of my subjectivity. As the past provides the foundation for facticity, so the future provides the foundation for possibility. The future constitutes the meaning of my present for-itself as a project of possibilities. The future is not a series of chronologically ordered nows which are yet to come. Rather, it is a region of my being, which circumscribes my expanding possibilities, and defines me as a for-itself who is always on the way.

The temporalized world of the for-itself is not an insulated world experienced in isolation. In the world of the for-itself the "others" (*autrui*) have already made their appearance. Hence, the being of the for-itself is always a being-for-others as well. The discussion of the problem of the interrelation of personal selves occupies a lengthy and important part of *Being and Nothingness*. The author begins with an examination and criticism of the views of Hegel, Husserl, and Heidegger, and then proceeds to a positive formulation of his own. The "other" is already disclosed in the movements of the prereflective, nonpositional consciousness. Shame affords an example of a prereflective, disclosure of the "other," as well as a disclosure of myself as standing before the other. Through shame I discover simultaneously the "other" and an aspect of my being. *I* am ashamed of *myself* before the "*other*." The "other" reveals myself to me. I need the "other" in order to realize fully all the structures of my being. It is thus that the structures of being-for-itself and being-for-others are inseparable.

In the phenomenon of "the look" (*le regard*) we find another example of the prereflective disclosure of the self and the other. It is through the look that the "other" irrupts into my world, decentralizes and dissolves it, and then by reference to his own projects reconstitutes it and the freedom which I experience. When I am "looked at" the stability of my world and the freedom which I experience as for-itself are threatened. The "other" is apprehended as one who is about to steal my world, suck me into the orbit of his concerns, and reduce me to the mode of being-in-itself—to an object or a thing. "Being-seen-by-the-other" involves becoming an object for the "other." When the movement of the look is completed I am no longer a free subject; I have fallen into the slavery of the "other." "Thus being-seen constitutes me as a being without defenses for a freedom which is not my freedom. It is in this sense that we can consider ourselves as slaves in so far as we appear to the other. But this slavery is not the result of a life in the abstract form of consciousness. I am a slave to the degree that my being is dependent at the center of a freedom which is not mine and which is the very condition of my being." It is in this way that the existence of the "other" determines my original fall—a fall which can be most generally described as a fall from myself as being-for-itself into the mode of being-in-itself. My only defense is the objectivization of the "other." Through *my* look I can seek to shatter the world of the "other" and divest him of his subjective freedom. Indeed I seek to remove the other from my world and put him out of play, but this can never succeed, because the existence of the other is a contingent and irreducible fact. I *encounter* the "other"; I do not *constitute* him. The "other" remains, threatening to counterattack my defenses with *his* look. Thus there results a constant cycle of mutual objectivization. I affirm my freedom by rendering the "other" into an object. Then the "other" affirms his freedom by rendering me into an object. Then I stage an existential counterattack, and the cycle repeats itself. According to the author there seems to be no end to this sort of thing. The upshot of all this is an irreconcilable conflict between the self and the "other," with a consequent breakdown of all communication. Alienation has the last word in Sartre's doctrine of inter-subjectivity. The reader who searches for a positive doctrine of community, searches in vain. All forms of "being-*with*" find their common denominator in an alienating "being-*for*."

In the relation of the for-itself with the "other" the body appears as a central phenomenon. The body is discussed in the context of three ontological dimensions: (1) the body as I exist it, (2) the body as utilized and known by the "other," and (3) the body as I exist it in reference to its being known by the "other." The body as I exist it is not the objectivized body constituted by nerves, glands, muscles, and organs. Such an objectivized body is present for the physician when he gives me a medical examination, but I do not apprehend my body in this way. I apprehend my body in its lived concreteness as that phenomenon which indicates my possibilities in the world. The body as *concretely lived* signifies a level of being which is fundamentally different from the body as *objectively known*. The body as concretely lived reveals an original relation to the world of immediate and practical concerns. I carry out my practical concerns through instruments or utensils.

Sartre, in the development of his concept of the world, draws heavily from Heidegger and defines the world of immediate experience as an instrumental world. Instruments refer to my body, insofar as the body apprehends and modifies the world through the use of instruments. My body and the world are thus coextensive. My body is spread out across the utensils which I use. My body is everywhere in the world. To have a body and to experience that there is a world are one and the same thing. However, not only do I exist my body, but my body is also utilized and known by the "other." This second ontological dimension indicates my body as a body-for-the-other. My body as known by the "other," and so also his body as known by me, is always a body-in-a-situation. The body of the "other" is apprehended within the movements of a situation as a synthetic totality of life and action. The isolated appendages and gestures of another's body have no significance outside the context of a situation. A clenched fist in itself means nothing. Only when the clenched fist is apprehended as an integral part of a synthetic totality of life movements is the lived body of the "other" disclosed. A corpse is no longer in a situation, and hence can be known only in its modality of death as an anatomical-physiological entity. The third ontological dimension indicates the reappraisal of my body as a body which is known by and exists for the "other." Thus alienation enters my world. My body becomes a tool or an object for the "other." My body flows to the "other," who sucks it into the orbit of his projects and brings about the dissolution of my world. This alienation is made manifest through affective structures such as shyness. Blushing, for example, expresses the consciousness of my body not as I live it for myself, but as I live it for the "other." I cannot be embarrassed by my own body as I exist it. Only a body which exists for the "other" can become an occasion for embarrassment.

In the concrete relation of the for-itself with the "other," two sets of contradictory attitudes make their appearance. On the one hand, there are the attitudes of love and masochism, and on the other hand, the attitudes of hatred and sadism. In the love relationship the beloved is for the lover not simply a thing which he desires to possess. The analogy of ownership breaks down in an explanation of love. Love expresses a special kind of appropriation. The lover wants to assimilate the love of the beloved without destroying his or her freedom. But this relationship of love ultimately founders because it is impossible to maintain an absolute subjectivity or freedom without objectivizing another as the material for one's freedom. This accounts for the insecurity of love. The lover is perpetually in danger of being made to appear as an object. In masochism the annihilation of subjectivity is deliberately directed inward. The masochist puts himself forward as an in-itself for the "other." He sets up conditions so that he can be assimilated by the "other"; thus, he deliberately transforms himself into an object. Hatred and sadism constitute the reverse attitude. Here there is an attempt to objectivize the "other" rather than oneself. The sadist seeks to "incarnate" the "other" by using his body as a tool. The "other" becomes an instrument in his hands and thus appropriates the freedom of the "other." But simplest form is an attempt to appropriate the freedom of the "other." But this attempt results in failure because the "other" can always turn back upon the sadist and make an object out of him. Thus, again, the reader is made aware of the futility of all attempts to establish harmonious relations with the "other." This inability to achieve genuine communication leads to a despair in which nothing remains for the for-itself but to become involved in the circularity of objectivization in which it passes from one to the other of the two fundamental attitudes.

The author concludes his phenomenological essay with a restatement and further elucidation of the nature and quality of human freedom, and a delineation of his program of existential psychoanalysis. Freedom is discussed in relation to the will, in relation to facticity, and finally in relation to responsibility. The will can never be the condition of freedom; it is simply a psychological manifestation of it. The will presupposes the foundation of an original freedom in order to be able to constitute itself as will. The will is derived or posited by reflective decision. It is a psychological manifestation which emerges within the complex of motives and ends already posited by the for-itself. Properly speaking, it is not the will that is free. Man is free. The will is simply a manifestation of man's primordial freedom. Freedom in relation to facticity gives rise to the situation. The situation is that ambiguous phenomenon in which it is impossible clearly to distinguish the contribution of freedom and the determinants of brute circumstance. This accounts for the paradox of freedom. There is freedom only in a situation, and there is a situation only through freedom. Sartre delineates five structures of the situation in which freedom and facticity interpenetrate each other: (1) my place, (2) my past, (3) my environment, (4) my fellow man, and (5) my death. Insofar as freedom always interpenetrates facticity, man becomes wholly responsible for himself. I am responsible for everything except for the fact of my responsibility. I am free, but I am not free to obliterate fully my freedom. I am condemned to be free. This abandonment to freedom is an expression of my facticity. Yet I must assume responsibility for the fact that my facticity is incomprehensible and contingent. The result is that my facticity or my final abandonment consists simply in the fact that I am condemned to be wholly responsible for myself. Although freedom and facticity interpenetrate, it remains incontestable that freedom is given a privileged status in the Sartrian view of man.

The touchstone of existential psychoanalysis is a concentration on man's fundamental project (*projet fondamental*). This fundamental project is neither Heidegger's *Sein-zum-Tode*, nor is it Freud's libidinal cathexis. The method of existential psychoanalysis resembles that of the Freudians in that an effort is made to work back through secondary and superficial manifestations of personality to an ultimate and primary project, but the existentialist differs with Freud concerning the nature of this project. The Freudian localizes the project in a libidinal attachment which is determined by the past history of the self. The existential psychoanalyst broadens the framework of explanation to include the future projects of the self as well. The fundamental project is thus understood in the context of man's temporalized being, which includes the ecstatic unity of past, present, and future. The irreducible minimum of this fundamental project is the *desire to be*. Quite clearly, it is impossible to advance farther than being, but in having advanced thus far one has undercut the simple empirical determinants of behavior. The goal of this desire to be is to attain the impermeability, solidity, and infinite density of the in-itself. The ideal toward which consciousness strives is to be the foundation of its own being. It strives to become an "in-itself-for-itself," an ideal which can properly be defined as God. One can thus most simply express the fundamental project of man as the desire to be God. But the idea of God is contradictory, for in striving after this ideal the self can only lose itself as for-itself. Man's fundamental desire to give birth to God results in failure. He must thus reconcile himself to the fact that his is a useless passion.—*C.O.S.*

PERTINENT LITERATURE

Grene, Marjorie. *Sartre*. New York: New Viewpoints, 1973.

Being and Nothingness is "one of the treasure-houses" of Western philosophy, according to Marjorie Grene. Even despite its distortion of realities through its obsession with nothingness, she contends, it reveals much about man through its occasionally brilliant phenomenological descriptions and particularly through the unusual subtlety of its arguments.

Grene's book is itself in many ways a masterful piece of argumentation. Actually, it is a critique of Jean-Paul Sartre's entire philosophy, from the early works on imagination and the emotions on through to *L'idiot de la famille*, Sartre's existential psychoanalysis of Gustave Flaubert which he never finished. The principal thrust of Grene's book is an attack on Sartre's Cartesianism. Yet she sees Sartre as a tragic figure to whom we can feel considerable indebtedness, since he, more than any other twentieth century thinker, has honestly faced the consequences of the crisis that Cartesianism has wrought in all of us. He thus may aid us in finally and completely evading those consequences ourselves.

Unfortunately, Chapter IV of Grene's book, which attempts to give a critical sketch of the whole of *Being and Nothingness* in barely thirty pages, can be followed only if the reader has the text of *Being and Nothingness* close at hand or fresh in mind; but it is here that she demonstrates most astutely that Sartre's "prereflective *cogito*," only a variant of the isolated Cartesian *cogito*, must, even as Sartre successfully overcomes all the traditional dualisms, lead him inevitably to espouse the dualism of all dualisms: the sheer surging forth of consciousness against a meaningless plenum.

In Chapter V, Grene's style is more expansive, as befits her subject matter. Here she retraces her steps to Parts III and IV of *Being and Nothingness* for a more thorough treatment of interpersonal relations, the body, and the emotions. She first points to the way in which Sartre's move out of solipsism, by way of shame, from the prereflective *cogito* to the *cogito* that reveals the Other, exactly parallels René Descartes' move, by way of reverence, from himself to the divine Other. Of course, the contrast between the God who founds all being and Sartre's "Other" who will not let him be "because *he* would be instead" is enormous, but Grene nevertheless finds Cartesian biases sustaining the adversary relationship that pervades all Sartrean community. First, Sartre's confining of the prereflective *cogito* to the nonthetic consciousness (of) *self* completely blinds him both to that "from-to" awareness that Edmund Husserl sees as an integral part of the self-world relationship and to the already-being-out-there-with-other-people that both Michael Polanyi and Martin Heidegger portray as fundamental to the structures of human existence and prior to methodological doubt. Second, Sartre's adherence to Descartes atomistic ideals of the instant and of freedom prevent him from seeing that both the for-itself and the for-others, although never derivable from each other, both depend for their being on what Grene refers to as the "among others." Third, and this is even more basic, Sartre's acceptance of the Cartesian division of consciousness from the body brings him to the impasse expressed in his statement, "The body is the instrument which I am." As a consequence of this, Sartrean man can never live in his own body as the vehicle of knowledge and of rational activity. In his perennial conflict with the Other, therefore, he strives to reduce the Other to body in order to put him out of action and so to defeat him. He never experiences the "among-others" as the bodily-being-together of persons.

In his discussion of the emotions Sartre reaches an even more serious impasse, Grene argues. She shows that passion for Sartre can have no authentic standing; it can only be deceptively emancipated from its role as the nonthetic other-side of reason. Reason, on the other hand, is empty. Only in nihilating choice can reason assert itself as free. In the final analysis, Sartre reduces Cartesian reason to will, depriving it of all content for the sake of its autonomy. But reason must have content as well as goal. And this, despite Sartre's pressing need to force the nonthetic mode of consciousness constantly in upon itself, he can discover only as a product of the passion to become God. Grene leads her reader to see that the irony and perhaps the tragedy of Sartre is to aspire, like his mentor Descartes, to a state "free of all cares and limited by no passions" only to discover and confess in the midst of that striving that he is nothing but a useless passion. For passion not to be useless, Grene contends, it must aim to be something less than the *causa sui*. It must have an end that is both lived and known, that is grounded both in history and in community, and that assents to the embodied being out of which it grows.

Anderson, Thomas C. *The Foundation and Structure of Sartrean Ethics*. Lawrence: The Regents Press of Kansas, 1979.

Thomas C. Anderson's book offers a counter to those many critics of Jean-Paul Sartre who contend that the ontology of *Being and Nothingness* will not support an ethics. Anderson, who believes that Sartre is one of the most misunderstood of modern philosophers, makes a careful textual analysis of sections of *Being and Nothingness* which he claims can ground a moral philosophy and calls on the later Sartrean writings as well as on the writings of Simone de Beauvoir and Francis Jeanson for aid in constructing a plausible moral theory which, to his mind, is truly representative of Sartre's views. His work contains many insights and cogent arguments, but he writes with a quite Pelagian bias that can blind him to the ineradicability of grounding ambiguities in Sartre's thinking and can therefore repeatedly lead him to an overly simplistic and vitiating interpretation of it.

A principal emphasis of Anderson is that the central goal for authentic Sartrean man is not to be God but to be free. It is true that for Sartre all men *desire* to be in-itself-for-itself or God; but that desire is on the prereflective or "lived" level. Reflection sees that being God is an impossible ideal. But more importantly, reflection is capable of acknowledging that this ideal has value only with respect to man as a contingent being. To Anderson it follows that this ideal need not be chosen as a goal. Only those, he says, who are prey to the debilitating spirit of seriousness expressly *choose* to be God. Good faith, in contrast, asserts human freedom as the highest value because freedom is itself the source of all values, including even the aim to be God. From all this Anderson concludes that life need not, after all, be a "useless passion." Sartre's readers too often forget, he claims, that the description in *Being and Nothingness* of man pursuing an unattainable end is intended only to portray man in bad faith. But here he himself fails to take seriously enough Sartre's repeated insistence that man must out of structural necessity always posit as his original choice some mode of the in-itself-for-itself.

Anderson believes that the reason why it is not sufficiently recognized that Sartre's ultimate value is freedom is that Sartrean authenticity has been too much stressed. The authentic person is simply one who accepts himself and his situation without fleeing from them. "Authentic," Anderson maintains, is an overly abstract and rather empty term used to designate the person who knows that his own freedom is the source of all values, who accepts responsibility for this, and thus makes freedom his ultimate value. The authentic person is simply one who accepts himself and his situation without fleeing from them.

Why does Sartre single out freedom as ultimate? Simply, Anderson says, because for him freedom is the source from which all meaningful values spring; and the choosing of any value logically entails the valuing of freedom as a more fundamental choice. But is not freedom, then, through this very logic, somehow elevated to the rank of an intrinsic value? On the contrary, Anderson insists. What has value has value because we choose it. It is precisely because nothing, including freedom, has intrinsic value, because all values, including the value of freedom, are created out of freedom, that freedom should be chosen first of all. Thus Anderson shows that, rather surprisingly, Sartre's very subjectivism regarding values grounds his ethics rather than rendering it impossible.

But what sense does it make to choose freedom, according it value, when, as Sartre everywhere insists, man is already fundamentally free? Critics who ask this question of Sartre, Anderson argues, forget that if something is a fact, that does not automatically make it valuable. Sartre is not guilty of the naturalistic fallacy. Quite to the contrary, he makes a distinction between freedom as an aspect of man's ontological structure and freedom as choice related to action. Men are quite free, for example, to reject or hide from their structural freedom as they do when they choose to believe in determinism. Furthermore, Anderson shows, Sartre insists repeatedly that although man is ontologically free, he should choose to realize his freedom ever more fully through striving to remove restrictions to choice and to the attaining of his goals. But, then, is freedom seen only negatively as "freedom-from"? No, Anderson answers, freedom once liberated has a goal. It aims at exercising and developing the multifaceted features of human life. Fundamentally, this goal is not external to man. Sartre can even speak of his ideal for man as "play," the pursuing of the free expansion of human existence. It is this, Anderson points out, that Sartre calls "true and positive humanism."

Anderson has a whole array of criticisms to make of the way Sartre grounds his ethics in *Being and Nothingness*. A most telling one involves pointing out that Sartre does not use the term "value" consistently. One result of this, Anderson believes, is that although Sartre successfully demonstrates that it is morally right for man to choose to value the capacity for choice, he has not established, as he believes, that a similar obligation exists for man to make free choice more real by changing his situation so as to increase his options for choice. Another criticism which is as important as any Anderson makes is that Sartre never explains convincingly why one must believe that logic and consistency are necessarily included in the choice of a meaningful life.

In the area of interpersonal relations, on the other hand, Anderson strongly defends Sartre, maintaining that Sartrean man is not nearly so estranged from the Other as Sartre's opponents claim. He contends that "conflict," taken in the strict sense, does not mean open hostility but means instead ontological distinctness and psychological objectification. These can, he acknowledges, be the basis for hostility; but they need not be. There is not even any necessity that men relate as being isolated against one another and striving to objectify one another. It is only those who attempt to be God who will end either by trying to dominate others or by being dominated by them. Thus, it is Anderson's firm if questionable opinion that *Being and Nothingness* leaves open the possibility for human relationships founded not on a precarious balancing of oppositions but on the uncontentious reciprocity that would allow positive harmony to prevail.

Manser, Anthony. *Sartre: A Philosophic Study*. London: The Athlone Press, 1966.

Anthony Manser's book has a way of making the analytically trained reader feel at home. The book makes a very special attempt to express Jean-Paul

Sartre's thought in language as close to that of contemporary British philosophical thinking; and it tries to demonstrate that there is a closer kinship between Sartre's thinking and the empirical tradition than is generally believed. With very little distortion, Manser brings Sartre onto Anglo-Saxon ground and clarifies his thought often by contrasting him with Bertrand Russell, Ludwig Wittgenstein, A. J. Ayer, or John Austin, sometimes by pointing to similarities between Sartre and thinkers such as Gilbert Ryle, Stuart Hampshire, Norman Malcolm, and Peter Winch.

One of the most important sections of Manser's book is his excellent discussion, based on a wealth of diverse passages culled mostly from *Being and Nothingness*, of Sartre's view of language. The following is a summary of a few of its dominant themes.

Manser shows that language is no less important for Sartre than for British philosophers. Indeed, it is precisely because Sartre considers language to be so central to human life that he is not attracted by abstract linguistic arguments that stay isolated within the boundaries of language alone. I am language as I am my body, is the Sartrean contention. The same problems and ambiguities that hold for the body hold also for language. Language differs in character depending on whether we look at it from the standpoint of the speaker or writer or from that of the reader or mere listener. Speaking resembles the body in action. One who speaks or who replies directly to speaking is situated within language. To him, words are a prolongation of sense like claws or antennae. A speaker feels them from inside and operates them as he does his body. It is as though he were possessed of a verbal body of which he is only indirectly aware, just as, when walking or running, he might be peripherally aware of his hands or feet. Sometimes, of course, he is uncertain about a part of his language and must reflect on what he is going to say, or he must call to mind some rule of grammar. In these cases he is like a person performing an unfamiliar action who has to concentrate on the way he moves his arms and legs. This is particularly true of speaking a foreign language. But in any sort of ordinary communication, language never seems to be something outside us as though it were an instrument that we are using.

On the other hand, words do have established meanings, and language does have rules. These latter have been *discovered*, however, *after* the spoken word, and basically they are in the forefront only for those standing outside living conversation, and then they cannot give entry to what is being said. Whenever we are mere listeners to the conversation of others, we may know all the rules and all the dictionary meanings of the words we are hearing, and yet, because we stand outside the interchange that is taking place, we will find that our attention to rules or meanings only blocks our understanding of it. Living language in which we participate, in contrast, is transparent; it never gets in the way. We can even find that after genuine participation in a conversation we know something that we learned through words, yet are unable to recall any of the specific words that conveyed it to us.

Too often we think of language as comprised of words that are mere units of discourse with rules that enable us to assemble them into sentences. Discourse, however, is made up of statements, questions, pleas, and commands. It is in sentences that these must be expressed; words are merely traces of the passage of sentences, in much the same way that highways were originally traces of the passage of caravans and pilgrims. Only in the sentence can the word function to designate. Outside it, it is a mere propositional function.

That language does exist independently of us is a fact. Yet being in a world full of linguistic rules and established meanings is part of what Sartre calls being in situation. Within my situation as the one speaking, I am free. *What* I say is never determined by the rules of language. When I am genuinely *saying* something, it is true that I take the orderings of grammar and meanings up into my speech, but I transcend them in my free act of speaking. In the same way, what I do physically is never dictated by my body, even though the ways in which I move are both restricted and helped along by the arrangement of my bones and muscles.—*C.W.L.*

ADDITIONAL RECOMMENDED READING

Caws, Peter. *Sartre*. London: Routlege & Kegan Paul, 1979. Caws takes as his first task the reconstruction of central arguments in Sartre's philosophy in order to bring criticism to bear on them. He gives particular attention to the development in *Being and Nothingness* of themes first found in the earlier works on the imagination and the emotions.

Champigny, Robert. *Stages on Sartre's Way: 1938-52*. Bloomington: Indiana University Press, 1959. In the belief that *Being and Nothingness* is a systematization of Roquentin's grounding experience in Sartre's novel *Nausea*, Champigny attempts to show that Sartre's entire philosophy is rooted in his sensibility.

Danto, Arthur C. *Jean-Paul Sartre*. New York: The Viking Press, 1975. Commending Sartre for the strength and vision of his philosophical system, Danto explains his thought in relation to other major philosophies as he examines the way Sartre relates reality to representation, language to consciousness, the world to the human structuring of it, and so forth.

Hartmann, Klaus. *Sartre's Ontology*. Evanston, Illinois: Northwestern University Press, 1966. Concerning himself with the basic premises of Sartre's ontology, Hartmann first traces its development from Husserlian phenomenology and then interprets *Being and Nothingness* within the framework of Hegel's dialectic.

Morris, Phyllis Sutton. *Sartre's Concept of a Person: An Analytic Approach*. Amherst: University of Massachusetts Press, 1976. Morris compares Sartre with Strawson, Ryle, Shoemaker, Russell, Austin, and others with respect to his treatment of the usual problems considered by Anglo-Saxon philosophers under the heading "philosophy of mind."

Stern, Alfred. *Sartre: His Philosophy and Psychoanalysis*. New York: The Liberal Arts Press, 1953. Giving a critical analysis in the first part of his book of the formative influences on Sartre's thought, Stern then moves on to an examination of the existential psychoanalysis found in *Being and Nothingness* and compares it with the doctrines of Freud, Adler, and others.

ETHICS AND LANGUAGE

Author: Charles Leslie Stevenson (1908-1979)
Type of work: Ethics
First published: 1944

PRINCIPAL IDEAS ADVANCED

Ethical disagreements usually involve both disagreement in belief and disagreement in attitude, but disagreement in attitude is the distinctive element in ethical disputes.

The judgment "This is good" usually functions both as the expression of an attitude and as an injunction; it is roughly equivalent to, "I approve of this; do so as well."

Ethical judgments are justified by the submission of reasons for acting; if the reasons do not appeal to the persons to whom they are addressed, and if there is no disagreement in belief, nothing can be done by the use of reasons.

No one explanation of the function of such a word as "good" is possible; emotive meanings are not so much defined as characterized, and they vary according to the context.

"This is good," according to a second pattern of analysis, means that the object has a particular set of qualities or relations in virtue of which the speaker approves of the object; the hearer tends to be encouraged to approve also. (Such a definition is normally persuasive; it alters descriptive meanings in order to redirect attitudes.)

Ethics and Language propounds what has been called the emotive theory of ethics, a theory often associated particularly with the logical positivists. Stevenson, however, explores an area largely ignored by those writers. Antipositivistic readers with a predisposition to disagree, on the basis that an emotive theory as previously propounded is oversimple, may be induced to set aside this judgment upon discovering Stevenson to observe human nature with acumen and to write with sensitivity and insight. One of Stevenson's avowed purposes is to remove from the term "emotive" any derogatory emotive meaning.

The work lies across several philosophical fields. While "the emotive theory" is a theory of ethics, emotive meaning is a feature of language, studied in semantics. The bases of emotive meaning, feelings, and attitudes, are objects of psychology. And as it combines these fields, the book is in large measure actually a rhetoric, following in a distinguished tradition founded by Aristotle. Stevenson himself calls the work "no more than a prolegomenon to further inquiry" in normative ethics.

Stevenson announces two chief objectives: to clarify the meaning of ethical terms, such as "good," "right," "just," and "ought," and to characterize the general methods by which ethical judgments are justified. He first examines the nature of cases of agreement and disagreement, the situations leading to ethical judgments. Disagreement, whose components are the more readily observed, is of two kinds, disagreement in belief and disagreement in attitude toward an object. "The former is concerned with how matters are truthfully to be described and explained; the latter is concerned with how they are to be favored or disfavored, and hence with how they are to be shaped by human efforts." What one believes to be the nature of an object will go far toward determining his attitude toward it. Furthermore, what one feels toward an object will also shape his belief of what its nature is. When an ethical controversy arises, almost always there is disagreement in both belief and attitude. Its resolution requires not only factual knowledge of the things involved but also recommendations of what is to be done, as well as consequent changes in the motivational attitudes of parties who will undertake pertinent action. Attitudes therefore earn constant attention in Stevenson's work. But since attitudes *alone* are not usually the sources of ethical disagreement, matters of establishing and testing beliefs, or organizing them practically, are vital in all normative discussion, and are likewise important in this exposition.

Efforts to approach ethical judgments as analogues of scientific judgments have been misleading, for, failing to take emotive meaning into account, they treat such judgments as expressive solely of belief. Rather than confine our attention to declarative statements of belief, we should be aware of the more emotion-laden imperative mode. An ethical judgment is closely related to an imperative: "You ought to defend your country" readily becomes "Defend your country." This clue gives Stevenson the working model for the first of two proposed patterns of analysis of ethical judgments. The judgment "This is good," he claims, roughly and partially means "I approve of this; do so as well." The first clause reports an attitude; the second is a command representing the speaker's effort to direct the hearer's attitudes according to his own. The formula should remind us explicitly that "good" is used "not only in expressing beliefs about attitudes, but in strengthening, altering, and guiding the attitudes themselves."

If ethical judgments have the significance of commands, how can they be justified? By the offering of a reason to obey. This may have the form of a description of the situation the speaker desires to alter, or of the new situation he desires to bring about, so that the hearer, upon realizing how obeying would satisfy a preponderance of his desires, will take the same attitude toward the object as the speaker. People who agree in belief generally agree in attitude, since most of us attain satisfaction in about the same things. It must be acknowledged at once that on some occasions two disputants could have precisely the same beliefs about an object, yet disagree radically in attitude, the one approving, the other not. As far as Stevenson's study is concerned, this situation is left as it is. "Those . . . who want to rule out the possibility of rival moral codes, each equally well supported by reasons, will find that the present account gives them less than they want."

Ethical judgments, however, do not have such a bald form in discourse as "I approve of this; do so as well." Neither do they function simply as the command of a superior to an inferior. Rather, they have the power of suggestion through emotive meaning, the "power that the word acquires, on account of its history in emotional situations, to evoke or directly express attitudes, as distinct from describing or designating them. In simple forms it is typical of interjections; in more complicated forms it is a contributing factor to poetry; and it has familiar manifestations in the many terms of ordinary discourse that are laudatory or derogatory."

In order to account for emotive meaning and to relate it to descriptive meaning, we must have a general theory of signs. One requirement of a good view of meaning is that according to its definition meaning must not vary in a bewildering way as emotional associations would do, depending upon the individual user and occasion. This requirement is met by adopting and developing a view of meaning as causal, on the pattern of stimulus-response, understood as complex. Even a seemingly simple instance of cause and effect such as the stimulating effect of drinking coffee is actually complex, joining together many factors of greater or less immediate or ultimate bearing on the outcome, which itself may be measured in terms of greater and less. Some of the factors are in the coffee, and some in the drinker. We say that the relevant cluster of factors in the person stimulated comprise his disposition to be stimulated by coffee. We may equally well say the coffee has a disposition to stimulate its imbibers. A disposition is realized only when its response concretely occurs along with its concrete stimulus, but for convenience we talk of dispositions existing regardless of whether they are being realized at the moment. A disposition is actually a collection of causal factors, known or unknown, involving both stimulus and response, sometimes said to "belong to" the one, sometimes the other, as a dispositional property. Some dispositions are causes of other dispositions.

The meaning of a sign, Stevenson now can say, is a dispositional property of the sign, whose response, varying with the circumstances, consists of psychological processes in a hearer stimulated by his hearing of the sign. Correspondingly, for the speaker it is the word's disposition to be used for a certain effect, the stimulus of his choosing it. *Emotive* meaning is a meaning in which the response of the hearer is a range of emotions. For *descriptive* meaning, the processes of response relate to cognition rather than emotion. Although the basis of the disposition is the psychological makeup of the hearer, it is convenient to refer still to the emotive meaning as "of" the sign just as we do its descriptive meaning. Thus it may be an abiding property of the sign rather than an aspect of individuals upon particular occasions.

Stevenson emphasizes the importance of linguistic flexibility. One and the same word may be used in different circumstances to express favor, disfavor, or indifference, having no one "real" sense present on all occasions. Rather than being able to provide a single definition of "good" or other ethical terms, he must on this account provide patterns for forming definitions of them as used in particular contexts. It is important to remember that these terms have both descriptive and emotive meaning. The patterns should serve to show when emotive meaning is dependent upon or independent of the descriptive meaning of the same term, or quasi-dependent upon indefinite or confused meanings. Emotive meanings, in fact, may need to be *characterized* rather than defined. Because of these complications, the first of Stevenson's two patterns for ethical definition is fashioned expressly to restrict severely the descriptive meaning of ethical terms. It consists simply in the employment, according to particular contexts, of working models of restatement, in the fashion after which "This is good," above, was restated.

A benefit of the first pattern is that it helps make evident the distinctness of the peculiarly moral attitudes, those usually associated with the ethical terms. Conduct morally disapproved leads to responses of indignation, mortification, or shock, or if it is one's own conduct, to guilt or bad conscience. If the conduct is merely disliked, it leads to displeasure but not of these sorts. What one simply likes brings an ordinary sort of pleasure, whereas one "may feel a particularly heightened sense of security" when something he morally approves prospers. "These differences in response, given similar stimuli, help to distinguish the attitudes which are moral from those which are not."

The first pattern also makes evident the methods one uses to support ethical judgments to which it is applied. The reasons are psychologically, not logically, related to ethical judgments, although deductive and inductive logic apply to their descriptive meanings, which express beliefs rather than attitudes. Ethical judgments are supported by such means as showing the nature of what is judged, or of its consequences, or motives that attend it, or origins of the attitude to which it testifies, and so on. Personal decisions, rising from inner conflicts of attitudes, are decided in the same ways as disagreements among individuals. Since emotive factors as reasons are connected only empirically and not in any necessary way to ethical judgments, when an ethical dispute is rooted in disagreement of belief, "it may be settled by reasoning and inquiry to whatever extent the beliefs may be so settled. But if any ethical dispute is *not* rooted in disagreement in belief, then no *reasoned* solution of any sort is possible."

Yet even in such cases of radical disagreement in belief, ethical agreement is sometimes reached, and Stevenson's study of methodology shows certain nonrational ways in which this occurs. The most important are the "persuasive" methods, in a broadened sense of that word. They use the direct emotional impact of the proponent's presentation—"emotive meaning, rhetorical cadence, apt metaphor, stentorian, stimulating, or pleading tones of voice, dramatic gestures, care in establishing *rapport* with the hearer or audience, and so on." Rational and nonrational, and indeed irrational, elements may be woven tightly together; but when we separate them by analysis, among the nonrational we may find emotive means in the supporting reasons as well as the thesis, or merely suggested elements rather than explicit ones. An appeal leading to an *Einfühlung* may bring the hearer to his own reasons for accepting the judgment. Self-persuasion exists and has its place, for persuasion is as ubiquitous as choice. The term "persuasion" has so many legitimate references that, like "emotive," it should not bear an opprobrious emotive meaning.

The question of validity of ethical judgments has often been raised. There can be nothing applying to attitudes and feelings corresponding to deductive validity or soundness of induction in the field of beliefs. Rather, determining what method to use to justify an ethical judgment is itself an ethical problem, whose outcome in turn is determined by an ethical judgment. A moralist may choose either rational or "persuasive" methods; the reasons for his choice, involving both his attitudes and his beliefs, will be as complicated as in any other case of ethical choice. The question of norms for ethical judgments is and remains a normative question. Similarly, the question of what means are to be adopted toward what ends is a normative question. Any combination of approval and disapproval of means and ends may occur. Hence, it is unwarranted for moralists to assume that they can leave the choice of means to others as long as they indicate what ends are worthy. The artificial division between intrinsic and extrinsic goods should be abandoned.

Further, A and B may both agree on the worth of X, but as a means to different ends, or one as a means and the other as an end. And one of them may approve of X both as an end and as a means to another end. Still further, what is first approved as a means may later be approved as an end, or vice versa. As our knowledge of the world increases, these interrelationships of ourselves with our objects of approval, and of other persons with their and our objects of approval, become multiplied to a great number and variety. It is therefore better to substitute the notion of a "focal aim" for "intrinsic good," as a major goal toward which one or many together may strive, for either final or mediate purposes. The whole consideration shows that a study of means is of the utmost importance to normative ethics.

According to Stevenson's second pattern of analysis, "This is good" means "This has qualities or relations X, Y, Z, . . ." and the term "good" also has "a laudatory emotive meaning which permits it to express the speaker's approval, and tends to evoke the approval of the hearer." This pattern permits rich and varied descriptive meaning (interpretations of X, Y, Z . . .) whereas the first pattern stringently restricted it. The explicit report of the speaker's attitude ("I approve of this") has dropped out, now only to be suggested. Like the first pattern, this description is to be treated as a pattern, not itself a definition, for language and contexts are various and we cannot fill in permanent interpretations of X, Y, and Z. The apparently greater "content" of the second pattern allows it to do much more justice to linguistic richness. It is useful where contrary predications of the ethical terms accompany contrary assertions about what they mean.

The definitions of the second pattern are normally *persuasive definitions*. These are definitions of familiar terms so as to alter the term's descriptive meaning, usually making the descriptive meaning more precise while retaining its previous emotive meaning. This is done, consciously or not, to redirect people's attitudes. For instance, we change the descriptive meaning of "temperance," a term with favorable emotive meaning for our opponent, from including only abstinence, which he admires, to including moderate imbibing, which he does not. When this procedure succeeds in redirecting his attitudes to some degree, the effect is not a rational but (in Stevenson's broad sense) a persuasive one. The definition not only clarifies but *participates in* moral issues. Hence great care is needed to keep separate the linguistic and moral aspects if one's purpose (unlike that of many moral philosophers, who are both analysts and moralists) is to achieve clarity and avoid confusion.

So far as norms are concerned, it is indifferent to the outcome of an ethical dispute whether the first or second pattern is used. With the second pattern, the definition itself is persuasive immediately. On the other hand, "instead of *defining* 'good' in terms of X, Y, and Z, as in the second pattern, one may use 'good' in a first-pattern sense and simply *predicate* it of X, Y, and Z. Either procedure will be persuasive . . ." and the choice of the linguistic mechanism to achieve the effect is only incidental.

To use an emotionally-laden word as a scientific term, we must first neutralize its emotive meaning. This may be done by carefully offsetting its emotive meaning with a compensating tone in its whole context, or by balancing particular laudatory terms and derogatory terms against one another, or by giving explicit admonition that emotive effects are to be resisted.

We have noticed that persuasive definitions change the descriptive meaning of a term while retaining the emotive meaning. The corollary process may also have persuasive effect; that is, creating a new emotive meaning without changing the descriptive meaning. Since changes in emotive meaning are not ordinarily said to be new definitions, Stevenson calls this latter process "persuasive quasi-definition." Most cases of persuasive definition exhibit this process to some extent also. Another class of definitions, including typically those of logic, are "detached." They are emotively neutral, persuasive only in the fact of their being the selection for others' attention of the authorities who give them. Related to these are "re-emphatic" definitions, which redirect attention forcibly by rhetorical means, such as a paradox or surprise. Some definitions indeed are both reemphatic and persuasive. Definitions should not be rejected out-of-hand on account of strong persuasive favor, for the emphasis may suggest useful inquiry.

Showing that the understanding of definitions is often "central to the for-mulation and outcome of highly important issues," Stevenson introduces as a sample the question of freedom versus determinism. The controversy be-longs to ethical methodology, involving as it does the relation of judgments and their reasons. Avoidability, not indeterminism, is what is required for responsibility for an action. "A's action was avoidable" means "If A had made a certain choice, which in fact he did not make, his action would not have occurred." (This does not say A's action was not determined. Avoidability has to do not with the causes of an actual choice, but with the effects of a different choice.) We do not assign blame for unavoidable action because ethical judgments are efforts to influence future actions, and blaming un-avoidable actions would not accomplish this end. But an ethical judgment of blame for a past act may serve to alter attitudes; hence, to alter both choices and subsequent action. Far from presupposing indeterminism, this view would seem to presuppose determinism, of the relation of attitudes, choices, and action. But while permitting full determinism, it *requires* only partial deter-minism, and may also permit partial indeterminism. The question of inde-terminism, then, is actually quite irrelevant to ethics.

In assessing the prospects of normative ethics, we may expect any writer presenting his own moral views to follow the long-existing ideal of examining both sides of a normative question and bringing to it as much knowledge as possible. "Our conclusions about how reasons *can* be used, when wedded to the above ideal, become an indispensable guide for deciding how they *should* be used." Such a writer, if he wishes to embody general unifying principles in the face of the great multiplicity of people's actual attitudes, must attend to "focal aims." He will be aware that the value of a goal depends on the still radiating consequences of it, once attained. Before reaching basic principles, he must start with specific judgments and lesser aims, using the sciences in a detailed manner, making empirical inquiry pervade his whole ethics. As far as he provides his norms with rational support, his inquiry will be confined to relevant factual conclusions about human nature and its environment. This writer will probably use persuasion to hasten the effects of his reasons, or to stimulate further inquiry, or to insure full and healthy exercise of the emotions; but these aspects of language must not be allowed to stultify the descriptive. Rather, both aspects must be made to work smoothly together, neither over-stepping its prerogatives. Normative writing and discussion "must draw from the *whole* of a man's knowledge, lending themselves very poorly to special-ization, and they demand a full but controlled emotional vitality."

With his last remarks, Stevenson makes it evident that he himself has been consciously using persuasive language in urging his views. To reject his doc-trine, it should probably be necessary to reject his early tenet that ethical experience has its being in the feelings (and is characterized by feelings of a certain sort as against others), and that therefore the ethical meanings of sentences are subsumed under their emotive meanings rather than those aspects which communicate belief. Stevenson has done a great service in showing the consequences of this tenet. Regardless of whether his contribution is an adequate prolegomenon to the art of morals, his study of emotive meaning is of great importance to rhetoric and semantics.—*J.T.G.*

PERTINENT LITERATURE

Aiken, Henry D. Review of Charles L. Stevenson's *Ethics and Language*, in *The Journal of Philosophy*. XLII, no. 17 (August 16, 1945), pp. 455-470.

This valuable early review focuses upon two or three of the most fundamental issues in Charles L. Stevenson's *Ethics and Language*.

Henry D. Aiken questions whether Stevenson is warranted in adding a second type of meaning to that usually acknowledged—descriptive or cognitive meaning—for Stevenson deals with the causes and effects of utterances, with respect to a hearer or speaker. Utterances have many kinds of effect besides the emotive, and Aiken sees no reason why these must be admitted as meanings or types of meaning of the utterance. Stevenson alleges that when a person is successful in an ethical dispute, he has changed his opponent's attitude, but not necessarily his belief. However, our ultimate purpose usually is starting or modifying action, and the normal way is first to change an opponent's belief by making statements having certain descriptive content. Then his new belief changes his attitude. Terms have emotive effect *by virtue of* descriptive content, not independently of it.

Aiken points out that actually belief itself is not cognition but an attitude, an affective process, a kind of *interest* in the truth or falsity of a proposition. Neither this attitude nor any other, however, determines the meanings of the terms expressing the content of the belief. To counter the view that emotive effects do not deserve the status of meaning, Stevenson has had to deny that *reference* exclusively constitutes the meaning of terms. Some words are apparently without reference but have emotive meaning, such as "alas" and "hurrah," although Aiken suggests that these actually have referents: namely, the distinctive states of the speaker's mind of which they are the sign.

Stevenson believes that meaning can be explained causally. The traditional objection to this view is that it fails to explain how a word can acquire and keep a stable meaning if it is the effect of ever-changing causes. Stevenson accounts for such a circumstance by means of the concept of dispositional properties: the meaning of a word lies in its activating our disposition to respond within a certain range of cognitive or emotive responses. Aiken asks for evidence, particularly that some important words evoke ranges of emotive meaning not prompted by a descriptive meaning; but there simply is no word having no descriptive meaning whatsoever. Stevenson ought to analyze cognition and its relation to attitude in order to strengthen his insistence that there is a dichotomy in which description and emotion are on a par. Instead, he begs the point of this main issue rather than demonstrating it.

Stevenson explains the meanings of ethical language in terms of the methods used to support or attack ethical judgments and hence to resolve ethical disagreements. Since this proposition rests wholly upon our admitting emotive meaning as a type of meaning comparable to and equally important with descriptive meaning, however, if we do admit emotive meaning and accept the consequence, we make the factors in adopting beliefs totally irrelevant to the content of the beliefs. We should not yield to such a theory. Rather, we should leave the way open for ethical judgments to be rationally justifiable propositions that are either true or false.

Black, Max. "Some Questions About Emotive Meaning," in *The Philosophical Review*. LVII, no. 2 (March, 1948), pp. 111-126.

It was C. K. Ogden and I. A. Richards in their influential book *The Meaning of Meaning* who first used the term "emotive meaning." Charles L. Stevenson, Max Black maintains, has kept in harmony with their linguistic theory yet has considerably remedied the weakness in their doctrine. Particularly valuable is his analysis of the "pragmatic" meaning of symbols, invoking a disposition to respond within a range of cognitions or emotions.

Black devotes the main part of his essay to Richards, and leaves only a short space for Stevenson, giving a "catalog" of doubts about the "pragmatic" analysis. First, he is inclined to resist calling emotive responses "meanings." Second, if the training or conditioning that all of us get to set up our ranges of responses accounts for emotive meanings of the words we hear, then since we respond to many other things besides words or symbols, a whole new category of nonlinguistic entities will have "meaning"—which goes against our usual ways of using particular words. Third, descriptive meaning needs a full clarification, and the claim that linguistic rules are the distinguishing characteristic of descriptive words seems mistaken and needs elucidation or correction. Fourth, Stevenson needs to take fully into account our usual understanding that a word or sign is a representative of something that it "means," rather than continuing to hold that a "sign" can have emotive meaning and yet not be a sign *of* anything—that is, have anything to which it refers. This point leads to another: that we will want to deny that the expressions having solely emotive meaning are words at all (are signs in our symbol system), they being on a par with ordinary physical stimuli of a nonsymbolic kind. In turn, we would be led to acknowledge only a single type of meaning, leaving the descriptive and emotive to be explained in terms of the referents of the signs comprising our language. The desired result of accounting for the liveliness of the predominantly emotive expressions in this modified linguistic theory will be accomplished simply by descriptive meaning in the more exciting expressions, which are more direct than the emotionally neutral expressions. Finally, the focus on the irrational aspects of ethical discourse, leaving ethical issues to be resolved principally by methods of changing persons' emotions or attitudes, not only would require us to revise considerably our ways of talking about them but might also have a definitely harmful effect. Insufficient credit is given to the cognitive; to reverse the emphasis even though acknowledging the strength of emotional factors might encourage a search for the more rational bases of agreement on ethical matters.

Urmson, J. O. *The Emotive Theory of Ethics*. London: Hutchinson University Library, 1968.

Charles L. Stevenson first considered emotive meaning for the sake of ethics rather than to explain ethics away, as A. J. Ayer had done. J. O. Urmson, admiring but not accepting the emotive theory, criticizes its development particularly in *Ethics and Language*, hoping thus to contribute further to value theory. He applies John Austin's concepts of expressive force in amending the emotive theory.

Urmson finds three serious defects in Stevenson: (1) no difference is shown between valid and invalid evaluations; (2) there are no logical irrelevancies in evaluations; (3) if evaluative language were successful, it would die out, having removed any need for itself, as it has no use where agreement is already present. Stevenson's greatest mistake, Urmson maintains, is in attempting to explain emotive meaning (and all meaning) in terms of cause. A speaker stirred by an emotion is impelled to express himself in an appropriate expression with an emotional meaning. This view taken narrowly has the odd consequence that one can never change one's own evaluations by taking thought, since they always follow stimuli impinging from outside.

How could "I approve of this" be part of the descriptive meaning of "This is good"? They are not identical. Approval is only one among the attitudes conveyed by judgments of goodness. Again, "I approve of this" is not necessarily most appropriately represented by "This is good," but sometimes by "This is right." Urmson rejects Stevenson's formulation of the meaning of the value judgment. Stevenson confuses (1) the *setting* of standards of evaluation with (2) *using* the standards once set, for judging individual cases. Under (2), a judgment is simply factual, can have validity, and may be either true or false. Stevenson's more flexible second pattern of analysis is a description listing important characteristics of an object with a tone of approval. Urmson finds that this alleges a separate definition for virtually every occurrence of "good," and is simply a mistaken view about what meanings of words are, thus perhaps explaining the process of *setting* standards, but not the far more numerous applications of "good" to instances when set standards already exist.

Stevenson argues that there is no distinction between valid and invalid ethical judgments. Urmson, however, rejects one of his premises: that the key to determining an ethical statement to be true is to see whether its speaker does in fact approve of what he calls good. Urmson, moreover, would reject the emotive theory rather than deny that there can be valid ethical argumentation.

It is important to distinguish two basic applications of the adjective "good": things good of a kind, and things good from a certain point of view. It is the latter that is commonly used in moral contexts. Urmson adverts to Austin's terms of expressive force: the *locutionary* force of a term is equivalent to the dictionary meaning of the term. Its *illocutionary* force is what its user is doing with it, such as commending, and its *perlocutionary* force is what he brings about by issuing the utterance. Now we find that there are occasions when a value term does not participate in illocutionary force in its clause, as when that clause is embedded in a long sentence, and also because empirical terms that are not ordinarily evaluative, can be given illocutionary force of favor or disfavor. Thus the occurrence of evaluative terms is neither a necessary nor a sufficient condition for evaluative illocutionary force. Illocutionary force, however, characterizes utterance *in a situation*, rather than independently of communication situations; thus it is not a part of the linguistic meaning of a term, although the linguistic meaning relates to illocutionary force, making some illocutionary forces possible and others not.

We can separate instances of expressions into those having *central*, and those having *peripheral*, illocutionary force. If, when a certain illocutionary force is present, a hearer would have to consent that that same illocutionary force is always present in all occurrences of that word, then its force is *central*; otherwise, it is *peripheral*. Thus we are helped to understand that the meaning of the word "good" is such that the illocutionary force of favor, commendation, approval, or the like is central to its employment. Urmson develops not a definition of "good" but several formulations that help us understand how it has a variety of illocutionary forces in its applications to things good of a kind and to things good from a point of view.

The emotivists did help us to escape the sterility of the conflict over whether "good" is a natural or a nonnatural quality. Their descriptions were early and imperfect formulations of insights of great importance. They placed too much stress on causality rather than on expressive force, too much on emotion with insufficient study and clarification of attitudes. The result was to make evaluation seem entirely nonrational, beyond considerations of truth or falsity, logical validity or invalidity. Yet they helped us recognize that to evaluate commits one to an attitude, that attitudes are formed not only by transitory emotions but also by words and acts, that attitudes can be altered rationally,

and thus can be the vehicles of agreements and of the resolution of disagreements through familiar sorts of reasoning. We could not advance beyond the
final stance of Stevenson and the other early emotivists if they had not made
their contributions.—*J. T. G.*

ADDITIONAL RECOMMENDED READING
Blanshard, Brand. "Emotivism," in *Reason and Goodness*. London: George
    Allen & Unwin, 1961. Severe criticism of the emotive theorists of ethics
    including, Ayer and the logical positivists; sections 16 to 32, concluding the
    chapter, are aimed primarily at Stevenson.
————————— . "The New Subjectivism in Ethics," in *Philosophy and Phe-
    nomenological Research*. IX, no. 3 (March, 1949), pp. 504-511. A sharp
    general criticism of the emotive theory, naming as its proponents Russell,
    Wittgenstein, Ayer, Carnap, Stevenson, and Feigl.
Brandt, Richard B. "The Emotive Theory of Ethics," in *The Philosophical
    Review*. LIX, no. 3 (July, 1950), pp. 305-318. Skillful analysis of Stevenson's
    chief principles and their interrelations.
Edwards, Paul. *The Logic of Moral Discourse*. Glencoe, Illinois: Free Press,
    1955. In constructing his own ethical theory Edwards largely incorporates
    Stevenson's interpretation of meanings of ethical terms while denying the
    adequacy of Stevenson's descriptive-emotive dichotomy.
Parker, De Witt H. "Reflections on the Crisis in Theory of Value. I. Mostly
    Critical," in *Ethics*. LVI, no. 3 (April, 1946), pp. 193-207. The "crisis" is
    represented by R. B. Perry, John Dewey, and Stevenson.
Robinson, Richard. "The Emotive Theory of Ethics," in *Proceedings of the
    Aristotelian Society*. XXII (1948), pp. 79-106. Variant of the emotive theory
    enforcing the independence of emotive from cognitive meaning and the
    unanalyzability of ethical (emotive) predicates.
Stroll, Avrum. *The Emotive Theory of Ethics*, in *University of California
    Publications in Philosophy*. XXVIII, no. 1 (1954), pp. 1-92. Berkeley:
    University of California Press. Through useful analyses of emotive, ex-
    pressive, and evocative meaning, and of four senses of "ordinary discourse,"
    Stroll endeavors to show that neither Ayer's nor Stevenson's version is new
    in philosophy and that neither emotive philosopher analyzes ordinary lan-
    guage correctly.

PHENOMENOLOGY OF PERCEPTION

Author: Maurice Merleau-Ponty (1908-1961)
Type of work: Existential phenomenology
First published: 1945

PRINCIPAL IDEAS ADVANCED

The world is not (as realism contends) the cause of our consciousness of it; but neither (as idealism contends) does our consciousness "constitute" the world by providing order and meaning to intrinsically meaningless "sensations."

The human body is no mere "physical body" which can be understood in terms of purely causal relations between its parts and between itself and objects; as "lived" it is, rather, the bearer of our most fundamental grasp of and orientation to the world, which provides the basis for our more conscious, personal activities.

The human mind is not sheer mind, possessing a pure rational comprehension of the world or of itself. Human rationality is rooted in human perception, and self-knowledge is mediated through bodily expression and action in the world and through time.

Man is not determined by his past, his temperament, his situation; but neither is he radically free in relation to these motivations. His freedom is found in accepting them and taking them up in free choices, in which one proferred motivation is refused only by accepting another, and which can only gradually modify the basic direction of personality.

Phenomenology of Perception is Maurice Merleau-Ponty's second book, following *The Structure of Behavior*, a critique of psychological behaviorism published in 1942. *Phenomenology of Perception* incorporates various insights from the earlier work, but also deals in depth with many matters which it did not treat, or treated only cursorily. This work defines the main lines of the philosophical position to which Merleau-Ponty held for most of the rest of his life, with significant changes in the direction of his thinking only clearly emerging in the various fragments which were published posthumously as *The Visible and the Invisible*.

Phenomenology of Perception is in some respects less, but in many respects more, than its title suggests. It is not a systematic orderly analysis, along Husserlian lines, of perception regarded in isolation from other modes of human consciousness. Rather, it is a kind of *ontology* of *human existence*, in which perception is shown to play a most fundamental role. In the range of its topics—which include embodiment, sexuality, the relation between self and other, self-knowledge, temporality, and freedom—the work is comparable to Jean-Paul Sartre's *Being and Nothingness*. Indeed, the influence of Sartre, who was Merleau-Ponty's friend and associate for many years, is often apparent, although Merleau-Ponty avoids the abstract oppositions and paradoxes of Sartre's thought and presents a subtler, more concrete conception of these matters.

In the working out of his position, Merleau-Ponty also comes to terms with such giants of modern philosophy as René Descartes, Immanuel Kant, and G. W. F. Hegel. His work reflects as well his familiarity with twentieth century French thinkers such as Henri Bergson, Léon Brunschvicg, and Gabriel Marcel, and with psychological literature, particularly that of the Gestalt school. But the most significant influence on his thinking is clearly phenomenology, as represented by Edmund Husserl, Martin Heidegger, and Max Scheler.

Merleau-Ponty's understanding of phenomenology is presented in the "Preface" to his work. Phenomenology, he says, involves an attempt to recall the prescientific experience of the world on which our scientific knowledge is based, but which is often passed over by an attitude that (mistakenly) takes scientific knowledge to be absolute. He credits Husserl with developing the method by which the absolutist pretensions of science could be criticized, but declines to follow Husserl in the idealistic direction that characterized much of his work. Phenomenological reflection does not lead, Merleau-Ponty says, to recognition of oneself as a "transcendental consciousness" somehow apart from the world, but to the revelation of our "being-in-the-world" ("being in" to be understood as meaning not simple spatial location, but "inhabiting," "being involved in"). Moreover, our reflection on "essences" does not disclose them as a separate sphere of being, but rather should serve as a means for clarifying concrete *existence*, our living experience of the world and ourselves.

The "Introduction" to *Phenomenology of Perception* is a section subtitled "Traditional Prejudices and the Return to Phenomena." Here Merleau-Ponty critically examines certain concepts and assumptions which have had the effect of obscuring, rather than illuminating, the true nature of our perceptual experience. Chief among such concepts is that of *sensation*. Sensations are usually conceived of as isolated, inner states which the perceiver undergoes as a result of external stimuli. The "constancy hypothesis" in psychology postulates that uniform stimuli produce uniform effects of this sort. But this attempt to construct a causal account of perception is inadequate, Merleau-Ponty argues; nothing in our actual experience corresponds to this concept of sensation. Our perceptual life is not composed of isolated states; in it, every element has some *meaning* in relation to the whole. Perceptual consciousness is not the sheer feeling of an inner state, but is (in the phenomenological sense) *intentional*, is directed *toward*, is consciousness *of* something other than itself. The empiricists' conceptions of "association" and "projection of memories" or the rationalists' conception of (for example) "judgment" as processes which remedy the deficiencies of sensations, only reflect the inadequacy of the concept of sensation. Association and memory must somehow be suggested, "motivated" by present experience, which thus *cannot* be a blind sensation. Judgment is *based on* a perceptual field having some *inherent* structure, which it seeks to make explicit.

The fundamental error of both empiricist and rationalist accounts of consciousness, Merleau-Ponty argues, lies in what he calls "the prejudice in favour of the world." They *presuppose* a conception of a fully determinate "objective" world and attempt to understand consciousness on this basis—either as a mere *effect* of this world or as objective *knowledge of* it—rather than beginning with an unprejudiced examination of that perceptual experience through which there *comes to be* a world *for me*. Such reflection will disclose perception as neither the passive undergoing of sensations, nor the active, rational "constitution" of the "objective" world, but as a living relation to an ambiguous, prescientific, perceptual world.

Having thus set the essential task of his work, Merleau-Ponty turns to the crucial topic of *the body*. His discussion—which occupies the first main division of *Phenomenology of Perception*—proceeds largely through reflection on scientific findings about the body, findings which he contends have been seriously misinterpreted by scientists themselves. He attempts to establish that the human body is not an object in the world (a mere "physical object"); *that* concept of the body is an abstraction from the concrete, *"lived"* body, which is one's point of view on, one's openness to, and the base of one's orientation toward the world. Because the theory of the body and the theory of perception are of necessity closely related, Merleau-Ponty's account of the body provides an avenue to disclosure of the concrete perceived world which underlies the "objective" world depicted by science.

Merleau-Ponty's reflections on the body are extraordinarily rich, and only some of their most basic themes can be indicated here. He points to a number of considerations which preclude the body's being adequately conceived as an "object"—as something which is related to other "objects," or whose parts are related to one another, only externally and mechanically. The study of the nervous system has shown, he says, that no *simple* localization can be assigned to the ability to perceive a specific quality. Sensible qualities are not mere effects of stimuli, but require that the body be somehow "attuned" for their perception, as the hand, in moving around an object, *anticipates* the stimuli which will reveal the object to it. Merleau-Ponty provides a particularly illuminating discussion of "phantom limb" experiences, in which a person seems to feel (for example) pain in an amputated limb. He argues that this phenomenon can be explained neither in terms of mere physical factors (such as stimuli affecting the nerves which had been linked to the limb) nor purely psychological factors (such as memory of the lost limb or refusal to face its loss). Rather, a phantom limb is experienced when objects are implicitly taken to be manipulatable as they were before loss of the limb. It is a matter of our projecting ourselves into a practical environment, of our embodied "being-in-the-world," of our ambiguous concrete existence at a level prior to the abstract distinction of the "physical" and the "psychological." The body is no mere "thing"; it is a "body-subject," the seat of our habits, of our innate and acquired capacities and orientation toward the world. As such it provides the general background from which our most conscious, personal, and rational acts emerge.

Merleau-Ponty subsequently deals with the nature of bodily movement and its relation to perception. Consciousness does not move the body as one moves an "object" through space, he argues; rather, the body moves insofar as it "inhabits" space, insofar as it is oriented in relation to objects. Our perceptual powers are themselves intimately interrelated. The unity of the living body is the unity of a "style," comparable to the unity of a work of art; our powers work together in disclosure of the world.

Merleau-Ponty's account of the body concludes with discussions of sexuality and of "the body as expression and speech." His discussion of sexuality—which involves some very subtle reflections on Sigmund Freud—depicts it as a general atmosphere which suffuses life in such a way that it can neither serve as a total explanation of our existence nor be isolated from the other modes of our being-in-the-world. Neither a matter of mere "physiology" nor of sheer consciousness, sexuality is a mode of our being-in-the-world, a basic manner in which one embodied being can exist in relation to another.

In his discussion of speech, Merleau-Ponty criticizes equally empiricist psychologies which construe our use of words as the mere result of physiological processes, and rationalist conceptions which take words to be merely external accompaniments of thought, linked to it by mere association. Both of these views deprive *the word itself* of meaning. But, he argues, thought and speech—either external or internal—are essentially bound up with each other. Contrary to most of the philosophical tradition since Plato, Merleau-Ponty denies that meaningful speech must be preceded or accompanied by a *separate* process of thinking. Rather, we think *in* speech; and although thinking sometimes seems to run "a step ahead" of speech, it nevertheless requires linguistic expression to establish itself. The phenomenon of speech must ultimately, he adds, be understood as of a kind with other modes of bodily "gesture"—their meaning is immanent in them. The whole expressive dimension of our embodied existence stands as one more proof that the rigid Cartesian dualism of thinking substance and extended substance is inadequate.

In the second main division of *Phenomenology of Perception*, Merleau-Ponty turns to an explication of the concrete structures of the *perceived world*. Again he attempts to delineate an alternative to both empiricism and rationalism. Both views, he argues, simply presuppose a fully determinate objective world. Empiricism locates the subject as a thing in that world, construes the relation of world to subject as causal, and constructs its account of experience on that basis. Rationalism takes the world to be *for* a knowing subject and analyzes experience accordingly. Neither takes its stand *within* that ambiguous living experience in which objects come to be for us. Accepting this task, Merleau-Ponty provides accounts of our concrete experience of sensible qualities, of spatial location, depth, and movement, of shape, size, the "natural thing" as a unity of sensible qualities, and finally of the *world* as that open unity which forms the ultimate horizon of all our experiences. Preeminent in all these experiences is the role of the body—its capacity to "merge into" a given perceptual situation (as when, without any thought, it manages to grasp the true colors of things despite abnormal lighting conditions which change the "objective" stimuli which are present), to respond to the solicitation of ambiguous data, to grasp through the unity of its perceptual powers the unity of qualities in a thing, to be present through the perceptual field to a world which is ever incomplete.

The last and perhaps most interesting chapter of Merleau-Ponty's account of the perceived world deals with "the other self and the human world" and draws on many of the basic insights developed in earlier sections. We are not only conscious of natural objects, he notes, but also perceive about us the artifacts and inhabitants of a cultural and social world—a *human* world. And the first, the most basic "cultural object," he argues, must be the *body* of the *other person*; only on the foundation of our perception of others is a cultural world accessible to us. But "objective thought" would make perception of the other impossible by construing all bodies as mere objects, and the subject as a pure "for itself," a sheer self-conscious, rational surveyor of the objective world. This would make it unintelligible that a body could ever be truly *expressive* of a subjectivity, and that there could ever be another for-itself *for me*. But, as Merleau-Ponty has shown, *I* am not a sheer for-itself—I am rather an embodied, perceiving, behaving subject—and thus the *other's* body is not for me a thing, a mere in-itself. *My* experience of embodied subjectivity allows me, prior to any sort of explicit analogy or judgment, to grasp another consciousness in *its* embodiment. The perceived world, as that unity which forever outruns my determinate grasp of it, is also crucial here; as my different perspectives "slip into" one another and are united in relation to the perceptible thing, so my perspective and that of the other "slip into" one another and are united in the world, in which our communication is possible.

Language and the experience of dialogue of course play an important role. Our thoughts are woven together in living, reciprocal speech. But, Merleau-Ponty adds, the plurality of consciousnesses, their difference from one another, is an inescapable fact. The anger or grief which I grasp in another's behavior, for example, do not have the same significance for both of us; he *lives* what I merely *perceive*. We have common projects, but each participates in it from his *own* perspective. Solitude and communication, Merleau-Ponty warns, must not be taken as exclusive alternatives; rather, they are two aspects of our ambiguous human condition. Thus I can recognize that the other is *imperfectly* known by me, only if I *do* have experience *of* the other. Merleau-

Ponty proceeds to criticize Sartre's claim that I must either make an object of the other, or allow his "gaze" to make an object of me; another person's gaze is felt as unbearable, he says, only if it replaces possible communication, and the latter retains its truth. He concludes by asserting that I am neither in society as one object among others, nor is society in me as an object of thought; rather, the social is a "dimension of existence" in which I live.

The third and final main division of *Phenomenology of Perception* deals with "being-for-itself and being-in-the-world." Here Merleau-Ponty discusses self-knowledge (the "*cogito*"), temporality, and freedom. Developing the position of Descartes, idealism has argued that objects must be *for* a subject which is *for itself*, which knows itself, which somehow contains within itself the key to every object that it could possibly encounter. But the mind is not a sheer for-itself, Merleau-Ponty maintains; the *cogito* does not involve an absolute and total self-knowledge. Thus he undertakes a critique of traditional doctrines of the *cogito*. He argues first that, contrary to Descartes, I can be no more certain *that* I see than the *thing* I see exists. Nor do I possess absolute self-knowledge in respect to my will or feeling; I can, for example, think that I am in love without truly being so. I do *not* know myself so much *in myself*, in some inner and immediate self-presence, as *in act*. It is by action and expression in the world and through the body that I achieve determinacy and clarity for myself, so that the *cogito* is inherently conditioned by temporality. Thus the "I think" is dependent on the "I am." Even in the sphere of so-called "pure thought"—geometrical thinking, for example—my grasp of truth is dependent on my bodily orientation to the world, through which I can fundamentally grasp what a "triangle" or a "direction" is. Moreover, thought is inherently dependent on speech, and the clarity achieved in a given thought is dependent on an always somewhat obscure context which has been formed by past acts of expression. The centrality of this phenomenon of "acquisition" in our mental life points again to the inherent temporality of all our grasp on truth.

These critical reflections on doctrines which would grant to the mind an absolute grasp of itself or of the world do not, however, lead Merleau-Ponty to reject the *cogito* altogether. There is, he says, a presence to self which precedes and conditions our explicit grasp of ourselves or of the world, a "tacit *cogito*" which precedes the "spoken *cogito*." But this tacit *cogito* is inchoate and must be expressed in a verbal *cogito* in order to attain clarity. The ultimate subject, Merleau-Ponty concludes, is not a sheer self-present nonworldly ego which "constitutes" the world, but a being which *belongs to* the world.

The fundamental role of time in relation to all sorts of phenomena is indicated throughout the *Phenomenology of Perception*, but it becomes the explicit theme of Merleau-Ponty's reflections only in the penultimate chapter of the work. He begins by arguing that time is inseparable from subjectivity;

without a subject, there is no *present* in the world, and without a present there can be no past or future. But what is the fundamental relation of time and subjectivity? The subject cannot, he says, be simply located in the "now," and its consciousness of past and future explained in terms of physiological or psychological "traces" of the past. Such "traces," being purely *present*, could not ground our opening onto past or future. But neither could time be a constituted *object* for a *nontemporal* subject before whom past, present, and future were equally arrayed; for if they were all alike *present*, there would be no time. Time, then, is inseparable from a subject, but this subject is *itself* inherently *temporal*, is *situated* in time, and grasps future and past on the horizon of a flowing present which accomplishes the transition between them. There is an essential interdependence between temporality and the "thrust" of concrete subjectivity toward a world and toward a future in which it can (in both senses of the term) "realize" itself.

The final chapter of *Phenomenology of Perception* is a subtly reasoned and eloquently expressed reflection on human freedom. Initially, Merleau-Ponty notes, the only alternative to a causal and deterministic conception of the relation between the subject and the world (a conception which would, in effect, make a thing of consciousness) is a view of human consciousness as *wholly* free, independent of all motives, of nature, of one's past temperament and history. In this view—which is essentially that expressed by Sartre in *Being and Nothingness*—even obstacles to our freedom are in reality deployed by it; it is my choice to reach a certain destination which *makes* certain objects into obstacles for me.

However, Merleau-Ponty responds, this abstract conception of freedom would in effect rule it out completely. A wholly indeterminate freedom would lack even the possibility of committing itself, since the next instant would find it again indeterminate and uncommitted. Rather, he argues, a choice once made must provide some impetus to personality, must establish a direction which tends to conserve itself. Because I am not a sheer self-conscious subject but an *embodied* being like other human beings, my free choices take place against a background of possibilities that have a kind of preliminary significance for me. Thus mountains appear high to me whether or not I choose to climb them. And because I am a *temporal* being, my established character and habits, although they do not cause, do *incline* me to certain choices.

Freedom is always, then, a taking-up of some meaning or some motivation which is offered by my situation in the world. I can reject one preferred meaning or motivation, Merleau-Ponty says, only by accepting another. And even if a man being tortured refuses to provide the information his torturers demand, this free action does not reflect a wholly solitary and unmotivated choice; it is supported by his awareness of unity with his comrades, his preparation for such an ordeal, or his long-established belief in freedom.

Man is neither a mere thing nor a sheer consciousness. Human life involves a continual synthesis of the for-itself and the in-itself, a taking-up and shaping of our finite situation, a reciprocity of self and world. We are truly free not by denying our natural and social situation, but by assuming it and living it. Thus philosophy recalls us to our concrete existence in the world, where— Merleau-Ponty suggests—our proper task is to commit our freedom to the realization of freedom for all.—*J.D.G.*

PERTINENT LITERATURE

Kwant, Remy C. *The Phenomenological Philosophy of Merleau-Ponty.* Pittsburgh: Duquesne University Press, 1963.

Remy C. Kwant's work is a good general study of Maurice Merleau-Ponty's philosophy. Nine of its thirteen chapters deal primarily with *Phenomenology of Perception*, although they also contain supplementary references to other works published during the philosopher's lifetime. The book is in large part expository and reflects sympathy for Merleau-Ponty's insights, although Kwant also criticizes seriously some basic aspects of his philosophical position.

The first three chapters concentrate on Merleau-Ponty's account of the "body-subject." Kwant discusses the sense in which the body can be described as "subject"—namely, in that it is "a meaning-giving existence," a source of meaning for various sorts of objects. But he is careful to add that Merleau-Ponty conceives the relation of the "body-subject" to objects as dialectical; the former does not stand apart from, but *is* in its relation to the latter. Kwant develops Merleau-Ponty's use of the question-answer relation as a metaphor for the relation of body and world. The body, he says, is permeated with "questioning orientations" which the world "answers" in various ways.

In reflecting on Merleau-Ponty's approach to the "body-subject," Kwant first notes the difficulty of describing his method precisely. One aspect of this method which he stresses is Merleau-Ponty's examination of instances of abnormality (for example, the case of a brain-damaged patient which is discussed at some length in the *Phenomenology of Perception*) in order to illuminate normal existence by contrast. Kwant comments, in a way with which most readers of Merleau-Ponty can sympathize, on the somewhat "obscure nature" of his philosophy. While granting important insights to Merleau-Ponty, Kwant suggests that his ideas cannot be systematized or very clearly formulated. But this is, he suggests, due to the nature of the subject matter— the "obscure basis," the "dark soil in which are the hidden roots of our existence."

Kwant regards Merleau-Ponty's attempt to show the dependence of thought on language, and of language on the body-subject, as an important aspect of a general attempt to establish the fundamental bodily nature of man. As Kwant understands Merleau-Ponty, the latter's position ultimately implies that "man is nothing but a body-subject"—although this claim is qualified in light of the fact that Merleau-Ponty uses the term "body" in different ways, sometimes as a term for our "fixed existence," but sometimes also as inclusive of the "self-transcending" capacities of human existence.

The sixth and seventh chapters of Kwant's book are closely related; they deal with Merleau-Ponty's "rejection of the absolute" and his account of "metaphysical consciousness." In the sixth chapter, Kwant indicates that Merleau-Ponty rejects any eternal, absolute truth, any truth transcending our "acquired" truths—those which have been established through human acts of expression. In the seventh, Kwant stresses a "revolutionary" aspect of Merleau-Ponty's thought—namely, that he does not take the "intelligibility of reality" to be true *in principle*, but regards it as a contingent *fact*, inseparable from our contingent, situated, bodily being-in-the-world.

Chapters nine and ten provide useful accounts of Merleau-Ponty's relation to the phenomenological tradition and the relation of his thinking to science. The twelfth chapter compares his philosophy to Jean-Paul Sartre's. While finding Merleau-Ponty's critique of the Sartrean conception of freedom to be sound, Kwant regrets that Merleau-Ponty's own account of freedom is framed so much in terms of criticism of Sartre, and he suggests that Merleau-Ponty lacks "a description of the inner essence of the thinking and free subject."

This latter point is related to criticisms suggested by Kwant throughout this work and brought together in the concluding chapter. In general, he suggests that Merleau-Ponty has given a good account of the *roots* of our existence but has not adequately treated its *heights*. He has not, for example, described the "inner character" of rational thinking *per se*, of the universality of rational truth, or of "conscious, free subjectivity." Kwant grants "great credit" to Merleau-Ponty for showing that the human body is no simple "thing," but suggests that traditional soul-body dualism *did* have a basis in certain aspects of our existence—such as our "universal openness" to truth and our capacity for unselfish love—to which Merleau-Ponty does not give sufficient attention. Finally, Kwant is critical of Merleau-Ponty's refusal to seek any ground outside contingent human existence in the world for the intelligibility of reality. Merleau-Ponty's thought "contains a very valuable vision," he says, but this vision is incomplete.

In general, Kwant's criticisms of Merleau-Ponty seem to be weighty, but not conclusive. *Phenomenology of Perception* did not give extended consideration to the structures of thinking *per se* or to the question of rational truth. But it is not wholly silent on these topics, and the fact that Merleau-Ponty did not treat them in more detail is partially to be explained by the fact that his primary concern was *perception*. It may not be so clear, as Kwant thinks, that Merleau-Ponty identified man with the body—even the body in a very broad sense of the term; but it must be admitted that, having shown how the traditional sharp distinction between mind and body distorts our concrete (and ambiguous) existence, Merleau-Ponty does not (perhaps in principle cannot) offer any precise account of their relation.

As for questions of the absolute, of rationality and truth, and of the spiritual dimensions of existence, it should be noted that Merleau-Ponty's later works (including some of his posthumously published writings) have much to say on these matters. On the whole, the horizons of the later works are somewhat broader than those of *Phenomenology of Perception*. It is true, however, that he never achieved a systematic or clear resolution of these most important and difficult issues.

Langan, Thomas. *Merleau-Ponty's Critique of Reason*. New Haven, Connecticut: Yale University Press, 1966.

Thomas Langan's book is a somewhat brief but intensive study of Maurice Merleau-Ponty's thought. Most of the chapters deal primarily with *Phenomenology of Perception* but attempt to integrate with it some of Merleau-Ponty's other writings. Langan interprets Merleau-Ponty as standing in, and making original contributions to, the tradition of "critical" or "transcendental" philosophy, which does not deal so much directly with objects as it reflects on the experience in which objects are given to us. More specifically, Langan sees Merleau-Ponty's thinking as a response to "internal tensions" in this tradition, which derives from René Descartes and has been developed by Immanuel Kant, G. W. F. Hegel, and Edmund Husserl, but which has also given rise to Søren Kierkegaard, Friedrich Wilhelm Nietzsche, Karl Marx, Martin Heidegger, and Jean-Paul Sartre.

Remy C. Kwant's first chaper, "The Transcendental Standpoint," reflects briefly on the tradition of transcendental philosophy, pointing to the difficulty of its attempts to put aside all commonsense presuppositions. With his interpretation, Merleau-Ponty attempted to go farther in this direction than either Hegel or Husserl, who presupposed (although in rather different ways) that reality is rationally knowable. Merleau-Ponty's distinctive contribution to transcendental philosophy, Langan suggests, lies in his elaboration of a "new notion of synthesis," a new account of the relation of experience and Being. According to this account, we "synthesize" or "make sense of" Being from a position *within* Being.

With this as his guiding theme, Langan sets out to explore various aspects of Merleau-Ponty's philosophy. His second chapter, entitled "Incarnated Intentionality: The New Transcendental Aesthetic," deals with Merleau-Ponty's account of embodied consciousness and perception. He first focuses on the problem of truth, noting that the way in which Merleau-Ponty originally poses the problem—asking how there can be an *"in-itself for us"*—indicates a basic attempt to surpass the traditional opposition of idealism and empiricism. Langan provides a helpful analysis of the way in which, according to Merleau-Ponty, our perception of a *figure* takes place (as the Gestalt psychologists had stressed) in the context of a background or *field*, with the *world* forming the ultimate background. This reference of perception to a background transcending it is important in Merleau-Ponty's account of experience as both *mine* and as pertaining to what lies *beyond* me. Langan proceeds to discuss the body as our opening onto this world, noting the impossibility of describing our embodied, living experience with clear and distinct concepts. Nevertheless, he provides an artfully constructed re-presentation of Merleau-Ponty's reflections on this topic, culminating in a discussion of intersubjectivity.

Langan's third chapter, "Analytica-Dialectica," begins with an account of Merleau-Ponty's treatment of the *cogito*, giving special attention to his conception of conceptual truth as dependent on human embodiment, perception, and expression. The fourth chapter, "Practica," discusses Merleau-Ponty's conception of finite freedom in the *Phenomenology of Perception* and then turns to his reflections on political action in later works. The fifth chapter— "Poetica: A New Montaigne"—centers around the opposition between "fascination" ("passive absorption in one's world") and "activism" (the attempt to achieve total domination of one's situation). That neither of these extremes is an adequate response to the human condition is clearly implied in *Phenomenology of Perception* but Langan finds in Merleau-Ponty's later works, particularly in his reflections on the varieties of human expression, a more developed depiction of the possibilities of existence in the tension between these polar opposites.

In his concluding chapter, "Toward the Rehabilitation of Reason," Langan resumes explicitly his discussion of the transcendental tradition and of Merleau-Ponty's place within it. In effect, he argues that, however significant Merleau-Ponty's advance over earlier philosophers in this tradition, he has failed in the task he set himself—that of explaining how there can be an in-itself for us, how we can grasp *as it is* a reality independent of ourselves. Can there be true objectivity of any sort, Langan asks, if—as Merleau-Ponty suggests—all our encounters with things are conditioned by the body and its acquisitions, culture and its "sedimentation" of past human expression? This is a complex question to which no simple answer ought to be made. It does not, however, seem that Langan has given quite enough consideration to those aspects of Merleau-Ponty's thought which point in a realistic direction— not to that scientistic "realism" which construes man and objects as causally related, but to a richer realism which attributes to human experience the power to transcend itself and grasp what is.—*J.D.G.*

ADDITIONAL RECOMMENDED READING

Bannan, John F. *The Philosophy of Merleau-Ponty.* New York: Harcourt, Brace & World, 1967. A useful general exposition of Merleau-Ponty's ideas.
Mallin, Samuel B. *Merleau-Ponty's Philosophy.* New Haven, Connecticut: Yale University Press, 1979. An ambitious, scholarly attempt at a synthesis

and reconstruction of Merleau-Ponty's philosophical position.

Merleau-Ponty, Maurice. *The Primacy of Perception*. Evanston, Illinois: Northwestern University Press, 1964. The title essay in this collection is a brief statement—read by Merleau-Ponty in 1945 to a gathering of French philosophers—of his major philosophical ideas, with the text of the (at times very interesting) discussion which followed. Other essays include a "prospectus" of work which he planned to do in the 1950's, and "Eye and Mind," a fascinating work written during the last months of his life.

Rabil, Albert. *Merleau-Ponty: Existentialist of the Social World*. New York: Columbia University Press, 1967. A solid account of Merleau-Ponty's thought which gives some attention to its development and to the political context of his work.

Sartre, Jean-Paul. "Merleau-Ponty," in *Situations*. New York: George Braziller, 1965. Sartre's eloquent and fascinating memorial essay on Merleau-Ponty.

THE OPEN SOCIETY AND ITS ENEMIES

Author: Karl R. Popper (1902-   )
Type of work: Social philosophy
First published: 1945

PRINCIPAL IDEAS ADVANCED

The Greek Enlightenment, exemplified by the Sophists and by Socrates, and the European Enlightenment, which found expression in the French Revolution, are part of man's often-interrupted attempt to break out of the closed society and fashion an open society.

This movement was opposed by Plato's efforts to resist change and by G. W. F. Hegel's doctrine that man's destiny is determined by historical laws.

Critical Rationalism, which is the application of the scientific method to practical problems, reaffirms the principles of the Enlightenment and shows how, by means of social technology, man can reshape society to further humanitarian ends.

The Open Society and Its Enemies was written during World War II while Karl R. Popper, a refugee from his native Vienna, was teaching in New Zealand. Although he called it a war book, he meant its strictures to apply to Marxists as well as to Nazis. Broadly speaking, it was directed against a mentality, found among both progressives and conservatives, which assumed that totalitarianism of one kind or another is inevitable. Popper's interest in scientific method had led him to examine contemporary holist and determinist tendencies in a later book called *The Poverty of Historicism* (1957). While preparing that work, he had collected notes with a view to showing that historicism and totalitarianism are deeply rooted in Western intellectual history; these notes became the basis for the present book.

In the Introduction to *The Open Society and Its Enemies*, Popper notes that civilization, which he represents as "aiming at humaneness and reasonableness, at equality and freedom," is always faced with difficulties. Strains develop from the shock of passing from tribal communities to open democracies, and these strains lead to reactionary movements. A nostalgia for the past combines with an apocalyptic view of history. Popper insists, however, that a proper sense of responsibility requires us to accept the strains of civilization as part of what it means to be human, and hence to reject escapist fantasies and to get on with the business of applying reason to the problems of social reconstruction.

Popper gives the name *historicism* to "the doctrine that history is controlled by special historical or evolutionary laws whose discovery would enable us to prophesy the destiny of man." Heraclitus, who combined his doctrine of universal flux with belief in the identity of opposites and in a fixed law which governs change, is said to be the first exponent of this doctrine.

Plato's philosophy is examined at length in the first volume of *The Open Society and Its Enemies*, subtitled "The Spell of Plato." Popper finds the key for understanding this philosophy in Plato's Seventh Letter. He, like Heraclitus, felt the strain of civilization: "Seeing that everything swayed and shifted aimlessly, I felt giddy and desperate." His whole philosophy was an attempt to arrest change. Plato was a historicist in holding that there are sociological laws which make it possible to predict social decline, but unlike most historicists he also believed that it is possible for man to influence his destiny. His doctrine of Forms provided him with the basis for an exact science of politics, and he became the first of a long list of social engineers.

Plato's philosophy of history (see *Republic* VIII) depicted the inevitable decline of a good city. This decline he viewed as an illness which, like a physician, he tried to diagnose. Anticipating Karl Marx, he found the cause in class struggle. Noting that deterioration inevitably begins within the ruling class, he undertook to design a society in which the ruling class would prove indefectible. His elaborate provision for selecting and educating suitable guardians was directed toward this end, as was his communism and his secret plan for developing a master race. Like other totalitarians, Plato built his state on "blood and soil."

Popper does not deny that Plato was a gifted sociologist. What he laments is that Plato turned his back on progress. Civilization was on the march. Athenian democracy under Pericles was a showcase of equalitarian individualism. The generation of thinkers which included Democritus, Protagoras, and Socrates was applying the principles of critical rationalism, as developed by Anaximander and his successors, to human problems. Unlike other forms of rationalism and empiricism, which suppose that the truth is somehow evident, critical rationalism proceeds by way of trial and error. The dialectic, as employed by the Sophists and by Socrates, was simply a device for testing hypotheses. It was part of the great revolution which took place when men broke with tradition and questioned all authority. Critical rationalism goes hand in hand with the theory called "critical dualism," Popper's name for the doctrine that decisions can never be derived from facts. "Nature consists of facts and of regularities, and is in itself neither moral nor immoral. It is we who impose standards upon nature, and who in this way introduce morals into the natural world." This, says Popper, was the import of the famous Sophist distinction between natural law and conventional law. Moral and social norms do not come from God and are not discovered in nature but are "man-made in the sense that we must blame nobody but ourselves." According to Popper, Socrates shared these views. If we want to see the true import of his teaching, we must turn to Antisthenes, the Cynic, whose teachings were equalitarian and democratic. Plato betrayed his master, putting into his mouth his own theory of the arrested society.

The remainder of the first volume is an attempt "to present Plato as a totalitarian party-politician, unsuccessful in his immediate practical undertakings, but in the long run only too successful." According to Popper, Plato was vain and ambitious. The beautiful portrait of the philosopher-king was a self-portrait. Plato was not willing to bid for popular support as Pericles had done, but as a natural ruler he was ready to descend from his heights if men came to him. Viewed in this light, Plato's political program can be understood for what it was intended to be: totalitarian rule.

What Plato has to say about justice bears no resemblance to what most of us, "especially those whose general outlook is humanitarian," mean by "justice." We mean individual self-determination, the elimination of privileges, and the principle that the state should prevent people from taking advantage of one another. Plato redefined justice to mean the opposite of all these things. It becomes for him identical with what is in the best interest of the state, which he interpreted to mean that everyone must perform the functions assigned to him by his caste-standing. Instead of the state's serving the individual, the individual must serve the state. The sole criterion of morality was to be what is in the best interest of the state.

The *Republic* was Plato's attempt to institutionalize his totalitarian moral system. In it everything turned on the principle of authority. The sovereignty of the state over the individual demanded a ruling class. The "lordly lie" was a means of convincing both rulers and ruled that some are superior to others by birth, and the mystique surrounding their education was intended to make them appear to themselves and others as "godlike if not divine." Apart from its propaganda function, the educational system was designed to produce docile leaders, men and women capable of subordinating their individual ambitions as well as their mental processes to the preservation of order. Happiness, like justice, Plato defined with reference to social functions. His state was not concerned with the happiness of individuals or of any one class, but only with the happiness, or more properly with the health, of the whole.

In expounding Plato's political views, Popper weaves back and forth between the closed society, which he identifies with Plato, and his own version of an open society, which he finds prefigured in the thought of Pericles, the Sophists, and Socrates. Popper makes it clear that what he calls "the open society" is a new faith—a faith in man, in human reason, in freedom, in brotherhood—"as I believe, the only possible faith, of the open society." In contrast to the closed society, which is a concrete, semiorganic unity, the open society is abstract, made up of competing individuals who form voluntary associations as their interests dictate. Economics, says Popper, is on the right track in its assumption that social institutions should be understood in terms of the decisions and actions of individuals and not in terms of so-called "real social groups." We can conceive of a society, says Popper, in which individuals never meet face to face; and in fact modern urban society is very close to this model.

Popper develops his conception of an abstract, or open, society along two lines: political and economic. His political theory he labels *protectionism*. "What I demand from the state is protection; not only for myself, but for others too." The difference between aggression and defense is fundamental. What we demand is a state organized to provide defense. "I am perfectly ready to see my own freedom of action somewhat curtailed by the state, provided I can obtain protection of the freedom which remains. . . . Thus I demand that the state must limit the freedom of the citizens as equally as possible and not beyond what is necessary for achieving an equal limitation of freedom." Because the state is based on men's decisions, there is no sense in reverting to the archaic notions of sovereignty and authority. Democratic theory, as long as it holds onto the obsolete notion that the people are sovereign and that the majority has a right to impose its will on the minority, will be embarassed by what Popper calls "the paradox of sovereignty"— namely, that any form of sovereignty has to be limited. Accordingly, what is important in a democracy is not the question "Who shall be rulers?" but "How can we tame them?" And the value of democratic institutions is that they constitute a system of checks and balances which prevent injustices and provide a means of ridding society of bad government.

Popper calls his economic policy *economic interventionism*. This means that the state must always be more powerful than economic interests. The need for the state to intervene in economic matters follows directly from the view that the state exists to protect the freedom of its citizens. Economic power may be as dangerous to these freedoms as physical violence. And there must be a political safeguard against this kind of abuse.

In this connection Popper unveils his concept of *social engineering*. Institutions are like machines in that they exist to serve human ends. The social engineer approaches institutions rationally, judging them according to their effectiveness and trying by experimentation to improve them. Plato's *Republic* is an example of what Popper calls *Utopian* engineering. There is an aesthetic element in it. Plato spoke of the necessity for his draughtsmen to clean their canvas before they start to work, and he suggested that one way would be to remove all citizens over the age of ten. The modern term for this, says Popper, is "liquidation." Popper rejects Utopian engineering for many reasons. "Dreams of beauty have to submit to the necessity of helping men in distress, and men who suffer injustice." In its place he argues for what he calls "piecemeal engineering." Recognizing that perfection is at best a distant goal and unwilling to sacrifice intervening generations, he proposes that we approach the problems of economic injustice by searching out and working to remedy the most serious evils of existing society. In this undertaking, reason will take the place of violence, and the freedoms of individual men and women will be respected. For, although it is wrong to suppose that one can devise institutional means to make people happy, there is abundant evidence that institutions can successfully attack the problem of helping those who are in distress. Moreover, institutions are not machines. Being made up of men, they are dependent ultimately on human decisions and can therefore be altered as mankind becomes more fully aware of what it demands of them. "We can tame them," Popper says. "We must realize this and use the keys; we must construct institutions for the democratic control of economic power, and for our protection from economic exploitation."

The substantial part of Volume Two, "The High Tide of Prophecy," is Popper's analysis of Marxism. This, however, is obscured by Popper's desire to show that everyone who has been infected with traditional metaphysics is a carrier of the totalitarian plague. G. W. F. Hegel, who imbibed freely from Aristotle, contaminated nearly everyone who came after him, including idealists, materialists, vitalists, voluntarists, phenomenologists, existentialists, and creative evolutionists.

Although Popper does not consider Artistotle a major thinker, he does regard him to be important as a transmitter. In the first place, Aristotle saddled Western scientific thought with the Platonic doctrine of universals. Popper calls this doctrine "essentialism" and maintains that the social sciences have not yet rid themselves of it. Like Aristotle, sociologists believe that it is necessary to grasp the universal in the particular and to frame definitions in order to attain knowledge—a method propagated in our time not merely by Edmund Husserl but also by Ludwig Wittgenstein. In contrast, scentific thought is nominalistic. Definitions are shorthand symbols; what matters is whether statements are refutable in terms of experience. In the second place, Aristotle is important because he gave Plato's historicism an optimistic turn, which made it possible for his modern disciples to combine essentialism with evolutionism. He did this by bringing Plato's ideas into the flux where they serve as essential and as final causes, guiding the processes of nature. Although he was not himself interested in history, his doctrine that the future is in the present contained the seeds of modern historicism, so that the fate of men and of nations may be read in advance.

Popper's sympathies with German philosophy terminate with Immanuel Kant (except for men like Jacob Fries and Arthur Schopenhauer, who clung to Kant in opposition to Hegel). Kant, for Popper, was a figure of the enlightenment, a defender of the ideas of 1789. J. G. Fichte, F. W. J. Schelling, and Hegel, on the other hand, were traitors to these ideas, much as Plato and Aristotle were traitors to the enlightenment of fifth century Greece. Popper has no respect for their intellectual ability nor for their moral integrity. Reading Popper, one gets the impression that Hegel worked out his philosophy after he moved to Berlin and became a lackey of the king of Prussia. In any case, Popper finds little in Hegel's philosophy that is not found in

Heraclitus and Plato.

According to Popper, the two pillars of Hegel's philosophy are his dialectic and his philosophy of identity. The former, according to which all things are contradictory, was adopted by Hegel in order to stop rational argument and end scientific progress. The latter, which declared that existence and essence are the same, that the real is rational and therefore good, was adopted in order to put down dissatisfaction with the Prussian state. Popper shows how Hegel used the dialectic as a means of perverting the ideas of 1789 by proving that freedom is obedience, that equality is difference, and that fraternity is strife.

Popper's chapter "Hegel and the New Tribalism" is as much concerned with German nationalism and with the rise of totalitarianism as it is with Hegel. Nearly half of it consists of quotations of assorted nationalists, racists, and statists whose opinions are assumed by Popper to have been influenced by Hegel. The idea of racial biology, Popper admits, was not invented by Hegel but by Ernst Haeckel; such an idea, he says, merely amounted to the substitution of blood for spirit, which "does not greatly alter the main tendency of Hegelianism." To give some direction to his argument, Popper discusses six typically Nazi themes, such as that the state is above morality, that war is good in itself, and that man is not a rational but a heroic animal; he then collates passages from Hegel with those of "his racialist followers." For example, Hegel in his *Logic* had said that the concept of pure being is identical with the concept of pure nothingness. Popper takes this to be the origin of Martin Heidegger's teaching that life can be understood only by understanding nothingness and of Karl Jasper's nihilistic doctrine that a person "really lives" only when he is facing death and destruction. "Human existence is to be interpreted as a 'Thunderstorm of Steel'; the 'determined existence' of man is 'to be a self, passionately free to die . . . in full consciousness and anguish.'"

Far more sober is Popper's discussion of Marx, whom he regards as a great humanitarian imbued with the principles of 1789 and, in his hope that the state would wither away, a devotee of the open society. In spite of this, Popper considers him a false prophet in that he was mistaken in his prophecies, but even more lamentably false in that his historicist methods have led people to believe that predicting the future is the correct way of approaching the solution of social problems.

Marx was not merely a historicist; fundamentally, he was a social analyst. And, according to Popper, his analysis was essentially correct. In contrast to John Stuart Mill, who tried to explain social behavior in terms of psychological laws, Marx recognized that the moral values of a society are bound up with social institutions and that the task of the social sciences is to analyze human actions within this framework. It is the method, long practiced by economists, of explaining behavior in terms of situational logic. Marx's error was that he exaggerated man's dependence on institutions to the point of denying that it is possible to bring about constructive change. For this reason, Marx opposed social engineering and placed his hope entirely in prophecy.

This prophecy Popper presents as a three-stage argument: the law of increasing misery, the inevitability of social revolution, and the emergence of a classless society. Popper treats each of these stages at length, showing in what way each is mistaken. Marx's main error lay in the fact that, contemptuous of politics, he refused to take account of the possibility of economic interventionism: namely, that popular governments might succeed in bringing capitalism under control. But he also neglected the possibility that, should revolution come, the workers might not win, and the further possibility that, should they win, class distinctions might not disappear. An interesting part of Popper's discussion is the blame which he places on Marxism for the success of fascism in central Europe, where Social Democrats as well as Communists were dominated by the conviction that class struggle would eventuate in victory for the working class and that nothing should be done that would postpone the day of decision. Guided by this prophecy, "scientific socialists" spurned democratic processes and poured contempt on any effort to relieve human suffering. Their policies created confusion among the poor and led to a reaction in favor of fascism. All of this leads Popper to speculate on what might have been the result had Marx encouraged democracy and turned his attention in the direction of social technology instead of trying to "shorten the birthpangs" of a new age.

Hegel's influence was not restricted to political thought. After Kant, modern man abandoned criticism for what Popper calls "oracular" philosophy. Philosophers ceased to argue and began to pontificate. Hegel led the way when he raised himself above the historical process and undertook to explain the thoughts of his predecessors in terms of the historical moment in which they had lived. This method, says Popper, was adopted by Karl Mannheim and the "sociology of knowledge school." According to Mannheim, every person, by virtue of his class, social stratum, and habitat, is invested with a total ideology which determines his thinking. Only by a kind of socioanalysis is it possible for a select few to transcend ideology and attain to objectivity. Like psychoanalysis, socioanalysis reveals the meaninglessness of what other people think and makes discussion with them impossible. Popper finds the same kind of intellectual arrogance in Arnold Toynbee's way of handling cultures and of placing men in their social habitats instead of considering the validity of what they have to say. Other examples of oracular philosophers are Henri Bergson and Alfred North Whitehead, who, dissatisfied with the kinds of explanations open to science, supplement them with profundities which are impossible to discuss. Popper calls all such philosophies "irrationalism," reserving the term "rationalism" for those which base their claims to knowledge on argument and experience.

In a final chapter, Popper asks whether history can be a science and concludes that its interests in specific events preclude it from ever being anything more than interpretation. In this respect, oracular history belongs to the class of "unveiling philosophies," along with psychoanalysis and socioanalysis. There is no such thing as history in the sense most people understand by it— a more or less definite series of facts. The realm of facts is infinite, and the selection which a historian makes is necessarily an interpretation. The notion that history is a kind of stage play in which freedom and brotherhood will eventually triumph is a superstitious relic of tribalism. The critical rationalist, who deliberately commits himself to the cause of equality and brotherhood, knows that history has only the meaning and purpose that men give it.

Originally this book was to have been entitled: "False Prophets: Plato, Hegel, and Marx." Obviously the book grew in Popper's hands. The terms "open society" and "closed society" were borrowed from Bergson and used to distinguish two types of planned society: that in which planning comes from the bottom and that in which it comes from the top. Popper makes a point of agreeing with Marx that government is an evil to be avoided as far as possible. But the paradox of freedom is that freedom must be limited. The vision of brotherhood and compassion requires positive steps not merely to equalize opportunity (Marx) but also to overcome disadvantages. And for this purpose, government must be large enough to secure citizens from as many of the unfortunate consequences of civilization as is possible. If bureaucrats have to submit their programs to popular criticism, mistakes will be corrected as they are in the scientific laboratory. Piecemeal engineering, which does not demand assent to an overall program but works selectively to overcome the most urgent evils of society, has a good chance of winning popular support.—*J.F.*

PERTINENT LITERATURE

Winch, Peter. "Nature and Convention," in *Proceedings of the Aristotelian Society*. N. S. LX (1959-1960), pp. 231-252.

In explaining critical dualism, Karl R. Popper mentions that the dualism of facts and norms is the same as that which Protagoras and other Greek Sophists had in mind when they distinguished between nature and convention. Peter Winch undertakes to show that social philosophy has moved a long way beyond the Sophists. There is a rough-and-ready sense in which it is true that "facts are *there*, whereas decisions have to be *made*." Investigating facts is quite different from deciding for or against a piece of legislation. But the philosopher is concerned not with particular facts or particular norms; rather, he is concerned with the concepts of factuality and normality. Both concepts, Winch maintains, "arise out of the way men live."

Winch argues, first, that Popper fails to establish his desired dualism. The claim that moral laws vary according to time and place, whereas scientific laws are always the same, is naïve, resting as it does on the assumption that there are scientific facts independent of the realm of scientific discourse. Winch quotes the physicist Robert Oppenheimer as saying, "The deep things in physics, and probably in mathematics too, are not things you can tell about unless you are talking to someone who has lived a long time acquiring the tradition." The tradition is man-made; but this is not the same as saying that physicists decide to talk the way they do. No more do we decide to talk about moral issues in the way that we do. In Abraham's day it was possible to talk meaningfully about child sacrifice; but this has, in William James's terms, ceased to be a "live option": what it meant to Hebrews at one time is not intelligible to us. We are no more free to decide for it than we are to decide against the Second Law of Thermodynamics.

This shows, says Winch, that decision is not fundamental in morality. What is fundamental is the "context of a meaningful way of life" which makes moral decisions possible; and this context, he holds, is quite analogous to the context which makes scientific judgments possible. Nor is the world neatly divided into two classes, scientists and nonscientists: instead of a dualism, the world is a pluralism in which there are many kinds of factual statements and many kinds of decisions. There are "business facts" which can be understood only by persons who make the kinds of decisions appropriate to the business way of life.

Winch's second point is that there are certain aspects of moral life which are not based on conventions but which are presupposed by any possible convention. Having argued that a scientific fact presupposes a scientific community, he goes on to show the difference between a scientific or business community on the one hand and that of the moral community on the other. Particular communities are voluntary; the moral community is not voluntary. Science can be described as a form of activity in which one chooses to engage; not so morality, for moral issues force themselves on everyone. There are certain moral conceptions without which human society could not exist.

Winch quotes Thomas Hobbes as representing the conventionalist point of view when in the *Leviathan* (II.17) he makes everything human rest on a covenant. As opposed to Hobbes, Winch quotes Giovanni Battista Vico's argument from *The New Science*, Paragraph 161, that "there must be in the nature of things a mental language common to all nations, which uniformly grasps the substance of things feasible in human social life." This presupposition of language, reason, convenants, decisions—everything that makes human community possible—Winch calls "integrity," meaning not one virtue among other virtues but a general commitment which everyone undertakes who acts in a social context. It is analogous to the commitment to truth undertaken by anyone who uses language with the intention of saying anything.

Kaufmann, Walter. "The Hegel Myth and Its Method," in *The Philosophical Review*. LX, no. 4 (October, 1951), pp. 459-486.

Walter Kaufmann expresses the opinion of many scholars when he says that Karl R. Popper's stimulating ideas about society and history are "amalgamated with a great deal of thoroughly unsound intellectual history." He is no doubt correct in holding that Popper is at his worst in dealing with G. W. F. Hegel. Gilbert Ryle, for example, while sharing Popper's hatred of Hegel, laments his use of the "blackguarding idiom characteristic of his enemies." In his article "The Hegel Myth and Its Method," Kaufmann uses Popper's book to correct several widely shared misconceptions about Hegel, which he calls "the Hegel myth." At the same time he protests against the tendency in Popper and in other progressive thinkers to distort history in order to promote their ideas; and this is what he means by "its method."

Kaufmann notes, to begin with, the inadequacy of Popper's scholarship. One who does not know the field, seeing nineteen pages of footnotes, will wrongly suppose that Popper has read a great deal of Hegel, together with the standard literature. But Kaufmann warns us that this is not the case. Popper says that he has used the translation in the Scribner's Selections, changing words here and there; but the fact seems to be that he relied on these selections instead of reading entire works, and that when he changed the translation he did so not in order to come closer to the German but for rhetorical reasons. Kaufmann's examples prove, at least, that one should not cite Popper as a source for what Hegel said.

Kaufmann calls attention to "quilt quotations," sentences picked from different pages and enclosed by a single set of quotation marks—a propaganda device which he compares to a composite photograph. And he notes the extensive use which Popper makes of anti-Nazi propaganda writings without checking the references and without proving the influence which he alleges Hegel to have had on proto-Nazi thinkers.

An extensive part of Kaufmann's article is directed against Popper's ignorance of nineteenth century thought. For example, Popper repeatedly speaks with favor of the Hegel-haters, Jacob Fries and Arthur Schopenhauer, presumably without knowing that both men were anti-Semites, which Hegel was not. Had Popper made his own survey of Nazi literature he would have discovered that Alfred Rosenberg, the official Nazi philosopher, denounced Hegel as being neither a racist nor a nationalist.

Turning from the method to the myth, Kaufmann reminds us that Hegel was not a historicist who tried to predict the future, that he nowhere said that the state is the march of God through the world, that his relations with the king of Prussia were not those of a lackey with his master, and that it was not Hegel's opinion that the only judgment upon a state is the success of its actions. Popper reiterates the popular belief that for Hegel "everything that now is . . . is reasonable as well as good," and mistakenly attributes to him the view that essences or ideas are identical with "things in flux." As Kaufmann explains, the real or actual was for Hegel that which fully realizes its nature; and he points out that Hegel did not hold that the ideal was actualized in Prussia or in any other existing state.

Hegel's view of the state as actualizing the ethical idea and as being the "basis and center of all the concrete elements in the life of a people: of art, law, morals, religion, and science," was popular with English Hegelians, and in the twentieth century has been a favorite target of liberal thinkers. But to confuse it with totalitarianism, says Kaufmann, is to misunderstand it. In fact it is the kind of view Pericles had of the Athenian democracy.

Rhees, Rush. "Social Engineering," in *Mind*. LVI, no. 224 (October, 1947), pp. 317-331.

According to Rush Rhees, Karl R. Popper's application of the metaphor "engineering" to human ways of life is confusing in theory and dangerous in practice. Typical of the confusion is the manner in which Popper sometimes suggests that the business of the social engineer is to ask whether a particular institution is well designed to serve its ends, while at other times he suggests that the task of the engineer is to reform institutions with a view to improving civilization, to "rationalizing" society. Popper likes to speak of "man" as having made institutions, which, says Rhees, can mean only that institutions have come into being along with man's social and mental development, and hardly supports the inference that the existence and operation of institutions is completely voluntary, "that the responsibility for them is entirely ours." Apart from the dubiety of saying that "man" does or decides anything, the generic term enables Popper to slip back and forth between the natural and voluntary aspects of society. The ambiguity reappears in Popper's attempt to account for social institutions. While he recognizes that there are facts of human nature which enter into the working of institutions and which can be described by means of sociological laws, he nevertheless insists that institutions are made by "establishing certain norms, designed with a certain end in mind." Consequently, he speaks sometimes as if institutions are machines and at other times as if they are rule books. In any case, Rhees objects to the view that all institutions can be understood in terms of ends and means; and he challenges the claim that they are controlled by their personnel.

Popper deludes himself, says Rhees, when he argues that there is an analogy between scientific experimentation and the control which the public exercises over its bureaucrats through free criticism. Raising objections to a policy differs from criticizing a scientific theory because in science there are common standards, whereas what justifies a social policy to one group may be no justification at all to another. We say that a compromise acceptable to all parties solves the problem, but this consensus is quite unlike that which exists when men succeed in solving a scientific problem.

Rhees is not impressed with Popper's distinction between piecemeal engineering and total engineering: the former is as much committed as the latter to a monistic view of society. According to Rhees, society as we know it is pluralistic. If there were not conflicting ways of living there would be no society. In this lies our freedom and our safety. Ours is not the closed society which Popper holds that civilized man should leave behind; but neither is it the abstract society of atomic individuals which Popper has named "the open society." And Popper's insensitivity to the difference poses the same kind of threat to meaningful human existence as does that of the Utopian.

Impatient with the world as he finds it, Popper wants to "further society" and "improve civilization." But, says Rhees, these expressions are meaningless in that neither of them describes a definite form of social activity. The same would be true of "serving humanity" if that expression were taken to include all classes of men. But Popper's humanitarianism is restricted to protecting the weak; and this is a specific form of activity which is capable of pitting the party of humanity against other conflicting ways of living. Popper does not envisage society controlling its own development but offers instead a new form of domination. The old dualism of facts and decisions reappears in the form of the still older dualism of those who decide and those who are protected because they cannot decide for themselves.—*J.F.*

Additional Recommended Reading

Acton, H. B. "Moral Futurism and the Ethics of Marxism," in *The Philosophy of Karl Popper* (The Library of Living Philosophers). Edited by Paul A. Schilpp. Vol. II. La Salle, Illinois: Open Court, 1974, pp. 876-888. A student of Marxism gives general approval to Popper's criticism of Marx's social theory.

Levinson, Ronald B. *In Defense of Plato*. Cambridge, Massachusetts: Harvard University Press, 1953. Detailed consideration of points raised against Plato by Popper and others.

Popper, Karl R. *Conjectures and Refutations: The Growth of Scientific Knowledge*. London: Routledge & Kegan Paul, 1963. A collection of papers by Popper on various subjects. See especially "On the Sources of Knowledge and of Ignorance," pp. 3-32.

Robinson, Richard. "Dr. Popper's Defense of Democracy," in *The Philosophical Review*. LX, no. 4 (October, 1951), pp. 487-507. A Plato scholar joins Popper's antitotalitarian crusade.

Winch, Peter. "Popper and Scientific Method in the Social Sciences," in *The Philosophy of Karl Popper* (The Library of Living Philosophers). Edited by Paul A. Schilpp. Vol. II. La Salle, Illinois: Open Court, 1974, pp. 889-

904. The relation between the concept of understanding an institution and the concept of improving an institution.

AN ANALYSIS OF KNOWLEDGE AND VALUATION

Author: Clarence Irving Lewis (1883-1964)
Type of work: Epistemology, philosophy of value
First published: 1946

Principal Ideas Advanced

Empirical statements, describing matters of fact, are equivalent in meaning to hypothetical statements to the effect that if one were to act in certain ways, then one would come to have experiences of a certain anticipated sort.

An empirical statement is verified by finding out whether what is presented in experience as a result of action is what one would expect.

A priori statements (statements whose truth is independent of matters of fact) are true by virtue of the meanings of their terms and the logical relations between terms.

Value statements concerning objects are empirical statements to the effect that if one were to be concerned with the objects, one would be satisfied or pleased by them; value statements expressive of the value-quality of experience do not admit of error and therefore, unlike value statements concerning objects, cannot be known to be true.

C. I. Lewis undertook an examination of basic topics in ethics in preparation for the Carus Lectures, the Seventh Series, to be delivered in 1945. But during the course of his philosophical inquiries he came to realize that problems of value take semantical priority over problems of moral rightness and duty, and that epistemological considerations, having to do with the knowledge of values, would have to come before further reflections on value. The problem for him became the problem of determining whether knowledge of values is possible. The conclusion he reached is that such knowledge is possible. The defense of his conclusion is *An Analysis of Knowledge and Valuation.*

The book begins with a pragmatic account of knowledge. "To know," he argues at the outset, "is to apprehend the future as qualified by values which action may realize." This theory of knowledge owes its basic character to Peirce and James. Statements describing matters of fact, whatever their grammatical form, are equivalent in meaning to hypothetical statements to the effect that *if* one were to act in certain ways, *then* one would come to have experiences of the sort anticipated. A statement is verified by acting and finding out whether what one receives in the way of experience is what one expected. "For example; this wall is hard: if I should bump my head against it, it would hurt." Knowledge, action, and evaluation are connected because knowledge is understandable only in terms of action; one seeks to know in order to inform action, and one seeks to act in a manner which will be satisfactory.

But this initial account of the nature of knowledge and of the relation of knowledge to action and evaluation is merely introductory in character. Lewis considers at some length problems of meaning and of analytic truth. His objective was to establish the point that *a priori* statements (statements whose truth is independent of matters of empirical fact) are dependent for their truth value on meanings alone. This involves the rejection of the synthetic *a priori* statement, for if a statement is synthetic and not analytic, it cannot be *a priori*. Empirical, synthetic statements, on the other hand, are true or false according to facts discoverable by sense experience; their truth values have no necessary connection with meaning and form. Since Lewis takes as his thesis the proposition that values are empirically knowable, it is relevant to his defense to consider whether other philosophers have been right who have said that the basic value and duty claims of ethics are synthetic *a priori* propositions.

Book I, then, following the two chapters of the Introduction, is devoted to "Meaning and Analytic Truth." The following book considers the most important problems relating to empirical knowledge: the bases of empirical knowledge, the nature of empirical judgments and beliefs, the justification of empirical beliefs, probability, and probable knowledge. This is a careful elaboration of the fundamental pragmatic thesis which relates empirical knowledge to predictions of sense experience.

The concluding book, Book III, presents an analysis of value, making the familiar distinction between instrumental value and intrinsic value and building up to the unifying claim that questions of value are empirical questions.

Lewis's account of value depends upon his basic assertion that values finally involve satisfaction, if not actually, at least potentially. Roughly speaking, something is valuable if it is such that under certain circumstances it will lead to someone's satisfaction. For a full understanding of various types of value judgments, one has to make distinctions of the sort Lewis clarifies—distinctions between the intrinsically good, the immediately good, the instrumentally good, and so forth. But for an understanding of the kind of defense possible for one who claims that values are empirically knowable, it is enough to realize that if value judgments can be expressed by hypothetical propositions, and if they relate to matters falling within the range of possible experience, then they are empirical judgments. To say that something is valuable is to say that *if* it were to have its effect on someone acting in regard to it, *then* it would satisfy or please him. It is possible to say even in regard to objects which are neither known to exist nor accessible to observation that some of them are worthwhile in that *were* they to be discovered, they would, in some way, satisfy. Thus, he writes that "the term 'valuable' is to be applied to objects and other existents solely with the meaning 'capable of conducing to satisfaction in some possible experience.'" To verify a value judgment, then, one has only to determine whether the object in question *does*, under the circumstances, *satisfy* the person or persons to whom reference is implicitly or explicitly made. The immediate content of experience can be worthwhile in the sense that the experience may be prized for its own sake.

Considering Lewis' argument in more detail, and turning back to the Introduction, we find that Lewis considers the following criteria of knowledge to be suggested by common usage of the term "knowledge": (1) knowledge involves belief in what is true; (2) knowledge involves meaning, a reference to some matter other than the experience of knowing; (3) knowledge involves a ground, or evidence; and (4) knowledge, in the strictest sense, is certain and not merely probable to some degree. However, if one were to define the term "knowledge" so as to include all these criteria, it would be difficult to find any instances of knowledge. A certain tolerance of the diversity of meanings and uses of the term "knowledge" is called for. Lewis decides to recognize three "types of apprehension": apprehension of "directly given data of sense," such as particular feelings, aches, conscious responses to light, and the like; apprehension of the empirically verifiable; and apprehension of what is involved in the meanings of terms. But of these three types of apprehension, only the latter two are called "knowledge" by Lewis; they are, then, empirical knowledge and the knowledge of meanings (or logical knowledge, analytic knowledge). The apprehension of feelings, since it involves no claims and thus gains no cognitive victories, is not called "knowledge" because the possibility of error is absent.

The discussion of meaning and analytic truth begins with an account of the four modes of meaning: *denotation*, the class of everything actual to which a term applies; *comprehension*, the class of everything possible to which the term could apply; *signification*, the property of anything in virtue of which the term applies; and *intension* (sometimes called "connotation" by other writers), the conjunction of all other terms applicable to anything to which the given term is correctly applicable. The most interesting and controversial claim made in connection with these distinctions is that the denotation of a propositional term, such as "Mary making pies now," is the actual world characterized by the state of affairs described. Every statement attributes a state of affairs to the actual world; true statements denote the actual world, but false statements denote nothing.

Since analytic statements are "certifiable from facts of intensional meaning," and thus can be known to be true by knowing nothing more than the definitions of the terms involved, they require nothing of the world in order to be true. Lewis calls the intension of an analytic statement considered as a whole its "holophrastic meaning"; and since all analytic statements have zero intension, the holophrastic meaning of an analytic statement is its zero intension. (For Lewis, the intension of a proposition is made up of whatever the proposition entails; since an analytic proposition entails nothing, it has zero intension.) The analytic meaning of an analytic statement is its meaning considered as a complex statement; that is, it is the meaning composed of the intensions of its terms. With this distinction, together with the distinction between implicitly analytic statements and explicitly analytic statements, Lewis is able to show that analytic statements are *a priori* since they can be known to be true by appeal to logic and to definitions. Since *a priori* truths are true independently of experience, they must be true by definition of terms; they must be analytic. The classes are equivalent; the *a priori* is the analytic; consequently there are no synthetic *a priori* statements.

Lewis does not accept the view that analytic truth merely expresses linguistic usage. The point is that once meanings are determined by use, the relationships of meanings are fixed and are not subject to linguistic stipulation. He maintains that language depends upon criteria for the applications of terms; the criteria are "sense meanings," understandable in advance of application in terms of "if . . . then . . ." propositions having to do with the experiential consequences of action. The source of analytic knowledge is to be found in the relations between sense meanings. "Such knowledge, like the meanings it concerns, is essentially independent of linguistic formulation. . . ."

Although all knowledge, whether of the analytic or of the synthetic, has reference to meanings which are "sense-representable," only empirical truth is such that one can acquire knowledge of it *only* through sense presentations. Analytic truths are known by the analysis of meanings; but synthetic, or empirical, truths are known only by the sense consequences of action. Lewis distinguishes three classes of empirical statements: *Formulations of the given* element in experience (such statements are expressive and involve no judgment); *terminating judgments* of the form, "Sensory cue S being given, if action A is undertaken, then experience E will occur"; and *non-terminating judgments* which present some state of affairs as being the case (such judgments have a significance which cannot be exhausted by any limited set of terminating judgments).

Lewis argues that perceptual knowledge involves two phases: the giving of some sense-datum or complex of data, "qualia," and the interpretation of the given. Interpretation is a function of past experience, and makes empirical belief or knowledge possible. If one expects a particular kind of experience to follow a particular kind of action, the perceptual judgment is terminating; if one states an objective state of affairs, the judgment is nonterminating, for there is no end to the ways in which, by action, one could confirm to some degree the objective claim. Objective beliefs, then, are never more than probably true. (Along the way there is an interesting discussion of the if-then relation in terminating judgments; the relation, Lewis claims, is neither material implication nor formal implication.)

In order to handle the question "In what sense can what is presently uncertain be called knowledge?" Lewis considers the meaning of "probability." The discussion is careful and involved but its point is fairly clear. According to Lewis, probability theory which attempts to make relative frequencies the final criterion of validity is intrinsically circular. Not the frequencies themselves, but "valid estimates" of frequencies, based on data, are the essential factors in probability judgments.

Passing on to a consideration of the justification of empirical judgments, Lewis argues that a body of empirical beliefs made up of beliefs which, considered singly, are of little weight, may nevertheless have considerable weight of probability as a result of the "congruence" of the beliefs. Congruence is described as a relationship somewhat stronger than consistency, and in Lewis' epistemology it takes precedence over coherency, the favorite of the idealists. "*A set of statements, or a set of supposed facts asserted, will be said to be congruent if and only if they are so related that the antecedent probability of any one of them will be increased if the remainder of the set can be assumed as given premises.*" If present memory can be trusted to afford some reason for counting on what is presumably remembered—and it is reasonable to assume that memory provides some evidential weight—then memory, together with the congruency of particular items of evidence, provides all that we need to make empirical knowledge of probabilities possible. The skeptic's reluctance to concede the reality of the objective world is a sign of a stultifying temperament with which Lewis has little sympathy.

Lewis' studies of meaning and empirical knowledge have prepared the way for the claims and arguments of Book III, "Valuation." "Evaluations are a form of empirical knowledge," he argues, and goes on to distinguish between "direct findings of value-quality in what is presented," the predictions of "a goodness or badness which will be disclosed in experience under certain circumstances and on particular occasions," and the evaluations of things, "appraisals of their potentialities for good or ill." The first—the direct findings of value-quality in experience—does not involve judgment. An expression of value found in experience is true or false, since lying is possible, but no judgment is involved since no predictions are made and one simply finds that the quality of experience is appealing or it is not. The second—the prediction that experience will have value if certain action is undertaken: "If I touch what is before me, I shall enjoy it"—involves terminating judgments, capable of verification, and of being known to be true. The most frequent kind of evaluation is the third—ascribing value to objects—and, as with any ascription of properties to objects, this form of judgment involves nonterminating judgments and is, consequently, never completely confirmable. But in regard to this third kind of evaluation, it is possible to acquire knowledge of probabilities, and such judgments, whether we know for certain that they are true, are either true or false.

For Lewis, then, the goodness of any good *object "consists in the possibility of [its] leading to some realization of directly experienced goodness."* The experience of goodness is simply the realization of some experience as being such that one likes it or, as is often said, "enjoys" it. Immediately realized values are described by Lewis as "subjective" when the prizing by the subject, the person, is a function more of his personality than it is of the quality of the experience. When the opposite is the case, the value is "objective," even though it is the value of an experience.

Immediate values are characterized as "intrinsic"; the values of objects are "extrinsic" or instrumental. When the object is such that in the presence of the object one realizes the value-quality of experience to which the object is conducive, the object is said to be "inherently" valuable. A beautiful object, for example, has inherent value because in contemplation of it a pleasant experience is realized; the experience itself is immediately, or intrinsically, valuable.

Developing his ideas of the aesthetic, Lewis argues that the object of aesthetic contemplation is what he calls "an aesthetic essence," contingent upon context and not merely subjective, a complexus of properties forming some kind of "configurational whole."

In commenting on the moral sense and contributory values, Lewis suggests that the life which serves as the norm in the activity of moral choice is the good life, a life in which individual experiences contribute, in virtue of their value-quality, to the worth of life as a whole. Choice is made on the basis of probabilities, and evidence as to the likelihood of achieving what one seeks through action is relative to past experience as remembered.

In the closing chapter, "Value in Objects," Lewis stresses a point which his analysis of empirical knowledge makes clear. A value property, like other empirical properties, need not be realized in order to be; something can be good in the sense that *were* it to affect someone, it *would* lead to satisfaction. He clears up various possible misconceptions: the fact that values are relative to circumstances and persons does not mean that they are subjective; the fact that a value is subjective does not entail that it is not genuine; the fact that something is of value to a person does not entail that it is objectively valuable (except as an object of his interest); and there are not simply one but several modes of value predication.

The closing remarks make the point that although determination of values is necessary to the application of ethical principles, it is not sufficient. Although valuation is always a matter of empirical knowledge, what is right and just cannot be decided by reference to empirical facts alone.

Lewis's presentation of important problems of meaning, knowledge, and value is both clear and convincing. Although he confines his attention to the empirical function of value terms, limiting his consideration of the expressive function to those occasions upon which one reports the value-quality of experience as immediately prized, his analysis stands as a credible addition to the literature of value theory. The fact that an analysis of this sort is possible and is able to withstand criticism across the years can serve to support the claim that value utterances are not always and exclusively the emotive expressions of attitudes.—*I.P.M.*

PERTINENT LITERATURE
Stace, W. T. Review of *An Analysis of Knowledge and Valuation*, in *Mind*. LVII, no. 225 (January, 1948), pp. 71-85.

W. T. Stace's critical review of *An Analysis of Knowledge and Valuation* does not challenge C. I. Lewis' claim that knowing—like deliberate doing—is subject to deliberate critique. Lewis maintains that the most vital aspect of knowledge is the *normative* constraint which it imposes on our conduct by guiding our actions in accordance with justified convictions and warranted expectations. He holds that this is the source of the most distinctive feature of human beings: our capacity to govern ourselves in thought, action, and belief. *An Analysis of Knowledge and Valuation* examines what Lewis takes to be the three vital correlative dimensions of this self-governance: logic, theory of knowledge, and value theory. In it he argues that such knowledge as we have of moral and aesthetic values is empirical knowledge, even though "what is right and just . . . can never be determined by empirical facts alone." In order to prove his thesis, Lewis first presents detailed analyses of *a priori* and of empirical knowledge. It is Lewis' analysis of empirical knowledge rather than his pragmatism which Stace finds questionable.

According to Lewis the only objects of *a priori* knowledge are analytic statements whose truth values are independent of matters of fact. He maintains that such statements are true (or else false) by virtue of the meanings of their terms and the logical relations among them. By contrast, he argues that all empirical knowledge—knowledge of synthetic statements whose truth values are dependent on matters of fact—must ultimately be grounded in perceptual knowledge. For Lewis, perceptual knowledge is constituted by combining the apprehension of some given qualia (sense-datum or aspect of a sensory experience) with an interpretation, based on past experience, of that which is "given." Lewis chose the term "the given" to refer to the experiential component of perceptual knowledge because he thought this term had "minimal implications of anything beyond the character of it [experience] as datal and immediate." Stace does not stumble over what Lewis accepts as "given"; however, later philosophers—notably Wilfrid Sellars, son of Lewis' friend and fellow philosopher, Roy Wood Sellars—brought much of traditional empiricist theory of knowledge into disrepute by showing that claims as to what is "given" in immediate experience themselves rest upon unwarranted assumptions. Although not addressed specifically to *An Analysis of Knowledge and Valuation*, perhaps the most important criticisms of this dimension of Lewis' theory of knowledge are Wilfrid Sellars' "Empiricism and the Philosophy of Mind," W. V. O. Quine's "Two Dogmas of Empiricism," and Saul Kripke's "Naming and Necessity." (See additional recommended readings.)

Even if Lewis is correct in attempting to ground empirical knowledge on what is perceptually "given," Stace argues that combining what is "given" with interpretation of it does not yield an analysis of our empirical knowledge of the objective characteristics of things. In general, Lewis maintains that empirical knowledge of presently perceived states of affairs (for example, my knowledge that I am now writing with a blue pen), as well as knowledge of presently unperceived states of affairs (for example, my knowledge that my car is gray in color), is essentially constituted by an open-ended set of true hypothetical statements of the forms—"If I should do so-and-so, then in all probability I would experience such-and-such" or "If this-or-that had been the case, then in all probability I would have experienced so-and-so." Roughly, Stace argues that this cannot be a correct analysis of the *meaning* of statements of empirical fact such as:

(1) I am now writing with a blue pen.
(2) My car is gray in color.
(3) Caesar was assassinated on the Ides of March, 44 B.C.

For, (1)-(3) refer to states of affairs which, in fact, exist or have existed, whereas the hypothetical statements suggested as their partial analyses could be true even if these states of affairs had never existed. Stace concludes that Lewis' analysis of empirical knowledge fails, since this argument holds with respect to any hypothetical statements which might be offered as analyses of the *meaning* of a statement of empirical fact.

Stace's criticism misses its mark if Lewis' theory of meaning is correct, for the theory includes both denotation and intension. For Lewis, the intension of a statement is the set of statements which it entails. He holds that the denotations of (1)-(3) are the actual world to which they attribute states of affairs which exist or have existed. Also, he holds that empirical truths like (1)-(3) entail—as partial analyses of their meanings in the sense of "intension"—that certain hypothetical statements are true. Hence, Lewis could respond to Stace by arguing that the entailments required by his analysis exist even though the entailed hypothetical statements could be true when (1)-(3) were false. What would be fatal to the claimed entailment relations would be the truth of (1)-(3) when the required sets of hypothetical statements were false. And, in fact, this criticism of *An Analysis of Knowledge and Valuation* was set forth by Roderick Chisholm, also in 1948.

Chisholm, Roderick M. "The Problem of Empiricism," in *The Journal of Philosophy*. XLV, no. 19 (September 9, 1948), pp. 512-517.

Roderick M. Chisholm's criticism of C. I. Lewis' theory of knowledge is based on the "relativity of perception." Crudely put, he argues that "the given" cannot be a philosophically sound foundation for claims to empirical knowledge, for what will appear as "given" when an object is perceived depends not only upon the object's actual characteristics but also upon the objective and subjective conditions in which it is perceived. Hence, no definitive set of hypothetical statements of what will be "given" to perception is entailed by statements describing an object's actual characteristics. Writing in the same issue of *The Journal of Philosophy*, Lewis responded by suggesting the possibility of developing a theory of the reliability of the connections between the qualia "given" to perception when objects are perceived under normal conditions and the objective characteristics of such objects. The development of this sort of theory, however, appears to belong to psychology rather than to philosophy; and, in fact, the founder of modern psychology, Wilhelm Wundt, sought such a theory. (See E. G. Boring, *A History of Experimental Psychology*, 2nd edition, New York, 1950).

The upshot of Chisholm's argument is that Lewis converts the philosophical problem of determining what the grounds and possible justifications for claims to empirical knowledge are into the psychological problem of determining what the nature of our experience is when we have empirical knowledge. That there is a psychologistic flaw in Lewis' theory of knowledge is revealed in his autobiographical foreword to Paul A. Schilpp's *The Philosophy of C. I. Lewis*. In recalling the conflict between Josiah Royce's idealism and Ralph Barton Perry's realism, Lewis wrote on page 10:

> What was being overlooked, I thought, were certain considerations which both parties should agree upon. For idealism, pragmatism, and realism, all three, it was the nature of knowledge and its relation to its subject which figured as the central problem. And all three of them might be said to take off from the Jamesian dictum, "The real is what it is known as. . . ."

This idea that what is real is somehow relative to our knowledge of it is now widely rejected by philosophers.

White, Morton G. "Value and Obligation in Dewey and Lewis," in *The Philosophical Review*. LVIII, no. 4 (July, 1949), pp. 321-329.

Morton G. White favorably contrasts C. I. Lewis' theory of value with John Dewey's. In short, he concludes that Dewey's attempt to define "desirable" results in a non-normative concept, one which cannot be equivalent with "ought to be desired." In effect, White finds Dewey guilty of the fallacy of inferring "X is desirable" from "X is desired"—although in a more sophisticated way than did the famous originator of this fallacious argument, John Stuart Mill (see Mill's *Utilitarianism*, London, 1863).

Lewis avoids the Dewey-Mill fallacy, although he too believes that objective value is "a potentiality of objects whose realization takes place in immediate experience, in immediate satisfactions." He does so by clearly separating the right and the good. Lewis holds that what experiences are found valuable and what objects are judged to give rise to valuable experiences are judgments of empirical fact. But he denies that such judgments can by themselves justify claims as to what ought to be found valuable morally (or aesthetically) speaking.

White shows that this way out of the Dewey-Mill fallacy leads Lewis into other problems since he exhaustively divides knowledge into just two kinds: empirical knowledge and *a priori* knowledge. Lewis holds that ethical knowledge—"knowledge of what is just, what is right, what ought to be"—"can never be determined by empirical facts alone." Hence, he cannot classify ethical knowledge as empirical knowledge. In Book I of *An Analysis of Knowledge and Valuation*, however, analytic statements can be known *a priori*, since *a priori* knowledge does not depend on experience. So, White argues, he also cannot classify ethical knowledge as *a priori*, for it is hardly possible that all ethical truths are analytic—that is, true solely by virtue of the meanings of their terms and the logical relations among them. To be sure, Lewis regards certain ethical statements as analytic truths; for example, "No rule of action is right except one which is right in all instances, and therefore right for everyone." But even if he were willing to regard all ethical statements, including, for example, "It was not right of Brutus to stab Caesar," as analytic, it seems unlikely that they are. So, on Lewis' account, ethical knowledge apparently can be neither empirical nor *a priori*. White concludes from this that although Lewis may have argued successfully that value statements do express empirical knowledge, he formulates a position in ethics which is closer than he thinks to noncognitivism—the view that there are no ethical truths to be known.

Lewis was not able to articulate successfully an alternative to noncognitive ethical theories in his published writings. However, J. Roger Saydah has argued that he did so in his unpublished manuscripts. (See additional recommended readings.)—*R.L.S.*

ADDITIONAL RECOMMENDED READING

Kripke, Saul. "Naming and Necessity," in *Semantics of Natural Language*. Edited by D. Davidson and G. Harman. Dordrecht and Boston: D. Reidel Publishing Company, 1972. Kripke argues that the references of terms and statements are not fixed by meanings. He emphatically rejects the idea that "the real is what it is known as" and argues that knowledge of the reference of a term does not depend in any way at all upon having a Lewis-like "criterion-in-mind" for application of the term.

Quine, W. V. O. "Two Dogmas of Empiricism," in *The Philosophical Review*. LX, no. 1 (January, 1951), pp. 20-43. Quine argues that it is "misleading to speak of the empirical content of an individual statement." He rejects the distinction between analytic and synthetic statements and contends that this leads to "a more thorough pragmatism" than that of Lewis.

Saydah, J. Roger. *The Ethical Theory of Clarence Irving Lewis*. Athens: Ohio University Press, 1969. Saydah expands upon the ethical theory found in Lewis' published writings by making use of his unpublished manuscripts. He argues that Lewis' theory is preferable to the more widely known but related theories of R. M. Hare and Marcus Singer. Finally, he concludes that Lewis' ethical theory is valid.

Schilpp, Paul A., ed. *The Philosophy of C. I. Lewis* (The Library of Living Philosophers). La Salle, Illinois: Open Court, 1968. This volume includes a complete bibliography, a brief autobiography, twenty-four descriptive and critical essays, and, finally, remarks on them by Lewis himself.

Sellars, Wilfrid. "Empiricism and the Philosophy of Mind," in *The Foundations of Science and the Concepts of Psychology and Psychoanalysis*. Edited by H. Feigl and M. Scriven. Minneapolis: University of Minnesota Press, 1956. Sellars argues that "the given" is a myth, and that our talk about things is logically more basic than the more subjective talk in which we express our perceptions.

SIGNS, LANGUAGE AND BEHAVIOR

Author: Charles W. Morris (1901-1979)
Type of work: Semiotic
First published: 1946

Principal Ideas Advanced

The study of signs (semiotic) is facilitated by the invention of a more useful vocabulary for discussing signs and sign-functioning.

The behavioristic approach to semiotic is adopted because it is more precise, interpersonal, and unambiguous than the appeal to the "mental."

When something controls the behavior of an organism in the process of satisfying a need in a way in which the actual object needed would have controlled the organism, it is a sign.

A symbol is a sign produced by its interpreter which acts as a substitute for a synonymous sign.

Among the conditions which must be met if a language is to be constituted by signs are the following: The signs must have common and constant signification, and they must be combinable.

Signs are used informatively, valuatively, incitively, and systematically.

Pragmatics is the study of the uses of signs, semantics is the study of the meanings of signs, and syntactics is the study of the modes of combining signs.

The publication of *The Meaning of Meaning* (1923), by C. K. Ogden and I. A. Richards, was only one indication of a rapidly increasing interest in the nature and role of signs in human and animal behavior. Studies appeared in such diverse areas as psychology, psychiatry, social science, linguistics, aesthetics, and logic. While there was unanimity in the conception of the problem involved, namely, the problem of what linguistic and nonlinguistic signs are and how they control and are controlled by human beings, there was no unity in the terminology in which such discussions were carried on. Words like "sign," "symbol," "meaning," "reference," "denotation," "connotation," and "expression" were used in almost as many ways as there were authors who used them. There was little evidence that the writers were examining essentially the same problem. The source material was distributed over so wide an area and the authors employed so diverse a terminology that cooperative effort was virtually impossible.

Morris attempted to remedy this situation by inventing a new vocabulary in which all of the basic terms used in discussing signs and sign-functioning are more or less precisely defined. His task, in some cases, involved taking over old words and giving them new and more precise meanings; but in the great majority of cases it required, as the reader will soon discover, devising new words to characterize heretofore unrecognized aspects of the sign-situation or aspects which had been recognized but had been named in such a variety of ways by different investigators that essential agreements in point of view had been more or less completely covered up. Morris is clearly aware of the fact that what he is presenting is simply a series of proposals; indeed, since his definitions are simply *stipulative* in character (let "*x*" mean such-and-such) rather than *legislative* ("*x*" *does* or *ought to* mean such-and-such), no one can reasonably object to what he has done. Whether such a term as "lansign-system," which he uses as substantially equivalent to "language," is or is not actually equivalent to it, is not his concern, and must be determined by the examination of actual languages; and whether his definition of "logic" in terms of analytic formative ascriptors would be accepted by logicians or authors of dictionaries in no way affects either the internal consistency of his scheme or its applicability to signs and sign-function as they exhibit themselves in our experience. He conceives his job to be simply one of examining the very complex situations in which signs occur, discriminating the various phases and aspects, hitherto either overlooked entirely or only confusedly recognized in these situations, and devising a terminology by which they can be accurately designated in such a way as to make cooperative study possible.

Of the possible approaches to the study of signs (semiotic) he chooses one—the behavioristic approach. This is based on his conviction that although the science of behavior (behavioristics) has not yet developed to the point where it can adequately explain either the more complex human actions or the signs which they employ, the only alternative, the "mentalistic" approach, is at a much greater disadvantage. The question is simply one of method, and reduces to the problem of whether such terms as "stimulus," "response-sequence," and "disposition to respond" are not, on the whole, much more precise, interpersonal, and unambiguous than such terms as "idea," "thought," and "mind." Morris makes it quite clear that he does not deny that such a term as "consciousness" is meaningful, nor that an individual can observe his feelings, or his thoughts, or his dreams in a way which is not possible to other individuals. He is therefore not taking sides on the metaphysical issue as to whether people have minds. He is simply recognizing that sign-functioning does occur in the case of animals, where mind in the usual sense of the word is undetectable, and that in studying this mode of sign operation we can learn much about the role of signs in human behavior.

Having adopted this approach to the study of signs, Morris begins by analyzing a case of animal behavior and a case of human behavior, both of which are instances of sign-behavior. A dog that goes to a certain place where food is seen or smelled is trained to go to this same place when a buzzer is sounded, even though the food is not seen or smelled. A person who is driving along a highway is stopped by another person who tells him that the road beyond is blocked by a landslide, and the driver turns off on a side-road and takes another route to his destination. In both cases something (the buzzer, the words of the informant) controls the behavior of an organism in the satisfaction of a need (hunger, desire to arrive at destination) in a way which is roughly similar to the way in which the object (actual food, actual landslide) would modify his behavior. Both are cases of goal-seeking behavior. Whatever exercises this type of control in such behavior is a *sign*, and the behavior which is thus exhibited is *sign-behavior*.

Important to this conception of sign-behavior is the notion that "sign" is defined not in terms of an actual response of the organism, but in terms of a "disposition to respond." This is described as a state of the organism which is such that under certain additional conditions the response *does* take place. The existence of this state in the organism is part of its goal-seeking behavior. But how shall we determine that an organism is *disposed* to act? Ideally, of course, by making the conditions available and showing that the organism *does* act. Another way is to define the response in terms of a wide *class* of responses (behavior-family) any one of which would constitute an instance of the disposition. Or we could introduce *partial* responses which are segments of the total response. Or we could define the response of the organism hypothetically, say, in terms of brain waves which have not yet been measured but may someday be recorded. Or we might, in the case of human beings, simply ask them whether the stimulus is a sign which produces the required disposition.

We are now ready to define the basis terms of semiotic. The organism for which something is a sign is called an *interpreter*. The disposition to respond in some way which is a member of a behavior-family is called an *interpretant*. That which would permit the termination of the responses to which the interpreter is disposed is called a *denotatum*, and the set of conditions satisfied by a denotatum terminating the responses is called a *significatum*. Thus in the case of the dog, the buzzer is the sign, the dog is the interpreter, the disposition to seek food in a specific way is the interpretant, the actual food in the proper place is the denotatum, and the condition of being an edible object of a certain kind in a certain place is the significatum. Other terms, such as *sign-vehicle, unisituational* and *plurisituational signs, vague signs, unambiguous* and *ambiguous signs*, and many others are defined by Morris. One distinction which he makes—that between *sign* and *symbol*—is important for his general thesis. A *symbol* is defined as "a sign produced by its interpreter which acts as a substitute for some other sign with which it is synonymous." Signs which are not so produced are called *signals*. It is clear from this that symbols are more autonomous and conventional than signals, for they may be created at will by interpreters, and they commonly vary considerably from interpreter to interpreter.

Morris now states the conditions under which signs constitute a language. He specifies five criteria. (1) A language consists of a plurality of signs. (2) Each sign has a signification common to a plurality of interpreters. (3) The

signs constituting a language must be producible and have the same signification to the producers that they have to other interpreters. (4) The signs
must have a relative constancy of signification in all situations in which they
occur. (5) Signs in a language must be combinable in certain ways so as to
form complex signs. Signs which possess these properties are to be called
lansigns and a system of such signs a *lansign-system*. Whether any actual
language possesses these characteristics and is therefore to be called a "lansign-system" is a matter to be decided by actual examination of the language
in question.

After examining further the social role of signs, and the way in which the
human use of signs may be differentiated from the animal use, Morris examines the very important problem of the modes of signifying. This problem
takes its origin in current attempts to distinguish between cognitive and noncognitive signs, referential and expressive signs, referential and evocative
signs, cognitive and instrumental signs, and many others. Illustrations of the
problem are found in the need for distinguishing from one another such
sentences as these: "What a fine fellow he is!" "Keep the wind ahead!" "There
is a deer." Morris reduces the problem to its simplest terms by indicating
three major factors which exhibit themselves in sign-behavior. These correspond, respectively, to the environment, the relevance of this environment
to the needs of the organism, and the ways in which the organism must act
upon the environment in order to satisfy its needs. The three parallel components of the sign-situation may be called the *designative*, the *appraisive*,
and the *prescriptive* components. In the case of the blocked road situation
the informant may designate the condition of the road, may appraise it as
preventing further progress, and may prescribe that the man discontinue
driving toward his destination. All sign-behavior contains components of these
three kinds, but their relative importance varies from situation to situation.
In sign-situations which are genetically early in the development of the organism, the components are not sharply distinguished; in symbol-situations,
and especially in situations which employ language symbols, the differentiation becomes sharp. The word "deer" may be purely designative. But if we
speak of a "fine deer" we are using language appraisively. And if we say that
when hunting a deer we should approach it against the wind, we are using
language prescriptively. What may be signified in a sign-situation is determined by the various dispositions to respond, and our ability to distinguish
these forms of behavior-response is a measure of our ability to identify the
modes of signifying.

The actual elements in the sign-situation which function in these different
ways may be called the *designators*, the *appraisors*, and the *prescriptors*. In
addition to these there are the *indicators*, which are distinguished from the
designators in that they direct responses to a certain spatiotemporal region.
These all influence the behavior of the interpreter in different ways, and may

be called *ascriptors*. They answer the questions of where what is signified is to be found, what characteristics it possesses, why it is relevant to the interpreter, and how he should respond to it. They may therefore be called "where," "what," "why," and "how," signs.

A special type of ascriptor, whose role in sign-behavior is difficult to explain, is the *formative ascriptor*. Signs of this type are best illustrated in language systems, and Morris exemplifies them by "or," "not," "some," "is," "plus," "five," variables, word order, suffixes, parts of speech, grammatical structure, punctuation devices, and the like. Whether these are properly to be called "signs" may be debated. Morris believes that since they do modify behavior-responses they should be so characterized, though this involves a more or less arbitrary decision as to how "sign" is to be defined. The most important aspect of formators is that they presuppose other signs and influence the significance of the specific sign combinations in which they appear. For example, given the signs "It will rain in Chicago" and "It will not rain in Chicago," we may use alternative formators in combining these signs, and thus produce different responses on the part of the interpreters: "Either it will rain in Chicago or it will not rain in Chicago," "It will rain in Chicago and it will not rain in Chicago," "If it rains in Chicago, it will not rain in Chicago." Or if we take certain arithmetical signs we may construct alternative complex signs by changing formators; for example, "2 plus (3 times 5)" may become "(2 plus 3) times 5." Or to return to the dog, we may train him to respond to two different signals in such a way as to permit us to characterize the signal as "S_1 or S_2 (at least one but not both)": in this situation the way in which S_1 and S_2 are combined by a formator produces a specific type of behavior response. Since formators are indicated usually by sign combinations, Morris contrasts them to *lexicators*, which are defined negatively as ascriptors which are not formators and which include indicators, designators, appraisors, and prescriptors.

Corresponding to the problem of the modes of signifying there is the parallel problem of sign use. This concerns the purpose for which an organism produces the signs which it uses and other organisms interpret. For example, a person may write a short story in order to earn money. There are so many purposes implied in the various usages of signs that no complete listing of them is possible. Some of the most common are: to gain prestige and power; to deceive or entertain; to excite or comfort; to record or to inform; to satisfy a need or arouse a need in another person; to induce action; to enlist the aid of other people; to "express" oneself, and so on. Morris summarizes these in the four categories: the *informative*, the *valuative*, the *incitive*, and the *systemic*. These terms are self-explanatory: they indicate, respectively, attempts on the part of a user to provide information, to aid in preferential selection of objects, to incite certain responses, and to organize behavior into a determinate whole. Signs which succeed in their informative use may be said to be *convincing*, in their valuative use to be *effective*, in their incitive use to be *persuasive*, and in their systemic use to be *correct*. (Morris grants that the last term, "correct," is not particularly appropriate; in the systemic use of signs emphasis is placed on their interrelationships and on the corresponding integrative, or lack of integrative, character of the behavior responses.)

Having examined signs from the points of view of their modes of signifying and their use, Morris then proceeds to combine these two aspects of signs. This becomes the problem of *types of discourse*. An illustration is to be found in a classification of books; books may be characterized as scientific, mathematical, poetic, religious, fictional, technological, propagandistic, metaphysical, and the like. All such schemes are very crude indeed, containing overlapping classes and subdivisions almost without limit. Morris believes that his double approach to signs in terms of mode of signifying and utility provides a scheme which will eliminate some of the ambiguities in the layman's solution to the problem, and he presents a table containing examples of the sixteen major types of discourse which result when each mode (Designative, Appraisive, Prescriptive, Formative) of signifying is combined with each use (Informative, Valuative, Incitive, Systemic) of signs.

In explaining the sixteen types of discourse, Morris makes it quite clear that he is not proposing that any one of these—say, religious discourse—is to be *defined* in terms of his table. On the contrary, what he is doing is defining a type of discourse, the prescriptive-incitive type, and then showing that much literature which is commonly called "religious" would fall loosely in this area and would thus constitute an *illustration* of prescriptive-incitive discourse.

1. *Scientific discourse* (Designative-Informative) is essentially designative since it does not evaluate or prescribe modes of behavior, and it is primarily informative, since its main concern is with truth. 2. *Fictive discourse* (Designative-Valuative) tells tales, usually about unreal persons and places, with the design not to inform but to evaluate (heroes and villains). 3. *Legal discourse* (Designative-Incitive) prescribes what a person should do, not by saying that it is good or bad, but merely by specifying rewards and punishments; it thus tries to incite action (or inaction) by informing the person of what the consequences of his behavior will be. 4. *Cosmological discourse* (Designative-Systemic) is not a clear-cut type but can be illustrated by certain kinds of metaphysics which describe the universe as one or many, mental or material, purposive or mechanical, yet are not primarily informative since they are concerned more with that organization of sign-behavior which is provided by the emphasis on the systemic use of the signs.

5. *Mythical discourse* (Appraisive-Informative) is appraisive since it evaluates actions, but its main purpose is to inform the reader of the way in which these actions are approved or disapproved by some group. 6. *Poetic discourse* (Appraisive-Valuative) is appraisive-valuative because the poet uses words

heavily charged with feeling to arouse feelings in the mind of the reader; thus, words which signify emotions are used to evoke emotions. 7. *Moral discourse* (Appraisive-Incitive) appraises actions as favorable or unfavorable from the standpoint of an individual or a group, and it tries to induce people to perform or avoid such actions. 8. *Critical discourse* (Appraisive-Systemic) consists of the measurement of appraisive judgments by their organization or lack of organization; it involves a grounded appraisal of appraisals, and may take the form of moral criticism, poetic criticism, religious criticism, or any other type.

9. *Technological discourse* (Prescriptive-Informative) may be popularly described as "how to" discourse; it provides information which is designed to make certain actions more effective in the production of certain desired ends. 10. *Political discourse* (Prescriptive-Valuative), exemplified by the Declaration of Independence, urges the adoption of a certain type of society which has a preferential status because of the rights, privileges, and happiness of its members. 11. *Religious discourse* (Prescriptive-Incitive), in its preoccupation with the "whole" man, both prescribes one type of personality as above all others and incites the individual to become this type of person. 12. *Propagandistic* (as Morris names it) *discourse* (Prescriptive-Systemic) consists of statements designed to produce action, but places emphasis on an integrated *program* of these statements, such as might characterize, for example, the policy of a newspaper, or the advertising techniques of a manufacturer, or the arguments of a speaker before Congress.

13. *Logico-mathematical discourse* (Formative-Informative) is illustrated by the syllogism, "If men are animals, and animals are mortal, then men are mortal." This is informative of a structural relation holding between propositions, but this relation is analytic in character, as shown by the formators— "if," "and," "then"; for example, to prove the validity of this argument one does not need to examine men, animals, and mortals to see whether the relation in question holds. 14. *Rhetorical discourse* (Formative-Valuative) is formative in mode of signifying but valuative in aim. If I say, "Children are children," I am using the formator "are" to create a sign-structure which is used for the purpose of expressing my approval of the actions of children when they behave in a manner contrary to that of adults. 15. *Grammatical discourse* (Formative-Incitive) incites the student, when he is given the conjugations of the verbs in a certain language, to use the language in accordance with these rules; thus it incites the individual to use formators properly. 16. *Metaphysical discourse* (Formative-Systemic) cannot be unequivocally placed in the category of formative-systemic discourse, since the term has so many meanings. But according to one commonly held conception, metaphysics consists of necessary truths having wide generality, and not being such as are refutable or irrefutable by the date of the special sciences. Judgments in this area will then be both formative, since their truth is determined merely

by their structure, and systemic, since they are characterized by their extreme generality.

Morris concludes with a discussion of the social and individual import of signs, in which he examines such questions as whether the arts can be considered a language, how language may be at times "healthy" and at other times "pathic," how signs are related to personality disturbances, and how signs may be used for social control. He examines the scope and import of the semiotic which he has developed, showing how it can be divided into *pragmatics* (which deals with the origin, uses, and effects of signs within behavior), *semantics* (which deals with all modes of signification), and *syntactics* (which deals with combinations of signs in abstraction from signification or behavioral connections). He believes that an adequate science of semiotic will do much to unify the sciences, to advance a scientific humanistics, and to increase the confidence of the individual in his own production and use of signs.—*A.C.B.*

PERTINENT LITERATURE

Black, Max. "The Limitations of a Behavioristic Semiotic," in *The Philosophical Review*. LIV, no. 2 (April, 1947), pp. 258-272.

In developing a theory of language which he considered scientific, Charles W. Morris deliberately chose for the foundation of his theory only concepts which he considered "behavioral." Max Black believes that Morris' vocabulary of "stimulus," "response," and "behavior" is too narrow to provide a basis for an adequate account of language. Black argues that the inadequacies of the vocabulary lead Morris in *Signs, Language and Behavior* to use his basic terms in vague, extended senses and that this vagueness enables Morris to make unsupported pronouncements on controversial issues.

An important feature of Morris' account is his view that words dispose the subjects who hear them to behave in certain ways. Morris believes that for every word in a language there is a distinctive goal-object or set of goal-objects denoted by that sign. A goal-object is related to the sign which denotes it such that when the goal-object is not present the presentation of the sign to a person disposes the person to be disposed to seek the goal-object. Black believes that this view is very implausible. The theory is not derived from empirical facts about how language in fact works, nor is it confirmed by these facts, Black writes. Rather, this theory is a product of an attempt to fit language into a preconceived mold; the theory arises from a simplistic assumption about what a theory of language must look like in order to be scientific.

Morris' view commits him to a belief in the existence of thousands of different human needs. There simply are not so many human needs, Black objects. There is no single goal which all persons hearing the word "black" are disposed to seek, nor is there a single goal or set of goals which is always sought by persons who hear such words as "deer," "taller," "stone," or any other word, Black writes. The word "black" does not necessarily dispose a person who hears the word to seek a black object, nor is there any other object that a person hearing the word necessarily is disposed to seek. The alleged needs corresponding to each word or sign, Black writes, are mere fictions or myths which Morris invents in order to be able to apply to human beings the same conceptual framework which he applies to rats.

Contained in Morris' account of signs is the claim that a stimulus is a *sign* of an object if the presence of the stimulus influences the responses of living creatures to the object. Black finds this view unsatisfactory. There are stimuli which influence behavior in this way but which are not "signs" in any established sense of the word. If a dog receives an injection of morphine and subsequently sees a rabbit, the behavior in response to seeing the rabbit may be influenced by the injection. Although the morphine brings about changes in the dog's behavior towards the rabbit, Black writes, it does not *signify* or *denote* the rabbit. Although the morphine in this situation satisfies Morris' conditions for being a sign of the rabbit, the morphine is not in fact a sign of the rabbit.

Black also writes that the meaning of the word *significatum*, another important term in Morris' account, is vague and unclear. Morris uses the term *significatum* to draw a distinction which parallels John Stuart Mill's distinction between a word's "connotation" and its "denotation" and Gottlob Frege's distinction between a word's "sense" and its "reference." With the term *significatum* Morris is attempting to explain the function which a sign has in a situation in which the denoted object is absent. Morris describes a *significatum* as a set of conditions or properties which an object must have in order to be denoted by a particular sign. Morris believes that for every word in a language there is a set of properties which corresponds to that word. Black objects to the assumption that *all* words are linked to such properties. Morris assumes, for example, that objects denoted by value words have the property he calls "valuata." The significance of the "either . . . or" sign Morris believes lies in "the property of alternativity." Black objects that it is doubtful that there are such properties as these. Black remarks that Morris has offered no argument in support of his controversial position on this matter.

Wild, John. "An Introduction to the Phenomenology of Signs," in *Philosophy and Phenomenological Research*. VIII, no. 2 (December, 1947), pp. 217-233.

In this article John Wild critically examines the two major theorists on signs, Charles W. Morris and C. J. Ducasse, and applies the insights he gains from this examination toward the development of his own theory of signs.

Wild presents many illuminating criticisms of Morris' theory.

Wild notices problems in Morris' use of the term *significatum*. For Morris, a *significatum* is that which is signified by a sign. Morris' use of this term is ambiguous, Wild writes, because at times Morris maintains that what a sign signifies is an organism's *behavior* in response to some object, while at other times Morris thinks of the *object* to which the organism is responding as that which is signified by a sign. Thus Morris is unclear about what it is that a sign signifies and is consequently unclear in his use of the term *significatum*.

An essential feature of Morris' *Signs, Language and Behavior* is that a sign exists in some relation to an organism that responds to the sign. Wild thinks this account depicts signs in a fashion that is too subjective. That a sign signifies an object is independent of any responses which organisms have to the sign, Wild argues. That smoke is a sign of fire is independent of all behavioral dispositions of animals and men toward fires. Smoke would be a sign of fire even if it had no influence on an organism's behavior, Wild writes. That a symptom of a disease is a sign of that disease is an objective relationship of the sign to the disease; the relationship is wholly independent of any responses which doctors or patients may have to the disease. A sign which signifies an event does so whether or not anyone is aware of the sign, the event, or the relation of the sign to the event, Wild writes. Although there may be ancient languages which no modern men can understand, the words in the language still have a significance, and it is possible for modern persons to uncover this significance.

That Morris deliberately explains the human use of language in the same way that he explains animal responses to sensory cues, Wild considers irresponsible anthropomorphism; Morris is thinking of nonhumans in a manner that can be literally true only of human beings. Although there are some signs (the snarl of an animal, for example) to which an animal may respond in the way that a person does, it does not follow that an animal *interprets* the signs in the way that a person does. There are important differences between "signs" to which animals respond and those to which people respond, Wild explains. The only "signs" which animals respond to are signs of particular things. Although an animal may respond to a moan of another animal, the moan is only a sign of a particular pain, of that pain which leads to the moan. Even if two animals respond in the same way to the groan of another animal, it does not follow that for these animals the groan has a universal significance. The groan would not have a universal significance in the way that a word in the English language does, Wild writes. The meaning of the word "pain," for example, extends beyond any particular sensation to which a person might refer with the word. Words have significances that are universal not because different people behave in the same way in response to them but because words represent universal concepts.

Wild rejects Morris' thesis that an essential feature of signs is that they cause those who interpret them to behave in certain fashions or to be disposed to behave in certain fashions. A thing which directly causes an organism to behave in a particular fashion is *ipso facto* not a sign, Wild writes. A wind which blows a person in a particular direction does not *signify* that direction. People act as they do only when they choose to do so; the presentation of a sign does not necessarily cause someone to be disposed to choose to behave in some fashion. The function of linguistic signs is not to cause behavior but simply to make signified objects *knowable*, Wild writes. Words are linked not to behavior but to knowledge.

Kattsoff, L. O. "What Is Behavior?," in *Philosophy and Phenomenological Research.* IX, no. 1 (September, 1948), pp. 98-102.

An important feature of Charles W. Morris' *Signs, Language and Behavior* is his attempt to understand the nature of signs by analyzing them by reference to the behavior of organisms that are presented with signs. Morris avoids direct references to internal, mental events in his account because, he argues, such events are not scientifically observable; behavior, on the other hand, is easily observed. L. O. Kattsoff believes that Morris' wish to explain language entirely by reference to behavior is doomed to failure. What is central to a correct understanding of signs—of human signs in particular—is not the behavior but the thoughts and ideas of those who are presented with signs, Kattsoff maintains.

Morris classifies signs into different types according to the alleged behavior which the signs produce. Since a word does not necessarily produce the same behavior on all occasions, Morris distinguishes that behavior which a word normally produces from that which it produces infrequently. For Morris the *informative* sense of a word, a sense which correlates with a broad and varied class of actions, is that sense of a word which is present when the word is used in order to cause someone to act as though a situation had certain properties. In contrast, a word is used in an *incitive* sense when it is used in order to direct someone's behavior into a more specific channel.

Kattsoff is not happy with this distinction between informative and incitive senses of a word, and he thinks that the distinction exposes major weaknesses in Morris' approach to understanding language. How can it be decided on a particular occasion which sense a person is attaching to his signs?, Kattsoff asks. This question, he writes, can be answered only by appealing to the *intentions* of a sign-user—that is, the thoughts and ideas in the mind of a speaker determine the sense which language has on any particular occasion. Thus Morris' desire to explain sign usage fully by appealing only to behavior is not in fact realized in his work, nor is it even in principle possible to satisfy this desire. Any attempt to explain sign usage within a framework where references to thoughts in the minds of sign-users are avoided necessarily will fail, Kattsoff maintains.

It is not by reference to the *actual* behavior of persons and animals in response to signs but rather by reference to *potential* responses that Morris analyzes language. Morris is aware that when people are presented with signs they often have no immediate behavioral response. (For example, students listening to a teacher's lecture generally have no immediate behavioral response to the words they hear.) This consideration leads Morris to say that the presentation of a sign causes a subject to be *disposed* to behave in a certain fashion under certain conditions, and it is by reference to such a behavioral *disposition* that Morris explains the significance of a sign.

That Morris is forced to resort to behavioral *dispositions* rather than to actual behavior in his account reveals a further problem in his approach to explaining language, Kattsoff explains. How is a disposition to behave *observed*?, Kattsoff asks. A behavioral disposition, like a mental phenomenon, is something which is *inside* a person and which is consequently not observable scientifically. Thus, here too Morris' wish to explain sign usage by reference only to what is scientifically observable is not satisfied.

Behavior is at most a sufficient condition for the presence of a sign, Kattsoff says. It is not a necessary condition. In contrast, a thought or an idea in the mind of someone who interprets a sign is both a necessary and sufficient condition for a sign's being present, Kattsoff writes. Thoughts and ideas in the minds of language-speakers and language-hearers are at the heart of language usage. Language usage cannot be adequately explained within a framework where references to the mental are studiously avoided.—*I. G.*

ADDITIONAL RECOMMENDED READING

Dewey, John. "Peirce's Theory of Signs, Thought, and Meaning," in *The Journal of Philosophy*. XLIII, no. 4 (February, 1946), pp. 85-95. Dewey discusses the relation of Peirce's views on the nature of signs to those of Morris.

Ducasse, C. J. "Some Comments on C. W. Morris's 'Foundations of the Theory of Signs,'" in *Philosophy and Phenomenological Research*. III, no. 1 (September, 1942), pp. 43-52. Many of these well-expressed criticisms which Ducasse directs at Morris' "Foundations of the Theory of Signs" are applicable to *Signs, Language and Behavior*.

Graham, Elaine. "Logic and Semiotic," in *Philosophy and Phenomenological Research*. IX, no. 1 (September, 1948), pp. 103-114. Graham examines Morris' account of "and," "or," "implies," and other logical signs.

Rynin, David. Review of Charles W. Morris' *Signs, Language and Behavior*, in *Journal of Aesthetics and Art Criticism*. VI, no. 1 (September, 1947), pp. 67-70. In this interesting review of Morris' book, Rynin gives special attention to Morris' discussion of art as a language.

THE CONCEPT OF MIND

Author: Gilbert Ryle (1900-1976)
Type of work: Philosophy of mind
First published: 1949

PRINCIPAL IDEAS ADVANCED

To suppose that the mind is a ghost mysteriously embodied in a machine is to commit the category mistake of confusing the logic of discourse about bodies and things with the logic of discourse about minds.

To talk of a person's mind is to talk of his ability to perform certain kinds of tasks; words such as "know" and "believe" are disposition words indicating that under certain circumstances certain kinds of performance would be forthcoming.

What are called mental processes are not processes; they are dispositions, or ways of acting, not themselves acts.

Pronouns, such as "I," do not function as proper names, but are index words; index words function in a variety of ways.

A man's knowledge of himself comes from observing his own behavior.

To imagine is not to look at pictures in the theater of the mind; it is to perform any one of a number of various kinds of acts (such as telling lies, or playing bears).

According to Gilbert Ryle, it is not the function of philosophy to furnish information about minds. Teachers, magistrates, historians, and plain people of all sorts already know the kinds of things that can be known about them, and knowing more is merely a matter of extending one's experience. The philosopher has access to no special facts. But if he rightly plies his trade, he can help "rectify the logical geography of the knowledge which we already possess."

As Ryle sees it, most people know how to make correct use of concepts which apply to mental situations but cannot state the "logical regulations governing their use." Consequently, they do not know how to correlate such concepts with one another or with concepts which refer to matters other than mental facts. The philosopher has the task of clearing up confusions and correcting mistakes which have their source in this kind of ineptness.

It is the more incumbent upon philosophers to do this because, in Ryle's opinion, most of the difficulties which have come to plague us when we talk about these matters—the mind-body problem, solipsism, our knowledge of "other minds," and so forth—have their origin in the errors of philosophers. In particular, modern European thinkers have great difficulty in throwing off the two-substance doctrine so forcibly stated by Descartes, according to which a man has immediate knowledge of his own mind by a kind of interior illumination, greatly superior to the kind of knowledge—never more than an inference—which he has of material things. According to this view, which Ryle calls "the official doctrine," minds dwell in bodies but share none of the characteristics of material things. He frequently stigmatizes it as "the dogma of the Ghost in the Machine."

In attacking this dogma, Ryle carries over into epistemology the battle which the logical positivists previously waged against metaphysics, and the lines of his attack, if not the weapons, are familiar. The first line of attack has to do with the logic of statements: whether the expressions are related to one another in a coherent fashion. The second has to do with the meaning of the statements: under which conditions they can be verified or confirmed. For the purpose of carrying through the former of these attacks, Ryle has set up a series of "categories," deliberately reviving the Aristotelian term, but relating the discovery of categories to linguistic analysis.

Ryle explains "the official doctrine" in terms of what he calls a "category mistake." To suppose that "the University" is an entity in the same sense that its component colleges, libraries, laboratories, and so forth are entities, would be to make a category mistake. Another would be to suppose that "team spirit" has the same kind of reality that batsmen, fielders, and umpires do. These extreme examples to one side, the danger is ever present, Ryle says, that people who know how to apply terms correctly in familiar situations will fall victims to the fallacy of mixing up terms of different orders when they try to think in abstract ways. In his opinion, most of our mistakes in thinking about "mind" are of this sort.

The categories which we use in describing the physical world are "thing," "stuff," "attribute," "state," "process," "change," "cause," and "effect." The error of philosophers, and of plain men when they try to theorize, consists in supposing that there are "things" called "minds" comparable to things called "bodies," except for having different attributes, and that there are mental "events," like physical ones, which have causes and effects. Ryle designates attempts to talk about minds in these terms as "para-mechanical." Mind is thought of as a ghost in the sense that it is regarded as immaterial; but it is believed to press levers, open windows, receive shocks, and exert reactions much as if it were material.

A special feature of "the official doctrine" which has impressed epistemologists is the teaching that mind knows itself in a peculiarly direct manner. Ryle supposes that this view reflects the strong influence upon seventeenth century European thought of the Protestant affirmation that men's minds are "illuminated" by divine truth—a mode of thought that was reinforced by a preoccupation with optical phenomena on the part of Galilean science. As a result, the paramechanical hypothesis of the mind's working was supplemented by a paraoptical hypothesis of its self-knowledge.

Ryle, on his part, does not admit that there is any such *thing* as mind. It is, he says, a solecism to speak of the mind as knowing this or choosing that. The correct thing to say is that a *person* knows or chooses. Some actions of men exhibit qualities of intellect and of character, and, says Ryle, the fact that a person knows or chooses can be classified as a "mental fact" about that person. But he regards it as "an unfortunate linguistic fashion" which leads men to say that there are "mental acts" or "mental processes" comparable to "physical acts" and "physical processes."

Ryle's book is an attempt to show how it is that, since there is no such thing as a mind, we sometimes talk as if there were. The fault derives from our failure to distinguish different types of statements, and from supposing that what is characteristic of words in one kind of sentence is also characteristic of words in other kinds of sentences.

Take, for example, words such as "know," "believe," "aspire," "clever," and "humorous." These are, in Ryle's terminology, *disposition-words*. Statements in which they occur do not assert matters of fact, but capacities, tendencies, propensities, and so forth. To say of a sleeping man that he knows French is not to affirm an additional fact about him comparable to saying that he has gray eyes and is wearing a blue suit. Dispositional statements correspond, rather, to the hypothetical propositions of modern logic: they are indicative sentences and may be true or false in the sense that they are verifiable under certain conditions. A man knows French *if*, when he is spoken to in French, he responds appropriately in French. But no one criterion of performance is sufficient. A mistake arises when it is supposed that every true or false statement is categorical and either asserts or denies that there exists some object or set of objects possessing a specified attribute.

Besides disposition-words there are *occurrence-words* which apply to the higher-grade activities of men which we call "mental." If, as suggested above, "knows" designates a disposition, "heeds" would seem to designate an occurrence, as, for example, when a person is said to heed what he is doing. A double-process misleadingly suggests itself in this instance, with the bodily activity (say, driving a car) going on more or less by itself and an intermittent mental process trying to parallel what is going on in the body. According to Ryle, however, there are not two processes, but one. Driving a car is an occurrence; paying heed is a state of readiness, or a disposition. To say that a person heeds what he is doing while driving is to make a semi-hypothetical, or a "mongrel categorical" statement. The heedful man drives differently, perhaps, in that he is alert to chuckholes and pedestrians; but the heeding is not itself an act in addition to the act of driving, and it presupposes no agent other than the one who is driving the car.

Ryle suggests that the wide currency of "the official doctrine" is due in great part to the "bogy of mechanism." The successes of physical science since the days of Galileo have excited in many theorists the expectation that the world may ultimately be explicable in terms of the motions of bodies according to laws which have the necessity of mathematical demonstrations. Hence, in the interests of human freedom, moral and religious thinkers have countered this prospect by asserting the autonomy of mind. According to Ryle, however, the fear is baseless.

In the first place, "laws of nature" are not "fiats." Law-statements are "open" hypothetical sentences—that is, hypothetical sentences in which the conditional phrase contains a universal term such as "any" or "whenever." Such sentences do not, like categorical sentences, affirm the existence of anything. "Causal-connections," in other words, do not exist in the same sense as, say, the existence of bacteria and the disease they are alleged to cause. To assume that they do is "to fall back into the old habit of assuming that all sorts of sentences do the same sort of job, the job, namely, of ascribing a predicate to a mentioned object." Statements about physical laws do not "mention" anything. They are merely predictive of behavior.

In the second place, according to Ryle, the mechanistic account of nature is no threat to human freedom because many questions concerning human behavior cannot be answered in terms of physical law. Suppose that physicists eventually find the answer to all physical questions, the plain fact is that "not all questions are physical questions." The same process, says Ryle, is often viewed in terms of two or more principles of explanation, neither of which can be reduced to the other, although one commonly presupposes the other. For example, if a child asks a chess player why he moves a certain piece (say, a knight) to a certain spot, the answer he requires is a statement of the rules of the game; whereas, if an experienced player asks the question, the answer required will be in terms of "tactical canons." Another example is the rules of grammar, which apply equally to all books in the language irrespective of style or content. Just so, says Ryle, the laws of physics apply to everything— animate as well as inanimate; but they do not explain everything. Even for describing a game of billiards, mechanical principles, while necessary, are not sufficient. The purpose of the game, its rules, and its tactics are equally important. These "appraisal concepts" are not in conflict with the law-statements; rather, they presuppose them, for there would be no place for planning if there were no predictability.

Ryle safeguards the meaning of purpose in human activity by distinguishing between questions about the *causes* of a man's acts and the *reasons* for it. Suppose the event to be explained is a man's passing the salt to his neighbor at the table. The question about causes demands to be answered in factual or categorical sentences such as, "He heard his neighbor ask for it," or "He saw his neighbor's eye wandering over the table." "Seeing" and "hearing" are events that may stand in the chain of causal explanations. The question about reasons does not admit of categorical answers. One might say, "He passed the salt from politeness," or, "He did it out of friendliness." These are reasons and not causes. They refer to motives or dispositional states, and are expressed in lawlike or hypothetical propositions. That we constantly appeal to them in explaining human behavior testifies to the incompleteness of "causal" explanations. Moreover, according to Ryle, they express all that we actually intend when we speak of man's acts as being free or voluntary.

Ryle finds that there is good sense in saying, "I know that I am free." To infer, however, that the pronoun "I" must be the name of a distinct entity is to misunderstand the true function of pronouns. They do not function like proper names, but are "index" words which point now to one thing, now to another. Because of the complexity of our experience, the pronoun "I" (with "me" and "myself") is used in a variety of ways. Sometimes the speaker uses "I" to refer to his body, as when a man says, "I was cut in the collision." He may even use "I" to refer to his mechanical auxiliaries, such as his car, as in the sentence, "I collided with the police car." These cases offer no particular difficulty. But it is different when one says, "I am warming myself before the fire." Here, "myself" could be replaced by "my body," but not "I." Even more complex are such statements as, "I was ashamed of myself," and "I caught myself beginning to dream." Ryle's explanation is that the pronouns are "used in different senses in different sorts of contexts." Human behavior frequently involves what Ryle calls "higher order actions"; that is to say, actions in which the second agent is concerned with actions of a first agent, as in spying or applauding. And a person's higher order acts may be directed upon his own lower-order acts, as in self-criticism. This, according to Ryle, is what we ordinarily mean by "self-consciousness." There is nothing here to support the view that one looks into his own mind and discovers its workings. What is known as "introspection" is in fact "retrospection." The attempt to glimpse ourselves in the act of thinking is hopeless.

The much-touted claims of introspective psychology, founded on the para-optical model of knowledge, are, therefore, rejected by Ryle. That we know our feelings immediately he does not deny. But he is careful to distinguish feelings, which are agitations, from moods and tendencies, which are dispositions. Of the latter we have no immediate knowledge. Only as they eventuate in actions can we form any estimate of them. A man's knowledge of himself, therefore, comes from observing his own *behavior* and is in principle no different from his knowledge of other persons. Ryle recognizes many grades of self-knowledge: a man may know that he is whistling "Tipperary" and not know that he is doing so to keep up his courage. Or, he may be aware that he is trying to keep up his courage without realizing that what makes him afraid is a guilty conscience. But in no case does he have "privileged access" to his own mental states.

Ryle continues: "No metaphysical Iron Curtain exists compelling us to be forever absolute strangers to one another, though ordinary circumstances, together with some deliberate management, serve to maintain a reasonable aloofness. Similarly, no metaphysical looking-glass exists compelling us to be forever completely disclosed and explained to ourselves, though from the everyday conduct of our sociable and unsociable lives we learn to be reasonably conversant with ourselves."

Ryle's treatment of sensation and observation is refreshing in that he candidly admits that his analysis is not satisfactory to him. He attributes his difficulty to contamination by sophisticated language. In ordinary language the words "sensation" and "feel" signify perceptions, but in philosophical language they refer to presumed bases for perceptual inference. Words like "hurt" and "itch" are not the names of moods, nor are they the names of certain kinds of perceptions, nor are they terms by which achievements are reported. Ryle confesses: "I do not know what more is to be said about the logical grammar of such words, save that there is much more to be said."

His discussion of imagination is perhaps the most provocative part of the book. The ordinary myth-view of imagination is that in the private box or theater of our minds we view private pictures. But the logic of discourse involving the word "imagination" does not entail any such fanciful assumption. To imagine is to lie, to play bears, to write a story, or to invent a machine. There is no need to suppose some one internal, private operation to which the word "imagine" calls attention; in fact, the word does no such thing; it calls attention to publicly observable behavior.

In his discussion of "intellect" Ryle rejects, as by now one might expect, any analysis which describes intellect as an organ, an internal lecturer, a private thinker. As a result of producing various kinds of things—such as sums, books, theories—men are said to have been engaged in intellectual processes. Confusing the grammar of intellect with the grammar of production, and working out an erroneous analogy, we tend to regard intellect as a hidden faculty of mind. Ryle's analyses—here, as elsewhere in the book, careful and illuminating—discredit such a notion. He makes the interesting suggestion that such words as "judgment" and "deduction" are words belonging to "the classification of the products of pondering and are mis-rendered when taken as denoting acts of which pondering consists." Such words, he argues, are "referees' nouns, not biographers' nouns"—that is, they are properly used to describe the products which men have produced; they are misleadingly used to talk about some hidden performances within the mind.

Ryle, in concluding his book, discusses the relation between his approach to the "concept of mind" and that which engages psychologists. It is his stated opinion that, with the collapse of the two-world view, psychology has ceased to have an identifiable aim and is more like medicine, a "fortuitous federation of inquiries and techniques." The wrong sort of promise, he feels, is being made when we are told that psychology will disclose causes of human actions which are hidden from such observers as economists, historians, anthropologists, and novelists. "We know quite well what caused the farmer to return from the market with his pigs unsold. He found the prices were lower than he had expected." The explanation of our competent mental behavior does not require a psychologist; it is apparent to ordinary good sense. Where the psychologist can be of service is in explaining why our competencies often fail. "The question why the farmer will not sell his pigs at certain prices is not a psychological but an economic question; but the question why he will not sell his pigs at any price to a customer with a certain look in his eye might be a psychological question."

Ryle recognizes a certain debt to behaviorism. Often confused by its practitioners with "a not very sophisticated mechanistic doctrine," it was originally a methodological program which insisted that the theories of psychologists "should be based upon repeatable and publicly checkable observations and experiments." This program, according to Ryle, has been of first importance in overthrowing the two-world myth. And it does not in any way entail mechanistic assumptions. For, says Ryle, the rise of the biological sciences and the fact that the Newtonian system is no longer the sole paradigm of natural science make it unnecessary for scientists to consider man as a machine. "He might, after all, be a sort of animal, namely, a higher mammal. There has yet to be ventured the hazardous leap to the hypothesis that perhaps he is a man."—*J.F.*

PERTINENT LITERATURE

Hampshire, Stuart. Review of Gilbert Ryle's *The Concept of Mind*, in *Mind*. LIX, no. 234 (April, 1950), pp. 237-255.

Stuart Hampshire begins his review of Gilbert Ryle's *The Concept of Mind* with a laudatory comment: "This is one of the two or three most important and original works of general philosophy which have been published in English in the last twenty years." Hampshire attributes the book's strength to Ryle's "distinction of style" and "simplicity of purpose," but he also refers to the book's weaknesses when he writes that "its argument seems somehow to fade and to lose some of its force when, laying the book down, one probes it again in some other and less powerful idiom." Hampshire refers to Ryle's tendency to write in epigrams; he declares that they "explode on impact," but he adds that they leave behind them "a trail of timid doubts and qualifications."

According to Hampshire, Ryle has here used the methods of linguistic analysis in the attempt to resolve a very important metaphysical problem— the problem of giving a credible account of mind. Hampshire gives Ryle credit for undertaking such a task, and he also gives him credit for expressing technical distinctions in plain prose; but he argues that the book contains the "radical incoherences" of a book in transition, if for no reason other than that Ryle was so carried away with the enthusiasm of his own rhetoric as to phrase his counterarguments (against mind-body dualism) in the language with which he finds fault.

Hampshire, of course, calls attention to Ryle's intention to dispel once and for all the myth of the "ghost in the machine," the idea that the mind (as John Wisdom put it in his critical comments on *The Concept of Mind*) is a "little man within" and that what the mind is within is a "mechanism," a machine. Hampshire refers to Ryle's disdain for the historical problem of discovering the origin of the idea that the mind is a "ghost" within us "the machine," and he ventures the suggestion that the conception was hardly born with the works of philosophers but is one of the most primitive and natural of myths. Hence, Hampshire claims, Ryle is not arguing against a philosophical concept of mind; he is arguing against "a universal feature of ordinary language itself . . ."—that is, against a universal, or fairly universal, faith. Ryle is arguing against ordinary language (which Ryle professes to respect) because not only is there the fairly common faith that somehow or other there is a ghost, little man, or soul in the machine; but there is also the concept of the machine built into ordinary language—with its talk of what "moves" us, of "impulses," "pushes and pulls," "stresses and strains."

To complicate matters, Hampshire continues, ordinary language is "firmly dualistic" in that it clearly distinguishes—or at least persists in distinguishing—between mental and physical states and events. To make matters even worse, Hampshire adds, Ryle purports to be appealing to ordinary language in his effort to clear up the myth of the ghost in the machine, in that Ryle appeals to what "at first look like distinctions in actual grammar," but which turn out, Hampshire claims, to involve some sort of linguistic ideal which Ryle is fostering.

Hampshire asks on what grounds Ryle decides that there are no acts referred to by such verbs as "see," "hear," "deduce," and "recall" in the way that there are acts meant by such verbs as "kick," "run," "look," and "tell." Ryle offers no convincing reasons for supposing that what he says is the case; his argument appears to consist only of the point that certain adverbs are conventionally attached to the latter set that would not conventionally be attached to the former. Hampshire suggests that for all his efforts to champion and to practice the contemporary method of linguistic analysis, Ryle writes as if there were "real" answers to his questions about verbs—"as though the world consisted of just so many distinguishable Activities (or Facts . . . or States or Things) waiting to be counted and named."

The general thesis of *The Concept of Mind*, according to Hampshire, is that there are no such things as "mental happenings." Ryle depends on the distinction between occurrences and dispositions, Hampshire points out, and thus the core of Ryle's argument is that to talk of someone's "mind" is to talk of that person's "abilities, liabilities and inclinations to do and undergo certain sorts of things, and of the doing and undergoing of these things in the ordinary world." But the "ordinary world" for Ryle is the world of the five senses, and what he requires of anyone who would make sense of talk about the mind is that he talk about what can be sensed—namely, certain telltale lines of behavior. Ryle would like—so Hampshire indicates—to recast ordinary categorical statements about the mind into hypotheticals having to do with what in the way of behavior would be perceived were such-and-such the case. But Hampshire contends that the distinctions between occurrences and dispositions and between categoricals and hypotheticals break down in almost every case of a statement about what the mind is or does. Hence, reformulation is needed.

Hampshire defends this latter point at considerable length—the point that the distinctions between occurrence and disposition and between categorical and hypothetical statements about mind are "pseudo-logical" distinctions. Hampshire goes further: he argues that Ryle attempts the impossible; that is, to convert epistemological distinctions (as to how we know) into logical distinctions (as to the forms of statements, the categories of things). Ryle confuses, so Hampshire claims, the truth-conditions of a sentence with the typical conditions under which some might claim to know what the sentence claims; he tends to identify the meaning of a statement with "*the*" method of its verification.

Hampshire's argument—or set of arguments—against much of what Ryle says is too lengthy and careful to be summarized. However, Hampshire does emphasize that in *The Concept of Mind* Ryle failed to decide whether what he wanted to claim is that what mental concepts "stand for" are not imperceptible states but perceivable behavior, or that statements having to do with the mind are testable only by reference to behavior. In his discussions of will, sensations, and images Ryle is said to exhibit what Hampshire calls "ambiguity of purpose, the conflict between general thesis and particular instance," and these, in turn, produce contradictions.

Hampshire contends that Ryle's urging the restriction of nouns to "solid objects" (so that he would deny, for example, "mental pictures") would be to allow "the fear of ghosts to drive us into pidgin English," and Hampshire suggests that if what we want is an ultimate literal language, perhaps pidgin English is the best we can achieve.

Hofstadter, Albert. "Professor Ryle's Category-Mistake," in *The Journal of Philosophy*. XLVIII, no. 9 (April 26, 1951), pp. 257-270.

Albert Hofstadter, Dickinson S. Miller, Hugh R. King, and Morris Weitz subject Gilbert Ryle's *The Concept of Mind* to searching critical examination in a single issue of *The Journal of Philosophy*. The principal contentions of each will be indicated in the following review.

Hofstadter describes Ryle's *The Concept of Mind* as a "brilliant attack on . . . mentalism," but he doubts whether it is philosophically successful or important. The central theme of Ryle's treatise, according to Hofstadter, is that the mind is not "another person" but a way of acting, a set of abilities and tendencies to act in certain ways. Hofstadter is especially critical of Ryle's effort to establish dualism as a logical mistake. In Hofstadter's opinion Ryle commits a "category mistake" (Hofstadter thereby borrowing one of Ryle's most characteristic weapons of criticism) in presuming that dualism, if it is mistaken, is *logically* mistaken; and Hofstadter attributes Ryle's mistake to his excessive nominalism, brought on by his supposing that logical analysis *is* philosophy.

The basic category mistake that Ryle identifies and attacks is the presumed one that he calls "the dogma of the Ghost in the Machine." Ryle spells out the mistake as that of mistaking references to *dispositions* as references to *occurrences*; instead of recognizing that a person's actions (of the kind we call "mental") are workings-out of various dispositions, the person who commits the category mistake of "Ghost in the Machine" supposes that such actions are the effects of inner occurrences, acts of an inner agent, the mind, a kind of "ghost." Thus the mistake, according to Ryle (as reported by Hofstadter), consists in supposing that "mental-conduct concepts" are concerned with the causation of behavior. The mistake is logical because mental-conduct concepts are concerned with the dispositional tendencies and abilities of a person, not with some presumed cause such as "will."

Hofstadter argues that a dualist would introduce references to "mind" in order to account for the behavioral dispositions that Ryle refers to. Although the dualist would agree with Ryle in maintaining that as far as language goes the mental concepts do refer to dispositional matters, the dualist wants in addition to *explain*, by venturing a theory about the world—that there is both body and mind in it—how such behavioral dispositions come about. Thus, Hofstadter argues, the dualist is not attempting a causal account of intelligent behavior; like Ryle, he understands intelligent behavior behaviorally; but, unlike Ryle, the dualist sets out to explain what makes intelligent behavior possible. Thus, again, it is not the dualist who makes the logical mistake: it is Ryle. Ryle mistakes the dualist's *explanatory theory* for a description of the facts to be explained.

In his essay "'Descartes' Myth' and Professor Ryle's Fallacy," Miller argues that by denying consciousness Ryle denies human selves, for there could not be what we call a "self" were there no states of consciousness. Although Ryle suggests that his behavioral accounts of "mental" matters are relevant in the account of his rejection of consciousness, Miller argues that Ryle never faces the issue directly, that he avoids considering the facts of consciousness, and thus he commits the fallacy of *ignoratio elenchi*. (Consciousness, Miller states in the process of calling attention to the facts that require the concept of consciousness, is what one loses upon falling into a dreamless sleep; it is what provides life with its content, the world-for-me; it provides the basis for a sense of self-identity.) Instead of entering the disputed area "in a jaunty spirit of paradox and hasty subversion," Miller writes, Ryle should have treated the subject with intellectual seriousness and taxing thought.

King argues, in "Professor Ryle and *The Concept of Mind*," that Ryle fails to distinguish between that sense of "intelligent" that enables us to describe action as "directed" action and another sense of the term by which we call attention to a "character of mind," *how* the performer undertakes his directed action. Accordingly, Ryle's discussion about dispositions, which relates to the latter sense of the term, is irrelevant to the consideration of mind, with which the former sense of the term is concerned. King is also critical of Ryle's claim that sensations are not mental, that facts about a person's having sensations are not facts about the mind. Ryle maintains that facts about observation are relevant in talking about the mind, for the making of observations is simply the exploitation of one's capacity to observe. Ryle suggests that the term "observe" is an achievement word. King's analysis calls attention to the role of sensations in observation and to the necessity of assuming observation before one can begin meaningfully to talk about the criteria of recognition.

King then challenges Ryle's denial of self-knowledge by introspection (Ryle supposes that the most one can know about oneself is how one does things), and he concludes his unsympathetic discussion of *The Concept of Mind* with a defense of the point that Ryle's analysis in no way accounts for purposeful and intelligent action. King's summary judgment of Ryle's book is that although Ryle destroyed the Cartesian myth of the "Ghost in the Machine," he ignored the fundamental problems and phenomena that gave rise to the myth. "And if he has succeeded in eliminating the bugaboo of the ghost-in-the-machine," King writes, "there still seems to me to be a skeleton in his epistemological cupboard."

The concluding essay in *The Journal of Philosophy* series concerning Ryle's *The Concept of Mind* is a lively and laudatory review of Ryle's basic contentions: "Professor Ryle's 'Logical Behaviorism,'" by Weitz. Weitz approves of Ryle's procedure of attacking the problems of mind by elucidating the logical character of certain model sentences in the language of everyday speech. Categorical sentences, such as "Jones solves the puzzle," are "simple narratives" that describe episodes. But a sentence such as "Jones is vain" is hypothetical or dispositional to the effect that *if* Jones *were* to be praised, he *would* do certain things—such as prolong the conversation; given half a chance, he *would* talk about himself . . . and so on. Finally, there are "mind-sentences" that are "mongrel-categorical or semi-dispositional," such as sentences containing what Weitz calls "heed" concepts—"noticing," "taking care," "concentrating on," and the like. The sentence "Jones is driving carefully," for example, is partly narrative and partly dispositional.

Weitz concludes that Ryle has offered a "logical behaviorism," an examination of the logic of the language of common sense; and Weitz judges Ryle's study of "mind-sentences" to be "essentially correct and profoundly first-rate. . . ." Ryle's logical behaviorism does not lead to the denial of factual assertions, for Ryle's book (Weitz contends) "stands or falls on the truth or falsity of his empirical claim that the world contains only episodes, about which certain categorical, mongrel-categorical, and purely dispositional statements can be made."—*I.P.M.*

ADDITIONAL RECOMMENDED READING

Addis, Laird and Douglas Lewis. *Moore and Ryle: Two Ontologists*. The Hague, The Netherlands: Martinus Nijhoff, 1965. Addis sets out to show that Ryle's materialism results from an inadequate ontology and the inability to solve the problems of intentionality. Lewis' essay is a discussion of G. E. Moore's realism.

Anscombe, G. E. M. *Intention*. Oxford: Basil Blackwell, 1957. A brilliant study.

Chappell, V. C., ed. *The Philosophy of Mind*. Englewood Cliffs, New Jersey: Prentice-Hall, 1962. An excellent anthology of outstanding essays published in British and American journals between 1950 and 1960. Contains an article by John Wisdom on Ryle's *The Concept of Mind*, as well as articles by B. A. Farrell, D. W. Hamlyn, Norman Malcolm, U. T. Place, Errol Bedford, P. F. Strawson, Paul Ziff, and J. J. C. Smart.

Hampshire, Stuart, ed. *Philosophy of Mind*. New York: Harper & Row Publishers, 1966. An excellent anthology of first-rate articles by some dozen contemporary philosophers.

Wisdom, John. *Other Minds*. Oxford: Basil Blackwell, 1952. Wisdom's articles exhibiting the uses of statements about mind and in that way illuminating the functions of such statements originally appearing in *Mind*. His lively, witty, and pertinent essays are important contributions to the philosophy of mind.

Wittgenstein, Ludwig. *Philosophical Investigations*. Oxford: Basil Blackwell, 1953. A modern classic that deals with problems of the mind as well as with the basic problem of philosophical method. (See the *Index* to locate the discussion of the book.)

ZEN BUDDHISM

Author: Daisetz T. Suzuki (1870-1966)
Type of work: Metaphysics, ethics
First published: 1956 (Selections by Editor William Barrett from works published during the years 1949-1955)

PRINCIPAL IDEAS ADVANCED

Zen is a way of life, of seeing and knowing by looking into one's own nature. The truth comes through active meditation, and enlightenment is sudden and intuitive.

Zen does not rely on the intellect, the scriptures, or the written word, but on a direct pointing at the soul of man, a seeing into one's own nature as making Buddhahood possible.

Zen masters make the moment of enlightenment (satori) *possible by referring directly to some natural and commonplace matter; the immediate recognition of the unity of being follows.*

The chief characteristics of satori *are irrationality, intuitive insight, authoritativeness, affirmation, a sense of the Beyond, an impersonal tone, a feeling of exaltation, and momentariness.*

The methods of Zen are paradox, going beyond the opposites, contradiction, affirmation, repetition, exclamation, silence, or direct action (such as a blow, or pointing).

Zen Buddhism shares with other philosophies and faiths which stress intuition and awareness the ironic condition of desiring to communicate what cannot be communicated. Like the theologies of the Middle Ages, it urges an understanding of true being by a kind of direct insight into one's own being, but it disdains any intellectual or formalistic methods of achieving that insight. The profession of conviction, then, is largely negative; the emphasis, insofar as discourse is concerned, is not on what can be said but on that concerning which we must be silent. A Zen master is not a lecturer; he is a director, or pointer, one who turns the attention of the disciple to some natural fact which, properly apprehended, reveals everything. Of those who have made the effort to explain Zen Buddhism, no one has been more successful than the Japanese philosopher and professor, Daisetz T. Suzuki, whose *Essays in Zen Buddhism* (1949, 1950, 1953), *The Zen Doctrine of No-Mind* (1949), and *Studies in Zen* (1955) provide the selections collected and edited by William Barrett under the title, *Zen Buddhism.* As an introduction to Suzuki's work and to Zen Buddhism, this volume is admirably suited; it deals with the meaning of Zen Buddhism, its historical background, its techniques, its philosophy, and its relation to Japanese culture.

According to the legendary account of Zen, given by Suzuki, Zen originated in India, and the first to practice the Zen method was Sakyamuni himself, the Buddha. He is reputed to have held a bouquet of flowers before his disciples without saying a word. Only the venerable Mahakasyapa understood the "silent but eloquent teaching on the part of the Enlightened One." Consequently, Mahakasyapa inherited the spiritual treasure of Buddhism.

According to historical accounts, however, Zen Buddhism originated in China in A.D. 520 with the arrival of Bodhi-Dharma from India (the twenty-eighth in the line of patriarchs of Zen, according to the orthodox followers). The message brought by Bodhi-Dharma became the four-phrase summation of the Zen principles:

"A special transmission outside the scriptures;

"No dependence upon words and letters;

"Direct pointing at the soul of man;

"Seeing into one's nature and the attainment of Buddhahood."

These are not the words of Bodhi-Dharma, but of later disciples who formulated his teachings. The method of "direct pointing," of referring to some natural thing or event as the focal point of meditation, preparatory to an instantaneous enlightenment, continues to be the most characteristic method of Zen Buddhism.

Dharma came to be known as the *pi-kuan* Brahman, the Wall-contemplating Brahman, because of his practice of contemplating a monastery wall—reputedly for nine years. One of the most familiar stories of his teaching has to do with the persistent seeker after truth, the monk Shen-kuang, described in legend as having stood in the snow until he was buried to his knees and as having cut off his arm in order to show the sincerity of his desire to learn. Finally, gaining audience with Dharma, he said, "My soul is not yet pacified. Pray, master, pacify it." Dharma replied, "Bring your soul here, and I will have it pacified." Suzuki finishes the story: "Kuang hesitated for a moment but finally said, 'I have sought it these many years and am still unable to get hold of it!'

"'There! It is pacified once for all.' This was Dharma's sentence."

The Chinese founder of Zen, Suzuki reports, was Hui-neng (638-713), who was so deeply touched by a recitation of the *Diamond Sutra* (*Vajracchedika-sutra*) that he made a month-long journey to beg the patriarch Hung-jen to allow him to study under him. Hung-jen recognized Hui-neng's spiritual quality and transferred the partriarchal robes to him. (The account may not be accurate, having been composed by the followers of Hui-neng.)

It was Hui-neng who taught that Zen is the "seeing into one's own Nature." According to Suzuki, "This is the most significant phrase ever coined in the development of Zen Buddhism." Allied with this idea was the "abrupt doctrine" of the Southern school of Hui-neng. According to the *Platform Sutra*, "When the abrupt doctrine is understood there is no need of disciplining oneself in things external. Only let a man always have a right view within his own mind, no desires, no external objects will ever defile him. . . . The ignorant will grow wise if they abruptly get an understanding and open their hearts to the truth." In opposition to the view that enlightenment can be achieved by passive or quiet meditation, Hui-neng emphasized apprehending the nature of the self while the self is in the midst of action. Hui-neng began the Zen tradition of getting at the truth directly, intuitively, not intellectually. "When the monk Ming came to him and asked for instruction," Suzuki recounts, "[Hui-neng] said, 'Show me your original face before you were born.'" Suzuki comments: "Is not the statement quite to the point? No philosophic discourse, no elaborate reasoning, no mystic imagery, but a direct unequivocal dictum."

Suzuki's essay "The Sense of Zen," which is Chapter I of Barrett's collection, states at the outset that Zen is "the art of seeing into the nature of one's own being." He argues that Zen Buddhism contains the essence of Buddhism, although it differs from other forms of Buddhism in not stressing rules, scriptures, authorities, and the intellectual approach to the truth. Zen Buddhism assents to the Buddha's "Fourfold Noble Truth" which is built on the basic claim that life is suffering and that to escape suffering one must overcome desire and find truth. There is a struggle in the individual between the finite and the infinite, so that the nature of one's being, which provides a clue to the resolution of the conflict within the self, must be directly grasped. But books are of no help, nor is the intellect; the only way to Buddhahood is through a "direct pointing to the soul of man," as one of the four statements claims. "For this reason," Suzuki writes, "Zen never explains but indicates. . . . It always deals with facts, concrete and tangible." Suffering is the result of ignorance, and ignorance "is wrought of nothing else but the intellect and sensuous infatuation. . . ."

Direct teaching or pointing is sometimes a silent reference, as with the Buddha's flower. But it may appear in the use of an apparently irrelevant, even ridiculous or apparently senseless remark. To appreciate the method of direct pointing, Suzuki cautions, one must regard the attempt to learn as no mere pastime; for Zen Buddhists, Zen is an ethical discipline, an attempt to elevate one's spiritual powers to their ideal limits. The brief answers of the masters to their students' questions were never intended to be intellectual riddles or symbolic utterances. To talk by the use of metaphorical imagery would not be to point directly. Perhaps one can say that although some of the statements attributed to the masters appear to be symbolic in import, there may very well be more direct meanings which are the significant meanings of the statements. Suzuki gives some illustrations of the Zen practice of uttering a few words and demonstrating with action: "What is Zen?" The master: "Boiling oil over a blazing fire." "What kind of man is he who does not keep company with any thing?" The master (Baso): "I will tell you when you have swallowed up in one draught all the waters in the West River."

There is perhaps no more difficult point to make than that such answers from the Zen masters are important not as charming and archaic riddles or irrelevancies, but as "direct pointings" to the truth. The tendency of the Western mind is to go at these remarks intellectually, to "make" sense out of them. But Suzuki argues with convincing sincerity that for the Zen Buddhist such remarks are instruments of enlightenment that can be comprehended simply and naturally with the "opening of a third eye," the sudden enlightenment by which one sees into the nature of his own being. The name for the moment of enlightenment or awakening is "*satori*," and the means to it is meditation of the proper sort. (As Mr. Barrett indicates, the term "Zen" comes from the Japanese term *zazen*, meaning "to sit or meditate," and is equivalent to the Chinese *ch'an* and the Indian *Dhyana*. The distinctive feature of Zen is that meditation and action are one. Suzuki says, "Zen has its own way of practicing meditation. Zen has nothing to do with mere quietism or losing oneself in a trance.")

To achieve *satori*, or enlightenment, involves "meditating on those utterances or actions that are directly poured out from the inner region undimmed by the intellect or the imagination. . . ." Again, examples from the masters are offered to suggest the direct method of Zen. Referring to his staff, Ye-ryo said, "When one knows what that staff is, one's life study of Zen comes to an end." Ye-sei said, "When you have a staff, I will give you one; when you have none, I will take it away from you."

Some suggestive remarks by Suzuki put the Zen method into a perspective accessible to Western minds. If we consider that the direct method is possible for the Zen masters because *any* point of meditation, properly caught in the fullness of its being, is infinitely illuminating, we can come to appreciate the pertinence of apparently irrelevant and abrupt remarks. If one's study of Zen ends with knowledge of the master's staff, it may be that it also ends, as Suzuki suggests, with knowledge of the flower in the crannied wall. Tennyson's image may have much the same significance as the Zen master's image. Referring to the Buddhist scriptures, Suzuki argues that "enlightenment and darkness are substantially one," that "the finite is the infinite, and *vice versa*," and that "The mistake consists in our splitting into two what is really and absolutely one." All of this is reminiscent of the philosophy of the metaphysical mystics; there is a close resemblance to the views of such men as Nicholas of Cusa and Giordano Bruno. Suddenly to appreciate the unity of all being and to recognize that unity in an illuminating moment of knowing one's own nature to be the nature of all being, and therefore the nature of whatever it is to which the master's abrupt remark calls attention, is surely not an act of intellect. For intellect to "work it out" would be to spoil the whole effect, as if one were to try to embrace the quality of a rug as a whole by tracing out its separate threads and their relationships to other threads. *Satori*, if it occurs, has to be a moment of "grasping," of knowing "all at once," and it is not at all surprising that the masters of Zen have come to rely on the abrupt remark as a sudden direct pointing.

In the essay, "Satori, or Enlightenment," Suzuki defines *satori* as "an intuitive looking into the nature of things in contradistinction to the analytical or logical understanding of it." It involves a new view, a new way of looking at the universe. The emphasis of the Zen masters, as with the patriarch Hui-neng, is not on direction or on instruction, but on seeing into one's own nature in order to see the nature of all, to achieve Buddhahood and to escape the cycle of birth and death.

Here again Suzuki emphasizes the masters' methods of bringing the seekers of enlightenment abruptly to *satori*. "A monk asked Joshu . . . to be instructed in Zen. Said the master, 'Have you had your breakfast or not?' 'Yes, master, I have,' answered the monk. 'If so, have your dishes washed,' was an immediate response, which, it is said, at once opened the monk's mind to the truth of Zen." Such remarks are like the strokes and blows, or the twisting of noses, which the masters sometimes resorted to, as if suddenly to make the disciple aware of himself and of the obscuring tendencies of his old perspectives. By referring to commonplace matters in the context of a desire to know all, the masters somehow refer to all. By being apparently irrelevant, they show the relevance of everything.

The chief characteristics of *satori*, Suzuki writes, are *irrationality*, the non-logical leap of the will; *intuitive insight*, or mystic knowledge; *authoritativeness*, the finality of personal perception; *affirmation*, the acceptance of all things; *a sense of the Beyond*, the loss of the sense of self together with the sense of all; *an impersonal tone*, the absence of any feeling of love or "supersensuality"; *a feeling of exaltation*, the contentment of being unrestricted and independent; and *momentariness*, an abruptness of experience, a sudden realization of "a new angle of observation."

In "Practical Methods of Zen Instruction," Suzuki discusses methods for arriving at the realization of the absolute oneness of things. A proper appreciation of these methods, even in outline, depends upon unabridged explanations and examples, but the methods can be mentioned. Zen sometimes utilizes *paradox*, but by concrete images, not by abstract conceptions. Another method is to attempt to think the truth without using the ordinary logic of affirmation and denial; it is the method of *"going beyond the opposites."* The third method is the method of *contradiction*, the method of denying what has already been asserted or taken for granted. The method of *affirmation* is the method frequently referred to: stating almost blithely some commonplace matter of fact in answer to an abstruse and apparently unrelated question. *Repetition* serves to return the self to what it has already seen and not recognized. *Exclamation*, particularly when used as the only answer and when the sound is meaningless, is sometimes used; and even the method of *silence* has provoked *satori*. But of all the methods, the *direct method* of illuminating action—even though the action be commonplace or almost violent, such as a blow on the cheek of a questioner—is most characteristic of Zen, perhaps because it is the action of everything to which Zen directs attention.

The *koan* exercise is the Zen method of teaching the uninitiated by referring them to answers made by Zen masters. The student is either enlightened or encouraged to "search and contrive" in order to understand the state of mind of the master whose *koan* he is considering. Suzuki devotes an interesting chapter to a discussion of the *koan* exercise, and he offers several examples.

The basic principles of Zen, particularly as related to the teachings of Huineng, are examined anew in the essay, "The Zen Doctrine of No-Mind," in which the emphasis on the No-Mind, the Unconscious, brings out the essential concern with active, nondiscursive, intuitive insight. By avoiding the conscious effort to understand intellectually and by participating in ordinary action, one prepares oneself for the moment of enlightenment.

Zen differs from pragmatism, Suzuki maintains, in that pragmatism emphasizes the practical usefulness of concepts, while Zen emphasizes purposelessness or "being detached from teleological consciousness. . . ." Suzuki describes Zen as life; it is entirely consistent with the nonintellectualism of Zen that Zen has implications for action in every sphere of human life. But Zen is concerned not so much with the quality or direction of action as with the perspective of the actor. The emphasis is on "knowing and seeing." Like existentialism, Zen recognizes the antinomy of the finite and the infinite and the possibilities which that relation of apparent opposition opens up; but unlike existentialism, Zen does not involve any conception of an absolute opposition and, consequently, does not entail any "unbearable responsibility," or nausea in the face of the necessity for action. Once the division of finite and infinite, individual and other, is seen to be the consequence of intellectual analysis, so that the idea of individuality is succeeded by the idea of oneness, there is no fear of plunging into the abyss.

In his discussion of Zen and Japanese culture Suzuki shows how Sumiye painting (ink sketching on fragile paper, with no corrections possible), swordsmanship, and the tea ceremony are expressions of Zen principles.

Suzuki's essays on Zen Buddhism are exotic material for the Western reader, but taken seriously—that is, as having some bearing on practice and perspective—they can contribute immeasurably to an appreciation of Oriental religion and philosophy. There is also the challenging possibility that these essays may lead to an understanding of the unifying intuitive mysticism which persistently runs through Western metaphysics despite its prevailing realistic and pragmatic directions. And the most hopeful possibility of all is that by a sincere effort to *learn by seeing* the Zen attitude, the Western mind may finally reach the enlightened freedom of finding that the opposition between realism and mysticism vanishes.—*I.P.M.*

PERTINENT LITERATURE

Watts, Alan W. *The Way of Zen*. New York: Pantheon Books, 1957.

Although acknowledging the value of Daisetz T. Suzuki's works on Zen Buddhism, Alan W. Watts maintains that not even Suzuki has written a work providing Zen's historical background in Chinese and Indian thought. Watts's book attempts to provide such an account; in the discussion of the background and history of Zen Buddhism he considers Taoism, Buddhism, Mahayana Buddhism, and the rise and development of Zen. The second part of his book is concerned with the principles and practice of Zen. According to Watts, Zen Buddhism is "a way and a view of life"; it does not fit into the categories of Western philosophy or religion. Zen defies classification, Watts writes, because it is *not* philosophy, religion, psychology, or science; the only way to explain what Zen is, he insists, is to make clear what it is not.

Watts begins the study of the historical background of Zen by turning to its Chinese origins; it is more Chinese than Indian, and although it has been a distinctive feature of Japanese culture since the twelfth century, its Taoist origins and its Chinese flavor must be understood if Zen is to be grasped at all. Hence, Watts's first concern is with "The Philosophy of Tao." Such a philosophy is difficult for the Western mind to comprehend, he suggests, because Western thinking is of the type a Taoist would call "conventional"— dependant upon conventional signs and modes of communication. Western thinking requires for its expression the use of an alphabetic language, and the words used call attention to abstractions; hence, Western thinking is "linear" and "one-at-a-time," Watts contends, and is hardly suitable for grasping a universe in which everything is happening at once, revealing a complexity that escapes analysis by the use of abstract terms. Watts contrasts Taoism to Western thinking: Taoism, he contends, is unconventional knowledge, a way of life that involves understanding life directly instead of by abstract, linear, representative thinking.

The author also contrasts Taoism to Confucianism: Confucianism attempts to order life according to conventional rules and standards; Taoism attempts to counter this restrictive tradition by developing "original spontaneity, which is termed *tzu-jan* or 'self-so-ness.'"

The common origin of Taoism and Confucianism, according to the Chinese, was not the *Tao Te Ching*, attributed to Lao-tzu, but the I Ching, or *Book of Changes*. Watts writes sympathetically about the use of the *I Ching* as a book of divination, a book by reference to which decisions can be made. He emphasizes the value of intuition, of what he calls the "peripheral vision" of the mind, and he suggests that perhaps the scientific way of discovery has serious limitations, at least when what one is deciding upon is a way of life.

In Taoism the mind is used but not forced. If the *tao*, the Way, the "world process," is to be grasped at all, it is by letting the mind go, by a kind of unconsciousness, a "no-mind" or un-self-consciousness.

The first principle of Taoism is the *tao* itself—the Way of life. The second is spontaneity: the *tao* operates in a spontaneous way, not according to plan. Accordingly, the intelligence that confronts the *tao* is itself spontaneous and intuitive. Watts explains *te* as a kind of "virtue" or "power" which one has who is of no-mind, whose mind is not conventional but spontaneous. The combining of Taoism, which Watts describes as "a liberation *from* convention and *of* the creative power of *te*," with Mahayana Buddhism resulted in Zen Buddhism.

In his chapter "The Origins of Buddhism," Watts explains the Four Noble Truths, the Eight-Fold Path, and the basic ideas of *karma* and *nirvana*. From the fundamental perspective that leads to the judgment "Life is suffering," or, Watts suggests, "frustration" (although, as always, no single Western term or even set of terms is sufficient), a way of life is derived that the Eight-Fold path prescribes. Everything depends on clear awareness, as in Taoism—an opening of the mind to what *is*; from such contemplation comes the right view, understanding, speech, action—and, in short, liberation, a condition of being that is *nirvana* or release from the limited ways and "desire" that inevitably involve suffering. Mahayana Buddhism concentrated on bringing about a cessation of the mind's tendency to think in a discriminative way; the effort was to find *upaya*, "skillful means" for eliminating discriminatory thought, thereby making *nirvana* accessible.

Watts declares that Zen Buddhism has a "special flavor" that resists descriptive identification, but he suggests that "directness" is the key to making the distinction between Zen and other forms of Buddhism. Zen relies on *chih-chih*, a direct pointing, a nonsymbolic action. He traces the historical development of Zen and gives numerous examples of the Zen way. His explanatory account to some degree relies on Suzuki, but his fresh and lively approach to the subject also illuminates Suzuki's writings and fills out the picture of Zen Buddhism.

Barrett, William, ed. "Introduction," in D. T. Suzuki's *Zen Buddhism: Selected Writings of D. T. Suzuki*. Garden City, New York: Doubleday & Company, 1956.

William Barrett's collection of selections from Daisetz T. Suzuki's works on Zen Buddhism is a convenient and dependable source of the most helpful of Suzuki's explanatory essays, and it is further distinguished by the quality of its introduction, in which Barrett makes the effort to connect the philosophical approach fostered by Zen Buddhism to the interests that in the West have led to a practical and cognitive effort to grasp the sense of the world of common experience and concern. The selections in *Zen Buddhism* are drawn from the following works published by Rider and Company, London: *Essays in Zen Buddhism, First Series* (1949), *The Zen Doctrine of No-Mind* (1949), *Essays in Zen Buddhism, Second Series* (1950), *Essays in Zen Buddhism, Third Series* (1953), and *Studies in Zen* (1955). (The latter work is also published in the United States by Philosophical Library.)

Barrett presents the selections under topics that provide a system of orientation for students unfamiliar with Zen Buddhism: I: The Meaning of Zen Buddhism; II: The Historical Background of Zen Buddhism; III: The Heart of Zen; IV: Techniques of Zen; V: Zen and the Unconscious; VI: Zen and Philosophy; and VII: Zen and Japanese Culture. For those familiar with Western philosophy, Chapter 9 (in Part VI, "Zen and Philosophy"), "Existentialism, Pragmatism and Zen" is especially helpful as providing a contrast that illuminates the difference between the Western philosophical method of analysis and experimentation and the Zen method of subjectivity.

Barrett regards Suzuki as unique in that Suzuki assumes that Buddhism is as pertinent and living a life spirit as it was over 2500 years ago when Gotama Siddhartha experienced enlightenment. Barrett testifies to the positive effect in his own life of his becoming acquainted with Zen through the writings of Suzuki, and he attributes much of the "freshness and vitality" of Suzuki's accounts of Zen to his having become thoroughly familiar with Chinese Buddhism.

The "practical and concrete Chinese spirit," Barrett writes, brings Buddhism more within the grasp of the Western mind than does the "soaring metaphysical imagination of the Indians." The paradoxes and anecdotes of the Zen masters exhibit the Chinese faculty of expression through concrete imagery that provokes the kind of intuitive response that makes understanding possible.

According to Barrett, the Western tradition, with its dominant Hebraic and Greek influences, has worked against the recognition of certain basic realities of life. Both influences have been divisive, Barrett believes: the Hebrew view distinguishes God from the world (and, accordingly, God from his creatures), the Law from fallible persons, and the spirit from the flesh; the Greek, by contrast, divides matters on intellectual, not moral and religious grounds, insisting upon a radical distinction between reason and the senses. The Orientals, on the other hand, by making intuition central, have avoided the divisions that plague the Western mind and spirit.

Medieval Christianity, as influenced by Aristotle, fosters a rational, logical, and hence humanized view of reality, Barrett maintains. But modern astronomy, physics, and even mathematics are more akin to the spirit and thrust of Indian thought, which emphasizes the vastness and ultimate irrationality of the universe.

Reason generates paradoxes; intuition grasps unity. If Being is to be known, it cannot be known by intellect. The Zen approach to understanding is by a form of subjective action that the term "no-mind" can only suggest. Barrett calls attention to Martin Heidegger's philosophy and its rejection of the dichotomizing intellect, and to D. H. Lawrence's call for "mindlessness" to correct the inhibiting and distorting influence of Western rationalism, which divides subject and object. These Western thinkers—the one, a philosopher, the other, an artist—approach but do not reach the revelatory attitude that Zen Buddhism encourages and exhibits.

The language of Zen involves concreteness of expression, the use of images and examples that incite intuition, Barrett writes; but this language is not simply a means: "On the contrary, the language of Zen is of the essence, the manner of expression is one with the matter." Zen is "Radical Intuitionism," Barrett suggests—not a philosophy of intuition but intuition "in the act itself." The task for the Zen master is to "awaken the third eye," the eye of intuition; language is used to get beyond language and concepts, even to get beyond distinguishable "facts" in order to know the unity of Being.

Zen itself is not a philosophy, Barrett warns—at least, it is not a philosophy in the Western sense; it is "a philosophy to undo philosophy," an attempt to avoid the divisive tendency of the emphasis on ideas as the objects of disciplined thought by achieving an "unmediated relation to reality. . . ."

Nor is Zen a kind of mysticism, Barrett insists. Although it works toward enlightenment, *satori*, it does not involve the conception of a reality beyond the world of sense experience and the consequent necessity of a radical experience by which one leaves the world of appearance and enters into the world beyond. Zen is matter-of-fact, Barrett contends; it is not philosophy, or mysticism, or pantheism, or theism; it is a way of achieving the actuality of unity, the living of Being. Zen is "the living fact in all religions East or West," Barrett declares. "Zen touches what is the living fact in all religions." He invites the reader to discover Zen through the writings of Suzuki.—*I.P.M.*

ADDITIONAL RECOMMENDED READING

Beck, Lily Adams. *The Story of Oriental Philosophy*. New York: Farrar and Rinehart, 1928. Beck covers Indian thought, Buddhism, Chinese thought, and finally, in Chapter XXIX, "Buddhist Thought and Art in China and Japan: The Teachings of Zen." Beck ties Zen to the teachings of Bodhidharma and the Yoga of the early Upanishads.

Hackett, Stuart C. *Oriental Philosophy: A Westerner's Guide to Eastern Thought*. Madison: University of Wisconsin Press, 1979. Hackett's account is intelligible and scholarly, and his remarks about Zen Buddhism, although brief, provide an excellent summary of the distinctive features of Zen.

Humphreys, Christmas. *Buddhism*. Harmondsworth, England: Penguin Books, 1951. A readable introduction to Buddhism with an account of the doctrines of the Southern and Mahayana schools, including a chapter on Zen Buddhism.

——————— . *Zen Buddhism*. London: Heinemann, 1949. As the title suggests, the author focuses on Zen Buddhism.

Koller, John M. *Oriental Philosophies*. New York: Charles Scribner's Sons, 1970. Chapter 13, "Zen Buddhism," explains Zen within the context of the history of Buddhism. Like Barrett, the author describes Zen Buddhism as neither a religion, a philosophy, nor a set of beliefs; it is an active way of achieving integrity and completeness in a moment of experience.

THE MYSTERY OF BEING

Author: Gabriel Marcel (1889-1973)
Type of work: Existential ontology
First published: 1950

PRINCIPAL IDEAS ADVANCED

The peculiar task of philosophy is to describe what it means to be in a particular concrete situation.

Existential thinking, the thinking of an involved self, is threatened by the interest in abstractions and by bureaucratic societies which reduce individuals to averages.

Primary reflection is analytical; secondary reflection is recuperative, allowing the self to discover its being in action.

The immediate encounter with the mystery of being is in terms of a lived participation; being is an internal relation; the self, or the body, is not an object of knowledge, but the subject who knows himself as he acts.

To know others existentially is to encounter them, not as things, but in acknowledgment of them as persons.

Freedom is found when the self turns inward and becomes aware of its capability for commitment and treason.

Gabriel Marcel is one of the main figures associated with existential thought in France. His two-volume work, *The Mystery of Being*, is the final product of a series of Gifford Lectures which were given in 1949 and 1950 at the University of Aberdeen. Volume I is subtitled "Reflection and Mystery." The subtitle of Volume II is "Faith and Reality." Characteristic of *The Mystery of Being*, and one might say of Marcel's writings in general, is a philosophical approach which is oriented towards concrete descriptions and elucidations instead of systematic delineations. In this respect the existentialism of Marcel has greater affinities to the thought of Kierkegaard and Jaspers than to that of Heidegger and Sartre. Marcel will have nothing to do with the system builders. A philosophical system, even though it may have an existentialist cast, as in Heidegger and Sartre, entails for the author a falsification of lived experience as it is immediately apprehended.

On every page of Marcel's writings the reader is forced to acknowledge the author's concentrated efforts to remain with the concrete. Existential thinking is the thinking of the "involved self." This involved self is contrasted by the author with the "abstracted self." The abstracted self, in its movement of detachment, escapes to a privileged and intellectually rarefied sanctuary—an "Olympus of the Spirit"—from which it seeks to formulate a global and inclusive perspective of the whole of reality. Marcel's concrete philosophical elucidations express a continuing protest against any such Olympian view.

"There is not, and there cannot be, any global abstraction, any final terrace to which we can climb by means of abstract thought, there to rest for ever; for our condition in this world does remain, in the last analysis, that of a wanderer, an itinerant being, who cannot come to absolute rest except by a fiction, a fiction which it is the duty of philosophic reflection to oppose with all its strength." Man as an "itinerant being" (or as a wayfarer, as the author has expressed it in the title of another of his works, *Homo Viator*, 1945) is always on the way, passing from one concrete situation to another. At no time can he shed his situationality and view himself and the rest of the world as completed. There is no *Denken überhaupt* which can tear itself loose from the concrete situation of the involved self and lay a claim for universal validity. This, for Marcel, as already for Kierkegaard, is the grievous fault in all varieties of idealism. Idealism fails to recognize the situational character of all human thinking. The philosophical reflection which the author prescribes is a reflection which retains its existential bond with the concrete situation. The peculiar task of philosophy is that of describing what it means to be in a situation. This task is a phenomenological one—phenomenological in the sense that it takes its point of departure from everyday, lived experience and seeks to follow through the implications which can be drawn from it.

Concrete existence is lost in the abstract movements of a detached reflection, but it is also threatened by the pervasive bureaucratization of modern life. In the chapter entitled, "A Broken World," Marcel develops a penetrating analysis of the dissolution of personality in the face of increased social regimentation. Man stands in danger of losing his humanity. Our modern bureaucratized world tends to identify the individual with the state's official record of his activities. Personality is reduced to an identity card. In such a situation man is defined in terms of replaceable functions rather than acknowledged as a unique and irreplaceable self. Creative activities are standardized and consequently depersonalized. Everything, including man himself, is reduced to a stultifying law of averages. In one passage the author speaks of an equality which is obtained by a process of "levelling *down*" to a point where all creativity vanishes. The language and theme are reminiscent of Kierkegaard's social critique in *The Present Age* (1846), in which he indicted the public for having effected a leveling process that virtually made the category of the individual extinct. This theme of depersonalization also links Marcel with the two German existentialists, Jaspers and Heidegger. Jaspers in his book, *Man in the Modern Age* (1931), has described how the masses have become our masters and reduced everything to an appalling mediocrity. Heidegger, in his notion of *das Man*, has expressed basically the same theme. In a later work, *Man Against Mass Society* (1952), Marcel gives special attention to this phenomenon, elucidating it in a descriptive analysis which is rich and penetrating.

The leading question in Marcel's philosophy of the concrete is the question,

"Who am I?" Only through a pursuit of this question can man be liberated from the objectivizing tendencies in modern thought, and return to the immediacy of his lived experience. Reflection will illuminate this lived experience only as long as it remains a part of life. The author defines two levels of reflection—primary and secondary. Primary reflection is *analytical* and tends to dissolve the unity of experience as it is existentially disclosed to the involved self. Secondary reflection is *recuperative* and seeks to reconquer the unity that is lost through primary reflection. It is only with the aid of secondary reflection that man can penetrate to the depths of the self. The Cartesian *cogito* is derived by primary reflection, and therefore it is viewed as a mental object somehow united with the fact of existence. But this abstract reflection is already at a second remove from the reality of pure immediacy. If the "I exist" is to provide the Archimedean point, then it will need to be retrieved in its indissoluble unity as an immediate datum of secondary reflection. Existence, as Kant had already shown in his *Critique of Pure Reason* (1781), is not a property or a predicate which can be attached to a mental object. Existence indicates an irreducible status in a given sensory context. Secondary reflection uncovers my existence as it is sensibly experienced *in act*. This apprehension of my existence *in act* is what Marcel calls the "existential indubitable." In asking about myself, I am disclosed as the questioner in the very act of posing the question. It is here that we find ourselves up against existence in its naked "thereness."

The living body is for the author a central phenomenon in secondary or recuperative reflection. Secondary reflection discloses my existence as an *incarnated* existence—an existence which is tied to a body which I experience as peculiarly and uniquely my own. The "existential indubitable" is manifested in the experience of my body as it actually lives. Primary reflection tends to dissolve the link between me and my body; it transforms the "me" into a universal consciousness and my body into an objectivized entity which is in fact only one body among many others. The original unity of the experience of myself as body is thus dissolved. Primary reflection takes up the attitude of an objectivizing detachment. The body becomes an anatomical or physiological object, generalized as a datum for scientific investigation.

It becomes evident that the Cartesian dualism of mind and body springs from primary rather than secondary reflection. The body in Descartes' philosophy is a substantive entity which has been objectivized and viciously abstracted from the concrete experience of the living body as intimately mine. Secondary reflection apprehends my body as an irreducible determinant in my immediate experience. On the one hand, my body is disclosed as something which I *possess*, something that belongs to me. But as I penetrate deeper I find that the analogy of ownership does not succeed in fully expressing the incarnated quality of my existence. The analogy of ownership still tends to define the relation of myself to my body as an external one. It defines my body as a possession which is somehow accidental to my inner being. But this is not so. My body is constitutive of my inner being. Properly speaking, it is not something which I have; it designates who I am. "My body is *my* body just in so far as I do *not* consider it in this detached fashion, do not put a gap between myself and it. To put this point in another way, my body is mine in so far as for me my body is not an object but, rather, I *am* my body."

It is at this point that the author's distinction between being and having becomes relevant. The phenomenon of being can never be reduced to the phenomenon of having. In *having* the bond between the possessor and the possessed is an external relation; in the phenomenon of *being* the bond is internal rather than external and is expressed by Marcel in the language of participation. Man has or possesses external objects and qualities, but he participates in being. The implications of this phenomenological distinction for the immediate awareness of the living body are evident. On one level of experience my body is something which I have or possess. It is a material complex which is attached to myself, and defines me as a self with a body. But on a deeper level of experience I *am* my body, and I am my body in such a way that the simple materiality of my body as a possession is transcended. I *exist as body*, as an incarnated being for whom the experience of body and the experience of selfhood are inseparable phenomena. Speaking of my body is a way of speaking of myself. The body in such a view is existentialized. It is no longer an object possessed by a subject. It is apprehended as a determinant of subjectivity.

The immediate encounter with the mystery of being is thus in terms of a lived participation. The idea of participation, says the author, had taken on importance for him even in the days of his earliest philosophical gropings. Although the language of participation would seem to betray a Platonic influence, the author makes it clear that the idea of participation includes more than an intellectual assent. Indeed, the foundational mode of participation is feeling, inextricably bound up, as we have seen, with a bodily sense. The Platonic dualism of mind and body, with its perfervid intellectualism and depreciation of the senses, could not admit the existential quality of participation which Marcel seeks to establish. Marcel's favorite illustrations of feeling as a mode of participation are his illustrations of the link between the peasant and the soil, and the sailor and the sea. Here, he says, we can grasp what participation means. The peasant's attachment to the soil and the sailor's attachment to the sea transcend all relationships of simple utility. The peasant does not "have" the soil as a simple possession. The soil becomes a part of his being. He becomes existentially identified with the soil. A separation of himself from the soil would entail a loss of identity and a kind of incurable internal bleeding. This bond through participation, expressed in the link between the peasant and the soil, points to the fundamental relation of man to the mystery of being.

In Marcel's philosophy of participation, the notions of intersubjectivity, encounter, and community are decisive. In the second volume of *The Mystery of Being* the author seeks to replace the Cartesian metaphysics of "I think" with a metaphysics of intersubjectivity which is formulated in terms of "we are." Philosophical reflection, he argues, must emancipate its inquiry from the solipsism of an isolated epistemological subject or a transcendental ego. My existence is disclosed only in the context of a "living communication" with other selves. "The more I free myself from the prison of ego-centricism," concludes the author, "the more do I exist." Imbedded in all my existential reflections is a preliminary and precognitive awareness of a communal horizon of which I am inextricably a part. *"I concern myself with being only in so far as I have a more or less distinct consciousness of the underlying unity which ties me to other beings of whose reality I already have a preliminary notion."*

The basic phenomenon of communal intersubjectivity is further elucidated in the author's use of the notion of encounter. The intersubjectivity of human life becomes apparent only in the movements of personal encounter. Now the phenomenon of personal encounter expresses a relationship which is qualitatively diverse from that which obtains in a relationship between physical objects on the level of *thinghood*. Selfhood and thinghood constitute distinct modes of being, correspondingly requiring different modes of apprehension or knowledge. Another human self cannot be encountered as a thing. Every human self is a "thou," and must be encountered as a personal center of subjectivity. Only through encounter does one attain knowledge of another self. The French verb *"reconnaître"* is peculiarly suited to express the movement of encountering. The range of meaning in *reconnaître* is restricted if it is translated in its usual manner as "to recognize." The French usage denotes *acknowledgment* as well as *recognition*. In an *encounter* another self is known when he is acknowledged as a person. Knowledge is acknowledgment.

Allied with notions of the encounter and *reconnaître* are the notions of *disponibilité* and *indisponibilité*, which are elucidated at some length in a previous work by Marcel, *L'Être et Avoir* (*Being and Having*, 1949). The two notions have been rendered into English respectively as *availability* and unavailability. Marcel suggests, however, that it would be more natural if one spoke of handiness and unhandiness. The self-centered person is unhandy. He does not make himself and his resources available to other selves. He remains encumbered with himself, insensitive to openness and transparence. He is incapable of sympathizing with other people, and he lacks a requisite fellow feeling for understanding their situation. "He remains shut up in himself, in the petty circle of his private experience, which forms a kind of hard shell round him that he is incapable of breaking through. He is unhandy from his own point of view and unavailable from the point of view of others." The handy and available self is that self who can transcend his private, individual life and become open to a creative communion with other selves. He is ever ready to respond in love and sympathy. No longer enclosed upon himself, he acknowledges the inner freedom or subjectivity of the other, and thus reveals both himself and the other as something other than object. It is Marcel's accentuation of the theme of creative intersubjectivity which most clearly contrasts his existential reflections with those of his fellow countryman, Jean-Paul Sartre. In the existentialism of Sartre the final movement culminates in a disharmonious and alienating ego-centricism. In the existentialism of Marcel the last measure and note is one of harmony—creative communality.

The existential reflections in the author's two-volume work are geared to an elucidation of various facets of the presence of being. Being discloses itself as a mystery—hence, the appropriate title of his lectures, *The Mystery of Being*. In the concluding chapter of Volume I the author erects a signpost for the philosophical wayfarer to help him in his metaphysical journeyings. This signpost is the distinction between problem and mystery. A mystery is something in which I myself am involved. A problem is something from which I detach myself and seek to solve. One is involved in mystery, but one solves problems. Mystery has to do with the experience of presence. Problem has to do with the realm of objects which can be grasped through the determination of an objectivizing reason. A problem is subject to an appropriate technique; it can be diagramed, quantified, and manipulated. A mystery by its very character transcends every determinable technique. Being is a mystery rather than a problem, and the moment that it is reduced to a problem its significance vanishes. By turning a mystery into a problem one degrades it. When the mystery of the being of the self is subject to a problematic approach, which by definition objectivizes its content, then the personal and subjective quality of selfhood is dissolved. When the mystery of evil is translated into a problem of evil, as is the case in most theodicies, then the issue is so falsified as to render impossible any existentially relevant illumination. In advancing his distinction between mystery and problem, however, Marcel is not delineating a distinction between the unknowable and the knowable. In fact, the unknowable belongs to the domain of the problematic. It points to the limiting horizon of that which can be conceived through objective techniques. The recognition of mystery involves a positive act or responsiveness on the part of self. It expresses a knowledge which is peculiar to its content—an immediate knowledge of participation as contrasted with an objectivizing knowledge of detachment. Knowledge is attainable both in the domain of mystery and in the domain of problem, but the knowledge in each case is irreducibly adapted to its intentional content.

In Volume II the author concludes his philosophical reflections by showing that his philosophy of being is at the same time a philosophy of freedom. Although the notion of freedom is not given as much attention in the existentialism of Marcel as in that of Kierkegaard, Jaspers, and Sartre, it plays a significant role in his elucidations of concrete experience. Freedom is disclosed in the domain of mystery rather than in the domain of problem. Freedom can never be found in a series of external acts. Freedom is found only when the self turns inward and becomes aware of its capacity for commitment and treason. Freedom is disclosed in the subjective movements of promise and betrayal. I am free to bind myself in a promise, and then I am free to betray the one who has taken me into his trust. Freedom is thus disclosed in both its creative and destructive implications. Both fidelity and treason are expressions of a free act. This freedom, which is experienced only *in concreto*, moves within the mystery of man's inner subjectivity. As a problem, freedom can be nothing more than a series of objectively observable psychological states. As a mystery, freedom constitutes the inner core of the self.

There is an inner connection between faith and freedom. In Volume II, which the author has subtitled "Faith and Reality," this inner connection is elaborated. Faith is itself a movement of freedom in the establishment of bonds of commitment—both with one's fellow man and with God. Faith is thus described as trust rather than as intellectual assent to propositional truth. Marcel distinguishes between *believing that* and *believing in*. Faith is not a matter of *believing that*. It is not oriented toward propositions which correspond to some objective reality. Faith is expressed through *believing in*. To believe in another person is to place confidence in him. In effect, this is to say to the other: "I am sure that you will not betray my hope, that you will respond to it, that you will fulfil it." Also, to have faith in God is to establish a relationship of trust in him. Man is free to enter into a covenant with God, invoking a bond of trust and commitment, but he is also free to betray him and revoke the covenant. Faith and freedom disclose the need for transcendence. Transcendence, for the author, is not simply a horizontal transcendence of going beyond in time—as it is for Heidegger and Sartre. Transcendence has a vertical dimension as well—a going beyond to the eternal. The experience of transcendence is fulfilled only through participation in the life of a transcendent being. Marcel's philosophy of being, unlike that of Heidegger and Sartre, is not simply a philosophy of human finitude. It seeks to establish a path which reaches beyond the finite and temporal to the transcendent and eternal.—*C.O.S.*

PERTINENT LITERATURE

Heinemann, F. H. "The Mysterious Empiricist," in *Existentialism and the Modern Predicament*. New York: Harper & Row Publishers, 1958.

There is a difference, says F. H. Heinemann, between talking about metaphysics and talking metaphysics; and he takes occasion to say that Gabriel Marcel was one of the few metaphysicians of our century. At the same time he points out the complexity of Marcel's nature—that he was a successful dramatist, a composer of music, and an *anima religiosa* as well as a philosopher.

Marcel's first philosophical studies were concentrated on German, English, and American idealism, culminating in what remains one of the best books on the philosophy of Josiah Royce. But he was put off by what seemed to him the false optimism of traditional metaphysics; and we read in his *Metaphysical Journal*: "A mind is metaphysical in so far as its position within reality appears to it essentially unacceptable. . . . It is in a false position. The problem is to correct this or to bring about a *détente*. Metaphysics is just this correction or this *détente*."

The tag "Mysterious Empiricist" does not do justice to the fullness of Marcel's thinking. In using it, Heinemann means to call attention to the turnabout which Marcel was one of the first to effect in the direction of contemporary philosophical enquiry. (Joseph Chiari reminds us that Marcel's *Journal* appeared in the same year, 1927, as Martin Heidegger's *Sein und Zeit*, and that many notions that have been popularized by Jean-Paul Sartre and Maurice Merleau-Ponty were introduced to the public in Marcel's dramas and other writings.) With but few exceptions, philosophers since the Enlightenment had tried to "explain away" anything that seemed mysterious. Idealism started with an abstract notion of consciousness; empiricism started with an equally abstract notion of sense data. Neither, according to Marcel, left any place for the concrete experience which a person has of himself in the everyday business of living, and, more particularly, in the relations, whether friendly or hostile or merely uncomfortable, which go to make up social life. The existence of man-in-the-world, which Marcel seeks to illuminate, is both problematic and mysterious.

Just as he transformed the concept of experience, so Marcel transformed the concept of reason, which ceases to be ratiocination and becomes reflection. As Heinemann reminds us, *réflexion* is not used in French in the same way that we use the English word "reflection." Rather, it has the technical sense of psychological reflection which "reflection" has in John Locke's *Essays*. Moreover, Marcel distinguishes between primary reflection, which is analytic, and secondary reflection, by means of which a person views his experience in a new, more authentic way. The latter ties in with Marcel's Bergsonian insight into the essentially progressive character of thinking which he catches in the title of his book *Homo Viator* ("Man the Wayfarer"). Man would like his thinking to stay put, but it is part of the task of living to remain on the move. Further, secondary reflection ties in with Marcel's emphasis on the manner in which thought is bound up with our bodies—what he calls incarnation. Our thought depends on sense experience; it has to embody itself in gestures, speech movements, sounds, and so forth, in order to be.

Finally, Marcel transformed the notion of metaphysics itself when he asserted that it is concerned with the metaproblematic—that is, with ontological mystery. These terms simply indicate that for Marcel, as for Søren Kierkegaard, the highest truth is subjectively conditioned. According to Marcel, man has two fundamentally different ways of addressing himself to his fellow creatures: he can view them in a problem context, in which they become objects, possessions, means to ends; or he can consider them as his fellows, participating in their hopes and disappointments, thereby remaining alive to the wonder and mystery of Being. Marcel develops these distinctions in his discussion of modern man's alienation, which he diagnoses as ontological deficiency. His argument is that to exist in the human sense is to coexist, to participate in the being of others, even to have the center of one's self in others—something that is particularly difficult in a technological society. Similarly, says Marcel, man can approach Transcendent Being either in the way he approaches a problem or in the way he approaches a mystery. Traditional metaphysicians take the former approach, distancing themselves from God and viewing his Being as a problem. But for Marcel, Transcendent Being must be approached through faith, hope, and love, which are not means of knowing in the objective sense but rather are modes of participation in Being.

Although Marcel is usually thought of as a Christian existentialist, this designation must be qualified. In the first place, Marcel was not reared as a Christian, and he developed his philosophy without any reference to the doctrine and practice of the Church, which he joined in 1929 at the instigation of the Catholic novelist François Mauriac. In the second place, from 1950 on, without changing his views, Marcel specifically rejected the title "Christian Existentialist." The reason is not entirely clear. Perhaps, says Heinemann, he wanted only to correct the impression that all that distinguished his philosophy from that of Sartre was that he was a believer and Sartre an unbeliever. On the other hand, Heinemann points out, a 1950 encyclical condemned existentialism as an aberration; and, although the condemnation was not directed against Catholic writers, it did put men like Marcel in an awkward position.

Hocking, William Ernest. "Marcel and the Ground Issues of Metaphysics," in *Philosophy and Phenomenological Research*. XIV, no. 4 (June, 1954), pp. 439-469.

Gabriel Marcel dedicated his *Metaphysical Journal* (1927) jointly to Henri Bergson and William Ernest Hocking. Bergson was the leading philosopher at the University of Paris, and his emphasis on creativity and openness had left Marcel dissatisfied with philosophical systems. Hocking, still early in his career at Harvard, was a fellow explorer with whom Marcel carried on correspondence following World War I. As appears from Hocking's article, both he and Marcel were fighting free of monisms, whether of the idealist or naturalist type, and both were exploring the possibilities of what Hocking calls "a higher-level or reflexive empiricism."

Hocking points out that when Marcel began keeping his *Journal*, he was not concerned with the problem of existence but with general questions of metaphysical method, such as were posed by the antithesis of subjectivism and realism and that of temporalism and the block universe. There was as yet no existentialist movement, and Marcel was not aware that his protest against systems paralleled that of Søren Kierkegaard, nor was he familiar with the work of Edmund Husserl, whose phenomenological method bears resemblance to what he called secondary reflection. It was by following his own trail, says Hocking, that Marcel was prompted to ask what we mean when we attribute existence to anything, particularly to ourselves.

Marcel's way of answering this question was to suggest that Being, Existence, the Actual, the Real, although they cannot be defined, can be experienced, and that the experience can be described. Human experience, as Hocking paraphrases Marcel's answer, is not subjective: it is experience of the real. Moreover, this experience includes a concern, a passion, which Marcel designates *exigence*, a word which, says Hocking, is both more primitive and more universal than Kierkegaard's *Angst*, but expressive of the same gravamen and inward flame. Such experience is antithetical to the experience cultivated by scientifically inspired philosophers who think of themselves as spectators rather than as parts of what is being observed. In exploring experience, Marcel was addressing the subconscious existence-awareness of our era in which man sees his own being and that of his race as threatened by nonbeing.

It was an important step, says Hocking, when Marcel chose the term "mystery" to denominate what is common to the numerous issues which confront us when we think about existence. A philosopher who, emulating the mathematician or the engineer, tries to deal with questions of existence as if they were problems is sometimes left with paradoxes—for example, the ancient quandary of self-consciousness—Epimenides truthfully knows himself to be lying. Marcel saw, on the contrary, that what appear to the objectivizing philosopher as paradoxes are better thought of as mysteries, to be investigated by less prejudicial methods. Unfortunately, says Hocking, the term "mystery" suggests mysticism and an end to clear thinking; but Marcel, he insists, used the term with the opposite intention.

Hocking takes the example of human communication, traditionally bound up with the mind-body "problem." This was a subject that Hocking and Marcel were investigating at the same time. Current theories recognized no mystery: all transmission of meaning from A to B was by way of a double-translation—from A's thought through physical signs to B's sense-receptors and through the nervous-system to his thought. No immediate passage was believed possible. But what if a person's experience belied the theory? What if B were convinced that on occasion he had direct access to some thought of A's? Recounting such experiences, Marcel put the question: "Admitting the hypothesis that direct communication is real, what are the conditions under which it is able to be real?" And his reply Hocking finds illuminating: "Human beings can be linked to each other in a real bond only because, in another dimension, they are linked to something that transcends them and comprehends them in itself."

In explaining Marcel's position, Hocking makes use of a statement made quite casually by Alfred North Whitehead in a Harvard seminar. "After all, *here we are*! We don't go behind that, we begin with it." (Compare Whitehead's *Process and Reality*, p. 6: "Our datum is the world, including ourselves.") What Hocking finds interesting in the expression "Here we are" is that without the "here" no "we are" is possible. Mutual awareness is by way of a field that binds us into a "we." This shared experience, which is presupposed in all human activity, Hocking calls latent or unfulfilled intersubjectivity, pointing out that it is present even when I think I am being most objective. For example, the physical world is never "my world," but always "our world"; to be aware in this way of a common field of being is a latent or partial intersubjective awareness.

Is there anywhere a direct intersubjective awareness? Presumably members of a seminar, or any other group engaged in a common undertaking, are not thinking about one another. But, says Hocking, indirect intersubjectivity, implied in such activities, is possible only because there is direct intersubjectivity somewhere: without direct knowledge of "we are" no gesture or speech could ever arise.

Moreover, intersubjectivity between persons points to higher things. For Marcel, thinking-a-world is a response. He rejects the view that sensations are effects and thinks of them as affects, as communicated and not caused. Human existence, dependent as it is on sensation, is a gift, in the receiving of which we are dimly aware of the Giver. Thus, when we respond to the sensibly given by thinking and commit ourselves to intersubjective truth-seeking, we encounter a Thou as our Creator.—*J.F.*

ADDITIONAL RECOMMENDED READING

Chiari, Joseph. "Religious Existentialism," in *Twentieth-Century French Thought: From Bergson to Lévi-Strauss*. London: Elek Books, 1975, pp. 117-133. Read with the chapter on Atheistic Existentialism, this chapter makes clear the importance of Marcel in French existentialism.

Farber, Marvin, ed. *Philosophic Thought in France and the United States*. Buffalo, New York: University of Buffalo Publications in Philosophy, 1950. See sections entitled "An Independent Phenomenologist: Gabriel Marcel" (by Jean Hering, pp. 74-75); "'I' and 'Thou'" (by Hering, pp. 79-82); and "The Christian Existentialism of Gabriel Marcel" (by Jacques Havet, pp.

22-24 and by Henry Douméry, pp. 227-232). See also Index, under "Marcel."

Gerber, Rudolph, S. J. "Marcel's Phenomenology of the Human Body," in *International Philosophical Quarterly*. IV (September, 1964), pp. 443-463. The body as perceived and lived illustrates the difference between a problem and a mystery.

Miceli, Vincent P. "Marcel: The Ascent to Being," in *Thought*. XXXVIII, no. 150 (Autumn, 1963), pp. 395-420. The role of the Christian philosopher as witness to communion.

THE PLACE OF REASON IN ETHICS

Author: Stephen Edelston Toulmin (1922-   )
Type of work: Ethics
First published: 1950

PRINCIPAL IDEAS ADVANCED

Traditional approaches to problems of ethics—the objective, regarding good-ness as a property; the subjective, relating goodness to a person's feelings or attitudes; and the imperative, focusing on the persuasive functions of language—are false and misleading.

A study of the logic of moral reasoning shows that what is central in ethics are good reasons for action.

A good reason is one that refers to the moral code of the community or to a principle that harmonizes interests and minimizes avoidable suffering.

The central problem of ethics, according to Stephen Edelston Toulmin of the University of Leeds, is that of finding a way for distinguishing good moral arguments from weak ones, good reasons from poor ones, and for deciding whether there comes a point in the course of moral argument when the giving of reasons becomes supererogatory. The inquiry he undertakes in *The Place of Reason in Ethics* centers around the question of what makes a particular set of facts that bear on a moral decision a "good reason" for acting in a particular way. The author contends that he has no interest in a circular argument to the effect that a "good reason" is one that supports the kind of act he would regard as a "good act"; his task is to clarify the nature of moral reasoning and the kind of logic that goes into it.

Toulmin's conclusion is that moral reasoning is a kind of inductive reasoning: one examines how various courses of action have worked out and determines to what degree those courses of action have reduced conflicts of interest and to what degree and in what respects certain ways of life lead to satisfaction and fulfillment and minimize or eliminate misery and frustration—and then one appeals to the results of empirical inquiry as providing good reasons for adopting certain principles (or following established ones) and for pursuing certain ways of life.

The discussion of the problem is divided into four major areas of inquiry: "The Traditional Approaches," "Logic and Life," "The Nature of Ethics," and "The Boundaries of Reason." The author begins with a discussion of the traditional approaches to ethics because the tradition has had a considerable influence, and there is the possibility that some traditional theories have something helpful to say about moral reasoning.

The traditional approaches, despite differences in details, fall into three classes, according to Toulmin: the "objective" approach is that of regarding such terms as "good" and "right" as attributing some property to whatever is so designated; the "subjective" approach is to regard such words as reports of feelings; and the "imperative" approach is to claim that value terms are without meaningful content ("pseudo-concepts") but are used as persuasive devices.

The critique of the objective approach begins with a classification of properties (characteristics). Toulmin uses the term "simple qualities" to refer to such properties as redness, blueness, softness, hardness—properties perceived by the senses, characteristics we become aware of through seeing, smelling, hearing, touching, tasting. "Complex qualities," such as that of a polygon's having 259 sides, for example, are recognized only by undertaking a complex procedure of sense observation involving the use of criteria of identification. Finally, "Scientific qualities" are those that cannot be directly perceived through the use of the senses but involve, in addition to sense observation, reference to scientific theory. Since philosophers generally have tended to regard goodness, if it is a property, as either a simple or complex quality, Toulmin confines his attention to those two possibilities.

Terms used to refer to simple properties are taught ostensively, Toulmin argues; one uses the term while giving examples or by pointing to things having the qualities. But, he argues, one certainly cannot teach the use of the term "good" in this way; hence, it is unlikely that goodness is a simple property. When two persons disagree in their descriptions of simple qualities they both clearly indicate, their difference is a linguistic one: they talk about the same simple quality but use different words in doing so. But those who use value terms, when it is clear they are talking about the same thing, do not regard a difference in the application of value terms as merely a linguistic difference. Again, it is unlikely that goodness is a simple quality.

Nor is goodness a complex quality, Toulmin argues. Ethical disagreements cannot be settled by agreeing on procedures of observation and translation rules. Hence, goodness is not a directly perceived quality at all. (And, Toulmin argues, it does not help matters at all to insist that goodness is a "non-natural" quality: such an expression is either meaningless or contradictory—like "non-tauroid bull.")

The objective approach fails because it cannot provide a method for agreeing on the identification of values as properties. Toulmin suggests that the objective view has had a hold on many thinkers because they suppose that "It is red" and "It is good" are alike in attributing properties to things and that when people disagree about values they are disagreeing about properties. But Toulmin accounts for disagreements about values—about the rightness of an act, say—by pointing to differences in the reasons given for doing or not doing the act or differences of opinion as to whether the reasons are good reasons. Accordingly, Toulmin rejects the objective approach as not only unhelpful but also "a positive hindrance" to anyone interested in understanding moral reasoning.

The subjective approach is also unsatisfactory, Toulmin argues. In contending that what is fundamental in moral disagreement, once there is agreement as to the relevant facts, is a difference in feeling or attitude, the subjectivist denies that moral reasoning can finally have criteria of validity other than by appeals to attitudes. It is not enough to know, Toulmin insists, what one's attitudes are toward various matters; one wants to know what they *ought* to be; and of the reasons that are given in support of moral judgments, one wants to know which are *good* reasons (not simply which of the reasons happens to appeal to one at the time).

Toulmin's conclusion is that such terms as "good" and "right" refer neither to objective properties nor to subjective relations; he contends that it is a mistake to ask, "Are values objective or subjective?" as if they had to be one or the other. The key terms of moral reasoning are to be understood by realizing what moral reasoning consists in.

The last and latest of the traditional approaches is the "imperative" approach, the defense of the doctrine that moral judgments are fundamentally ejaculations or commands. The imperative theory, holding as it does that moral judgments are calls for agreement in feeling or attitude, does not allow for reasons; it finds no place for reason in ethics and consequently cannot account for the kind of dialogue that ensues when there are ethical disagreements. Like the objectivists and the subjectivists, the imperativist appears to be led into fallacy by the idea that if ethical judgments are to be true, they must be "about" some feature of the object or subject; hence, those who hold the imperative view argue that since there is no identifiable feature of object or subject with which moral terms are concerned, no moral judgment is true. (The result, writes Toulmin, is a kind of pessimism.)

The bright side of Toulmin's criticism of traditional views is that he recognizes an important emphasis in each of the three kinds of theories rejected: the objectivist theory emphasizes the need in moral argument for good reasons; the subjectivist emphasizes the importance of the feelings of approval and obligation; and the imperative approach calls attention to the rhetorical force of moral judgments.

In Part II, entitled "Logic and Life," Toulmin examines reasoning and its uses, experience and explanation, and reasoning and reality. He argues at the outset of his extensive discussion that the logic of utterances is inseparable from the point of the activity in which the utterances are used. He warns against supposing that there is but one kind of activity called "reasoning"; there are many ways of using language other than the descriptive use, and if close attention is paid to the variety of uses to which language is put (like a set of tools, to use Ludwig Wittgenstein's image, which Toulmin mentions), it becomes credible that the kind of reasoning involved in a purposive activity may involve for its expression a number of various uses of language. (This point is in line with Toulmin's insistence upon looking afresh at ethical reasoning to discover what is happening there—a great deal more than simply describing objects and expressing feelings.)

Toulmin offers an analysis of scientific reasoning to make the point that what serve as "good reasons" in science—namely, "those which are predictively reliable, coherent and convenient"—are bound up with the purposes of science. There is, thus, a relativity of reasons and of the value of reasons to the purpose of the activity in which the reasons play a part. For the same reason, as he argues in "Reasoning and Reality," it is nonsense to ask what is "really real"; scientific "reality" and artistic "reality" are not incompatible: each relates to the distinctive purposive activity that generates talk about the real.

The question of whether ethics is a science is best approached, according to Toulmin, by noticing the difference in function between scientific and moral judgments. Scientific judgments are intended to alter expectations in experience; predictions are made that certain kinds of responses will follow from the activity of sensing various kinds of objects. Moral judgments, on the other hand, are intended to alter feelings and behavior. But it has been a mistake to suppose that science involves the use of reason while ethics (or moral judgment) involves the use of rhetorical techniques and methods of rationalization. Both activities involve reason and the use of reasons; both may involve rhetoric and rationalization. What is important is to discover the difference between the two.

By examining the kinds of reasons given in support of moral claims, Toulmin concludes that two fundamental kinds of reasons (not necessarily distinct) count as "moral" reasons: those reasons that relate an act said to be a duty to the moral code of the community in which the reasons are advanced, and those reasons that relate to the avoidance of the suffering, annoyance, or inconvenience of members of the community.

Accordingly, Toulmin argues that the idea of moral duty is intimately bound up with the practices adopted by a community to make living together possible and agreeable. Reasons relating to the moral code and reasons relating to human welfare come to the same thing: concern about harmonizing the interests and actions of the members of a community. Harmonizing interests requires procedures for settling conflicts of interest, and morality provides such procedures.

In the early stages of the development of a community's ethics, sets of principles are devised to regulate action. But as it becomes evident through experience that some principles are not effective in harmonizing interests while in particular situations moral principles may conflict, a critical stage enters in which attention is paid to the "motives" of actions and the "results" of social practices. The consideration of consequences leads to modification of principles and hence to a more satisfactory moral code—that is, a moral code that is more successful in regulating conduct so as to prevent or minimize the suffering inflicted on persons. (Toulmin's emphasis is not on action intended to increase happiness, as with the utilitarians, but on action intended to settle conflicts of interest and reduce suffering.)

In his exposition of the "Logic of Moral Reasoning," Toulmin first explains that questions concerning whether a contemplated action is or is not right amount to questions about whether the action does or does not conform to a principle embedded in the community's moral code. Giving reasons in support of one's moral decisions, then, amounts to referring to a principle that governs action in such cases. The principle, of course, according to Toulmin, embodies accepted social practice.

Where there are conflicts of duties relative to principles, it may turn out that only by a comparison of estimated consequences can it be decided what would be the right thing to do. Rightness, however, is determined by the consideration of reasons, not by direct reference to consequences. The fundamental question is always whether a way of action is in accord with a principle established by conventional practice or is likely to harmonize interests or prevent suffering.

When the justice of a principle is called into question, it is relevant to consider the utility of the principle in harmonizing interests and preventing avoidable suffering, but it is not proper moral reasoning to decide whether an act in accordance with principle is likely in a given case to have utility; there is already a reason for acting in a certain way, and it is a sufficient moral reason: namely, that the action is required by principle.

It is possible that alternative courses of action might both satisfy the requirements of moral choice, either by both being in accord with the same principle (code) or having probable equally beneficial effects; in such a case, writes Toulmin, moral considerations no longer apply: if a choice is made, it is made on other grounds.

Toulmin argues that there is no need for a general answer to the question, "What makes a reason a good reason or an ethical argument a valid argument?" It is sufficient to consider what would constitute a good reason in a particular case. To be "reasonable" in the making of moral decisions is to decide on the basis of good reasons; that is, reasons that are based on principles derived from social practice. To be reasonable in the appraisal of existing practices is to consider the effects of such practices on those who comprise the community. It would be a mistake in definition, Toulmin argues, to define the term "right" either by reference to principles or to utility; "right" is to be understood by reference to what is reasonable.

In arguing with a person whose self-love has "overpowered his sense of right," Toulmin declares, you find yourself in a logical difficulty: if the sense of right has been overpowered, the appeal to reasons is futile. It does happen sometimes, however, that good reasons will weaken the hold of self-love and in that way restore the sense of right.

Toulmin discusses what he calls "equity in moral reasoning" and maintains that an ethical argument is an instance of moral reasoning only if it is worthy of acceptance by anyone; there must be a corresponding equity of moral principles—that is, the principles serve as general guides for anyone in the kinds of situations governed by the principles.

In Part IV, "The Boundaries of Reason," Toulmin writes about philosophical ethics and then about reason and faith. Some ethical theories are "disguised comparisons," Toulmin argues; the debate between objectivists and subjectivists, although based on the mistake of thinking that the term "good" must refer either to an objective property or to a state of the speaker, nevertheless invites consideration of the degree to which the use of "good" is like (or unlike) property words and like or unlike words expressing feelings. Perhaps some illumination is provided by this kind of philosophical exercise (as exhibited by John Wisdom in his philosophical essays).

But there is no need for ethical theories to be excursions into paradox, Toulmin contends. The study of moral reasoning yields explanatory accounts that are true and helpful; such accounts can correct whatever misconceptions may result from philosophical attempts to answer questions that themselves spring from mistaken assumptions.

Toulmin distinguishes between ethics and religion in this way: ethics provides *reasons* for choosing an action as "right"; religion uses concepts "spiritually"—to inspire us, enkindle our hearts, and give us the will to do the right thing.—*I.P.M.*

PERTINENT LITERATURE

Kerner, George C. *The Revolution in Ethical Theory*. New York: Oxford University Press, 1966.

George C. Kerner, of Michigan State University, describes his objective in this book as that of making intelligible "the radical change that ethical theory has undergone during the course of the present century." He concentrates on the views of four outstanding thinkers in ethics: G. E. Moore, Charles L. Stevenson, Stephen Edelston Toulmin, and R. M. Hare.

These thinkers have in common the tendency to handle problems of ethics by examining the language of morality. Thus, ethical theory has become "the logical analysis of ordinary moral language." Kerner points to Moore's *Principia Ethica* as the beginning of the linguistic emphasis in philosophical ethics, and he explains that by examining the views of Moore, Stevenson, Toulmin, and Hare one can get a good idea of the issues and methods that revolutionized ethical theory in the twentieth century.

The idea that more than any other epitomizes the radical change in ethics, according to Kerner, is the proposition clearly advanced and defended by

Stevenson: namely, that there are two kinds of meaning involved in moral judgment, *descriptive* meaning (a matter of belief) and *evaluative* (or emotive) meaning (a matter of attitude). Kerner maintains that it is misleading to regard moral language as having a kind of meaning all its own. What distinguishes moral language from other kinds of language is the distinctive "performative" use to which language is put. What is needed, then, he maintains, is a more useful and subtle philosophy of language, along the lines suggested by J. L. Austin in his philosophical investigations into speech acts. But it is not to be expected that ethical work in the new spirit will produce some grand and durable system, Kerner warns; what is to be hoped is that philosophers will continue to do what they tend now more and more to be doing: examining moral language in its varied uses to clarify the meanings and functions of moral utterances.

In his discussion of Toulmin's views, Kerner first of all emphasizes Toulmin's effort to develop an account of moral validity by concentrating not on the meanings of terms of moral discourse but on the kinds of reasons that are acceptable as "good" reasons. In opposition to Moore, who believed that moral intuition depends on the existence of moral qualities, and also in opposition to Stevenson, who regarded moral arguments as neither valid nor invalid but as expressions of fundamental emotive attitudes, Toulmin nevertheless took something from each of these revolutionary philosophers. He agreed with Moore that moral arguments can be valid and that moral judgments can be true, and he agreed with Stevenson that moral judgments have persuasive force and that there are no distinctive moral properties.

Toulmin's procedure, as Kerner describes it, was to abandon the attempt to define certain key terms (such as "good" and "right") and instead to turn analytic attention to moral reasoning and to the kinds of reasons involved in such reasoning. Kerner then refers to Toulmin's claim that one kind of good reason for claiming an action to be morally right is that the action conforms to a prevailing moral code, and that another kind of good reason is that the action would tend to harmonize interests. But this account of "good reasons" could be accepted by Stevenson, Kerner argues; Toulmin's task remains that of showing that the connection between a moral judgment and the reasons given in support of it is a *logical* connection.

Toulmin's account of moral reasons is not entirely clear, Kerner claims; not only is it not clear how many fundamental kinds of "good" reasons there are, but also it is not clear how the principles of a moral code relate to principles or standards by which such principles are called into question and appraised. In effect, Kerner argues, Toulmin regards both truth and validity as based not on facts that can be described but on good reasons; but he fails to make clear how the good reasons determine truth and validity.

Toulmin's difficulty, Kerner contends, stems from his failing to distinguish "performative uses" of moral language (to assert, command, encourage, condemn, and so forth) from "causal uses" (such as to persuade, gratify, horrify, and, in particular, according to Toulmin's emphasis, to *harmonize*).

Accordingly, Toulmin's thesis that the function of moral language is to reduce conflicts of interest (to "harmonize" interests) misrepresents the performative function of value terms (that of approving, endorsing, entitling, and so forth) with Toulmin's own tendency to approve of the harmonization of interests. Thus, according to Kerner, Toulmin's thesis is not a logical thesis at all but, in effect, a moral recommendation: that the harmonization of interests be made a fundamental moral standard.

Rawls, John. Review of Stephen Edelston Toulmin's *An Examination of the Place of Reason in Ethics*, in *The Philosophical Review*. LX, no. 4 (October, 1951), pp. 572-580.

It is always instructive and sometimes exciting to find out what one distinguished philosopher of ethics has to say about the major work of another outstanding thinker in the same field. As the author of *A Theory of Justice* (1971) John Rawls has come to the forefront of ethical debate with his view of justice as fairness. Writing in 1951 as a reviewer of Stephen Edelston Toulmin's book, Rawls not only offers a number of telling criticims of Toulmin's ethical theory but also comments generally and provocatively about the task of ethics itself.

Rawls begins by taking note of Toulmin's reasons for rejecting what Toulmin calls the "traditional" theories: that the traditional theories fail to explain what a "good reason" is in moral judgment and, consequently, fail to give an account of valid moral reasoning. Although Rawls believes that Toulmin is misinformed about traditional theories, he concedes that Toulmin is correct in rejecting the subjectivist notion that good reasons are simply those reasons one is psychologically disposed to accept.

Rawls also agrees with Toulmin's contention that it is useless to seek for the criteria of good reasons in general; one has to ask what are good deductive reasons, inductive reasons, and moral reasons. Again, Rawls agrees that to find the criteria of good reasons one has to examine instances of the kind of reasoning under examination. But he points out that one has to have some criteria for selection of the instances to be examined. Finally, as to agreements, Rawls agrees that reasoning is finite, that there comes a point at which it no longer makes sense to ask for a further reason.

Rawls then begins systematically to find fault with the details of Toulmin's account of moral reasoning. But first Rawls agrees that there are a variety of types of moral reasoning: reasoning about rightness in a specific case where there is an accepted social rule; reasoning about rightness where there is a conflict of rules; reasoning where there is no rule; reasoning about the validity of social practices, disputing the justice of a principle (here, no doubt, Rawls was incited to ponder about justice, if he was not already doing so); and reasoning about the comparative worth of different ways of life. The procedure endorsed by Toulmin, as reported by Rawls, appears to be that of referring to principles when principles (relating to the general welfare) are available and referring to relative risks and consequences when principles are not available or when they conflict.

As to the faults found by Rawls: First of all, Rawls denies that there are generally accepted, well-known moral codes to which appeal can be made. (He regards rules such as that promises must be kept, or that one must drive on one side of the road rather than on the other, as hardly proving the case: the first rule is a favorite of moral philosophers, while the second is a legal, not a moral rule.)

Rawls's second objection is that Toulmin limits the range of good reasons by requiring that they be either relative to socially recognized rules or that they be defensible by reference to consequences relating to the social welfare. Rawls cites examples of moral reasoning which involve reference to particular circumstances that modify instances, and he concludes that "a reason is any consideration which competent persons in their reflective moments feel bound to give some weight to. . . ." Rawls contends that it is possible and reasonable to go against a rule in a particular case and to defend doing so sometimes by reference to another general rule, while he suspects that Toulmin regards exceptions as calling into question the general rules to which the exceptions are exceptions.

The next point of criticism made by Rawls is that the appeal to accepted rules varies in force according to circumstances, while Toulmin appears to think that the appeal to rules always has the same force. Rawls then finds fault with Toulmin's "appeal to consequences." Rawls calls attention to the general acceptance of utilitarian rules as important in moral reasoning and to the fact that even utilitarians regard the basic rule as in need of modifications. He objects to Toulmin's ignoring the whole problem of modifying utilitarianism.

Finally, Rawls finds fault with Toulmin's idea of traditional ethics. He contends that Toulmin is mistaken in supposing that traditional ethics can be appreciated by taking G. E. Moore, A. J. Ayer, and Charles L. Stevenson as prime examples. He concludes by remarking that if Toulmin's remarks about "traditional moral philosophy" are an "expository device," the remarks could be dispensed with.—*I.P.M.*

ADDITIONAL RECOMMENDED READING

Baier, Kurt. *The Moral Point of View: A Rational Basis of Ethics.* Ithaca, New York: Cornell University Press, 1958. Baier acknowledges Toulmin's help and encouragement; Baier's views are a distinctive development of the ethics of good reasons.

Frankena, William K. *Perspectives on Morality*. Edited by K. E. Goodpaster. Notre Dame, Indiana: University of Notre Dame Press, 1976. Frankena's philosophical explorations include searching examinations of the ethics of reasons, with references to Baier and Toulmin.

Sacksteder, William. Review of Stephen Edelston Toulmin's *The Place of Reason in Ethics*, in *Ethics*. LXII, no. 3 (April, 1952), pp. 217-219. Sacksteder, of the University of Chicago, takes Toulmin to task for his use of limiting questions and for permitting his covert faith to be influential in the development of his ideas.

Toulmin, Stephen Edelston. *The Uses of Argument*. Cambridge: Cambridge University Press, 1958. Toulmin's essays about logic call into questions many prevailing assumptions about deduction and throw some light on the perplexing problem of the logic of ethics.

THE REBEL

Author: Albert Camus (1913-1960)
Type of work: Ethics
First published: 1951

Principal Ideas Advanced

When a person who is slave to the absurd conditions about him declares that there is a limit to what he will endure or approve, he becomes a man, he exists.

In creating value through rebellion, the rebel creates values for all men and makes himself part of the community of men.

Those who attempt to rebel by becoming nihilists or utopians fail to achieve authentic rebellion.

The genuine rebel combines the negative attitude of one who recognizes the relativity of values with the positive attitude of one who makes an absolute commitment which gives rise to spiritual values.

From Robespierre to Stalin, lovers of justice and equality have fallen time and again into contradiction and ended by outraging the humanity they were committed to save. *The Rebel* seeks to understand the failure of a century and a half of revolution and, by returning to its source in the spirit of revolt, to recover the ideal which has eluded the ideologues.

Camus' book is, in one respect, a history of the whole anti-God, anti-authoritarian movement in literature, philosophy, and government. This is clearly indicated in the subtitle, *An Essay on Man in Revolt*. The historical study is divided into three parts. The first, entitled "Metaphysical Rebellion," examines a gallery of "immoralist" authors beginning with the Marquis de Sade and ending with André Breton. A longer section, called "Historical Rebellion," traces the fortunes of political nihilism both in its individualist and its collectivist forms. A third part, "Rebellion and Art," briefly indicates the manner in which the same analysis may be carried over into the fine arts, particularly the history of the novel. Thus, the body of this considerable work is a series of essays in literary and historical criticism.

But the introductory and concluding essays are of a different sort. In them Camus conducts a phenomenological investigation into the data of Revolt, analogous to Max Scheler's study of Resentment and his own earlier analysis of the Absurd. These essays, which are the most original part of the book, provide the norm by which the failures of nihilism are judged, and point the direction of a more humane and creative endeavor.

The essay *The Myth of Sisyphus* (1942) was addressed to the problem of nihilism which engrossed the minds of intellectuals at the close of World War I. In it we are offered Camus' variant of existentialism, according to which the person who has been confronted with the meaninglessness of existence gives his own life a modicum of dignity and significance by holding the posture of revolt. An honest man, says Camus, acts according to his belief. If he affirms that the world is meaningless, he is bound to commit suicide, for to go on living is to cheat. According to Camus in this youthful work, the only honest reason for a man's putting up with the irrationality of things is to be able to feel superior to the forces that crush him—like Pascal's Thinking Reed. To the man of the Absurd, the world becomes as indifferent as he is to the world. He bears his burden without joy and without hope, like Sisyphus, who was condemned to roll his rock up the hill anew each day; but he preserves a titanic fury, refusing any of the palliatives offered by religion or philosophy or by the distractions of pleasure or ambition.

When *The Rebel* was written, ten years later, the fashionable nihilism of the period between the wars was no longer relevant. The fall of France led to the taking of sides by many intellectuals, including Camus. The problem of suicide gave way to that of collaboration. People who had cultivated indifference suddenly found that they could not overlook the difference between Pierre Laval and Charles de Gaulle.

The new concern is plainly evident in Camus' novel *The Plague* (1947), where it is abundantly clear that those who are strong ought to bear the burdens of the weak. In this pest-hole of a world, no man can stir without the risk of bringing death to someone. But although we are all contaminated, we have the choice of joining forces with the plague or of putting up a fight against it. The immediate objective is to save as many as possible from death. But beyond this, and, in Camus' eyes even more important, is the task of saving men from loneliness. It is better to be in the plague with others than to be isolated on the outside.

In *The Rebel*, Camus tries to show that solidarity is logically implied even in the absurdist position; for to perceive that life is absurd there must be consciousness, and for there to be consciousness there must be life. But the moment human life becomes a value, it becomes a value for all men. In this way, absurdism may be extended to prohibit murder as well as suicide. But it offers no creative solution to an age of wholesale exportation, enslavement, and execution. We must turn, instead, to a different kind of revolt—that which on occasion is born in the heart of a slave who suddenly says, "No; there is a limit. So much will I consent to, but no more." At this moment a line is drawn between what it is to be a thing and what it is to be a man. Human nature is delineated, and a new value comes into being. To be sure, the universe ignores it, and the forces of history deny it. But it rises, none the less, to challenge these; and in so doing so creates a new force, brotherhood. Out of rebellion Camus wrenches a positive principle of politics as Descartes had found certitude in the midst of doubt. "I rebel," says Camus, "therefore *we* exist."

Although the first stirrings of rebellion are full of promise, the path they mark out is straight and narrow, and few there be that follow it to the end. Like the moral virtues in Aristotle's *Ethics*, it is a mean between two extremes. The rebel, if he thinks out the implications of the impulse which moves within him, knows that he must never kill or oppress or deceive his fellow man. But in the actual world such a policy makes him accessory to the crimes of others. Therefore, he must on occasion perform acts of violence in the interest of suffering humanity. The difficulties of taking arms against oppression without becoming an oppressor are so great that it is small wonder most would-be rebels slip into one false position or another.

In *The Myth of Sisyphus*, Camus went to great lengths showing the inauthentic responses to the Absurd made by the existentialists Søoren Kierkegaard, Franz Kafka, and Jean-Paul Sartre, who, according to Camus, rejected literal suicide, but substituted a kind of "philosophical suicide" by making believe that it is possible to escape Absurdity. Just so, in *The Rebel*, Camus' chief line of argument is to show that the great heroes in the literature of revolt and in the history of revolution, almost without exception, fall away from authentic rebellion. For some, the dominant impulse is to negate the forces that frustrate man's development: with them rebellion passes into hatred, and they can think of nothing but destruction. For others, the impulse is to enforce order and realize a standard good: love of their fellow man gives place to an abstract goal which they must achieve at any cost. The former are nihilists, the latter utopians.

Camus' discussion in "Rebellion in Art" provides a clear instance of the two kinds of false rebellion. All art, in his opinion, is essentially a revolt against reality. Art both needs the world and denies it. But contemporary art has allowed itself to be sidetracked. Formalism gravitates too exclusively toward negation, banishing reality and ending in delirium. Realism, however (he specifies the "tough" American variety), by reducing man to elemental and external reactions, is too eager to impose its own order on the world. Both arise, in a sense, out of the spirit of revolt, protesting the hypocrisy of bourgeois conventionality; both fail, as art, inasmuch as they lose touch with the springs of revolt. Proust is Camus' example of a genuine artist: rejecting those aspects of reality which are of no interest to man while lovingly affirming the happier parts, he re-creates the universe by redistributing its elements after the heart's desire. This suggests that the creative way is not that of "all or nothing" but that of moderation and limit. The order and unity which make for genuine art do minimal violence to the matter they undertake to re-form. And the artist remains, above all, a friend of man.

Camus' classification of rebels into world-deniers and world-affirmers provides only a rough basis for division when he comes to consider the great figures in the history of revolt. The difficulty is that the contradictions into which their extremism leads renders them at last almost indistinguishable. Nevertheless there is merit in retaining the groupings. Under "Metaphysical

Rebellion," Sade's advocacy of universal crime and Alfred de Vigny's Satanism exemplify rebellion which took the way of negation. With them we may place Rimbaud, who made a virtue of renouncing his genius, and the surrealist Breton, who talked of the beauty of shooting at random into a street crowd. On the other side are the partisans of affirmation—Max Stirner with his absolute egotism, and Nietzsche with his deification of fate. When we turn to "Historical Rebellion," there are the anarchists and nihilists such as Michael Bakunin and Dmitri Pisarev, for whom destruction was an end in itself. But they are more than balanced by the revolutionaries, whose ambition in overthrowing the present order was but a means toward fulfilling the destiny of a race or of mankind—Robespierre and St. Just, Mussolini and Hitler, Marx and Lenin.

The section on Metaphysical Revolt deals with those whose revolt was centered in the realm of imagination. Camus finds their archetype not in Prometheus but in Cain; because rebellion presupposes a doctrine of creation and a personal deity who is held to be responsible for the human condition. Their temper is rather that of blasphemy than of unbelief; and when they go so far as to deny that there is a God, their protest, lacking an object, turns into madness. Here Ivan Karamazov is more instructive than real-life rebels. Indignation causes him to reject God on the grounds that a world that entails suffering ought never to have been permitted. But he discovers that, having rejected God, there is no longer any limit—"everything is permitted." And Ivan acquiesces in the murder of his father—before going mad. Ivan rejects *grace* and has nothing to put in its place. This is the tragedy of nihilism.

Historical Revolt was directed less immediately against God than against the absolutism of divine right kings and the prerogatives of feudal lords and bishops. But it has its metaphysical dimension. In rejecting the old order, the revolutionaries too were rejecting grace, without, however, falling into nihilism; for instead of concluding that all things are permitted, they immediately divinized *justice*. They repudiated Christ, but retained the apparatus of an infallible institution within which alone salvation is possible. And in place of the madness of Ivan Karamazov, they find themselves swallowed up in Chigalov's despair. Their conclusion is a direct contradiction of their original premises: starting from unlimited freedom they arrive at unlimited despotism.

In Camus' opinion, just as the nineteenth century revolted against *grace*, the twentieth must revolt against *justice*. The kingdom of men which the revolutionaries sought to substitute for the kingdom of God has retreated into the distance and the goal has been brought not a step nearer. The fault is in the nature of revolution itself, which, as the word indicates, describes a full cycle. In rebellion, the slave rises against his master; in revolution, he aspires to take his master's place. Thus, the champions of justice have merely substituted a new domination for the old. And in many ways the new is less tolerable than that which it replaced. For the rule of God at least allowed man to preserve the human image; but when the sacred disappeared, man's dignity disappeared with it. Ivan Karamazov said that "everything is permitted"; Chigalov, the human-engineer, calculated that nine-tenths of the human race must be reduced to herd animals. This is what takes place when God is overthrown. It is a principle of all revolutions, says Camus, that human nature is infinitely malleable; in other words, that there is no special human nature. Under the kingdom of grace there was; and the rebel insists that there still is. This is the limit that he opposes to Caesarism. Rebellion rediscovers man, affirms that he is not a mere thing, insists that a distinctive nature sets him off from all other beings and, at the same time, unites him with every other man. From this point of view, the only alternative to grace is *rebellion*.

No doubt enough has been said about the defections into which rebels are prone to fall. Like many a preacher, Camus finds it easier to criticize the failures of others than to present a clear-cut statement of what authentic rebellion entails. We have, of course, his stories and dramas to fill out the picture. But so far as the present essay is concerned, the only vivid illustration of genuine revolt is found in his account of a group of Russian terrorists (the most exemplary were brought to trial in 1905) who combined nihilism with definite religious principles. Camus calls them "fastidious nihilists." "In the universe of total negation, these young disciples try with bombs and revolvers and also with the courage with which they walk to the gallows, to escape from contradiction and to create the values they lack." They did not hesitate to destroy; but by their death they believed they were re-creating a community founded on love and justice, thus resuming the mission the church had betrayed. They combined respect for human life in general with the resolution to sacrifice their own lives. Death was sought as payment for the crimes that the nihilists knew they must commit.

Transposed into a more moderate key, what Camus seems to be advocating is a life of tension in which contradictions may live and thrive. There must be a way between that of the Yogi and that of the Commissar, between absolute freedom and absolute justice. In this world, man has to be content with relative goods; but he does not have to give them anything less than his absolute commitment. This is humanism, though hardly of the Anglo-Saxon utilitarian variety. The values born of the spirit of rebellion are essentially spiritual. The rebel wills to serve justice without committing injustice in the process, to use plain language and avoid falsehood, to advance toward unity without denying the origins of community in the free spirit.

Politically, Albert Camus takes his stand with syndicalist and libertarian thought: as opposed to the revolutionists who would order society from the top down, he favors a society built out of local autonomous cells. Far from being romantic, he holds that a communal system is more realistic than the totalitarian, based as it is on concrete relations such as occupation and the village. Nor is it new. From the time of the Greeks, the struggle has been going on (especially around the Mediterranean) between city and empire, deliberate freedom and rational tyranny, altruistic individualism and the manipulation of the masses. It is the endless opposition of moderation to excess in man's attempt to know and apply the measure of his stature, his refusal to be either beast or god.—*J.F.*

PERTINENT LITERATURE

Brée, Germaine. *Camus*. New Brunswick, New Jersey: Rutgers University Press, 1959.

At the age of forty-four, Albert Camus received the 1957 Nobel Prize for literature. Germaine Brée believes that Camus' international reputation rests primarily on novels such as *The Stranger* (1942), *The Plague* (1947), and *The Fall* (1956), but she also includes *The Rebel* (*L'Homme révolté*) in her distinguished list. Like Camus' fictional works, however, this essay in moral and political thought has attracted far less attention from professional philosophers than the work of his famous French contemporary and rival, Jean-Paul Sartre.

Although Camus will continue to be counted among the existentialists, he actually disclaimed connection with them. Brée finds that Camus' study of Edmund Husserl, Martin Heidegger, and Karl Jaspers did not run very deep. The thought of Friedrich Nietzsche and Søren Kierkegaard was better known to him, but Brée surmises that neither attracted him strongly. In fact, she suggests, Camus had relatively little interest in philosophical scholarship.

Brée notes that the appearance of *The Rebel* provoked a major controversy in France. Concerned with what she calls "the monomaniacs of revolt," Camus' book was in part a critique of the French political left, arguing that Marxist ideology could destroy freedom and result in Stalinist terror. At this time, Sartre and some of his followers were striving to combine existentialism and Marxism. Stung by Camus, they attacked him as a sentimental idealist. The ensuing debate, rancorous at times, left the friendship of Sartre and Camus in ruins. Brée stresses that the issues at stake in *The Rebel* transcended the personal disputes that split French intellectuals in the 1950's, but she does defend Camus and underscores how characteristic it was for him to root his literary concerns in the soil of his particular time and place.

The Rebel is a reflection provoked by politically inspired mass murder in the twentieth century. According to Brée, Camus argues convincingly for the book's central thesis: When revolution in the name of human freedom becomes an unlimited demand for liberty, the result is tyranny; likewise, when revolution against social injustice turns into an unbounded claim for justice, the outcome is terrorism against individual existence.

Grasping for absolutes, Camus thought, leads to madness. To avoid that tragic waste, there must be moderation. In making these claims, Brée points out, Camus was neither preaching accommodation nor rejecting his own inheritance from the left. He did, however, question some of the latter's Marxist axioms. Camus, for example, doubted that history is predetermined to move toward one particular form of human liberation, and thus he denied that all actions are justifiable so long as they lead to the emergence of a socialist state. Camus' criticism of Marxist ideology, Brée asserts, unmasked the fallacy of sacrificing the present happiness of individuals, for whom justice was supposedly being sought, in order to pursue ends that were nebulous and problematic.

Such criticism, Brée admits, was not original with Camus. She asserts, however, that the "eminently sane" conclusion to *The Rebel* takes a more distinctive position. Dealing with broad moral considerations more than with specific political policies, it delineates Camus' democratic idea of rebellion as moderation. Freedom and justice ought to be preserved and extended, but modern men and women must recognize how life imposes limits that cannot be violated with impunity. Quite rightly, Brée implies, Camus affirms the need for law to define basic human rights and for governments to honor them as inalienable. Only by doing so will there begin to be assurance that people can enjoy "the daily measure of happiness which, in Camus's eyes, is man's greatest treasure."

Wilhoite, Fred H., Jr. *Beyond Nihilism: Albert Camus's Contribution to Political Thought*. Baton Rouge: Louisiana State University Press, 1968.

If Albert Camus has never taken center stage in academic philosophy, Fred H. Wilhoite, Jr., acknowledges that his is not often mentioned by political theorists either. Yet Wilhoite agrees with Germaine Brée in holding that political concerns were never far from Camus' attention. This book, therefore, explores whether ,Camus had an explicit political philosophy. The answer, Wilhoite states, must be negative if one is looking for a systematic view that discusses all the major questions that normally occupy political theory. On the other hand, he thinks Camus' sensitive reflections do contribute significantly to recent social thought.

Wilhoite says that two themes are especially important in his study of Camus. First, there is Camus' "existential method." Here the author is not pointing primarily to a set of substantive conclusions, but rather to the fact that Camus tried hard to avoid vague abstractions. Wilhoite finds Camus "existential" because he worked from his own experience, not from *a priori* truths, and because the characters in his stories, novels, and plays give his ethical inquiry a realistic texture. The second theme, more directly applicable to *The Rebel*, is Camus' struggle to develop a normative response to contemporary nihilism, which Wilhoite describes as an outlook that finds existence bereft of intrinsic meaning and, in particular, devoid of intellectually authoritative moral standards.

The Rebel, Wilhoite claims, contains the core of Camus' existential ethic. Moving from Camus' observation that rebellion says "No!" to exploitation and thereby says "Yes!" to limits that must not be overstepped, Wilhoite holds that Camus' rebel uncovers a shared common good that transcends one's individual fate. True, rebellion may be motivated by egoistic concerns; but the rebel's willingness to die in resisting oppression implies a commitment to rights for all. Thus, the form of rebellion advocated by Camus does not seek to conquer or to destroy its opposition. Mutual respect for life is its goal instead.

Camus was impressed by the fact that men and women, at least sometimes, simply recognize wrongdoing and act to stop it. This insight, Wilhoite insists, is especially important because Camus also recognized that apparently timeless moral truths have repeatedly been negated by twentieth century history, which seems to permit anything. According to Wilhoite, Camus discovered that even in a wasteland of moral skepticism and metaphysical absurdity, rebellion assumes and reveals that human existence itself still contains a firm foundation for establishing differences between right and wrong and thus for building human solidarity.

Although Camus never wrote a systematic treatise on the subject, Wilhoite holds that his entire literary output consists of observation and comment on human nature. *The Rebel* in particular affirms universal human qualities, thus helping to explain Camus' rejection of "existentialism," which he tended to equate with the Sartrean formula that where human life is concerned existence precedes essence. On the other hand, Wilhoite also thinks that Camus' own existential leanings account for his reluctance to describe human nature as though it could be encompassed by the abstract categories of traditional philosophy. Camus chose instead to illuminate humanity's shared predicament in striving after meaning and justice. The most vital result of that effort, Wilhoite concludes, shows that even without the "certainty of divine guidance or of consensus on a metaphysical system, we need not float adrift on a sea of nihilism."

Masters, Brian. *Camus: A Study.* Totowa, New Jersey: Rowman and Littlefield, 1974.

On January 5, 1960, while traveling to Paris in a fast car driven by Michel Gallimard, Albert Camus died instantly when the vehicle crashed into a tree. He was only forty-six, and thus Brian Masters reminds us that *The Rebel* was the work of a relatively young man. Praising Camus' writing as a "hymn to life," Masters notes that Camus was joyful and not one to be downcast. He reports, too, how Camus once stated that if he were to write a book on ethics it would consist of a hundred pages. Ninety-nine would be blank, but the last one would say, "I know of only one duty, and that is to love."

The Rebel, it seems to Masters, may not stand up to rigorous philosophical scrutiny because it is less a careful study of moral and political theory than it is an autobiography. Masters views the work as Camus' attempt to solve an intolerable paradox posed by history: that people are more good than bad and yet they do more evil acts than good ones. Camus believed that this tragedy emerged from the human propensity to go to the extremes of absolutism or nihilism. He thought that his description of authentic rebellion might be the needed corrective, but as far as the political climate of Camus' own day was concerned, Masters observed that Camus was overly optimistic. The book provoked stormy attacks not only from the left but also from the political right.

Masters calls Camus a "stern moralist" who struggled to renew humane values that are under threat. Especially significant in this battle is Camus' argument that even when one starts with the Absurd, with the conviction that all transcendental values have fled from a world that is ridiculous and senseless, and unshakable conviction remains. This conviction holds that existence lacks justice, an undeniable realization that is precious to Camus because it implies that men and women do possess a common basis for understanding what justice is. The Absurd, suggests Masters, is thus seen by Camus as an affront to an inherent moral sensitivity that points toward what Camus cautiously designates as a shared human nature.

Recognition of human solidarity, however, does not solve the practical problems that remain. For example, Masters argues, Camus' rebel cannot condone injustice; but in combatting wrong, further injustices may be committed. Masters finds that Camus "is not a successful theoretician" when it comes to handling satisfactorily all the difficulties that an authentic rebel must confront in pursuing a path of moderation, a middle way between the extremes of all or nothing that absolutism or nihilism involve. He does find, however, that Camus himself was consistently guided by the rebel's aim of seeking greater *degrees* of justice, freedom, and happiness—not everything or nothing at all. Thus, Masters concludes, he also chose means for action that were faithful to his beliefs, exhibiting a determined honesty that "opposed force from whatever quarter it came and exposed intolerance under whatever name it was cloaked."

In common with other interpreters, Masters affirms that Camus did not regard himself as the leader of a school of thought or even as a philosopher. The author thinks Camus was motivated to write *The Rebel* and all of his other books mainly because he wanted no one to live deceived or oppressed. This "transparent sincerity," Masters maintains, gives Camus' writings their special distinction.—*J.K.R.*

ADDITIONAL RECOMMENDED READING
Barnes, Hazel E. *The Literature of Possibility: A Study in Humanistic Exis-*

tentialism. Lincoln: University of Nebraska Press, 1959. Although she finds that Camus' allusions to human nature present many problems, Barnes acknowledges that *The Rebel* stakes out a dynamic middle ground where one must live with the recognition that violence may at times be morally necessary even though it can never be fully legitimate.

Copleston, Frederick. *A History of Philosophy*. Vol. IX. Garden City, New York: Image Books, 1977. *The Rebel*, says Copleston, is not intended to be a political blueprint but rather a moral reflection that explores the tensions between the spirit of moderation and the passion of revolt.

Cruickshank, John. *Albert Camus and the Literature of Revolt*. New York: Oxford University Press, 1960. Although *The Rebel* reveals Camus' ethical sensitivity and nobility of mind, Cruickshank finds the book unsatisfactory because of its "lyrical flights" at the end.

Doubrovsky, Serge. "The Ethics of Albert Camus," in *Camus: A Collection of Critical Essays*. Edited by Germaine Brée. Englewood Cliffs, New Jersey: Prentice-Hall, 1962, pp. 71-84. Doubrovsky holds that Camus' writings, including *The Rebel*, speak most clearly about what persons ought *not* to do. Thus, they form an ethical prolegomenon rather than a fully developed moral theory.

Hanna, Thomas. *The Lyrical Existentialists*. New York: Atheneum, 1962. Asserting that Camus' thought is best summed up as a "philosophy of revolt," Hanna sees *The Rebel* as an extraordinary reflection on the tragic aspects and redemptive possibilities within modern European history.

Meagher, Robert E., ed. *Albert Camus: The Essential Writings*. New York: Harper Colophon Books, 1979. Meagher's commentary in this anthology interprets *The Rebel* as itself an act of rebellion, one that reveals Camus' own protests and the affirmations implicit in them.

Murchland, Bernard C. "Albert Camus: The Dark Night Before the Coming of Grace?," in *Camus: A Collection of Critical Essays*. Edited by Germaine Brée. Englewood Cliffs, New Jersey: Prentice-Hall, 1962, pp. 59-64. Citing *The Plague* and *The Rebel* as perhaps Camus' best works, Murchland underscores Camus' use of rebellion to protest against absurdity.

Olafson, Frederick A. "Albert Camus," in *The Encyclopedia of Philosophy*. New York: Macmillan Publishing Company, 1967. Olafson stresses that the taking of human life is inconsistent with Camus' true rebellion, but he thinks that Camus failed to sufficiently clarify how his rejection of violence is to be interpreted.

Thorson, Thomas Landon. "Albert Camus and the Rights of Man," in *Ethics*. LXXIV, no. 4 (July, 1964), pp. 281-291. This article finds Camus' insights about political philosophy especially pertinent for the second half of the twentieth century.

Woelfel, James W. *Camus: A Theological Perspective*. Nashville: Abingdon Press, 1975. Calling *The Rebel* Camus' "definitive philosophical essay,"

Woelfel sees Camus setting himself in opposition to Sartre by postulating a universal human nature.

NATURE, MIND, AND DEATH

Author: Curt John Ducasse (1881-1969)
Type of work: Philosophy of philosophy, metaphysics, epistemology
First published: 1951

PRINCIPAL IDEAS ADVANCED

Philosophy can proceed scientifically from data statements in which terms crucial to philosophical problems are used to theorize concerning the meanings of such terms; the terms central to the philosophic enterprise are value-terms.

Causation is understandable in terms of a single change (the cause) prior to another event (the effect) in a specific environment.

Sensations are not objects of acts of sensing, but kinds of sensing, ways of responding sensibly.

Mind is a substance capable of receiving impressions, causing bodily action, and causing events in consciousness.

Although life after death cannot be proved, it is possible: what could survive is not personality, but individuality.

Nature, Mind, and Death is a comprehensive summary of the author's views concerning causality, nature, matter, mind, and the possibility of life after death. Its importance lies in the fact that its conclusions are presented not simply as metaphysical statements, but as illustrations of a general method which is applicable to all philosophical problems. The book consequently falls both in the area of metaphysics and in the area of epistemology, or theory of knowledge. It restates the author's view on philosophical method, which was earlier described in *Philosophy as a Science* (1941), and elaborates his views on causation, perception, and symbols, previously published in monographs and periodical articles.

The first section of this work is devoted to a discussion of the method of philosophy, with an illustration of its application to the problem of the nature of reality. Ducasse believes, contrary to the tenets of certain modern philosophers, that metaphysics is, or can be, a legitimate and profitable study. The reason for its being held in disrepute is that its problems, in general, have been so badly stated that it has been unable to avoid looseness of inference, ambiguity of terms, confusion of issues, and inadequate testing of its hypotheses. The tacit assumption has apparently been that one can attain satisfactory knowledge in this area by using the vague terms of ordinary language, and without bothering to introduce the technical apparatus of logic and the scientific method. The two maxims of a scientific philosophy are that the data with which it deals should be stated clearly and explicity and that the problem whose solution is being sought should be defined as sharply and unambiguously as possible.

More explicitly, the philosophical method is substantially the same as the scientific method. It consists of data which are disclosed through observation and experimentation, formulations of these data in language appropriate to the problem, empirical generalization, analysis and confirmation of hypotheses, and practical application of the knowledge thus obtained. There are, in fact, two kinds of problems in science: problems "for" science, and problems "of" science. The former are the practical or technological problems; these have to do with means and ends, provided the ends are not the purely theoretical ends identified with mere knowledge. The latter are theoretical or epistemic problems, which characterize science as an explanation or understanding of nature. Problems of this kind are themselves of two sorts: those which concern, on the one hand, what is observable, what is primitive, and what must be taken as initial or empirical basis; and, on the other hand, the abstract theories which are derived from the primitive data and constitute their explanations and interpretations.

Ducasse believes that philosophy differs from science, not in method, but in the special character of its practical and theoretical problems and in the nature of its primitive data and its derived hypotheses. Practical philosophy always concerns itself with problems of *values*; it is therefore much interested in means and ends, as is science, but it goes beyond science in raising questions concerning the values of the means and the values of the ends, and whether acts *ought* or *ought not* to be performed in certain circumstances where value judgments are involved. Theoretically, philosophy centers its attention on procuring the knowledge which will permit us to make reliable judgments of value having the forms, "This syllogism is (or is not) valid," "This act is (or is not) moral," "This consideration is (or is not) important." These are the primitive, initial, and basic facts of philosophy. Theoretical philosophy then goes on to explain these data. Here its character is sharply distinguished from that of science, for its problems now become semantical; its task is to discover the meaning or meanings of terms. The data from which it starts are actual statements in which value-terms are used, and its problem is to formulate a linguistic hypothesis which will attempt to answer the question: "What does the value-term as employed in these statements mean?" The test of such a hypothesis lies in observing whether the proposed definition is actually substitutable in these assertions without altering any of their standard implications. If it is, then its validity is proportionate to the number of the original statements or to their representative character as samples of a large group; if it is not, it has to be rejected or revised. This procedure constitutes empirical confirmation, for the meanings are empirically discoverable. Furthermore, Ducasse's theory does not in any way reduce philosophy to a mere study of language, for statements *in* language can also be statements *of* extralinguistic facts; this is no more paradoxical than saying that a mathematical problem which is solvable by purely formal techniques may also be a problem about nature.

As an illustration of his philosophical method, Ducasse examines the problem of explaining what may be meant by an individual who utters a number of true judgments containing the word "real." That that *is* a value-predicate is not explicitly stated by Ducasse, though in the earlier book referred to above he makes this point quite clear: to be *real* is to be *interesting*, and "interesting" *is* a value-predicate. The problem of discovering the possible meanings of the word "real" is an *ontological problem*, and the solution may be termed as an *ontological hypothesis*. Four hypotheses, each proposing a meaning for the word "real," are examined: (1) "real" as opposed to "apparent": a dog is not really ferocious though apparently so; (2) "real" as opposed to "nonexistent": black swans are real but green swans are not: (3) "real" in the sense of physical existence as opposed to mathematical or psychological existence: black swans are real but numbers are not, or ideas are not; (4) "real" in the sense of what is relevant to our purposes or interests as opposed to what is not: a table is really a cloud of minute particles at relatively vast distances from one another, not a hard and solid object. Solving the philosophical problem consists in substituting each of these meanings of the word "real" in the statements initially uttered by the individual to see whether their implications would be altered. Any meaning which does not permit this substitution must be eliminated as a disconfirmed hypothesis; any meaning, if any, which permits the substitution is to that degree confirmed and constitutes a solution of the ontological problem.

In Part II of his book Ducasse turns to an application of his method to the clarification of some of the fundamental categories of philosophy. One of these is *causation*. The procedure to be used in examining this concept should not be that adopted by Russell when he collects a number of philosophical definitions of "cause" and tries to determine which is right; these are philosophical hypotheses, not data, and one cannot decide whether they are good or bad unless he has something on which to base his decision. The data must be a series of statements made by a certain individual (we should probably try to eliminate at the outset an individual who employs odd usages, or who is crude or careless in his speech, or who is a deliberate innovator) when he asserts, say, that the New England hurricane of 1938 caused the death of a number of persons and that its tidal wave caused a number of yachts to become lodged on the top of a bridge.

Ducasse finds that the meaning of "causation" which will best explain these statements, and similar ones, is a complex one, but one which can be rendered precise through careful formulation of its properties. Distinction must be made between "cause of" and "condition of," the first being synonymous with "sufficient to" and the second with "necessary to." We are permitted to speak of a cause *necessarily* producing its effect, but we must not confuse the necessity holding between natural events with the necessity holding between the premises and conclusion of a valid argument. Causes are never substances or forces, but always events or happenings. Causation is a relation in which only two changes occur, the earlier one being the cause, and the later one the effect; but it is a triadic rather than a dyadic relation, because there must also be present an environment in which the changes take place. Also, although causation is a relation between concrete, individual events, it may be generalized into a relation between *kinds* of events and may then be formulated as a causal law. Causal relations are empirically observable, but since the cause must be detected in every case as the *only* change in a certain neighborhood, and since to do so requires us to be sure that *no other* change is present, we can easily make mistakes and believe that we find causal relations when they are not really present.

The solution to the problem of whether the will is free is dependent upon the results of Ducasse's previous analysis of causation, which showed that while causal laws are *possible* in the case of repeated causal connections, the universality of causation does not of itself entail that there *are* such causal laws, or that every event which occurred was theoretically predictable. Since a cause is a cause only within a given state of affairs, it will produce its effect when it recurs only if this given state of affairs also recurs. Determinism, therefore, if it means universal predictability, cannot be proved to apply to our world. Freedom of the will exists in the sense that man can do, within limits, what he wills; this may be called "freedom of efficacy." Freedom *to will*, as distinguished from freedom *to act as one wills*, is a special case of freedom of efficacy; in some cases man can will what he wants to, and in some cases he cannot. A volition is determined by the circumstances which a man believes himself to be facing at a certain time and by the consequences which he judges that volition to have. Without this determination moral acts would be irrational and erratic, and rewards and punishments would be senseless. Freedom of choice consists in awareness of alternative possible courses of action, the choice being determined by one's preference. There is no such thing as acting against one's will, for all such cases involve choosing among alternatives, all of which are repugnant, and what one does is merely to choose the *least* unpleasant. Furthermore, although one's choice in a given situation depends on his volitional nature, which is itself dependent on his heredity, upbringing, and social environment and seems therefore to be external to him, yet his volitional nature is still his own. This conclusion is established by the fact that his volitional nature is not fixed forever, but can be changed as a result of self-observation and self-appraisal. Finally, the predictability of a person's future acts is not in any way incompatible with the freedom which we believe him to possess.

Part III deals with nature, matter, mind, and the problem of perception. The naturalistic theory of mind argues that mind is not a special, psychical entity, which is the antithesis of everything that is material. On the contrary, it is simply the name for the way in which the biological organism behaves when it is adapting itself to its environment, or adapting its environment to itself, in a cognitive manner. Such a theory describes mind as a part of nature, if we mean by this term whatever is perceptually public and whatever is existentially implicit therein. The most extreme form of naturalism involves a radical behaviorism which denies the existence of mental events observable only by introspection.

This form of radical behaviorism Ducasse rejects, on the grounds that the meaning which it gives to the word "mind" is quite different from that given to it by the ordinary man. Thus, the behavioristic conception of mind is to be rejected because it clashes with the preexisting, commonly accepted use of the term "mind." It does not represent a *fact* which naturalism has discovered, but only a deep-seated *resolution* to make the term applicable to something in the perceptually public world. Introspective knowledge, indicated by statements such as "I am conscious of such-and-such" must be interpreted by the behaviorist as a special kind of behavior response. But we do not ordinarily *mean* a behavior response when we are aware of our own consciousness, and there is no reason whatsoever why this awareness should always be *expressed* in this kind of statement.

The solution which Ducasse offers to the problem of perception seems to depart from, rather than to be in accord with, ordinary usage. But he permits the philosopher, in cases "where ordinary language hesitates," to "purge it of defects." He begins by making a linguistic distinction between two kinds of accusatives, illustrated by "I jumped an obstacle" and "I jumped a jump." He calls the former an "alien accusative" and the latter a "connate accusative." Then he proceeds to subdivide each of these accusatives into special kinds: coordinate and subordinate. For example, a jump is coordinate with jumping, but a leap is subordinate to it; and an obstacle is coordinate with jumping, but a fence is subordinate to it. We then have four cases:

(1) coordinately alien accusative: jump an obstacle;
(2) subordinately alien accusative: jump a fence;
(3) coordinately connate accusative: jump a jump;
(4) subordinately connate accusative: jump a leap.

Now it is obvious that the accusatives in cases (1) and (2) may both exist independently of the processes, in that both obstacles and fences may exist without being jumped. But in cases (3) and (4) the accusatives cannot be independent, for a jump could not exist without the jumping, and a leap, since it is a special case of jumping, could not exist without the jumping. Now let us translate the problem into one of *perception*, and examine the distinction between "I see blue" and "I see lapis lazuli." Ducasse refers to G. E. Moore's argument that these are both cases of alien accusatives, that in both instances I am aware of a content, through *different* contents, of consciousness or experience. Ducasse disagrees with Moore. He insists that the lapis lazuli is an alien accusative because its nature is such that whenever I turn my eyes upon it in daylight it causes me to experience something called "blue." However, the blue is not an alien but a connate accusative. When I see blue I do not see a blue content; I see "bluely." Furthermore, when I see blue I am seeing a subordinate accusative, not a coordinate one; seeing blue is a special *kind* of seeing, not seeing a special *kind of content*. We are now ready for the final conclusion. Since in the case of connate accusatives the object cannot exist independently of the awareness, the blue which I see cannot exist independently of my awareness of it; to assert that it could exist independently would be as absurd as to say that leaping could exist without jumping.

The view of mind which Ducasse develops on the basis of these and similar considerations is that mind is a *substance*. This view is arrived at inductively from what introspection reveals, and it discloses that mind, like other substances, exhibits itself by its properties and capacities. The minimal properties which a mind would have to exhibit are three: the capacity for *impressions* of a certain kind, caused by physical stimulation of sense organs, by telepathy, by clairvoyance, or otherwise; the capacity for *causation of external effects* in the body or in the outside world *by means of impulses*; and the capacity for *causation of psychical events by other pyschical events*, as in the case of causing an impulse by an impression.

If mind is this sort of thing it must have a certain kind of relation to the body, and the nature of this relation will determine the possibility of life after death. This is the topic of Part IV of the book.

What are the characteristics in terms of which I identify my body as my own, rather than that of someone else? Ducasse lists four. (1) It is the only physical object in which certain bodily changes can be caused or inhibited by my mind: *my* blushing can be caused only by *my* feeling of shame. (2) It is the only physical object in which certain changes can cause changes in my mind: sticking a pin in *my* finger causes *me* to feel pain. (3) It is the only physical object in which mutilations of brain or sensory nerves causes alterations in my conscious mind: cutting *my* optical nerve causes *me* to lose my capacity for vision. (4) It is the only physical object in which structural connections among brain neurons can be brought about by my willing to acquire certain habits and skills: *my* brain pattern can be changed by *my* decision to learn a certain foreign language and *my* developing the skills which are required.

Ducasse thus concludes that there must be direct causal interactions between two different substances, mind and body. There is no more mystery about this causal interdependence than there is about physicophysical causation. Since minds and bodies are substances, and causal actions have been shown above to hold between certain kinds of events which are changes in substances, there is no reason for denying causal interaction between mind and body; the fact of interaction does not depend on the *kinds* of events interacting, but only on the *form* of the interrelation.

Life after death cannot, according to Ducasse, be either proved or disproved. The fact that some people believe in it and some do not can be explained by many factors: human credulity (the readiness to believe without having investigated); such human bias as the unfounded conviction that only the material can be real; the existence of certain phenomena—the so-called "Psi" phenomena, including clairvoyance, precognition, retrocognition, and telepathy—which, supposing them to be genuine, have not yet been explained and *could*, therefore, constitute evidence for survival; the variations in the beliefs as to *what* survives death, in case anything survives; and the admitted existence of fraud and trickery on the part of certain people who had previously claimed to demonstrate immortality.

It is only the *possibility* of life after death that Ducasse proves. This he does by showing that the arguments against survival contain certain loopholes. To show, for example, that mind and body interact, and therefore that many psychical events are caused by physical events, does not establish the impossibility of psychical events which are not thus caused; hence, a disembodied mind *may* exist. And to show that mind cannot exist without body because mind is *defined* in terms of behavioral responses is to prove nothing, but only to attempt to make our language legislate over nature and thus prescribe what can and what cannot exist. On the positive side, Ducasse argues that certain forms of survival are perfectly consistent with what he has shown mind to be, with what he has shown the mind-body relation to be, and with all empirical facts, whether normal or paranormal, now known. Furthermore, these forms, in addition to being possible, are *significant* enough to us now to be of interest.

The form of survival which Ducasse considers to be both possible and significant is the following: What survives in not man's *personality* (his habits, skills, and memories) but his *individuality* (his native aptitudes, instincts, and proclivities). This could be the distillation from a number of different personalities. For some time after death the personality could persist in a dreamlike consciousness, and during this interval, through recollection of the acts and events of the preceding life, new dispositions and deep changes in attitude could be generated much as they are in life when experiencing a deep tragedy produces a change in values. Finally, our desire that the injustices of life should be redressed in the afterlife would be satisfied not only because a man's individuality shapes his personality but also because his personality shapes his individualilty; therefore justice is immanent in the entire process.
—*A.C.B.*

PERTINENT LITERATURE

Demos, Raphael. "Nature, Mind and Death," in *The Review of Metaphysics*. VI, no. 4 (1953), pp. 563-582.

Raphael Demos begins his critical study of C. J. Ducasse's *Nature, Mind, and Death* by noting that it divides into four parts. The first deals with philosophy and philosophical method, the second with some of the basic concepts of philosophy (such as causality, freedom, substance), the third with how the mental and the physical are to be understood and with the relationship between sensing and our knowledge of a physical, external world, and the fourth with the relation between mind and body and the issue of survival after death.

Demos does not find these topics to be tightly related, and while he grants that Ducasse thinks that the parts of the book fit into a single structure of argument and perspective, basic to which is an attempt to clarify the relationship between mind and body, he finds the links of the book to be more closely related to the interests of the author than to any intrinsic connections between the topics themselves.

Demos characterizes Ducasse's position in terms of an "attitude" which he (admittedly inadequately) characterizes as "a combination of empirical analysis and common sense." But what is being analyzed, Demos says, is not mere words, but ideas or concepts. (Presumably, insofar as the overall program is successful, one is also offered an account of what these ideas or concepts are ideas or concepts of.) Thus Ducasse espouses such "commonsense categories" as *substance* and *property*, and he objects to behaviorism on the ground that "observation" includes the meaning of "introspection" as part of its meaning.

Putting them ultimately as questions to the author (to which Ducasse responded in the *Review of Metaphysics*, VII, 1953-1954, pp. 290-298), Demos raises various objections to Ducasse's line of reasoning, including objections concerning the meaning of "reality," the analysis of causation, the issue of freedom, the doctrine of substance, and the question of survival.

Ducasse maintains, Demos reports, that "what we call real is wholly relative to our purposes" and that "to be real is to be relevant to the purposes or interests which rule at the time." To this, Demos, in effect, raises three objections. This doctrine is false, because there are many things which are real at any given time which are not relevant to whatever purposes or interests currently rule. It is false, furthermore, because, however relevant to our interests or purposes they might be, unicorns and headless horsemen are not real. To be real is to exist, independent of relevance to interests or purposes.

Regarding causality, Demos offers this criticism. Demos reports that Ducasse holds that (1) causality is a relation between similar events; (2) causality is a relation of (etiological) necessity; and (3) we can observe causal connections. Suppose C and E are singular events, and in a given situation S, one observes that the only change in S immediately prior to E's occurrence is C's occurrence. One observes, that is, S at a certain time, t (which contains neither C nor E). Then (according to Ducasse) one can say that C is E's cause. But, Demos continues, according to Ducasse, if C causes E in situation S, then, given *C*, *E* was *inevitable* in *S*. But while one observes *S* and *E*, Demos contends, one does not observe *E's inevitability, given C*. So either (2), or else (3) is mistaken, if (1) is true.

Demos also has deep reservations regarding Ducasse's views on freedom and responsibility, which he reports as including the following: (1) to be *free* (with respect to an action) is to be self-caused or self-determined (regarding that action); (2) any self-determined action (choices counting as actions) is determined in such a manner that the agent could not have done otherwise under the then-prevailing conditions; and (3) reward and punishment (including praise and blame) are appropriate with regard to self-caused actions and are relevant only to future effects of the reward or punishment.

To these claims by Ducasse, Demos replies as follows. If I am appropriately rewarded or punished for doing A, then, under the then-prevailing conditions, I both could have refrained from doing A and could have done A, so that it was genuinely up to me whether I did A or not. Under the conditions Ducasse lays down for being self-caused, I am not able to act other than as I do, so I am not free after all, and hence I am not responsible. This, Demos in effect suggests, is why Ducasse must deny the view that anyone *deserves* punishment (or reward) for what he has done, independent of consideration of future effects; this important element of *desert* is left out of Ducasse's view, which is hence at best partially correct.

Concerning the topic of substance, Demos indicates that Ducasse's views include the claim that items have dispositional properties, or capacities, such as combustibility or solubility (or memory, for that matter). Then Ducasse, correctly according to Demos, claims that events do not have dispositional properties or capacities. For that, you must have enduring items which have properties and are not themselves properties and which endure through time—that is, substances. But then Ducasse, Demos reports, goes on to say that substances are merely sets of properties. If so, Demos argues, there was no need to introduce substances at all; events and properties are enough to account for what there is in the world. If, though, as Ducasse holds and Demos agrees, they are not enough, then substances are not simply sets of dispositional properties, but are what *have* such properties (and other sorts of properties as well).

Concerning the topic of evidence concerning survival of death, Demos notes that Ducasse "pays careful and respectful attention to the mediums" but dismisses the mystic. He ignores the religions of mankind but listens carefully to the occult. Why? Demos finds two reasons in Ducasse, such as they are. One is a tendency to explain religious belief and experience psychologically—Ducasse suggests that belief in a Supreme Being is "born . . . of a remembered comfort of the young child's relationship to the father." But, Demos points out, one can offer this sort of psychological explanation for a scientist's belief in order as "born of remembered respect for a beloved policeman from one's childhood." Independent of an assessment of the reasonableness of the belief itself, such "explanation" is worthless, and Demos goes so far as to use the term "prejudice"; he also notes that, given the remarks, earlier treated, on "reality," Ducasse is peculiarly ill-placed to offer such "explanations." The other reason Demos finds Ducasse offering for not referring to religious evidence is that mystical (and other religious) experiences are private rather than public, "not shareable" by others than the ones who have them. But, Demos says, to the degree that this is so of religious experiences, it is also true of occult. Hence, neither of Ducasse's reasons, Demos argues, is sound.

Pap, Arthur. "A Note on Causation and the Meaning of 'Event,'" in *The Journal of Philosophy*. LIV (February 28, 1957), pp. 155-159.

Arthur Pap begins by noting that critics of the regularity theory of causation—of the theory that to say that an event A is the cause of another event B is to say that A belongs to a class K1 and B belongs to a class K2 and that the members of K1 are in a one-to-one correspondence with the members of K2—usually themselves follow a certain pattern. They point out that two events can be regularly conjoined without being causally connected, as will be the case with two clocks which are nearly synchronized and run at the same rate (their being only *nearly* synchronized will allow one clock to "say" *one o'clock* just before the other does, accommodating the clock example to those cases where the cause occurs prior to, rather than simultaneous with, the effect). But, he continues, they do not go on to offer some improvement on, or replacement of, the regularity theory, and some even hold causation to be a category which is unanalyzable.

Pap finds C. J. Ducasse's *Nature, Mind, and Death*—a book that Pap says contains "a veritable mine of thorough, sober analyses of fundamental concepts"—an exception to the usual pattern, but he thinks that the analysis Ducasse offers is "completely untenable." Pap defends this contention, in part, by criticizing the argument by which Ducasse defends his analysis of causation. Ducasse proffers this account: to say that an event C·causes another, later, event E in a situation S is to say that C is the only change in S which immediately preceded C. Ducasse, Pap indicates, reports an experiment he ran at various times with his students. He would place a paper parcel on the desk at the front of his classroom. Then he would put his hand on the parcel, at which point the end of the parcel nearest the students would begin to glow. Upon asking his students what caused it to glow, Ducasse would receive the answer that the glowing was caused by his touching the parcel. The procedure, then, illustrates, if it does not confirm, Ducasse's analysis of causation.

Pap contends that Ducasse's procedure and argument, contrary to Ducasse's intent, confirms rather than disconfirms the regularity account of causation which Ducasse is criticizing. Pap's reasoning goes as follows. The observation of a solitary change preceding an effect may require a tacit argument which eliminates alternatives. The structure of Ducasse's argument, Pap suggests, is this. Suppose that (1) at time t_1, A does not have Q; (2) at time t_3 A does have Q; and (3) the only property A has at t_2 which it did not have at t_1 is P. Then, according to Ducasse's analysis, we should conclude that: (4) the cause of A's having Q at t_3 is A's having had P at t_2. But then, Pap argues, this presumably will be the case only if it is the case that A has P at t_2, acquired Q at t_3 and, for any time t and any item X, if X has P at t then X will acquire Q at time t^*, where t^* is related to t as t_3 is related to t_2. (No doubt some conditions would have to be placed on A and the items whose names replace "X," but Pap ignores this for the sake of simplicity.) Thus, Pap suggests, it is the case that: (5) were there some property R such that A has R at some time between t_2 and t_3, but not at t_2, then it is A's having R at (say) $t_{2.5}$ that, on Ducasse's analysis, is the cause of A's having Q. Suppose, then, that one believes in universal causation (roughly, that every event has a cause, and like causes have like effects) and accepts the facts about A, Q, and P recorded in (1)-(3). Then one can claim that there is no property R that A has and which meets the conditions specified in (5), and hence that (4) is true—that is, that A's having Q at t_3 is indeed caused by A's having P at t_2. So, Pap contends, the example Ducasse offers as a fair example of causation is one quite in accord with the regularity analysis Ducasse wishes to replace.

Another way in which all this raises a problem for Ducasse, Pap suggests, is this: Ducasse, in criticizing the regularity account of causality, supposes that if the regularity theory is correct, then the only way to discover causal connections is induction by enumeration—by arguing that since $A1$ at t is followed by $E1$ at t_1, and $A2$ at t_4 is followed by $E2$ at t_5, and so on, then probably every E is preceded (and presumably caused) by an A. This suggests that, according to a regularity view, one cannot discover causal connections from a single case. Pap contends, however, that one can accept the regularity thesis and proceed to discover causal connections by eliminating alternative hypotheses in such a manner as to discover causal connections from a single case.

Further, Pap argues, whatever the force of Ducasse's argument, his analysis of causation is mistaken. Suppose that an event C is preceded by two events A and B which are quite independent of each other. Then, Pap claims, given Ducasse's analysis, it is logically impossible to suppose that C is caused at all, for the cause of C (in Ducasse's analysis) is *the* event in C's situation which has changed. Ducasse, Pap notes, considers this sort of objection, offering the example of a situation in which a well-thrown stone strikes a window at the same time at which air waves caused by the singing of a bird reach it. The window breaks, and the cause we know to have been the stone, not the song or the air waves. To fit this fact into his account, Pap reports, Ducasse distinguishes between concrete events and kinds of events. Ducasse says he intends the term "cause" to stand for a relation between concrete events which are identifiable only in terms of their temporal and spatial locations. The breaking of a window pane at t_2 is not a concrete event, but part of one (call it E) which also consists in the arrival of the air waves at the pane at the same time as the stone. Further, Pap continues, the position of the stone at t_1, just prior to the pane's breaking, is also part of another concrete event (call it C) which, in part, consists in the air waves almost having reached the window. If there is no time gap between them, (all of) C is the cause of (all of) E. Thus, Pap says, in Ducasse's view the approach of the air waves is part of the cause of the pane's breaking. But then, Pap contends, since the only way, according to Ducasse, to specify concrete events is by way of temporal and spatial location, the answer to "What caused E, which happened at place P at time t_2?" will be "What happened at P at t_1." This will make causal propositions nearly vacuous. Now Ducasse had claimed, Pap notes, that he was offering us an analysis of causality which accorded with common sense and (what Pap calls) an "ordinary and significant" use of the terms "cause" and "effect." But, Pap continues, in any "ordinary and significant" sense of these terms, they apply to definite kinds of events; the denial that they do so arose only when Ducasse endeavored to answer the objection noted above. Pap in effect concludes that the answer to the objection saves Ducasse's view from falsehood only by removing it from any genuine contact with the ordinary concept of causality.

(Ducasse wrote a reply to Pap's criticism, which appeared in *The Journal of Philosophy*, LIV, 1957, pp. 422-426.)—*K.E.Y.*

ADDITIONAL RECOMMENDED READING

Badham, Paul. *Christian Beliefs About Life After Death*. London: Macmillan and Company, 1976. A contemporary treatment, with historical background, of the topic the title specifies.

Brand, Myles, ed. *The Nature of Causation*. Urbana: University of Illinois Press, 1976. An anthology of many views regarding causation, including that of Ducasse.

Ducasse, C. J. *A Critical Examination of the Belief in a Life After Death*. Springfield, Illinois: C. C. Thomas, 1961. A discussion of the topic the title indicates, heavily influenced by psychical research.

——————. *A Philosophical Scrutiny of Religion*. New York: The Ronald Press, 1953. An introductory-level treatment of various topics in the philosophy of religion.

Lewis, H. D. *Persons and Life After Death*. London: Macmillan and Company, 1978. A discussion of life after death which is not so heavily influenced by psychical research.

Mackie, J. L. *The Cement of the Universe: A Study of Causation*. London: Oxford University Press, 1974. A contemporary discussion of causation which includes a discussion of Ducasse.

SYSTEMATIC THEOLOGY
(Volume One)

Author: Paul Tillich (1886-1965)
Type of work: Theology
First published: 1951

PRINCIPAL IDEAS ADVANCED

Man was created to be oriented by an ultimate concern; such a concern may be either for God or for some finite object.

Philosophy is the cognitive approach to reality in which reality is the object; theology is concerned with the meaning of being for men.

The sources of systematic theology are the Bible, tradition, and the history of religion and culture; these sources are perceived through the medium of experience.

Revelational answers are taken by the theologian from the source, through the medium, and under the norm (the New Being in Jesus as the Christ).

Revelation transcends the subject-object distinction; usually in a moment of "ontic shock," the abrupt confrontation with the power of being, one's finiteness is overcome by anticipation: this is salvation.

Religious symbols need not be true; it is enough that they be existentially effective, that they evoke awareness of the power of being.

There is little doubt that two of the greatest Protestant theologians are Paul Tillich and Karl Barth. These stand far above all others in originality and creativeness of thought; yet they stand near opposite ends of the theological spectrum. At one time or another they have both been classified as "neo-orthodox," presumably because both generally concur in their pessimistic doctrines on man. Yet their fundamental contrasts make such a designation meaningless. Theologically, Barth belongs solidly in the orthodox tradition of Luther and Calvin, and with Kant philosophically; Tillich, on the other hand, stands clearly in the liberal theological tradition of Schleiermacher and Otto, and philosophically in the train of such Idealists as Schelling and Hegel. The fittingness of the designation "neo" in both cases rests on the influence of Kierkegaard and the existentialists as well as the biblical critics upon them.

Barth's greatness rests fundamentally on his ability to resurrect the orthodox dogma of Christendom in all its Reformation centrality in the aftermath of an epoch of liberalism that had largely undermined biblical authority, the unique miracles of the Incarnation and Resurrection, the metaphysical significance of the Atonement, the necessity of special revelation, the legitimacy of original sin as a descriptive category, the indispensability of the "new birth," and the utter uniqueness of Christianity. Thus, Barth stated a radical rejection of all compromise with culture. In his opinion, Protestant theology since Schleiermacher has been what he called "Kultur-protestismus," or what H. Richard Niebuhr calls the "Christ of Culture" position; that is, instead of Christendom standing against culture, against the faith of secularism, it has become its product. Cultural concern has become cultural capitulation, for since the days of Kant Protestant theologians have seen their task as being one of defending the faith on culture's own terms; it was inevitable that culture should become Christianity's criterion of truth. Such is the irony of the impotent Christianity of the present.

Barth's solution is to have no dealings with culture; theology is strictly *Church* theology, or as he prefers to call it, Church dogmatics. He who would know the Truth must enter the community of the faithful, must participate in the action and liturgy that only believers understand. Here the Holy Spirit enters the human soul with the power to overwhelm and cure. If the faith be "proven," "defended," or "argued," the spirit relied upon is finite, and the word spoken is not the Word of God but the word of man.

It is here that the tremendous gulf between Barth and Tillich is most visible. Tillich is, above all, a theologian to, for, and of culture; in fact, the new enterprise called "theology of culture" is largely of his making. Tillich has been from the beginning an activist in politics, social work, art, and culture in general. It was his work with the Christian Socialists in Germany and his outspoken attitude toward the rising totalitarianism which drove Tillich from his homeland to permanent residency in the United States. Since then he has been actively writing in almost every area of the social sciences, defending Christianity in the categories of and from the problems of culture. In his well-known work entitled *The Religious Situation* (1929), Tillich early clarified his task—his concern is not with the religion of the churches but with the faith contained in and being witnessed to by every culture in every aspect of its work and product. Tillich's insistence is not upon any special revelation in Christianity, but upon the Christian faith, rightly reinterpreted, as the clue to the universal revelation of the eternal God-man relation, universally available and universally perceived.

Tillich's lifetime of thought and activity is presently being crystallized in a celebrated three-volume *Systematic Theology*. Volume One is by far the most important, for in it Tillich lays out his system as a whole, defines his basic categories, and develops his fundamental theological method. Characteristic of Germans, but especially characteristic of Tillich, is the tendency to create new terminology with abandon. This makes his work particularly difficult to understand. For the reader not well versed in philosophical theology, it is suggested that he begin his reading of Tillich with *The Courage to Be* (1952), *The Religious Situation* (1929), or *The Dynamics of Faith* (1957). Although Volume One of *Systematic Theology* is by far his most important work, *The Dynamics of Faith* is the most lucid presentation of his basic approach which is available to the general reader; in its own right, it is a classic of clarity and simplicity, traits usually uncommon to Tillich.

Tillich's system is contained in his unique theological method, the "method of correlation." Theology must exist in the tension of revelational truths and the questions implied in man's concrete situation. This "situation" to which theology must respond is "the totality of man's creative self-interpretation in a special period." Underlying Tillich's thinking here is the Augustinian conception of community. For St. Augustine, man was created to be oriented by a supreme "love," or what Tillich calls an "ultimate concern." This concern is either for "God" or for some finite object, being, idea, or goal made "god." Communities are formed on the basis of their ultimate loyalty to some common object of love. For Tillich, every epoch, generation, people, and nation is so characterized, drawing from this ultimate concern its vitality, values, and destiny.

Consequently, this ultimate concern permeates all of a culture's products, giving them their unique "style"; this is most true of art. The theologian must analyze these works, ascertaining through this style the "faith" of each cultural situation. Thereby the questions haunting a particular situation are seen expressed in the categories which that situation can understand; only by finding these can the theologian make revelation relevant and intelligible. As Tillich says, the only proper theology is "answering theology."

For Tillich, every attempt to understand human existence must begin with "an a priori of experience and valuation." That is, every such attempt is a circle, beginning and ending with a "mystical a priori," an immediate intuition of something ultimate in value and being that transcends the distinction between subject and object. This intuitive foundation is the common basis which Tillich sees between the realms of question and answer and which makes the correlating dialogue possible. This basis applies to the Christian theologian, but his circle is smaller, for he is committed to the Christian message as the criterion of all other circles.

The distinction between philosophy and theology appears here. Philosophy is *"that cognitive approach to reality in which reality as such is the object,"* that is, the structure which makes reality a whole. *The* philosophical question concerns the "general structures" which make experience possible. The Kantian influence here is obvious. Theology, having as its object that which concerns man ultimately, raises the same question as philosophy, but in a manner of involvement, not detachment. While philosophy is interested in the *structure* of being, theology is concerned with the *meaning* of being *for us*. Although these two may be distinguished, the philosopher of necessity operates from an ultimate concern, and the theologian must assume the structure of being. Yet they cannot contradict each other, for "no philosophy which is obedient to the universal *logos* can contradict the concrete *logos*, the Logos 'who became flesh.'"

The sources of systematic theology are threefold. The Bible is the basic source, interpreted not infallibly but as human response to historical events. The second source is tradition. The third is the history of religion and culture, for herein are the means of expression, their confirmation, and the formulations of the existential questions. These sources are perceived through the medium of "experience." In this regard, Tillich sees Christianity as divided between the Augustinian-Franciscan tradition and that of Aquinas and Duns Scotus. For the former there was an immediate awareness of being-itself, a mystic intuition underlying all human operations; the latter tradition, however, replaced such mystical immediacy with "analytical detachment," not experiencing the divine but inferring it from sense-data regarded as prior and more certain.

The Augustinian-Franciscan approach, on which Tillich insists, he sees classically formulated by Friedrich Schleiermacher, who defined religion as the "feeling of absolute dependence." This experience, having its religious roots in pietism and its philosophical roots in Spinoza and Schelling, Tillich sees as being "rather near" to his experience of "ultimate concern." The sources become revelatory only when in them one experiences the power of being as one's ultimate concern.

Over against the sources and medium Tillich places a "norm" by which these are formulated. This norm must be the basic existential question of an age. In the early Greek Church it was the question of finitude, death, and error; in the Reformation this question concerned a merciful God and the forgiveness of sins. In our age, Tillich insists, it is the question of "a reality in which the self-estrangement of our existence is overcome, a reality of reconciliation and reunion, of creativity, meaning and hope." Such a reality Tillich calls "the New Being." For the Christian, while the critical principle is that of ultimate concern, the norm is the New Being in Jesus as the Christ. The former judges all religion as to "form," the latter judges it as to "content."

Systematic theology is essentially a rational discipline, but rational in two special senses. For Tillich there are two types of reason—"ontological" and "technical." The former is reason as the capacity to participate in immediacy, for transcending the subject-object bifurcation—this is the experience which is revelation, whereby the whole man is grasped by an ultimate concern. Hereby the "content" of faith is received. "Technical" or formal reason is man's capacity for logical procedure; hereby the content of faith is systematized into theological concepts. This relation of form and content is always dialectical; thus theology is always changing, for since its method is that of "correlation," its formulations change with the situation. The revelational answers are taken by the theologian *from* the source, *through* the medium, *under* the norm. The content is revealed; the form is dependent on the structure of the questions.

For Tillich, such a method "escapes" one of the basic religious quarrels. By considering only the *existential* validity of religious symbols, he "tran-

scends" the inadequacies of supernaturalism, naturalism, and dualism or natural theology. As we shall see more clearly, Tillich rejects any supernatural
realm and any theistic "object"; his concern is only with the existential nature
of finite reality.

Having established his theological method and the ontological presuppositions implied by this method, Tillich develops his three-volume theology
logically. The work is composed of five parts, each of which analyzes one
portion of finite existence and provides an exposition on the basis of sources,
medium, and norm. These parts are: "Reason and Revelation," "Being and
God," "Existence and Christ," "Life and the Spirit," and "History and the
Kingdom of God." Volume One consists of an introduction and the first two
parts.

In Part One, "Reason and Revelation," Tillich attempts to analyze reason
in terms of the two types indicated. He insists that our age has made technical
reason supreme, reducing reason to reasoning, concerned only with means
to ends. The classical idea of ontological reason as the source of structures,
values, and meanings, has been totally dismissed, and the "ends" are provided
by nonrational forces. Religion has become the instrument of technical reason.
In such a situation, the task of Christian theology, for Tillich, is to exhibit
"the essence of ontological reason" as identical with "the content of revelation," thereby indicating the difference between ontological reason in its
perfection and its predicament in the different stages of its actualization. It
must show that such perfection rests in its unity with being-itself, and that its
weakness is a result of the conditions of existence. Reason thereby raises the
question of revelation.

Tillich defines ontological reason as "the structure of the mind which enables it to grasp and to shape reality." Such reason has its receptive side
(constituted by a cognitive and aesthetic polarity) and its reactive side (constituted by an organizational and organic polarity). The affinity between the
objective structure of reality and the structure of the mind points to something
in both which transcends both; this Tillich calls "being-itself," that "power"
which manifests itself inexhaustibly in everything. Each realm points to this
in its own way, whether as Truth-Itself, Beauty-Itself, and the like.

This "depth of reason" which apprehends the depth in all things can be
expressed only in terms of myth and symbol; but the fact that these contradict
reason witnesses to reason as "fallen" in its existential condition. Herein
reason raises the question of revelation. This Tillich sees exhibited in Kant's
near-perfect description of finite reason. Finite reason cannot grasp being-
itself, for the mind's categories are finite. But Kant's doctrine of the categorical
imperative points to the depth of practical reason, just as his doctrine of the
teleological principle in art and nature points to the depth of "ontological
reason." Thus, since the component elements (polarities) of reason operate
in relative isolation and conflict, they raise the question of revelation, "the

reintegration of reason."

Further, knowing is a form of union between knower and known. Yet finite knowledge is characterized by detachment, separation, the chasm between subject and object. Likewise, knowledge is desired in order to heal, to reunite; yet in finite knowing the alienation remains even more strongly. Thus, what is asked for is a type of "knowing" which transcends such conditions. And last, knowledge which is certain is not ultimately significant, while that which is ultimately significant cannot be given certainty. This dilemma likewise gives rise to the desperate search for revelation in which ultimate significance and certainty are present.

Revelation is the answer for this existential dilemma of reason, for it transcends the subject-object distinction in immediacy. It is the ecstatic, mystic, intuitive experience of the "ground of being" as that which is our ultimate concern. It is usually derived through an "ontic shock," through being driven to the boundary of human capacity where one is still sustained in a "nevertheless" by the power of being beyond him. This is revelation, and it is "salvation," for one's finiteness is "overcome in anticipation."

Reason is grasped from beyond itself, yet the beyond is the mystery in reason's own depth. In it the person is grasped as a whole, and the polarities of reason are sustained in a unitary function. This is revelation, for the mind is made one with itself. The "objective" event or "source" with which such experience is correlated is a "miracle," but not miracle in the sense of supernatural interference. For Tillich, "miracle" is a special constellation of elements whereby they become a "medium" of the ground of being, becoming "transparent" by pointing beyond themselves to the power of being which sustains them. They are miracles only for those who receive them as such, who enter into a subject-subject relation of immediacy.

Because, for Tillich, revelation is the correlation between mind and the ground of being, and since all things exist through their participation in this ground, all things may become media of this power; that is, all things may be seen as transparent, as revelational. This is the meaning of sacraments: that bread, stone, a book or person, may become the instrument of the revelational correlation. And yet a distinction may be made between original and dependent revelation. Men may come into a revelational relation with a constellation seen as miracle by other men in the past; the same power is experienced, but the medium ("source") is derived. In this sense Jesus is revelatory; unlike orthodox Christians, Tillich understands Jesus himself as not the revelation, but as the *medium* of revelation for any who accept him *as the Christ*. In this fashion Tillich attempts to escape (his word is "transcend") the problem of biblical historicity. As he says in other works, if it could be shown with probability that the historical man Jesus never lived, it would not change Christianity. The basis of Christian revelation is not Jesus Christ, but Jesus *as* the Christ. For all those moved by the power of being *through* the biblical "portrait" of Jesus as the Christ, this "revelation" is valid; that is, the power of being is existentially efficacious. So with all "knowledge" of the divine—all designations are "symbolic" in the sense that their "truth" is their capacity to evoke awareness of the power of being. Since they provide no "knowledge" of the divine, their "truth" comes into being and dies. Symbols are born of the collective unconscious of believers and are valid only as long as they retain this connotative capacity.

For Tillich, the uniqueness of the Christian revelation rests in the insistence on Jesus as the *final* revelation, "final" meaning the criterion of all other revelational correlations. The criteria of finality are these: awareness of uninterrupted unity with the ground of being and constant negation of self to this ground. This is to be completely transparent, therefore the most complete medium, for it witnesses to what all things are ontologically. The Christ is Christ only because he was constantly conscious of God and was denied equality with God, who sacrificed through the Cross "the Jesus who is Jesus to Jesus who is the Christ." This means that an object or being is "redeemed," restored to its essential being, when it rejects all claims for the finite to be absolute and points beyond itself to its true source of power.

As his other volumes make clearer, to stand in such transparency is to know oneself as a "new being," for one knows that despite the fact that he is unacceptable, he is nevertheless sustained in being—he is "accepted." This, for Tillich, is the meaning of the Protestant norm of justification by faith, reinterpreted as norm for our contemporary situation. Being so redeemed, one can apprehend all things with the "vision of the New Being," that is, can enter into "I-Thou" relations with all of reality, perceiving in all things the power of being which permeates all things. This is the vision of universal salvation of which such revelation makes promise.

In regard to culture, the final criterion judges all cultures, determining the degree to which the products of each are transparent to their ground. The ideal is a "theonomous" culture, as opposed to the "autonomous" culture of the twentieth century in which its bankrupt products witness only to the hollowness of "self-sufficient finitude." Such judgment drives a culture to the "abyss" whereby in disillusionment it may apprehend the power of being operative even when denied. This is the positive function of theology of culture, the fullest completion of Tillich's method of correlation.

This "ground of being" towards which the symbol "God" points cannot be known, only experienced. The only literal statement possible is that "God is being-itself"; all other declarations are symbolic. For example, God is both "cause" and "substance," yet transcends both. Perhaps Tillich's most indicative statement is that God can be thought of only through a double negative— God is the negation of the negation of being. Here we see the fuller significance of Tillich's rejection of supernaturalism. God is neither an object nor a subject—"He" transcends both. It is not even true to say that God exists.

All affirmations of God are only affirmations about finite existence. To say, for example, that "God is good" means that God is the ground of finite good. God as "living" means he is the ground of life.

This is why Tillich's section on God begins with the questions of finite Being from which the affirmation of God arises. It is from the awareness of anxiety that man's affirmation of God begins. God is the name for the ultimate concern which answers this question of existence. The tension in *man's* ultimate concern is the basis for the different types of ideas of God in history.

It is here that the radicalness of Tillich's conception of both metaphysics and theology can be seen. When living and nonliving, personal and nonpersonal, free and determined, static and dynamic, unity and diversity, potentiality and actuality, and the like, are all finite polarities which the divine transcend, truth in both the philosophical and theological senses is radically reinterpreted. Theologically, dogma provides not knowledge of the divine being, but symbols of *finite* experience in relation to an undifferentiated ground. Metaphysically, ontology is not knowledge of the structures of Being Itself, but knowledge of the *structures* of finite existence. It is for this reason that the label "religious naturalist" is not completely inappropriate for Tillich.

In effect, what Tillich has done is to affirm the ontological argument, not as argument but as finite experience. No longer is Christian revelation understood as divine activity in history, but the Christian doctrine of God is reinterpreted in terms of symbols having the power to effect the experience of absolute dependence and exhibit it in human and cultural action. Nowhere has the "liberal" tradition of Schleiermacher, Otto, and Bergson been so consistently developed as an explication of Christianity.—*W.P.J.*

PERTINENT LITERATURE

Roberts, David E. "Tillich's Doctrine of Man," in *The Theology of Paul Tillich*. Edited by Charles W. Kegley and Robert W. Bretall. New York: Macmillan Publishing Company, 1952, pp. 108-130.

Despite his expressed antipathy for any theological system, David E. Roberts shows himself to be an able apologist for Paul Tillich in discussing his doctrine of man. He begins by characterizing Tillich's thought as "a combination of objective and existential thinking" and then shows how it is open simultaneously to attack from revelationists and objectivistic naturalists alike. In the process of delineating Tillich's strategy in resisting these attacks, Roberts defends Tillich's position on both fronts.

On the objectivist front, for example, Roberts shows how Tillich's anthropology, while itself open to scientific findings, finds science and philosophy irrelevant because of their inability to deal seriously with man's basic inner concern for the structure, meaning, and aim of life and opposes them outright when they become "cryptotheological" in their attempt to exclude theology.

Roberts then adds both symmetry and argumentative force with his own observation that although Tillich's view of revelation is not demonstrable, simply by virtue of the fact that it does justice to existential concern it is probably less arbitrary and more complete than any so-called objective theory.

On the revelationist front, Roberts points to Tillich's insistence that although the norm of systematic theology is given through revelation and not found in any kind of reflection, still, Karl Barth notwithstanding, there is no revelation-in-itself apart from human reception of it. In manifesting himself to man, God is dependent upon how man receives his manifestation. Central always is the dialectic in which question (human existence) meets answer (revelation). Roberts poignantly adds that for Tillich man's very *ability* to ask about this unity testifies to a link between God and essential human goodness, just as the *necessity* that he ask is a sign of his estrangement.

Roberts continues in the advocate role even as he criticizes Tillich. To him, Tillich's rigid definition of theology and philosophy makes "existential philosophy" a contradiction in terms—an unfortunate consequence, since some of the recent developments in philosophy that are the most promising are attempts by people such as Gabriel Marcel and Karl Jaspers to show that metaphysics realizes itself only by including an existential element. Still, Tillich's affinity with these thinkers and his own approach to ontology by way of anthropology are evidence that he does not actually intend to rule out existential philosophy.

In fact, the very cornerstone of Tillich's ontology is existential. Man possesses an awareness of the basic self-world correlation, and this implies a capacity to know all levels of life both through their incorporation in himself and through his differentiation from them in self-and-world transcendence. Tillich's three sets of polar elements—individualization and participation, vitality and intentionality, freedom and destiny—are *a priori* structures of man and world; and his four categories—time, space, causality, substance—are analyzed entirely from the standpoint of human finitude.

Like the typical existentialist, Tillich makes finite freedom the fulcrum of his doctrine of man. In a way that overcomes the freedom-determinism dilemma, Tillich situates human freedom—the other side of the coin from responsibility—in action determined by the centered totality of a person's being. As such a centered totality, the human person is aware of himself as finite, as a mixture of being and nonbeing. Yet this very awareness—exemplified in the grasping of his life as a whole as moving toward death—is itself the key to man's transcendence of finitude and the mark of his essential belonging to infinity and to Being itself. Nothing finite whatever can hold him. Still, man's essential belonging to Nothingness is the source of his fundamental anxiety (*Urangst*). The latter is ineradicable. Yet it too can be accepted and freely used to create and manifest personhood.

Anxiety over the possibility of being estranged from one's true self in "existential disruption" is different from the original anguish accompanying finitude. It occurs when man oscillates between one polar element and its opposite, as when excessive individualization in the form of self-centeredness produces the threat of loneliness, while excessive participation produces the threat of complete collectivism, or when excessive assertion of freedom defies destiny, while accommodation to destiny makes possible the surrender of freedom. At what point does sin occur? Tillich maintains that the transition from the possibility of existential disruption to its actuality is universal in human life, although it is not necessary. It is mediated by human freedom. Yet, paradoxically, the transition is nontemporal. All human history and every individual life is characterized by both the goodness of creation and the universality of sin. But how, Roberts asks, is it possible for God to be at once the ground of essense *and* existence, of creation and the fall, without being enmeshed in the conflict that these pairs intrinsically involve? Furthermore, how can the actualization of human freedom be from one standpoint the aim and end of creation and from another standpoint its ruination? Again Roberts comes to Tillich's defense, at least in regard to the second of these questions. The grandeur and the misery of man are better described and accounted for in Tillich's way than by mere logical niceties. We should understand Tillich to mean that man matures as a responsible person only by passing beyond innocence or potentiality, and that leaving innocence requires that man enter the domain of conflicts and moral distinctions in which one sins and is guilty.

Finally, Tillich's doctrine of sin is related to his Christology. Man is in despair because he is unable to overcome the estrangement of sin. He cannot lift himself to harmony between himself and God. Man's fundamental quest and need is for a healing of disruption coming from Essential Being but actualized under the conditions of existence. In the Christ the needed "New Being" is made manifest and accessible. Despite Tillich's unorthodox approach and formulations, Roberts can maintain that his doctrine of man presupposes a Trinitarian structure.

Randall, John Herman, Jr. "The Ontology of Paul Tillich," in *The Theology of Paul Tillich*. Edited by Charles W. Kegley and Robert W. Bretall. New York: Macmillan Publishing Company, 1952, pp. 132-161.

Rather surprisingly, John Herman Randall, Jr., the functionalist naturalist, finds Paul Tillich's *Systematic Theology* quite congenial. No one with any interest in philosophy, he says, can fail to be stimulated by Tillich's ability to delve beneath the symbolic forms in the theologies and philosophies of the past and confront the problems of human destiny at issue in them. He lauds Tillich as the foremost exponent of existentialism, which is not far from pragmatism in many of its emphases; and he counts Tillich among his allies in the campaign to revive metaphysical inquiry.

According to Randall, Tillich's central enterprise is the construction of a realism that involves vision and participation. Standing in the Augustinian or Christian Platonic tradition, Tillich learned well the lesson of the *Symposium*. With Martin Heidegger, he protested against Edmund Husserl's preoccupation with the description only of essences; his own concern with existence reaffirms both *eros* and the Platonic quest for true being, setting him apart from Aristotle's inclusion of science in wisdom and Saint Thomas Aquinas' separation of the realms of faith and natural reason. It also sets him against any kind of Kantian dualism.

Yet Randall finds just such a dualism, involving the existential (the practical) and the theoretical, insinuating itself into the heart of Tillich's own system, and some of his most telling criticisms are directed against it. Tillich identifies "being as such" with "reality as a whole." But for Randall these two are very different notions. The first refers to the generic traits predicable of any subject matter, while the second means "objective reason," the unifying principle of the universe, "universal *logos*." The first is Aristotelian, the object of an ontological inquiry that has no religious significance and is therefore of no existential concern. The second is Platonic or Neoplatonic and is often identified with God. Tillich regularly equates both with "the structure of being," although only the second is fully compatible with this concept which arises out of the Augustinian tendency in his thought.

The same questionable dualism mark's Tillich's portrayal of the supposedly essential divergence he finds between the cognitive attitudes of the philosopher and the theologian. The one is detached in his search for the structures of universal being, while the other is committed in his search for structures that manifest themselves in particular historical events and in religious institutions. However, Tillich grants that these attitudes also converge, so that there is always something of the theologian in the philosopher and something of the philosopher in the theologian. Ultimately, indeed, Tillich's Christian Platonism reasserts itself; and in the last analysis it becomes impossible for him even to distinguish the emphases of the two attitudes. Any distinction, then, simply varies with the situation; far from being structural, it is relative or "existential."

Randall notes that a major contribution of the movement in philosophy that includes existentialism and pragmatism was the undercutting of Kantian and Aristotelian dualisms. "Pure reason" should not be considered the opposite of the practical or the existential; rather, theory must be seen as a stage in the broader context of "practice." Disciplines vary in the degree of their approximation to universality and detachment, but metaphysics, which seeks to encompass every possible situation, aims at being the most highly theoretical of all disciplines and for that very reason is the most instrumental or existential. Tillich in his covertly dualistic attempt to distinguish between philosophy and theology and concomitantly to relate the two through his method of correlation does not, Randall believes, give serious enough attention to theory as existential in nature.

Randall considers Tillich's epistemology to be the least adequate part of his system, primarily because it is not sufficiently elaborated but also because it again harbors the same dualism. As philosophy prepares for theology, so reason prepares for revelation. For Tillich reason or *nous* or *intellectus* points always one step beyond the intelligible structures that it discovers in experience to something like the Neoplatonic One or the Augustinian Original of the Copy, which Tillich locates in the depths and calls "Being itself." Yet this "ground of being" and ground of all knowing which is present in all the operations of reason nevertheless remains mysterious and usually gives expression to itself only in myth and ritual. Thus ordinary reason as encountered in existence remains finite and self-contradictory. It grasps only relativities. All of its antinomies—autonomy *versus* heteronomy, the static *versus* the dynamic element, formalism *versus* emotionalism—press on toward revelation, which is the only source of their resolution. Randall here insists that these are not intellectually insoluble antinomies. There is no evidence that an adequate intellectual method faces ultimate self-contradiction. Therefore, if it is "revelation" that provides solutions, it must be revelation as discovery by means of the intellect. With characteristic facetiousness Randall invites Tillich to strike up a relationship with intelligence, since in Randall's eyes Tillich's own combining of the experiential and the intuitional for philosophical purposes already seems very close to the American instrumentalists' "method of intelligence," a method close to Randall's own.

Tillich claims that all the principles, categories, and ultimate notions in his system are *a priori* conditions of experience itself. Randall views this Kantian language as nonessential to Tillich's position and ultimately incompatible with it. Since Tillich grants that the structures of experience are discovered *in* experience, why does he call them "presuppositions," as though they were brought to experience from somewhere outside? Tillich is attempting to combine his epistemological realism with the contrary view that the object of knowledge is determined by the knower. Fortunately Tillich avoids a strictly static *a priori* through his [Duns] Scotist voluntarism, which allows for indeterminacy in the structure of being. Thus, although man is by definition a *historical* being, the structures of human nature do change within history. The one exception is the subject-object distinction, which for Tillich remains absolutely ultimate. As Aristotle would put it, it remains both "prior for us" and "prior in nature." Why does Tillich never consider the possibility of the emergence of that distinction also from the natural conditions of life, both organic and social?

Randall closes on a completely different note. He doubts whether either "anxiety" as the self's immediate experience of its finitude or "ground of being" is a genuine philosophical *concept*. Both seem to him to be solely theological *symbols*. Finitude is for him simply a natural condition of human life, which rarely produces such "anxiety" as existentialists describe. The real horror to contemplate would be man as *not* finite. Usually men have felt much more poignantly the moral limitations of humanity than they have the "ontological anxiety" of temporal and spacial determinateness. For Tillich, however, and for other continental existentialists who have lived through two major wars, anxiety may understandably be an "existential commitment."

As for "being itself" and "the ground of being"—ironically the only terms that Tillich himself insists are *not* symbols—Randall notes that they are often used interchangeably with "structure of being" and "power of being" in Tillich's system. A structure, however, is scarcely the same as a power. How does Tillich distinguish "ground" from "cause," which is admittedly a symbol for him, at least when used of the relation of being itself to finite beings? What about Being itself? This is the most illusive of all phrases. It is incapable of being conceptualized through any sort of ontological analysis. Hence, Being itself, for Tillich as well as for past ages, is actually nothing more than a great unifying symbol or myth, one by means of which men bring the world into focus in relation to their systems of values and meanings that are their ultimate concerns.

Niebuhr, Reinhold. "Biblical Thought and Ontological Speculation in Tillich's Theology," in *The Theology of Paul Tillich*. Edited by Charles W. Kegley and Robert W. Bretall. New York: Macmillan Publishing Company, 1952, pp. 216-227.

Paul Tillich's *Systematic Theology* will be "a landmark in the history of modern theology," Reinhold Niebuhr predicts. This is true, in the first place, because it is more rigorous and deals more imaginatively with all the disciplines of culture than any other speculative religious work in the last several decades and, second, because Tillich's *Systematic Theology* is more mindful of the limitations of reason in its attempts to penetrate the divine mystery as well as the mystery of human existence. Hence it is more open to a kerygmatic dimension than were the natural theologies inspired by Immanuel Kant and Georg Wilhelm Friedrich Hegel.

Still, there is a peculiar significance to Niebuhr's contrasting Tillich with Karl Barth by referring to them as the modern Origen and the modern Tertullian, respectively, considering that both Church Fathers were proclaimed heretical. Clearly Tillich's heresy, for Niebuhr, is his forthright picturing of the Fall as one aspect of creation.

When Tillich maintains that man's existence is not the same as his essence, he means that man is outside the divine life as well as within it: "Man has left the ground in order to 'stand upon' himself, to be actually what he essentially is, in order to be finite freedom." It is at this point that creation joins the

Fall, for in Tillich's words, "fully developed creatureliness is fallen creatureliness." The freedom of the creature is actualized just insofar as it is outside the divine life in an existence which has ceased to be one with an undifferentiated essence.

In analyzing Tillich's position here, Niebuhr shows that Tillich himself traces the ambiguity of the concept of "essence" back to Plato. Essence is the nature of something or the quality in which something participates; it is also that from which something has fallen. This ambiguity, in turn, is rooted in the ambiguity associated with the concept of "existence," which both expresses being and contradicts it. In saying that "the structure of man's *essential* nature is the structure of finite freedom," Tillich means "essential" in the first sense. Man's nature or character is to be both finite and free. On the other hand, when he says that existence stands in contradiction to essence, "essence" is "that from which existence has fallen." Every existing creature imperfectly embodies its essence at the same time that it also partially contradicts it. However, there is no contradiction of the creature's *own* essence, which in man's case is to be both finite and free: the reference is to essential being or being *per se*. The creature is suspended between being and nonbeing. When used in this context, then, "existential" can refer to the creature only in its capacity for being estranged from its divine ground, and not to real, concrete creatures or things as they actually exist in time, since real things retain their essential element through their relationship, only partially dissevered, to the divine ground.

If, however, "existential" is meant to apply thus to particularity and discreteness, Niebuhr asks, then how can it be used also to define man's unique possibility of contradicting his own nature, in the way that the brutes cannot, by perversely centering his life around self, sex, or glory? How can "existential" be consistently applied to "sin" in the biblical sense as Tillich frequently applies it? Tillich's answer is that there are two dimensions to sin corresponding to a "transcendent fall" on the one hand and an "immanent fall" on the other, to destiny and to freedom. Seen from one perspective, solely because of his separation from the divine ground, man is "subject to the impossibility of not sinning." Seen from another perspective, because he is free to contradict his own essential being, man is subject to the possibility, but not the necessity, of sinning. Sin as ontological fate, as *Sonderung* or separation, is simply the other side of the shield from the sin portrayed in the Bible as historic corruption born of unbelief.

What here appears to be a maze of terminological confusion is not so troubling to Niebuhr as the fact that when Tillich's two kinds of sin are coupled in this way ontological sin clearly outweighs historical sin. One evidence of this is Tillich's refusal to acknowledge that the myth of Adam's innocence prior to the Fall is a *historical* symbol. Tillich's Adam is, as he writes, at "a stage of infancy before contest and decision," and this implies a state that "is neither potential being nor actualized being in time." But what, Niebuhr asks, is infancy without historical connotations? Both the individual and the community remember early periods of simple harmony which were disturbed through increasing freedom, only to open up on the possibility of more complex and inclusive harmonies. To be sure, it is absurd to attribute to Adam before the Fall both innocence and perfect love toward Christ as orthodox theology has done; but this absurdity does more justice to "essential" man as a historic creature than Tillich's "dreaming innocence" does. According to Niebuhr, "the 'perfection before the fall' is the higher possibility of self-realization through self-giving which exists before every act in which the self actually resolves its problem by seeking itself more narrowly than it should."

In contradistinction to Tillich's view, it is of great significance, Niebuhr believes, that the myth of creation and the myth of the Fall found in Genesis are *two* stories and not one. Creation symbolizes the beginning of history, and the Fall symbolizes the corruption of freedom in history. The one points to a historical state characterized less by separation than by life in unity with life, and it shows that, even as a particular, separate existence, man has a nature open to the possibility of harmonious relationships. The other affirms that every act of estrangement is a fall from a higher possibility of life's relating to life in love.—*C.W.L.*

ADDITIONAL RECOMMENDED READING

Alston, William P. "Tillich's Conception of a Religious Symbol," in *Religious Experience and Truth*. Edited by Sidney Hook. New York: New York University Press, 1961. Maintains that an important weakness in Tillich's theory of symbols is his failure to give an adequate account of the interrelation of "symbolizing" and "pointing to."

Emmet, Dorothy M. "Epistemology and the Idea of Revelation," in *The Theology of Paul Tillich*. Edited by Charles W. Kegley and Robert W. Bretall. New York: Macmillan Publishing Company, 1952, pp. 198-214. Appreciative of Tillich's description of the interrelation of technical and ecstatic reason, but takes Tillich to task for his idealist view of ontological reason.

Hartshorne, Charles. "Tillich's Doctrine of God," in *The Theology of Paul Tillich*. Edited by Charles W. Kegley and Robert W. Bretall. New York: Macmillan Publishing Company, 1952, pp. 164-195. A challenge to Tillich's system from one of the most eminent representatives of process theology.

Macleod, Alistair M. *Paul Tillich: An Essay on the Role of Ontology in His Philosophical Theology*. London: George Allen & Unwin, 1973. Claims to detect an incoherence at the heart of Tillich's philosophy based on several very different conceptions of ontology.

Martin, Bernard. *The Existential Theology of Paul Tillich*. New York: Bookman Associates, 1963. Generally faithful to Tillich, this analysis of the first two volumes of *Systematic Theology* nevertheless attempts to demonstrate that the method of correlation as Tillich describes it does not square with his actual procedure.

Rowe, William L. *Religious Symbols and God: A Philosophical Study of Tillich's Theology*. Chicago: University of Chicago Press, 1968. A systematic and lucid analysis of the close relationship in Tillich's system between his view of the role of religious symbols and his conception of God as being itself.

THE COURAGE TO BE

Author: Paul Tillich (1886-1965)
Type of work: Ontology, ethics
First published: 1952

PRINCIPAL IDEAS ADVANCED

Considered from the ethical point of view, courage in a man is a sign of his caring for something enough to decide and to act despite opposition; considered in terms of its effect on his being (ontologically), courage is the self-affirmation of one's being.

These points of view are united in the conception of courage as the self-affirmation of one's being in the presence of the threat of nonbeing; anxiety is the felt awareness of the threat of nonbeing, and courage is the resolute opposition to the threat in such a manner that being is affirmed.

Three types of anxiety—ontic, moral, and spiritual (the anxiety of fate and death, of guilt and condemnation, of emptiness and meaninglessness)—are present in all cultural ages, but spiritual anxiety is predominant in the modern period.

Existential anxiety cannot be removed; it can be faced only by those who have the courage to be.

The courage to be involves the courage to participate, to be oneself, and to unite the two by absolute faith in the God above God, "being-itself."

The material in Tillich's book, *The Courage to Be*, was first presented in the form of a series of lectures given at Yale University in 1950-51, under the sponsorship of the Terry Foundation. The central task which the author has assumed in these lectures is that of a dialectical analysis and phenomenological description of courage as a structural category of the human condition.

Courage, as understood by the author, is both an ethical reality and an ontological concept. As an ethical reality courage indicates concrete action and decision which expresses a valuational content. As an ontological concept—that is, as illuminating a feature of being—courage indicates the universal and essential self-affirmation of one's being. Tillich argues that these two meanings of courage must be united if a proper interpretation of the phenomenon is to be achieved. In the final analysis the ethical can be understood only through the ontological. Courage as an ethical reality is ultimately rooted in the structure of being itself.

These two meanings of courage have been given philosophic consideration throughout the whole history of Western thought. The author provides a brief historical sketch of the attempt to deal with the phenomenon of courage by tracing its development from Plato through Nietzsche. There is first the tradition which begins with Plato and leads to Thomas Aquinas. In the thought of Plato and Aristotle the heroic-aristocratic element in courage was given priority. Plato aligned courage with the spirited part of the soul, which lies between reason and desire, and then aligned both courage and spirit with the guardian class (*phýlakes*), which lies between the rulers and the producers. The class of guardians, as the armed aristocracy, thus gave the Platonic definition of courage an indelible heroic-aristocratic stamp. Aristotle preserved the aristocratic element by defining the courageous man as one who acts for the sake of what is noble. However, there was another current of thought developing during this period. This was the understanding of courage as rational-democratic rather than heroic-aristocratic. The life and death of Socrates, and later the Christian tradition, gave expression to this view. The position of Thomas Aquinas is unique in that it marks the synthesis of a heroic-aristocratic ethic and society with a rational-democratic mode of thought. With Stoicism a new emphasis emerges. Taking as the ideal sage the Athenian Socrates, Stoics became the spokesmen for an emphatic rational-democratic definition of courage. Wisdom replaces heroic fortitude and the democratic-universal replaces the aristocratic ideal. The "courage to be" for the Stoics was a rational courage, indicating an affirmation of one's reasonable nature, or Logos, which countered the negativities of the nonessential or accidental. But this courage to be, formulated independently of the Christian doctrine of forgiveness and salvation, was ultimately cast in terms of a cosmic resignation. The historical significance of the ethical thought of Spinoza, according to the author, is that it rendered explicit an ontology of courage. This ontology of courage was one which made the Stoic doctrine of self-affirmation central, but which replaced the Stoic idea of resignation with a positive ethical humanism. Nietzsche stands at the end of the era, and in a sense is its culmination. Nietzsche transforms Spinoza's "substance" into "life." Spinoza's doctrine of self-affirmation is restated in dynamic terms. Will becomes the central category. Life is understood as "will-to-power." Courage is thus defined as the power of life to affirm itself in spite of its negativities and ambiguities—in spite of the abyss of nonbeing. Nietzsche expressed it thus: "he who with eagle's talons *graspeth* the abyss: he hath courage."

Tillich, in formulating his ontology of courage, keeps the tradition from Plato to Nietzsche in mind. His definition of courage, as the universal self-affirmation of one's being in the presence of the threat of nonbeing, receives its final clarification only in the light of the historical background which he has sketched. In the author's definition of courage the phenomenon of anxiety is disclosed as an unavoidable consideration. Courage and anxiety are interdependent concepts. Anxiety is the existential awareness of the threat of nonbeing. Courage is the resolute facing of this anxiety in such a way that nonbeing is ultimately embraced or taken up into being. Thus, the author is driven to formulate an ontology of anxiety. There is first a recognition of the interdependence of fear and anxiety. Fear and anxiety are distinct, but not separate. Fear has a determinable object—a pain, a rejection by someone who is lived, a misfortune, the anticipation of death. Anxiety, on the other hand, has no object, or paradoxically stated, its object is the negation of every object. Anxiety is the awareness that nonbeing is irremovably a part of one's being, which constitutes the definition of human finitude. Anxiety and fear are thus distinct. Yet they are mutually immanent within each other. Fear, when it is deepened, reveals anxiety; and anxiety strives toward fear. The fear of dying ultimately ceases to be a fear of an object—a sickness or an accident—and becomes anxiety over the nonbeing envisioned "after death." And conversely, anxiety strives to become fear, because the finite self cannot endure the threatening disclosure of nonbeing for more than a moment. The mind seeks to transform anxiety into fear, so that it can have a particular object to deal with and overcome. But the basic anxiety of nonbeing cannot, as such, be eliminated. It is a determinant of human existence itself.

The author distinguishes three types of anxiety: (1) *ontic anxiety* or the anxiety of fate and death; (2) *moral anxiety* or the anxiety of guilt and condemnation; and (3) *spiritual anxiety* or the anxiety of emptiness and meaninglessness.

Fate threatens man's ontic self-affirmation relatively; death threatens it absolutely. The anxiety of fate arises from an awareness of an ineradicable contingency which penetrates to the very depth of one's being. Existence exhibits no ultimate necessity. It manifests an irreducible element of irrationality. Behind fate stands death as the absolute threat to ontic self-affirmation. Death discloses the total ontic annihilation which is imminent in every moment of our existence. For the most part man attempts to transform this anxiety into fear, which has a definite object. He partly succeeds but then realizes that the threat can never be embodied in a particular object. It arises from the human situation as such. The question then is posed: "Is there a courage to be, a courage to affirm oneself in spite of the threat against man's ontic self-affirmation?"

Nonbeing threatens on another level. It threatens by producing moral anxiety—the anxiety of guilt, which threatens relatively, and the anxiety of condemnation, which threatens absolutely. The self seeks to affirm itself morally by actualizing its potentialities. But in every moral action nonbeing expresses itself in the inability of man to actualize fully all of his potential. He remains estranged from his essential being. All of his actions are pervaded with a moral ambiguity. The awareness of this ambiguity is guilt. This guilt can drive man toward a feeling of complete self-rejection, in which he experiences the absolute threat of condemnation. The question then arises whether man can find a courage to affirm himself in spite of the threat against his moral self-affirmation.

Lastly, there is the anxiety of emptiness and meaninglessness, which reveals the threat to man's spiritual self-affirmation. Emptiness threatens this self-affirmation relatively, meaninglessness threatens it absolutely. Emptiness arises out of a situation in which the self fails to find satisfaction through a participation in the contents of its cultural life. The beliefs, attitudes, and activities of man's tradition lose their meaning and are transformed into matters of indifference. Everything is tried but nothing satisfies. Creativity vanishes and the self is threatened with boredom and tedium. The anxiety of emptiness culminates in the anxiety of meaninglessness. Man finds that he can no longer hold fast to the affirmations of his tradition nor to those of his personal convictions. Truth itself is called into question. Spiritual life is threatened with total doubt. Again, the question arises: Is there a courage to be which affirms itself in spite of nonbeing—in this case, nonbeing expressed in the threat of doubt which undermines one's spiritual affirmation through the anxiety of emptiness and meaninglessness?

These three types of anxiety find a periodic exemplification in the history of Western civilization. Although the three types are interdependently present in all cultural ages, we find that ontic anxiety was predominant at the end of ancient civilization, moral anxiety at the end of the Middle Ages, and spiritual anxiety at the end of the modern period. The anxiety of fate and death was the central threat in the Stoic doctrine of courage; it received expression in the transition from Hellenic to Hellenistic civilization, which saw the crumbling of the independent city states and the rise of universal empires, introducing a political power beyond control and calculation; and it is present on every page of Greek tragical literature. In the Middle Ages the anxiety of guilt and condemnation was dominant, expressed in the theological symbol of the "wrath of God" and in the imagery of hell and purgatory. Ascetic practices, pilgrimages, devotion to relics, institution of indulgences, heightened interest in the mass and penance—all witness to the moral threat of nonbeing as it manifests itself in guilt and condemnation. Modern civilization, born of the victory of humanism and the Enlightenment, found its chief threat in the threat to man's spiritual self-affirmation. Here the anxiety of emptiness and meaninglessness becomes dominant. Democratic liberalism calls into question the security and supports of an absolute state; the rise of technology tends to transform selves into tools and thus displace man's spiritual center; skepticism replaces philosophical certitude. All cultural contents which previously gave man security no longer afford satisfaction and meaning. Modern man is threatened with the attack of emptiness and meaninglessness.

The author concludes his ontology of anxiety by distinguishing existential anxiety, in the three types discussed, from pathological or neurotic anxiety. Existential anxiety has an ontological character and is thus understood as a universal determinant of the human condition. Existential anxiety cannot be removed; it can only be courageously faced. Pathological anxiety, on the other hand, as the result of unresolved conflicts in the sociopsychological structure of personality, is the expression of universal anxiety under special conditions.

It is the consequence of man's inability to face courageously his existential anxiety and thus take the nonbeing which threatens into himself. The neurotic self still affirms itself, but it does so on a limited scale. Such affirmation is the affirmation of a reduced self which seeks to avoid the nonbeing that is constitutive of his universal finite condition. But in thus seeking to avoid nonbeing the neurotic self retreats from the full affirmation of his being. Hence, the author's definition of neurosis as *"the way of avoiding nonbeing by avoiding being."* The neurotic personality always affirms something less than what he essentially is. His potentialities are sacrificed in order to make possible a narrow and intensified affirmation of what remains of his reduced self. The neurotic is unable to take creatively into himself the universal existential anxieties. In relation to the anxiety of fate and death this produces an unrealistic security, comparable to the security of a prison. Since the neurotic cannot distinguish what is to be realistically feared from those situations in which he is realistically safe, he withdraws into a castle of false security so as to insulate himself from all threats of existence. In relation to the anxiety of guilt and condemnation, pathological anxiety expresses an unrealistic perfection. The neurotic sets up moralistic self-defenses against all actions which would widen the horizons of his reduced and limited actualized state, which he considers to be absolutely perfect. In relation to the anxiety of emptiness and meaninglessness, which expresses itself in a radical existential doubt, pathological anxiety drives the self to an unrealistic certitude. Unable to face the doubt regarding the contents of his cultural tradition and his personal beliefs, the neurotic constructs a citadel of certainty, from which he fends off all threat of doubt on the basis of an absolutized authority. This absolutized authority may be either a personal revelation, a social or religious institution, or a fanatical leader of a movement. In any case, he refuses to accept doubt and rejects all questions from the outside. He is unable courageously to accept the reality of meaninglessness as a universal phenomenon in existential reality.

The courage to be is the movement of self-affirmation in spite of the threat of anxiety as the existential awareness of nonbeing. This courage is conceptually clarified by the author through the use of the polar ontological principles of participation and individualization. The basic polar structure of being is the polarity of self and world. The first polar elements which emerge out of this foundational polar structure are the elements of participation and individualization. The relevance of these elements to Tillich's doctrine of courage is evident. Courage expresses itself as "the courage to be as a part," exemplifying the polar element of participation, and as "the courage to be as oneself," exemplifying the polar element of individualization. Finally, these two polar exemplifications of courage are transcended and united in "absolute faith." Absolute faith, grounded in transcendence, provides the final definition of the courage to be.

First the author examines the manifestation of courage as the courage to be *as a part*. This is one side of man's self-affirmation. He affirms himself as a participant in the power of a group, a historical movement, or being as such. This side of courage counters the threat of losing participation in his world. The social forms which embody this manifestation of courage are varied. The author briefly discusses four of these forms: *collectivism, semi-collectivism, neocollectivism,* and *democratic conformism.*

All of these forms attempt to deal with the three types of anxiety—ontic, moral, and spiritual—by channeling their individual expressions into an anxiety about the group. Thus, it becomes possible to cope with these existential anxieties with a courage that affirms itself through collective or conformal participation. The individual anxiety concerning fate and death is transcended through a collective identification. There is a part of oneself, belonging to the group, which cannot be hurt or destroyed. It is as eternal as the group is eternal—an essential manifestation of the universal collective. So, also, a self-affirmation is made possible in spite of the threat of guilt and condemnation. Individual guilt is translated into a deviation or transgression of the norms of the collective, and the courage to be as a part accepts guilt and its consequences as public guilt. The anxiety of emptiness and meaninglessness is dealt with in the same way. The group becomes the bearer of universal meaning, and the individual derives his personal meaning through a participation in the group. The ever present danger in the radical affirmation of the courage to be as a part is the absorption of the self into the collective, with the consequent loss of the unique, unrepeatable, and irreplaceable individual.

The courage to be *as oneself* expresses the other side of man's self-affirmation. This movement is made possible through the ontological polar element of individualization. The courage to be as oneself has found a concrete embodiment in *romanticism, naturalism,* and *existentialism.*

Romanticism elevated the individual beyond all cultural content, and conferred upon him a radical autonomy. In some of its extreme expressions, as in Friedrich von Schlegel, the courage to be as oneself led to a complete rejection of participation.

Naturalism, whether of the "philosophy of life" variety or of the American pragmatic variety, follows basically the same path. Nietzsche, in his definition of nature as the will-to-power, granted priority to the individual will and made it the decisive element in the drive toward creativity. In Nietzsche individual self-affirmation reaches a climactic point. American pragmatism, in spite of its roots in democratic conformism, shares much of the individualistic attitude characteristic of European naturalism. It finds its highest ethical principle in growth, sees the educational process as one which maximizes the individual talents of the child, and seeks its governing philosophical principle in personal creative self-affirmation.

It is in *existentialism* that the courage to be as oneself is most powerfully presented. Tillich distinguishes two basic expressions of existentialism—as an attitude and as a philosophical and artistic content. Existentialism as an attitude designates an attitude of concrete involvement as contrasted with an attitude of theoretical detachment. Existentialism as a content is at the same time a point of view, a protest, and an expression. But in all of its varieties existentialism is the chief protagonist for the reality of the individual and the importance of personal decision. It is concerned to salvage the individual from the objectivization of abstract thought, society, and technology alike. The existentialist struggles for the preservation of the self-affirmative person. He fights against dehumanization in all of its forms. The task of every individual, according to the existentialist, is to be himself. Heidegger has profoundly expressed this existentialist courage to be as oneself in his concept of resolution (*Entschlossenheit*). The resolute individual derives his directives for action from no external source. Nobody can provide for one's security against the threat of ontic annihilation, moral disintegration, or spiritual loss of meaning. He himself must decide how to face his imminent death, how to face his moral ambiguity, and how to face the threat of meaninglessness which strikes at the root of his existence.

We have seen that the danger in the courage to be as a part is a loss of the self in the collective. The opposite danger becomes apparent in the various forms of the courage to be as oneself—namely, a loss of the world as a polar structure of selfhood. The question then arises whether there can be a courage which unites both sides of man's self-affirmation by transcending them.

Courage understood as absolute faith exemplifies this union through transcendence. A courage which can take the three types of anxiety creatively into itself must be grounded in a power of being that transcends both the power of oneself and the power of one's world. The self-world correlation is still on this side of the threat of nonbeing; hence, neither self-affirmation as oneself nor self-affirmation as a part can cope successfully with nonbeing. The courage to be, in its final movement, must be rooted in the power of being-itself, which transcends the self-world correlation. Insofar as religion is the state of being grasped by the power of being-itself, it can be said that courage always has either an explicit or implicit religious character. The courage to be finds its ultimate source in the power of being-itself, and becomes manifest as absolute faith. As long as participation remains dominant the relation to being-itself is mystical in character; as long as individualization remains dominant the relationship is one of personal encounter; when both sides are accepted and transcended the relation becomes one of absolute faith. The two sides are apprehended as contrasts, but not as contradictions which exclude each other.

This absolute faith is able to take the threefold structure of anxiety into itself. It conquers the anxiety of fate and death in its encounter with providence. Providence gives man the courage of confidence to say "in spite of" to fate and death. Providence must not be construed in terms of God's activity, but as a religious symbol for the courage of confidence which conquers fate and death. Guilt and condemnation are conquered through the experience of divine forgiveness which expresses itself in the courage to accept acceptance. The courage to be in relation to guilt is "the courage to accept oneself as accepted in spite of being unacceptable." In relation to the anxiety of emptiness and meaninglessness the courage to be, based on absolute faith, is able to say "yes" to the undermining doubt and to affirm itself in spite of the threat. Any decisve answer to the question of meaninglessness must first accept the state of meaninglessness; this acceptance constitutes a movement of faith. "The act of accepting meaninglessness is in itself a meaningful act. It is an act of faith." Through his participation in the power of being-itself man is able to conquer emptiness and meaninglessness by taking them into himself and affirming himself "in spite of."

The content of absolute faith is the "God above God." Tillich rejects the God of theological theism, who remains bound to the subject-object structure of reality. A God who is understood as an object becomes an invincible tyrant who divests man of his subjectivity and freedom. This is the God whom Nietzsche pronounced dead, and against whom the existentialists have justifiably revolted. Theism must be transcended if absolute faith is to become a reality. The "God above God" is the power of being-itself, which, as the source of absolute faith, is not bound to the subject-object structure of reality. Being-itself transcends both self and world and unites the polarities of individualization and participation. The courage to be, which is ultimately grounded in the encounter with the "God above God," thus unites and transcends the courage to be as oneself and the courage to be as a part. This courage avoids both the loss of oneself by participation and the loss of one's world by individualization.—*C. O. S.*

PERTINENT LITERATURE

Randall, John Herman, Jr. "The Philosophical Legacy of Paul Tillich," in *The Intellectual Legacy of Paul Tillich*. Edited by James R. Lyons. Detroit: Wayne State University Press, 1969.

John Herman Randall, Jr.'s lecture was the first of three given at Wayne State University under the Slaughter Foundation commemorating the first anniversary of Paul Tillich's death. Randall, who was closely associated with Tillich from the time of his arrival in this country—for many years they conducted a joint seminar on Myth and Symbol—mentions his own delight at being able to observe a true-blue German Romantic at first hand. As a historian, Randall notes that in his student years Tillich was introduced to philosophy by an expert on Johann Gottlieb Fichte, and that, having bought a set of F. W. J. Schelling at a bargain, he made Schelling the subject of both his Th.D. and Ph.D. dissertations. Martin Heidegger, his colleague at Marburg, contributed to his philosophical vocabulary.

Randall views Tillich as primarily a philosophical theologian, engaged in the perennial task of interpreting the symbols of religion in terms of contemporary philosophical thought. Tillich said that philosophy formulates an analysis of the human situation and asks the questions to which it gives rise, leaving to theology the task of finding the answers in the revelatory message. Randall, however, doubts whether the matter is that simple. In fact, the philosophy to which Tillich was attuned was that which he found in Schelling, Søren Kierkegaard, and the early Karl Marx, who were in revolt against Hegelian essentialism and the optimistic assumption that man is realizing his essence in the world process. Convinced that existential man, caught in his situation, is estranged from his essential nature, these thinkers were already giving expression to the Christian interpretation of man's fallen condition. Hence, in Randall's opinion, it is only those philosophers who are hidden theologians who will ask questions which theologians find significant.

Tillich's existentialism is, however, only one aspect of his thought. More fundamentally, he must be understood as a modern representative of the Augustinian tradition of Christian Platonism, as against the Thomistic tradition of Christian Aristotelianism. Like St. Augustine, he could admit no clear distinction between philosophy and theology. Faith is not a weaker form of knowledge, but an ontological commitment; truth is not a quality of propositions, but the power of being; knowing is not abstraction, but participation. For Tillich, no cosmological argument for the existence of God is possible because any being whose existence demands proof is finite. On the other hand, the ontological argument, although not a proof, reveals God as the Ultimate presupposed in all our encounters with reality.

Philosophically, Tillich stands in the tradition of Platonic realism. As he sees it, reality possesses a structure (*Logos*), and it is this structure which makes reality a whole. This logical realism, which affirms that subjective reason grasps the objective structure of things, says Randall, is "designedly not in the fashion of much recent nominalist philosophizing," although Randall looks favorably upon it. A more serious problem for the modern mind is that the reason (*nous*) which grasps these higher structures by a kind of direct participation does not admit of verification in the way that technical reason (*dianoia*) does. And Tillich, aware of the problem, carefully described what he called an "experiential" (as distinct from experimental) method. What he intended, says Randall, seems close to what American pragmatism calls the method of intelligence.

On the whole, says Randall, Tillich's philosophy is so difficult for English-speaking philosophers to take seriously that his legacy is likely to consist in his wealth of specific insights rather than in his system as a whole.

Boas, George. "Being and Existence," in *The Journal of Philosophy*. LIII, no. 23 (November 8, 1956), pp. 748-759.

John Herman Randall, Jr. relates that when G. E. Moore's time came to comment on a paper read by Paul Tillich, he said, "I don't think I have been able to understand a single sentence of your paper. Won't you please try to state one sentence, or even one word, that I can understand?" George Boas is more attuned than most English-speaking philosophers to Tillich's language. His book *Dominant Themes of Modern Philosophy* (1957) concludes with a chapter entitled "The Rise of Existentialism." Boas remains, however, an unreconstructed American; and in this paper, part of a symposium of existentialist thought in which Tillich was the first participant, he holds out for the language of John Dewey and George Santayana.

Boas develops his subject, "Being and Existence," in quite traditional terms, equating being with the realm of essence and existence with the realm of fact. The realms are opposed to each other as universal is opposed to particular; but they are further opposed in that the former, which is set up by human reason in order to make sense of the latter, often fails, as when scientific theories prove false and our best-laid plans "gang agley." Such headaches, however, are no reason for despair. Boas himself is convinced that the universe is not completely intelligible, but he agrees with Dewey that what people like to call mysteries can be dissipated if we revise our assumptions—that is, adjust essence to existence.

Against the background of this kind of reasoning, Boas asks what Tillich can mean when, in *The Courage to Be*, he says that nonbeing is contained in being. First, nonbeing can refer only to what the ancients called becoming. It is not, of course, the logical negation of being; hence, it must stand for coming-into-being and ceasing-to-be. That it is eternally present in "the process of the divine life" can mean only that cessation of being is always a possibility, but not an actuality; hence, it is not, strictly speaking, nothing. To say, however, that man is threatened by nonbeing when he thinks of death or guilt or meaningless is mistaken. "To be" is either a copula or a synonym for existence: taken either way, the negation of being is not what threatens us; it is the positive associations that go with our ideas of death or guilt or fate. That a person may be depressed when he thinks of any of these is understandable, but to talk as if such feelings are rationally connected with the recognition of man's finitude is wrong-headed. On the contrary, it is possible, with the Buddhists, for example, to accept nonbeing as the highest good.

Having disposed of nonbeing, Boas turns to being, in which nonbeing is said to be contained. We tend, says Boas, to hypostatize essences, and we then fall into the trap of supposing that anything that can be named, such as universe or being, can be subsumed under a more comprehensive genus. This tendency explains not merely how Tillich comes to speak of nonbeing as a correlative of being but also how he arrives at the more general concept of being-itself. But how, asks Boas, can anything be predicated of that which is supposed to transcend being and nonbeing since that which is beyond this distinction is beyond meaningful discourse? In Boas' opinion, it cannot; hence, all talk about being-itself, or the ground of being, or unconditional transcendence is literally nonsense.

Hook, Sidney. "The Atheism of Paul Tillich," in *Religious Experience and Truth*. Edited by Sidney Hook. New York: New York University Press, 1961, pp. 59-64.

There is no reason to think that Paul Tillich's denial of the God of theism, specifically the personal God of liberal Protestantism, would have scandalized either Martin Luther or St. John of the Cross. Sidney Hook is right, however, in believing that when the ordinary person reared in the Western tradition professes to believe in God, he thinks of God as a being who exists alongside the world that he has created; therefore he would call Tillich an atheist if he heard him deny that such a being exists and say that to worship such a being as God is superstitious idolatry. Hook mentions that Benedictus de Spinoza and G. W. F. Hegel, who took a somewhat similar stand, were denounced as atheists; but neither of these was a professor in a church seminary.

Hook makes no bones about his own opposition to religion, explaining that he does not belong to the Jamesian school of pragmatism which holds that "the warmth and light radiated by the beaming countenance of a cosmic confidence man is to be preferred to the stern and cheerless visage of the truth about man's tragic estate." Yet he can almost approve Tillich's kind of religion; for worshipers who hold that God is not *a* being but *being* itself would surely not persecute one another; nor would they oppose science. Moreover, on the positive side, they might well devise symbols that would provide aesthetic and emotional support for various ethical and cultural societies, whose outlook is often funereal. Nevertheless, reminding himself that there is an irreconcilable difference between even the highest religion and the secular, rational way of approaching human problems, Hook sees the danger that religious professionals will take advantage of the obscurities of Tillich's language and use it to support the very superstitions which Tillich opposed.

Hook owns that he is tired of arguing and hearing others argue with Tillich about ontology, explaining that to do so is like punching an eiderdown. When he had polemized against Tillich, with his customary mildness to be sure, always Tillich had replied, "I agree with everything you have said," and embraced him as a fellow seeker of the Grail. To an outsider, however, it seems possible that Tillich may have grown tired. Anyway, it is hard to believe that he could have given assent when Hook argued, as he does here, that being is nothing but an abstraction. Tillich, he says, sees plainly enough that, just as what all men have in common is not another man, so what all beings have in common is not another being. (This is the metaphysics lying behind his theological talk about God not being *a* being but *being*-itself.) Still, says Hook, Tillich fails to see that any answer we may give to the question "What do different beings have in common?" can never be anything but a universal or essence or definition. Furthermore, this fact is fatal to his concept of being itself as some sort of unconditioned ground of all beings: first, because an essence, no matter how purely conceived, has no ontological standing; and, second, because an essence must be differentiated from other essences, whereas Tillich's being itself is supposed to include all differences.

Unable to accept Tillich's ontology as philosophy, Hook casts a glance at German Romanticism and concludes that the unconditioned transcendent is simply the all-in-all of pantheistic spiritualism. It was typical of the Romantics, he says, to think of our individual egos as part of the Cosmic Ego, from which it is painful to be separated and in which we find peace and security when our egos are reintegrated into the whole.—*J.F.*

ADDITIONAL RECOMMENDED READING

Kelsey, David H. *The Fabric of Paul Tillich's Theology*. New Haven, Connecticut: Yale University Press, 1967. Kelsey explores Tillich's ontological analysis in Chapter 3 as providing the framework within which Christian symbols are meaningful.

McLean, George F., O. M. I. "Paul Tillich's Existential Philosophy of Protestantism," in *Paul Tillich in Catholic Thought*. Edited by Thomas A. O'Meara and Celestin D. Weisser. Dubuque, Iowa: The Priory Press, 1964, pp. 42-84. Critical although not unsympathetic exposition of Tillich's religious philosophy, particularly the polarity between individuality and participation. Part of the Catholic-Protestant dialogue.

Margolis, Joseph. "Existentialism Reclaimed," in *The Personalist*. XLII, no. 1 (Winter, 1961), pp. 14-20. Suggests qualifications which must be made in Tillich's existentialism if it is to qualify as a philosophy.

May, Rollo. *Paulus: Reminiscences of a Friendship*. New York: Harper & Row Publishers, 1973. Tillich was one of May's advisers while he was writing his graduate thesis, later published as *The Meaning of Anxiety*. Tillich told May that *The Courage to Be* was his reply to that book.

Randall, John Herman, Jr., "The Ontology of Paul Tillich," in *The Theology of Paul Tillich*. Edited by Charles W. Kegley and Robert Bretell. New York: Macmillan Publishing Company, 1952, pp. 131-161. An earlier and more technical version of the discussion of topics treated in his Slaughter Lecture.

THE LANGUAGE OF MORALS
and
FREEDOM AND REASON

Author: R. M. Hare (1919-   )
Type of work: Ethics, philosophy of language
First published: 1952 and 1963, respectively

Principal Ideas Advanced

Moral judgments have two kinds of meaning, prescriptive and descriptive.
As prescriptive, moral judgments give directions for action.
As descriptive, moral judgments are universalizable.
Moral principles can specify exceptions for kinds of cases, but not for individual cases.
Moral reasoning proceeds by looking for moral principles which one can honestly accept for all cases to which the principles apply, even when one's own interests are at stake.
Moral reasoning is like applying the golden rule: "Do unto others as you wish that others would do unto you."
Moral conclusions cannot be deduced from nonmoral premises.

R. M. Hare is the Professor of Moral Philosophy at Oxford. In numerous articles and reviews, and in three books, he has developed a theory of moral reasoning which he calls "universal prescriptivism." Two of these books are reviewed here; the third, *Moral Thinking: Its Levels, Method, and Point*, is to be published shortly.

Moral reasoning is reasoning used to arrive at moral judgments. A moral judgment is (with unimportant exceptions that are "moral" only by an equivocation) a kind of value judgment. There are also other kinds of value judgments, such as aesthetic ones. To understand moral reasoning, one must first understand the logical structure of value judgments.

Value judgments, according to Hare, are universal or (when not universal) universalizable prescriptions. Universalizability will be discussed later. We turn first to prescriptivity.

To *prescribe* is basically to give directions for action. By contrast, to *describe* is basically to make a report. If I say "Shut the door," I am telling someone what to do, and this sentence expresses a prescription. If I say "The door is shut," I am making a report, so this sentence expresses a description or descriptive statement. If I say "You are about to shut the door," I am not literally telling anyone to do anything. I am expressing a prediction, and a prediction resembles a report, not a directive. We might say that a prediction is an attempt to report the future. Hare says that such a sentence expresses a descriptive statement. One broad kind of prescription is that expressed by sentences in the imperative mood. Hare calls prescriptions of this kind *commands*. Commands, in Hare's sense, include not only orders such as "Forward march!" but also instructions in cookbooks, such as "Take four eggs. . . ," as well as requests, pieces of advice, exhortations, and so on.

Commands tell someone what to do without implying anything about what other people, to whom the command is not addressed, are to do. Commands are therefore singular (as opposed to universal) prescriptions. To assent (sincerely) to a command that is addressed to oneself is to agree to do what is commanded. By contrast, to assent (sincerely) to a descriptive statement is to agree that the facts are as reported. A command is therefore not the same as any possible descriptive statement. For example, a command is not the same as a report of the speaker's wishes, because assenting to the command is agreeing to act in a certain way, not agreeing to believe that the speaker has certain wishes about how one might act.

According to Hare, value judgments resemble commands in that they give directions for action, but differ in that they are not solely applicable to particular audiences. For example, to judge that a particular apple is a good apple is to recommend that *anyone* who is choosing apples choose that apple or one like it (or, of course, one of some other good kind). To judge that a particular action is right is to propose or require that *anyone* in that kind of circumstance do that kind of action.

Value judgments are therefore prescriptions, although not of the same kind as commands. To agree with Hare about this is to be a *prescriptivist*. By contrast, a *descriptivist* is one who holds that a value judgment is a kind of report. Descriptivists have a hard time explaining what it is that value judgments report. Perhaps they must say that a moral judgment reports a special kind of fact, called a "moral fact," which has a strangely close connection with action, but is strangely distant from observation. According to Hare, descriptivism involves such a fundamental confusion that it makes it impossible to understand how reasons can support moral judgments.

One might wonder at first whether Hare's prescriptivism has the same result. Prescriptivism holds that moral judgments resemble commands in an important way. Commands, however, are neither true nor false; and since validity for arguments is often defined in terms of the possible combinations of truth and falsity among premises and conclusion, it might seem to follow that commands cannot be supported by reasons. If moral judgments resemble commands, one might then suspect that they, too, cannot be supported by reasons.

Hare rejects this conclusion on two counts. First, he asserts that commands can occur as premises and conclusions in valid arguments. "Take all the boxes to the station" and "This is one of the boxes" together entail "Take this to the station." The conclusion and one of the premises are commands, and so are neither true nor false, but this does not upset the entailment.

Second, even though moral judgments resemble commands in being pre-scriptive, and commands are neither true nor false, Hare does *not* say that moral judgments are neither true nor false. (He seems to regard this as a question about whether to adopt an extended sense of "true" and "false"; nor does he seem particularly hostile to the adoption of such an extended sense.) Hare's point here is about prescriptivity, not about truth and falsity. One could, of course, go beyond Hare and maintain that moral judgments are neither true nor false without undermining Hare's account of the way in which reasoning can be used to arrive at moral judgments. Although moral judgments can occur in arguments as premises and as conclusions, we cannot validly deduce a value judgment from descriptive premises alone. Basically, this is because you cannot get more information out of a valid argument in the conclusion than you put into it in the premises. Thus, we cannot argue from facts to values without relying on additional premises that express value judgments.

For example (this example is not Hare's), we cannot deduce "Jones did wrong" from "Jones kicked the baby under the car" without relying on an additional premise such as "One ought not to kick a baby under a car," or on several additional premises including one like "One ought not to cause gross injury." This point is sometimes expressed by saying that you cannot deduce an "ought" from an "is." Hare calls this philosophical claim "Hume's Law," after David Hume. Whether or not Hume himself accepted "Hume's Law" in its most uncompromising form, Hare certainly does. He considers it a truth of fundamental importance for understanding moral reasoning.

What Hume's Law shows is that moral views cannot be justified by what Hare calls "linear inference." (Hare's objection to reliance on linear inference must not be confused with the objection to "linear thinking" which one some-times hears from confused people. Such people object to clarity itself; Hare, on the other hand, is chiefly concerned to clarify.) "Linear inference" is reasoning which moves from premises assumed to be secure to conclusions assumed to depend on them. The alternative to such reasoning is reasoning which says, "This conclusion follows from these premises; the conclusion is unacceptable; therefore at least one of the premises must be rejected." Sci-entists reason in this way; so, too, according to Hare, do thoughtful moralists.

If linear inference were the only procedure available to moral inquirers, then the only way to use reason to support a moral judgment would be to deduce it from some more general moral judgment (or value judgment). This in turn would have to rest on a still more general value judgment, and so on to the most general value judgment which one cared to propose. Then the chain would stop, and there would be no way at all of giving rational support to the most general value judgment, on which all the others depended. Be-cause of Hume's Law, the chain of moral reasons could not finally be derived from any claim about the nature of the world.

Fortunately, one is not limited to linear inference. Suppose that you are wondering whether to accept a certain moral principle. You can deduce its logical consequences for various kinds of cases. If some of the consequences are unacceptable to you, you must reject the principle.

The search for moral principles all of whose logical consequences one can accept is, according to Hare, the fundamental procedure of moral reasoning. The most important part of the procedure has not, however, yet been mentioned. Because of universalizability, every moral judgment carries with it (in fact, logically entails) commands addressed to the person making the judgment. For this reason, one cannot rationally accept the judgment without accepting the associated commands also. It is the difficulty of assenting to certain commands about one's own case which chiefly limits the moral views one can rationally accept.

Moral judgments (like all value judgments) are *universalizable*. This means that if I make any value judgment about one case, I am logically committed to making the same kind of judgment about any other case which is precisely similar in its descriptive (nonevaluative) features. If a painting is beautiful, then any other painting which looks exactly like it must be beautiful also. If it is wrong for you to steal from me, then it must also be wrong for me to steal from you, if the cases are precisely similar.

To say that moral judgments are universalizable is therefore to say that they must rest on principles which are universal in form. "Universal" in this context does not mean "universally accepted"; it has nothing to do with whether people accept it. "Universal" means "able to be expressed without the use of proper names (or demonstratives or the like)." A universal principle is one which specifies the cases to which it applies by describing them rather than by singling them out as individuals. It applies to all cases of a specified kind.

If I judge that it is morally right for me to steal from you, I am committed to accepting some universal moral principle about all cases of the same kind. Otherwise, I did not mean what I said when I used the moral term "right." It may require some thought to decide what principle it will be, but whatever it is, it will have to make the same prescription for any two cases which differ only in the identity of the individuals involved. Otherwise, it would not be universal. Therefore, if I judge that in the present case it is right for me to steal from you, I am logically committed to judging that in the hypothetical case in which I am in your position, and have all your descriptive characteristics (including your needs and desires), it would be right for someone to steal from me. If I cannot accept this, I must, in order to be logically consistent, give up the claim that it is right for me to steal from you in the present case.

Moral reasoning is therefore required by its logic to proceed by the reasoner's putting himself/herself imaginatively in the place of the other persons whose interests are involved in the case. Imaginative sympathy is therefore necessary for intelligent moral reasoning. The required procedure is reminiscent of the "golden rule": "Do unto others as you wish that others would do unto you." The logical analysis behind the procedure is reminiscent (although less closely) of Immanuel Kant's "categorical imperative." The result of using the procedure will be to weight everyone's interests as equally important, given that they are equally strong—a view which is typical of utilitarianism. So, Hare's semi-Kantian analysis has led him to become a utilitarian—a result, he has said, which he did not expect when he started his inquiries.

According to Hare, moral language expresses judgments which are universalizable, because moral words (like other evaluative words) have both descriptive and prescriptive meaning. Descriptions, in Hare's account, are inherently universal, so a prescription that is coupled with a description is a prescription that is universalizable to cover all the cases that fit the description. For example, "Jones is courageous" both describes Jones and commends him/ her. The description is, approximately, a report that Jones hardly ever backs down when threatened. The commendation is a prescription; it is, approximately, a recommendation that one try to be like Jones. The word "courageous" expresses the description and the prescription simultaneously, thereby suggesting that whoever fits the description is to get the commendation.

The word "courageous" therefore has a substantive moral judgment built into its meaning. So do many other evaluative words, such as "blasphemous" and "industrious." If we disagree with the judgment, we shall not wish to use the word (seriously and in its currently standard sense). Hare fully understands (it is amazing but true that he has philosophical opponents who seem not to understand) that the mere presence in our language of a word which has a certain moral judgment built into it does not require us to agree with the judgment. The question of whether the cases that fit the description are to be prescribed for in that way has to be answered independently of the question of whether we have in our language a word which presumes so.

If we wish to do moral reasoning without assuming in advance that we shall wish to accept those moral judgments which happen to be incorporated into the current meanings of our words, we need a different kind of evaluative word. Such a word would have a fixed prescriptive meaning, and it would be part of the meaning-rule for using the word that it have some descriptive meaning or other on every occasion of its use, but *what* descriptive meaning it has would be variable without limit. Such words are "good," "bad," "right," and "wrong." A related account applies to "ought." Hare calls such words "primarily evaluative words." He calls words such as "courageous," which are used evaluatively but whose descriptive meaning is (relatively) fixed, "secondarily evaluative words."

On Hare's account of "good," if someone says "Jones is a good man," the prescriptive meaning has to be commendatory, but the descriptive meaning could be anything. Hare maintains, however, that it would be a mistake to say that "good" had *no* descriptive meaning when used in this way, because we can ask, "What do you mean, 'good'?" and get back a descriptive answer. Depending on the speaker's principles, the answer might be "I mean that he does what he's told," or "I mean that he makes up his own mind what to do," or any other description at all. When making up our minds what moral principles to adopt, we need to use the primarily evaluative words, because they are flexible in this way. (This does not mean that the principles themselves will be flexible; it means that they will not be deduced from the meanings of words.)

By this account, to think morally is inevitably to prescribe universally. In our ordinary moral thinking, however, we go beyond universalizability and say that cases must be judged alike even if they are not precisely similar, so long as they are similar in all morally relevant respects. To go beyond universalizability in this way is to *generalize* our moral judgments, extending a judgment about one case to other somewhat similar cases even though the descriptive similarity is not complete. It is useful to do this, because then we can use our principles to guide our decisions about new cases. Any two actual cases will differ in some descriptive features, and if we did not generalize our principles at all, then each one would apply to at most one actual case in our lifetimes. On the other hand, we must not generalize too far, since this would commit us to making moral judgments (and therefore to doing certain actions in hypothetical cases) which we would not really be prepared to accept if we thought about it. For such cases, we make our principles more specific; that is, we discern a morally relevant difference.

The need to balance, in our moral thinking, the convenience of generality (or of simplicity) against the need to say only what we can seriously mean, explains in a striking way both the importance of tradition in morality, and the importance of sometimes rethinking and changing our principles (for example, when circumstances change). Hare's discussion of this topic (*The Language of Morals*, Chapter 4) is most illuminating.

To generalize in ethics is, then, to leave out, as irrelevant, from the moral principle which one applies to a situation some of the descriptive features of that situation. To decide which features to leave out is virtually to decide what principle to adopt. The features that are mentioned in the principle one adopts are the ones one has decided to count as morally relevant; in fact, this is what "morally relevant" means. The specification of which features count as morally relevant cannot be part of the logical analysis of moral language, because this would be to smuggle bits of one's substantive moral views into one's pretended logical analysis. It has to be decided in the course of the substantive inquiry.

Although Hare does not put details of his substantive moral views into his theory of moral reasoning, there is a certain general outlook which may possibly be said to be implicit in the theory. This outlook is personally austere, socially tolerant, very ready to acknowledge duties to others, and very ready to make decisions and take responsibilities on oneself. It is individualistic, but not self-indulgent. It is, in one traditional sense of the word, a *liberal* outlook. Hare's critics sometimes say he has built such liberalism into his theory. Perhaps Hare would reply that the theory is required by the logical structure of moral judgments, and that liberalism is indeed a likely consequence of understanding that structure.

Hare's theory is challenged at every point by contemporary critics. His response is often to extend and deepen the theory, and sometimes to make corrections in it, but seldom if ever to shift his ground. Like Socrates in Plato's *Gorgias*, Hare goes on saying the same things. Perhaps he is entitled to his tenacity, since his theory, unlike its contemporary rivals, has very great scope and power.—*J. C.*

Pertinent Literature

MacIntyre, Alasdair. *Against the Self-Images of the Age: Essays on Ideology and Philosophy*. New York: Schocken Books, 1971.

This collection of essays by Alasdair MacIntyre contains several which criticize R. M. Hare's theory. Chapter 12, "What Morality Is Not," is a well-known paper which first appeared in *Philosophy* in 1957 and which is also reprinted in G. Wallace and A. D. M. Walker, eds., *The Definition of Morality* (London: Methuen, 1970).

MacIntyre argues that Hare's analysis of moral language builds into it several features which are characteristic not of all moral thinking but only of some. For example, Hare says that all moral judgments are universalizable. According to MacIntyre, it is true that we frequently make moral judgments of this kind; such judgments are the ones that rely on maxims (universal moral principles) applying the same judgment to a whole class of relevantly similar cases. However, sometimes we resolve a moral problem created by conflicts among maxims by making a moral decision about the particular case, without intending it to apply to other situations of the same kind. We commit ourselves, but refrain from prescribing for others (or even, it may be, for ourselves in future cases).

According to MacIntyre, to resolve moral conflicts in this particular way is not to rely on maxims, but to pay attention to details (including "phenomenological," that is, introspective, details) of the particular case. This, he says, is why existentialist philosophers such as Jean-Paul Sartre, who are interested in such cases, must use novels rather than logical analyses to "present their insights."

Hare has replied that regardless of how we approach actual cases, the situations presented in novels can be known to us *only* by their descriptions.

Therefore any moral claim which is capable of being conveyed in a novel is absolutely guaranteed to be universal in form. It may be about a very specific kind of case, but a specific kind is still a kind, not an individual. MacIntyre adds that Hare's claim that moral judgments must always be universalizable expresses a bias in favor of treating different people (oneself and others) as equals. It builds into the logical analysis of moral judgments the "liberal" requirement that one not make an exception in one's own favor.

Another "liberal" bias which MacIntyre discerns in Hare's analysis is connected with Hare's separation of fact and value. To say, as Hare does, that descriptive facts do not in themselves have moral implications is, MacIntyre remarks, to imply that we get our moral views by deciding on them rather than by discovering them. In effect, then, Hare has boldly made individual autonomy a defining feature of moral thinking.

Another argument of MacIntyre appears to go like this. In some historical periods, it does not occur to people to challenge the moral rules adopted by, or the human goods acknowledged by, their society. In other, later periods, because of conflicting rules or alternative goods, it occurs to them. Prescriptivism is, therefore, a correct analysis of *part* of the thinking of the *later* periods (provided it is a "reformed" prescriptivism which does not construe as intelligible every possible moral principle but only those among which people are forced to choose). On the other hand, for the earlier periods, and for most of the moral thinking of the later ones, various naturalist analyses (analyses which hold that value judgments are implicit in descriptions) are correct, and prescriptivism is incorrect. It is incorrect because it counts more views as logically coherent than are conceivable to the people whose thinking is being analyzed. One may well reply on Hare's behalf that a philosophical analysis should avoid giving to people's lack of imagination the status of logical necessity.

Foot, Philippa. *Virtues and Vices and Other Essays in Moral Philosophy*. Berkeley: University of California Press, 1978.

This convenient collection of essays by a leading moral philosopher, Philippa Foot, contains several which are important as criticisms of R. M. Hare's views. Chapter 7 is her article "Moral Arguments," first published in *Mind*, Volume LXVII (1958). Chapter 8 is "Moral Beliefs," first published in *Proceedings of the Aristotelian Society*, Volume LIX (1958-1959). Chapter 9 is "Goodness and Choice," first published in *Aristotelian Society Supplementary Volume* XXXV (1961).

Foot argues, against Hare, that moral inquirers are not in principle free to select any descriptive characteristic they like as morally relevant. It is laid down for us independently of our choices, by the logic of moral thinking, that certain things can count as evidence for the rightness or wrongness of an action, and that other things cannot. Moral views which purport to base a moral judgment on an ineligible principle are logically incoherent. For example, it is logically incoherent, according to Foot, for anyone to judge that someone is a good man because he clasps and unclasps his hands and never turns north-northeast after turning south-southwest. At least, it is logically incoherent until some further background is given which explains why this behavior matters in this case. If it seems conceivable that some moral eccentric might actually make this judgment, that is probably because a special background linking this behavior with ordinary human interests has been surreptitiously assumed.

Hare has replied that Foot's analysis confuses our great *surprise* that anyone should make such a judgment with *inability to understand* it. (Whatever is logically incoherent is unintelligible, but we have no trouble in understanding these views which Foot alleges to be incoherent.) One can go further than this reply. Not only would one *understand* judgments such as these; one actually *hears* them. For example, one has heard judgments like "Jones is a good man because his hair is cut short," supported by principles like "One ought to try to look like everyone else."

Since this is a real case, there is inevitably a background; that is, a collection of surrounding facts and causes. Not just any background, however, will give support to Foot's theory. What is required is that the surprising judgment be shown to bear a reasonable relationship to ordinary human needs, given the special facts of the case. But there is no reason to suppose that the background will show this, in this case.

Turning to imaginary cases, this reviewer finds it easy to imagine a religious movement that inculcates hand-clasping as virtuous, without alleging any reason for its being so; neither that it conduces to health, nor that it helps to avoid divine wrath, nor any other reason at all. Some people would not willingly join such a movement, but others would.

Foot's positive suggestion about what is required in order for moral judgments to be logically coherent is that they must be connected with human good or harm, which in turn must be conceived in certain specific ways. That this suggestion is a mistake can be seen immediately from the fact that it excludes from the sphere of morality the classic objections to vivisection, which are based on nonhuman interests. Of course one can easily see how to correct the analysis to take care of this particular objection: just remove the word "human." But how did that word get in there in the first place, if not by a general confusion of logical with substantive requirements?

Taylor, C. C. W. Review of R. M. Hare's *Freedom and Reason*, in *Mind*. LXXIV, no. 294 (April, 1965), pp. 280-289.

According to R. M. Hare's theory, a moral reasoner, in deciding whether a proposed action is right or wrong, must (if investigating the question down to the bottom) put himself/herself imaginatively in the place of each other person whose interests are affected. This is because moral judgments are universalizable. To judge that an action is right is to commit oneself logically to judging that any other precisely similar action would be right also. It requires that one accept the principle (universal prescription) that in all cases having the same complete description as the present case, an action of the same kind would be right.

The description of each of the persons involved is part of the description of the case. However, the identity of the individuals is not part of their description. (The difference between describing and identifying is the difference between what is universal and what is singular.) Therefore, in order to prescribe universally, one must prescribe the same way for the present actual case and the hypothetical case in which one has changed places with someone else concerned. ("Turnabout is fair play.") The exchange must be an exchange of all descriptive features; so, one must imagine oneself not only as being in the other person's circumstances, but also as having the other person's interests and desires.

Hare uses the critical scrutiny of racist principles as an example. Suppose I, being white, take the view that blacks should have fewer political rights than whites. Is this view morally acceptable? To decide this, I find out whether I can universalize it. If I can accept it as applying even to the hypothetical case in which I am black, then I have accepted it universally. In fact, I cannot sincerely accept it for that case. Therefore, I cannot without logical inconsistency adopt it as my moral view, since the moral words have it as part of their meaning that moral judgments are universalizable. Hare suggests that by following this strategy an inquirer will be forced to abandon all racist principles whatever.

Hare's procedure for thinking moral problems through to the bottom makes great demands on the moral imagination. (Therefore, we must not always try to do this. Much of the time, we must rely on our existing moral assumptions.) However, it cannot, if Hare's theory is to be correct, demand that we imagine something that is logically impossible.

In one part of his review, C. C. W. Taylor argues that Hare's theory does just that. In the case which I am asked to imagine, I have cultural and physical characteristics which differ pervasively from my present ones, and I am in different circumstances, and I have different needs and desires and ideals. Taylor suggests that in that case I would no longer be the same person that I now am. So, according to Taylor, I cannot prescribe what should be done by or to myself in that hypothetical case, because I (who am doing the prescribing) am not *in* that case (am not identical with anyone in the imaginary case).

It may perhaps be thought that there are unresolved puzzles somewhere in Hare's use of the logical property of universalizability to require us to sympathize with our neighbor. The particular puzzle noted here, however, has in Hare's view been cleared up by Zeno Vendler in his article, "A Note to the Paralogisms," published in Gilbert Ryle, ed., *Contemporary Aspects of Philosophy* (Boston: Oriel Press, 1976). Referring his readers to Vendler for details, Hare meets Taylor's challenge head on and maintains that there is no absurdity in my imagining, and prescribing for, a case in which I have radically different characteristics from my present ones.—*J.C.*

ADDITIONAL RECOMMENDED READING

Hudson, W. D. "Prescriptivism," in *Modern Moral Philosophy*. Garden City, New York: Anchor Books, 1970. An extensive critical discussion of Hare's theory and its relation to other issues in contemporary philosophy.

_____ . "A Rationalist Kind of Non-descriptivism," in *A Century of Moral Philosophy*. New York, St. Martin's Press, 1980. The best brief critical summary.

Kerner, George C. "R. M. Hare," in *The Revolution in Ethical Theory*. Oxford: Oxford University Press, 1966. An outline explanation and criticism of Hare's theory, emphasizing *The Language of Morals* more than *Freedom and Reason*.

Mortimore, Geoffrey, ed. "Hare's Paradox," in *Weakness of Will*. New York: St. Martin's Press, 1971. A group of articles by different authors on difficulties in the prescriptivist claim that there is a close logical connection between assenting to a moral judgment and acting on it.

Rowson, Richard. "Richard M. Hare," in *Moral Philosophy*. Milton Keynes, England: Open University Press, 1973. An introductory workbook for beginners designed to be used in conjunction with *The Language of Morals* and *Freedom and Reason*. In some libraries, this book is not catalogued under "Rowson" but under "Open University. Problems of Philosophy Course Team."

Warnock, G. J. "Prescriptivism," in *Contemporary Moral Philosophy*. Section IV. New York: St. Martin's Press, 1967. An unfriendly interpretive summary relating Hare's theory to other stages in the history of ethics in the twentieth century.

PHILOSOPHY AND PSYCHO-ANALYSIS

Author: John Wisdom (1904-   )
Type of work: Philosophy of philosophy
First published: 1953

PRINCIPAL IDEAS ADVANCED

Philosophical questions are verbal in the sense that they turn upon unconventional uses of language; but they are not merely verbal, for, in virtue of their oddity, in the process of justifying their use, one's attention is called to matters obscured by conventional language.

Metaphysical paradoxes and platitudes function as penetrating suggestions as to how language might be used to reveal what is hidden by the actual use of language.

In philosophical analysis penumbral facts (matters to which certain conventional sentences call attention) are compared to nonpenumbral facts (matters to which the penumbral are presumably reducible) in order to determine whether the switch from one kind of statement to another is advisable and illuminating.

The goal of philosophy is the clarification of the structure of facts.

Philosophers do not uncover new facts, but they show us old facts in a new way.

The title of this book is somewhat misleading. Only two of the fifteen essays are concerned with psychoanalysis. Even these two do not face squarely the question as to the sense, if any, in which the perplexities which the ordinary man experiences when he wonders about the universe and is led to the philosopher for help are like the perplexities which the psychotic and the neurotic experience when they develop conflicts and are directed to the psychoanalyst for treatment. The author does show that there are certain similarities between the approach of the metaphysician and the approach of the psychoanalyst, but he also shows that there are similarities between the approach of the metaphysician and that of the lawyer, or the mathematician, the logician, the scientist, the art critic, or even that of the novelist. Thus his design is really to clarify the term "metaphysics." He suggests in one place that his task is one of "meta-metaphysics," that is, one of determining the status of metaphysical problems and metaphysical judgments. The essays are united only in their common concern with this problem. They extend in time of publication from 1932 to 1953 and are arranged, roughly, in chronological order. Several are critical book reviews. Only one, the last, is not indicated as having been previously published.

The importance of the book lies in the fact that it clarifies the position of the author in relation to the current attempts to define philosophy as some form of linguistic analysis. Though Wisdom was strongly influenced by the late Ludwig Wittgenstein, he does not believe, as Wittgenstein and many of the logical positivists did, that metaphysics is nonsense of some sort which becomes evident when its statements are properly analyzed; nor does he believe that metaphysical statements are *merely* linguistic and that all difficulties can be eliminated by substituting clear words for vague ones and precise grammatical constructions for ambiguous ones; nor does he follow the Oxford School in stressing either the *language* of man in the street or his *beliefs* on certain philosophical matters as the final court of appeal for settling all philosophical disputes. He examines these views, as well as others which associate philosophical problems with their mode of expression and endeavors to state his own view in contrast to them.

Let us begin by taking some typical philosophical problems: "Can we really know what is going on in someone else's mind?" "Can we really know the causes of our sensations?" "What is a chair?" These are the kinds of questions philosophers ask, and we must attempt to determine what they are seeking when they ask them, and what they mean when they reply, "We can never really know what is going on in someone else's mind," "A chair is nothing but our sensations," or, "A chair is something over and above our sensations."

In a sense, Wisdom says, philosophy gives rise to verbal disputes. To state that we cannot know what is going on in someone else's mind is to utter something which is obviously untrue unless we adopt an unusual meaning for the word "know." Thus we might say that one who makes a statement of this kind is uttering nonsense. Or suppose a philosopher asks whether two plus three can ever equal six? Again the question becomes nonsense unless we adopt unconventional meanings for some of the words which it contains. But the fact that both statements are nonsensical does not mean that they are nonsensical in the same way. And in order to determine how they differ in their portrayal of nonsense we should have to make a study which would be at least partially verbal. Thus, philosophical clarification is achieved through an examination of language. Similarly, if a philosopher says that a chair is something over and above our sensations he is not proposing a new definition of "chair," nor a new use for chairs, but he is suggesting the need for a clarification of the meaning of a word. Hence, philosophical questions and answers seem to be verbal.

But although the philosopher's statements are formulated *in* words, his intention is not to raise verbal issues; he is not taking over the role of the translator. A translator substitutes a sentence S for a sentence S', for the purpose of telling us the meaning of S'. The philosopher does not wish merely to substitute one statement of a fact for another; he wishes to transmit insight—insight into the structure of the fact which is asserted by S'. He equates S with S' because he believes that S better indicates the structure of a certain fact than does S'. This is not a verbal matter.

The nature of philosophical statements can be further clarified by distinguishing their *content* from their *point*. Suppose we have a philosophical statement containing the word "monarchy." Now anybody who knows that "monarchy" means the same as "set of persons ruled by the same king," and who also knows the meaning of *either* of these expressions, will find that the philosophical statement becomes clarified if one is substituted for the other. But this involves merely clarification in *content* and is the concern of the decoder rather than of the philosopher. The philosopher achieves his clarification (the *point* of his utterance) only if his hearer already uses and understands the meaning of *both* "monarchy" and "set of persons ruled by the same king." Philosophical statements thus appear to be very curious; they provide information only if the hearer already knows what is to be told him. Philosophy is trying to show the "structure" of a monarchy by bringing together the sphere in which "monarchy" is used, and the sphere in which "set of persons ruled by the same king" is used. These are different categories, and the philosophical problem is that of showing by means of the structure of the statement how these are related. Wisdom suggests a certain mnemonic device: "It's not the stuff, it's the style that stupifies." It is not *what* the philosopher talks about that makes him unique, but the *form* in which he expresses himself. Wisdom apologizes for a suspicion of smartness when he says, "Philosophers should be continually trying to say what cannot be said."

What is really involved in this disclosure of "structure" can be understood only by an examination of what Wisdom means by *analysis* as the method of all philosophy. But since his use of this word is somewhat technical, the way may be prepared by an examination of the conception of the world which, according to Wisdom, is held by all metaphysicians. They believe, in his words, "that the actual world is made up solely of positive, specific, determinate, concrete, contingent, individual, sensory facts." But they also believe in an apparent "penumbra of fictional, negative, general, indeterminate, abstract, necessary, super-individual, physical facts." This penumbra is only apparent because we have not penetrated deeply enough. Now philosophers feel that there are not two ways of knowing—one for the nonpenumbral facts and another for the penumbral. Yet they also feel that since the nonpenumbral and the penumbral are not identical, there *must* be two ways of knowing. This produces philosophical perplexity.

Let us take some examples. "The height of the average man is simply the sum of the heights of the individual men divided by their number." "A chair is simply a collection of sense-data." "A person's mind is nothing more than his behavior." "The State is something over and above the individuals who make it up." "The statement 'Not three people are interested in mathematical logic' may be expressed in the form: 'If x is interested in mathematical logic, and also y is interested, and also z is interested, then x is identical with y, or y is identical with z, or x is identical with z.'" "'All men are mortal' can be reduced to 'John is mortal, and George is mortal, and James is mortal, and so on.'" "*Time* means (G. E. Moore) that lunch is over, supper to come, that Smith's anger is past, and so on." "Analytic propositions are merely verbal propositions."

In all of these examples what is given first may be designated as the penumbral fact, and what is given second as the nonpenumbral fact. Then average men, physical objects, minds, States, numerical statements, general statements, time, and analytic propositions are all penumbral. And actual men, sense-data, behavior, individual citizens, identity of *x*'s and *y*'s, John and George being mortal, supper following lunch, and verbal propositions are nonpenumbral. Call the former "X facts," and the latter "Y facts." Then the question becomes simply this: Are X facts ultimate or are they reducible to Y facts? If they are reducible, are they *completely* reducible, that is, are X facts *equivalent to* Y facts? If they are not completely reducible, are X facts something *over and above* Y facts?

Wisdom believes that it is misleading to formulate the problem in terms of *facts*, for it suggests that the issue can be decided simply by examining the world, either the logical world or the natural world. This is not the case. The question should therefore be expressed in terms of propositions or sentences: Do X sentences stand for the same proposition as any combination of Y sentences? Are X sentences used in the same way as some combination of Y sentences? When we have an X sentence can we find a Y sentence which serves the same purpose?

This approach suggests that we examine the sentences to see under what circumstances we would be inclined to answer the question, "Yes," and under what circumstances, "No." There is no right or wrong answer to these questions. But dispute can be resolved by explaining what induces each disputant to claim what he does. Thus, statements which are metaphysical paradoxes, and statements which are metaphysical platitudes are revealed to be not simply false statements and true statements, but penetrating suggestions as to how language *might be used* to reveal what is completely hidden by its *actual use.* "Thus it appears how it is that, to give metaphysicians what they want, we have to do little more than remove the spectacles through which they look at their own work. Then they see how those hidden identities and diversities which lead to the 'insoluble' reduction questions about forms, categories and predicates, have already been revealed, though in a hidden way."

We are now ready to turn to an examination of what Wisdom means by *analysis*. A distinction must first be made between *material* analysis and *philosophical* analysis. To give a material analysis is simply to give a definition: "*Wealth* is defined as *what is useful, transferable, and limited in supply.*" A definition of *wealth* as *riches* would not be materially analytic, for it does nothing to render explicit the connotation of the word defined. But a philosophical analysis is given by a rule for translating sentences about any abstraction ("the State") into sentences about what it is an abstraction from ("the individual citizens"). A second distinction must be made between *formal* analysis and *philosophical* analysis. A formal analysis is the replacement of a sentence by another which more clearly indicates the form of the fact asserted: "'*Two horses passed him*' means '*A horse passed him and then another.*'" This would not be a material analysis for *two* is not an adjective, and it is not a philosophical analysis for it merely exhibits clearly the structure of something whose structure was not clear. The distinction between the three types of analysis can be illustrated by the statement, "Two men are good." A *formal* analysis would be, "A man is good and another man is good"; a *philosophical* analysis would be, "A *mannish* pattern of states contains a high proportion of good ones and another *mannish* pattern does so also"; and a *material* analysis would be, "A *mannish* pattern of states contains a high proportion of states likely to cause approval and another does so also."

Analysis (philosophical analysis) cannot be understood without explaining *ostentation*. Philosophers have always employed ostentation, though because of their preoccupation *with* philosophy they have had little time to *talk about* ostentation. Ostentation is a kind of substitution; we use ostentation on a sentence S' when we substitute for S' another sentence S which more clearly reveals the ultimate structure of the fact they assert. Let us take the sentence, "England invaded France." This has a dyadic structure exhibited by "EIF" where "E" is a term, "I" is a relation, and "F" is another term. But the sentence "EIF" does not exhibit the *ultimate* structure of its fact. In order to show this we should have to formulate sentences about Tom, Dick, and Harry, and about Henri, François, and Jean, and about the former being sent threateningly into land owned by the latter, and so on. We can say that "EIF" *directly* locates a fact of which England is an element; but it *indirectly* locates a fact of which Tom, Dick, and the rest, are elements. The analysis of the sentence "EIF" into sentences about Englishmen and Frenchmen is a philosophical analysis because the predicates which are applicable to England are definable in terms of the predicates which are applicable to Englishmen. They are, of course, different *kinds* of predicates because they are exhibited in different *kinds* of structure. The sentences about Englishmen and Frenchmen become an ostentation of the sentence about England and France; S is an ostentation of S'. When this is the case the facts displayed, though not two, are not identical. Thus the distinction between the penumbral and the non-penumbral facts has been recognized, and the question as to whether the former can be "reduced" to the latter (whether the former are "logical constructions out of" the latter) can be intelligently discussed, pro and con. What is introduced by ostentation is not merely a clearer understanding of the structure of a fact, but an increased clearness in the apprehension of the *ultimate* structure of the fact. We should not say that S is merely a translation of S' but that S displays directly what S' displays indirectly, or that S' displays a fact which is secondary to the fact which S displays. The sentence about Tom, Dick, and the others displays directly what the sentence about England and France displays indirectly, or the fact displayed by the sentence about England and France is secondary to the fact displayed by the sentence about Tom, Dick, and the others. Wisdom concludes the discussion of this topic by stating that the philosopher makes a prayer: "*Please give me clearer apprehension of the Arrangement of the Elements of the Fact finally located by the sentence* 'aRb.'" (In this statement Wisdom uses capital letters to indicate that what the philosopher is seeking is the *ultimate* arrangement of the *ultimate* elements of the *ultimate* fact, not merely the structure which is obviously exhibited by "aRb.")

The question of whether the penumbral can be reduced to the nonpenumbral has divided philosophers into two schools. On the one hand are the naturalists, empiricists, and positivists. They accept the Verification Principle. On the other hand are the realists and the transcendentalists, who accept the Idiosyncrasy Platitude. The former maintain such statements as "A cherry is nothing but sensations and possibilities of more," "A mind is nothing but a pattern of behavior," "There are no such things as numbers, only numerals." The latter argue that every statement has its own sort of meaning, and "everything is what it is and not another thing." Examples can be found in "Ethical propositions involve value predicates and are ultimate," "Mathematical propositions are necessary synthetic propositions—an ultimate sort of proposition," "Statements about nations are not to be reduced to statements about individuals, they are about a certain sort of concrete universal."

Wisdom's contention with regard to both of these principles is that we should examine what we mean when we say that either of them is true. To say this is to suppose that the principles in question can be confirmed or disconfirmed. But this is not the case; neither principle is a scientific theory. The issue should, therefore, be formulated in terms of the question whether we should accept the Verification Principle, or the Idiosyncrasy Platitude. But now what has the issue become? Can we say that the Verification Principle is a metaphysical theory? Yes, says Wisdom, in a certain sense. It is not so much a metaphysical theory as a recipe for framing metaphysical theories; it is a mnemonic device which tells those who accept it how to proceed in settling certain metaphysical issues. It draws their attention to "the deplorably old-fashioned clothes in which it presents itself," since it appears in the disguise either of a scientific discovery which removes a popular illusion or of a logical proposition from which deductions can be made. Furthermore, the principle serves to draw the attention of those who reject it to the fact that underneath its disguise it has obvious merits. The principle, therefore, has the characteristics of all metaphysical statements in that it covers up what it really intends to say. The same is true of the Idiosyncrasy Platitude. Whether either of these is called "metaphysical" is of no great importance; the point is that in examining the reasons for or against accepting one of these principles we are led into the activity which is designed to eliminate metaphysical perplexities, and to arrive at that clarification of structure which is the goal of philosophy.

Finally, Wisdom attempts to show in what sense philosophical difficulties are like psychopathic difficulties. Wittgenstein said that he held no opinions in philosophy but tried to remove "a feeling of puzzlement, to cure a sort of mental cramp" which is associated with philosophical problems. Wisdom gives an example in which an individual wrestles with the problem of whether he can or cannot know what other creatures are thinking about. He points out that such an individual, first skeptical about the minds of other people, is led inevitably into skepticism about his senses, and finally into a skepticism about everything. But this is obviously an absurd position, and he develops a stress which is quite analogous to that of the businessman who is trying to meet his financial obligations and becomes neurotic as a result. In what respects are these stresses alike, and in what respect is the cure which the philosopher might administer to the puzzled thinker like the cure which the psychoanalyst might administer to the neurotic businessman?

Philosophy has never been a purely psychogenic disorder and it is not ordinarily considered to be a therapy. But when philosophers proceed by trying to show us "not new things but old things anew," they are adopting procedures much like those of the psychoanalyst. Philosophical discussion aims to bring out latent opposing forces, and not to teach what is behind closed doors or whether 235 times 6 equals 1410. Philosophy often shows that behind the latent linguistic sources of confusion there are much more deeply hidden nonlinguistic forces, and that a purely linguistic treatment of philosophy cannot therefore be adequate. Philosophy also shows that the nonlinguistic sources are the same as those that trouble us elsewhere in our lives; hence, that the philosophical riddles are the true "riddles of the Sphinx."

Philosophy is concerned with what is paradoxical and unconventional. Such matters are not to be settled by experiment and observation. Many philosophers have said that questions which cannot be settled by experiment and observation are questions merely of words. In saying this they are speaking wildly. But so are those "scientists, philosophers, or poets who say one cannot stir a flower without troubling of a star. What they say is mad but there's method in it."—*A.C.B.*

PERTINENT LITERATURE

Bambrough, Renford. "Principia Metaphysica," in *Philosophy*. XXXIX, no. 148 (April, 1964), pp. 97-109.

Between 1931 and 1933, John Wisdom, then a young Cambridge philosopher, published a series of five papers entitled "Logical Constructions." In these papers he produced a complete development of the ideas and practice of philosophy as *analysis*, a conception of philosophy, derived from George Edward Moore and Bertrand Russell, which dominated philosophy (much more so in England than elsewhere) especially in the 1920's and 1930's. With these papers Wisdom became the foremost philosophical analyst. (The first two papers in *Philosophy and Psycho-Analysis* are specimens of this period of his thought.) Meanwhile, Ludwig Wittgenstein, the most famous name in philosophy in the 1920's, had returned to Cambridge to teach in 1930. In approximately 1933 (at about the time when Wisdom was finishing his logical construction papers), Wittgenstein's philosophical ideas and practice underwent that radical change which produced "the later philosophy of Wittgenstein." It was that change which decisively influenced Wisdom. As a younger colleague of Wittgenstein, those new ideas were available to him; as someone who had gone as far along the road of analysis as anyone could, Wisdom was in a unique position to appreciate instantly the value of Wittgenstein's new ideas and their relevance to the work he had just finished doing. Wisdom's own radical change in philosophical outlook began with that. In terms of published work it begins with "Philosophical Perplexity" (1936), and the development of this new conception of philosophy runs through the remainder of the essays in *Philosophy and Psycho-Analysis*. (Notice the footnotes in both "Philosophical Perplexity" and in "Metaphysics and Verification" mentioning the existence and nature of his debt to the new work of Wittgenstein.)

In "Principia Metaphysica," Renford Bambrough presents a theory (consisting of twenty-one interconnected theses) about the nature of metaphysics which he claims to find in both the later Wittgenstein and the later Wisdom. It would be much easier to prove that the entire theory is to be found in Wisdom than to prove it is in Wittgenstein. For that reason Bambrough's account is here treated as an important and clearly rendered exposition of Wisdom's later thought. (For another somewhat different account, see the essay by D. A. T. Gasking included in the Bambrough book mentioned in the bibliography following these essays.)

The theory in question is not about metaphysics as distinct from, say, aesthetics, both considered as "sub-areas" of philosophy. Rather, it is a theory about the nature of philosophy. It is a philosophy of philosophy. The central thesis is that metaphysics (philosophy) is an inquiry into the ultimate ways in which propositions are to be justified: it is an investigation into the nature of reasons. To illustrate this, consider the following questions: What is the ultimate justification for claiming that there is a cherry over there? In what way, if any, is "John sees a cherry there" a reason for saying "There is a cherry over there"? What is the nature of reasoning that goes from "John sees a cherry" to "There is a cherry"? According to the theory, all significant issues in philosophy, no matter what the subject matter, turn out to be that kind of problem. Further, the chief philosophical positions (Transcendentalism, Reductionism, Skepticism) are types of answers to that kind of question.

The theory, as Bambrough describes it, does more than just say that philosophy is a study of the nature of reasons. The theory itself includes a substantive view about reasons and reasoning, especially about reasons in metaphysics. The view is that human reasoning is ultimately not deductive— and ultimately not inductive either. (See especially theses 1, 2, 9, 12, and 20.) At bottom, reasoning is concerned with particular cases, and general statements are only ways of bringing some particular cases to bear on other particular cases.

Lazerowitz, Morris. "The Nature of Metaphysics," in his *The Structure of Metaphysics*. London: Routledge & Kegan Paul, 1955.

John Wisdom's work has strangely received little attention from those whose philosophical views and practices are the objects of his criticisms. Several reasons might be offered for this absence of attention of potential critics. For example, it might be held that Wisdom's style of philosophizing is so much different from prevailing modes of philosophical thinking and writing that outsiders, traditionalists, are not able to see how his work has a bearing on their own styles and views. Whatever the explanation for the unwillingness of those who do not take to his ideas to become serious critics of his work, one consequence of the fact that there exists no body of serious criticism is inescapable: if one wants to examine writings dealing with Wisdom's thought, one must look at what his students have had to say, both in exposition and in furtherance of his thinking.

Of a number of themes arising from Wisdom's writing and teaching, one is concerned with connecting philosophy with psychoanalysis. The book *Philosophy and Psycho-Analysis* is misleadingly titled since that connection is by no means the central object of the various papers collected in it. Yet it is one such topic. It arises for Wisdom in the following way. Wisdom's interest is in the philosophy of philosophy, and one of his techniques for revealing something of the nature of philosophy is to explore how philosophy is like and also how it is unlike other disciplines: science, logic, law, poetry—and also psychoanalysis. This topic is worth pursuing, precisely because it may have something to do with the fact that critics of Wisdom have not appeared. It is one of Wisdom's students, Morris Lazerowitz, who has carried the discussion of this topic the farthest. Although his work has been carried out in a number of papers and books over some years, perhaps the proper starting place is with "The Nature of Metaphysics." (It will not be possible here to bring out how his account relates to Wisdom's own employment of the ideas.)

There are two broad ways of seeing philosophy as like psychoanalysis: one might think of the philosopher as the therapist or as the patient. Lazerowitz shows little interest in the first line of thought; he treats philosophers and their theories as patients while he performs as the analyst. The need for such a practice is determined by his belief that a metaphysical (philosophical) dispute is never settled. No one position on any given philosophical issue is ever accepted by all philosophers as the right one (as happens in science). Lazerowitz's project consists in his attempt to *explain* why philosophical disputes are never resolved, why there is no body of accepted truth in philosophy.

He rejects out of hand the explanations that philosophers are incompetent and (more plausible) that the problems are enormously difficult. The only plausible explanation is that disputes are not settled because they are not *resolvable*; we do not find one to be true because philosophical views are neither true nor false. But what can a theory be if it is undecidable, yet capable of protracted thought and argument? Lazerowitz examines and rejects the four major interpretations of the nature of philosophical views (that they are high-level empirical theories, that they are *a priori* theses, that they are concealed linguistic claims, and that they are nonsense). None will do, for all (even the last) presuppose that philosophical problems can be settled.

His own account of philosophical views is that they have three layers. There is first a rationalized surface, which conceals a hidden linguistic change, which in turn is produced by an unconscious desire to talk in that new way.

Dilman, İlham. "Wisdom's Philosophy of Religion: Part I: Religion and Reason; Part II: Metaphysical and Religious Transcendence," in *Canadian Journal of Philosophy*. V, no. 4 (December, 1975), pp. 473-495 and 497-521.

Although most of John Wisdom's work has been concerned with the philosophy of philosophy and with elucidating basic patterns of reasoning, his eye has been attracted to other issues of philosophical substance. Some of these arise in the course of illustrating his theses about the nature of philosophy and reasoning. Others, however, get much more extended treatment. While the problem of other minds is the one which has drawn his most intense interest (see his collection of essays *Other Minds*), he has also recurrently considered questions about the nature of religious belief. In fact, the best-known essay in *Philosophy and Psycho-Analysis* is "Gods" (1944). İlham Dilman discusses Wisdom's philosophy of religion as a friendly critic: he takes Wisdom's work on the topic to be very important and on the whole importantly correct. Nevertheless, it is not wholly correct, and the areas of falsity are significant.

Throughout his philosophical work Wisdom has opposed all the standard, historically recurrent positions on philosophical questions—Transcendentalism, Reductionism, and Skepticism. Transcendentalism is the idea that philosophically significant notions—for example, the notion of another mind, or of a material object—are notions of objects which exist above and outside human experience, and which are thus knowable only by an inference (be it deductive or inductive) from what we do experience—namely, behavior, appearances. Wisdom regards the belief that (the Christian) God is a transcendent being existing outside this world as another instance of philosophical Transcendentalism. As a consequence, Wisdom does with "God talk" what he does with talk about other minds and material objects: he tries to show how it is a certain kind of talk about this world. On the one hand, Dilman agrees that (the Christian) God is not to be conceived of as an entity, knowable only by inference; that conception of religious language is seriously impoverished. On the other hand, he holds that (Christian) talk of God as transcendent *must* be intelligible (although it is a further question whether it is true) since it has functioned in a pattern of life for centuries. Dilman thus concludes that Wisdom must have erred in taking the believer's or theologian's idea that the deity is transcendent to be just another instance of Transcendentalism, to be simply a philosophical theory. Dilman then has to work out what the real point of the claim that God is transcendent is. Since the claim does not refer to a being outside this world, Dilman interprets it as a claim about this world.

That line leads on to the other half of Wisdom's philosophy of religion. Wisdom defends religious language against positivists who hold that it is either literal nonsense or else is nothing but an expression of a commitment to a way of life; in either case religious beliefs could be neither true nor false, nor even rationally defensible. A large part of Wisdom's writings on religion are an elucidation of the pattern of reasoning to be found in religious disputes. (That pattern is one which Wisdom holds to be central to all metaphysical problems.) With all the facts known, one person will see things one way, another person will see them differently, and the reasoning involves bringing out those features of the situation which incline one person one way and others, the other.

Dilman agrees that that is the form of religious rationality, but he holds that there is a flaw in Wisdom's account. The religious case is not analogous to the one in which we come to see that Alice is lovable; rather it is like the case where we see something new about love itself.—*M.R.*

ADDITIONAL RECOMMENDED READING

Bambrough, Renford, ed. *Wisdom: Twelve Essays*. Totowa, New Jersey: Rowman and Littlefield, 1974. The only collection of essays about Wisdom; includes a list of his published writings.

Dilman, İlham. *Induction and Deduction*. New York: Harper & Row Publishers, 1973. Although technically a study of topics in Wittgenstein, this book has been influenced by Wisdom and discusses several themes central to his work.

Lazerowitz, Morris. *Studies in Metaphilosophy*. New York: Humanities Press, 1964. A continuation of the investigations discussed above.

PHILOSOPHICAL INVESTIGATIONS

Author: Ludwig Wittgenstein (1889-1951)
Type of work: Philosophy of philosophy, philosophy of language
First published: 1953

PRINCIPAL IDEAS ADVANCED
Language is best conceived as an activity involving the uses of words as tools.

Words are used in a multiplicity of ways and are to be understood by engaging in the language "games" in which they are employed; words are not labels for things.

For a large number of cases in which the word "meaning" is used, the meaning of a word is its use in the language.

Discourse about sensations is understandable because there is a grammar of the word "sensations," and of such words as "pain" and "remember," which can be grasped by anyone acquainted with the relevant language games; no reference to what one has in mind or feels privately makes sense unless it makes sense in this way.

Expecting, intending, remembering—these are ways of life made possible by the use of language; and language is itself a way of life.

Philosophical Investigations, published posthumously, contains in Part I a body of work completed by Wittgenstein by 1945. This material includes a preface in which he comments on the book, characterizing it as an "album" of "sketches of landscapes," in virtue of its being a collection of philosophical remarks by the use of which Wittgenstein attacked the problems with which he concerned himself. Parts II and III, written between 1947 and 1949, were added by the editors, G. E. M. Anscombe (who translated the work from the German), and R. Rhees. The German and English versions appear side by side.

Although the work has been in translation only a few years, discussion of its contents preceded the publication of the work because of the appearance of the "Blue Book" and the "Brown Book," collections of typescripts and notes based on Wittgenstein's lectures at Cambridge. In part, the author's interest in the publication of the work during his lifetime came from a reluctance to rest his reputation on second-hand reports of his philosophical remarks.

An aura of mystery, then, surrounded *Philosophical Investigations* when it finally appeared—and something of the aura yet remains as arguments having to do with the interpretation of the sense and direction of Wittgenstein's remarks tend to condition the understanding of the book. Nevertheless, there is little argument about the central theme; in spite of Wittgenstein's erratic and peripatetic method, the purpose of his remarks manages to become clear.

The point of the book appears to be that language is best conceived as an activity involving the uses of words as tools. There is a multiplicity of uses to which words can be put. To understand the meaning of an utterance is to understand the use to which it is put. Consequently, it is misleading and confusing to think of language as being made up of words which stand for objects. Understanding the uses of words is like understanding the rules of games, and just as confusion results when a player in a game makes up new rules as he goes along, or misapplies the rules, or conceives of the game in some static fashion—so it causes confusion and perplexity when a user of language creates new rules, violates old ones, or misconceives language. To be clear about language, one must look to its uses.

But if all that Wittgenstein meant to do with his remarks were to say this, he could have done the job with a great deal less effort and at considerably less length. The *Investigations* is not so much a report of the results of Wittgenstein's philosophical investigations, as it is itself an investigation *in progress*—and what it deals with and exhibits are philosophical investigations. In other words, Wittgenstein's remarks are used to show that certain philosophical problems arise because language is misconceived; and because of the author's adroit uses of language we are lead to conceive of language as instrumental. In a sense, then, the book *is* what it is *about*; its process, as a proof, is its evidence.

What is it to investigate *philosophically?* Wittgenstein's answer is: It is *not* to seek theses or theories, and it is *not* to find static meanings (objects) for which words are permanent labels; it is, rather, to understand by attending to the uses of language relevant to the problem at hand in order to discover how philosophical problems arise "when language *goes on holiday*"—that is, when a user of languages takes off in new, unpredictable directions as a result of failing to abide by the rules of a particular "language game." One might support Wittgenstein at this point by saying that what poets do intentionally, in order to be poets, philosophers do in ignorance—and hence are philosophers.

In the Preface to the book, Wittgenstein declares that he had hoped to bring the remarks of the book into some coherent whole, but such an attempt—he came to realize—could never succeed. He suggests that philosophical investigation involves coming at a problem from a number of different directions.

On the point concerning coherence one may justly dissent. Though it is true that escape from a static conception of language is made possible by a series of relevant demonstrations of the uses of language, there is no reason why the points of the book could not have been clearly made seriatim—even if, to do so, eccentric uses of language would have been necessary. A number of problems could then have been dealt with in the Wittgenstein fashion, a fashion which would have illuminated the eccentric uses of language. In fact, that is what *almost* happens in the *Investigations*: now and then we catch the author presenting a thesis, and it is clear that the problems he considers— suggested by his own odd uses of language in the expression of his theses— are intended to illustrate and support his points. Yet Wittgenstein had a streak of philosophicl coyness—sometimes disguising itself as a kind of insight— which led him, presumably for theoretical reasons, but more likely for effect, sometimes to withhold the moral of the tale, the destination of his philo- sophical wanderings.

There are two principal metaphors by the use of which Wittgenstein has sought to make his meaning clear: the metaphor of language as a game and the metaphor of language as a tool. Or, to be more accurate, the metaphors of languages as games or as tools. After describing a primitive language which could be described as involving a process of calling for objects by the use of words, Wittgenstein writes: "We can . . . think of the whole process of using words . . . as one of those games by means of which children learn their native language. I will call these games 'language-games' and will sometimes speak of a primitive language as a language-game. . . . I shall also call the whole, consisting of language and the actions into which it is woven, the 'language-game.'" (7) (In Part I, which comprises the largest section of the work, the remarks are numbered. For convenience in referring to the work— since there are no chapters, section headings, or other devices for locating oneself—these numbers are mentioned here.)

Then, in 11, Wittgenstein writes: "Think of the tools in a toolbox: there is a hammer, pliers, a saw, a screwdriver, a rule, a glue-pot, glue, nails and screws.—The functions of words are as diverse as the function of these ob- jects."

But what is the point of using the expression, "language-game"? Wittgen- stein answers: "Here the term 'langue-*game*' is meant to bring into promi- nence the fact that the *speaking* of language is part of an activity, or of a form of life." (23) He then presents a list of some of the functions of language— for example, giving orders, describing, reporting events, making up stories, translating—and comments: "It is interesting to compare the multiplicity of the tools in language and of the ways they are used, the multiplicity of kinds of word and sentence, with what logicians have said about the structure of language. (Including the author of the *Tractatus Logico-Philosophicus*.)" (23) Here the reference is to his own earlier work (1921) in which he defended a logical atomism—a philosophy which would elucidate problems by devising an ideal language in which for each simple object or property there would be a fixed, unambiguous symbol—ironically, the very conception of language which the *Investigations* examines and rejects.

The simile that using an utterance is like making a move in a game suggests the problem, "What is a game?" If language involves simply the use of names as labels, then there is a definite answer to that question. But if the word "game" is used in various ways, it may very well be that there is no "object," no essential nature, to which the word "game" calls attention. Indeed, this conclusion is what Wittgenstein argues. In response to the supposition that there must be something common to the proceedings called "games," he urges everyone to "*look and see* whether there is anything common to all," and he ends a survey of games by remarking: "And the result of this examination is: we see a complicated network of similarities overlapping and criss-crossing: sometimes overall similarities, sometimes similarities of detail." (66) He introduces the expression "family resemblances" to characterize the similarities.

The point is that just as games form a "family," so do the various uses of an expression. To look for common meanings, then, is as fruitless as to look for the essential nature of games. The only way of making sense out of a problem having to do with the essence of language (or the meaning of a word) is by examining language as it is actually used in a multiplicity of ways.

The theme of the *Investigations* is introduced shortly before the philosophical investigation into the essence of games: "For a *large* class of cases—though not for all—in which we employ the word 'meaning' it can be defined thus: the meaning of a word is its use in the language." (43)

To understand this critical sentence is to understand the *Investigations*. At first the claim that, as the word "meaning" is often used, the meaning of a word is its use in the language might appear to be a variant of the familiar pragmatic claim that verbal disputes are resolved by decisions as to the practical use of language. William James considered the question "Does the man go round the squirrel?" in an imagined situation in which, as the man walks round a tree, the squirrel moves about the tree trunk, keeping the tree between himself and the man. Some persons would be inclined to say that the man *does* go round the squirrel, since the man's path enclosed the squirrel's path; but others would say that the man does *not* go round the squirrel since the squirrel keeps the same part of its body turned toward the man. James would settle the issue by deciding how to use the word "round." He did not *answer* the question, but he settled the problem; he settled it by resolving the issue as a problem. In an analogous fashion, it might seem, Wittgenstein proposed resolving problems, not by answering them, but by showing that they involve confusions concerning the use of language.

But to interpret "the meaning is the use" in this manner is to fail to understand the function of the sentence in Wittgenstein's remarks. For Wittgenstein is not suggesting that meanings be determined by reference to use, or that meanings be explicated by reference to human attitudes in the use of language. What he suggests is what he says (but he says it oddly): the meaning of a word is its use in the language. For anyone who takes the word "meaning" as if the meaning of a term were an object, or a class of objects, or a property of a class of objects—in other words, something to which a word, as a label, refers—it is nonsense to say "the meaning of a word is its use." If the word "man" means rational animal, for example, what would be the sense of saying, "The meaning of the word 'man,' namely, rational animal, is its use in the language"? That is indeed philosophic garble. But if, now, we take the word "meaning" as it is used in discourse about the *meaning* of conduct, the *meaning* of an act, the *meaning* of a form of life—then it makes sense (even though it is *new* sense, since we do not usually talk about the meaning of a word in this sense of the word "meaning") to talk about the meaning of a word as being the use of the word in the language: it makes sense if by the "use" of something we mean what we would mean—more or less—in talking about the "purpose" of something. To understand a word, then, is much like understanding an act which makes no sense until one notices what the act does and, consequently, realizes what the act is *for*, what the purpose of it is, what *meaning* it has.

There is no more difficult demand upon philosopher accustomed to the sign-referent way of analyzing language than this demand that philosophers stop thinking of words as names for objects (a conception that has some use only in reference to a primitive language quite different from ours) and start thinking of words as tools that can be used in various ways and can be understood as bringing about certain changes in behavior or in ways of looking at things. Figurative description of language as a game is meant to stress "the fact that the *speaking* of language is part of an activity, or of a form of life": one does something with the use of a word that is much like what one does in making a move in a game; and just as it would be senselss to ask what the move *stands for* or *represents* (as if somehow it were a symbol for the victory toward which the player moves), so it is senseless to ask what the word, as used, *stands for* or *represents*. To be sure, conventional answers can be given to questions of the latter sort, but conventional answers are not illuminating; one comes to understand what language is and what language means in noticing (seeing) what is done with it (just as one can come to understand a machine by watching its operation).

This interpretation of Wittgenstein's remark that "the meaning of a word is its use in the language" gains strength with the realization that a considerable number of the remarks are directed against the idea that the meaning of a word is whatever the speaker has in mind or feels privately. Here again the problem "What is the essential nature of games?" is illuminating. By a survey of the various activities to which attention is called by various uses of the word "game," one comes to understand the word "game" and games; and the problem dissolves because one is satisfied with the survey of the family of games, and there is nothing more to wonder about. Similarly, to understand the meaning of the word "pain" is to have acquired the technique of using the word; there is nothing hidden or private to wonder about.

But this conclusion—that discourse about sensations is meaningful because the word "sensation" has a use in our language, and that the word "sensation" cannot be part of a private language significant only to the speaker—is intolerable to philosophers who like to say that "Sensations are private," "Another person can't have my pains," or "I can only *believe* that someone else is in pain, but I *know* it if I am." (These are Wittgenstein's examples—which he discusses in a series of related remarks.) Wittgenstein realized that much of what he had to say is intolerable to some philosophers, but he writes that philosophers have the habit of throwing language out of gear; and sometimes the philosophical use of language is so extreme, so abnormal, that what is called for is *treatment* by one who understands that philosophical problems arise and philosophical theories are advanced when philosophers develop the disease of taking expressions that fit into the language in one way and then using the expressions in some other, problem-provoking, paradox-generating way. Hence, "The [enlightened] philosopher's treatment of a question is like the treatment of an illness." (255)

Thus, if someone comes forth with the philosophical "discovery" that "Sensations are private," what he needs is treatment: a philosopher who talks about private sensations has made the error of confusing a discovery about the "grammar" (the systematic use) of the *word* "sensation" with a nonlinguistic fact. "The truth is: it makes sense to say about other people that they doubt whether I am in pain; but not to say it about myself." (246) But it does not follow from the grammatical point—that it would be senseless to *say* that I doubt whether I am in pain—that therefore I *know* that I am in pain: the expression "I know I am in pain" has no use in our language—except, perhaps, to emphasize (do somewhat better) the job that is done with the expression "I am in pain." To confuse the use of the word "know" in such an expression as "I know he is in pain" (for he is writhing, clenching his teeth, and the like) with its use in the expression "I know I am in pain" is to breed perplexity which only an investigation into the multiplicity of uses of the word "know" can resolve.

In his discussions of understanding, memory, and sensations, Wittgenstein characteristically sketches the range of uses of the terms "sensations," "understand," and "remember." He resists the tendency to settle upon one use, one way of looking at things, one definition as somehow settling anything. For even if one considers what one takes to be a "single" use of a term, it soon develops that there are borderline cases, areas in which one use imperceptibly merges into another, so that any decision as to the use of language by way of definition settles nothing (the complex network remains) and may lead to further paradox. Philosophical difficulties in this area (as well as in others) arise when one kind of grammar is mistaken for another, when an expression appropriate in one context is used in another: "Perhaps the word 'describe' tricks us here. I say 'I describe my state of mind' and 'I describe my room.' You need to call to mind the differences between the language-games." (290)

Expecting, intending, remembering—these are ways of life made possible by the use of language; and language is itself a way of life. What we find when we try to find the criteria of these states are the uses of various expressions— or by noticing the uses of various expressions we come to learn what kind of behavior prompts our use of these terms. No reference to *inner* thoughts, sensations, intentions, or memories is necessary.

For Wittgenstein "*Essence* is expressed by grammar." (371) To understand the nature of something is to acquire the technique of using the language which prompted the question and the investigation concerning it. There are, however, no simple answers; in a sense, there are no answers at all. One gets acquainted with the multiplicity of uses and one surveys the scene accordingly: there is nothing left to wonder about.

Wittgenstein does not deny the existence of feelings, of pains, memories, and expectations. In response to the charge that "you again and again reach the conclusion that the sensation itself is a *nothing*," he responds, "Not at all. It is not a *something*, but not a *nothing* either! The conclusion was only that a nothing would serve just as well as a something about which nothing can be said. We have only rejected the grammar which tries to force itself on us here." (304) Again, in response to the query "Are you not really a behaviorist in disguise? Aren't you at bottom really saying that everything except human behavior is a fiction?" he replies, "If I do speak of a fiction, then it is of a *grammatical* fiction." (307) The effort throughout is to argue against the tendency philosophers sometimes have of studying "inner processes" in order to acquire knowledge about sensations, memory, and so forth; the proper procedure, according to Wittgenstein, is to attend to the use of the relevant terms. If we do observe the uses of such terms as "sensation," "pain," "think," "remember," and so forth, we come to see that the technique of using these terms in no way depends upon introspecting private processes. An analagous mistake is made when it is assumed that to mean something is to think something. We can say that we meant a person to do one thing, and he did another—and we can say this even though we did not think of the possiblity in question: "'When I teach someone the formation of the series . . . I surely mean him to write . . . at the hundreth place.'—Quite right; you mean it. And evidently without necessarily even thinking of it. This shows you how different the grammar of the verb 'to mean' is from that of 'to think.' And nothing is more wrong-headed than calling meaning a mental activity!" (693)

In Part II of the *Investigations* the theme of the latter section of Part I is made perfectly clear: meaning, intending, understanding, feeling, and seeing (whether it is visual apprehension or the understanding of something; and these are related) are techniques, forms of life, modes of action about which we could be clear were we not confused by misleading parallelisms of grammar. To understand, to see clearly, is to master techniques to which our attention is called when language is used; and the use of language is itself a technique.

Philosophical Investigations is Wittgenstein's mature discourse on method. It corrects the basic error of the *Tractatus Logico-Philosophicus*—the error of supposing that there are atomic facts involving unanalyzable simples, an error which arose from the mistaken conception of language as a naming of objects. This book not only makes the correction by conceiving of language as a tool and of the use of language as a form of life involving techniques, but it also exhibits the multifarious character of philosophical investigations by showing them as criss-crossing sight-seeing excursions made possible by tracing out families of similarities to which the multiplicity of language uses calls attention.

If there is a weakness in this revolutionary work, it is the weakness of glossing over the multiplicity of *limited* philosophical concerns. Not all philosophers can be satisified with the restless philosophical excursions which so delighted Wittgenstein and at which he was so adept; many philosophers are more content to stay at home with their limiting and precising definitions, their fanciful speculations, their penchants for single uses of single terms. Nevertheless, Wittgenstein's work can serve as a foundation for argument against philosophic dogmatism; it makes possible an *enlightened* staying-at-home. From it a philosopher can learn that there is more between heaven and earth than can be seen by the use of his vocabulary; and there is then some hope that, though he spends his days looking at the world from his single window, he will not confuse the complexity of the world with the simplicity of some grammatical fiction.—*I.P.M.*

PERTINENT LITERATURE

Pitcher, George. *The Philosophy of Wittgenstein*. Englewood Cliffs, New Jersey: Prentice-Hall, 1964.

Anyone who turns to look at the *Philosophical Investigations* must have, if he is to make sense of that work at all, a few key background facts in mind. First, Ludwig Wittgenstein was, as George Pitcher says, one of the greatest of twentieth century philosophers, if not the greatest. Second, this work, the *Investigations*, is one, but only one, of two books upon which that judgment is based; his earlier book, the *Tractatus Logico-Philosophicus*, is as important in making that claim about his historical importance. Third, the *Philosophical Investigations* rejected most of the views Wittgenstein held in the *Tractatus*. This last fact is crucial. The *Tractatus* established Wittgenstein as one of the central philosophers of the century; but later he came to form philosophical views quite at odds with those which had elevated him to international recognition. And that fact, that he rejected the views of his youth to work out a wholly different set of ideas which became equally important, creates one of the strongest reasons for a claim to greatness. The reader of the *Investi-*

gations must realize that in that work one of Wittgenstein's aims is to show how misdirected his earlier ideas had been.

It is thus very helpful for a beginning student of the *Investigations* to know something of Wittgenstein's ideas in the *Tractatus* in order to know what forms the background of the detailed work in the later book. That is where a book like Pitcher's is very helpful. By including a discussion of both books under the same cover, Pitcher is able to make the relevant connections that assist the beginning reader of the *Philosophical Investigations* to understand the course of Wittgenstein's thinking.

Since the concern of this review is with the *Investigations*, only a few brief words about the earlier part of Pitcher's book are in order. He begins with a short sketch of Wittgenstein's life and character (and there is no doubt that Wittgenstein was a fascinating and exasperating character), and he then moves off into a discussion of the *Tractatus*. His aim in that discussion is to give the reader the broad picture of what Wittgenstein was up to, and so he omits all mention of the technical material on logic. Most briefly, the *Tractatus* is shown as a book which presents a metaphysical system based upon reflections on language and logic. Pitcher's aim is to show, in an introductory way, what Wittgenstein's views of language and logic were at that time and how those views acted to produce an account of what the world must be like in its broadest and deepest features.

It seems clear that upon finishing the *Tractatus*, Wittgenstein thought that he had solved all the central philosophical problems, and so he gave up philosophy. Other philosophers, however, deeply impressed by the book, sought him out to discuss it with him. Some of those conversations led him to start thinking about the problems once more. The upshot was that he returned to philosophy in 1929 in order to think and teach. Within the next decade he came to see that he had been radically wrong in his earlier thinking. The *Philosophical Investigations* is his attempt to work out a new set of ideas.

Pitcher organizes his discussion of the *Investigations* around several of Wittgenstein's themes, including that of the rejection of the doctrines of the *Tractatus*. The topic that Pitcher treats at greatest length is that of the nature of philosophy, allocating two different chapters to it; and there is no doubt that Wittgenstein had original things to say about what philosophy is.

Whereas metaphysicians, including Wittgenstein in the *Tractatus*, had thought of philosophy as rather like logic or as either a super-science or a study subservient to science, Wittgenstein came to the point of not accepting any of those models. For him, philosophical problems came to be best seen as puzzles (although as he says they are very *deep* puzzles.) The traditional ways of describing philosophy, including that which held philosophy necessarily to involve failure, took philosophers to be trying to answer problems *about the world*. Wittgenstein, looking back upon his own superb piece of metaphysics, came to talk of philosophical puzzlement as something not needing an *answer* but as something requiring help in finding one's way about. For Wittgenstein, in philosophy we are not faced with the problem of dealing with the unknown and our ignorance of it; rather, the pieces of the puzzle are all there if we can but see that they are there and how to put them together.

How does it come about that we get ourselves into such a baffled condition? Wittgenstein spends a good deal of time on that question. Pitcher notes that Wittgenstein found several different sources for such a condition, but thinks that there is one which Wittgenstein emphasizes throughout the *Investigations*. Wittgenstein found there to be a very fundamental tendency in human thought toward uniformity. This craving for similarity is an attempt to smooth out or ignore differences among related objects, to make people, things, and ideas as much alike as possible. For Wittgenstein in his later work, the metaphysician is one who allows that common human tendency free rein. Philosophy is the desire to *assimilate*, and philosophical puzzlement arises simply because the phenomena which philosophers try to assimilate exhibit great and basic differences, differences which in the long run really cannot be overlooked.

With that analysis of the nature of philosophy, one can see why so much of Wittgenstein's method is that of getting people to break down the blinders with which they view the world. The *Investigations* is a work on differences in the uses of language and in the world, on how to see variety where before one saw similarity.

Cavell, Stanley. "The Availability of Wittgenstein's Later Philosophy," in *The Philosophical Review*. LXXI, no. 1 (January, 1962), pp. 67-78.

The *Philosophical Investigations* is so close to us in time and, because of the very forcefulness of its ideas, has engendered so much passion and partisanship, that there are a great number of seriously conflicting interpretations of the aim, meaning, and truth of Ludwig Wittgenstein's work. In the absence of anything approaching consensus about how to understand the book, the general reader can become lost in a sea of perspectives from which to regard it. These circumstances make Cavell's essay "The Availability of Wittgenstein's Later Philosophy" very helpful. Not only does Cavell develop a definite and important interpretative line, he also sets his view in direct contrast to another way of reading the *Investigations*. Cavell's essay is a critical review of a book by David Pole entitled *The Later Philosophy of Wittgenstein* (London: The Athlone Press, 1958.) Since the type of interpretation offered by Pole is not unusual, a reader of Cavell's essay can see two very opposed views standing face to face. Finally, one can see in this discussion a vigorous defender of Wittgenstein replying to a strong critic of the views expressed in the *Investigations*.

Cavell's essay has two sections covering two notions crucial to an interpretation of Wittgenstein; then two sections in which he examines questions concerning "ordinary language philosophy"; and, finally, a consideration of Wittgenstein's style of writing.

Cavell takes it that Pole's aim is to show that Wittgenstein's ideas about language are wrong. Cavell argues that Pole (like other commentators) reads Wittgenstein as having held that language is essentially a system of rules which govern our linguistic behavior. On the contrary, Cavell writes, it was Wittgenstein's aim to reject just that picture of language, to show that language is not a calculus comprised of a set of rules. The consequence of such a rejection is that Wittgenstein had to spend a great deal of time trying to show how language could function without being bound everywhere by rules.

If, according to Cavell's line of interpretation, Wittgenstein did not hold rules to be the ultimate components of human understanding, what *did* he suggest is at the bottom of our language? This is where Wittgenstein's idea of a *form of life* is introduced. Following a rule is itself one kind of human activity, one form of life, or one aspect of the human form of life; the activity of following a rule cannot itself be understood as governed by rules.

An interpretation such as Pole's, which places rules at the center of the story, must also emphasize the notion of *decision*. Since a given system of rules cannot cover every relevant possible happening, it seems that occasions must arise in which the system plugs a hole in the set of rules and does so by way of a decision as to how the rules should apply to a given and anomalous case. However, Cavell argues that the concept of decision plays quite a different and less crucial role in Wittgenstein's thought. In fact, he holds that the central theoretical concepts in the *Investigations* are not rules and decisions but rather the related notions of "grammar" and (less centrally) "criteria."

A second major topic on which such critics as Pole have attacked Wittgenstein is on his views about ordinary language. The one group of interpreters will regard remarks to the effect that philosophy can only describe ordinary language and not change it as being deeply conservative and wholly opposed to the entire spirit of rationalism built into the philosophical tradition. Cavell, in this brief essay, is deliberately tentative in replying to that line of interpretation and criticism. In part, he says that interpretation of the meaning of the appeal to ordinary language on Wittgenstein's part is simply mistaken: Wittgenstein meant only that mere philosophizing cannot change language, not that the results of philosophizing cannot help in linguistic reform.

That is not a full answer to Pole's view, however, for it is plain that the philosophical tradition importantly seems to come into conflict with "common-sense" beliefs at various crucial places. And there is a clear sense generated by Wittgenstein's remarks on ordinary language that he is somehow arguing in defense of common beliefs and in opposition to the philosophical views which conflict with them. Cavell tries to work out what is going on in this dispute. Basically, he argues that Wittgenstein denies that philosophy has the upper hand in seeming conflicts with commonsense beliefs; what Wittgenstein does not do, however, is assert, like George Edward Moore, that common sense has the upper hand. Instead, he denies that there is really any conflict between philosophy and common sense; and that is because philosophical propositions are not strictly propositions at all—they are a kind of remark which has no grounding in our form of life.

Cavell wants Wittgenstein's aim in this matter to be seen as *Kantian*. Immanuel Kant maintained that the persistence of certain philosophical troubles arises because philosophers attempt to know what is beyond the limits of any conceivable experience. Many philosophical propositions for Kant are produced by misunderstanding the limits of human understanding. It is Cavell's contention that Wittgenstein's attack on the philosophical tradition is very much like Kant's (although clearly there are also differences). The appeal to ordinary language, then, is not a conservative claim, or one holding philosophy to be impotent—it is rather a claim that there are conditions of human understanding, that these are embodied in a complex way in language, and that metaphysical propositions violate them.

Cavell finds it necessary to conclude with a few remarks on the style of the *Investigations*, a style that has perplexed many readers because it seems so unphilosophical. Cavell's aim is to show that the style is not wholly new to philosophy: it is a form of the confessional style incorporating aspects of the dialogue. Moreover, Cavell holds that it was *forced* upon Wittgenstein by the nature of the argument rather than adopted out of perversity or idiosyncrasy.—*M.R.*

ADDITIONAL RECOMMENDED READING

Baker, G. P. and P. M. S. Hacker. *Wittgenstein: Understanding and Meaning.* Chicago: University of Chicago Press, 1980. A detailed commentary of the first 184 sections of the *Investigations* (to be Volume One of a sequence.)

Cavell, Stanley. *The Claim of Reason: Wittgenstein, Skepticism, Morality, and Tragedy.* London: Oxford University Press, 1979. A brilliant but idiosyncratic application of Wittgenstein's ideas.

Fann, K. T., ed. *Ludwig Wittgenstein: The Man and His Philosophy.* New York: Dell Publishing Company, 1967. More essays from various perspectives, some stressing the biographical.

Pitcher, George, ed. *Wittgenstein: The Philosophical Investigations.* Garden City, New York: Anchor Books, 1966. A good collection of essays.

THE MORAL POINT OF VIEW

Author: Kurt Baier (1917-   )
Type of work: Ethics
First published: 1958

PRINCIPAL IDEAS ADVANCED

Moralities are forms of social control and practical reasoning.

The fact that an act is right implies that there are conclusive reasons for doing it.

Moral reasons overrule reasons of self-interest because a system of self-interested reasons would impoverish life.

We should be moral because following rules in the interest of everyone alike protects everyone alike in that such rules overrule reasons of self-interest.

The question, "Should I follow reason?" is nonsensical in that the question itself is a call for reasons.

The subtitle of Kurt Baier's *The Moral Point of View* is "A Rational Basis for Ethics." Baier's central theme is that a moral question is a call for reasons for doing one thing rather than another; a moral judgment is a claim to the effect that the act said to be right is one for which compelling reasons can be given for doing it.

Accordingly, Baier's primary problem is that of explaining how moral reasons can count as reasons for one whose inclination is to consider self-interest. Moral interests, Baier claims, are social interests; moralities are devised to achieve social control, and the kind of reasoning they encourage is a form of practical reasoning. How, then, can moral reasons strike a person interested only in his own well-being as reasons for acting?

Baier's answer is that moral rules are designed to adjudicate in cases in which there is a conflict of interests in order to prevent one rival from eliminating the other or from satisfying his interests at the expense of the other. Although operating on the basis of rules of self-interest might benefit a person on one occasion, a reversal of rules is possible, and only moral rules can provide fair and equitable ways of resolving conflicts, thereby preventing society from disintegrating and falling into a state of nature that is "nasty, brutish, and short," as Thomas Hobbes described it.

Baier contends that moral judgments have four principal logical features that traditional theories of ethics cannot accommodate: (1) moral judgments can be mutually contradictory; (2) moral judgments can guide moral agents; (3) there are always good reasons for doing what is morally right; and (4) we can know whether an act is morally right.

Emotive theories which contend that moral judgments merely express feelings or attitudes cannot account for the first of the four distinctive logical features of moral judgments, Baier argues. Theories that insist that moral judgments report facts cannot explain the second feature—namely, that moral judgments can guide conduct. (Baier contends that facts are logically compatible with behavior of any kind.) Those who regard morality as based on ideal law cannot account for the third feature—that there are always good reasons for doing right—for such persons cannot provide reasons for taking the ideal as ideal. Finally, according to Baier, all traditional theories fail to explain how knowledge of moral rightness is possible. (Baier, on the other hand, can explain—so he claims—by relating the rightness of an act to the moral reasons for doing it. We can know that an act is right, he insists, because we can appreciate the weight of moral reasons behind it.)

Baier begins his treatise with an account of value judgments. He distinguishes between theoretical and practical judgments. Theoretical judgments make factual claims through the exercise of special skills, such as judgments of speed or distances. Practical judgments are logically related to action; they are action-guiding in that they give reasons for doing one thing rather than another.

Baier rejects the view that value judgments are distinct from factual judgments. Not only do value judgments make factual claims, but they are also empirically verifiable. Just as practical judgments may involve empirically verifiable comparisons and rankings, so value judgments, as forms of practical judgment, may involve verifiable comparisons and rankings. Whatever the form of judgment, Baier points out, criteria and standards are involved; and although criteria and standards may conflict with each other, verification is possible as long as a specifiable standard is alluded to in judgment. One can learn about values through experience, Baier reminds us, and if one is oneself ignorant, there are experts who know enough to verify value claims.

Value judgments involve matters of opinion as well as matters of taste, Baier points out. But although value judgments have a factual dimension, they are able to give rational guidance because they relate matters of fact to interests, wants, desires, and needs.

Problems may arise, however, concerning the rightness of the criteria of judgment. Baier argues that criteria of judgments may be validated by considering, in the first place, the purpose (if there is one) of the kind of object being evaluated. Other human aims direct our attention to aspects other than basic purpose. An automobile is a means of transportation, but safety, comfort, and reliability are also to be considered because such features matter to human beings. One simplifies the problem of validation by narrowing the basis of comparison and by adopting some method for ranking objects of the same kind. Baier's conclusion on this point is that criteria can be validated by reference to human interests and needs; judgment is possible by comparison and ranking.

To consider what *ought* to be done, Baier argues, is to consider what course of possible action is supported by the best reasons. It is not enough to ask which is the best way to gain an end already decided upon; in asking what ought to be done, proposed ends may themselves be called into question. To decide what is the best thing to do one considers everything that bears on one's interest.

Baier distinguishes between doing what is personally beneficial and in that respect "in the interest" of the agent and what would be beneficial to any agent in that position and hence "in *one's* interest." Whatever an agent may want and whatever might satisfy a current interest the agent has, the best thing to do is whatever is supported by the best reasons—and reasons function socially only by reference to matters, including interests, that are not, as he puts it, "person-relative."

Baier concludes that all "consideration-making beliefs are person-neutral." However, a particular person in a particular situation may have a reason for acting that would not be a reason for someone else in the same situation. Such a fact is person-relative. But judgment is made by relating the person-relative fact to a generalization identifying "one's" taking an interest in something or enjoying something as a "reason" for doing it. An argument leading to a person-relative conclusion as to what ought to be done depends, then, on a major premise establishing the relationship of anyone's interest to reasons for acting; and such a major premise is person-neutral.

In deliberation, Baier contends, one looks for *facts* that are *reasons*; one does not look for features that are appealing, that one knows will motivate action. The alternative supported by the best reasons may not be something one wants to do at all; nevertheless, the act ought to be done because it is supported by the best reasons. Deliberation and justification are concerned with reasons; explanation refers to motives. One can explain how it comes about that an agent does what ought to be done even though the agent does not at the time care to do it by calling attention to the sort of training most persons have received which establishes the habit of doing whatever is supported by the best reasons even in cases when to do so goes against one's current inclinations.

Baier next considers individual, social, and moral "rules of reason." He characterizes the rules of reason as "beliefs," and he asks initially what these beliefs are and later considers which of them are true. The individual rules of reason are those concerning individuals—that is, individual persons. Baier distinguishes rules concerning *self-regarding* persons (those concerned only about their own well-being) and rules concerning *other-regarding* persons (those concerned about the well-being of others as well). He also distinguishes between short-range and long-range rules. The first of the short-range self-regarding rules of reason may be summarized by the formula: *If* one *would enjoy* doing something or would enjoy continuing doing what one is doing, then one has a reason for action. The primary consideration is the factor of *enjoyment*. The second short-range self-regarding rule of reason is: If an action *would satisfy a desire*, then there is a reason for doing it.

Baier then calls attention to the fact that each person has a distinctive "point of view"; that is, certain aims or goals such that some acts are in one's interest and others are not. The fact that something is *in one's interest* provides a reason for action. Long-range individual self-regarding rules of reason relate to one's interest: if an act is in fact (and not simply mistakenly believed to be) in one's interest, there is a reason for doing it.

Short-range and long-range other-regarding individual rules of reason involve reference to someone else's enjoyment, desire, or interest: the fact that something one might do would please someone else, satisfy the other's desire, or be in the other's interest provides a reason for doing it (or if the act would displease the other, a reason for *not* doing it).

Baier contends that one always attaches greater weight to the self-regarding reason in cases in which the self-regarding reason and the other-regarding reason are in conflict but are of the same sort. Where there is a significant difference, as when the benefit to oneself would be small and the disadvantage to others great, either the "decent" or the "selfish" course would be in accordance with reason.

Baier introduces his discussion of social rules by distinguishing six senses of the word "rule." A rule may be a regulation, a matter of social mores, a maxim or principle, a canon, a regularly repeated practice ("As a rule, he does such-and-such"), or a determination of procedure whereby an activity is defined (as in "rules of chess").

In the examination of social rules Baier concentrates on *mores* (customs, rules of etiquette) and *regulations* (enforced requirements, as for example traffic regulations). Accordingly, social rules of reason relate to laws, customs, manners, conventions, and traditions. If an act would be required by any of these social "rules" (in any of the senses relating to mores and regulations), then there is a reason for doing it. (Baier calls a reason for doing something a "pro" and a reason for not doing something a "con.")

Laws and customs provide the conditions that make for a common way of life, Baier points out. Points of view and particular practices are made universal through the formalization of social pressure. Religion makes sense as a system of belief operating within a legal framework; in the Christian religion, for example, God is the perfect ruler and legislator; He reveals laws and passes judgment. Baier describes religious considerations as "nothing but special sorts of legal considerations."

As he closes his discussion of social rules of reason, Baier makes an interesting comment concerning the question as to whether customs, conventions, rules, or laws are true. Although it makes sense to say that an action is or is not in accordance with customs or rules, it does not make sense, he claims, to ask whether the customs or rules are themselves true. "The only question we can ask at this level is whether the custom, convention, rule, or law is good or bad, civilized or uncivilized, desirable or undesirable," he concludes. Moral reasons make reference to morality, Baier writes; if a moral rule declares a certain way of acting to be wrong, then there is a moral reason for not doing it.

Baier objects to the view that moral beliefs are merely expressions of feelings or attitudes. Although he agrees that moral convictions have imperatival force, he denies that they are neither true nor false. Unless moral reasons make reference to a morality involving conceptions that are true, the reasons are not reasons for acting. Baier argues that we do in fact ask such questions as, "Is what that morality forbids *really* wrong?" and "Are the moral convictions of that group true?"

But if moral beliefs must be true to serve as the reference in moral reasons, what is the test of their truth? According to Baier, moral beliefs are true "if they can be seen to be required or acceptable *from the moral point of view.*" Once again he emphasizes the difference between, say, a personal point of view or a practical point of view and the moral point of view. To make the matter clear, however, he develops his idea of what he calls "the moral point of view."

By the moral point of view, Baier means a point of view that provides a method of arbitration between conflicting interests. Accordingly, the moral point of view cannot be identified as that of self-interest. The egoist acts on the principle of doing only what will be in his interest; the agent with the moral point of view refers not to his own interest but to moral rules. By definition of the term "moral point of view," Baier makes it contradictory to consider that reference to self-interest could constitute the moral point of view.

Moral rules differ from laws and regulations, Baier contends, in that they are not "administered" by the police and civil judges. Furthermore, moral rules do not originate with someone's decision; moral rules are not "laid down." Finally, laws and regulations provide the conditions that make for exceptions, but in the case of moral rules the only exceptions are "morally deserving cases" that are seen to be morally deserving in that they come under the rule. The distinguishing feature of moral rules is that moral rules are "meant for everybody." A personal rule to which one holds faithfully, never making exceptions in one's own interest, is not a moral rule unless it is to be acted on by everyone.

If moral rules are meant for everybody, the teaching of morality must be universal and open, Baier contends. Furthermore, moral rules are not frustrated if everyone acts in accordance with them; as Baier puts it, moral rules are not "self-frustrating." Nor are they "self-defeating," as rules would be that, when openly acknowledged, cease to work (such as the rule, "Make promises only when you do not intend to keep them"). Finally, since moral rules must be teachable, any rule that rules out the conditions of teaching would be a "morally impossible rule." Baier gives as an example of a morally impossible rule, "Always assert what you think not to be the case." Following such a rule, he contends, would make communication and hence teaching impossible.

The last distinguishing feature of moral rules, unlike the features previously discussed by Baier, is not purely formal; it is a matter of content: moral rules are so constituted that, when observed, they are "for the good of everyone alike." It is immediately apparent that any principle or rule that aims at the satisfaction of self-interest alone could not possibly be a moral rule. The moral point of view, Baier insists, is that of "an independent, unbiased, impartial, objective, dispassionate, disinterested judge." He informally characterizes such a point of view as a "God's-eye point of view." The point is that anyone adopting the moral point of view would not give priority to his own interests or those of a selected few but would, to the extent that it would be relevant to do so, take the interests of all concerned into account.

Baier objects strongly to the claim made by deontologists (moral philosophers who regard formal principles as fundamental in moral judgment) and utilitarians (those who regard the end of moral action to be an increase in the balance of happiness over unhappiness of all concerned) that one's moral duty involves doing the *optimific* act; that is, the act that would produce the greatest good for the greatest number. One is morally required to help one's neighbor when the neighbor is in need, but one is not morally obligated always to be striving to maximize the well-being of everyone.

Moral reasoning necessarily involves the social context, according to Baier. A single person on a desert island would have no need to reason morally. The social factor is implied by the adjudicative function of moral rules; where there is no conflict of interests, there is no need of moral rules. Baier considers the question of whether morality is prior to or after society. He distinguishes between true moralities and "absolute morality." By absolute morality is meant the set of true moral convictions that must be embodied in any particular morality if that morality is to be "true." Particular moralities, if true, are applications of absolute morality to specific social conditions. Society contributes to absolute morality in that it provides established patterns of behavior; social positions, status, and the division of labor; and, often, the provision for the makings of contractual agreements.

Baier distinguishes between "primary" moral rules, such as "Thou shalt not kill," and "secondary" moral rules that enable persons to restore the moral equilibrium, to act morally in response to a violation of moral rules. The task for any society, if it is to function in conformity with absolute morality, is to provide specific ways of restoring equilibrium when violations occur, ways that are themselves justifiable by reference to moral rules.

Furthermore, a society can be in conformity with absolute morality only by prohibiting courses of action such that they would work against the common good if everyone followed them, provided that any such course of action is such that anyone would be entitled to engage in it and engaging in it would be an "indulgence," not a sacrifice. (For example, a society might be justified in prohibiting walking across the lawn or using gas for nonessential purposes during peak hours.)

Baier concludes his account of the moral point of view by considering the question, "Why should we be moral?" He begins with a discussion of what he calls "our most elementary consideration-making belief"; namely, that the fact I would enjoy something is a reason for doing it. To ask whether such a reason is a true reason is to ask whether it is better that we act from such reasons or from their contradictories or contraries. Since the best course of action relates to the good life, to what would satisfy us, it would run counter to reason *not* to do something because one would enjoy it (other things being equal). One might even, Baier suggests, call persons who replace this fundamental consideration-making belief with its contrary or contradictory "mad." In any case, they certainly would not fare as well as those who adopt the belief.

When there is a conflict between reasons based on self-interest and moral reasons, the moral reasons should prevail, argues Baier, because they are superior reasons. Since moral reasons overrule reasons of self-interest when action prompted by self-interest would be harmful to others, it is better for society and hence for those in it that moral reasons prevail; hence, they are superior in that they make for a better life generally. As to the question, "Why should I follow reason?" Baier claims that it does not make sense. The word "should" is itself a call for a reason; hence, the question is tautological, like asking, "Is a circle a circle?"—*I.P.M.*

Pertinent Literature
Frankena, William K. *Perspectives on Morality*. Edited by K. E. Goodpaster. Notre Dame, Indiana: University of Notre Dame Press, 1976.

In arguing for the view that moral judgments can be distinguished from nonmoral normative judgments not by the normative terms used in moral judgments but by reference to the kinds of reasons given in support of moral judgments, William K. Frankena lends support to the views of Kurt Baier and Stephen Toulmin, among others. Frankena has made the effort to explain the distinctive "moral point of view," and he argues that the moral point of view can be distinguished from other normative points of view by the "kinds of considerations it takes account of."

His essay "The Concept of Morality," 1966 (not to be confused, he warns, with another, earlier essay—but published later—having the same title and reprinted in *The Definition of Morality*, 1970, edited by G. Wallace and

A. D. M. Walker), as well as "On Defining Moral Judgments, Principles, and Codes," 1973, presents and defends his proposal for distinguishing moral judgments (or the moral point of view) from nonmoral judgments and points of view. A number of the essays included in this volume fill out Frankena's ideas on this subject, but the two cited are endorsed by him as statements of his position and are worth careful attention, particularly by anyone interested in the comparable (although not identical) views of Baier and Toulmin. (Another essay included in this volume, "'the principles of morality,'" also examines the distinction and specifically comments on Baier.)

In "The Concept of Morality" Frankena considers the question, "When is a code or action-guide to be called a moral one, a morality?" He begins by distinguishing between a "*wider* formal concept" of morality and a "*narrower* material and social one." According to the formal concept, an "action-guide" (code to direct action) is a morality if and only if it is taken as prescriptive and universalized and regarded as "definitive, final, over-riding, or supremely authoritative." According to the material concept, an action-guide as a morality must involve some kind of social concern, some principles or rules that relate the value of actions and agents to the feelings or interests of "others"—described by Frankena as "persons or centers of sentient experience."

The author then defines four conceptions of morality: the purely formal conception, the material conception (involving a rejection of the formal requirement that the action-guide be supremely authoritative), a view combining the formal and material requirements (but settling for the ambiguity of "moral"), and another kind of combination view that accepts both the authoritative condition of the formal position and the social condition of the material view.

The view of morality defended by Frankena is the material (or social) conception, one he shares, so he contends, with Toulmin, Baier, Marcus Singer, P. F. Strawson, and John Kemp. (Frankena mentions that View IV, as he calls it, also appeals to him—the *other* paper entitled "The Concept of Morality" is a defense of View IV—but his main objection to attempting to combine the requirement of authoritativeness with the social criterion is that the question, "Why should I be moral?" thereupon becomes "senseless.")

Frankena objects to View I (the formal view) on the ground that to call an action guide a "morality" *suggests* (he does not write "implies") that it is socially important and worthy of social sanction; hence, there must be a material condition added to the formal conditions of prescriptiveness, universality, and authoritativeness (or at least to the first two). The reverse side of this point is that we ordinarily regard a prudential code as either "nonmoral" or "immoral"; yet the formal view would have to accept such a code (provided that it satisfied the three conditions) as a "morality." (He has a number of other objections to the formal view, but for the most part Frankena's objections appear to stem from his sense of what the term "moral" is ordinarily used to mean or call attention to: namely, the social point of view.)

As to the arguments against the "material" view (the idea that morality must embody some form of social concern), Frankena argues that the material condition does not build utilitarianism into the definition of "morality" because his version of the material view, at least, allows for deontological action guides (moral codes involving fundamental principles specifying forms of right action). As to so-called "moralities" that *appear* to be nonsocial (such as those defended by the Greeks, Benedictus de Spinoza, Friedrich W. Nietzsche, and the Navaho—to mention Frankena's examples), Frankena suggests that they may not be "consistently and thoroughly" nonsocial.

The material view also allows for the possibility of self-referential duties, for the possibility that altruism may require egoism (as a practical consideration it *could* turn out that the best way to serve others is to do what is to one's own self-interest), and for the possibility that morality is *in fact*—although not by definition—the final arbiter of right and wrong. Frankena denies that the material view—which he describes as a proposal about the *future* use of "moral"—is naturalistic; his view does not, he claims, settle normative questions by definition.

Frankena contends that the idea of morality is traditionally the idea of an action guide that is both rational and social. There is no way of proving this to be the case, he admits, but he argues that the rationality of the social point of view should be postulated. He suggests that the moral point of view is one that a "rational, informed, and nonevasive" person would choose—and he contends that it would be a view that involved social concern.

In his essay "'the principles of morality'" Frankena again makes the point that the expression "the principles of morality" (like such terms as "morality" and "moral ideal") in effect makes reference to action-guides that a clear-headed, informed, rational person would choose. There is truth, then, he claims, in talking about "true morality" and in claiming that an action-guide accepted from the moral point of view (as specified above) is "objectively or absolutely valid. . . ."

Finally, in the essay "On Defining Moral Judgments, Principles, and Codes," Frankena concludes tentatively that the material view of morality requires that normative judgments, principles, and codes involve reference to the effects of actions on "sentient lives," including persons other than the agent when others are involved. Furthermore, moral reasons are "moral" because they are important in the consideration of action from a "certain point of view that includes having a certain conative disposition" (presumably the disposition to take certain kinds of facts as relevant in the determination of right and wrong conduct).

Frankena categorically rejects ethical egoism as a moral position; he claims that it would not "seem natural for anyone to call it a morality." Certainly Frankena's material view is such that for him to call egoism a morality would be to contradict himself, for egoism does not require the consideration of others and Frankena's carefully composed set of arguments supports Baier's contention that the "moral point of view" is one involving social concern.

Hospers, John. "Baier and Medlin on Ethical Egoism," in *Philosophical Studies*. XII, nos. 1 and 2 (January-February, 1961), pp. 10-16.

Although Kurt Baier regards ethical egoism as resting upon a reasonable foundation—namely, that the fact that an act serves the agent's self-interest is a good reason for undertaking the act—he nevertheless has sought to win acceptance for the societal or communal point of view (the point of view relating to the interests of everyone involved in a moral situation) as constituting *the* moral point of view. The primary reason for regarding the social point of view as the moral point of view, he has argued, is that there must be a way of resolving conflicts of interests. In *The Moral Point of View* Baier not only argues that this primary reason can be appealed to in the effort to discredit ethical egoism as a moral point of view but also attempts to disprove ethical egoism altogether. John Hospers, although acknowledging that Baier's book is "excellent," challenges the rejection proof that Baier offers.

Baier's proof (in radically condensed form) runs something like this: If B and K are candidates for the presidency of a certain country and the only way for B to gain his objective is to liquidate K, while the only way for K to secure his objective is to liquidate B, then B ought to liquidate K while K ought to liquidate B. But since the same act cannot be both right and wrong (each would be working against what it would be right for the other to do), ethical egoism is refuted. (Baier concludes that "morality is designed to apply in just such cases: namely, those where interests conflict." Thus, the moral point of view cannot be that of self-interest.)

Hospers first of all states that it would not be a contradiction to speak of right and wrong in the case cited because it is not *one* act that is being considered but *two* acts—the act by B (of liquidating or attempting to liquidate K) and the act by K (of attempting to liquidate B).

In discussing Baier's criticism that a self-interest theory is inadequate as a basis for settling conflicts of interest, Hospers first of all distinguishes between what he calls the "personal" egoist and the "impersonal" egoist. The personal egoist thinks that his duty is to promote his own interests, but he says nothing about what others ought to do. The impersonal egoist says that it is everyone's duty to pursue his own interests exclusively.

Hospers then considers how Baier's inadequacy argument would affect the personal egoist. He concludes that it would not affect the personal egoist at all, for he has no interest in anything (such as the task of resolving conflicts of interest) that does not relate to his interests. Baier's argument does not refute *personal* ethical egoism, then, because the personal egoist does not concede that a morality should arbitrate conflicts of interest.

As to the *impersonal* ethical egoist, although his ethical view is a generalization to the effect that it is everyone's duty to pursue his own interest and hence B's duty to pursue his interest and K's duty to pursue his interest, he has no obligation to make his ethical position known, to stress the duty of an individual to that individual if to do so would in any way threaten his own position, work against his own interests. The only problem for the impersonal egoist is what Hospers calls the "tactical" problem of deciding when to or whether to encourage someone by assuring him that pursuing his own interest is a moral right and obligation.

Hospers next considers a difficulty that appears to stem from ethical egoism, the difficulty that consists in the egoist's appearing to support A's position in urging A to do what is to A's interest and appearing to support B in urging B to do what is to B's interest (in a case in which the interests of A and B conflict). The charge against egoism is that egoism is guilty of "issuing *inconsistent directives*" and is attributed to Brian Medlin (among others). Medlin's point is that, in effect, the egoist is at one point saying "I want *you* to come out on top," while later on, to one working against the interests of the first person addressed, the egoist will be saying, in effect, "I want *you* to come out on top."

Hospers notes that if the egoist claims that probably people will be happier generally if each follows his own interests, the egoist is making an empirical claim (not enunciating an ethical theory), a claim that is highly dubious. In any case, to make such a claim would be to be a utilitarian, not an egoist. Hospers points out, however, that the egoist need not be guilty of the duplicity consisting in assuring each of the contesting parties that he is the egoist's favorite. The egoist can be an impartial spectator who says something like, "I hope each of you tries to come out on top." In this way there would be no inconsistency in his pronouncements of ethical egoism. Just because the egoist is inconsistent in some formulations of his doctrine, writes Hospers, there is no need to assume that he is always inconsistent. (Of course, one is inclined to return to Hospers' earlier point: the ethical egoist need not proselytize his theory at all—unless it is to his interest to do so—and he need not go about encouraging other people to be ethical egoists.)—*I.P.M.*

ADDITIONAL RECOMMENDED READING

Kerner, George C. *The Revolution in Ethical Theory*. New York: Oxford University Press, 1966. Kerner examines the ethical theories of G. E. Moore, Charles L. Stevenson, Stephen Toulmin, and Richard M. Hare. His criticism of Toulmin relates to an appraisal of Baier.

Toulmin, Stephen E. *The Place of Reason in Ethics*. Cambridge: Cambridge University Press, 1950. Baier acknowledges that his views are closest to those of Toulmin, and it is instructive to compare the two.

Warnock, Mary. *Ethics Since 1900*. Oxford: Oxford University Press, 1960. An excellent survey of twentieth century developments in ethics.

WORD AND OBJECT

Author: W. V. O. Quine (1908-　　)
Type of work: Philosophy of language
First published: 1960

PRINCIPAL IDEAS ADVANCED

Translation from one language into another is indeterminate. Two schemes of translation, incompatible with each other, might be equally adequate and acceptable.

Two kinds of entities exist: physical objects and sets of objects.

Entities are posited to exist if they are empirically attested to or have theoretical utility.

First-order predicate logic with identity is a canonical notation.

A canonical notation—that is, a logically perspicuous language—makes clear the ontological commitments of a theory.

Word and Object is W. V. O. Quine's *magnum opus*. Although it is neither his first word about the topics that have dominated his philosophical life nor his last word, it is the most complete expression of his views in a single place and was written when he was at the height of his philosophical powers, roughly between 1955 and 1959.

The book continues the themes of his earlier articles in *From a Logical Point of View* (1953), of which the two most famous are "On What There Is," which discusses criteria for ontological commitment, and "Two Dogmas of Empiricism," the first dogma being that there is a clear distinction between analytic sentences, which are true by virtue of their meanings, and synthetic truths, which are made true by facts; the second dogma being that each meaningful sentence is reducible to an equivalent sentence, all the terms of which refer to immediate experience. As these two articles make clear, Quine is equally interested in the problems of ontology and language, problems that he thinks are intertwined. Quine further elaborated and refined the views of *Word and Object* in *Ontological Relativity and Other Essays* (1969). In the title essay, which constitutes the first of the John Dewey Lectures, given at Columbia University in 1968, Quine admits his debt to Dewey; in *Word and Object* and other essays he expresses his debt to C. S. Peirce and his commitment to a kind of pragmatism. By his own admission Quine is in the mainstream of traditional American philosophy.

Word and Object can be seen to consist of three projects: one concerns words; one concerns objects; and one concerns the conjunction of words and objects. The first project is an attempt to give empirical foundations to language, to explain the human use of language in terms of human behavior and the perceptual environment. Quine restricts the theoretical terms of the explanation to these two because, he claims, they are the only available resources for the evidence upon which human beings learn language; thus Quine is very much concerned with reconstructing how a person—typically, but not invariably, a child—might come to learn a language. The second project concerns the classic problem of metaphysics: What kinds of objects are there? What really exists? Quine's short answer to these questions is that there are two kinds of objects that really exist: physical objects and sets or classes of objects. These first two projects come together in his discussion of the kind of language that is appropriate for expressing what there is. According to Quine, it is science that says what there is, and the language for science, what he calls "a canonical notation," is first-order predicate calculus with identity.

Quine's most famous or infamous thesis about language is what he calls "the indeterminacy of translation." The thesis is this: two systems of translating one language into another can be devised such that each system is compatible with all the speech dispositions of those who know the language; yet the two systems are not equivalent. Quine develops his thesis in the course of describing the situation with which a linguist would be confronted when first coming upon a culture wholly alien to his own. How can the linguist correlate sentences of his language with sentences of the native speaker? That is, how can the linguist come to translate between his own language and that of the native? This is the problem of radical translation.

Suppose a rabbit hops by and the native says, "Gavagai." The linguist might plausibly guess that the utterance means, "There's a rabbit," or "Look at that rabbit." Of course the linguist might be wrong; in order to determine that, the linguist has to test his guess or hypothesis by interrogating the native in some way. But how can he do this? One way is for him to say "Gavagai" the next time a rabbit appears and observe the reaction of the native. The linguist wants to see whether the native will assent to or dissent from the utterance. Assuming that a linguist can ask a native whether a given sentence is appropriate, Quine defines "affirmative stimulus meaning" as the class of stimulations that would prompt assent, "negative stimulus meaning" as the class that would prompt dissent, and "stimulus meaning" as the ordered pair of the two. Further, two utterances are stimulus synonymous just in case they have the same stimulus meaning; that is, when they would produce assent or dissent in the same situations. Although the notion of stimulus meaning is well-defined, the linguist is still faced with a cluster of problems, to which Quine is attentive. Which utterances of the native are to count as assent and which dissent? Given that "evok" and "yok" are the utterances expressing each, which is which? Another problem is that a native will not always be willing or able to respond to the query. His glimpse of the object may not have been long enough to allow him to respond at all. So, in addition to the assents and dissents there will be some lack of response. The native will sometimes make mistakes; perhaps he was looking in the wrong direction or

attending to the wrong object. Or he might lie. Because of all of these possibilities for skewed results, stimulus synonymy is not what is ordinarily meant
by "synonymy."

This partial catalogue of the linguist's problem is not meant to imply that
the linguist's task is impossible. The point is rather to indicate what difficulties
one faces in learning a wholly alien language, what resources are available
to learn it, and the strategy the linguist will employ in matching utterances
with behavior. Given enough data, time, and imagination, the linguist will
surely succeed in writing a manual of translation.

Quine helps us understand how the linguist will proceed with his job of
translation beyond those utterances whose use is most closely tied to observation by explaining how the linguist might move from translating observation
sentences like "Gavagai" to truth-functional sentences. The linguist comes
to translate a linguistic element as expressing negation when and only when
adding it to a short sentence causes a native speaker to dissent from a sentence
previously assented to; the linguist comes to translate a linguistic element as
conjunction when and only when it produces compounds from short component sentences that the native is disposed to assent to when and only when
he is also disposed to assent to the components separately. The qualification
"short" is added to guard against the native's becoming confused by a sentence
of extreme length. And it applies only to the language-learning situation;
once the terms are learned, there is no restriction on the length of the sentences to which the terms are applied.

After the observation sentences, the truth-functional ones, and some other
related sorts are translated, how does the linguist proceed? Roughly, he
divides the sentences he hears into those segments that he hears often repeated; these he counts as the words of the language. His task is then to
correlate these words with words of his own language in such a way that the
correlation conforms to his translation of the earlier sentences. Quine calls
these correlations "analytical hypotheses." A further constraint on analytical
hypotheses is that stimulus-analytic ones, those sentences that receive unanimous assent among the natives, should, if possible, be correlated with sentences that are stimulus-analytic for members of the linguist's own speech
community; *mutatis mutandis* for stimulus-contradictory sentences. The par-
enthetical "if possible" is an escape clause. It is not always possible, without
sacrificing the simplicity of the analytical hypothesis, to match a stimulus-
analytic sentence of the natives with one of the linguist's community. It may
be necessary, in the interests of simplicity, to translate a stimulus-analytic
sentence of the natives as, "All rabbits are men reincarnate." Such translations, however, are a last resort. By the principle of charity, one should always
avoid attributing absurd or bizarre beliefs to foreigners.

There is another problem, or rather another result, of the thought experiment involving radical translation. The most fundamental relation between

language and the world, the relation of reference, is infected by a kind of indeterminacy, which Quine calls "the inscrutability of reference." Suppose that one linguist has determined that "Gavagai," whatever its other uses, translates "rabbit" when it is used as a term. It remains a possibility that a second linguist, acting on the very same evidence as the first, will determine that "Gavagai" translates "rabbit stage" and a third that it translates "undetached rabbit part." Each of these preferred translations is consonant with all of the empirical evidence, yet the references of "rabbit," "rabbit stage," and "undetached rabbit part" are different. In other words, there is no one correct answer to the question, "What does 'Gavagai' refer to?" Reference is inscrutable.

The situation of radical translation implies that the translator has a language and attempts to correlate the sentences of his own language with the sentences of a language foreign to him. In this regard the problem of radical translation is different from the situation that the infant is in when he begins to acquire his language. However, there is an important respect in which the infant is in the very same situation: he has the very same resources available to him as the linguist does. Like the linguist, the infant must learn his language on the basis of perceptual stimulation and human behavior and must construct and test hypotheses about what an utterance means just as the linguist, but self-consciousness is not essential to the learning process.

The babbling of human beings during the end of their first year of life becomes transmuted into an incipient language by selective, positive reinforcement. Among the randomly produced verbal sounds of the infant will be "mama" and "papa," which for the infant have no significance. They acquire significance when its mother and father reward the infant for producing those vocal sounds. Like a chicken learning to pull a lever for a pellet of food, a child first acquires language. The comparison of a child with a chicken is neither facetious nor unfair. Quine's model for the first steps of language acquisition is a stimulus-response model, and he approvingly refers to the work of his Harvard colleague B. F. Skinner in this regard. In an oblique response to the criticisms of Noam Chomsky, who trenchantly criticized Skinner's work, Quine concedes that, in addition to the stimulus-response mechanism, such innate forces as the natural tendency for an infant to smack its lips in anticipation of nursing and thereby to utter "mama" and a "basic predilection for conformity" play some role in a total causal account of infant language acquisition. Chomsky, however, is not satisfied by such meager concessions; he demands a more full-blown innatism and he discusses Quine's views in his contribution to *Words and Objections*, edited by Donald Davidson and Jaakko Hintikka.

Among the most important things that the infant needs to learn are the distinctions among various types of terms. Quine distinguishes between singular terms, such as "Cicero" and "the orator who denounced Catiline," and general terms, such as "orator" and "apple." General terms, unlike singular terms, divide their reference among a number of objects. Definite and indefinite articles, "the" and "a(n)" respectively, and the plural ending, are devices for the use of general terms in English. A person does not know how to use a general term in English if he does not know how to use such expressions as "an apple," "the apple," and "apples." Mass terms, such as "gold" and "water," are a kind of middle case, a kind of grammatical hermaphrodite. Syntactically, they are like singular terms in resisting indefinite articles and plural endings; semantically, they are like singular terms in not dividing their reference. But they are like general terms in not naming one thing. The double role of mass terms extends to predication. In the subject position they are like singular terms ("Water is wet"); in the predicate position, they are like general terms ("That puddle is water").

Quine's second project is to answer the question, "What is there?" His answer that there are physical objects, that is four-dimensional spatiotemporal entities, and abstract objects, sets or classes of objects, is perhaps less interesting than his answer to several related questions, such as "What isn't there?" or, to put the question more perspicuously, "Why does Quine refuse to countenance various sorts of purported entities?" On the ground of economy, Quine does not accept sense-data; they are not needed for science. Physical objects cannot be eliminated from science, and they do all the work that sense-data do. Sense-data are not needed even to account for reports of illusions and uncertainty. Quine accounts for them with the phrase "seems that" prefixed to a sentential clause about physical objects, and he then paraphrases them away in the same way he paraphrases away propositional attitudes towards sentences. Sense-data are excess baggage.

Quine's rejection of sense-data brings his standards for adjudicating conflicting claims for thinghood into high relief. Something has a claim to being an entity if it is empirically attested to or is theoretically useful. Competing claims to thinghood have to be weighed against both considerations. Sense-data have empirical support but no theoretical use. Physical objects have at least some empirical support and a great deal of theoretical utility. Even if physical objects are not completely observable, or not "all there," positing the unobservable parts involves more conceptual continuity than inventing an abstract entity. Theoretical utility also recommends classes or objects for thinghood. Classes account for numbers and numbers for mathematics. Hence, there are classes.

There are no properties or attributes because, in contrast with classes, they do not have clear identity. Classes are identical just in case they have the same members. There is nothing similar to be said for properties. The same set of objects might have two different properties; all and only creatures with hearts are creatures with kidneys; but the property of having a heart is different from the property of having a kidney.

Also, there are no facts. Like properties, facts do not have well-defined identity conditions. There is no answer to the question, "Is the pulling of the trigger the same entity as the killing of the man?" Facts are objectionable on other grounds. "Fact" is a stylistic crutch; it helps support the word "that" in some grammatical constructions, such as "The fact that he left is no excuse," and the phrase "that fact" is a kind of standard abbreviation for a previously expressed assertion. As such, however, facts can be eliminated or altogether avoided by simple paraphrase; it also helps invigorate a prose style, as William Strunk, Jr., and E. B. White show in *The Elements of Style*.

Another question is, "Are objects given?" Quine says, "No." They are posits. To call something a "posit" is not, for Quine, to be derogatory. Although some posits are bad—theoretically unjustified—some posits are really real; we posit entities of certain sorts in order to explain phenomena. For Quine, our beliefs are replete with posits. If a posit fails to explain a phenomenon or if another posit explains it better, then its justification fails. But the best explanatory posits are justified and have the status of being real. In short, for Quine, two sorts of objects have this status: physical objects for natural sciences, and sets or classes for mathematics.

Quine's third project is to explain how a person's ontological commitments can be clearly expressed in language. His explanation is that what is required is a canonical notation which is clear, precise, and unambiguous. Such a notation is the first-order predicate calculus with identity. A canonical notation has two purposes. The first is that it allows for simplification of theory. It allows a person to iterate a few constructions a large number of times to the same effect as the use of a larger number of constructions a small number of times. The use of a larger number of constructions may allow for psychologically simpler constructions, but not a theoretically simpler one; and that is what is demanded. The second purpose of a canonical notation is clarity. There are no ambiguities and no hedged entities in a canonical notation. Everything that is meant is up front.

Quine's notion of philosophical explication is an important one in itself and important historically in contrast with some traditional notions of analysis. A philosophical explication does not purport to uncover or bring to light the hidden or implicit ideas of the people who use the problematic notion; and it does not purport to be synonymous with the problematic notion. In one stroke, Quine cuts the Gordian knot of G. E. Moore's paradox of analysis. Philosophical explication is informative because it replaces the problematic notion with unproblematic notions that serve the same purpose. The notions of the explication may well be unfamiliar to and difficult for the ordinary user, but that is irrelevant. Familiarity should not be confused with intelligibility. Philosophical explication requires philosophically acceptable notions, not familiar ones.

This view of philosophical explication introduces a certain latitude into the standard of correctness. A correct explication may not be a unique one; several nonequivalent explications may be equally acceptable, no one of which is more or less correct than the others, so long as each explication meets scientific standards and serves the original purpose. For example, it is indifferent whether one accepts Gottlob Frege's, John von Neumann's, Ernst Zermelo's, Richard Dedekind's, or someone else's definition of number—so long as the chosen one does the job. In short, explication is elimination: out goes the bad air of familiar but unacceptable notions; in comes the good air of intelligibility. Quine thinks that his view of philosophical explication is in line with Ludwig Wittgenstein's doctrine that the goal of philosophy is to dissolve a problem by showing that, contrary to appearances, there really was no problem.—*A.P.M.*

PERTINENT LITERATURE

Harman, Gilbert. "Quine on Meaning and Existence," in *The Review of Metaphysics.* XXI, nos. 1 and 2 (September and December, 1967), pp. 124-151, 343-367.

Gilbert Harman's article has two parts. The first part is an exposition of W. V. O. Quine's views about meanings and propositions. The second part explains how Quine goes about answering the question, "What is there?"

Harman explains that Quine's objections to the existence of meanings and propositions is not ontologically based. Quine does not reject them because they are abstract entities; sets are abstract entities, and Quine believes that they exist. The difference between meanings and propositions on the one hand and sets on the other is that sets have explanatory value and the others have none; this is the reason why Quine rejects them. He rejects them because they do not in fact explain what they purport to explain. Believing that there are such entities as meanings or propositions is similar to believing in phlogiston or witches; such beliefs are part of an inadequate scientific theory. Worse, appeals to meanings and propositions are not simply incorrect explanations; they explain nothing, although they may give the false appearance of explaining something. Instead of saying that "Copper is a metal" is true by virtue of the meanings of its words, there is nothing to prevent one from saying with equal justice that it is true by virtue of the fact that copper is a metal. Similarly, instead of saying "Copper is copper" is true by virtue of the meanings of its words, there is nothing to prevent one from saying with equal justice that it is true by virtue of the fact that everything is self-identical. The phrase "by virtue of the meanings of its words" does no explanatory work.

One argument for the existence of propositions is this: The same belief can be expressed by different sentences; thus beliefs cannot be sentences; they are what is expressed by sentences—namely, propositions. Quine claims that the postulation of propositions plays no explanatory role. What is believed are sentences, and ordinary talk allows the same belief to be identified with several sentences. The phenomenon of belief can be accounted for solely in terms of attitudes toward sentences, and hence no postulation of propositions is necessary and no postulation is justified.

In the second part of his article, Harman explains how Quine answers the question, "What exists?" Philosophy, for Quine, is continuous with science. Philosophy differs from science only in being methodologically more self-conscious and in being applied to problems more general than those which any particular science investigates. In order to answer the question "What exists?" we need to know something about science; to do this is to do philosophy of science, and, for the purposes of ontology, that is all philosophy needs to be.

These views put Quine at odds with logical positivists, for whom there is a sharp division between philosophy, which in large part consists of practical decisions about the language of science, and science. Should one choose the physical object language of science or the language of sense-data? For Quine, to choose a language is to choose a theory. A person makes decisions about what kind of language to speak on grounds of practicality, convenience, and simplicity; but these are the very same sorts of considerations that go into decisions about what scientific theory a person should accept. One can, if one likes, formulate talk about things as talk about language. And this is sometimes a useful device. The sentence "Grass is green" can be reformulated as "'Green' is true of what 'grass' is true of." Quine calls such reformulations "semantic assent." These reformulations are legitimate; they are especially helpful for parties who are arguing about ontological commitments. But at some stage a person must go down the mountain and talk about nonlinguistic things.

Scientific theory needs a regimented language, and regimentation of language serves the same purpose as scientific theory: systematization. Two marks of systematization are definiteness and regularity. Regimented language has a definiteness and regularity that ordinary language lacks; and, because the better a scientific theory the more definite and regular it is, regimented language can express sophisticated scientific theories with an ease and accuracy that is ill-suited to ordinary language. This view of regimented and ordinary language does not entail a conflict between the two. Each is well-suited to its own purposes, but it is important not to mistake those purposes nor to deny the legitimacy of either.

Strawson, P. F. "Singular Terms and Predication," in *Words and Objections: Essays on the Work of W. V. O. Quine.* Edited by Donald Davidson and Jaakko Hintikka. Boston: D. Reidel, 1969, pp. 97-117.

A central part of W. V. O. Quine's theory of a canonical notation is his distinction between singular terms (for example, "Leo" and "that lion") and general terms in the predicate position (for example, "tawny" in "Leo is tawny"). P. F. Strawson thinks this distinction rests upon concepts that Quine has not made explicit. These concepts are: first, a hierarchy of types of entities, where spatiotemporal particulars are of type 0 and their properties type 1; second, the function of singular terms to identify particulars, where identifying is to be understood as bringing it about that the audience knows what object is to receive the predication. A singular subject/predicate statement is true, then, just in case the predicate applies to the object identified by the subject term; it is false if the predicate does not apply. When the subject term fails to identify any object at all, then there is nothing for the predicate to be judged either true of or false of, and the result is what Quine calls a truth-value gap.

The existence of truth-value gaps is not the important point; it is just a consequence of what is important—namely, that singular terms and general terms in the predicate position play different roles, and that consequently their failure to function properly leads to different results. General terms, according to Quine, have the role of being true of the object that the singular term refers to; and reference is the role of the singular term. But, Strawson objects, the terms "is true of" and "refers to" are as obscure as the distinction they are intended to explain; and, worse, Quine sometimes uses them interchangeably.

The need for an adequate account of the distinction is acute because of Quine's views about canonical notation; he holds that all singular terms get eliminated in favor of variables, quantification, and general terms in the predicate position. Such elimination, however, masks the fact that we understand the role of variables only because we understand the role that singular terms have. It is important, then, to see that the elimination of singular terms, if in fact it can be carried out, does not dispense with the notion of identification, which is inextricably tied to them.

There is a further point to be made about predication. In correct predication, the predicate expresses a property that is of a type that groups or collects the object identified by the subject; and there are levels of properties that form a kind of hierarchy. First-order properties, such as being human, group spatiotemporal particulars; properties of properties, such as being a color, group properties of the first type. This fact explains Quine's choice of quantification as a test of ontological commitment. Because he is ontologically committed to spatiotemporal entities as the basic entities, he looks for a criterion that picks them out to the exclusion of other things. Quantification in first-order predicate logic offers him such a criterion, because of the type-hierarchy implicit in predication; spatiotemporal entities are of type 0; that is, they and only they can be the values of bound variables and are not things that might be expressed by a general term in the predicate position. All other kinds of entities, properties, properties of properties, and so on, can introduce entities expressed by general terms in the predicative position. Strawson wants to remind Quine, however, that such entities can also be identified by singular terms in the subject position; and this means that they too count as entities, although they are not, of course, the same type of entity as spatiotemporal particulars.

Strawson, P. F. "Entity and Identity," in *Contemporary British Philosophy*. Edited by H. D. Lewis. London: George Allen & Unwin, 1976, pp. 193-220.

P. F. Strawson claims that W. V. O. Quine's slogan, "No entity without identity," does not express a philosophically valuable principle. The slogan is susceptible to various interpretations: (1) everything is identical with itself; (2) everything belongs to some sort or kind of thing such that instances of each sort or kind are identifiable by a common or general criterion; (3) some things belong to sorts or kinds of things such that instances of each sort or kind are identifiable by a common or general criterion; and some things do not belong to such sorts or kinds. The former things are entities; the latter are not.

Strawson holds that (1) says too little to be of value; (2) says too much to be of value; and (3) is stipulative at best. (1) merits no further discussion. (2) is shown to be false by considering universal or general things. Neither character traits (wit, cheerfulness, amorousness), nor smells, nor musical *timbres*, nor ways of walking, talking, and gesturing, nor literary and architectural styles, have statable identity conditions, although competent speakers have no problem correctly applying the terms for them and saying whether, with respect to them, something is the same as or different from another thing.

Concerning (3), it is the case that there is a distinction between instances of those kinds of things for which there are specifiable criteria or identity—call them "substances"—and instances of those kinds of things for which there are not—call them "nonsubstances." This fact, however, cannot be used to establish that the former instances are entities and the latter are not. For, while it is true that identification of some nonsubstances depends upon the identification of substances, it is also true that substances themselves depend upon forms that do not themselves have specifiable criteria of identity. So, to honor substances alone with the title of "entity" is simply to stipulate what an entity is.

Why then should Quine, or anyone else, find (3) appealing? Strawson thinks it is due to conflating two very different considerations. The first consideration is that substances, material individuals, are the original entities of our acquaintance and undeniably entities; this is an ontological consideration. The second consideration is that material individuals are the subject of first-order predication; this is a logical consideration. It is not surprising, however, that the two considerations should have been conflated; each reinforces the other. Material entities are eminently predicate-worthy in the sense that they are the indispensable objects of first-order predication; and we understand first-order predication by our practice of predicating things of material entities. Material individuals, however, are not the only subjects of predication and not the only things that have specifiable criteria of identity. Earlier, Strawson had made clear that any concept expressed in a predicate can be shifted into the subject position of a sentence and thereby made a suitable candidate for predication. "Green" in "Grass is green" can be promoted to the subject position, as in "Green is my favorite color." Usually, the shift from predicate to subject position requires some grammatical readjustment—concrete common terms in the predicate position become abstract singular terms in the subject position—but that is logically unimportant. What is important is the fact that these abstract objects can be subjects for predication, and yet they do not have specifiable criteria of identity. Thus (3) fails to capture fully our notion of an entity.

There is at least one additional way in which Quine's slogan can be interpreted; namely, as saying that everything that can be sensibly talked about can be, at least in principle, identified. This, however, is not an interpretation that Quine ever intended to be put on it. It is, rather, Strawson's own view, and it is with rare immodesty that he refers to this interpretation as an admirable maxim. The immodesty is tempered, however, when he goes on to explain that the maxim has a different application for each different class of ontological kinds, and should either be dropped from the philosophical vocabulary or severely restricted in sense.—*A.P.M.*

ADDITIONAL RECOMMENDED READING

Davidson, Donald and Jaakko Hintikka, eds. *Words and Objections*. Boston: D. Reidel, 1969. A collection of essays, inspired by *Word and Object*, by first generation Quinians and many of Quine's most important contemporaries.

Harding, Sandra G., ed. *Can Theories Be Refuted? Essays on the Duhem-Quine Thesis*. Boston: D. Reidel, 1976. A collection of essays discussing Quine's view that individual sentences of a scientific theory are not refuted piecemeal.

Orenstein, Alex. *Willard Van Orman Quine*. Boston: Twayne, 1977. A comprehensive introduction to Quine's philosophy.

Strawson, P. F. "Positions for Quantifiers," in *Semantics and Philosophy*. Edited by Milton K. Munitz and Peter K. Unger. New York: New York University Press, 1974, pp. 63-79. A further attack by Strawson on Quine's ontological use of quantification theory.

Shahan, Robert W. and Chris Swoyer, eds. *Essays on the Philosophy of*

W. V. O. Quine. Norman: University of Oklahoma Press, 1979. A *Festschrift*, the contributors of which are second-generation Quinians and critics.

SENSE AND SENSIBILIA

Author: J. L. Austin (1911-1960)
Type of work: Theory of perception
First published: 1962

PRINCIPAL IDEAS ADVANCED

The "argument from illusion" fails to establish the existence of sense-data in illusory experiences, and, a fortiori, *fails to establish their existence in all perceptual experiences.*

Neither the objects of perception nor the circumstances of illusions constitute a homogenous class; many different kinds of things are perceived, and the ways in which perceptions are illusory are many.

Philosophers must use words in their ordinary sense because that is the only sense that is intelligible, unless the word is given a technical meaning; and it is not always easy to introduce a technical meaning for a word.

Neither the term "sense-datum" nor "material object," as used by philosophers, has been introduced in a meaningful way.

Underlying the argument from illusion is a desire for incorrigible knowledge; underlying the desire for incorrigible knowledge is a theory according to which certain propositions describing certain experiences are evidently true and all other knowledge is built upon the evident knowledge by inference. This theory of knowledge is false; there are no such privileged experiences or propositions.

Sense and Sensibilia is a reconstruction of J. L. Austin's notes for the undergraduate lectures that he first gave at Oxford in 1946 and several times after that until 1959. They also form the bulk of his lectures at the University of California, Berkeley, where he was a visiting professor in the fall of 1958. The general doctrine that Austin wishes to attack is formulated by him as follows: ". . . we never see or otherwise perceive (or 'sense'), or anyhow we never *directly* perceive or sense, material objects (or material things), but only sense-data (or our own ideas, impressions, sensa, sense-perceptions, percepts, etc.)." Baldly stated, this doctrine may seem odd; Austin concedes that its proponents may not mean it literally or even at all. But, Austin thinks, it is not relevant whether they mean it literally or not. Philosophy, in a normative sense, is rigorous, and part of being rigorous is being exact, being willing to be evaluated on the basis of what you say. So Austin relentlessly attends to the actual words used by his opponents, the actual arguments they present, and finds them wanting. He is less concerned with whether their conclusions are true than with whether the statements of their premises are strictly intelligible and logically compelling.

However it is to be taken, the general doctrine is a hoary philosophical view: Plato, René Descartes, George Berkeley, David Hume, and Bertrand

Russell, to mention the most prominent and dear to British philosophy, espoused it. So, if Austin's attack is successful, he has refuted an important doctrine. He does not, however, aim his arrows at Plato and company; he forgoes philosophical patricide for fratricide; he takes as his quarry some books of his brothers at Oxford: H. H. Price, Wykeham Professor of Logic (1935-1959); A. J. Ayer, then Grote Professor of Metaphysics at the University of London and later Price's successor; and G. J. Warnock, Principal of Hertford College, Oxford. Ayer's book *The Foundation of Empirical Knowledge* is dealt with most severely, and there are some who claim that Austin selected that book because he thought that Ayer had not deserved the professorship at London, a position Austin himself had turned down. They are not convinced by Austin's own disclaimer that he selected these books "for their merits and not for their deficiencies," since he virtually never mentions any merits. And Ayer has protested that Austin's criticisms are not always fair. A more likely reason why Austin chose these books is that he was very much concerned about philosophical method or style, correct philosophical style, as opposed to the standard way of doing philosophy; and since his colleagues were those most likely to influence the actual philosophical style of his students, he probably thought it his duty to say exactly what he did not like about their style. Austin's book is most valuable, then, as an attack on a traditional way of doing philosophy, as an illustration of philosophical criticism, and as a demonstration of an alternative style of philosophy. There is another way to express this point. The title of Austin's book is by design similar to that of a novel by Jane Austen, *Sense and Sensibility*. Just as Austen's book is a criticism of British social manners, Austin's book is a criticism of British philosophical manners.

One of the philosophical manners that Austin finds objectionable is the practice of positing a dichotomy that is either inadequate to the phenomenon under investigation or downright unintelligible—what he calls "the bogus dichotomy." Such a dichotomy is the one between sense-data and material objects, a dichotomy that Austin thinks is presupposed by Ayer and Price and never argued for except tendentiously. Ayer introduces the dichotomy at the opening of his book; he contrasts the ordinary man's supposedly naïve belief that he can perceive material objects directly and the philosopher's belief that human beings directly perceive not material objects but "sense-data," a term requiring explanation. Austin is dubious about both terms of the dichotomy. Concerning the beliefs attributed to the ordinary man, Austin points out that not only would the ordinary man not say that he perceives material objects, because these terms are not part of his *modus dicendi*, but also he would not restrict the class of perceptual objects to the "moderate-sized specimens of dry goods," pens, tables, and desks, which Ayer cites as paradigms of material objects. For the ordinary man, sounds, odors, flames, rainbows, cinematic images, paintings, and vapors are perceptual objects.

Are they material objects also? Ayer does not say, and, Austin claims, he could not easily say, for "material object" has no independent meaning of its own; it is simply a term of contrast for "sense-datum." What, then, does "sense-datum" mean? It is introduced as a term of contrast for "material object." It is what is named as being immediately perceived once the ordinary man is persuaded that he is mistaken that material objects are immediately perceived. "Sense-datum" and "material object" are mutually parasitic; each simultaneously hosts and feeds upon the other; or, to use Austin's metaphor, they "live by taking in each other's washings."

Lurking beneath Austin's criticism is a positive doctrine; he thinks that "what is spurious is not one term of the pair [sense-datum/material object], but the antithesis itself." That is, there is "no *one* kind of thing that we 'perceive' but many different kinds." This is the full force of his catalogue of disparate perceptual objects. Philosophers should attend to the multiplicity of kinds of things; in another work he recommends that philosophers proceed like entomologists who have taxonomized tens of thousands of kinds of insects. Austin always opposed the philosophical penchant for monism and dualism; "Why, if there are nineteen of anything, is it not philosophy?" he once asked. Russell and William James thought that they had cut through the Gordian knot tied by the equally unattractive, and seemingly exhaustive, alternatives of materialism, idealism, and dualism by espousing neutral monism, according to which there is only one kind of thing, neither mental nor material, of which mind and matter are constructions. Austin might be said to have espoused neutral pluralism: there are many kinds of things, of which being mental or material are merely dimensions of some of them.

The ordinary man is supposed to be jarred out of his naïve belief that he directly perceives material objects, and eventually taken down the garden path of the causal theory of perception or phenomenalism by what is known as "the argument from illusion." The argument has two stages. The first stage is designed to establish that human beings on some occasions and in some situations do not directly perceive material objects. The second stage is designed to establish that the result of the first stage should be generalized to all occasions and all situations. Many different versions of the first stage could be devised; Ayer presents three of them. The first is the stick-in-the-water version. A straight and otherwise normal stick, if partially submerged in water, will appear to be bent. Since it is assumed that the stick in the water remains straight, the person does not see the stick directly. What he sees directly is the appearance of a bent stick; call it a "sense-datum." So sometimes people do not perceive material objects directly. The second version is the mirage version. Under certain physiological conditions, a person will seem to see an oasis. Since the oasis does not in fact exist and yet something is seen which is not a material object, what the person directly sees is not a material object, but a sense-datum. A third version is the mirror version. A person seeing himself in a mirror does not see his body directly; what he sees directly is his reflection, which is not material, but a sense-datum.

The second stage of the argument proceeds by claiming that the experiences of the sense-data just discussed are qualitatively identical with experiences caused by material objects in standard perceptual situations. So, it is philosophically uneconomical to say that the entity perceived in these situations is different in kind from the sense-data; hence, sense-data are immediately perceived in every perceptual situation. If a different kind of entity were involved, a different kind of experience would be involved. This line of reasoning is buttressed by the consideration that perceptions often gradually shift from being nonveridical to veridical. The apparent size of an object may change from being misleadingly small to its correct size through a series of gradual and imperceptible stages.

Austin likes virtually nothing about "the argument from illusion," including its name. The "the" in its name indicates that there is one kind of illusion, and that is false. There are many kinds, which should be distinguished, although typically they are not; some arise from defects in the subject of perception, some from defects in the medium, some from the object, and some from faulty inferences. An adequate taxonomy of illusions would take all of these aspects into account. Also, many of the purported illusions are not illusory at all. Mirror reflections are not; and the appearance of a stick in water is not just like the appearance of a bent stick out of water. For one thing, water can be seen in the one case and not in the other. Further, seeing a bright green after-image on a wall is not exactly like seeing a bright green patch on the wall, nor is seeing the world through tinted glasses like seeing the world without them. So much for the first stage of the argument.

Sometimes the appearances of objects x and y are qualitatively identical; but from this it does not follow that x and y are identical. Why shouldn't perceiving one sort of thing be just like perceiving another, so long as there is some independent means of distinguishing them? Even if we should admit the existence of sense-data for the abnormal cases, why should we also admit them for the normal ones? So the attempt to generalize the argument in stage two fails. Finally, Austin objects to the metaphorical phrase "deceived by our senses." Our senses are dumb; they do not say anything and hence cannot deceive us; similarly, there is no testimony of the senses, *pace* Descartes and other philosophers.

Another of the philosophical manners that irritates Austin is the practice of taking an ordinary word that has a very restricted use and gradually extending that use "until it becomes, first perhaps obscurely metaphorical, but ultimately meaningless." An example of this practice is the word "direct" as it is used by philosophers in connection with perception. It sometimes might make sense to say that one has seen an object "directly" or "indirectly," but it is either an obscure metaphor or meaningless to talk about touching something indirectly—does it mean using a stick or gloves?—or smelling, tasting, or hearing something (an echo?) indirectly. The problem is that we cannot take the word, as used by philosophers, in its ordinary sense; and if we cannot take it in that sense, then it is not immediately clear in what sense we are to take it. And if we do not know what sense to attach to the word, then we can hardly judge the truth or falsity of the purported propositions in which the word appears. Thus Austin's scruples against misusing words are not based upon a love of the ordinary but upon a love of the intelligible and the true. He is not casting his lot with the vulgar against the philosophers. An ordinary word can be given a technical sense, a new word coined, and Austin has no objection to the invention and use of technical terms in philosophy, as his *How To Do Things with Words* amply shows. But, he complains, philosophers have not succeeded in giving a technical meaning to such terms as "sense-datum" and "material object," and so their use of them is unintelligible; the purported propositions in which they occur are neither true nor false. The upshot is that Austin is lobbying not for the average and mediocre, but for the traditional high standards of philosophy; and he is not a little incensed that the generally accepted quality of philosophizing does not measure up to them.

Another word abused by philosophers is the word "real." Austin wants to make two basic points about "real." First, it is a normal word; second, it is not a normal word. It is normal because it is not "new-fangled" or technical; its use is firmly established in ordinary speech and, in this way, its meaning is fixed. This has the consequence that a philosopher cannot simply mean by it whatever he chooses. It is, at the same time, although not of course in the same way, an abnormal word. It is not ambiguous, but it also does not have a single specifiable meaning. What "real" means in a given context of use depends upon the substantive which it modifies. A real duck is one that is not a decoy; a real gun is not one that is not a decoy, but one that is not a toy or model. Austin calls words like "real" "substantive hungry." A consequence of substantive hunger is that there is no general criterion for being real or distinguishing what is real from what is not. What procedure should be followed to determine whether something is real depends upon the substantive that "real" is attached to. It might seem to be axiomatic that if something is not real, then it does not exist. But that is not the case. A decoy duck exists but is not a real duck; a toy gun exists but is not a real gun. Conversely, the decoy and toy are respectively a real decoy and a real toy. In general, one and the same thing can be a real *x* and not a real *y*. Austin is only half facetious when he calls his minute investigations of the use of the word "real" a discussion of "The Nature of Reality."

Philosophers purport to posit sense-data to account for the facts of perception and to provide a nonambiguous term for perceptual experiences. Austin does not think these reasons, unsupportable in themselves, constitute their deepest motives. He thinks they are posited because, as described by philosophers, they provide a foothold on certainty. For Ayer, sense-data are those objects which, when sensibly experienced, really exist and really have the properties they seem to have. Thus, statements about sense-data, given in good faith, are incorrigible. Austin does not think much of the idea of incorrigibility, about which he says, "The pursuit of the incorrigible is one of the most venerable bugbears in the history of philosophy."

The search for the incorrigible is bound up with a certain general doctrine about knowledge, and it is knowledge, as the title of Ayer's book attests, not perception, that moves philosophers. The doctrine is that empirical knowledge has foundations upon which all other knowledge is built by inference as one ascends the various tiers. The foundations must be absolutely secure in order to guarantee that the edifice of knowledge cannot crumble. Sense-data are embedded in the foundations. Statements about them are incorrigible; so all other knowledge is built upon them. Statements about material objects and beliefs about them depend upon inductive inferences from statements about sense-data; such statements and beliefs go beyond the immediate evidence and for that reason are fallible.

Virtually all of this general doctrine is false, says Austin. It is not the case that statements about sense-data are incorrigible. A person might misuse the word he selects or misreport his perception because he insufficiently attends to it. Not all statements about sense-data are evidence for other statements; "It appears blue" may or may not be evidence for a thing's being blue, depending upon the circumstances. Conversely, not all statements about material objects require evidence or stand in need of verification. If a person sees that something is a pig, he does not need evidence for its being a pig; if the pig is not in view, evidence may be in order. And sometimes some sentences about material objects are conclusively verified and incorrigible, "in the sense that, when they are made, the circumstances are such that they are quite certainly, definitely, and un-retractably true." Seeing, smelling, poking at a pig, a person might incorrigibly know that he sees a pig. It all depends upon the circumstances. So, it is not true that knowledge in general has a specific structure; and, according to Austin, if the Theory of Knowledge is the search for such a general structure, then there simply is no such theory.—
A.P.M.

Pertinent Literature

Ayer, A. J. "Has Austin Refuted the Sense-Datum Theory?," in *Synthese*. Vol. XVII, no. 2 (June, 1967), pp. 117-140.

The initial reception of J. L. Austin's *Sense and Sensibilia* was phenomenal, so to speak. A. J. Ayer thought that that reception was undeserved and wrote this article in order to defend the honor of the sense-data theory against

Austin's numerous criticisms. Ayer selects seventeen of them, which he discusses seriatim, not all of which can be mentioned here. The first one is that the contrast between sense-data and physical objects is an oversimplification. Ayer concedes this criticism but hopes to show in his replies to the other criticisms that this does not adversely affect the validity of the arguments for the existence of sense-data.

Austin's second criticism is that it only makes sense to talk about certainty and uncertainty in abnormal situations, where there is some reason to doubt one's perceptions. But philosophers use the notions of certainty and uncertainty in an unrestricted way, to apply to every situation; so this use makes no sense. Ayer disagrees; he thinks the main point about certainty with respect to sense-data is a logical one; it is that the occurrence of the perceptual experience that gives rise to the judgment that a certain physical object exists is logically consistent with the falsity of that judgment. This point implies that it is possible to formulate statements that do not go beyond perceptual experience, whether the experience is veridical or not. And Austin does not address himself to this point at all. His sensitive discussions of how we ordinarily use a word and what-we-should-say-when are all to be commended in themselves but not insofar as they are supposed to bear on the matter of sense-data; it remains true that judgments about physical objects go beyond the data upon which they are based. Consider the judgment that I see an apple. I assume that it is tangible and has a certain texture, smell, and taste; I make further assumptions about the material out of which it is made, its origin, its causal properties, and many other things. All of this is inferred from past experience and the current visual experience of a circular patch of red, and it all exceeds the evidence of my current experience.

Let "the argument from illusion" be a misnomer, as Austin maintains. The assumption has no logical force against its conclusion that appearance and reality do not coincide. Even if there are many types of illusions and many of the discrepancies between appearance and reality are incorrectly called "illusions," the fact of illusion and these discrepancies are sufficient to prove that perceptual judgments go beyond the evidence upon which they are based.

Concerning incorrigibility, Ayer thinks that a nonempty class of incorrigible statements is important in order to stop a regress that threatens to go on infinitely. If to know that a proposition *p* is true normally involves knowing some other proposition *q*, which supports *p*, then either *q* itself requires support from further propositions *ad infinitum* or, at some stage, a proposition is reached that does not require additional support but is knowable in itself, that is to say, incorrigible. And the obvious candidates for such incorrigible statements are those that report a person's current thoughts and perceptions. Perhaps Austin is right in holding that not even these experiences are always correctly reported, but at least this weaker thesis is true: the person having the experience is the final judge of the truth of his reports; no one else can gainsay his verdict as to the accuracy of his reports of his own experiences.

Ayer concedes that his saying that no statements about physical objects are ever conclusively verified is objectionable; but he nevertheless insists that the point he had in mind was correct—namely, that material object statements stand to experiential statements as theoretical statements stand to observation statements.

In short, most of Austin's arguments are bad, according to Ayer; those that are good are irrelevant to the existence or nonexistence of sense-data; and since the main point of Ayer's arguments for them is untouched, the standing of sense-data is secure.

Graham, Keith. *J. L. Austin: A Critique of Ordinary Language Philosophy.* Brighton, England: The Harvester Press, 1977.

Keith Graham is frank about his general attitude toward J. L. Austin's philosophical work. He thinks it is "stultifying" and typically has a bad influence on those who study it, especially if they are converted to Austin's method of doing philosophy. Graham's chief objection is that Austin's attentiveness to the minutiae of ordinary language gives ordinary language undue weight. There may be a reason for each distinction drawn in ordinary language; but is there a *good* reason for each? Austin uncritically accepts what ordinary language dishes out, claims Graham. Austin's overreliance on ordinary language, Graham also believes, hinders him from recognizing distinctions that are not to be found in it.

Graham, in his book, which is a comprehensive examination of Austin's philosophical work, devotes one long chapter to *Sense and Sensibilia*. He is not concerned with how fairly Austin has criticized A. J. Ayer but with what, if any, enduring merit there is in Austin's attitude toward phenomenalism and the causal theory of perception. Yet many of Graham's criticisms are *ad hominem* arguments. He claims that Austin holds that scientists, if anyone, not philosophers, should attempt to reduce the number of kinds of perceptual objects, and yet he himself reduces that number by rejecting the existence of sense-data; and, while recognizing the possibility that different persons may have alternative conceptual schemes, Austin rejects Ayer's suggestion that some people may say different things about perception because they have alternative conceptual schemes. But, Graham continues, commitment to sense-data is a commitment to an alternative conceptual scheme.

Austin's position in *Sense and Sensibilia* is best described not as a refutation of the arguments of H. H. Price and Ayer but as a refusal to accept the terms of their arguments, and this is due to his philosophical conservatism, his commitment to preserve ordinary language and ordinary beliefs unchanged. His conservatism makes him fearful even to countenance arguments that might upset his beliefs; and that is what lies behind his refusal to let the argument from illusion get started. He charges philosophers who espouse the argument from illusion with begging the question about the existence of sense-data; but it is Austin himself who is begging the question, Graham counters, by denying their existence.

In two matters, Graham defends Austin. He does think that Austin's attack on the philosophical belief in the incorrigibility of some statements is successful. All description, insofar as it involves classification and memory, is fallible; it could be false, even in those cases in which the likelihood of falsity is very small. Yet Austin fails to see that there is a difference between sense-data reports, which, when true, do not require evidence, and material object reports, which do.

Graham also agrees that Austin's analysis of "real" is on the right track. Since the idea of existence is at least as problematic as the notion of reality, the latter cannot be analyzed in terms of the former. Reality is, indeed, a peculiar notion, and quite different from a concept like redness, which is very informative. To say that something is real is to say the minimum. Virtually all the content expressed by a phrase of the form "real X" is contributed by the noun filling the place marked by "X"; it is in this sense that "real" is substantive hungry. So, if philosophers want to know more about reality, they should study concrete instances of real X's.

Grice, H. P. "The Causal Theory of Perception," in *Proceedings of the Aristotelian Society*. Supplementary Volume XXXV (1961), pp. 121-152.

J. L. Austin's attacks in *Sense and Sensibilia* dampened the enthusiasm of those proponents of sense-data who accepted the force of his characteristic form of argumentation, which has come to be called "ordinary language analysis." Austin's attacks had virtually no effect on the direction or manner of thinking of those who would have no truck or trade with ordinary language analysis. This lack of commerce did not, however, prevent the proponents of sense-data from purporting to answer Austin's criticisms. Most of these replies amount to no more than indignant harumphings, no matter how articulate or sophisticated they are. This is the case whenever the defender of sense-data concedes that Austin's criticisms, taken as applying to what was literally *said* about sense-data and the argument from illusion, are correct, but not about what the proponents *meant*. For philosophy, as a rigorous science, stands or falls by what is exactly said. For those who stand on the same battlefield as Austin, two of the casualties of his attacks are phenomenalism, the view, roughly, that there are no unknowable entities behind appearances—only appearances are real—and the causal theory of perception, the theory that the notion of perceiving a material object includes the notion of a material object as playing a causal role in the having of a sense-datum and that perceiving is an inference from effect to cause. For each of these views, as described by A. J. Ayer and H. H. Price, respectively, depended upon arguments for the existence of sense-data, arguments that Austin had exploded.

An exception to the standard course of replying to Austin's kind of argumentation is that of H. P. Grice, whose defense of sense-data was radically new. He accepts Austin's way of doing philosophy as an important and legitimate way, but thinks that a way remains open not to outflank Austin's arguments, but to silence one of them as it is deployed against sense-data. So Grice meets Austin on his own ground. Before sketching the argument, it is advisable to mention the consequences if Grice is right. One is that there is at least one successful attempt to establish the existence of sense-data and that this one way prevails even in the face of an infinite number of unsuccessful attempts. A further consequence is that phenomenalism and the causal theory of perception are resurrected. These two consequences are impressive enough; but there is another. Contrary to the accepted view that phenomenalism and the causal theory of perception are competitors, Grice pointed out that they are consonant with each other; one can hold both by first giving a causal analysis of "*S* perceives *O*" and then paraphrasing this analysis into phenomenalistic terms.

Austin's main strategy against arguments for the existence of sense-data was to prevent them from getting off the ground by showing that the purported premises of those arguments made no literal sense, that they were meaningless. Against the contention that sense-data are referred to by such sentences as "It seems (appears) to be red," Austin and his followers typically argued in this way: It makes no sense to *say* "It seems (appears) to be red" unless there is some reason to deny or doubt—Grice calls this "the D-or-D conditions"—that the object is red. But since proponents of sense-data try to assert this when there is no reason for doubt or denial, their words make no literal sense. Notice that this line of argument turns on tying the D-or-D condition to the meaningfulness of the words used. Grice's way of refuting this line is to untie this connection. He does this by first distinguishing between what a speaker means and what his words mean, and, second, by distinguishing between what a speaker implies and what his words imply. He points out that while a speaker might imply and hence mean that the D-or-D condition is fulfilled, his words do not; for the speaker's implication can be canceled or detached by some added disclaimer; it is not contradictory to say "It seems (appears) to be red; and no one could doubt or deny that it is truly red." Implications that depend upon what the words mean cannot be nullified in this way. So, while asserting that "It seems (appears) to be red" may be misleading, it is meaningful and possibly true; and this is what is critically needed in order to establish the existence of sense-data.—*A.P.M.*

ADDITIONAL RECOMMENDED READING

Bennett, Jonathan. "'Real,'" in *Mind*. LXXV, no. 300 (October, 1966), pp. 501-515. Bennett charges that Austin's own account of how "real" is used is unclear, inaccurate, and irrelevant to the traditional problem about appearance and reality.

Firth, Roderick. "Austin and the Argument from Illusion," in *The Philosophical Review*. LXXIII, no. 3 (July, 1964), pp. 372-382. A sympathetic yet critical discussion of Austin's attack on the argument from illusion.

Forguson, L. W. "Has Ayer Vindicated the Sense-Datum Theory?" in *Symposium on J. L. Austin*. Edited by K. T. Fann. London: Routledge & Kegan Paul, 1969, pp. 309-341. A defense of Austin against Ayer's response; a reply by Ayer is also included in this volume.

McGreal, Ian P. *The Art of Making Choices*. Dallas, Texas: Southern Methodist University Press, 1953. Chapter Nine, "What Is Real Really?" argues that "real" is an emphasis word and, accordingly, has no meaning of its own.

Price, H. H. *Perception*. London: Methuen, 1932. One of Austin's prime targets in *Sense and Sensibilia*; it contains a classic statement of the causal theory of perception.

Stroll, Avrum and Robert Foelber. "Talk About Talk About Surfaces," in *Dialectica*. XXXI, nos. 3 and 4 (1977), pp. 409-430. A discussion of surfaces and their relation to sense-data that measures up to Austin's standards for rigor and detail.

HOW TO DO THINGS WITH WORDS

Author: J. L. Austin (1911-1960)
Type of work: Philosophy of language
First published: 1962

PRINCIPAL IDEAS ADVANCED

There appears to be a contrast between merely saying something and doing something; this is the contrast between "constative utterances," such as stating, and "performative utterances," such as promising.

Detailed examination of this contrast shows that it is not fruitful: to say something is to do something; in fact it is to do many things.

Locutionary acts consist, among other things, of uttering words with a sense and reference.

Illocutionary acts are governed by conventions and include such things as promising, swearing, and stating.

Perlocutionary acts are natural acts, such as persuading or angering, consequent upon illocutionary acts.

How to Do Things with Words is a reconstruction of J. L. Austin's William James Lectures at Harvard for 1955; it was first published posthumously under the editorship of J. O. Urmson. Austin's views on the matters discussed in the lectures were first formed in 1939, and he made some use of them in his address, "Other Minds," to the Aristotelian Society (1946). Between 1952 and 1959, he lectured on the same topic, sometimes under the title "Words and Deeds." Much of Austin's philosophical reputation rests upon his incisive and acerbic criticism of the views of other philosophers, for example his withering attacks on the views of A. J. Ayer and G. J. Warnock in *Sense and Sensibilia. How to Do Things with Words*, however, is a first-class piece of constructive philosophy. Austin invented speech act theory; before him there was no such theory; and his theory has been used, revised, and extended not only by philosophers, but also by linguists, linguistic anthropologists and sociologists, cognitive psychologists, and speech communication theorists.

Austin begins his lectures in a remarkably modest way: "What I shall have to say here is neither difficult not contentious; the only merit I should like to claim for it is that of being true, at least in parts." Coming from most philosophers, such modesty would hardly be disarming; coming from Austin, it is simply the first of those many parts that are true. He then recounts with approval the attempts to recognize that some purported statements are strictly nonsense and to account for why they are nonsense. He also lauds the discovery that some apparent statements do not purport to state facts but to evince emotion or to prescribe or otherwise influence conduct. These efforts and discoveries have developed piecemeal, he thinks, but also amount to a revolution in philosophy, about which he says, "If anyone wishes to call it the greatest and most salutary in its history, this is not, if you come to think of it, a large claim." What he proposes to offer the revolution is a manifesto, or, to drop the metaphor, a theory that describes the utterances that masquerade as statements. He calls such utterances "performatives."

Performatives have two characteristics: (a) they do not describe or "constate" anything at all and are not true or false; (b) to utter the performative sentence is not merely to say something. Austin's first examples of performatives are "I do," uttered by a bride or groom; "I name this ship the *Queen Elizabeth*," uttered by someone smashing a bottle of champagne against the bow; "I give and bequeath my watch to my brother," as occurring in a will; and "I bet you sixpence it will rain tomorrow." Based upon these examples, it might be tempting to think that to say the right words is the same as to do the action at issue. But that is not correct. In general, the words have the proper effect only if uttered in appropriate circumstances, and only if the participants are doing certain other physical or mental things; for example, breaking the bottle of champagne. Further, for some acts, words are not necessary at all. Marrying might be accomplished by cohabiting, betting accomplished by inserting a coin into a slot machine.

Austin's examples of performatives are sufficient to prove that there is some distinction to be drawn between them and constatives: "But now how, as philosophers, are we to proceed? One thing we might go on to do, of course, is to take it all back: another would be to bog, by logical stages, down. But all this must take time."

Constatives are true or false; performatives are not; rather, because they are types of actions, they can be done well or badly. Austin, in his doctrine of infelicities, concentrates on how they can be performed badly; for one way to learn how a machine works is to see in what ways it can break. As a kind of action, performatives are subject to all the defects that any action is; as linguistic acts, they have some special problems. Without pretending that the list is exhaustive or that its items are mutually exclusive, he mentions three conditions on performatives, conditions which, if contravened, give rise to infelicities:

> (A) A conventional procedure having a conventional effect must exist, and it must require that certain words be uttered by certain persons in certain circumstances; and the persons and circumstances must be the right ones for invoking the conventional procedure.
> (B) The procedure must be performed correctly and completely.
> (C) When the procedure requires certain thoughts, feelings, or intentions to act subsequently in a certain way, the participant must have them and in fact perform the intended action.

If an action is infelicitous for contravening either (A) or (B), the action is a misfire; the attempted performative is a failed attempt; the act is null and void. If an action is infelicitous for contravening (C), then the performative is successful but defective for "abusing" the procedure. This classification is helpful and instructive even though the borders between (A), (B), and (C) are not always clear, and it is not always possible to decide whether an infelicity belongs to one kind or another. It is important to be attentive to these deficiencies in the classification. "And we must at all cost avoid over-simplification, which one might be tempted to call the occupational disease of philosophers if it were not their occupation."

Although performative utterances are not true or false if they are felici-tously, that is, nondefectively, performed, they are related to statements that are true. For example, if a person felicitously utters, "I apologize," it is true that he apologizes, true that the person had offended or otherwise injured the addressee, true that he commits himself to not repeating the injury, and so on. The way in which a performative is related to some true statements is analogous to the way in which constatives are related to some true state-ments. The sentence "All men blush" *entails* "Some men blush." Saying "The cat is on the mat" *implies* that the speaker believes that the cat is on the mat. And "All Jack's children are bald" presupposes that Jack has children (see P. F. Strawson's *Introduction to Logical Theory*). So constatives are more like performatives than first appeared to be the case; they are being assimilated.

There are other reasons for assimilating constatives. The truth of "I am stating that John is running" depends upon the felicity of the speaker's saying or having said, "John is running." So at least some constative utterances have felicity conditions. On the other side of the distinction, some performatives are false: The warning "I warn you that the bull is about to charge" is a false warning if the bull is not about to charge.

These matters raise doubts about the performative/constative distinction. Is there a way to make the distinction in grammatical terms, by grammatical criteria? Many, but not all, performatives have their main verb in the first person singular, present tense, active, indicative mood, but "You are hereby authorized. . . ," "Passengers are warned. . . ," "Notice is hereby given . . ." and "Turn right" are exceptions. Thus, neither person, number, tense, voice, nor mood can be used as a simple criterion. The first-person, active, present tense remains, however, an attractive base upon which to build a criterion. For notice that there is an asymmetry between a performative verb in this form and the same verb in other persons, tenses, and moods. If I utter "I had bet," "He bets," or "They (might) have bet," I describe a certain action; but no action is described if I utter the words "I bet." Rather, to say, "I bet" (in the right circumstances, frame of mind, and so on) is, roughly, to bet. Austin's strategy for devising a criterion is, then, to make a list of verbs having this asymmetry and to "reduce" other performative utterances to this form, which Austin calls "explicit performative" form.

Explicit performatives should be considered a development of language that evolves out of "primary performatives," which are vague and less explicit because they serve more than one purpose. "I will," in contrast with "I promise that I will," can be used either for a prediction, expression of intention, or promise. Explicit performatives do the work that mood, tone of voice, cadence, adjectives, adverbs, particles, and sundry other things do in primary performatives. The imperative mood is indeterminate between giving an order, advice, permission, or consent, where the corresponding performative verb is determinate. Depending upon how the sentence "It's going to charge" is uttered (depending upon its phonological contour), the act is either a warning, a question, a charge, or a statement. The particles "therefore," "although," and "moreover" become, respectively, "I conclude that," "I concede that," and "I add that" in explicit performative form.

Although all this is instructive, it fails to serve the purpose of yielding a criterion of explicit performatives. For it is not always easy to determine whether an utterance is performative. "I assume that . . ." can be performative but may not be, and one can assume things without saying anything at all; and "I agree that . . ." may be performative or merely descriptive of the speaker's attitude. Another problem is that "I state that . . ." seems to be performative and yet is paradigmatically constative. The performative/constative distinction, then, cannot be sustained as a fruitful one, and it has, as promised, bogged down.

Up to this point Austin has been contrasting saying and doing. A new approach is required, one that focuses on the senses in which saying can be doing. Austin notices that every case of saying something, in the full sense, what he calls "the locutionary act," is a case of doing something. Every locutionary act consists of a *phonetic* act, a *phatic* act, and a *rhetic* act. The phonetic act is the act of merely uttering noises; a parrot is capable of performing a phonetic act. The phatic act is the act of uttering certain words in a grammatical sequence, that is, noises that belong to a language, and of uttering those words *as* belonging to a language. The *as* requirement is important; a parrot utters words but because it is not aware of them *as* words or *as* having a meaning, it does not perform a phatic act. The rhetic act is the act of uttering the words with a more or less definite sense and reference. The terms "sense" and "reference" are those of Gottlob Frege, but the doctrine is Austin's. For Frege, all meaningful words have both a sense and reference; for Austin, reference belongs to words that are correlated to objects by "demonstrative conventions"; sense belongs to those words that are correlated to general things by "descriptive conventions." For more about this see his articles "Truth" and "How To Talk: Some Simple Ways."

The difference between the phatic act and the rhetic act is brought out by the different ways of reporting them. A phatic act is reported by direct quotation: He said, "The cat is on the mat." A rhetic act is reported by indirect quotation: He said that the cat is on the mat. The difference is critical. A person who reports a phatic act is claiming, in effect, to be offering a verbatim report of the speaker's words; he is not committed to the proposition that its speaker had achieved any reference; there might have been no cat at all to refer to. A person who reports a rhetic act is not claiming that its speaker used the very words in which the report is cast; the speaker might have said, "The feline pet is lying upon the fabric used for protecting the floor." The person is committed to the proposition that the speaker's words had a definite sense and reference.

To report a rhetic act is not to report a speech act fully; for such a report leaves out the force of the utterance. Was his saying that I was to go to the store an order or merely advice or a suggestion? The force of a speech act is its "illocutionary force"; the act is an *illocutionary* act. The illocutionary act is governed by and conforms to conventions, and it should not be confused with something else that is done in a speech act, a *perlocutionary* act, which is not. A perlocutionary act is an act that produces certain effects on the feelings, thoughts, or actions of the audience, or even the speaker, as a consequence of the illocutionary act. These effects are natural consequences and not conventional ones, such as follow illocutionary acts. Although it is only a rough linguistic guide, we commonly report illocutionary acts as things done *in* saying something and perlocutionary acts as things done *by* saying something. In saying it, I *warned* him (illocutionary act); by saying it, I *persuaded* him (perlocutionary act). These linguistic formulas do not, however, yield a criterion. *By* saying something, a person might have been joking or insinuating, but joking and insinuating are not perlocutionary acts. And *in* saying something, a person might have made a mistake; but making a mistake is not an illocutionary act.

The original contrast between performatives and constatives was a false dichotomy. Illocutionary acts are performative, in Austin's original sense of that term, and some of them have truth-values. "I state that . . ." is on a par with "I argue that . . ." and "I promise that . . ." Like performatives, statements also have felicity conditions. A statement often presupposes the existence of a referent; so if no referent exists, the attempted statement fails. Further like performatives, statements require that the speaker be in a certain position; without evidence, the speaker cannot state when the world will end, although he may guess or prophesy it. Stating, it appears, is not *sui generis*; it is just one of many kinds of evaluation, and statements are not simply to be evaluated in terms of truth and falsity. Statements can be correct or incorrect, fair or unfair, exaggerated, precise, apt, misleading, or rough.

Statements belong to one category of illocutionary acts. Austin tentatively distinguishes five such categories: *verdictives, exercitives, commissives, behabitives*, and *expositives*. Verdictives, as the name implies, are typified by the kind of judgment issued by a jury, judge, umpire, or arbiter; they include estimates and appraisals. Exercitives are exercises of power; they include appointing, voting, ordering, and warning. Commissives commit the speaker to a course of action; they include promising, swearing, and declaring. Behabitives concern attitudes and social behavior; they include apologizing, congratulating, and condoling. Expositives indicate how an utterance fits into a conversation; they include arguing, replying, objecting, and stating.

Austin ends his lectures by commenting on his failure to relate his theory to traditional philosophical problems. The failure was deliberate; "I have purposely not embroiled the general theory with philosophical problems . . . ; this should not be taken to mean that I am unaware of them. . . . I leave to my readers the real fun of applying it in philosophy."—*A.P.M.*

PERTINENT LITERATURE

Searle, John R. "Austin on Locutionary and Illocutionary Acts," in *The Philosophical Review*. LXXVII, no. 4 (October, 1968), pp. 405-424.

John R. Searle thinks that J. L. Austin's distinction between illocutionary acts and locutionary acts is unhelpful and proposes to replace it with another: namely, the distinction between an illocutionary act and a propositional act. Searle's alternative distinction has, he thinks, important consequences for a number of the issues Austin discussed, including the relationship between truth (and falsehood) and statements, and the relationship between what a speaker means when he says something and what the sentence means.

Searle's first objection to Austin's distinction is that the terms are not mutually exclusive. There are some sentences in which the meaning exhausts its potential illocutionary force; for example, "I hearby promise that I am going to do it," which has the meaning of a promise. This entails that the locutionary act would be the same as the illocutionary act. And a description of the locutionary force, the meaning of the sentence uttered, would be a description of the illocutionary force of that utterance. Searle does not deny that the concepts of locutionary act and illocutionary act are different; rather, he is pointing out that the classes they denote overlap; some of their members are the same.

Searle's second objection concerns the *way* Austin tries to distinguish between locutionary and illocutionary acts. Austin holds that locutionary acts should be reported by direct quotation, while illocutionary acts should be reported by indirect quotation. Contrast this report of a locutionary act: He said, "Shoot her," with this report of the illocutionary act: He urged (advised) me to shoot her. This means that direct quotation should be wedded to locutionary acts; indirect quotation should be wedded to illocutionary acts. Austin, however, violates this; for he again deploys the difference between direct and indirect quotation to make out the distinction between the phatic and rhetic acts. Phatic acts, he holds, should be reported by direct quotation, rhetic acts by indirect quotation. Report of phatic act: He said "Get out!"

Report of rhetic act: He told me to get out.

There is a further problem here. Notice that the report of the rhetic act above contains a verb expressing an illocutionary act, "told." In general, all reports of rhetic acts will contain some verb expressing some illocutionary act, even if the verb is a generic one; for example, "told" is a generic term; "order," "request," and "command" are more specific terms of that class. What this means is that the notion of an illocutionary act leaks into the notion of a locutionary act. Why does that happen? Searle's answer is that it is because every sentence has, as part of its meaning, some illocutionary force potential. The grammatical moods of indicative, interrogative, and imperative express this force. The upshot is that while phonetic acts and phatic acts can be separated from illocutionary acts, there is no rhetic act separate from an illocutionary act. There is a distinction between the literal meaning of a sentence and the intended force of its utterance, but this is only a special case of the distinction between literal meaning and intended meaning, and it has no special relevance for speech act theory. As a consequence of Searle's criticism of Austin's distinctions, he proposes to eliminate the notions of locutionary act and rhetic act. What remains are three equally primary concepts of a phonetic, a phatic, and an illocutionary act.

Behind Searle's objections to Austin's distinction are three linguistic principles: The first, which he elaborated in his book *Speech Acts*, is the principle of expressibility, according to which whatever can be meant can be said. Often we mean more than what we say because we do not know the words or constructions to say all that we mean, sometimes because the language itself lacks the resources. Nevertheless, in theory all that we mean could be said; we could improve our knowledge of the language, or, if the language itself is deficient, improve its resources. Austin has overstressed the distinction between a sentence and the speech acts performed, to the neglect of the Principle of Expressibility. Since it is possible for a speaker completely to express what he means by uttering a sentence, what he says can include the force he means; so Austin's attempt to distinguish the force of an utterance from its meaning was wide of the mark. More importantly, the study of the meaning of sentences and the study of the illocutionary acts which are performed in uttering those sentences are not two different studies, but one and the same study from two different perspectives.

The second principle, which might be called "The Fundamental Principle of Language," is that the meaning of a sentence is a function of the meanings of its parts. The parts of a sentence include, in addition to its constituent words, syntactic and phonetic structure, roughly, the order in which the words occur and their intonation patterns. If Austin had considered this he would have been less likely to separate the illocutionary force of a sentence from its meaning. He might have seen that sentence structure, intonation, and the mood of the main verb express force and hence would have seen that the force is an inseparable part of meaning.

The third principle is that the illocutionary force of an utterance can be more or less determinate, and illocutionary acts are distinguishable by virtue of several dimensions. An illocutionary act might have the generic force of soliciting action without having the more specific force of being either a request, entreaty, or plea. Neglect of this third principle may have misled Austin into thinking that such generic illocutionary force expressions as "say that," "tell someone to do something," and "ask whether" are expressions for another kind of act: namely, locutionary acts.

The defects of Austin's distinction between locutionary and illocutionary acts notwithstanding, an important insight underlies it, Searle argues. It is the insight that most illocutionary acts can be divided into a propositional content, which consists of a sense and reference, and the force with which that content is put forward. This distinction between propositional content and force can be parlayed into accounting for why the concept of the act of making a statement has been confused with the concept of a statement, the object or product of the act of stating. A statement is a propositional content, put forward with stated force. Statements are the results or products of a particular kind of act, an illocutionary act of stating. The act of stating occurs in time and takes time to perform. The resulting statement is neither in time nor takes time. The act of stating is neither true nor false. The statement *is*.

Strawson, P. F. "Intention and Convention in Speech Acts," in *Logico-Linguistic Papers*. London: Methuen, 1971, pp. 149-169.

J. L. Austin explicity and repeatedly says that an illocutionary act is a conventional act: that is, an act done in accordance with a convention. This claim is true about a great many illocutionary acts: declarations of guilt and innocence, umpire calls, surrendering. But it is not true of all. Stating, questioning, and warning are illocutionary acts, but they are not, or at least not always, conventional acts in the sense Austin means. The only conventions associated with these acts are the conventions governing the use of the words uttered in performing the act. But these conventions determine what locutionary act has been performed; they do not make the illocutionary act conventional.

Working on the supposition that Austin did not simply overgeneralize, P. F. Strawson wants to understand what insight lay behind Austin's mistake; he finds a clue in Austin's qualified remark that an illocutionary act is conventional in the sense that it could be made explicit by the performative formula. The clue is the notion of explicitness. All illocutionary acts are communicative acts; this means that for a successful illocutionary act, it is not enough that the speaker mean something when he performs his act; it is also necessary that the audience understand what the speaker means. Further, and this is the crucial point, the mechanism by which the speaker transmits his message and the audience understands it must have a certain overtness; it must, in other words, be avowable. This point is best explained in terms of H. P. Grice's account of "nonnatural meaning," according to which, in a speech situation, a speaker nonnaturally means something just in case he intends to produce a certain response in an audience by an utterance, intends his audience to recognize his intention, and, further, intends that the audience's recognition will be part of its reason for having the response. Strawson then complements Grice's analysis with a tentative analysis of audience uptake. For human communication is successful only when the audience recognizes the speaker's intentions. An audience understands something by an utterance only when it recognizes that the speaker intends that the audience is to recognize that the speaker intends to produce a certain response.

Strawson then uses this analysis of audience uptake to explain two features of Austin's theory: (1) Austin's view that all illocutionary acts are conventional in the sense that they can be made explicit by the performative formula, and (2) Austin's attempt to characterize illocutionary acts as something we *do*, in saying something. Concerning (1), Strawson begins by pointing out that because nonnatural meaning concerns a speaker's own intentions, he can speak of those intentions with a special kind of authority: they are his own-most. Further, the speaker has a motive for doing so; it is one of his intentions that the audience recognize them; so, if there is a way to facilitate that recognition, the speaker will want to avail himself of it. One of these ways would be to add to the content of the message a conventional device that would signal the type of force that the message has. To the message that the audience should move, the speaker might add what looks like another comment: That's a warning (I'm warning you) or That's an order (I am ordering you). But this appearance of two comments, message and comment on message, disappears when the latter assumes its performative form: I hereby warn you; I hereby order you. When the explicit performative formula precedes the message (the that-clause), it no longer appears to be a comment on a message but a convention-governed device for *making explicit* the type of communicative force that the speaker intends. Concerning (2), Strawson contrasts illocutionary acts with showing off and insinuating, which, although not illocutionary acts, are things that are done in saying something. Showing off and insinuating are not illocutionary acts because they lack the requisite openness. It is not part of the speaker's intention to have his audience recognize his desire to impress the audience, in the one case, or to instill a belief, in the other. And such recognition may in fact frustrate the speaker's intention.

While the openness required of communicative meaning is instructive, it does not explain everything. How, for example, can "Don't go" have, on one occasion, the force of a request, and, on another, the force of an entreaty? Strawson's answer is that such cases call merely for enriching the intentional scheme already devised. In an entreaty the audience is to understand that the speaker intends it to recognize that he passionately or desperately desires something to be done and to understand that the speaker intends it to have this understanding; the same applies to requests *mutatis mutandis* except that the desire is less passionate or desperate. Orders or commands call for a further, although still quite manageable, complication. The audience is supposed to recognize, *via* the communicative intentions, the right sort of social requirements.

There is, however, a limit to how much can and should be packed into the intentions of the speaker. At a certain stage of conventionalized behavior, the requirement that the speaker have certain intentions drops out, and its work is performed, in a certain context, by mere physical gesturing. Umpires, juries, judges, bridge players, priests, and civil servants perform their assigned illocutionary acts unfettered by the requirement that they have the complex kind of intention to secure a certain response in their audience. The convention governing the gesturing behavior in a certain context is sufficient to guarantee the act.

The upshot is that there is a spectrum of cases. At one end, the illocutionary act depends heavily on the intentions of the speaker and their recognition by the audience; and the illocutionary act is in no way conventional except in the sense that the words of the utterance are bound by conventions. At the other end of the spectrum are the fully convention-governed illocutionary acts that dominated Austin's thinking. This is not to say that intentions play no role in the illocutionary act; in the standard case, they are present. But they are not necessarily present in each case, and, when they are not, the convention supplies what is lacking. The conventionalized and nonconventionalized illocutionary acts are, then, alike in possessing wholly overt and avowable intentions. They are also unalike. In a conventionalized illocutionary act, whenever the audience understands what the speaker intends, the illocutionary effect is achieved. If a runner understands that the umpire intends him to be called out, he is out. This is not the case for *non*conventional illocutionary acts. The audience might understand what response the speaker intends and yet not respond in that way. The audience might recognize that the speaker intends it to believe something and yet not believe it; or the audience might recognize that the speaker intends it to do something and yet not do it.

Strawson ends his article with a caveat. Conventionalized and nonconventionalized illocutionary acts are merely the extremes of a spectrum. There are many intermediate cases, and it is important not to lose sight of them; yet a general account of linguistic communication cannot supply every qualification that the facts might require without risking the audience's failure to understand the main point.—*A.P.M.*

ADDITIONAL RECOMMENDED READING

Fann, K. T., ed. *Symposium on J. L. Austin*. London: Routledge & Kegan Paul, 1969. A volume containing contributions by many of Austin's colleagues, students, and friends, on a wide range of subjects, including several biographical accounts.

Furberg, Mats. *Saying and Meaning: A Main Theme in J. L. Austin's Philosophy*. Totowa, New Jersey: Rowman and Littlefield, 1971. The first book-length discussion of Austin's theory.

Holdcroft, David. *Words and Deeds*. Oxford: Clarendon Press, 1978. A recent attempt at a comprehensive theory of speech acts that takes into account the work of Austin, Grice, Searle and others.

Searle, John R. *Speech Acts: An Essay in the Philosophy of Language*. London: Cambridge University Press, 1969. The best and most adequate extension and revision of aspects of Austin's theory of speech acts.

Vendler, Zeno. *Res Cogitans*. Ithaca, New York: Cornell University Press, 1972. In Chapter 2 Vendler uses transformational grammar to provide theoretical support for Austin's classification of illocutionary acts.

A THEORY OF JUSTICE

Author: John Rawls (1921-   )
Type of work: Moral and social philosophy
First published: 1971

PRINCIPAL IDEAS ADVANCED

The principles of justice are whatever would be agreed to by rational, self-interested, and unenvious persons who knew they were to enter a society structured according to their agreement but did not know what positions they would have nor what their natural endowments and particular interests would be.

Justice is fairness.

The principles of justice are: First, equal and maximum feasible liberty for all. Second, power and wealth to be distributed equally except where inequalities would work for the advantage of all and where all would have equal opportunity to attain the higher positions.

The most ambitious and influential work in social philosophy of the later twentieth century, this book attempts to show what the principles of social justice are and why they can be satisfied only in a liberal society which partially redistributes income and wealth for the benefit of its least advantaged members. John Rawls revives the social contract tradition of John Locke, Jean Jacques Rousseau, and Immanuel Kant, in opposition to utilitarianism.

Justice, the author declares, is the first and indispensable virtue of social institutions, as truth is of theories. Even the welfare of society as a whole cannot morally override the inviolability that each person has, founded on justice. This is the reason why utilitarianism, which looks only to the sum of welfare and permits the sacrifice of the few for the good of the many, is not a tenable moral theory.

In this book Rawls is concerned with social justice only, not with the justice that individuals may display in private dealings. Society is a cooperative venture for mutual advantage: that is, if people cooperate in the production of goods, there will be more goods than if every person produces things only for his own consumption. But people do not only cooperate in the production of social goods, they also compete for them. Everyone prefers more rather than less. These facts give rise to the problem of distributive justice: On what principles should these benefits be distributed?

There is scope for the operation of justice whenever many individuals coexist in a territory and are similar enough so that no one is able to dominate the rest. The social goods must be moderately scarce so that there will be conflicting claims that cannot all be satisfied.

Rawls makes a distinction between the *concept* of justice, on which all agree, and different concep*tions* of justice. The concept, he says, is that "institutions are just when no arbitrary distinctions are made between persons in the assigning of basic rights and duties and when the rules determine a proper balance between competing claims to the advantages of social life." Different conceptions are generated when people differ in their interpretations of what distinctions are arbitrary and what balances are proper.

The social justice of which Rawls writes has to do with the basic structure of society: the way in which major social institutions, chiefly governmental, distribute fundamental rights and duties and divide up the product of social cooperation. This is the distributive aspect of the basic structure of society, not a complete social idea. Rawls claims that his conception of distributive social justice tallies with the traditional Aristotelian notion that justice consists in giving everyone his due; for notions of what people are entitled to are ordinarily derived from social institutions.

Rawls's basic idea is that the correct principles of justice are what free and rational people, concerned to further their own interests, would agree to accept as defining the fundamental terms of their association, if their agreement were made under conditions that were fair to all parties. This is "justice as fairness." The conditions of fairness obtain when no party to the agreement is in a position where he can have any advantage over other participants in furthering his own interests. Such a fair position, which Rawls calls "the original position," demands that all participants be equal: this corresponds to the "state of nature" in traditional contract theory. But Rawls requires in addition that no contracting party shall know what his place will be in the society he is to enter, nor what class he will belong to, nor what his social status will be, nor even his fortune in the distribution of natural assets and abilities: his intelligence, strength, and particular psychological traits. This is the "veil of ignorance," drawn to prevent the parties from pressing their particular selfish interests. It would not be "fair" if the parties could be influenced in their deliberations by the morally irrelevant contingencies of natural chance (to which natural endowments are due) or social circumstances. Rawls assumes, however, that all parties know the "laws" of psychology and sociology and the general facts about social life. They are also to be mutually disinterested—that is, they take no interest in the interests of other people; and rational in the sense that they take the most effective means to whatever they put before themselves as their ends. Rawls assumes, finally, that they are not motivated by envy; that is to say, they will not forgo goods for themselves merely to prevent others from enjoying them. Although the parties are not allowed knowledge of what their particular conceptions of the good will be, they are assured motivation by a "thin theory of the good": they all want to pursue rational plans of life, in which rights, liberty and opportunity, income and wealth, and the bases of self-respect are primary goods; for it is rational to desire these things, and good is the object of rational desire.

Principles of justice, then, are to regulate the distribution of these primary goods.

No actual person, of course, is ever ignorant in the ways specified, nor are actual persons equally rational, disinterested, and envy-free. But the restrictions of the original position are not arbitrary or fantastic but serve to rule out of discussion factors that we are convinced are irrelevant to justice. The conception of justice that results must be one that validates our strongest intuitions—for example, that religious and racial discrimination are unjust. We must aim for "reflective equilibrium" in which our intuitions about justice are harmonized with our principles. This may require adjustment in either or both. The conditions of the original position are those we do in fact accept, Rawls avers—or that we could be "persuaded" to accept.

There are certain formal constraints embodied in the concept of right: principles should be general, universal in application, public, capable of ordering conflicting claims, and final. These conditions are satisifed by the notion of deliberation in the original position: since the individuals cannot identify themselves, they cannot tailor principles to their own advantage; nor would there be any point in their trying to strike bargains with one another. Rawls assumes, furthermore, that as everyone is equally rational and similarly situated, each is convinced by the same arguments. Anyone—any actual person—can enter the original position at any time by arguing in accordance with its restrictions.

The parties in the original position would agree, Rawls claims, in choosing two principles of justice. The first is that everyone is to have equal right to the most extensive basic liberty (political, intellectual, and religious) consistent with equal liberty for others. The second is that social and economic inequalities are to be arranged so that they are (1) to everyone's advantage (this is called "the difference principle") and (2) attached to positions open to all. The first principle is prior to the second—that is, it must be fully satisfied before the second comes into play; no tradeoffs of liberty for economic or social advantage are to be permitted.

The general conception of justice behind this is that all social values should be equally distributed unless an unequal distribution turns out to be to everyone's advantage—for example, by providing incentive for greater production to be shared by all. Rawls defines injustice as "inequalities that are not to the benefit of all."

It is supposed to follow deductively from the specifications of the original position that the parties will vote unanimously for the two principles. The argument is this: The voters not only do not know what their position in the society they are forming will be; but they also do not even have any basis on which to calculate the likelihoods of alternatives. Moreover, Rawls claims, a person in the original position will care little for what he might gain above the minimum he can be sure of. And the situation is one of grave risk: that is, if the principles of justice allow unacceptable positions to exist in the society, every voter runs some risk—the magnitude of which he cannot even guess—of ending up in it. Under these conditions the theory of rational choice is said to dictate a "maximin solution": choose principles such that their worst outcome for the chooser will be better than the worst possible under alternative principles—in other words, choose as if your enemy is to assign you your social place.

The maximin strategy would lead to choice of equal distribution of all social goods, were it not for the fact that some inequalities may be such as to bring about the production of more social goods to be distributed, so that by permitting these inequalities it will be possible for everyone, including the worst off, to have a larger share of goods than if the distribution were equal. Since the choosers want more rather than less, and are not envious, there is no reason why they should not adopt this, the difference principle: inequalities to be permitted when everyone, including the worst off, benefits from them. This principle, being chosen under fair conditions of equality, is just.

The social good of liberty is to be distributed equally. People in the original position must adopt a principle of equal religious liberty if they are to adopt any principle at all. As for toleration, the principle is that limitations on liberty must be for the sake of preventing even greater violations of it and must be supported by arguments capable of convincing any rational person. Applying this principle to the question of tolerating the intolerant, Rawls holds that it cannot be unjust for the tolerant to suppress the intolerant in self-defense; but when the intolerant do not constitute a real threat they must be tolerated. Paternalism—governmental protection of ourselves against our own weakness and irrationality—is acceptable, as the rational persons in the original position would foresee that they might become irrational and need such help.

Only in the distribution of wealth, income, and authority are inequalities to be allowed. Here too equality is the "benchmark"—equal distribution would not be unjust, only inefficient. Rawls recognizes that people are born with unequal natural endowments, physical and mental, and that social and familiar conditions may accentuate them. But these inequalities are "arbitrary from the moral point of view"—no one deserves his natural endowments, and even a sober and industrious disposition is dependent on the accidents of nature and nurture. The "system of natural liberty," which rewards people in proportion to what they have the talent and industry to produce, thus permits distribution to be improperly influenced by the "natural lottery." The difference principle represents an agreement to consider the total pool of natural talents as a common asset in which everyone shares. While the natural lottery is neither just nor unjust, societies that base distribution of goods on it are unjust. There must be redress for the undeserved inequalities of birth and natural endowment. It is unjust that people should get more because they are born with more.

Under the difference principle, those who are less favored by nature have no ground for complaint of inequalities, for they benefit from their existence. The more favored should realize that their well-being depends on cooperation, which must be obtained on reasonable terms which the difference principle specifies. Thus the difference principle promotes fraternity, making society more like a family.

The only sense in which people can be said to deserve anything is this: if in accordance with the difference principle it has been announced that those who produce more will get more, then the higher producers deserve their differential and it would be unjust to withhold it from them.

The background institutions for distributive justice may be either democratic capitalist or socialist, but they must include a public school system, equality of economic opportunity, a social minimum, and social security. Rawls recommends a governmental organization including four branches: Allocation, to keep prices competitive and to prevent too much economic concentration, by adjusting taxes and subsidies. The Stabilization branch will guarantee full employment. The Transfer branch will correct competitive pricing (which by itself ignores need) to see that total income is allocated according to need. The Distribution branch, by taxes and adjustments in the rights of property, corrects the distribution of wealth. A proportional expenditure tax (the more you spend the higher your tax rate) is preferable to a graduated income tax.

Rawls claims that his theory is in the spirit of Immanuel Kant, who held that moral principles are the objects of rational choice by free and equal rational beings. The original position is devised in accordance with this conception. One acts autonomously when action is the expression of freedom and rationality. In the original position it is impossible to choose heteronomous principles. Moreover, the Rawlsian principles of justice are categorical imperatives: they do not assume that anyone has any particular aims. But justice as fairness improves on Kant by showing how in choosing principles of justice we are fully expressing our natures as rational and free individuals— our noumenal selves. In justice as fairness, moreover, the basis of equality is being a moral person, which means having the capacity to have a conception of one's own good and a sense of justice. Moral persons are all persons who would be capable (contingencies aside) of taking part in the initial agreement.

To give people really fair opportunities, the family ought to be abolished; but this reform, Rawls allows, is not urgent.

The most important social good, Rawls avers, is self-respect, which he defines as "a person's sense of his own value, his secure conviction that his conception of his good, his plan of life, is worth carrying out," together with confidence in his ability to carry it out. Justice as fairness furthers the equal distribution of the bases of self-respect.

Although the assumption that persons in the original position are not motivated by envy is contrary to present facts about real persons, Rawls holds that in the just society there will be little occasion for or incitement to envy. It is not right to claim, as conservative writers do, that the modern tendency to equality is based on envy. In any case, the two Rawlsian principles of justice cannot be so based, for by hypothesis they are chosen by envy-free people.—*W.I.M.*

PERTINENT LITERATURE

Nozick, Robert. *Anarchy, State, and Utopia.* New York: Basic Books, 1974.

This book shares honors with *A Theory of Justice* as a seminal work in social and political philosophy. The view advanced is the antithesis of John Rawls's: only a minimal state, one which limits its functions to common defense and protection against crime, is morally justifiable; and distributive justice is satisfied whenever a person is entitled to his holdings, which is when he produced them or acquired them through voluntary exchanges from people who were entitled to them.

At page 183 Robert Nozick pays a handsome tribute to the importance and elegance of the work of Rawls, his colleague in the Harvard philosophy department; he then offers forty-nine pages of criticism. What, Nozick first asks, is Rawls's problem? Is it how the total product of a cooperative society ought to be distributed? Or is it only how to distribute the surplus produced over what would have been produced if there had been no cooperation? Apparently the former; but this might give some persons less than they would receive if they worked only for themselves. How can this be fair?

Why, indeed, does social cooperation create a problem for distributive justice? People who did not cooperate—who lived, for example, each on his own island—might still make Rawlsian claims to get more than they produced because they did not "deserve" their natural endowments of poorer soil, greater need, and the like. Then justice would have to counteract this "natural lottery." But such claims would obviously be without merit, since in these situations it would be clear who was entitled to what. How does social cooperation change things so that entitlement is no longer an applicable or appropriate criterion? Because everything then becomes a joint product in which individual contributions are indistinguishable? But Rawls admits that individual contributions to the social product can be identified, for he allows unequal incomes to be paid to specified persons as incentives.

Rawls says that it is not just for some to have less in order that others may prosper. But could this not be said when, in order to satisfy the difference principle, funds are transferred from a previously prosperous group to a previously depressed one? In any case, from the mere fact that A has more than B it does not follow that B is badly off *because* A is well off.

   The difference principle indeed offers terms on which the less well endowed would be willing to cooperate: what better terms could there be for them? But it does not offer terms on which the better endowed would be willing to cooperate. Although everybody gains from cooperation, the difference principle does not assign the results symmetrically to the better and worse endowed. In Rawls's scenario it is proposed on behalf of the worse endowed that they should get so much that any attempt to give them more would result in their actually getting less. Why is this any fairer than if the better endowed made the reverse proposal? Rawls's explanation of why the less well favored should not complain of inequalities is that they get more than they would under equality. But he says about the more favored only that they should not complain because only thus could they expect willing cooperation from the less favored. This is not enough.

   If social products fell like manna from heaven, the difference principle might be a suitable rule for their distribution. But this is not the appropriate model for deciding how to divide up the pie when the contributors to the pie are known. How do people in the original position get the *right* to make this kind of decision? Rawls assumes without argument that no entitlement theory of justice can be correct—that is, the right theory of justice must be one in which the pattern of distribution is settled in advance. This assumption, furthermore, clashes with Rawls's contract theory, for such a theory is one according to which *anything* emerging from a certain process is just.

   Noting that much of Rawls's theory depends on the belief that it is the business of a just society to neutralize the baleful workings of "the natural lottery," Nozick finds an ambiguity in the claim that natural endowments are "arbitrary from a moral point of view." Is this supposed to be part of a positive argument to show that the distributive effects of natural endowments ought to be nullified, or of a negative argument to rebut any claim that they ought *not* to be nullified? A positive argument, Nozick claims, could not involve the notion that goods should be distributed according to desert, since Rawls explicitly rejects desert as a distributive basis. Hence the supposition underlying Rawls's position must be that people ought to be treated equally unless there is a moral reason why they need not be. Equality is the "benchmark"; deviation from it needs to be explained by moral forces. But why? Differential treatment of citizens by their government does indeed need moral justification; but elsewhere, it is not so clear. No moral reason need be produced to justify my patronizing one theater owner and not another. The assumption of the argument consequently fails.

   Finally, Nozick questions Rawls's proposal to deal with natural assets as a pool for the benefit of all. To do so *is* to treat persons as mere means, contrary to Kant's prohibition. Envy of the better-endowed does after all underlie the Rawlsian conception of justice.

Matson, Wallace I. "What Rawls Calls Justice," in *The Occasional Review*. Autumn, 1978, pp. 45-57.

Wallace I. Matson contends that despite the title, John Rawls's book is not about justice. Rawls said that the concept of justice, on which there is agreement, is that of not making arbitrary distinctions between persons in the assigning of basic rights and duties and the determination of a proper balance between competing claims to the advantages of social life. Matson disagrees. Balancing claims and assigning rights and duties are primarily the business of politicians and arbitrators, not of the paradigmatic institutions of justice—namely, courts. Judges are concerned with awarding persons what is *due* them. The concept of justice is that of giving every man his due. Conceptions of justice differ as to what in particular is a person's due.

Rawls's two principles do not constitute a conception of justice, either a right one or a wrong one. The first principle, equal liberty, cannot be part of a conception of justice, since liberty and justice are independent notions—either can exist without the other: in a monastery there might be justice without liberty, and in an anarchical society, liberty without justice. Nor is the difference principle a principle of justice: it does not award people their due, nor does Rawls claim that it does. Rawls holds, rather, that except for what follows from governmental promises, no one deserves anything.

Matson concedes that a Rawlsian might admit these points but dismiss them as irrelevant on the ground that Rawls was writing explicitly about social justice, not the justice one individual shows in his private dealings with other persons. The author replies that institutions and societies can be just only in the derivative sense that they further just dealings of individuals with other individuals. The notion of "social justice" as different from, and even in opposition to, individual justice is mere cant.

Why did Rawls overlook so obvious a point? Because, Matson conjectures, he accepted a genetico-social deterministic account of human behavior, as a consequence of which the notion of desert becomes vacuous. Rawls has attempted to construct an ethics without desert. The first principle of such an ethics must be that there can be no moral reason to treat one man any differently from another: the equalitarian "benchmark." And equality would remain the principle if Rawls did not recognize the dismal fact that the intelligent and industrious cannot in practice be motivated to produce without hope of selfish gain. Hence the difference principle, the Rawlsian analogue of the Apostle Paul's grudging allowance for sex, "It is better to marry than to burn."

In the desertless ethics, fairness, which dictates distribution when desert is not in question, becomes the substitute for the vacuous notion of justice. Rawls's astonishing assertion that "Injustice is simply inequalities that are not to the benefit of all" begins to make sense once "unfairness" replaces "injustice." But it is important for Rawls to retain the *word* "justice." Such emotively appealing pronouncements as "Justice is the first virtue of social institutions" and "Each person possesses an inviolability founded on justice that even the welfare of society as a whole cannot override" lose their plausibility and attractiveness if in each case rewritten as, for example, "The *difference principle* is the first virtue of social institutions."

Johnson, Oliver A. "The Kantian Interpretation," in *Ethics*. LXXXV, no. 1 (October, 1974), pp. 58-66.

Oliver A. Johnson takes issue with Rawls on his claim to have produced a theory of justice in the spirit of Immanuel Kant's ethics. Three concepts that play a central role in Kantian ethics are autonomy, the categorical imperative, and rationality. Johnson argues that the Rawlsian theory clashes with Kant with respect to all three.

Kantian autonomy of the will refers to action done from the motive of respect for the moral law. In autonomous action the agent's wants and inclinations play no part. Rawls interprets this as meaning that the autonomous agent acts according to principles chosen by him as expressing his nature as a free and equal rational being, not because of his peculiar endowments, wants, or social position. The veil of ignorance is supposed to guarantee autonomous action. However, Johnson notes, the veil of ignorance does nothing to alter the motivation of Rawls's parties, which Rawls explicitly states to be the desire to promote their own interests. Their actions therefore remain heteronomous, since for Kant only the motive counts, not the circumstances.

Rawls's misconstruction of the autonomous/heteronomous distinction leads him to misinterpret the categorical imperative, which he supposes to be obeyed by the parties in the original position because they do not act in order to obtain particular ends but only because they desire "primary goods." But (says Johnson) that only makes their principles into what Kant calls "counsels of prudence," which are hypothetical, not categorical imperatives.

Both these Rawlsian misinterpretations stem from the misconception of Kant's notion of the role of reason in ethics. Rawls's notion of rational choice is that of taking the most effective means to given ends. It is exemplified in the choice of a rational plan of life that will further the primary good of self-respect, thus producing happiness for the agent. But Kant explicitly rejected the notion that the role of reason in morality is to produce happiness, and he denied that in fact it could efficiently do so. He conceived the role of reason as quite different and higher: to produce a will good in itself. This is not merely different from but opposed to the role assigned by Rawls. A "Kantian interpretation" of Rawls's theory is therefore impossible. Rawls is not Kantian but anti-Kantian.

Replies to Johnson's paper were published by Bernard H. Baumrin (in

Midwest Studies in Philosophy, I) and Stephen Darwall (*Ethics*, LXXXV). Rejoinders by Johnson appeared in Vols. II and LXXXVII of the same journals, respectively. Conclusions similar to Johnson's will be found in "Rawls' Kantianism" by Andrew Levine, *Social Theory and Practice*, III.— W.I.M.

ADDITIONAL RECOMMENDED READING

Barry, Brian. *The Liberal Theory of Justice: A Critical Examination of the Principal Doctrines in 'A Theory of Justice' by John Rawls*. Oxford: Clarendon Press, 1973. First book-length critique of Rawls.

Daniels, Norman, ed. *Reading Rawls*. New York: Basic Books, 1975. Fourteen essays selected from the enormous Rawls literature. Contains a Rawls bibliography, 1971-1974.

Gauthier, David. "Justice and Natural Endowment: Toward a Critique of Rawls' Ideological Framework," in *Soical Theory and Practice*. III, no. 1 (Spring, 1974), pp. 3-26. Argues that parties in the original position, who according to Rawls would know the general facts about natural endowments, would adopt not Rawls's principles but principles approximating those of a free market economy.

Urmson, J. O. "A Defence of Intuitionism," in *Proceedings of the Aristotelian Society*. N. S. LXXV (1974-1975), pp. 111-119. A metatheoretical argument to show the implausibility of *any* ethics such as Rawls's based on a single principle or a few principles with a decision procedure.

AUTHOR INDEX

ABELARD, PETER
Glosses on Porphyry, The, II-643
ALEXANDER, SAMUEL
Space, Time, and Deity, IV-1735
ANAXAGORAS OF CLAZOMENAE
Anaxagoras: Fragments, I-52
ANAXIMANDER OF MILETUS
Anaximander: Fragments, I-1
ANSELM, SAINT
Monologion *and* Proslogion, II-632
AQUINAS, SAINT THOMAS
Summa contra Gentiles, II-693
Summa Theologica, II-704
ARISTOTLE
Ethica Nicomachea, I-369
Metaphysics, I-359
On the Soul, I-348
Organon, I-329
Physics, I-340
Poetics, I-400
Politics, I-381
Rhetoric, I-391
AUGUSTINE, SAINT
City of God, The, II-571
Confessions, II-560
AUSTIN, J. L.
How to Do Things with Words, V-2513
Sense and Sensibilia, V-2502
AVERROËS
Incoherence of the Incoherence, The, II-652
AVICENNA
Book of Salvation, The, II-621
AYER, ALFRED JULES
Language, Truth and Logic, V-2127

BACON, FRANCIS
Advancement of Learning, The, II-795
Novum Organum, II-805
BAIER, KURT
Moral Point of View, The, V-2478
BARTH, KARL
Knowledge of God and the Service of God, The, V-2160
BAYLE, PIERRE
Historical and Critical Dictionary, The, II-935
BELL, CLIVE
Art, IV-1680
BENTHAM, JEREMY
Introduction to the Principles of Morals and Legislation, An, III-1166
BERDYAEV, NIKOLAI
Destiny of Man, The, IV-1979
BERGSON, HENRI
Creative Evolution, IV-1616
Introduction to Metaphysics, An, IV-1582
Time and Free Will, III-1484
Two Sources of Morality and Religion, The, IV-2013
BERKELEY, GEORGE
Three Dialogues Between Hylas and Philonous, II-980
Treatise Concerning the Principles of Human Knowledge, A, II-946

BLANSHARD, BRAND
Nature of Thought, The, V-2186
BOETHIUS
Consolation of Philosophy, The, II-582
BONAVENTURA, SAINT
Journey of the Mind to God, II-681
On the Reduction of the Arts to Theology, II-673
BOSANQUET, BERNARD
Principle of Individuality and Value, The, IV-1660
Three Lectures on Aesthetic, IV-1702
BRADLEY, FRANCIS HERBERT
Appearance and Reality, III-1493
Ethical Studies, III-1418
BRIDGMAN, PERCY WILLIAMS
Logic of Modern Physics, The, IV-1858
BROAD, CHARLES DUNBAR
Mind and Its Place in Nature, The, IV-1824
BRUNNER, HEINRICH EMIL
Revelation and Reason, V-2222
BRUNO, GIORDANO
Dialogues Concerning Cause, Principle, and One, II-786
BUBER, MARTIN
I and Thou, IV-1801
BÜCHNER, LUDWIG
Force and Matter, III-1333
BUTLER, JOSEPH
Fifteen Sermons Preached at the Rolls Chapel, III-991

CAMUS, ALBERT
Rebel, The, V-2392
CARNAP, RUDOLF
Introduction to Semantics, V-2259
Philosophy and Logical Syntax, V-2102
CASSIRER, ERNST
Philosophy of Symbolic Forms, The, IV-1789
CHUANG CHOU
Chuang Tzu, I-422
COLLINGWOOD, ROBIN GEORGE
Essay on Metaphysics, An, V-2197
COMTE, AUGUSTE
Course on the Positive Philosophy, III-1246
CONFUCIUS
Analects of Confucius, The, I-21
CROCE, BENEDETTO
Aesthetic, IV-1571

DEMOCRITUS OF ABDERA
Democritus: Fragments, I-135
DESCARTES, RENÉ
Discourse on Method, II-816
Meditations on First Philosophy, II-828
DEWEY, JOHN
Art as Experience, V-2068
Human Nature and Conduct, IV-1763
Logic, the Theory of Inquiry, V-2172
Quest for Certainty, The, IV-1909
DIDEROT, DENIS
Thoughts on the Interpretation of Nature, III-1050

I

II

AUTHOR INDEX

PERTINENT LITERATURE REVIEWED

LITERATURE FOR ADDITIONAL RECOMMENDED READING

Aaron, Richard I.
John Locke   II-933
Acton, H. B.
"Bosanquet, Bernard," in *The Encyclopedia of Philosophy*   IV-1669
"Moral Futurism and the Ethics of Marxism," in *The Philosophy of Karl Popper*   V-2322
Adam, Antoine
Grandeur and Illusion   II-884
Addis, Laird and Douglas Lewis
Moore and Ryle: Two Ontologists   V-2358
Adler, Mortimer
Saint Thomas and the Gentiles   II-703
Afnan, Soheil Muhsin
Avicenna, His Life and Works   II-631
Alexander, Hubert G.
Language and Thinking: A Philosophical Introduction   IV-1822
Alexander, Ian W.
Bergson: Philosopher of Reflection   IV-1591
Alexander, Peter
"Ernst Mach," in *A Critical History of Western Philosophy*   III-1457
Allen, Alexander V. G.
Jonathan Edwards   III-1070
Allen, Edgar L.
Creation and Grace: A Guide to the Thought of Emil Brunner   V-2232
Allen, Gay Wilson
William James: A Biography   IV-1648
Allen, R. E.
"Law and Justice in Plato's *Crito*," in *The Journal of Philosophy*   I-178
Allen, R. E. and David J. Furley
Studies in Presocratic Philosophy   I-9
Allison, Henry E.
Benedict De Spinoza   II-897
Alston, William P.
"Tillich's Conception of a Religious Symbol," in *Religious Experience and Truth*   V-2430
Ambrose, Alice and Morris Lazerowitz, eds.
G. E. Moore: Essays in Retrospect   V-1787
Ames, Van Meter
Proust and Santayana: The Aesthetic Way of Life   III-1525
Anderson, Fulton H.
Philosophy of Francis Bacon, The   II-815
Annas, Julia
Aristotle's Metaphysics, Books M and N   I-368
Anschutz, R. P.
Philosophy of J. S. Mill, The   III-1382
Anscombe, G. E. M.
"Aristotle: The Search for Substance," in *Three Philosophers*   I-368
Intention   V-2358

Introduction to Wittgenstein's Tractatus, An   IV-1761
Aquinas, Saint Thomas
Basic Writings of St. Thomas Aquinas   II-716
On the Unity of the Intellect Against the Averroists (De Unitate Intellectus contra Averroistas)   II-662
Arberry, A. J.
Revelation and Reason in Islam   II-662
Aristotle
De Anima   I-357
De Anima Books II and III   I-357
Politics of Aristotle, The   I-390
Armstrong, A. H.
"Plotinus," in *The Cambridge History of Later Greek and Early Medieval Philosophy*   II-558
Armstrong, D. M.
Berkeley's Theory of Vision   II-957
Perception and the Physical World   V-2042
Arnold, E. V.
Roman Stoicism   II-513
Aron, Raymond
"August Comte," in *Main Currents in Sociological Thought*   III-1255
Ashforth, Albert
Thomas Henry Huxley   III-1515
Atwell, John
"Ross and *Prima Facie* Duties," in *Ethics*   IV-1967
Aune, Bruce
Kant's Theory of Morals   III-1165
Averroës
Destructio Destructionum Philosophiae Algazelis, in *the Latin version of Calo Calonymos*   II-662
Avicenna
Liber de Anima seu Sextus de Naturalibus   II-631
Liber de Philosophia Prima sive Scientia Divina   II-631
Métaphysique du "Shifā", La   II-631
Avineri, Shlomo
Hegel's Theory of the Modern State   III-1268
Ayer, A. J.
Origins of Pragmatism: Studies in the Philosophy of Charles Sanders Peirce and William James, The   IV-1648
Part of My Life: The Memoirs of a Philosopher   V-2137
Ayer, A. J., ed.
Logical Positivism   V-2113, 2137
Ayres, Clarence E.
Huxley   III-1515

Badham, Paul
Christian Beliefs About Life After Death   V-2414

Bevan, Edwyn R.
Bhagavad-Gītā, The   I-133
Bhagavad-Gītā: An English Translation and Commentary, The   I-134
Bhagavad-Gītā: With a Commentary Based on the Original Sources, The   I-134
Bhagavad-Gītā as It Is   I-134
Stoics and Sceptics   II-504, 534
Bibby, Cyril
T. H. Huxley: A Scientist, Humanist, and Educator   III-1515
Bidney, David
Psychology and Ethics of Spinoza, The II-897
Bilsky, Manuel and Holley Gene Duffield, eds.
Tolstoy and the Critics: Literature and Aesthetics   IV-1535, 1930
Birley, Anthony
Marcus Aurelius   II-523
Biro, J. I. and Robert W. Shahan, eds.
Spinoza: New Perspectives   II-898
Bitterman, H. J.
"Adam Smith's Empiricism and the Law of Nature," in *The Journal of Political Economy*   III-1080
Black, Max, ed.
Importance of Language, The   IV-1823
Blackham, Harold J.
Six Existentialist Thinkers   IV-1989
Blake, R. M.
"Paradox of Temporal Process, The" in *The Journal of Philosophy*   I-82
Blanshard, Brand
"Emotionism," in *Reason and Goodness*   V-2298
"Kierkegaard on Faith," in *The Personalist*   III-1305
Nature of Thought, The   III-1427; IV-1637
"New Subjectivism in Ethics, The" in *Philosophy and Phenomenological Research*   V-2298
Blau, Joseph L.
Men and Movements in American Philosophy   V-2147, 2159
Blum, Alan F.
Socrates: The Original and Its Images I-158
Boas, George
"Santayana and the Arts," in *The Philosophy of George Santayana*   III-1525
Boase, Alan M.
Fortunes of Montaigne: A History of the Essays in France, 1580-1669, The   II-785
Bocheński, I. M.
Contemporary European Philosophy   IV-1591
History of Formal Logic, A   III-1292
Boehner, Philotheus
Collected Articles on Ockham   II-742
Bolman, Frederick de W.
"Kierkegaard in Limbo," in *The Journal of Philosophy*   III-1305

Bonar, James
Moral Sense   III-1081
Bonaventura, Saint
Itinerarium Mentis in Deum   II-691
Souls Journey into God, The Tree of Life, The Life of St. Francis, The   II-691
Boring, E. G., *et al.*
"Symposium on Operationism," in *The Psychological Review*   IV-1868
Bosanquet, Bernard
Philosophical Theory of the State, The III-1268
Bosanquet, Bernard, *et al*
"Do Finite Individuals Possess a Substantive or an Adjectival Mode of Being?," in *Proceedings of the Aristotelian Society* IV-1669
Bougerol, Jacques Guy
Introduction to the Works of Bonaventure   II-680
Bourgeois, Patrick L. and Sandra B. Rosenthal
"Lewis, Heidegger, and Kant: Schemata and the Structure of Perceptual Experience," in *The Southern Journal of Philosophy*   IV-1943
Bowman, Archibald
Sacramental Universe, Being a Study in the Metaphysics of Experience, A   IV-1896
Bowne, Borden P.
Kant and Spencer; a Critical Exposition   III-1371
Boydston, Jo Ann and Kathleen Poulos
Checklist of Writings About John Dewey   IV-1
Bradley, Francis Herbert
Appearance and Reality   III-1427
Ethical Studies   IV-1908
Bradley, J.
Mach's Philosophy of Science   III-1458
Brand, Myles, ed.
Nature of Causation, The   V-2414
Brandt, Frithiof
Thomas Hobbes' Mechanical Conception of Nature   II-862
Brandt, Richard B.
"Emotive Theory of Ethics, The" in *The Philosophical Review*   V-2298
Bréhier, Émile
Hellenistic and Roman Age, The   II-504
Brémond, Henri
Sir Thomas More. The Blessed Thomas More   II-763
Brezik, Victor B., C. S. B., ed.
One Hundred Years of Thomism, Aeterni Patris and Afterwards, A Symposium   IV-1999
Brightman, E. S.
Philosophy of Religion, A   III-1352
Britton, Karl
John Stuart Mill   III-1383
Broad, C. D.
"Berkeley's Denial of Material Substance," in *The Philosophical Review*   II-989
Five Types of Ethical Theory   III-1141

Centre International de Synthèse
Pierre Gassendi, 1592-1655, sa vie et son oeuvre   II-873
Chadwick, Owen
Secularization of the European Mind in the Nineteenth Century, The   IV-1558
Chai, Ch'u and Winberg Chai, eds. and trs.
Humanist Way in Ancient China: Essential Works of Confucianism, The   I-420
Chai, Winberg and Ch'u Chai, eds. and trs.
Humanist Way in Ancient China: Essential Works of Confucianism, The   I-420
Chambers, Raymond W.
Thomas More   II-763
Champigny, Robert
Stages on Sartre's Way: 1938-52   V-2285
Chang Ch'i-chün,
Lao Tzu che hsueh (The Philosophy of Lao Tzu)   II-482
Chang Chung-yüan,
Creativity and Taoism: A Study of Chinese Philosophy, Art, and Poetry   II-482
Chapman, John W.
Rousseau: Totalitarian or Liberal   III-1092
Chappell, V. C., ed.
Philosophy of Mind, The   V-2358
Chen, Ellen Marie
Tao, Nature, Man: A Study of the Key Ideas in the Tao Te Ching   II-482
Chenu, M. D.
Toward Understanding Saint Thomas   II-703
Chevalier, Jacques
Henri Bergson   III-1491
Chiari, Joseph
"Religious Existentialism," in *Twentieth-Century French Thought: From Bergson to Lévi-Strauss*   V-2380
Chisholm, Roderick
Perceiving: A Philosophical Study   V-2042
"Sextus Empiricus and Modern Empiricism," in *Philosophy of Science*   II-534
Chisholm, Roderick M., ed.
Realism and the Background of Phenomenology   V-2066
Chisholm, Roderick M., Archie Bahm, et al.
"Symposium in Honor of Roy Wood Sellars, A" in *Philosophy and Phenomenological Research*   V-2066
Christensen, Niels Egmont
On the Nature of Meanings: A Philosophical Analysis   IV-1823
Christian, William
Interpretation of Whitehead's Metaphysics, An   IV-1955
Church, Alonzo
"On Carnap's Analysis of Statements of Assertion and Belief," in *Analysis*   V-2268
Church, Ralph W.
Study in the Philosophy of Malebranche, A   II-909
Clark, Gordon
Karl Barth's Theological Method   V-2171

Clive, Geoffrey
Romantic Enlightenment: Ambiguity and Paradox in the Western Mind (1750-1920), The   IV-1547
Cobb, William S., Jr.
"Anamnesis: Platonic Doctrine or Sophistic Absurdity?," in *Dialogue: Canadian Philosophical Revue*   I-231
Cobban, Alfred
Rousseau and the Modern State   III-1092
Cohen, Arthur A.
Martin Buber   IV-1811
Teachings of Maimonides, The   II-671
Cohen, Carl
Civil Disobedience   I-178
Cohen, G. A.
Karl Marx's Theory of History: A Defense   III-1483
Cohen, Morris R. and Ernest Nagel
Introduction to Logic and Scientific Method, An   III-1292
Collins, James Daniel
History of Modern European Philosophy, A   IV-2023
"Jaspers' Quest of Transcendence," in *The Existentialists*   V-2125
Mind of Kierkegaard, The   III-1318
Philosophical Readings in Cardinal Newman   II-1404
Collins, W. L.
Butler   III-1001
Commager, Henry Steele
American Mind: An Interpretation of American Thought and Character Since the 1880's, The   IV-1658
Comte, August
August Comte: The Founder of Sociology   III-1255
Confucius
Analects   I-31
Analects of Confucius, The   I-31
Wisdom of Confucius, The   I-31
Conkin, Paul K.
Puritans and Pragmatists: Eight Eminent American Thinkers   IV-1547
Connell, Desmond
Vision in God: Malebranche's Scholastic Sources, The   II-909
Conze, Edward, ed. and tr.
Buddhist Wisdom Books: The Diamond Sutra and the Heart Sutra   II-599
Cooper, Lane and Alfred Gudeman, eds.
Bibliography of the Poetics of Aristotle, A   I-410
Copi, Irving M.
Introduction to Logic   III-1293
Copi, Irving M. and James A. Gould
Readings on Logic   I-338
Copi, Irving M. and James A. Gould, eds.
Contemporary Readings in Logical Theory   IV-1734; V-2114
Copi, Irving M. and Robert W. Beard, eds.
Essays on Wittgenstein's Tractatus   IV-1761

Duffield, Holley Gene and Manuel Bilsky, eds.
Tolstoy and the Critics: Literature and Aesthetics   IV-1535, 1930
Duncan, Alistair R. C.
Practical Reason and Morality
III-1141,1165
Dunn, John
Political Thought of John Locke: An Historical Account of the Argument of the "Two Treatises of Government," The
II-934

Eames, S. Morris
"Meaning of Truth in William James, The" in *The Philosophy of William James*
IV-1658
Earle, William James
"William James," in *The Encyclopedia of Philosophy*   IV-1648
Eckstein, Jerome
Platonic Method: An Interpretation of the Dramatic-Philosophic Aspects of the Meno, The   I-199
Edwards, Paul
Logic of Moral Discourse, The   V-2298
Edwards, Paul, ed.
Encyclopedia of Philosophy, The   III-1342; IV-1558
Eiseley, Loren
Man Who Saw Through Time, The
II-803
Eliot, T. S.
Knowledge and Experience in the Philosophy of F. H. Bradley   III-1503
Elliot, R. K.
"Unity of Kant's 'Critique of Aesthetic Judgement, The" in *The British Journal of Aesthetics*   III-1187
Elliston, Frederick and Peter McCormick, eds.
Husserl: Expositions and Appraisals
IV-1679
Elrod, John W.
Being and Existence in Kierkegaard's Pseudonymous Works   III-1331
Elwood, Douglas J.
Philosophical Theology of Jonathan Edwards, The   III-1070
Emmet, Dorothy M.
"Epistemology and the Idea of Revelation," in *The Theology of Paul Tillich*
V-2430
Epictetus
Epictetus   II-513
Epicurus
Letters, Principle Doctrines, and Vatican Sayings   I-440
Epp, Ronald H.
"Some Observations on the Platonic Concept of Katharsis in the Phaedo," in *Kinesis*   I-232
Epstein, Isadore, ed.
Moses Maimonides, 1135-1204; Anglo-Jewish Papers in Connection with the Eighth Centenary of His Birth   II-671

Erdmann, J. E.
History of Philosophy, A   III-1352
Evans, Joseph W., ed.
Jacques Maritain: The Man and His Achievement   IV-2031
Ewing, A. C.
Definition of Good, The   IV-1967
Idealism: A Critical Survey   IV-1637
"Pursuit of the Good, The" in *Ethics*
IV-1967

Fann, K. T., ed.
Ludwig Wittgenstein: The Man and His Philosophy   V-2477
Symposium on J. L. Austin   V-2523
Farber, Marvin, ed.
Philosophic Thought in France and the United States   V-2380
Farquharson, A. S. L., ed.
Meditations of the Emperor Marcus Antoninus, The   II-523
Farrington, Benjamin
Faith of Epicurus, The   I-440
Francis Bacon: Pioneer of Planned Science   II-815
Philosophy of Francis Bacon, The   II-803
Faust, Clarence H. and Thomas H. Johnson
Jonathan Edwards   III-1070
Feibleman, James K.
Introduction to the Philosophy of Charles S. Peirce, An   IV-2012
Fell, Joseph P.
Heidegger and Sartre: An Essay on Being and Place   IV-1883
Feurstein, G. A.
Introduction to the Bhagavad-Gītā: Its Philosophy and Cultural Setting   I-134
Field, G. C.
Plato and His Contemporaries   I-207, 298
Figgis, J. N.
Political Aspects of St. Augustine's City of God, The   II-581
Findlay, John N.
Hegel: A Re-examination   III-1224, 1235
"Time: A Treatment of Some Puzzles," in *Logic and Language*   II-569
Firth, Roderick
"Austin and the Argument from Illusion," in *The Philosophical Review*   V-2512
Fisch, Mat H. and T. G. Bergin, eds.
Autobiography of Giambattista Vico, The   III-1023
Flew, Antony
"Survival and Immortality," in *An Introduction to Western Philosophy: Ideas and Argument From Plato to Sartre*   I-232
Flower, Elizabeth and Murray G. Murphy
History of Philosophy in America, A
IV-1648
"Josiah Royce," in *A History of Philosophy in America*   IV-1570
Foelber, Robert and Avrum Stroll
"Talk About Talk About Surfaces," in *Dialectica*   V-2512

"Marcel: The Ascent to Being," in *Thought* V-2381

Michel, Paul Henri
Cosmology of Giordano Bruno, The II-793

Micklem, N.
Reason and Revelation: A Question from Duns Scotus II-730

Miel, Jean
Pascal and Theology II-884

Mill, John Stuart
Utilitarianism IV-1908

Miller, Perry
Errand into the Wilderness III-1070

Milne, A. J. M.
"T. H. Green's Theory of Morality," in *The Social Philosophy of English Idealism* III-1437

Monist, The III-1417

Moody, Ernest A.
Logic of William of Ockham, The II-742
"Ockham, Buridan, and Nicholas of Autrecourt," in *Franciscan Studies* II-742

Moore, A. W.
Reviews of *The Life of Reason*, Vols. I-IV and Vol. V, in *The Journal of Philosophy* IV-1615

Moore, Donald J.
Martin Buber: Prophet of Religious Secularism IV-1811

Moore, Edward C. and Richard S. Robin, eds.
Studies in the Philosophy of Charles Sanders Peirce, Second Series IV-2012

Moore, George Edward
"Refutation of Idealism, The" in *Philosophical Studies* II-990
Some Main Problems of Philosophy III-1427

Moore, John M.
Theories of Religious Experience with Special Reference to James, Otto, and Bergson IV-1721

Moravcsik, Julius M. E.
"Forms, Nature, and the Good in the *Philebus*," in *Phronesis* I-307

Moravcsik, Julius M. E., ed.
Aristotle: A Collection of Critical Essays I-339, 380

Morewedge, Parviz
"*Metaphysica*" of Avicenna, The (ibn Sīnā) II-631

Morgan, George A.
What Nietzsche Means III-1448, 1470

Morgenbesser, Sidney, ed.
Dewey and His Critics IV-1773; V-2079

Morrall, John B.
Aristotle I-390

Morris, Charles
Pragmatic Movement in American Philosophy, The IV-1648

Morris, Phyllis Sutton
Sartre's Concept of a Person: An Analytic Approach V-2285

Morrow, G. R.

Plato's Cretan City: A Historical Interpretation of the Laws I-327

Mortimore, Geoffrey, ed.
"Hare's Paradox," in *Weakness of Will* V-2454

Mossner, Ernest C.
Bishop Butler and the Age of Reason III-1001
Life of David Hume, The III-1117
"Religion of David Hume, The," in *Journal of the History of Ideas* III-1117

Mourelatos, A. P. D.
Route of Parmenides, The I-51

Muelder, Walter G., Lurence Sears, and Anne V. Schlabach, eds.
Development of American Philosophy, The V-2159

Muirhead, John H., ed.
Contemporary British Philosophy III-1352
Platonic Tradition in Anglo-Saxon Philosophy, The III-1503
Rule and End in Morals IV-1967

Mulgan, R. G.
Aristotle's Political Theory: An Introduction for Students of Political Theory I-390

Murchland, Bernard C.
"Albert Camus: The Dark Night Before the Coming of Grace?," in *Camus: A Collection of Critical Essays* V-2401

Mure, Geoffrey R. G.
Introduction to Hegel, An III-1235

Murphy, Arthur E.
"Alexander's Metaphysic of Space-Time," in *Monist, The* IV-1747

Murphy, Jeffrie G.
Kant: The Philosophy of Right III-1165
"Socratic Theory of Legal Fidelity, The" in *Violence and Aggression in the History of Ideas* I-178

Murphy, Murray G. and Elizabeth Flower
History of Philosophy in America, A IV-1648
"Josiah Royce," in *A History of Philosophy in America* IV-1570

Murray, Gilbert
Five Stages of Greek Religion I-317

Murty, K. Satchidananda
Revelation and Reason in Advaita Vedānta II-610

Musgrave, Alan and Imre Lakatos, eds.
Criticism and the Growth of Knowledge V-2100

Musil, Robert
Man Without Qualities, The IV-1761

Nagel, Ernest and Morris R. Cohen
Introduction to Logic and Scientific Method, An III-1292

Naravane, V. S.
Modern Indian Thought V-2055

Naravane, V. S. and Robert A. McDermott, eds.
Spirit of Modern India: Writings in Philosophy, Religion, & Culture, The V-2054

"Some Questions on Dewey's Esthetics," in
  The Philosophy of John Dewey
  V-2079
Perkins, Jean A.
  "Diderot and La Mettrie" and "Voltaire and
  La Mettrie," in *Studies on Voltaire and the
  Eighteenth Century*   III-1034
Perry, Charner M.
  "Some Difficulties in Current Value The-
  ory," in *The Journal of Philosophy*
  IV-1856
  "Value as Any Object of Any Interest," in
  Ethics   IV-1857
Perry, Ralph B.
  Present Philosophical Tendencies   III-1342
Persons, Stow
  American Minds   V-2159
Peterfreund, Sheldon P.
  *Introduction to American Philosophy,
  An*   V-2159
Peters, Richard
  Hobbes   II-850
Peterson, Houston
  Huxley: Prophet of Science   III-1515
Pfeutze, Paul E.
  Social Self, The   V-2090
Pilkington, A. E.
  *Bergson and His Influence: A Reassess-
  ment*   III-1491; IV-1592
Pintard, René
  *Libertinage érudit dans la prémière moitié du
  xvii₌ siècle, Le*   II-873
Pitcher, George, ed.
  *Wittgenstein: The Philosophical Investiga-
  tions*   V-2477
Plamenatz, J. P.
  English Utilitarians, The   III-1383
Plato
  *Euthyphro, Apology of Socrates and
  Crito*   I-168
  Gorgias   I-207
  Banquet, Le, in *Oeuvres complètes*   I-219
  Phaedrus of Plato, The   I-253
  Protagoras and Meno   I-94
  Symposium   I-220
  Theaetetus   I-269
Podro, M.
  *Manifold in Perception: Theories of Art from
  Kant to Hildebrand, The*   III-1187
Pollock, Sir Frederick
  Spinoza: His Life and Philosophy   II-898
Pollock, Robert C.
  "Process and Experience," in *John Dewey:
  His Thought and Influence*   V-2184
Pompa, Leon
  "Vico's Science," in *History and
  Theory*   III-1023
Popkin, Richard H.
  *History of Scepticism from Erasmus to Spi-
  noza, The*   II-785
Popper, Karl R.
  *Conjectures and Refutations: The Growth of
  Scientific Knowledge*   V-2100, 2322
  Open Society and Its Enemies, The   I-244

"Three Views Concerning Human Knowl-
  edge," in *Conjectures and Refutations: The
  Growth of Scientific Knowledge*
  III-1458
Poritzky, J. E.
  *Julien Offray de La Mettrie, sein Leben und
  seine Werke*   III-1035
Poulos, Kathleen and Jo Ann Boydston
  *Checklist of Writings About John
  Dewey*   IV-1773, 1919
Prabhavananda, Swami and Christopher Ish-
  erwood, eds. and trs.
  Shankara's Crest-Jewel of Discrimination
  II-610
Pratt, J. B.
  Adventures in Philosophy and Religion
  V-2147
  What Is Pragmatism?   V-2147
Price, H. H.
  Belief   V-2043
  Perception   V-2512
Prior, A. N.
  Formal Logic   III-1293; IV-1734

Quine, W. V. O.
  "Two Dogmas of Empiricism," in *The Philo-
  sophical Review*   V-2333
  Ways of Paradox, The   V-2269
Quinn, John Francis
  *Historical Constitution of St. Bonaventure's
  Philosophy, The*   II-680

Rabil, Albert
  *Merleau-Ponty: Existentialist of the Social
  World*   V-2310
Raines, J. C.
  "Sin as Pride and Sin as Sloth: Reinhold
  Niebuhr and Karl Marx on the Predica-
  ment of Man," in *Christianity and
  Crisis*   V-2247
Raju, P. T.
  Idealistic Thought of India   II-610
Ramsey, Paul
  "Love and Law," in *Reinhold Niebuhr: His
  Religious, Social, and Political
  Thought*   V-2247
Randall, John Herman, Jr.
  Aristotle   I-358, 368, 399, 410
  "Ontology of Paul Tillich, The," in *The The-
  ology of Paul Tillich*   V-2443
  "Romantic Faith in Mechanistic Evolution,
  in *Philosophy After Darwin*   III-1372
Ransom, John Crowe
  "Art and Mr. Santayana," in *The Virginia
  Quarterly Review*   III-1525
Raven, J. E. and G. S. Kirk
  "Anaxagoras of Clazomenae," in *The Pre-
  socratic Philosophers*   I-61
  Presocratic Philosophers, The   I-10, 20,
  51
Reck, Andrew J.
  "Authority of Morality over Aesthetics in
  Santayana's Philosophy, The," in *The
  Southern Journal of Philosophy*

XXXVII

"Role of Theory in Aesthetics, The," in
  Problems in Aesthetics   IV-1690
Werkmeister, W. H.
  *Theories of Ethics: A Study in Moral Obli-
  gation*   IV-1845
West, Thomas G.
  Plato's Apology of Socrates   I-158
White, Alan
  "Causal Theory of Perception (2), The," in
  The Philosophy of Perception   V-2043
White, H. and G. Tagliacozzo, eds.
  *Giambattista Vico, an International Sympos-
  ium*   III-1023
Whitehead, Alfred North and Bertrand Rus-
  sell
  Principia Mathematica   IV-1734
Whittaker, Thomas
  Neoplatonists, The   II-559
Wiener, Philip P.
  "Method in Russell's Work on Leibniz," in
  The Philosophy of Bertrand Russell
  III-1105
Wiener, Philip P. and Frederic H. Young, eds.
  *Studies in the Philosophy of Charles Sanders
  Peirce*   IV-2012
Wild, John
  *Radical Empiricism of William James,
  The*   IV-1547
Williams, Bernard
  Descartes: The Project of Pure Enquiry
  II-827
Williams, Donald C.
  "Of Essence and Existence and Santayana,"
  in *The Journal of Philosophy*   IV-1897
Wilshire, Bruce, ed.
  William James: The Essential Writings
  IV-1659
Wilson, John Cook
  Statement and Inference   III-1427
Wilson, Margaret D.
  Descartes   II-838
Winch, Peter
  "Popper and Scientific Method in the Social
  Sciences," in *The Philosophy of Karl Pop-
  per*   V-2322
Wing-tsit Chan
  "Evolution of the Confucian Concept of *Jen*,
  The," in *Philosophy East and West*
  I-31
Wing-tsit Chan, ed. and tr.
  Source Book in Chinese Philosophy, A
  I-113, 123, 450, 472; II-492, 599
Winspear, Alban

Genesis of Plato's Thought, The   I-289
Wisdom, John
  Other Minds   V-2358
Wittgenstein, Ludwig
  Notebooks, 1914-1916   IV-1762
  Philosophical Investigations   IV-1762;
  V-2358
Woelfel, James W.
  Camus: A Theological Perspective   V-2401
Wolfson, Harry A.
  "Maimonides on Negative Attributes," in
  Louis Ginzberg Jubilee Volume   II-671
Wollheim, Richard, ed.
  "Introduction," in *Hume on Religion*
  III-1117
Wolter, Allan B., O. F. M.
  *Transcendentals and Their Function in the
  Metaphysics of Duns Scotus, The*
  II-730
Woo, Catherine Yi-Yu Cho
  *Characters of the Hexagrams of the I
  Ching*   I-113
Wu, Joseph
  "Son Being Witness Against the Father—A
  Paradox in the *Confucian Analects*, The,"
  in *Clarification and Enlightenment: Essays
  in Comparative Philosophy*   I-31
  "Understanding Taoism: A Chinese Philos-
  opher's Critique," in *Clarification and En-
  lightenment: Essays in Comparative
  Philosophy*   II-483

Yates, Frances A.
  "Bruno, Giordano," in *The Encyclopedia of
  Philosophy*   II-794
Yolton, John W.
  *John Locke: Problems and Perspectives: A
  Collection of New Essays*   II-922
  *Locke and the Compass of Human Under-
  standing: A Selective Commentary on the
  "Essay"*   II-922
Young, Frederic H. and Philip P. Wiener, eds.
  *Studies in the Philosophy of Charles Sanders
  Peirce*   IV-2012

Zimmerman, R.
  "Kant: The Aesthetic Judgment," in *Kant:
  A Collection of Critical Essays*
  III-1188
Zyskind, Harold and Robert Sternfeld
  *Plato's Meno: A Philosophy of Man as Ac-
  quisitive*   I-199

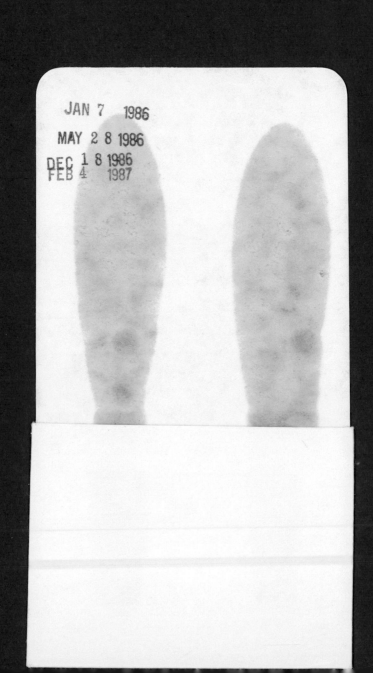

JAN 7   1986

MAY 2 8 1986

DEC 1 8 1986
FEB 4   1987